CW01654727

All Shapes and Sizes

An illustrated history of film in cinema and television

Grant Lobban and Jim Slater

This book is a highly readable and copiously illustrated technical presentation of the history and technology of film as it has been used in the cinema and television industries since their inception.

The authors have taken great pains to explain the many different technologies involved in a manner that is understandable to the novice whilst providing sufficient detail to satisfy the expert and the enthusiast seeking an in-depth understanding of the many and varied topics that are covered. Each chapter focuses on a particular facet of film or television, and clear explanations are given as to how the two sciences have been mutually dependent from the earliest times.

The mass of technical information is made readily understandable by the many illustrations which accompany the words, many of these being actual clips from films in the formats being explained, and the whole book is leavened by the inclusion of many personal stories and experiences from the authors which make it enjoyable to read. Although encyclopaedic in its coverage, the book is also a treat to dip into to read its various parts for particular items of information.

It is hoped that young graduates wanting to pursue a career in film preservation and restoration will find the wealth of historical information of great value as they seek the best ways of restoring films to their original glory, but the book will appeal to a much wider range of readers, including film students and cinema enthusiasts seeking a deeper insight into the history of the cinema.

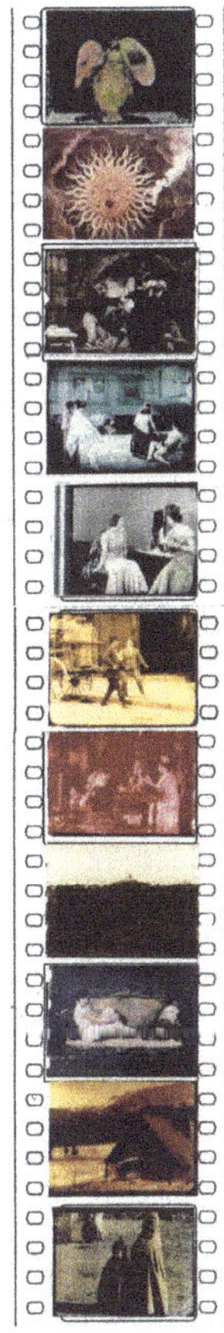

This edition published in 2019 by
AG Books, an imprint of
Andrews UK Limited
under exclusive license from
Slater Electronic Services
17 Winterslow Road, Porton,
Salisbury SP4 0LW UK
www.slaterelectronics.com
© 2018 Grant Lobban and Jim Slater

British Library Cataloguing in Publication Data
A catalogue record for this book is available from the British Library

Acknowledgement:
In an encyclopaedic book like this the copyright of many of the historic illustrations is unclear, the authors having gathered their material over many years from many different sources. Most of the illustrations in this book are from Grant's personal archive and his collection of all shapes and sizes and colour film frames dating back to the 1890s. Every effort has been made to establish the rights to use this material, but the authors fully recognise and acknowledge the rights of any owners of material that appears in this publication and are grateful for the opportunity to have included it.

All rights reserved. This book or any portion thereof may not be reproduced or used in any manner whatsoever without the express written permission of the publisher except for the use of brief quotations in a book review.

© 2018 Grant Lobban and Jim Slater

Contents

Introduction

Hand Crafted - the making of a 'masterwork'!

This book is the result of a decades long collaboration between the authors, a labour of love from both. It is lavishly illustrated and has lots of fascinating stories that it is hoped will appeal to a wide range of cinemagoers and cinema enthusiasts as well as to professionals involved in film preservation and restoration.

A key factor in wanting to put this book together was a desire to do as much as possible to help the preservation of old film, both the physical film stocks and the wealth of wonderful programming that cinema has provided over the last 120 years, as well as to provide detailed information to aid those who are striving to restore long-forgotten gems from the past.

Art and Craft

Preservation and restoration involve far more than the skilled craftsmanship that we take for granted from restorers at places like the UK's BFI National Archive, which collects, preserves, and restores old films. The authors have been privileged to visit the J. Paul Getty, Jr. Conservation Centre in Berkhamsted, Hertfordshire, and are lost in admiration for the craft skills of those who undertake high precision tasks like repairing damaged sprocket holes and 'floating' film images from a damaged base onto a new film stock. Important as these aspects of preservation and restoration are, for films to be restored to as near as possible their original format, those involved must have an in-depth understanding of how the films were originally made, the different film types, how they were intended to be shown, and how they would have been shown in practice.

Technology

The book begins with an examination of the chemistry and the physical composition of film, both black and white and colour, and provides a historical background detailing the many different methods that were used to bring colour to the cinema screen, from the incredible hand-colouring of over 100 years ago to today's superb multi-layer film stocks. The Technicolor 3-Strip dye-transfer process is explained in detail.

Ethics

Restoration is a complex business, closely related to the equally important art of long-term conservation of film, and several chapters consider not only the technical aspects of both but also the ethical aspects, such as whether a restorer should improve the images to be better than they would have originally been, just because digital techniques allow this, or whether the restored image should be as close as possible to the original, even if the original colours seen by the audience would have been less than true to life. Sadly, in some cases, restorers may no longer have the choice. Even for relatively recent colour films, which are found to be suffering from severe dye-fading, it may no longer be possible to recreate the brilliance and quality of their original images.

Frame rates

The importance of showing films at the 'correct' frame rate is explained, as are the difficulties of knowing exactly what that 'correct' rate would have been.

Aspect ratios

When a restorer has various different prints of the film being worked on, the importance of determining the 'definitive' version is explained, and much information is provided as to how to identify the different types of film and the multiple image sizes and aspect ratios that have been used by the industry over the years. Alternative (non-standard) movie formats that have been used over the years are detailed, in case restorers come across them, and both large format and smaller 'home movie' formats are included.
The enormous confusion surrounding aspect ratios is examined in detail - a restorer needs to understand precisely what the director's intentions were and the version of the film print being used, if anything like the original pictures are to be restored, and examples are given as to how many movies have historically been shown at the wrong shape, often with parts of the picture missing, either due to lack of care or a lack of understanding of what the images should have looked like. Reasons why the industry hasn't reached agreement on a single aspect ratio are debated- although with today's 'Scope and 'Widescreen' alternatives we are probably as close to a near-universal agreement as we shall ever be!

Film and Television

Film has been associated with Television since TV's earliest origins, and the book gives much detailed information about their historical relationship, moving from black and white systems where 'live' TV programmes were originated from 35mm film within seconds of its emerging from a developing tank to discussions of the different aspect ratios used and the technologies involved in providing today's 16:9 high definition colour pictures. The stories of how TV and cinema have been regarded as competitors over the years are given, with up to the minute explanations as to how cinema is currently using Premium Large Format technologies to distinguish itself from the ever larger TVs being made available to the home viewer.

Keeping the Magic

Cinema has always aimed to more than compete by providing a totally different experience from watching TV at home, and from the earliest times cinemas have used various forms of 'showmanship' to ensure that customers get something extra special from their visits. The book shows how cinema owners in the 1920s used a wide range of tricks and gimmicks, from skeletons on wires above the audience to 'guarantees' to pay out thousands of pounds in insurance if an audience member died of shock during a particularly scaring horror movie! Modern cinemas use technology to increase the sense of wonder and of involvement - 'Keeping the Magic' - today's equivalent of the old 'showmanship' in many ways, as well as offering food, drink and special hospitality to make each visit a special 'going out' event to be remembered - something you can't get from the TV at home.

And a little bit extra

We have included an extra section at the end of the book, somewhat whimsically entitled 'Grant's Gems'. It is a fairly random collection of technical pieces that don't quite fit into the main sections, but which provide look at some of the technical factors that affect how we see images on our cinema screens, from lenses with strange, previously unexplained distortions to he technology of film soundtracks to somewhat scurrilous stories of life as a BBC projectionist. Quite a range of topics for one book - we hope you will enjoy it as well as finding it useful and educational!

Bringing the book together

The collaboration between Grant and Jim turned out to be serendipitous and the resulting synergies between the two led to this book, which neither could have completed alone. Much, though not all of the material was published as articles in *Image Technology* and *Cinema Technology* magazines over the years, but the collaborators had long cherished the idea of eventually publishing this book.

Although you won't find any more complete or up to date information about the topics he writes about, there is certainly nothing digital about Grant's major contribution to the history of colour film preservation and restoration, apart from the fingers that he uses to provide the type-written copy that is often heavily annotated by hand, with other bits stuck-on, before being posted to Jim. This involved over 300 closely-typed (not word-processed!) pages, accompanied by dozens of 35mm slide frames, many of which contained carefully assembled collages of different types of film to illustrate a particular point being made in the article. Each of the slides was taped to a paper containing accompanying captions, sometimes with special instructions ('make sure this one is printed emulsion side up', or 'the fading is supposed to mean that the faces are yellow and the background is blue', with an occasional 'this is the only frame that still exists - guard it with your life!'). Such instructions are often very necessary, since colour scanners are notorious for 'doing their own thing' and introducing unwanted colour corrections. There were also over 100 colour prints for scanning, comprising posters, newspaper cuttings, even the box of a very old reel of film.

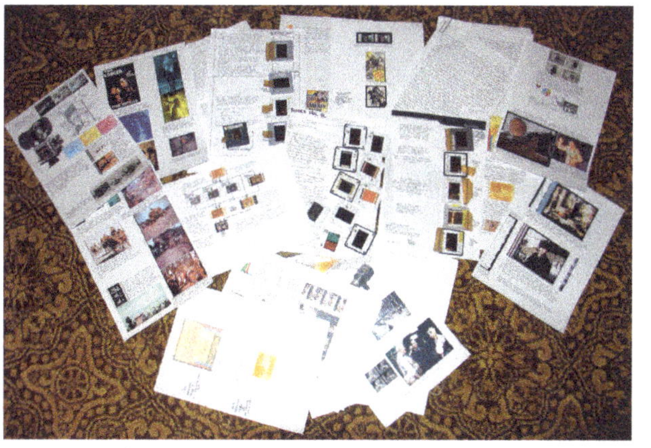

The raw materials for just one chapter

Putting the pieces together, working with all this precious material, makes you feel like those who worked on the 'Dead Sea Scrolls' must have done. Some of the images are, not surprisingly, less than perfect and betray traces of their 'cut and paste' (literally) origins, but I do hope that we have managed to do reasonable justice to Grant's remarkable research work.

Jim did his best to make sense of the piles (the photo above shows just a part of the collection sent for one chapter) and eventually turned it into a chapter of the book, having made further suggestions, collected extra illustrations and had long discussions with Grant. Eventually a pdf of each draft chapter was printed it out in colour and sent to Grant. After a period for cogitation by Grant, Jim received a marked up draft in the post, and it isn't unknown for each of these drafts to be accompanied by another set of slides ("I have just come across this extra information, and it really will help to make the chapter better - could you please squeeze it in.....") which require substantial changes to the layout before we can start on the iterative editing process all over again. No surprise, then that Jim sometimes missed out a slide or two, and Grant had to say 'whatever happened to my slide with the 9.5mm film clip inside?'. But eventually we did get things into a state that both found acceptable (did I mention the discussions on where we might fit in another last minute 28 pages....?)

Worth waiting for...

The time involved in this whole process is interesting. Grant is a complete enthusiast for film and can spend as long as a couple of years researching and gathering together information on a specialist topic. Years ago he said 'don't try and rush me, I can't tell you when my next chapter will be ready', and experience has shown this to be good advice, and also that the results are always worth waiting for.

About the authors

Grant Lobban FBKS is an ex-BBC projectionist and a total film enthusiast who has spent his life learning and researching about all aspects of film history and has become a world-renowned expert on the history of film and on the conservation and preservation of this wonderful material whose known archival properties still exceed anything that even the latest digital imaging techniques can offer. He has been a regular (and irregular!) contributor to the magazines of the British Kinematograph Sound and Television Society (re-named the International Moving Image Society in recent times) for many years, and was responsible for several of the society's informative wallcharts on all aspects of film. Grant is a regular, hard-working and hands-on volunteer at London's Cinema Museum in Kennington, which is, as he is, devoted to keeping alive the spirit of cinema from the days before the multiplex.

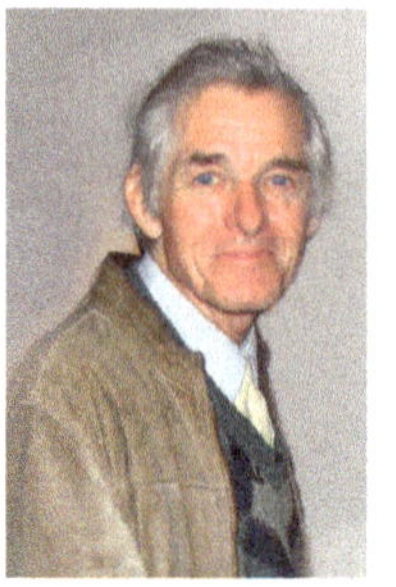

Jim Slater FBKS I.Eng. MIET began his career as a BBC broadcasting engineer, later moving into research, with a background in digital television, and his books, lectures and published articles on Satellite Broadcasting, Cable Television, HDTV and Digital TV led many to a deeper understanding of the subjects. He became Managing Editor of Cinema Technology magazine back in 1979, and, from a background where, as he confesses, his only real knowledge of film (apart from owning a trusty old 16mm B&H projector) was from putting it onto telecine machines and tweaking the results to suit (anathema to cinema people, of course!), he learned from colleagues in the cinema industry and developed a deep appreciation of the very special qualities of film and of the skills of those who strive to provide the best possible cinema shows. He has visited the projection boxes of hundreds of cinemas around the world and the factories of the major projector manufacturers, and after an in-depth training course, gained recognition as a qualified digital projector installer, but has been far too busy writing to ever put these skills into practice in the cinema.

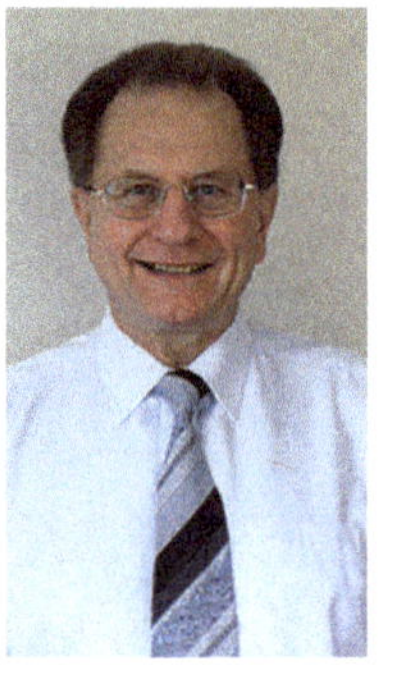

The historical background of colour film processes

A plethora of ideas and technologies preceded the commercial adoption of colour in the cinema

Colour in film

The cinema industry had well over a century of making 'black and white' movies, but the aim of providing moving images in colour existed for decades before it became practically possible on an everyday basis. Over the years hundreds of different techniques have been experimented with, tried and tested, and this short history documents the many and various ways that colour films have been photographed, processed and printed, and goes on to suggest the types of original material which may still be available for making new copies and which if necessary may be restored to ensure the future survival of much of this historical film content.

Historical Background and Technology

From the birth of motion pictures, colour films of different types have existed alongside those in black and white, although the earliest would be better described as 'coloured'.

Hand Painting

The established method of hand-painting lantern slides was soon extended to moving pictures, using fine brushes to apply transparent colour dyes to each frame. The earliest surviving example is probably the Kinetoscope 1896 subject, *The Serpentine Dance* by Annabelle-the-Dancer. [Frame 1 on the facing page. Other numbers throughout this chapter in square brackets refer to images in subsequent frames of the 'film strips'].
Some of the black and white prints were coloured by the wife of one of Edison's associates, who hand painted all 800 frames of the 50 foot 35mm films. Other films from the early 1900s, which can still be seen today, include coloured versions of Georges Méliès' trick and fantasy films [2], and the hand-coloured gun flashes in *The Great Train Robbery* (1903), shown in the centre picture at the bottom of the page.

Stencil Colouring

To speed up the process, stencils were sometimes cut to colour areas which remained the same shape and size over a large number of frames. This skilled, but laborious task, was later fully mechanised, with up to six different colour tints applied through 'moving' stencils. Each of these was cut by an electrically powered stylus guided by an operator tracing around the chosen area on an enlarged image of each frame.
A single set of stencils could then be used to colour a large number of prints, with the dyes applied through the cut outs using dye soaked ribbons. **Pathécolor** [3] (known as **Pathéchrome** in the USA) was the best known system of this type, with Gaumont [4] offering a similar service.

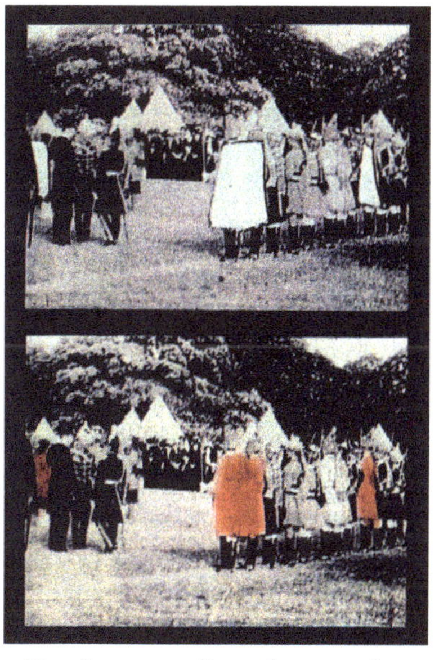

Hand cut stencil used to speed up the colouring process

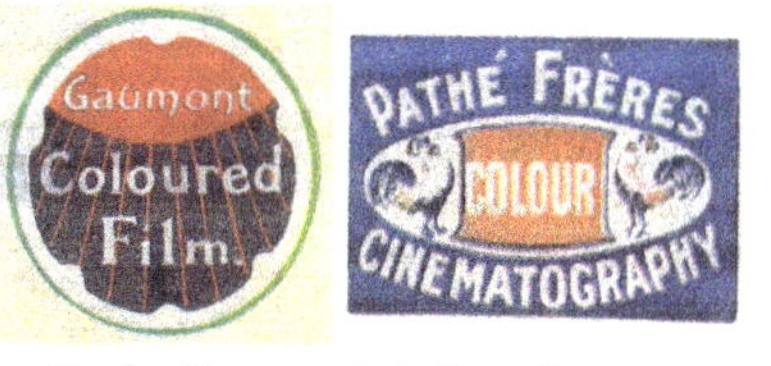

Early film-can labels indicating a possible stencil-coloured treat inside

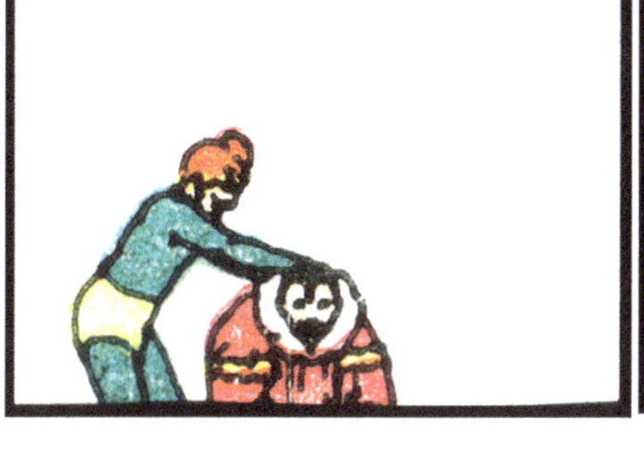

An earlier method of adding colour is shown in this tiny clip of a cartoon loop for a toy projector that was hand painted then printed in colour by lithography, a method that wasn't suitable for longer cinema films.

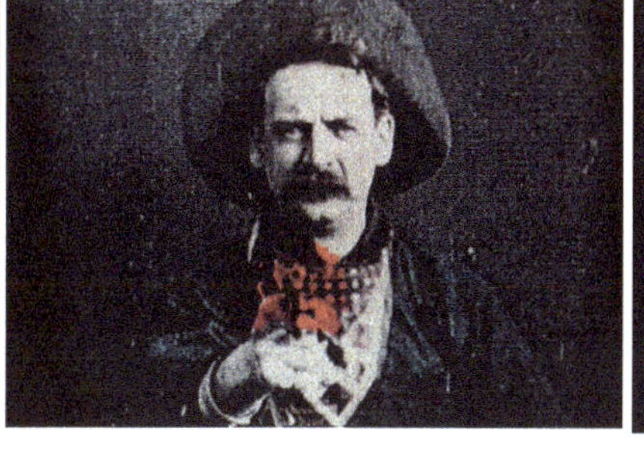

From a hand-coloured print of 'The Great Train Robbery' (1903)

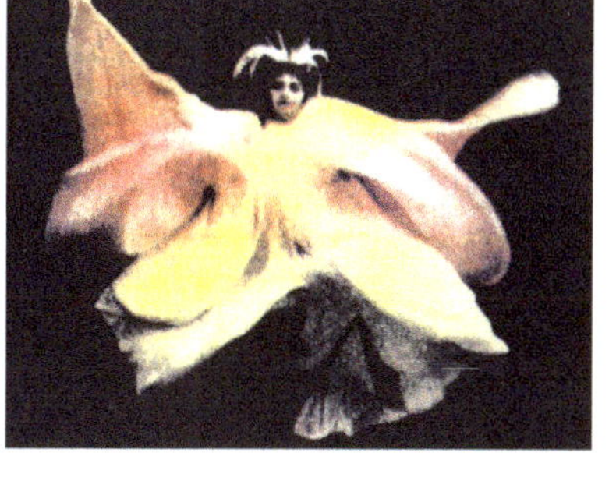

Hand-coloured 'Butterfly Dance' (1907)

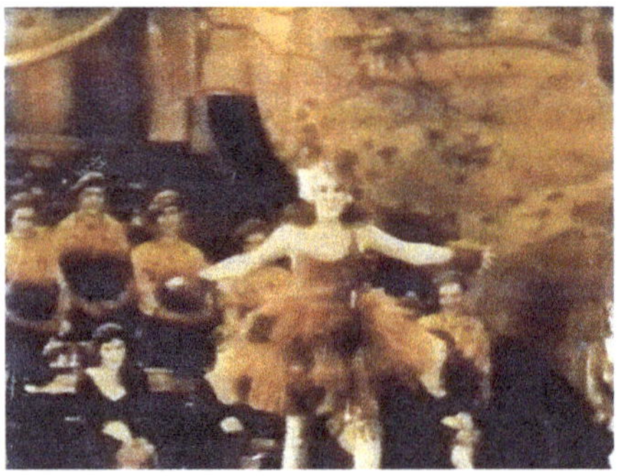

One of the last examples of stencil colouring by Gaumont - a colour sequence from 'Elstree Calling' (1930)

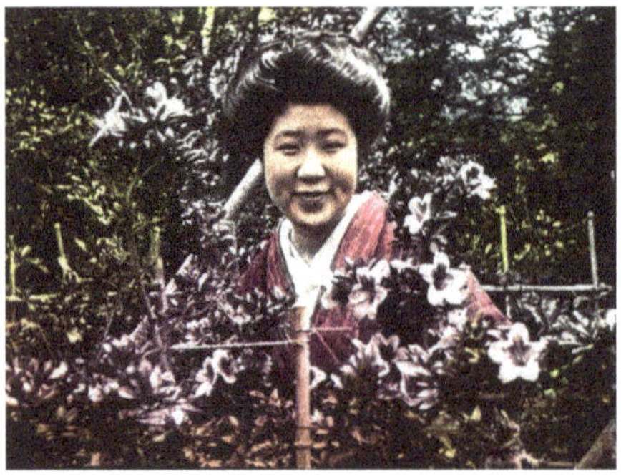

Stencil colour (above) and its modern equivalent (below) colorisation

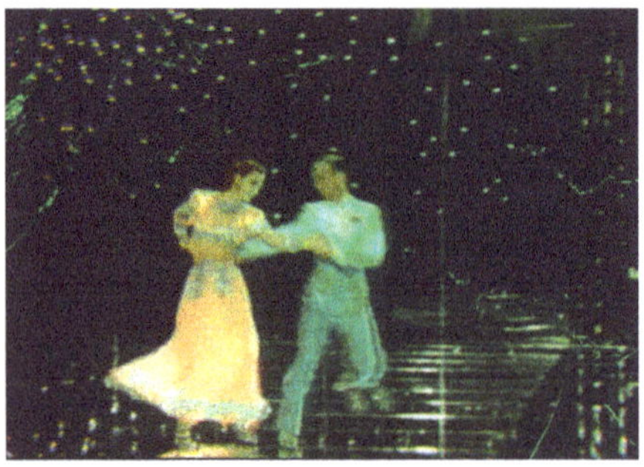

Mechanical Colouring

Mechanical colouring began around 1907, making the process more practical as films were becoming longer. A different approach to adding the colour was the **Handschiegl** system, introduced in 1915, which transferred the dyes via a separate 'matrix' film, acting like a printing plate. For each colour, up to four, a print of the film was used as a source to make the matrix. The areas chosen to receive the colour were painted out with opaque ink and a duplicate negative printed. This was developed in such a way to produce an image made up of differentially hardened gelatin. The blocked out unexposed areas were softer than the rest of the emulsion and able to absorb the dye which was then transferred in register onto the final print. Up to 40 prints could be coloured with the same set of matrices.

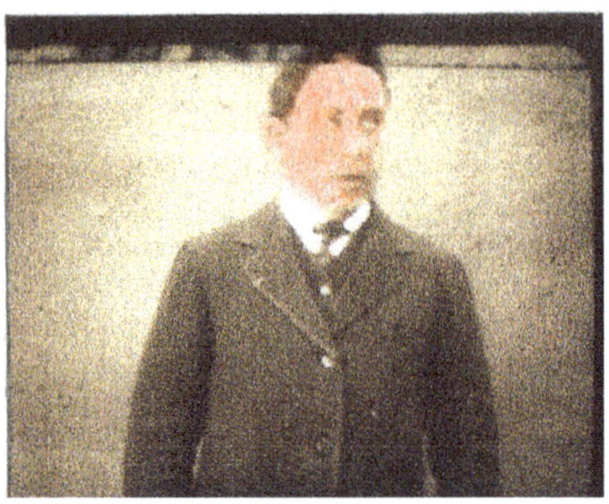

Clip using the Handschiegl process

Pathécolor remained the most successful method and many films were stencil coloured up to the end of the 1920s. A regular user was Pathé themselves, who added colour to many of their dramatic films, together with its Pathé Revue, a supplement to its newsreel. Popular subjects included fashion and travel items and they are available again in colour from the present Pathé News library. Back in the 1920s, Pathé also managed to stencil colour some of their 9.5mm printed films for sale or loan to the home cinema showman.

Stencil colour survived just into the start of the sound era. The British all-star revue, *Elstree Calling* (1930), picture top left, had some of its musical numbers coloured by Gaumont, in an attempt to rival the many Hollywood musicals of the time which included Technicolor sequences.

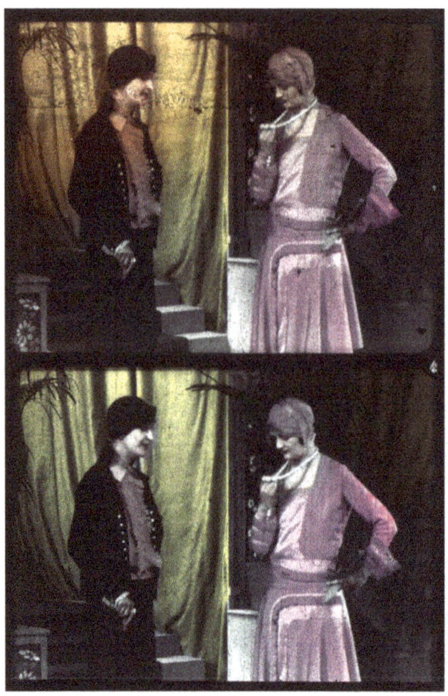

Stencil colour fashion item from a Pathécolor short topical film (1920s)

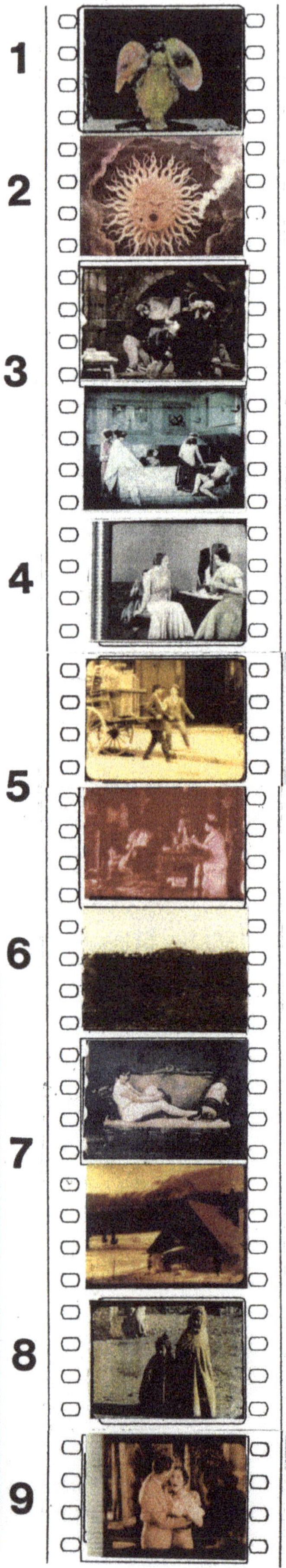

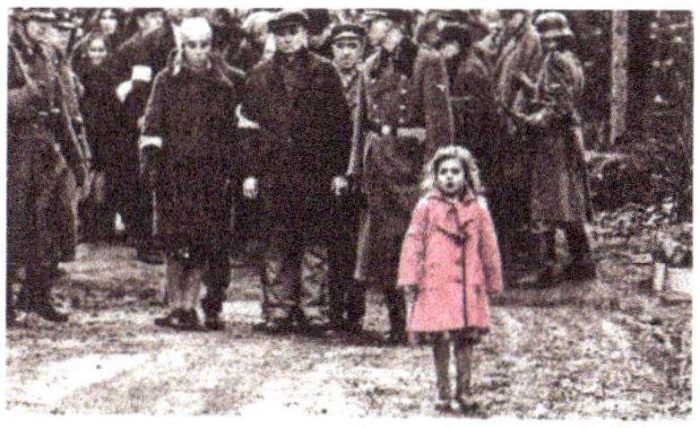

Red coat in 'Schindler's List'.

The practice of colouring local areas of black and white films has been revived from time to time since then, often for its shock effect. Red has proved to be the most popular colour, as in *Jack The Ripper* (1958), used when the villain is crushed under a lift, complete with a spurt of red blood. *The Tingler* (1959), went one better with a whole bath full! Also memorable, was the gun shot flash in Hitchcock's *Spellbound* (1945) and the little girl's red coat in *Schindler's List* (1993). For most of these later films, the effect was usually created on modern colour stock and joined into the black and white print. In the case of the British feature, *Jack The Ripper*, some colour short-ends left over from a previous production were used to give the film its oozing red blood finale. Unfortunately, it was all too gory for the British censor, so only appeared in the American prints. When shown on TV over here, there is no sign of the colour ending. If it still exists, tracing and reinstating it would make an interesting project for a film restoration student.

Tinting and Toning

Hand and mechanically coloured prints cost between two and five times that of the equivalent black and white copies. A simpler and cheaper alternative to put colour up on the screen was tinting and toning, with the colours chosen to match the mood of the subject e.g. blue for night scenes and red for fire. **Tinting** [5] produces an overall uniform veil of colour, similar to placing a coloured filter in front of the projector's lens. **Toning** [6] converts the actual black and white image into a coloured one, retaining its tonal values e.g. clear highlights remain uncoloured. Tinting was achieved by dyeing the final prints, or making them on previously tinted stock. Toning methods include chemical toning, which converts the silver image into a coloured metallic compound, such as iron for blue, or uranium and copper for red.

Tinting (top) and tinting and toning (bottom)

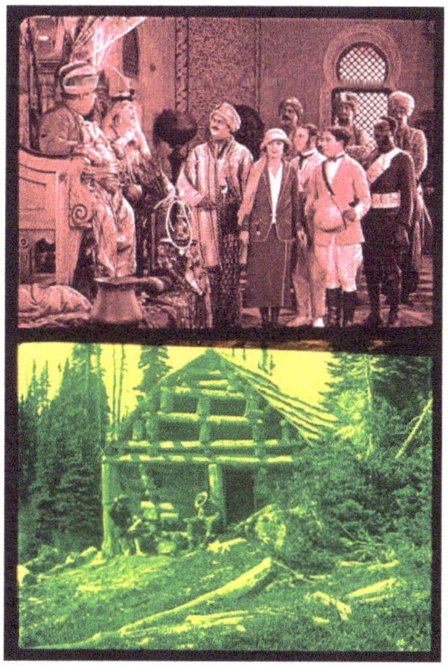

Dye-toning first bleaches the silver image, which will not accept a dye, and converts it to a new form which can then be coloured using any of a wide range of basic dyes. Tinting and toning could be combined, producing a two tone effect, with the overall tinted colour being more apparent in the highlights [7]. A popular combination was a blue toned image, together with a pink tint, ideal for the 'we say farewell to...' sunsets at the end of many travelogues. Other techniques which extended the art, included dissolving back and forth from one colour to another, for example to simulate changing stage lighting during a variety act. The section of the print to be treated was wound around a rack or drum and was only partially immersed in the first bath of dye, before being turned to tint the rest of the film in another colour. Another variation was double-toning, in which the process was started to produce one colour, then interrupted and completed in another. The dominant colour depended on the image density, and when combined with an additional overall tint in a third colour, a skilled lab worker could produce a result to rival stencil colour.

It has been estimated that up to 80% of silent films were either wholly or partly coloured in one way or another. During the heyday of tinting, chemical companies satisfied the high demand from the film industry by supplying special 'cine' dyes with exotic names like *fire-glow, azure, nocturn, peach-glow and inferno.*
The practice rapidly declined after the introduction of sound, as many of the methods which were employed interfered with the optical sound track. Tinting was still

The old tradition of adding artificial colour to black and white films continues with today's 'colourisation'.

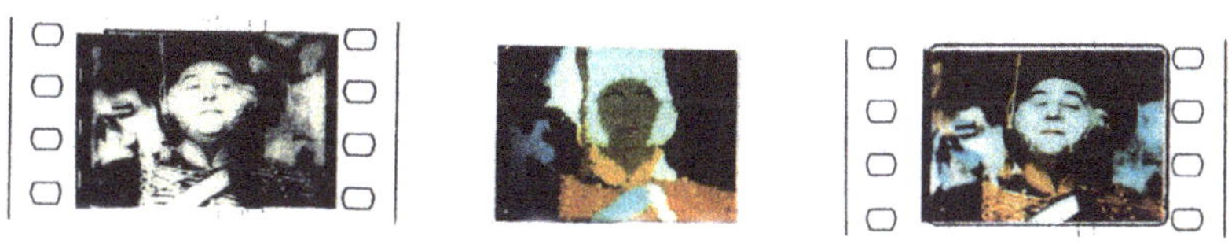

Original B&W version | *Electronically generated colour* | *'Now in Colour' version*

Dye-toning

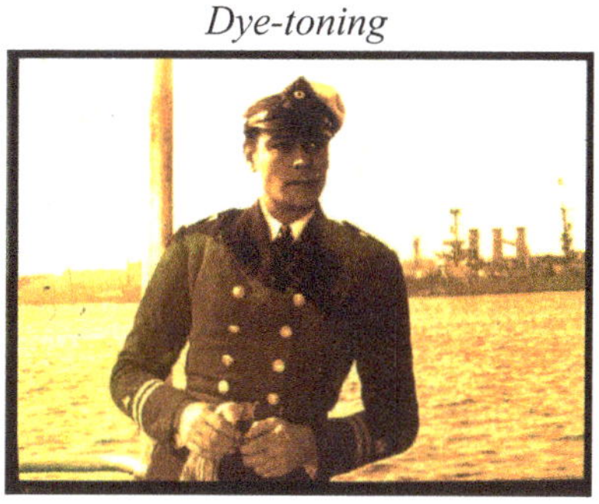

Sonochrome tinted stock for sound films

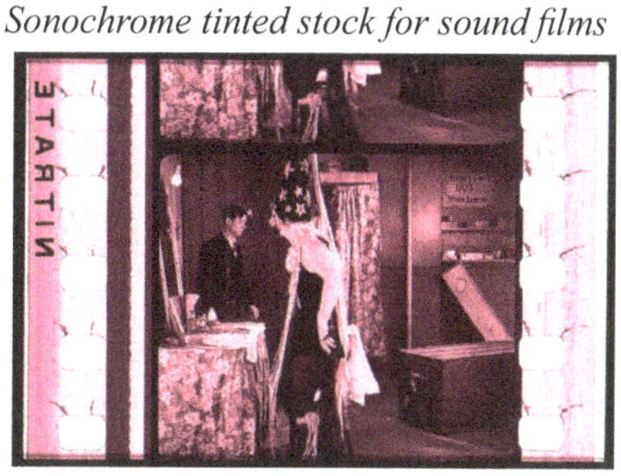

Sepia toned sound film

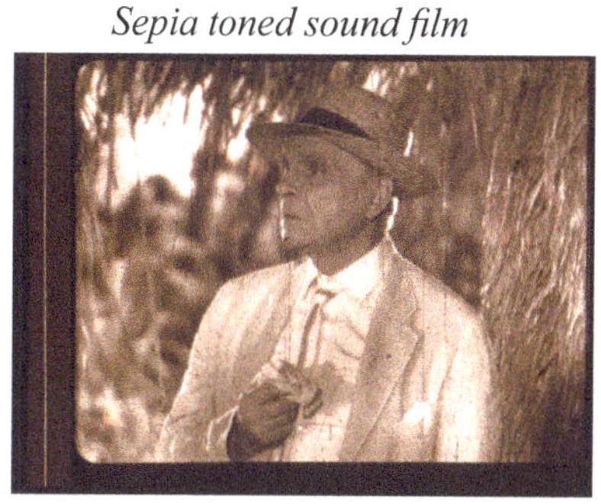

occasionally used for sound films, some printed on special pre-tinted stock, such as **Eastman 'Sonochrome'**, which offered a range of 16 tints, chosen not to upset the sound reproduction. Other solutions included having coloured lacquer coated on the film's base, avoiding the track area [9].

Early systems didn't always survive

By the mld-1930s, Sonochrome and most other pre-tinted stock had been discontinued, any remaining supplies used up by printing adverts, announcements and trailers, in usually arbitrarily chosen colours. The fact that a trailer was tinted didn't mean that the actual feature was too. Those that were had fewer changes of colour, or were tinted the same colour throughout, which could be done in a continuous processing machine. Among the few examples of its continued use were the sepia toned or amber tinted B-westerns from the 1930s and 1940s. MGM's exclusive **'Sepia Platinum'** process was used to tone the entire *The Good Earth* (1937), and just the opening and closing Kansas sequences in *The Wizard Of Oz* (1939) with, in the original prints, the transitional frames hand-coloured to smooth the change to the wonderful Technicolor land of Oz.

Interesting method of adding colour to the projector.

'Colour your own' with a multi-colour filter attachment in front of the projection lens

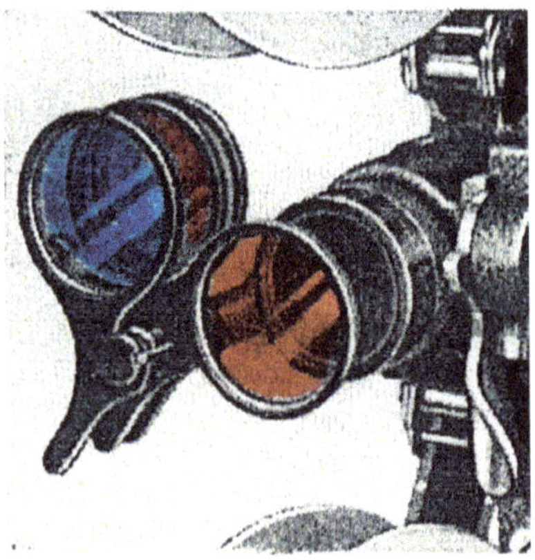

Colour via the projector

For those who liked to see their films tinted, it could still be done at the time of projection. Multi-colour filter wheels and holders were available for both amateur and professional projectors for use in front of the lens. As late as 1961, yellow filters were provided along with the black and white prints of *The Day The Earth Caught Fire* to tint the opening and closing 'it ain't half hot' scenes.

Not natural

Of course, all the efforts to add colour to films described so far only produced 'artificial' colour, and although the art lives on in the form of today's electronic colourisation, the ultimate goal was to perfect a 'natural' colour process, which could record and reproduce the actual colours of the subject. However it was to be a slow and difficult task, with more money spent and lost trying to come up with a workable perfected colour process than in any other technical aspect of film making.

Capturing The Hues of Nature

Colour photography was made possible by the discovery that, like the receptors in the eye, any colour of the spectrum can be created by mixing proportions of only the three primary colours of red, green and blue. **The practical ways of using this principle fall into two categories, additive and subtractive.** The first 'natural' colour processes for motion pictures were additive. If three separate black and white images are taken of the scene through red, green and blue filters and then projected back through the same filters and superimposed in register on the screen, a full colour image is reproduced. No light represents black and equal amounts of red, green and blue produce white and shades of grey.

Lee and Turner

An early example was the Lee and Turner system from 1902. The three 'separation' images were recorded in sequence along the length of the film and shown using a triple lens projector equipped with filters. Although it projected the three frames at once, the film ran at normal speed with each frame shown three times, with the filters changing to the correct colour as each passed behind the three lenses in turn.

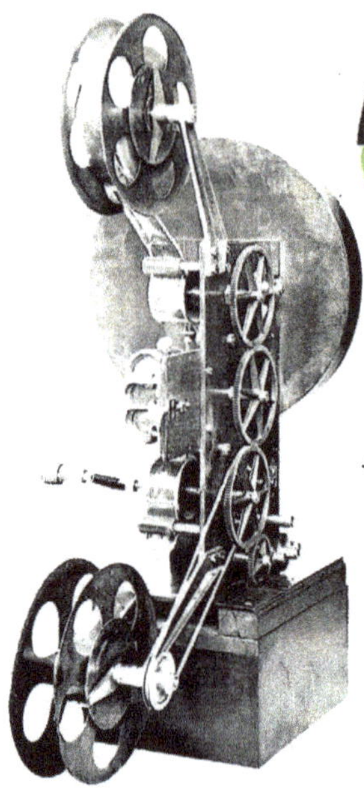

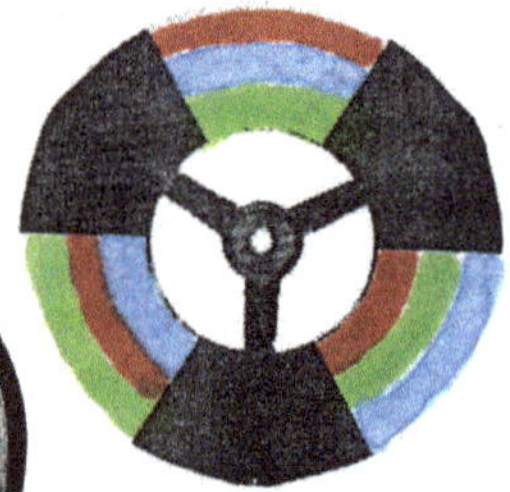

Lee & Turner three-colour additive projector (1902) with three 'sawn-off' lenses for simultaneous projection of its triple black and white filtered images on special 38mm film. The combined shutter and stepped colour filters (above) followed their appropriate frames as they passed in turn behind each of the lenses.

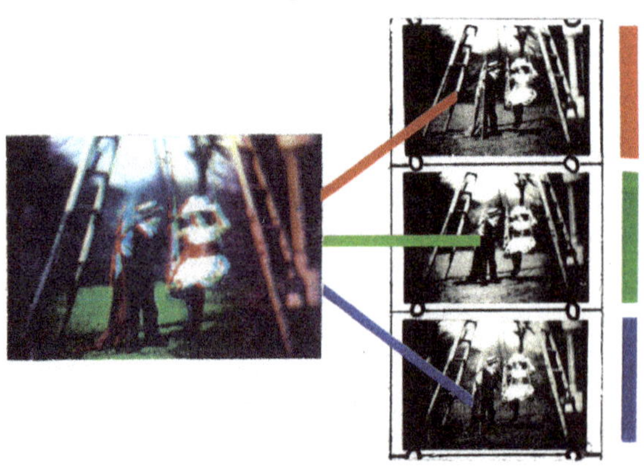

Although unsuccessful, the Lee and Turner process led on to the development of the much simpler and commercially successful Kinemacolor

Chronochrome

The later Gaumont **Chronochrome** process [10] used a similar triple lens projector, but the pull-down distance was increased to advance all three frames at once, which were reduced in height to lessen the strain imposed on the film. Demonstrated in 1912, it was to have only limited showings up to around 1920 with the added attraction of sound coming from a disc on a synchronised phonograph.

There was still difficulty registering the images coming from three separate lenses. One great obstacle for those working on the first colour processes was that cine film stock at the time was only sensitive to blue and a little green light. To make it sensitive equally to all colours, it had first to be bathed in special sensitising dyes before being exposed in the camera. If a green sensitising dye is added, it is 'excited' by green light and the released energy is able to 'expose' the otherwise only blue sensitive emulsion, extending its range to include green (**orthochromatic**). Similarly, if a red sensitising dye is also included, the film becomes '**panchromatic**' and can now record all colours. (A very-simplified explanation of the theory.) At first, it was difficult to achieve a consistent and predictable result. It was not until 1912 that Kodak could supply a ready sensitised panchromatic negative stock. Initially available on an experimental basis for colour processes, it was first used for ordinary black and white films in 1922, becoming universal by 1927.

Two colours - good enough for some

With attempts to produce full three-colour additive systems proving difficult, the task was simplified when it was realised that a limited, but adequate range of colours could be reproduced using only two filters, red and blue/green. This was particularly so, if viewed in a darkened cinema when unable to see the true colours of nature for comparison.

Kinemacolor

The first successful process to exploit this was **Kinemacolor** [11], in which the film was photographed and projected at double the normal speed through alternat-

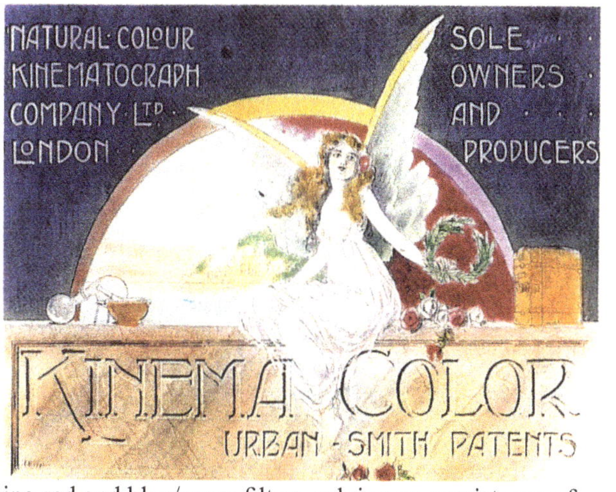

ing red and blue/green filters, relying on persistence of vision to fuse the images together on the screen.

Although the colour reproduction would not impress today's audiences, Kinemacolor was a big hit when first shown in 1910. Most of the films were outdoor non-fiction newsreels and travel subjects, including their greatest success, the 2½-hour coverage of the 1911 Delhi Durbar. This was an ideal subject for Kinemacolor, with lots of brightly coloured pageantry shot under the sun in India. There were a few dramatic productions, such as *The World The Flesh And The Devil*, shown in 1914, followed by the first 'natural' colour versions of *Robin Hood* and *Dr Jekyll And Mr Hyde*.

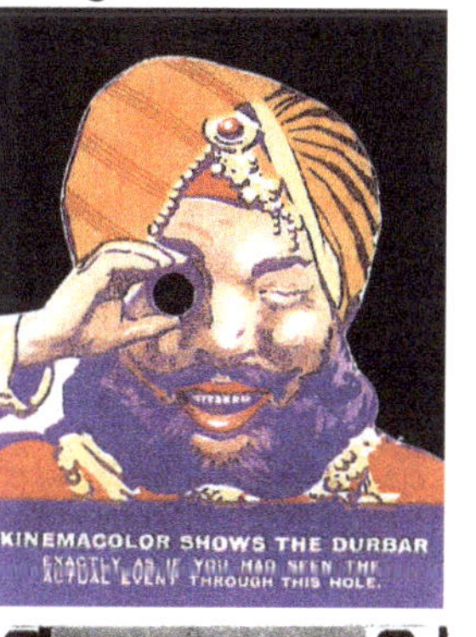

The projection of Kinemacolor at double the usual speed (32 frames per second) was an extra strain on both man and machine. If the film broke, care was needed during the repair to ensure that the colour records remained in sequence. Although credited as a British invention, Kinemacolor was equally successful around the world. To help avoid breakdowns, special heavy duty motor driven projectors had to be hired for the performance. In America, many states had banned the use of electric motors on projectors to prevent the operator from wandering off and not being able to deal with a fire or

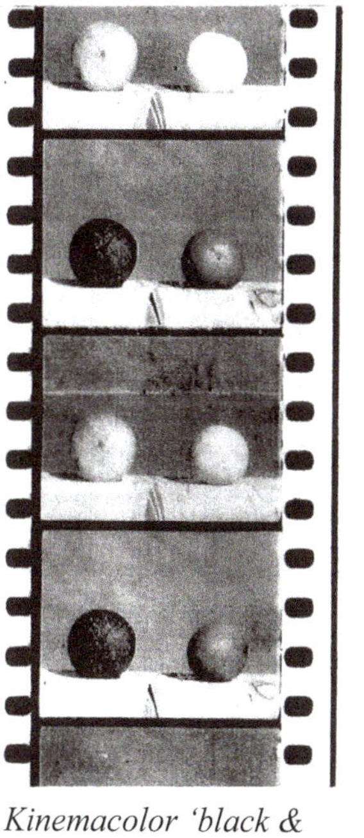

Kinemacolor 'black & white' print showing the subject's colour represented as the different tones recorded as alternate frames along the film

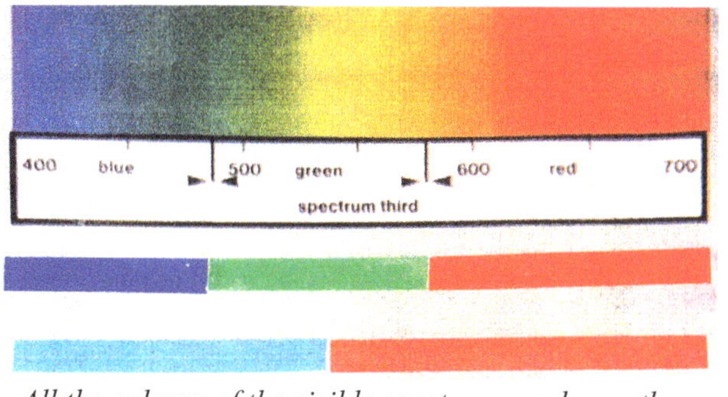

All the colours of the visible spectrum can be synthesised by recording only three regions, using red, green and blue filters. Using only two compromise filters, red-orange and blue-green, an adequate but limited range of colours can be produced

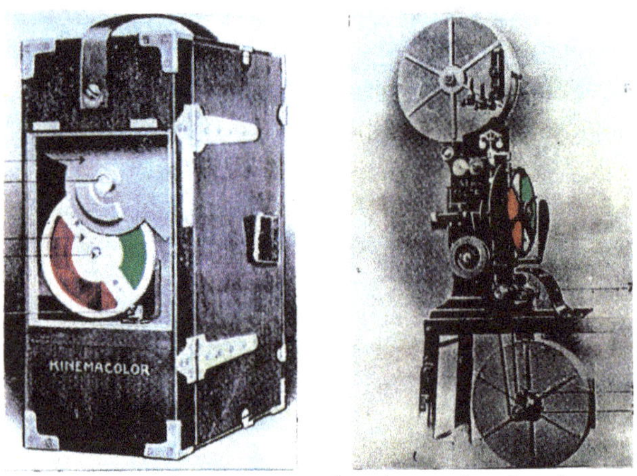

Kinemacolor camera and projector showing the alternating red and green filters

other emergency. For them, a hand turned version was available, specially geared to reduce the fatigue, but even so the projectionist still needed a strong right arm. All this extra trouble and expense for exhibitors, together with the novelty wearing off, led to the closure of the Kincmacolor Company in 1916.

Biocolor

British pioneer William Friese-Green tried to compete with Kinemacolor, using a similar process, but staining the alternate frames on the print the appropriate colour, to eliminate the need for filters on the projector. Unsuccessful when first proposed in 1911, as Biocolor [12] it was later re-launched in the mid-1920s by his son Claude. Some travel films were made in the process and footage showing everyday life in Britain between the two world wars has been restored in colour and seen again in recent TV documentaries.

Colour fringing

Although both Kinemacolor and Biocolor were photographed and projected using a single lens, colour fringing was often noticeable due to the subject moving between exposures. Other systems tried to reduce the effect by cutting the time interval between the taking of the successive red and blue/green records, or photographing them simultaneously using a double lens camera, but fringing was still evident, particularly at closer distances, due to parallax between the two lenses.

For simultaneous images with identical geometry a single-lens beam-splitting optical system was preferred, but was more difficult to construct. Before parting with any money, a prospective investor in early additive colour processes was advised to ask the inventor or promoter to give a demonstration featuring a performer dressed in a rainbow coloured suit juggling red, green and blue balls.

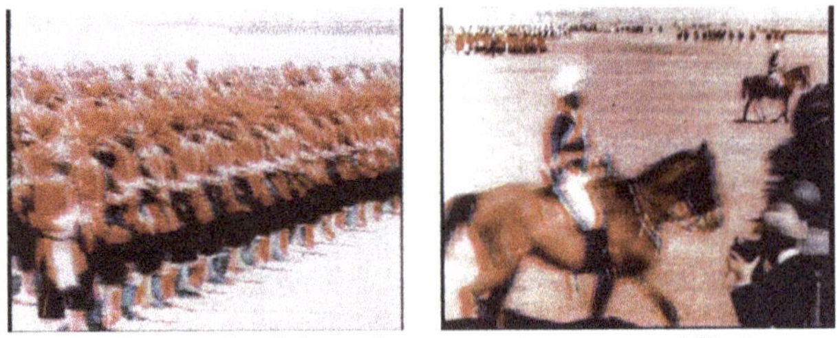

The result of the subject moving too rapidly in front of a Kinemacolor camera

Raycol and Rouxcolor

Additive systems continued to be promoted, most placing the two or three separation black and white images reduced in size within the space of a normal 35mm frame and projected through special multiple lens attachments incorporating filters. Examples, which had some commercial application, include the British **Raycol** (two-colour) system, used for *The School For Scandal* (1930) and the short, *Skipper Of The Osprey* (1933). **Realita** [14] (three-colour) was the British version of the French **Franchita** process. A number of short films were made using it, including a colour record of George VI's Coronation procession in 1937. One of the last attempts to introduce an additive process was another French system, **Rouxcolor**, used for *The Millers Daughter* (1948). All the systems suffered from poorer definition due to the reduced sized images, together with the inevitable colour fringes becoming too apparent.

Lenticular Systems

One solution, without inherent fringing problems, was the lenticular additive process. A vertical or horizontal series of very fine (22 to the millimetre) parallel lenticular lens elements was embossed into the film's base. These (facing the lens), combined with a tri-colour banded filter placed over the camera lens, split the image up into three narrow interlaced strips behind each lenticle representing the red, green and blue components of the picture. After reversal processing, the positive print was projected through a matching filter on the projector's lens, with the lenticles directing each of the image strips back through their correct colour band in the filter, creating a full-colour picture on the screen. The need for reversal processing, and the difficulty in making lenticular copies, made the process more suitable for amateurs, who only needed one print.

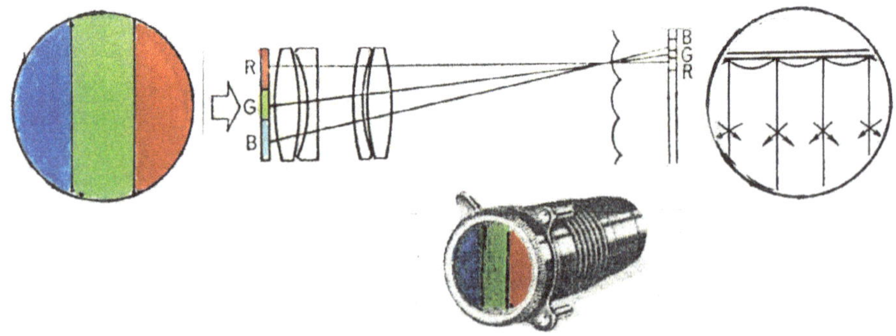

The lenticular process records three B&W filtered images as narrow interlaced stripes, using a combination of a tri-colour banded filter with lenticular lens elements (22 to the mm) embossed on the film's base

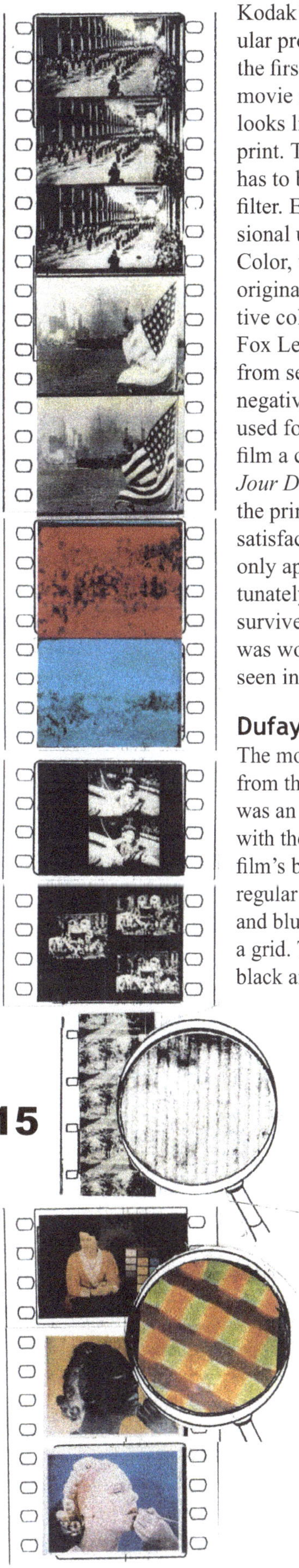

10

11

12

13

14

15

16

17

Kodacolor and Thomson Color

Kodak's Kodacolor [15] 16mm lenticular process was introduced in 1928, the first colour film available for home movie makers. When found today, it looks like an ordinary black and white print. To reveal the hidden colour, it has to be shown through the 'magic' filter. Examples of attempted professional use include the French Thomson Color, which used a lenticular camera original as a source for making subtractive colour prints, and experimental Fox Lenticular release prints made from separation negatives or colour negatives (1952). Thomson Color was used for an unsuccessful attempt to film a colour version of Jacques Tati's *Jour De Fete* in 1948. At the time, the printing method failed to produce satisfactory colour prints, so the film only appeared in black and white. Fortunately, the lenticular camera original survived and, after a means to copy it was worked out, the film can now be seen in colour, over 50 years late.

Dufaycolor

The most successful additive system from the 1930s, was Dufaycolor [16]. It was an integrated colour screen process with the colour filters built into the film's base, which was coated with a regular pattern of microscopic red, green and blue filter elements in the form of a grid. The base faced the lens and the black and white emulsion was exposed through the colour screen (reseau). After reversal processing, the positive image was projected back through the filter elements which, viewed from a distance, blend together in the eye to form the colour picture on the screen. The principle was later exploited in the form of colour TV picture tubes and other types of video displays.

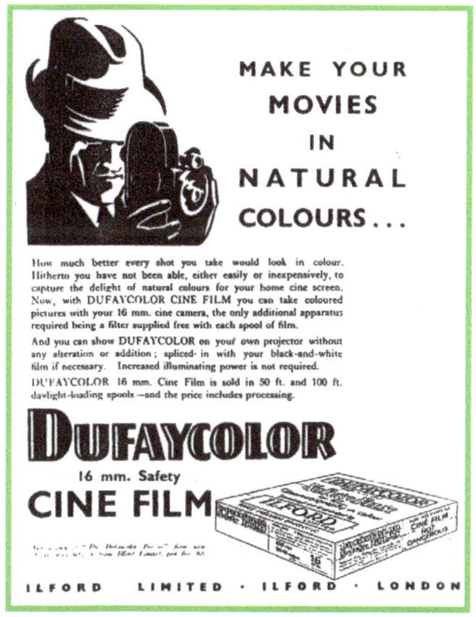

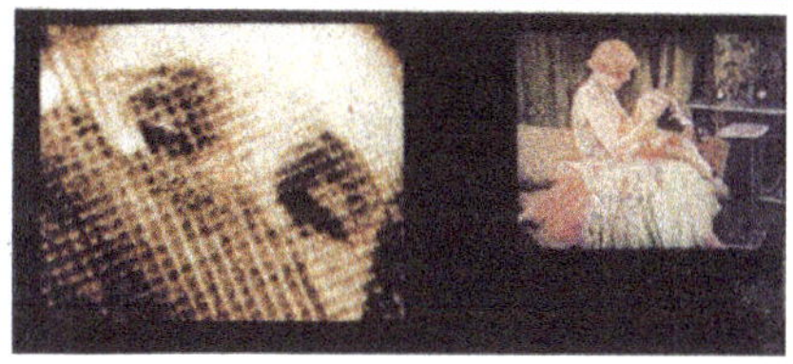

Enlarged portion of a Dufaycolor frame with the minute grid of tri-colour filters on its base removed

At first (1932), Dufaycolor was only a direct to positive reversal process, so again best suited to amateurs, and was available in both 16mm and 9.5mm sizes. However, a 35mm professional version was also introduced, after a way was worked out to make satisfactory reversal prints, without too much loss of saturation, and avoiding interference patterns between the two reseaus. It was used to add colour sequences to the British *Radio Parade of 1935*, and King George V's Silver Jubilee celebration's filmed by Movietone News, who ordered 150 prints for showing in cinemas the next day.

In 1937, Dufaycolor in its 35mm form became the first ever colour negative/positive process [17] and went on to be used for over 80 short films. One of the most successful was the Pathé News

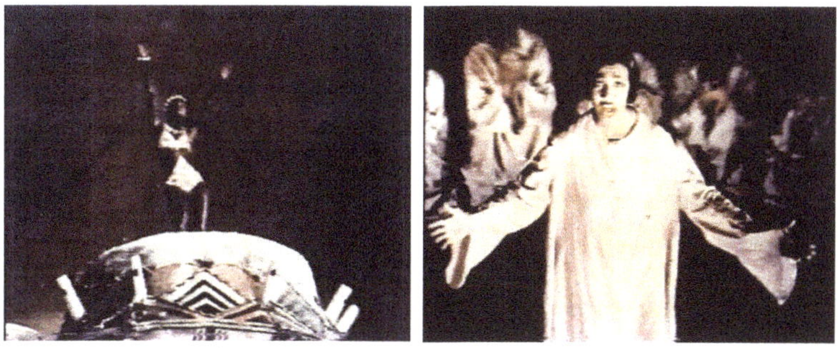

From a Dufaycolor sequence in 'Radio Parade of 1935'

coverage of King George VI's Coronation. Among the last Dufaycolor films was the only full-length feature shot entirely in the process, *Sons of the Sea* [18] (1939).

Both lenticular Kodacolor and Dufaycolor had fixed registration, so were free from fringing problems.

18
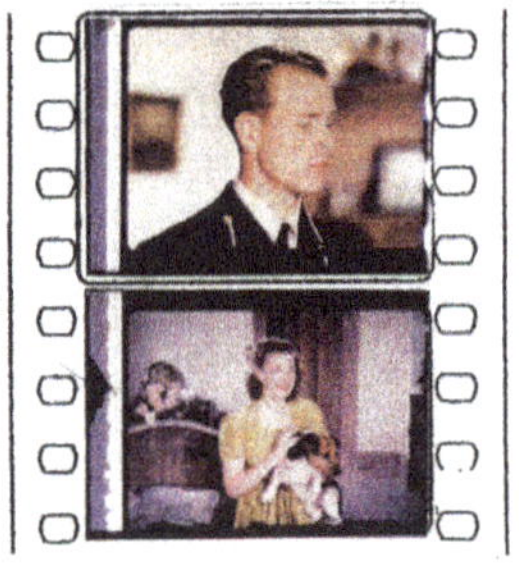

Dufaycolor was a fully integrated additive system, with all the elements of the process built into the film itself, which could be viewed in colour by the naked eye or projected normally like black and white films, although much more light was required to maintain the same screen brightness. Even if the colour picture was not marred by fringes, the greatest disadvantage remained that of all the early additive processes, being the high absorption factor of the colour filters, with only about a quarter of the total available light ever reaching the screen. Most modern methods employ a combination of low-loss dichroic filters/reflectors to divide the light into its primary colours

Polaroid Instant Movies

The integral colour screen principle returned in the 1970s as the basis of Polaroid's instant movies. The loss of light was even greater as the final positive Super-8 image also included the remains of a weak negative. The film was so dense it stayed in its cassette and could only be viewed using a small-screen back projection unit equipped with a very bright light.

Even the old Kinemacolor idea of sequential black and white colour records shown through changing filters never died. It reappeared as part of the first proposed colour television systems.

Subtractive techniques

It was always appreciated that subtractive colour prints would be the most convenient for exhibitors, but the technology proved to be more daunting. The prints have to have the red, green and blue components of the scene reproduced as three superimposed transparent images

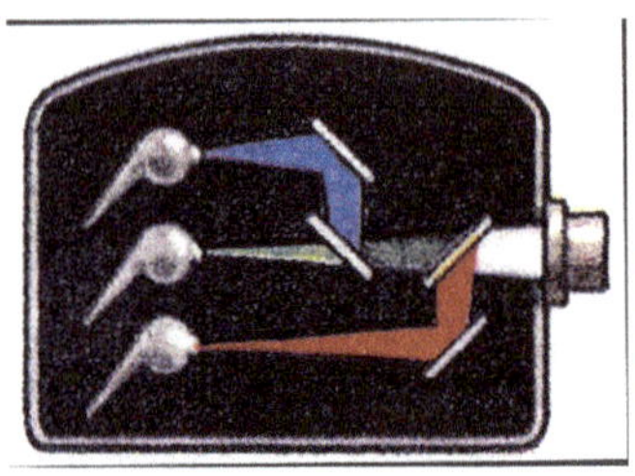

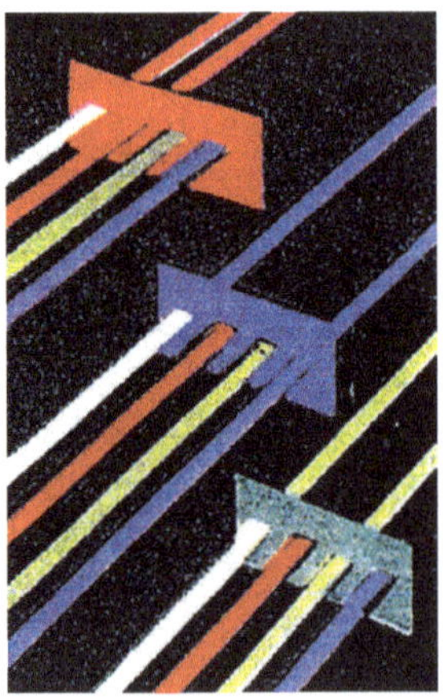

The greatest disadvantage of using traditional tri-colour filters as part of a light-splitting optical system is their high absorption, resulting in severe loss of light.

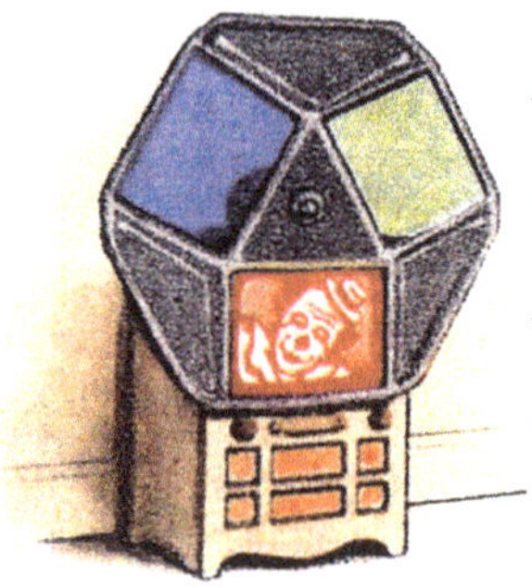

Early proposed sequential frame colour TV system with spinning red green and blue filters in front of a B&W CRT. Best viewed from a safe distance!

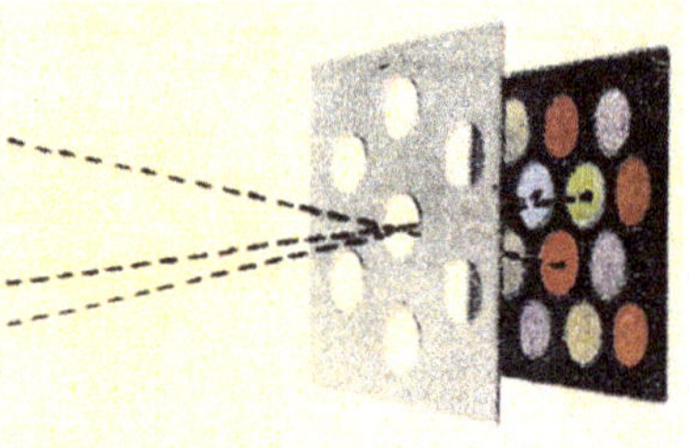

The 'shadow-mask' colour TV became the most popular form of TV display device in the latter part of the 20th century. This uses the same principle as Dufaycolor, with the pattern of dots or lines on the screen blending together to form a full colour image when viewed from a distance.

coloured in their complementary colours of respectively, cyan, magenta and yellow. These act as filters subtracting proportions of the white light passing through them, resulting in a colour image which can be viewed directly by transmitted light, or projected without the need for additional optical attachments, or extra light. On the print, white is represented as clear film, and black by maximum density of all three colours.

To make things easier, the first subtractive processes were also only two-colour, using the compromise colours of red/orange and blue/green. Not all the actual colours could be reproduced accurately, but fortunately flesh tones could be quite pleasing. To help compensate for the shortcomings, the pair of colours could be adjusted to match the subject matter, although they must remain complementary to maintain the proper grey scale.

The pair of separation negatives was obtained using various methods, from a simple Kinemacolor type camera, to more elaborate twin-lens or beam-splitting optics. For cartoons or other static subjects, a normal camera could be used to photograph the filtered images successively along the film. Like negatives from other single-film colour cameras, with adjacent pairs of colour records, the printing was done using a skipping step-printer. Later, the most popular means of providing the two negatives was a bi-pack camera, which ran two black and white films emulsion to emulsion together through the gate. Examples are shown.

The front film nearest the lens (exposed through its base) was orthochromatic and recorded the blue/green image. On its surface was a red filter layer which stopped all but red light passing through to the rear panchromatic film to expose the red negative. To make the final colour prints, the pair of separation negatives were usually printed onto either side of double-coated (duplitized) stock. This had a black and white blue-sensitive emulsion on both sides of the film, with a yellow filter layer

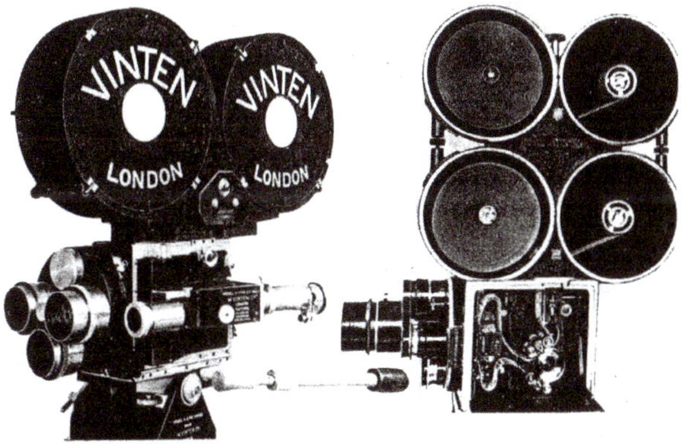

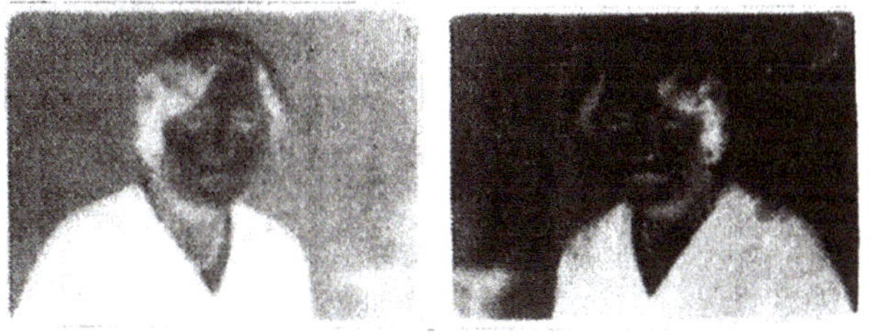

Pair of bi-pack negatives for making two-colour prints. Produced in a normal 35mm film camera adapted to run two films together through the gate, with special magazines to accommodate the two rolls of film, either side by side or under and over

in between to allow each negative to be printed separately without the printer's light passing through the base.

After processing, the two positive black and white images were subtractively coloured using various methods depending on the individual process. The ways chosen to treat each side separately also varied. The film could be run over rollers which picked up the dye and transferred it to one side only. It could also be wound tightly around a rubber-faced drum to prevent the chemicals reaching the rear emulsion. Among the other methods employed was to either float the strands of film on the surface of the solutions, or protecting one side by varnishing before immersion and then removing the varnish for the second treatment.

The first Kodachrome

An early process from 1915 was the first to be called Kodachrome [19]. An adjacent pair of separation red and green filtered images were photographed simultaneously using a twin-lens camera. An intermediate positive print was made, and using a special optical printer, the pair of images was printed at the same time onto opposite sides of double-coated stock. This was then processed in a special developer and bleach, which hardened the emulsion where development had taken place. Each side was then dyed the appropriate red-orange and blue-green, with the 'negative' images turning to a positive as the dyes were absorbed into the softer unexposed areas. Two-colour Kodachrome was only used for short films including one featuring the world of haute couture fashion [20], which could exploit the colour. Later, in 1929, the process was briefly adopted by the Fox studio, who re-named it Fox Nature Colour, and among the few examples was The London Revue of 1930.

Prizma Colour

Another early two-colour process, which achieved commercially acceptable results, was Prizma Colour. Like many others which followed, it coloured each side of the film, using the established methods of toning black and white films. Metallic toning with uranium was available to produce the red-orange side, often also dyed to add brilliance to the image, and iron-toning for the blue-green. The silver images could also be bleached and dye-toned with a basic dye, which gave a greater control over the final colour than metal-toning. Prizma Colour was launched in 1919 with a short travelogue Everywhere With Prizma. It was impressive enough to encourage producers to eventually produce over 100 short subjects in Prizma Colour, together with a number of features including *The Glorious Adventure* in 1922 [21], followed in 1923 by *Vanity Fair* and *The Virgin Queen*. In 1928, Prizma was acquired by Consolidated Labs and returned to the screen later as Magnacolor.

Magnacolor & Multicolor

Magnacolor was used first for the series of shorts, *Unusual Occupations* and *Popular Science*, and then some of Republic's westerns, including the suitably titled *Man From Rainbow Valley*, although not all the colours of the rainbow were present.
Magnacolor films of the 1940s were shot using bi-pack cameras, but this method of obtaining the pair of negatives was first used back in 1928 by another descendant of Prizma Colour, Multicolor [22]. This appeared as sequences in a few early sound films, including The Fox *Movietone Follies Of 1929* and *The Great Gabbo* (1929). It was also used for the cartoon *Goofy Goat*, claimed to be the first colour cartoon, in 1931. Multicolor seemed to have a great future when it was taken over by Howard Hughes, but, despite this, it was little used and sold off in 1932 to Cinecolor Inc. As Cinecolor [23] it was to become the most popular and well known two-colour system.

Cinecolor

After a modest start in the 1930s with shorts and cartoons, including Ub Iwerks Comicolor series, Cinecolor was used for its first feature, *The Gentleman From Arizona*, in 1940. After this, it was used extensively by many Hollywood studios for their lower budget colour

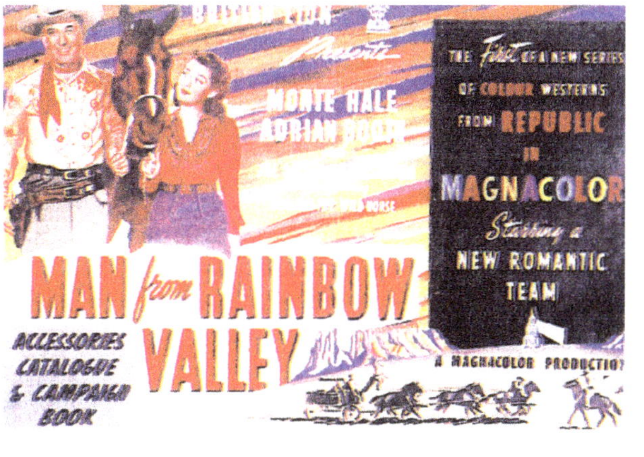

westerns and costume dramas. At its peak, Cinecolor labs were turning out 120 million feet of two-colour prints a year. Cinecolor used a red-orange dye-toned image on one side of the film, and a blue-green iron-toned image, plus the sound track, on the other. This arrangement produced the best possible track, as it had a high density to infra-red light, to which photocells of the time were most sensitive. A pure dye track would have been almost transparent to IR, resulting in low level and distorted sound. If an old colour print is found today with a bright blue sound track it is likely to be in a two-colour process. Having emulsion on both sides of the base is also a good clue. This also made them more vulnerable to damage, so a worn copy may now have brilliant red or blue scratches appearing on the screen.

UK two-colour versions

As well as the American two-colour prints shown in Britain, there were a few home-grown processes available in Britain during the 1930s. They were similar, using double-coated prints carrying various combinations of dye or metal-toned images. There was the choice of **Polychromide** [24], **Brewster Colour** and **Dunningcolor**, the latter used to make Britain's first colour cartoon, Sam and his Musket in 1935.

Also on offer, was **Chemicolor** [25], used for part of *Pagliacci* starring the opera singer Richard Tauber. The process was a version of the German **Ufacolor**, employing Agfa bi-pack negative and duplitised print stock.

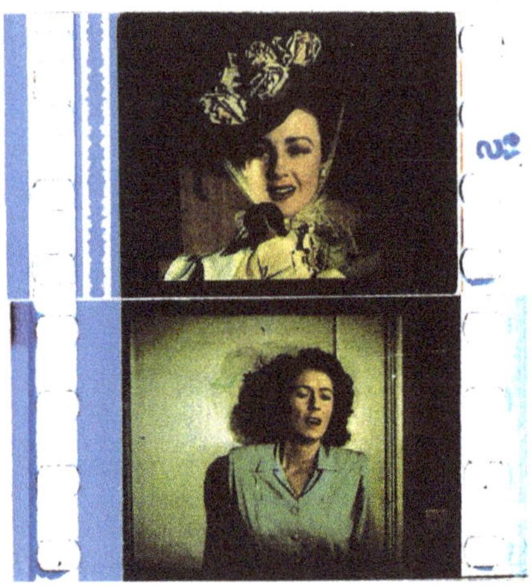

Cinecolor two-colour prints used a blue-green image and sound track on one side of the film's base and a red-orange image on the other

The same process was called **Spectracolor** when it was used to film *Faust* [26] and *Railroad Rhythm*, both in 1936. The prints had dye-only images, so to solve the sound track problem, the original silver track was retained by coating it with a ribbon of varnish to prevent it from being bleached and dyed along with the picture.

Moves to three colours

All this activity in British two-colour during the 1930s has only left us a relatively few colour films, mostly shorts and cartoons, usually sponsored by advertisers. In an attempt to make them more attractive, efforts were made to add the third colour to the basic two-colour prints, but were held back by the lack of three-colour cameras. The third colour record could readily be added to the single-film sequential frame negatives used for cartoons and other 'static' subjects, but live-action remained a problem.

For a three-colour version of Brewster Colour [27], an elaborate 3-strip beam-splitting camera was constructed using a pair of spinning mirror shutters to divide and direct the image coming from the single lens to three separate films. The double-coated prints had a cyan dyed image on one side of the film and a magenta image on the other. The third, yellow image was added to the magenta side as a separate operation using a matrix. Other methods included re-coating one side of the film with a new layer of emulsion, before printing and colouring the third image, or re-sensitising one of the existing already printed and processed sides to receive the third colour, as in **Super Cinecolor** [28].

Gasparcolor

Another printing process, which had some success during the 1930s, was Gasparcolor [29]. It was conceived as a full three-colour system, having the dyes already included in the emulsion layers during manufacture. The print stock had a blue-sensitive magenta-dyed layer

A frame of a three colour version of Super Cinecolor

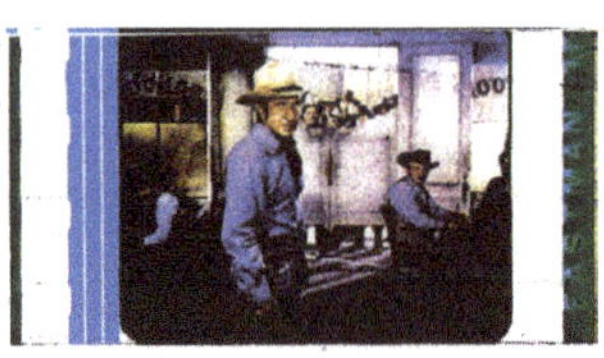

19
20
21
22
23
24
25
26
27
28
29
30

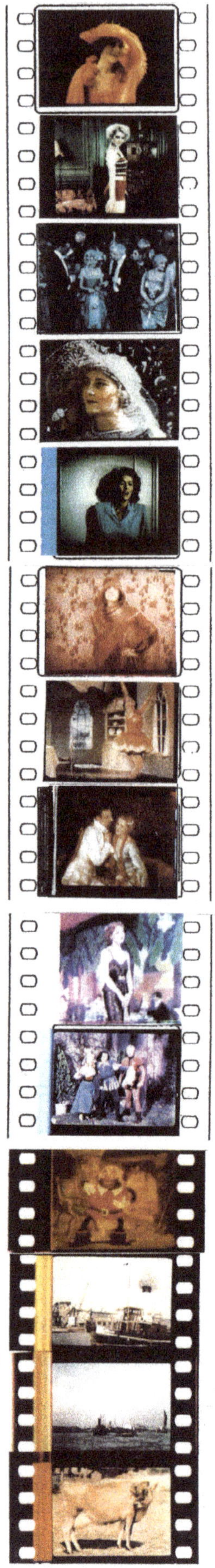

and a red-sensitive yellow-dyed layer coated on one side of the film's base, and a blue-sensitive cyan-dyed layer on the other. It was a direct positive process requiring three separation positives, which were printed on their correct layer using red or blue light. During the processing, the dyes were destroyed in the exposed areas and replaced by the negative silver images, which after being removed, left the remaining dye to form a highly saturated positive colour print. Unfortunately, this dye-destruction principle was not sensitive enough to be used as an original camera film, so most Gasparcolor prints were of animation. These included, Len Lye's *Rainbow Dance* and George Pal's *Puppetoons*. As described in a subsequent section, a few live-action films were photographed using a conventional camera running at three times the normal speed and recording the separations in sequence on a single film, avoiding subjects with rapid movement. An example was the slow-moving river craft in *Colour On The Thames* [30], a Gasparcolor short from the 1930s. No features were released using Gasparcolor, and like the other British systems on offer during the 1930s, it was swept away by the arrival of the all-conquering Technicolor in its two and three colour versions, and a subsequent chapter describes in more detail how the various competitors for the early commercial market for colour films in cinemas fought their various corners with differing degrees of success.

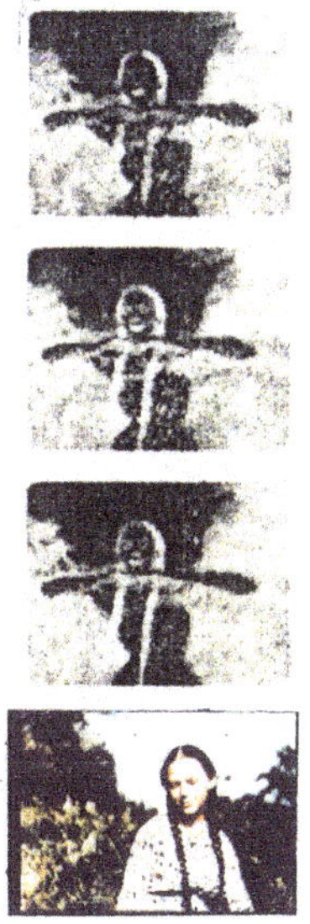

Gasparcolor high-speed sequential frame negative which ran at 72 frames per second

The Triumph of Technicolor

Technicolor began in the USA back in 1916 as a short-lived additive process. A single-lens camera with a beam-splitting prism simultaneously produced an interlaced pair of red and blue-green separation full-size images spaced two frames apart. This arrangement allowed the resulting print to be projected through two separate normal aperture lenses without any restriction to their diameter. Both the camera and the projector still only advanced the film two frames at a time, so no stock was wasted. Only one feature, *The Gulf Between*, was shown using the first additive system in 1917, but registering the images from the widely spaced lenses proved almost impossible, so it was abandoned in favour of a second subtractive process. Again only two-colour, a new camera with a more compact beam-splitting optical system produced a pair of adjacent images with one inverted, placed toe-to-toe along the single film. At first, these were printed as two rows of positive images on specially perforated double-width film which was folded over and glued with the images on the outside. Later, the printing was onto two separate films which were cemented back to back in register.

The silver images now on both sides of the film were first bleached, which also hardened the gelatin where the original exposure and development had taken place. Then relief images were formed by washing away the softer unexposed areas in hot water to leave the various tones reproduced as varying thicknesses of hardened gelatin. These could then be dyed in the appropriate subtractive colours, blue-green from the red negative and red from the blue-green.

The first feature made in the new 'cemented-positive' process was *The Toll of The Sea* in 1922. Other films, wholly or partly in this early Technicolor included *The Ten Commandments* (1923), *Ben Hur* (1924) and, the most successful of all, Douglas Fairbanks' *The Black Pirate* (1926) [31].

Although made using thinner based stock, the cemented prints were still thicker than normal and, like other colour prints with emulsion on both sides, tended to get scratched more easily. They were also prone to buckle during the heat of projection and to going out of focus. To literally iron out the problem, the prints had to be regularly returned to Technicolor to be flattened out before being reused. To put an end to all this aggravation the process was changed in 1928 to a dye-transfer system. The same camera negative was again used to print the two films with their relief images, but now they were kept separate and used like printing blocks to first absorb the appropriate dyes and then transfer them in turn on top of each other in register onto the same side of a third clear gelatin-coated blank film to create the final colour print.

The same pair of transfer films, known as matrices, could be re-dyed and the transfer process repeated to produce multiple copies [32]. With the arrival of sound, the blank receiving film could first be printed with a silver optical sound track giving the same quality as those on normal black and white films [33]. This wasn't needed for the first all-talking, all-singing, all-Technicolor feature *On With The Show*, shown in 1929 with the sound coming from Vitaphone synchronised discs. Its success was the start of a mini-boom for colour with Technicolor being used for many complete films and inserts, mostly musicals.

Although over 60 million feet of release prints were made in 1930, interest in colour, both by producers and audiences, waned due to the added cost and often indifferent colour, resulting from both technical and artistic shortcomings. Even the best examples couldn't overcome the inherent restrictions when using only a two-colour system. The last two Technicolor two-colour features, *Doctor X* (1932) and *The Mystery of The Wax Museum* (1933) were considered to be the best that could be achieved, with the not quite real colour range more suited to horror films.

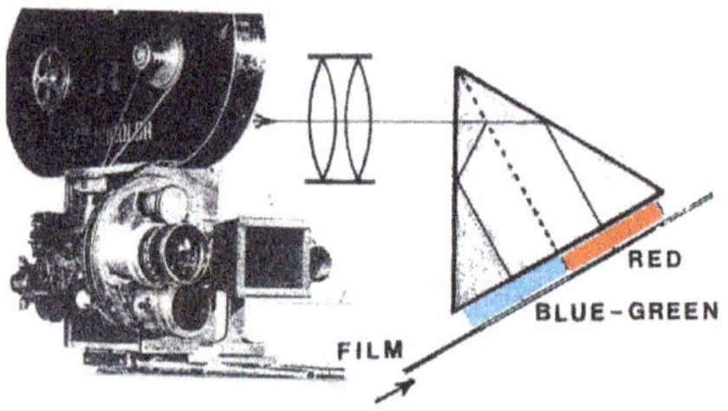

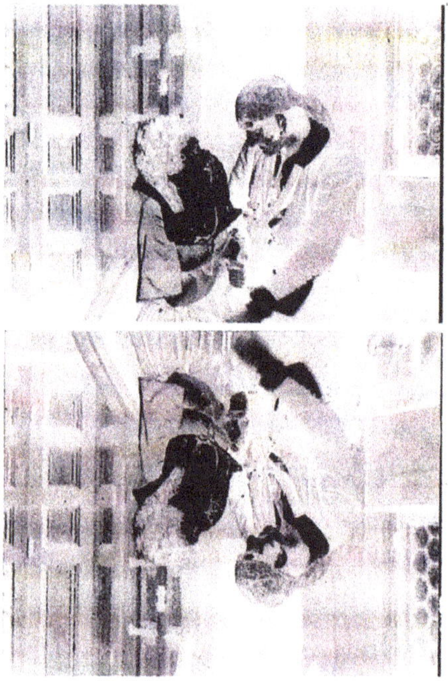

The Technicolor two-colour system showing beam splitting prism and the resulting pair of 'toe to toe' negatives

Three-colour Technicolor

To revive interest, Technicolor finally added the third component to the system and could now provide a true 'full-colour' process. The dye-transfer method of making the prints continued, the conversion to three-colour made possible by the construction in 1932 of the renowned three-strip camera, and this system, which exposed the three black and white separation negatives simultaneously via a beam-splitting prism, is detailed in a subsequent chapter.

One of the first three-strip cameras was given to Walt Disney, together with the exclusive use of the three-colour process in the field of animation for three years. His first colour cartoon Flowers and Trees (1932) was a success, and after mickey Mouse appeared in colour in 1935, all Disney's output turned into Technicolor, beginning a long association with the company.

The three-strip camera was rather cumbersome for animation so was replaced by the successive-frame method in time for the start of production of the first feature-length cartoon Snow White and the Seven Dwarfs (1937).

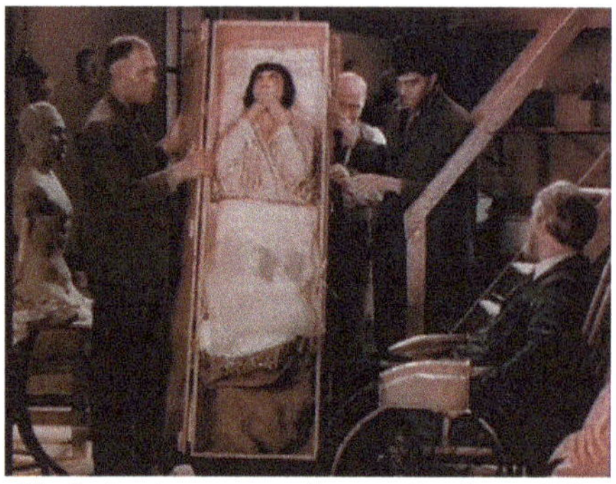

Technicolor two-colour print from 'The Mystery of the Wax Museum' (1933)

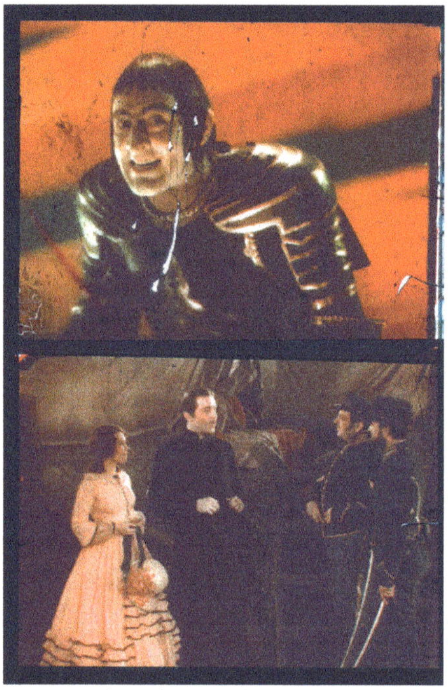

Examples of two-colour Technicolor

The first examples of live action photographed with the three-strip camera appeared as a Technicolor insert in the black and white feature *The House of Rothschild* and the all-colour short *La Cucaracha*, both released in 1934. The continued success of three-colour Technicolor was assured after the first full-length feature *Becky Sharp* was shown in 1935 to great acclaim, both artistically and for its use of colour.

By the end of the 1930s, many of the films which were to become regarded as classic examples of three-strip Technicolor had already reached the screen, including *The Garden Of Allah* (1936), *The Adventures Of Robin Hood* [35] (1938), *The Wizard Of Oz* [36] (1939) and *Gone With The Wind* [37] (1939).

Technicolor set up a lab in Britain

31

32

33

34

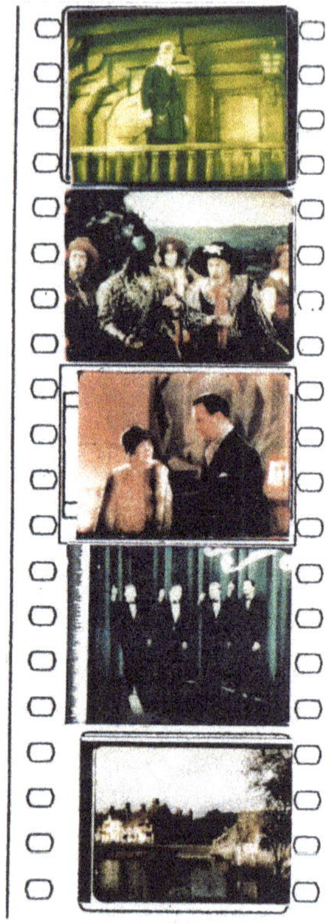

35

36

37

38

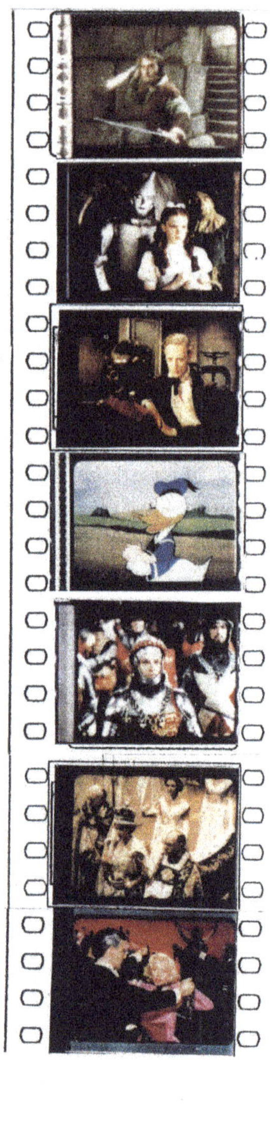

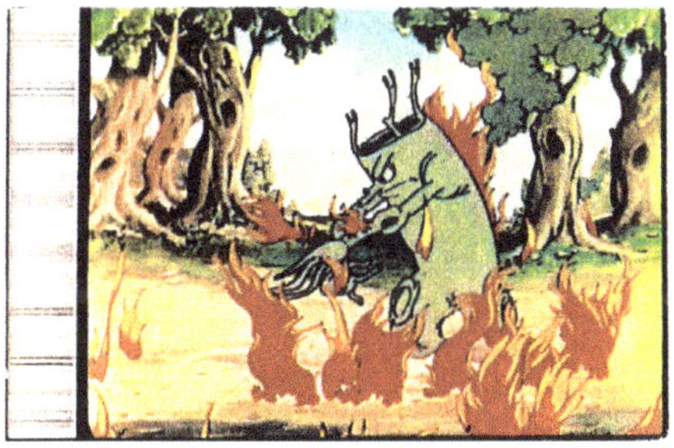

First Technicolor three-strip film 'Disney's 'Flower& Trees' (1932)

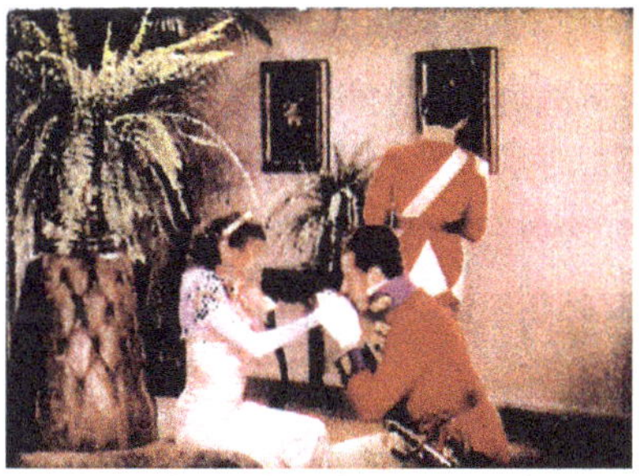

First Technicolor three-strip feature film 'Becky Sharp' (1935)

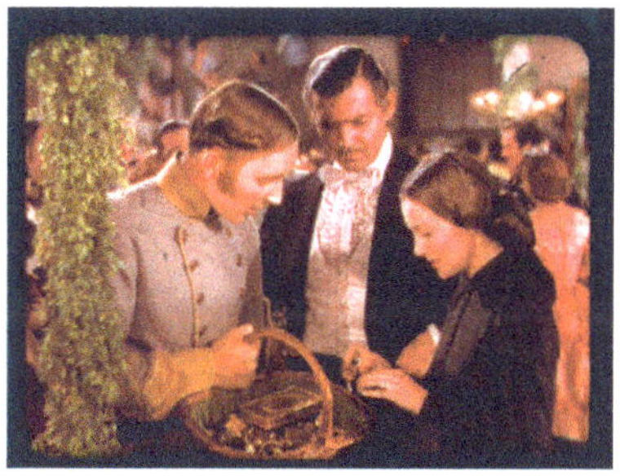

'Gone with the wind' in Technicolor (1939)

which started operations during 1937. This was not in time to service the first British Technicolor feature, the horse racing drama, *Wings Of The Morning* (1937), which had to be processed in America. Over here, Alexander Korda's London Films was an early user giving us the still popular *The Four Feathers* (1939) and *The Thief of Bagdad* (1940).

Two-colour Technichrome - a one-off

The two-colour process continued to be on offer for a couple more years, used mostly by animators having to wait to use the new three-strip version. The last two-colour live-action film was a tale filmed on Bali, *Le Gong: The Dance of the Virgins*, in 1935. As explained in more detail in a subsequent chapter, Technicolor later revived an improved version of its old two-colour system for a special one-off job in 1948. Given the name Technichrome [34], it was devised to help make a Technicolor film of the London Olympic games. There were not enough three-strip cameras available to cover all the various events, so most were shot using two-colour bi-pack cameras, with only the opening and closing ceremonies known to have been filmed in proper three-strip to avoid giving the game away with the inaccurate colour reproduction of the national flags and banners. The completed film, *XIVth OLYMPIAD - The Glory of Sport*, was printed using the normal transfer machines with, for the two-colour footage, both the magenta and yellow matrices made from the same blue/green bi-pack negative.

Reducing costs - and quality?

From the 1930s to the 1950s, the credit 'Colour by Technicolor' became synonymous with colour motion pictures [38]. The only competition came from the surviving two-colour processes like Magnacolor, Trucolor and Cinecolor, which were used for lower budget productions, mostly westerns. If carefully handled, their limited range of colours wasn't noticed by most of the audience, with many thinking the film was also in Technicolor. In fact, to cut the cost, a few original Technicolor features were later re-issued using cheaper Cinecolor prints derived from only the red and green negatives.

Another way to cut the cost of colour was to use it for only part of the film, and the early idea of inserting Technicolor sequences into black and white films was

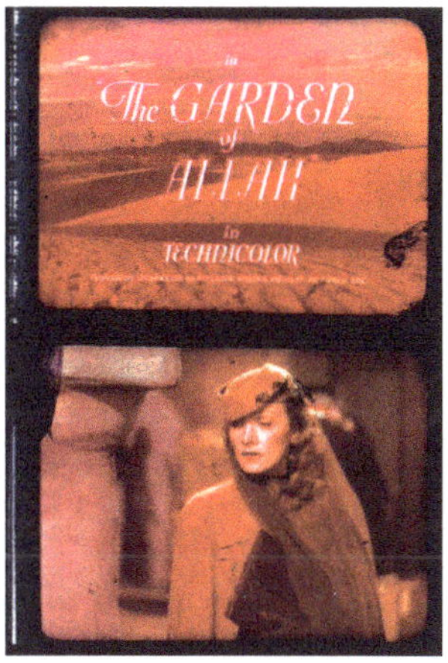

Early Technicolor 3-strip 'The Garden of Allah' (1936)

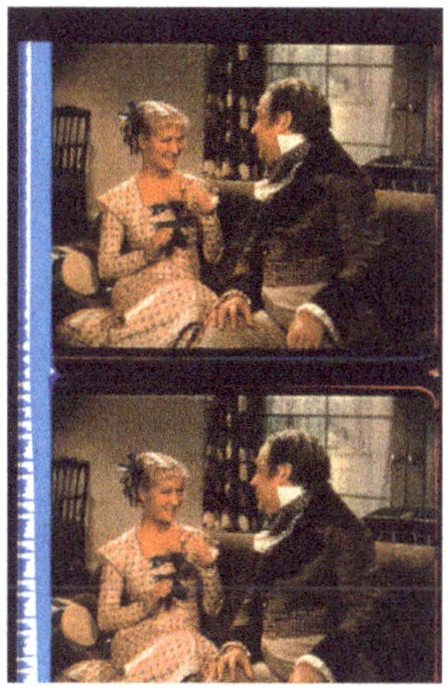

Cinecolor re-issue of 'Becky Sharp' (1944)

again used occasionally to surprise the audience. To ensure their maximum impact, colour inserts in black and white films usually appeared unannounced, but in the case of The Angry Red Planet (1959), the film's trailer hyped 'Cinemagic', which, in the feature itself would give the audience the experience of actually being on Mars. For those tempted to see it, the film was in colour, but the Martian scenes only seemed to be in red-tinted monochrome with a solarisation effect added, producing a surreal cartoon look.

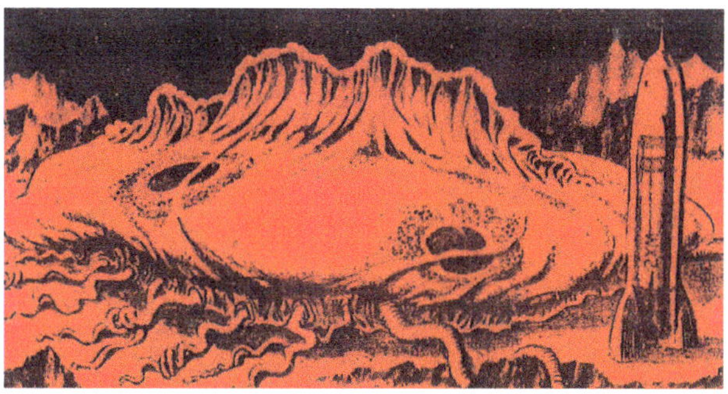

It is interesting to reflect that today, when practically all films are in colour, it is now black and white sequences that are used in order to indicate events which may have happened in 'the old black and white days'.

Colour as a novelty

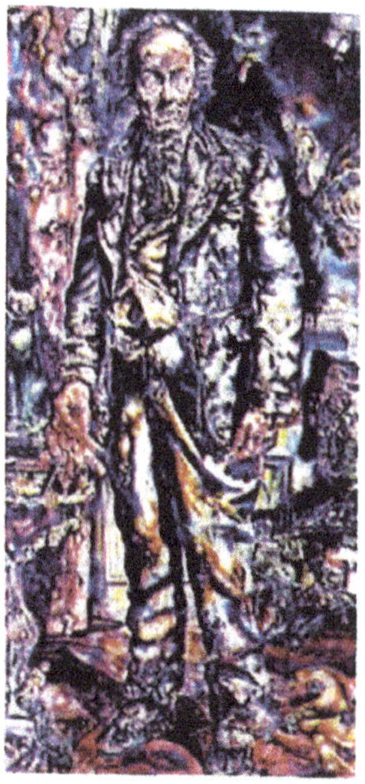

Not a faulty print, but a clip from 'The Picture of Dorian Grey' which appeared as a Technicolor insert in the otherwise B&W feature film

Inserting colour sequences into otherwise black and white films became quite a novelty. A popular excuse was to highlight paintings, such as those included in *The Moon And Sixpence* (1942), *The Private Affairs Of Bel Ami* (1947) and, perhaps the most famous of all, the glimpses of *The Picture Of Dorian Grey* (1945) as it slowly changes to show the horrific results of his dissolute life.

Technicolor finales were another added novelty from *Kid Millions, and The Little Colonel* in the 1930s, followed by others including *Victoria the Great* (1937), *Shine On Harvest moon* (1944), *Solid Gold Cadillac* (1956) and into the 1960s with *Is Paris Burning?* (1966). Sometimes, the sudden burst into Technicolor at the end of the film only made you wish that the whole thing had been in colour. *A Matter Of Life And Death* (1946) alternated from colour to black and white, with the down to earth part of the story in full Technicolor and the heavenly but rather dull afterlife in 'dye-monochrome'. As one of the characters on a visit to the land of the living laments, 'we are starved of Technicolor up there'.

Real Competition

At the beginning of the 1950s, there was a risk that everybody would be starved of Technicolor for good. Its virtual monopoly was at last broken by the appearance of its first serious competitor, Eastman Color. Its introduction was the culmination of all the efforts made to provide professionals with a perfected single-strip negative/positive colour film process, which could be exposed in a normal camera and then processed and printed by any laboratory with no more difficulty than black and white.

In the event, the only casualty at Technicolor was to be its complex 3-strip camera, which was phased out during 1955. Its last outing in the USA was for *Foxfire* (1955) and in Britain at Ealing Studios for *The Ladykillers* (1955) and *The Feminine Touch* (1956).

Some of the cameras were given a new lease of life by being converted to run colour negative in the horizontal 8-perf. Vistavision and Technirama formats. Others kept the beam- splitting optics to make colour travelling mattes.

Although Technicolor was among the first labs to install facilities for processing colour negatives and printing rush prints in Eastman Color, they decided to stick with dye-transfer for their release prints.

'New Improved' versions

At first, three separation positives had to be made from the colour negative which in turn were used to make the equivalent of the original 3-strip camera negatives. Later, the old blue sensitive matrix film was replaced with a new higher definition panchromatic stock to allow the matrices to be made directly in one step from the colour negative by printing through the appropriate red, green or blue filters. The increased sharpness enabled the final dye-transfer prints to successfully compete with the initially higher resolution of Eastman Color print film. This was important as the introduction of the easier to use colour negative had also helped to start the cinema's widescreen revolution with the associated larger screens needing greater magnification of the image. The 'new improved Technicolor' could now be shown on screens over 50 feet wide and could also exploit the benefit of using a larger area camera negative, like VistaVision's 35mm double-frame horizontal 8-perf. format [39]. The resulting optically reduced standard 4-perf. vertical release prints, together with reductions from the various 65mm processes which followed, were some of the finest dye-transfer colour prints ever produced. The richer grain-free images fully justified VistaVision's credit byline, 'Motion Picture High Fidelity'.

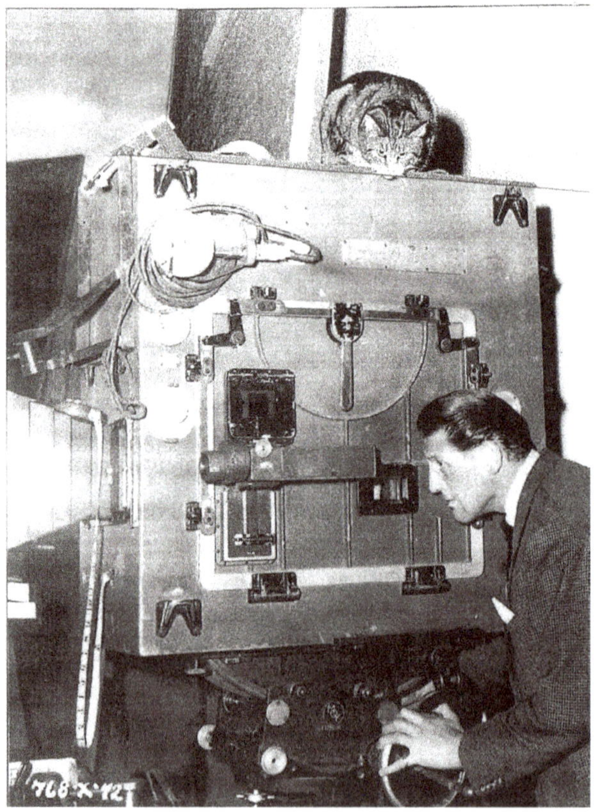

One of the last outings for the Technicolor 3-strip camera in Britain was for 'Touch and Go' (1955). The cat on top of the camera's huge blimp was a member of the cast.

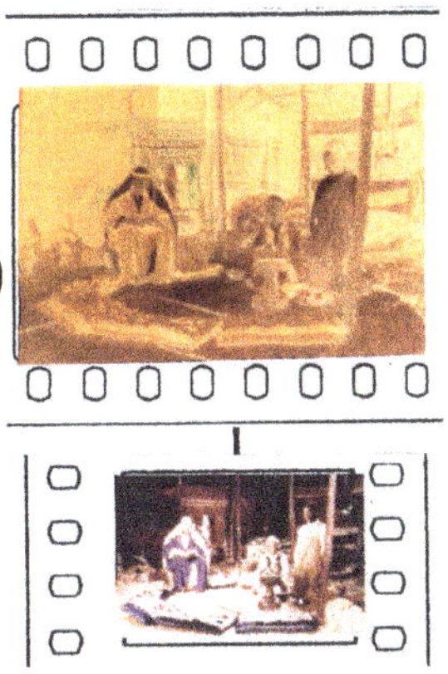

39

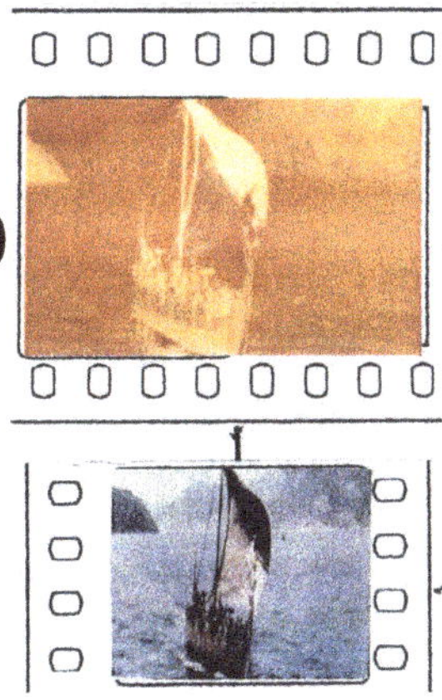

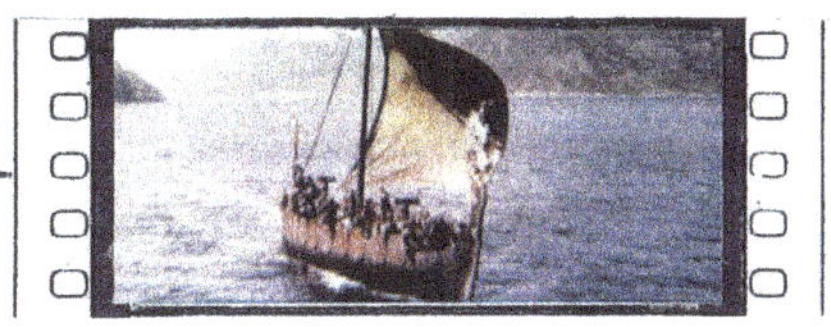

40

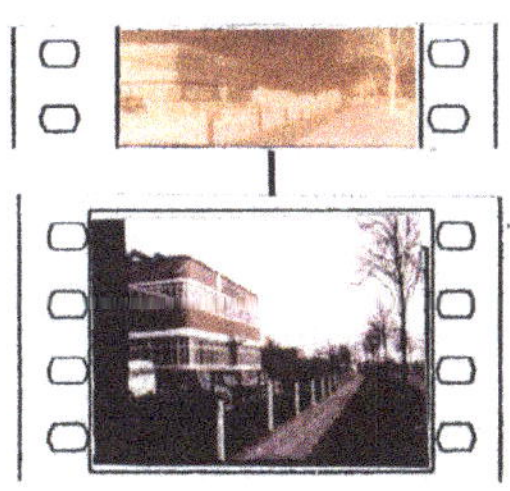

41

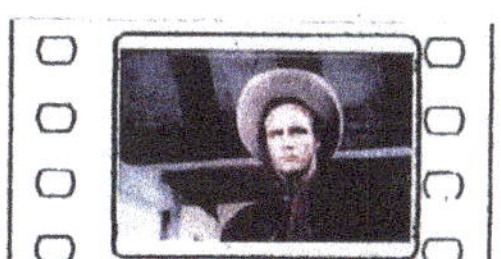

43

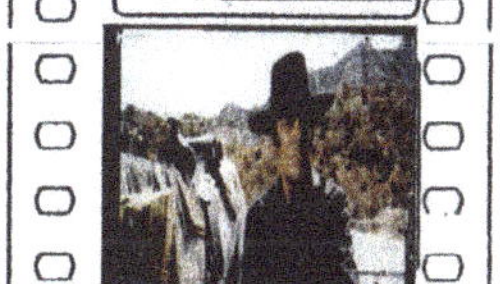

42

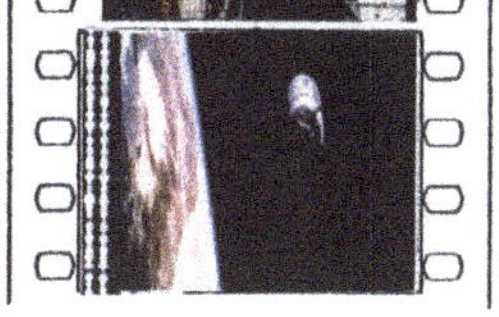

44

Technicolor went on to introduce its own Technirama large-area negative widescreen process, which added an anamorphic lens to the VistaVision format, making it more suitable for providing-higher quality CinemaScope-type prints [40]. Technicolor was to specialise in the optical conversion between all the various widescreen formats, done without any loss of picture quality as the matrices were printed. These had always needed to be optically printed through the film's support, to keep the exposed areas adjacent to the base, rather than at the surface of the emulsion which was dissolved away during the formation of the relief image.

All these developments, together with the increased use of colour during the 1950s, secured the use of dye-transfer prints which were now being ordered in even greater numbers than before the challenge from Eastman Color. Given the choice, many in the industry and colour conscious movie-goers still preferred the more saturated and consistent colours of Technicolor, compared to its often pale imitators, whose prints didn't always look their best, as laboratories new to colour gained experience handling the new colour stocks.

Expansion

Technicolor expanded by opening a new laboratory in Rome and another, albeit short-lived, in Paris. Extra sets of matrices were made and exchanged between Technicolor's plants, ensuring that audiences around the world enjoyed the same high quality images as the domestic prints. The only difference was the addition of subtitles or a foreign language track pre-printed onto the local blank. As an example, *Snow White and The Seven Dwarfs* could be transferred with a choice of 10 alternative soundtracks.

Technicolor In Disguise

During the 3-strip camera era, productions were exclusively serviced by Technicolor keeping control of the process from the original photography through to the final release prints. With the change to the origination on colour negative, there was to be greater co-operation with other laboratories, leading to confused credits.
'Print by Technicolor' was meant to indicate that the negative had been processed by another lab, with the dye-transfer release prints manufactured by Technicolor. However, on occasions, only the other lab or process name was given the whole credit, helping to enhance its reputation with the viewer, who was led to think it was just as good as Technicolor. One of the first features shot on Eastman Color in the USA, Warner Bros, *The Lion And The Horse* (1952), was printed by Technicolor but only carried the studio's own WarnerColor logo on the credits. When Eastman Color arrived at the doors of Technicolor in London, London Films was again first in the queue for their *The Constant Husband* (1954) and *A Kid For Two Farthings* (1954), both being early British productions shot on Eastman Color and serviced by Technicolor providing dye-transfer prints complete with a Technicolor credit. In the years to come, un-credited dye-transfer prints would often come out of the London and Rome plants as a result of accepting contracts to make the British and European copies of Hollywood features printed by rival laboratories on Eastman Color in the USA.
For another 20 years or so, dye-transfer print making co-existed alongside colour print film. Further developments included changing the mixed formula dyes for purer single component versions which were transferred at ever greater speed and precision from more stable polyester matrices. The increased output of sharper prints more than kept pace with improvements made to colour negative and print film. As grain size reduced, so did the advantage of reduction printing. Marlon Brando's *One Eyed Jacks* [43] was the last chance to appreciate the largely underrated VistaVision process. Unfortunately, from its introduction back in 1954, with *White Christmas*, its advantages were never fully understood by the average cinema-goer, who preferred the more obvious attraction of the CinemaScope format.

Farewell Technirama

Technirama bowed out in 1967 after leaving us with beautiful dye-transfer prints of around 50 films, including *El Cid, Spartacus, Zulu,* and finishing with *Custer of the West*. Still on offer was the more economical Techniscope 2-perf 'half-frame' camera negative widescreen system [41]. Introduced in 1963 to encourage film makers on a tighter budget to use Technicolor, the smaller, but wider aspect ratio image, was vertically stretched during the optical printing of the matrices to end up with a standard anamorphic print. In terms of the number of films produced, it was even more successful, with nearly 150 being released well into the 1970s. The admittedly rather grainy image suited the many gritty and dusty 'spaghetti westerns' shot in the process, such as *A Fistful Of Dollars* (1964) and *Once Upon A Time In The West* (1969) [42]. Here in Britain, Michael Caine's *The Ipcress File* (1965) and *Alfie* (1966) helped showcase the system.

Release prints

The bulk of Technicolor's output was always 35mm cinema release prints, but the transfer machines also turned out many millions of feet of 16mm prints together with 8mm, Super-8 and even some 35mm still educational film strips. The only major format not catered for was 70mm, with all the copies having to be made on Eastman Color print film, including those from Technirama negatives (Super Technirama 70). Technicolor could if necessary print other gauges onto ordinary print film, usually for smaller batches which didn't justify the making of matrices. Although in Hollywood a few early colour television programmes made on film, like Disney's *Wonderful World of Color*, used dye transfer prints, it was more usual to distribute them on Eastman Color, often with the contrast and colour saturation reduced to make them more suitable for telecines.

Although continually updated, the photo mechanical 'lithographic' dye transfer process remained as much an art as a science, operated by skilled craftsmen who, for example, judged the colour balance and density by eye as the film passed through the transfer machine, making any corrections by washing off some of the dye from the matrix before it came into contact with the receiving film. Efforts were made to avoid having to print and process the sound track as a separate operation and include it along with the picture transfer, but time ran out for dye transfer with economics finally leading to its demise.

The process was withdrawn in the USA during 1975, after making copies of *The Godfather Part II* and a re-issue of Disney's *Swiss Family Robinson* using previously made matrices. The transfer machines kept going for another two years at the London and Rome plants, with *Star Wars* [44] being one of the last big orders. Francis Ford Coppola, one of the many admirers of dye transfer prints, hoped to have the European copies of his *Apocalypse Now* printed this way at Technicolor's Rome lab, but production delays meant the film missed the closing date. Twenty years later, he had better luck for the film's most recent re-issue, which coincided with a trial re-introduction of the process in Hollywood during the late 1990s. It was among others printed again in dye transfer, including old Technicolor classics like *Gone With The Wind* and *The Wizard Of Oz*, before the experiment was suspended again in 2002.

Part of the language

As explained elsewhere in this book, the process had already been given a second chance when, back in 1978, Technicolor equipment from London was shipped off to China where the large number of prints required continued to make it viable until the mid 1990s. In practice, from 1978, Technicolor had ceased to be a unique individual process, but the name remains familiar to today's audiences, as well as taking its place in cinema history. It will never be forgotten, as Technicolor has become part of the language, found in many dictionaries, quoted not only as a trade name for colour motion pictures, but as a colloquial term to describe anything brightly coloured, not least, *Joseph's Amazing Technicolor Dreamcoat.*

The wonders of modern colour film

Eastman Color, which was to have such an impact in the field of professional colour motion pictures, belongs to the category of so called 'modern' colour film. The basic principles and ways of producing a single multi layer film with the colour chemically created in the film itself as it is being processed (chromogenic development) had been described and even patented long before breakthroughs in coating techniques and film chemistry made it all feasible. Modern colour films are based on the use of integral tri-pack stock with three thin emulsion layers coated one on top of the other on the same side of a single film. Each layer is sensitive to either red, green or blue light. The most common arrangement is to have a blue sensitive emulsion on top. Below this is a yellow filter layer (which is removed during processing) to prevent any blue light reaching the next orthochromatic layer, which now only records the green. The final bottom layer has a blue and red sensitive emulsion, but with no blue present, it is exposed just to the red. Tri-pack film can be used in a normal camera and one short lived idea was, after the exposure, to peel the layers apart and treat them as separation negatives. Only one feature, the 3D *The Stranger Wore A Gun*, gave 'stripping negative' a try, and was released in 1953 as a pair of left and right eye Technicolor dye transfer prints.

Colour couplers

The other important innovation, which made modern colour film possible was the use of 'colour couplers'. First proposed as an alternative means of toning black and white prints, they allow the colour dye images to be created in each of the emulsion layers as they are being developed. Couplers are substances which react with the chemical changes and by-products produced as the silver black and white image is being developed to generate another corresponding dye image along with it. After helping to form the dye, the silver image is removed, leaving only the coloured version made up of pure transparent dye. Different couplers are available to produce dyes complementary in colour to the original sensitivity of the emulsion layers, cyan in the red sensitive layer, magenta in the green, and yellow in the blue. They can either be dissolved in the processing solutions, which requires each layer to be treated separately, or included in the individual emulsion layers, allowing them to be processed together.

Kodachrome again

Kodak revived the name Kodachrome [45] for the first process to adopt these principles. It was a direct to positive colour reversal film introduced in 1935 and used until around 2009. The processing was complex, using the couplers in the solutions method. The film was first processed in a normal black and white developer, producing negative silver images in each layer. At this stage, the film was not fixed, the unexposed and undeveloped emulsion being retained to help form the final positive image. This was fogged with an overall exposure to light and the film processed again with a colour developer containing a cyan forming coupler, resulting in cyan images in all three layers. As this was only required in the bottom red-sensitive layer, the others in the layers above were removed using a slow controlled penetrating bleach. The bleached silver images are capable of being re developed and this was done again, this time in a magenta forming developer. This left magenta images in the upper two layers with the cyan below unaffected. As the magenta image was only needed in the middle green-sensitive layer, the top blue-sensitive layer was bleached and re developed in the third yellow forming developer. Finally, the film was fixed and all the silver images bleached away, leaving only the positive full colour image in pure dye. In 1938, the procedure was changed to a slightly less involved method. Each layer is still treated separately in turn using its own colour developer containing the appropriate coupler, but now turned directly to its correct colour after being individually fogged with coloured light. First red through the base for the red sensitive layer, then blue to the front for the blue-sensitive layer and finally white light to give the remaining and now only un-exposed and un-developed middle green-sensitive layer its second 'reversal' exposure.

Kodachrome, with its bright faithful colours soon became the first choice for amateur film making in colour with the earlier additive Kodacolor and Dufaycolor falling out of favour. Lenticular Kodacolor was withdrawn in 1937, but Dufaycolor refused to give in until the 1950s, particularly for 9.5mm enthusiasts, who had to wait until 1951 for Kodachrome to arrive in their gauge. Like all reversal processes it remained more suitable for amateurs, with the original camera film being processed directly

A micrograph of the edge of a processed Kodachrome film showing the yellow, magenta and cyan layers

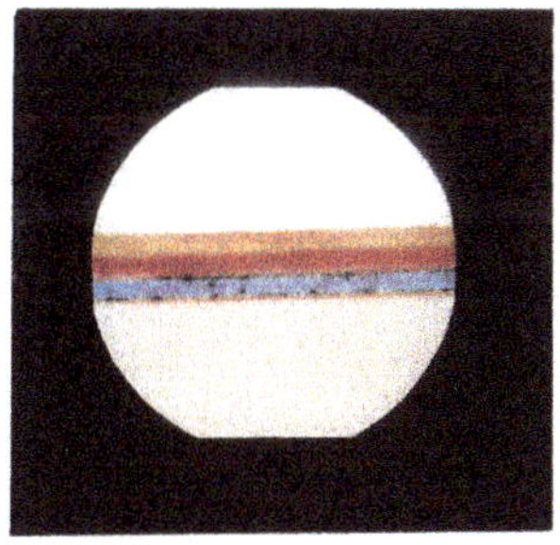

The total thickness of the multiple layers is only 15 microns. (1 micron is a thousandth of a millimetre).

A later type II version, introduced in the early 1960s, reduced the thickness to 9 microns.

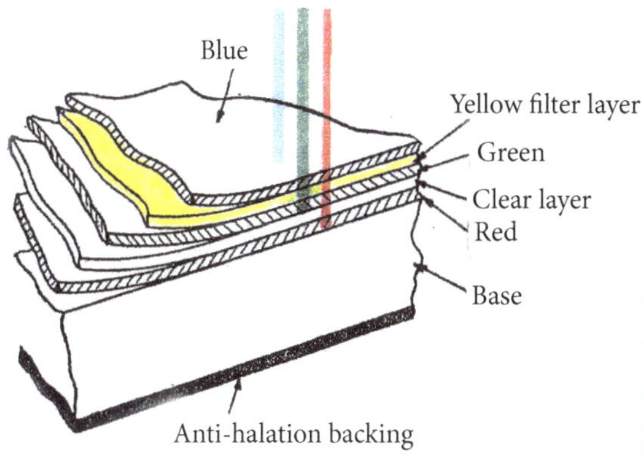

Kodachrome was the first integral tri-pack colour film with three thin layers coated on top of each other on the same side of a single film. Each layer is individually sensitive to either red, green or blue light and their total thickness is little more than that of a single black and white emulsion layer.

to a positive ready for projection. If necessary, copies could be made on reversal colour film, but it was difficult to match the quality of the original. Although initially launched as a home movie film, Kodachrome rapidly gained acceptance for making 16mm non theatrical educational, scientific and industrial colour films. To make it more suitable for professional use, a 'commercial' type was introduced with lower contrast to provide the best possible copies. Many documentaries shot on 16mm Kodachrome were blown-up to 35mm for cinema release, including Disney's True Life Adventure series and Conquest of Everest (1953). These were among the many printed by Technicolor in dye-transfer with the matrices produced from a set of enlarged separation negatives made from the 16mm positive colour original.

Monopack

A 35mm version, known as 'monopack', was also adopted for a while by Technicolor [46]. The quality could never equal the 'taken from life' negatives from their normal 3 strip camera, but it was occasionally used as a more convenient and less bulky source in sometimes difficult situations.

45 47

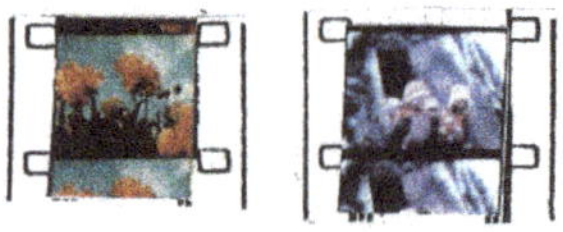

46 48 49

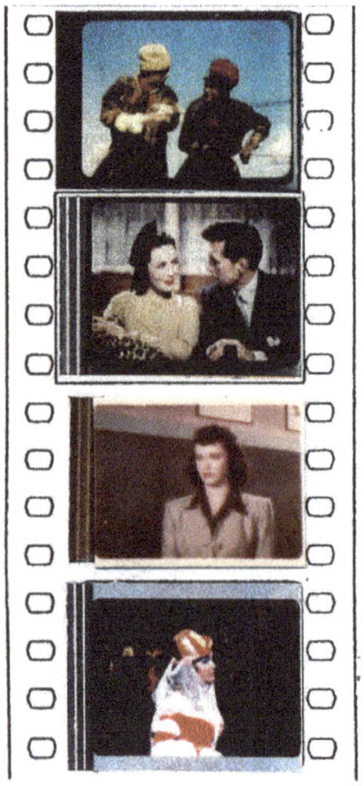

Monopack was first used for location work on *Lassie Come Home* (1943) and the complete *Thunderhead - Son Of Flicka* (1945). The special reversal camera original could only be processed in Hollywood, so the inevitable delays discouraged its use in Britain. In spite of this, monopack sequences appeared in the Technicolor WWII drama documentary *Western Approaches* (1944) when, unlike the cast and crew, the Technicolor 3 strip camera was far too valuable to risk venturing into enemy waters. Monopack film was discontinued by Kodak and Technicolor during 1952 after being used to make a few 3D features, including RKO's *Second Chance*.

Couplers in the layers

The couplers in the layers approach was pioneered by Agfa in Germany, and first introduced as Agfacolor Neu [47] reversal colour film in 1936. (The 'New' designation was to distinguish it from a then still available Agfacolor lenticular additive colour film, which was abandoned soon after.) This arrangement allowed the second colour development of the layers to be achieved simultaneously in a single step. To this end, Agfa split the constituents of the coupler substances up

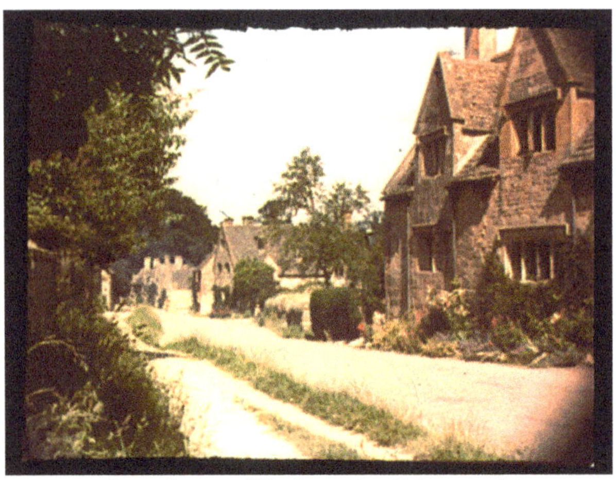

British use of Technicolor 'Monopack' (35mm Kodachrome) - 'English Village (1943)

and dissolved the common parts into a special developer and placed the colour dependent components in their appropriate layers. During the development, this combination produces the insoluble dyes wherever the silver image is being developed in each layer, which after being removed, leaves only the yellow, cyan and magenta dye versions of the images to build up the final colour picture. All this was only made possible after a way was found (using larger molecules than the gelatine emulsion) to make the normally soluble couplers stay put in their respective layers without wandering into the others or being washed out into the solutions during the processing.

Kodachrome, Agfacolor, Ektachrome

In essence, Kodachrome uses a relatively simple multi-layer film in the camera, but requires complex processing by the manufacturer, whereas Agfacolor's film is more complicated, with its incorporated couplers, but the more straightforward processing can be undertaken by any independent laboratory or even the user.
In time, Kodak came up with Ektachrome, its own alternative reversal colour film with the couplers in the layers (kept in place using resin binders) for simpler user-friendly processing. The lower contrast 'Commercial' version replaced the previous equivalent type of Kodachrome as a camera master for professional users. It was to prove popular with TV companies for in-house processing of 'useless if delayed' news items and topical programmes.

Agfa's American associate Ansco introduced their version of Agfacolor in 1938. During World War II, the company was put under guard by the U.S. Government and all its output was used by the military. After the war when the film was again also available to civilians, a 35mm colour reversal system was offered to the cinema industry. It consisted of a lower contrast camera and intermediate duplicating multi-layer stock, and a projection contrast print film. They could be used together or individually. The camera film could be used like monopack for printing using other processes. Some films shot on reversal Ansco Color, like *The Man on the Eiffel Tower* [48] (1948), were also printed by Technicolor in dye transfer. At the end of the 1940s, a couple of coupler-containing print stocks were marketed for printing from black and white separation negatives.

For two colour processes, Kodak could supply a duplitised stock with a cyan coupler in the emulsion on one side of the base, and a mixture of magenta and yellow in the layer on the other. This combination gave the required red-orange and blue-green images which could be produced simultaneously using a single colour development step in conventional processing machines. It was adopted by Consolidated Film Laboratories for Republic Studios' first Trucolor process, printed from bi-pack negatives. It supplemented their much more true to life Technicolor output and was chosen mostly for B-westerns, including the few from the Roy Rogers series which were made in colour. The American DuPont company introduced a full three colour print film in 1949, for making colour copies from black and white separations [49]. The multi-layer stock incorporated couplers in layers made of synthetic polymer instead of gelatine to protect them from diffusion. It was also adopted for Trucolor to expand the process into three colour. As the means of producing the three colour negatives was limited, the first film released on DuPont's colour print film was a cartoon *Beyond Civilisation To Texas* (1949), which was skip printed from a sequential frame negative. The credit line for these three-colour prints was 'Trucolor by Consolidated'.

A Negative Move to More Colour

Like traditional black and white film making, a negative-positive system is preferred when a large number of prints are required. By the end of the 1930s, a negative-positive version of Agfacolor was being used in Germany for feature films. The film exposed in the camera was basically the same as the reversal stock but now processed with only one development step in the colour-forming developer to produce a colour negative, with both the tones and colours reversed. This could then be printed onto similar multi-layer film to produce the positive colour prints.[50].

One early snag was that although the yellow, cyan and magenta dyes generated by the couplers appear satisfactory visually, they do not act as perfect tri-colour filters, absorbing light of other colours. In practice, the yellow dye is fairly good at stopping only blue light, but the magenta, which should only stop green light, has an unwanted yellow component which stops some blue as well. The cyan dye is even worse, as it has unwanted portions of both yellow and magenta. This degrades the purity of the colours, particularly when printing onto other multi layer dye coupling stock.

At the beginning, to keep the build up of errors in the colour reproduction to a minimum, all the prints had to be first-generation copies made from the original negative, despite the risk of damage. As a precaution, more than one original negative was shot, with one left untouched and the others used to make the release prints. Also revived from the early days of the cinema was the practice of creating the fades, dissolves and special effects in the camera. Also, 'chemical' fades could be added to the processed negative by progressively bleaching away the image at the start or end of the chosen scenes, again with extra takes provided in case of mishaps. One of the most famous of Germany's wartime colour features was the fantastic *Adventures of Baron Munchausen* (1943), with its remarkable special effects achieved despite the restrictions of early Agfacolor. After WWII, the technical details of Agfacolor were disclosed to other film manufacturers, who eventually

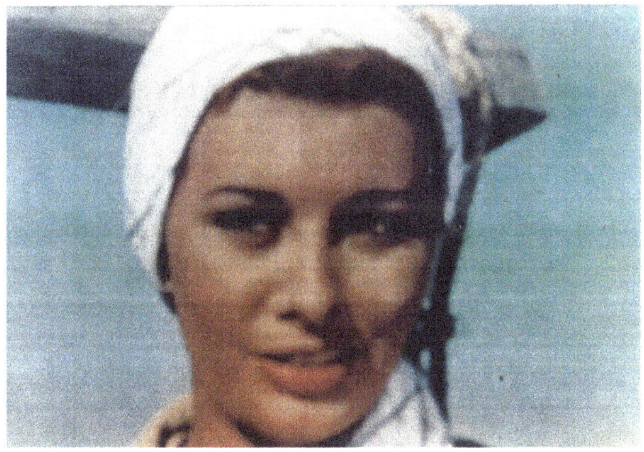

Early appearance of both Sophia Loren and Ferraniacolor, 'Africa Sotto I Mari' (1952) - Africa Under the Seas.

introduced their own versions. The first was Belgian **Gevacolor** in 1947, not widely seen in Britain until it was chosen to film British Movietone News coverage of the Coronation in 1953, although its colour was put in the shade by the competing 3-strip Technicolor *A Queen Is Crowned* from Gaumont British News. From Italy came **Ferraniacolor**, its first feature, *Toto A Colori*, appeared in 1952, as did pre-Hollywood Sophia Loren in *Africa Sotto I Mari* (Africa Under the Seas), followed by Aida in 1953, both shot on early Ferraniacolor negative. Out of Japan, came **Fujicolor**, with its first full length film *Adventure Of Natsuko* judged a successful debut in 1954. In the coming years, Japanese film makers were to gain a high reputation for their artistic use of colour.

Agfa itself had ended the war with its main manufacturing plant at Wolfen, then in the Russian-controlled zone. It continued to produce its colour stocks with a new name **ORWOcolor** (Original Wolfen), which was to become the principal colour process used in Russia and Eastern Europe.

The original Agfa company re organised in the West and Agfacolor was back on the market again in 1949. Prints of Agfacolor and ORWOcolor films from the Soviet Union were sometimes given the tag line **Sovcolor** when shown in the West. Ansco, no longer linked to Agfa, went on to intro-

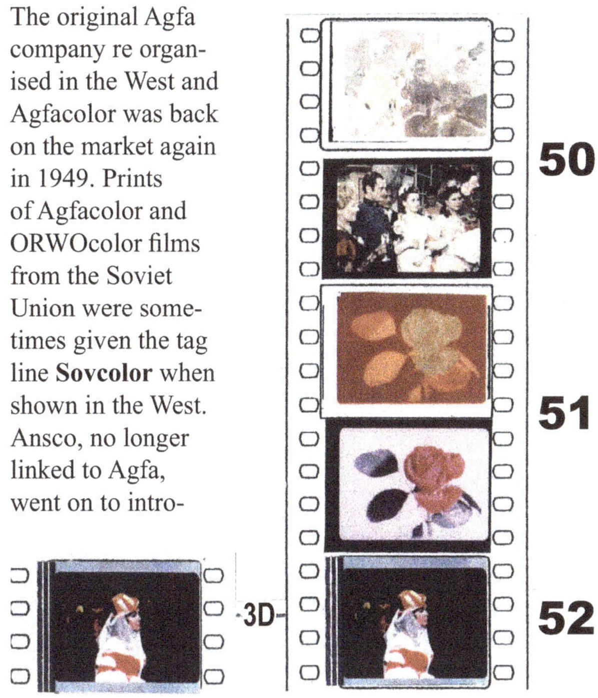

duce its own negative-positive version of **Anscocolor**. An early use was to supplement the Technicolor 3-strip camera for shooting some of the scenes in *Plymouth Adventure* (1952). It was also used for a low budget jungle drama called *Bwana Devil*, which is only remembered today because it was also shot in 'a lion in your lap' 3-D, and was such a box office hit that it sparked off Hollywood's stereoscopic craze of 1952/3.

Making a longer lasting impact behind the screen was Kodak's contribution to the new negative-positive colour processes, Eastman Color [51]. Although having much in common with all the other Agfacolor type films, it included further innovations which allowed the colour negative to match the quality of 3-strip photography.

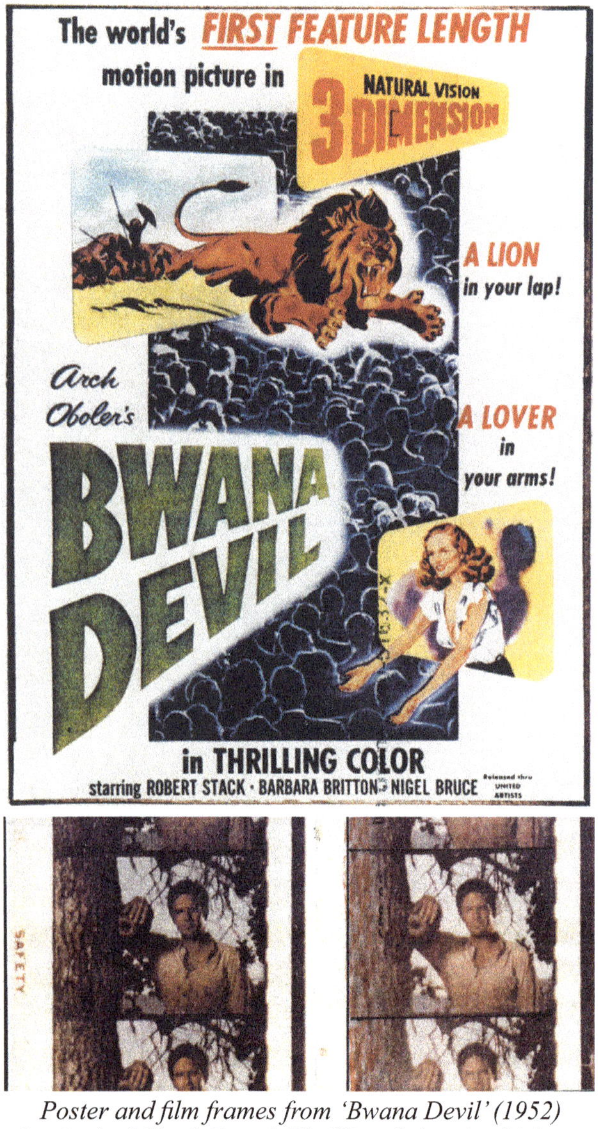

Poster and film frames from 'Bwana Devil' (1952) shot in dual-film 3-D and 'Thrilling Colour', which was in fact Ansco Color with the US domestic prints being struck on DuPont colour print film.

It's Eastman Color that finally catches up with Technicolor.

Eastman Color was still a multi-layer coupler-incorporated film, but Kodak was able to use their smaller resin protected coupler structure, which gave a finer grain looking image than the larger long-chain molecules in the layers of its Agfacolor-type competitors. However, the most important advance was the exclusive integral colour masking system, which automatically corrects the absorption deficiencies of the dyes, to improve the fidelity of the final printed colour.

The coupler substances in the least satisfactory magenta and cyan layers were themselves coloured to match the unwanted absorption of the dyes they produced. In its raw undeveloped state, the magenta forming coupler is yellowish and the cyan, reddish.

They lose their own colour when generating the negative dye image, leaving the unused and still coloured coupler to form a corresponding positive colour correcting mask. The negative image combined with the mask produces an overall uniform density in the unwanted colour which is filtered out during printing.

The satisfactory yellow forming coupler is colourless, so the counterbalancing effect of the other two layers gives the negative its familiar orange-red appearance.

This is of no consequence in a negative, which is only a means to an end, but the print film has to have colourless couplers to enable it to reproduce natural looking colours. The same integral masking system was also included in the intermediate colour duplicating films needed to make duplicate negatives for protection, and to create the opticals and special effects.

Later, by the 1970s, the colour mask became noticeably less orange-looking with the introduction of an additional colour-correcting technique. Dye forming inhibitors are now produced along with the dye images which are able to move between the layers to reduce an amount of dye produced in one colour layer to compensate for the unwanted absorption in another. Known as the inter-image effect, it was also incorporated into colour reversal films to improve the fidelity of the colours.

Kodak's coloured correcting mask was a patented feature, so was denied to other manufacturers. Some of these made limited use of a separately printed, or an internally generated black and white silver positive mask. When combined with the colour negative image, it could not counterbalance the absorption failings of the dyes, but reduced the contrast in some or all of the layers which, when restored during the printing, also increased the colour saturation, which helped to obscure the deficiencies. For maximum sharpness, it was the common practice to re arrange the order of the layers on colour print film. The yellow dye-forming layer was placed next to the base, with the cyan in the middle and the visually most important magenta on the top. In the final image, this contributes 60% of the apparent sharpness, with the cyan 30% and the yellow only 10%.

How it works - Schematic showing the colour and chemical changes which take place during the development of the three basic sensitive layers of Eastman Color and similar colour negative and positive film

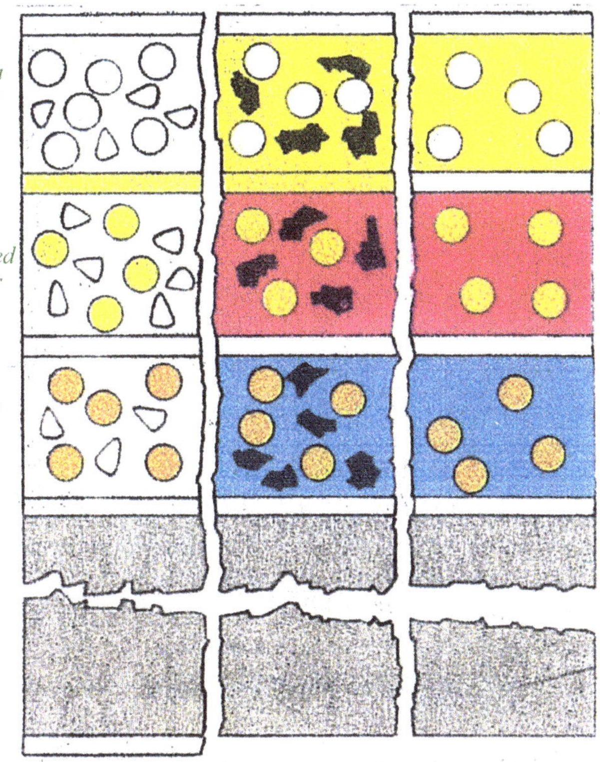

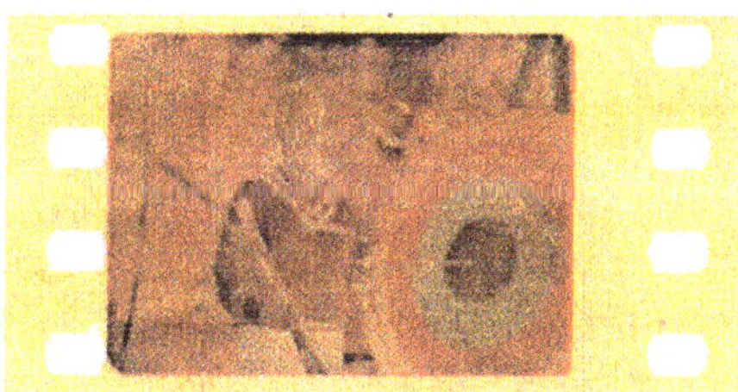

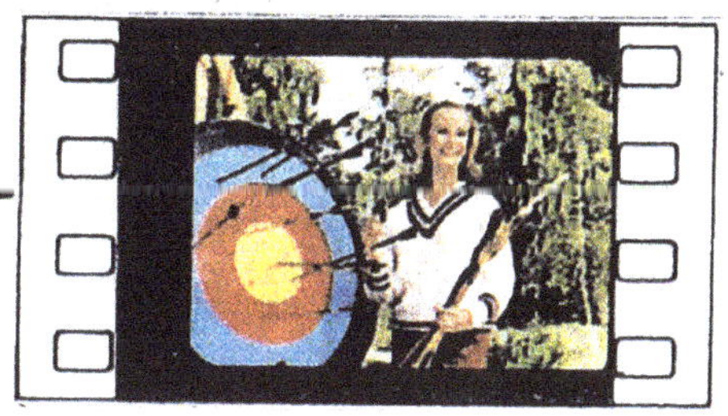

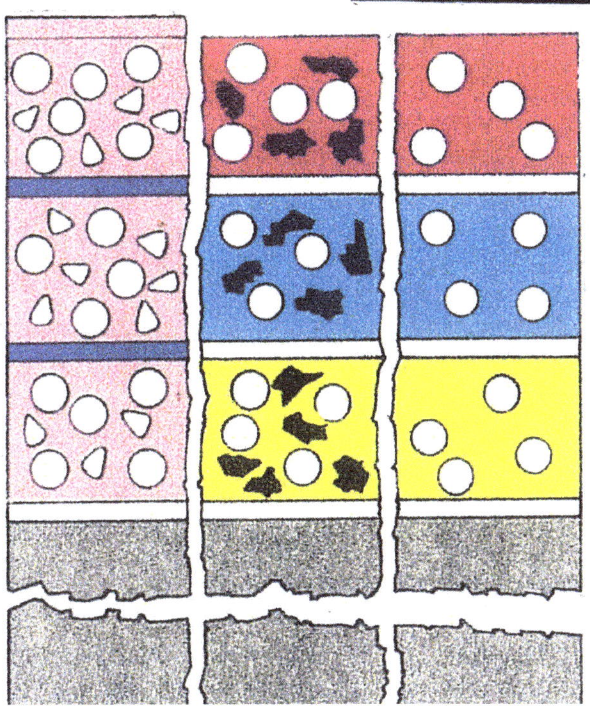

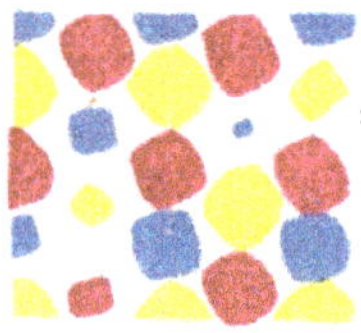

Although the final images are made up of pure dye, they still have a grain structure. This is because the dye is generated in the form of clumps or spots adjacent to and in proportion to the developing silver grains, which, although later removed, still show their effect.

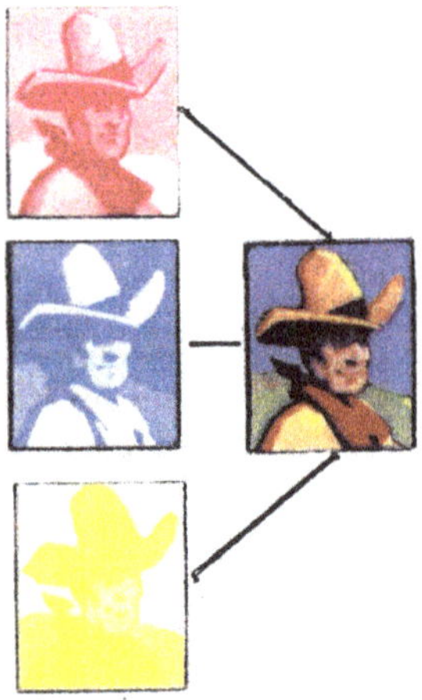

For maximum sharpness, the order of the layers on colour-print film is re-arranged, with the yellow layer next to the base, the cyan in the middle, and the visually most-important magenta on the top. This contributes 60% of the apparent sharpness, with the cyan 30% and the yellow only 10%.

Normal Printing Route from camera negative through to the release print, which helps to protect the original

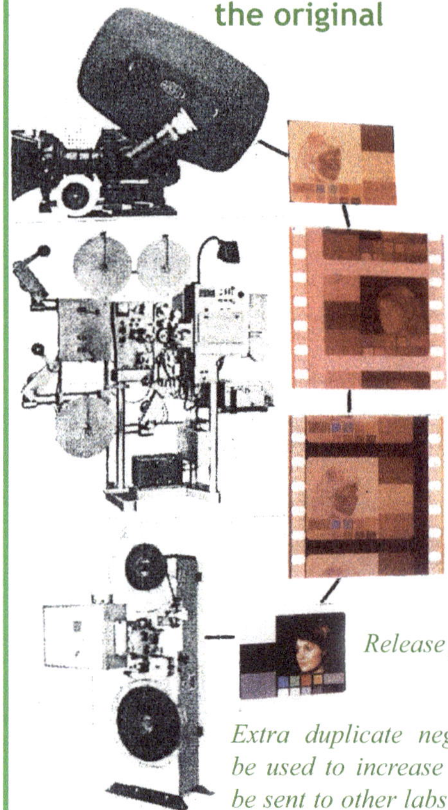

Extra duplicate negatives can be used to increase output and be sent to other labs for making locally produced prints

Although the images in modern colour film are formed in pure dye, they still have a grain structure. This is because the dye is generated in the form of clumps or spots adjacent to and in proportion to the developing silver grains, which, although later removed, still show their effect.

When introduced in 1950 the Eastman Colour system didn't include any colour duplicating film, so at first the negative alone was seized upon as a convenient source for making black and white separations and for release printing using the established processes which already used them as part of their systems. *The Sword of Monte Christo* and *When the Redskins Rode* were released in 1951 using 3-colour Super Cinecolor, together with *Honeychile* and *This is Korea* in the 3-colour version of Trucolor. Eastman Color negative rapidly replaced Technicolor's monopack (35mm Kodachrome) as an alternative to its three-strip camera, and in a few years replaced it altogether.

After about a year, a special multi-layered duplicating colour negative stock became available for making duplicate negatives. These still had to be produced via three separation positives made in turn by printing through tri-colour filters from the original colour negative. These were combined back through the appropriate filters onto the duplicating film, adding any opticals that might be required. For these it was usual to keep the visible loss of quality to a minimum by only duplicating the length of the actual optical effect and then joining it into the original. The cut negative could then be used to produce all the release prints on the companion Eastman Color print stock. A safer route, although sacrificing some of the potential quality, was to make the prints from a full length duplicate negative. Sometimes, the domestic prints were produced from the original negative with a duplicate sent to foreign labs for world wide distribution. One of the first adopters of Eastman Color was Warner Bros for their new WarnerColor process, first used for *Carson City* (1952) and others including their 3-D movies *House Of Wax* (1953) and *Dial M For Murder* (1954). Not all the prints were on Eastman Color. Like other early users, still gearing up to produce large numbers of colour prints, they did the initial negative developing and rush printing, but handed over the cut negative or duplicate to Technicolor to manufacture the release prints in dye transfer without an additional credit. This duo lab co-operation was to remain a common arrangement for many years.

Eastman Colour complete system

Finally in 1953, Eastman Color became a complete all-colour stock single strip process with the introduction of an additional colour intermediate film which could be used as a master positive as well as the duplicate negative. In theory there was no longer any need for the black and white separations, but it was still recommended that they be made of the completed film, with their more stable silver images guarding against the possible future fading of the dyes in the original colour negative. Although not fully appreciated at the time, this threat would lie in wait to cause problems in the years to come.

Own Brands

Now, any studio or laboratory had the means to launch their 'own brand' colour systems. The new Eastman Color and other colour negative/positive films could he handled with little more difficulty than black and white, differing only in the need for printers which could vary the colour of the light to control the colour balance and processing machines with the extra baths required for colour. The once ubiquitous 'Color by Technicolor' was now joined by, not only **WarnerColor**, but by **Color by DeLuxe, Movielab and Metrocolor**. Pathe's laboratory revived the name **Pathécolor** from the old stencil colour days, but later gave its true origin away with a new credit 'Eastman Color by Pathe'. **Trucolor** by Consolidated also abandoned printing on DuPont colour print film, switching to the use of Eastman Color throughout. The barrage of new colour processes included a few which were only inventions of the studios' advertising departments and poster designers. Audiences were to be treated to subject related '**LunaColor**', '**Blushing Color**', '**Monster Color**' and '**TerrorColor**'.

Although its days were numbered, Technicolor's 3-strip camera was still busy around the world until 1955, after which time it was re-deployed or became a valued museum exhibit. The only other serious competition to Eastman Color in the USA was Ansco's new colour negative. It seemed to have a bright future when it was adopted by MGM, being in the camera for films like *Escape From Fort Bravo* (1953), *Kiss Me Kate* (1953) [52] and *Seven Brides For Seven Brothers* (1954).

The prints were mostly made by Technicolor in dye transfer or on Eastman Color print film. MGM also used Eastman Color negative for some of their other colour features, including the British shot *Knights of the Round Table* (1953) and *Bad Day At Black Rock* (1954). After making its last Ansco Color film, *Lust For Life*, in 1956, MGM was to use the Eastman Color system exclusively under the Metrocolor banner. After this, Ansco largely abandoned the theatrical market to concentrate on supplying its traditional best customer, the US Government. Their Anscochrome reversal films were some of the fastest available, and chosen by NASA for the first 16mm space flight films. Kodak could also provide a special version of its Ektachrome stock on a thinner base to save weight and bulk in space craft, with 600 feet of film fitting into a 400 ft magazine.

Before Eastman Color print stock became generally available in sufficient quantities outside Hollywood, the first Eastman Color shot films were printed in Britain and Europe using the more readily available Gevacolor, Agfacolor or Ferraniacolor. The first full length Eastman Color film, *Royal Journey*, a documentary about

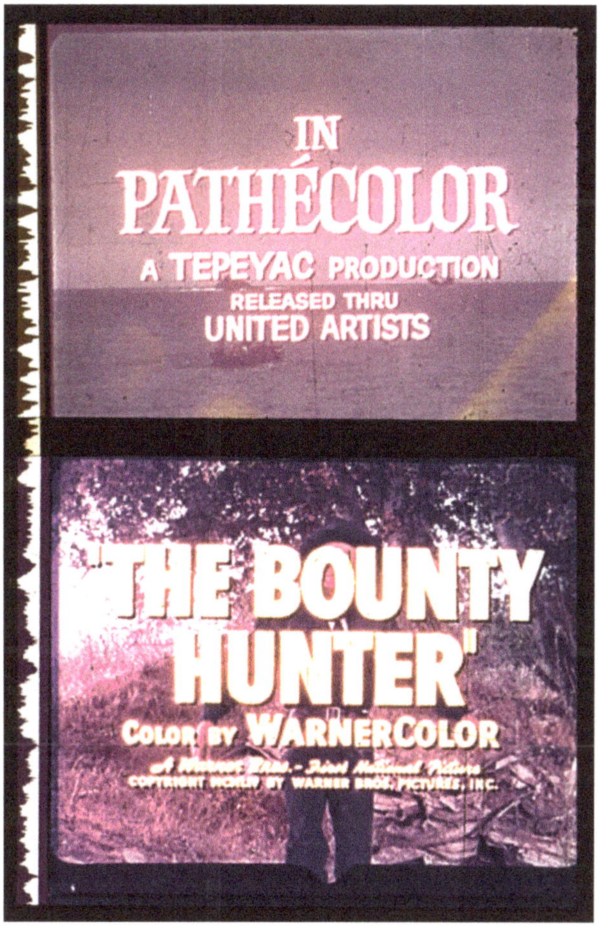

At the beginning of the 1950s the names of many new colour processes began to appear on the credits, almost all of them being re-branded Eastmancolor.

Princess Elizabeth's tour of Canada in 1951, was printed on Gevacolor here in Britain. MGM's first Ansco Color feature, *The Wild North* (1952), was released here with both Gevacolor and Ferraniacolor prints.

Technicolor was contracted to make dye transfer prints in London of the early WarnerColor and Trucolor productions. Cinecolor's British lab at Slough also played its part by making both two colour and three colour copies via separations made from the Eastman Color negatives. The resulting double sided prints included *Jack And The Beanstalk* (1952) [28] in three-colour Super Cinecolor, and *Invaders From Mars* (1953) in only the cheaper two colour version.

Colour becomes universal

At the beginning of the 1950s, movie goers were seeing more colour than ever, with it being used to back up other anti-TV innovations. Of these, the shape of the screen changed to wider formats for good, but 3D soon went flat and stereo sound wasn't generally accepted, by exhibitors at least, until the arrival of Dolby SVA in the mid 1970s. Even filming in black and white made a comeback for many A grade features during the late 1950s and 1960s, before colour became virtually universal by the 1970s.

Print film competitors

Although Kodak's Eastman Color dominated colour filming since the mid 1950s, there was to be more competition in the print film market until the other stock manufacturers could use the same integral colour masking and compatible processing. After being used to produce over 200 features, Ferrania gave up supplying Ferraniacolor camera negative in 1966, but continued making colour print film. They were eventually taken over by the 3M company in America during 1974. Agfa and Gevaert joined forces in 1964, producing masked colour films in 1968, which became fully compatible with Eastman Color in 1974. Agfa Gevaert has since left the field of professional colour motion picture camera films, but Agfa remained a major supplier of colour release print stock for many years.

Kodak and Fuji continued to offer the film industry a full range of colour camera, intermediate and print stocks which were all compatible and interchangeable when printing and processing. The introduction of ever improving films resulted in a dramatic gain in image quality with finer grain, higher resolution and colour fidelity. 16mm film now looks like a typical 35mm production from the 1960s, and 35mm is able to fill the largest cinema screen, without the need for 70mm, which is now only to be found running in Imax and other special venue theatres.

Technical complexity

Modern colour film is very complex. Advances in coating techniques allow up to nineteen separate layers to be applied to the film's base in one go. The original red, green and blue sensitive layers are now sub divided into separate fast and slow emulsions to increase the exposure latitude and colour saturation. Making the individual layers thinner has reduced light scatter and improved the definition. The actual light sensitive grains are now specially shaped and orientated in the emulsion to capture the maximum amount of light for a given grain size.

Perhaps the most welcome advance for those concerned with colour film restoration and preservation was the inclusion, from the 1980s, of improved colour-forming couplers which generate dyes with a greater degree of stability and permanence. This is of enormous importance to those of us who want to understand how the heritage of colour films can best be preserved and restored.

The Cinema Museum - Everything about film

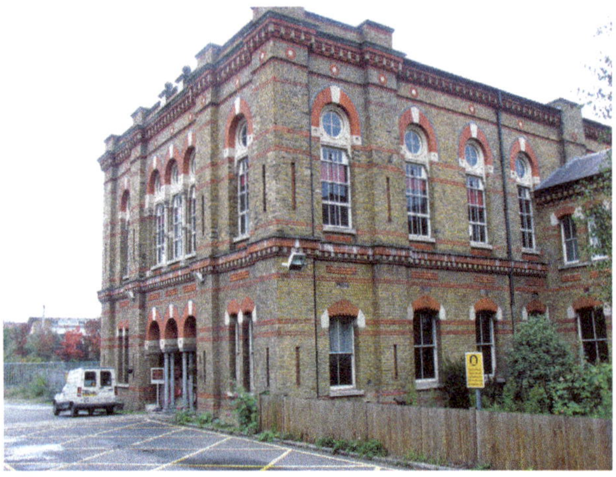

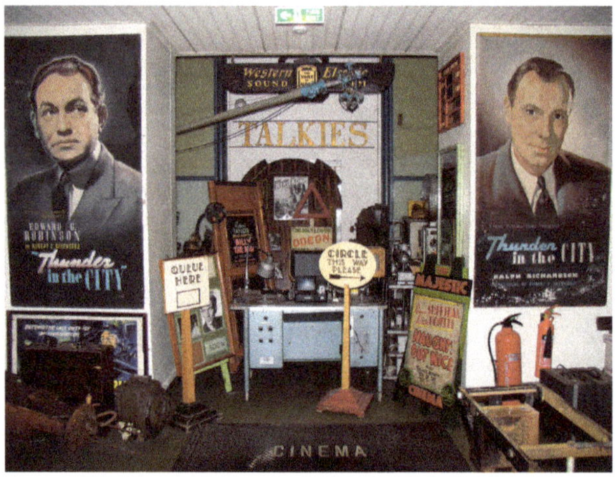

London's Cinema Museum is devoted to keeping alive the spirit of cinema from the days before the multiplex. Set in historic surroundings in Kennington, close to the Elephant & Castle, the Cinema Museum houses a unique collection of artefacts, memorabilia and equipment that preserves the history and grandeur of cinema from the 1890s to the present day. The Cinema Museum is culturally very important to the history of movies and gives insight into how things have changed. It is housed in a building that was the workhouse where Charlie Chaplin went as a child and is a monument of great importance to anyone interested in Cinema.

Also housed in the museum, which really does contain 'everything about cinema', is the Ronald Grant Archive, a library of more than a million photographic stills and slides, all related to aspects of film or cinema. The photo library is a separate business from the Cinema Museum, and its sole purpose is to provide financial support for the museum. The library is well-known for its enormous range, and for the expertise of its workers, who have a deep knowledge and understanding of what their archive contains and can often make suggestions that help radio, TV and film researchers to come up with exactly the images they need for any particular programme.

The museum is open for pre-booked visits and hosts a varied programme of ticketed events for cinema history enthusiasts. For further information contact The Cinema Museum, 2 Dugard Way, London SE11 4TH
Tel.: +44 (0)20 7840 2200 Email: *info@cinemamuseum.org.uk* Website: *http://www.cinemamuseum.org.uk/*

A closer look at some of the early colour film processes

Dufaycolor and Cinecolor were the major contestants, but many others also challenged Technicolor as modern colour films became the norm

Quite a history!

Cinema guru Adrian Hopkinson told an interesting tale that illustrates well the sheer cut-throat competition that there was between different colour systems in the early days of the movie business. In 1936 Alan Gundelfinger, a senior executive with the Cinecolor Corporation, was sent to London to establish the London Cinecolor plant, being put up (as he described it - expense accounts must have been generous in those days!) at the Savoy. One evening at dinner he was approached by a very upright and pompous English gentleman called Adrian Cornwell Kline who described himself as the Managing Director of the Dufay company, which he claimed was about to launch its motion picture product. In so many words he advised Alan not to try to set up Cinecolor in London because his Dufay product was going to be much superior, so why did he not go back to Hollywood and stay there?! Alan was not a man to be easily put off, and went ahead with his plans. He not only established the London plant but he also met and married an English girl before returning to the US. Cinecolor was in operation until the mid 1950s - the last Cinecolor prints were made in 1955, the final ones from America carrying the credit 'Color by The Color Corporation of America'.

Numerous other colour processes came and went over the decades, and it is interesting to compare them technically and to see how and why they fared commercially.

The contestants

Cinecolor was a two-colour process providing prints with a ferric-toned blue-green image and soundtrack on one side of the film's base and a dye-toned orange-red image on the other. This combination provided an adequate, if restricted, range of colours and the metallic-toned track reproduced satisfactorily on conventional sound-heads.

Dufaycolor, on the other hand, was a full three-colour additive process which enabled black and white film to reproduce colour by exposing and projecting its images through a microscopic pattern (reseau) of red, green and blue filter elements printed on the film's base. In 1931 it was demonstrated to the Royal Society and to a new organisation recently formed for film technical people - The British Kinematograph Society. Its major disadvantage was the severe loss of light, with the built-in colour screen absorbing two-thirds of the available light. This made the prints look dim when compared with black and white and with subtractive colour prints like Cinecolor. Also, the mosaic of filters (pixels!) was clearly visible to those close to the screen, even though it was very fine, with about one million to the square inch. When first introduced, Dufaycolor was a reversal direct-positive process, which was no problem for its amateur 9.5mm and 16mm sizes, but made making copies difficult. In spite of this, a number of 35mm short films were produced, including King George V's Silver Jubilee celebrations filmed by Movietone news who ordered 150 prints for showing in cinemas the next day. Dufaycolor sequences also appeared in the British musical Radio Parade of 1935, shown in 1934.

Negative-Positive version

In 1937 a negative-positive version of Dufaycolor was launched, making it more suitable for professional motion pictures. The density of the filter layer was reduced a little to improve the light transmission; achieved without the loss of too much colour saturation. Eventually, over 80 short films were to be made in Dufaycolor, one of the most successful being the Pathé News coverage of King George VI's Coronation in 1937. The only full-length feature in Dufaycolor was *Sons of the Sea* in 1939. It was probably the improved neg-pos Dufaycolor which was used as the weapon to see off Cinecolor,

Prints from the CINECOLOR two-colour process. Note in the left hand frames the colour of the images on the opposite sides of a Cinecolor print.

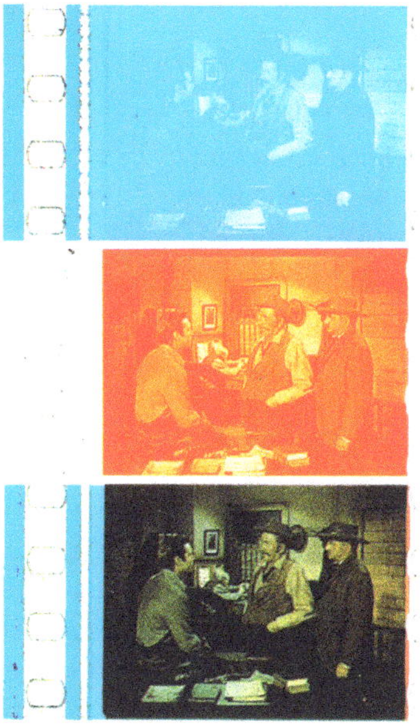

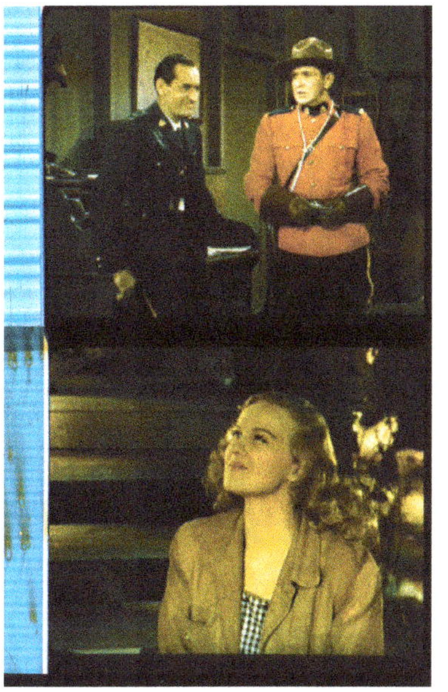

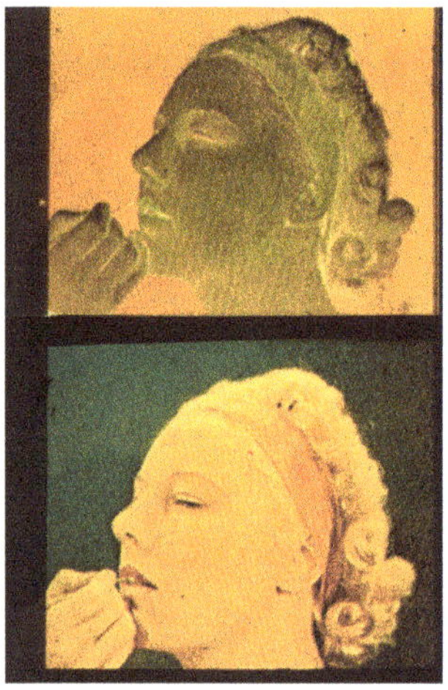

Dufaycolor was the first negative / positive colour film system

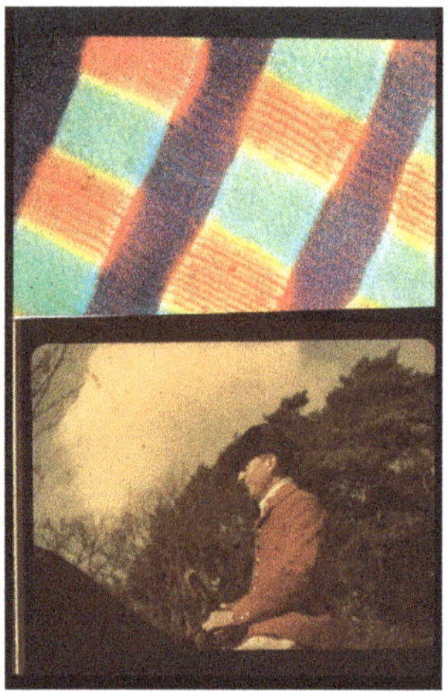

Dufaycolor print, showing (top) the highly magnified 'reseau' filter mosaic.

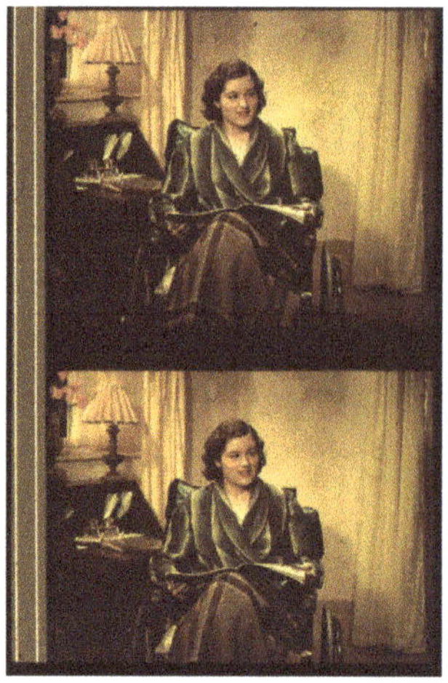

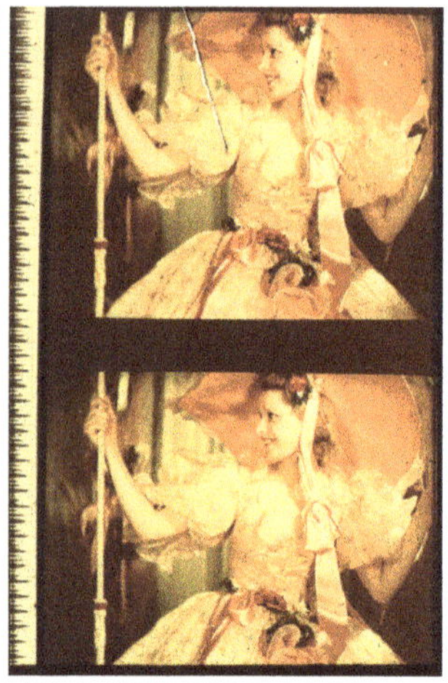

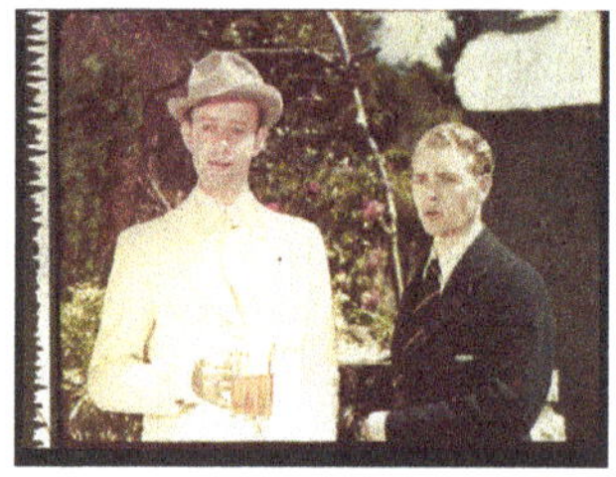

Dufaycolor prints. The only full length feature in Dufaycolor was Sons of the Sea (1939) - right.

but in the event, it was to be the outbreak of a real war, World War II, which delayed Cinecolor's own invasion plans for over 10 years.

Even without Cinecolor to do battle with, Dufaycolor still had other rivals. Perhaps the least to worry about, were other additive systems using the traditional separate black and white images photographed and projected through colour filters and superimposed, hopefully in register, on the screen. (The principle was later used in some triple-lens video projectors.)

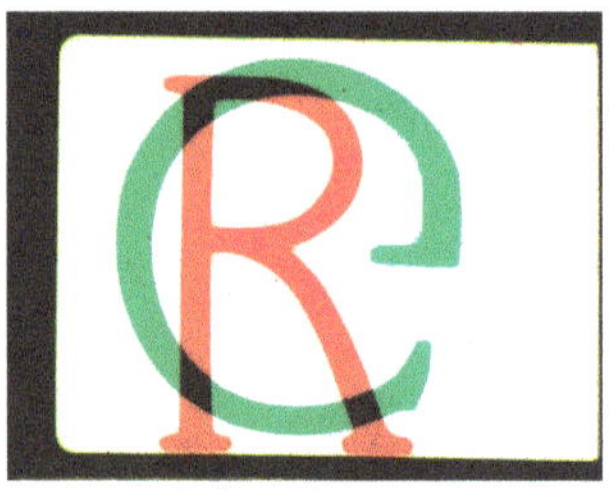

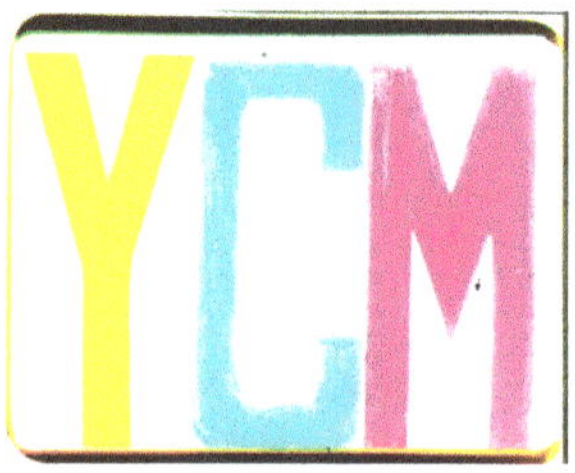

Colour layers on two and three colour prints

Raycol Process

The British Raycol process was only two-colour, with a pair of one quarter size images stacked within the space of a normal 35mm frame. It was interesting as it used a red filter to project the red record, but NO FILTER for the green. Strangely, it still worked, due to the subjective contrast phenomenon in the eye. One feature was filmed in Raycol colour, *The School for Scandal* in 1930, followed by a short (29 min) *Skipper of the Osprey* in 1933 (below).

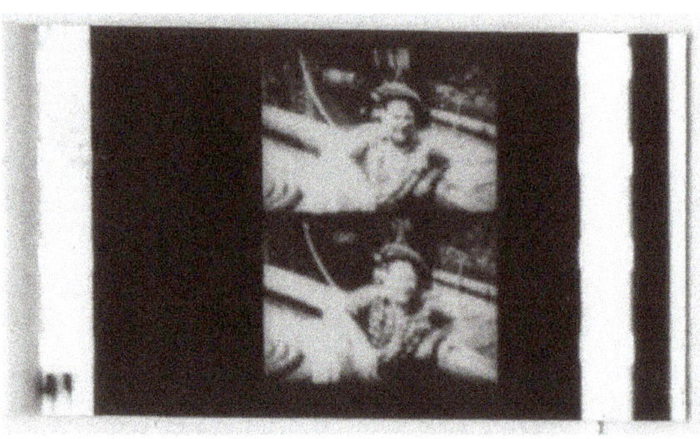

Realita

British Realita was a three-colour additive system, again with the smaller images fitted within a standard frame. It was also used to make a colour film of the 1937 Coronation of King George VI (photo below). The process was described in only the second issue of the BKS Journal in 1938 but, like Raycol, it was abandoned because, unlike Dufaycolor, it required special lenses or attachments fitted to the projector. Some of the early additive films were later reprinted as subtractive prints.

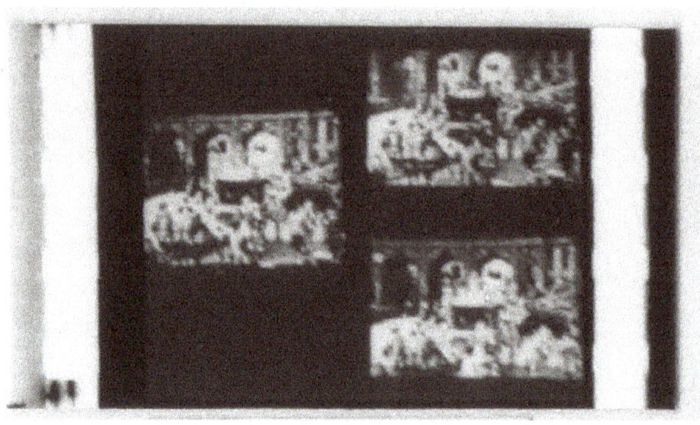

Dufaycolor was still to have many subtractive challengers during the 1930s.

Gasparcolor

Major Cornwell-Kline had, in fact, previously deserted from his post at Dufay in favour of another process, Gasparcolor, named after its Hungarian inventor, Bela Gaspar, who had perfected his three-colour multi-layer subtractive printing process at the Geyer labs in

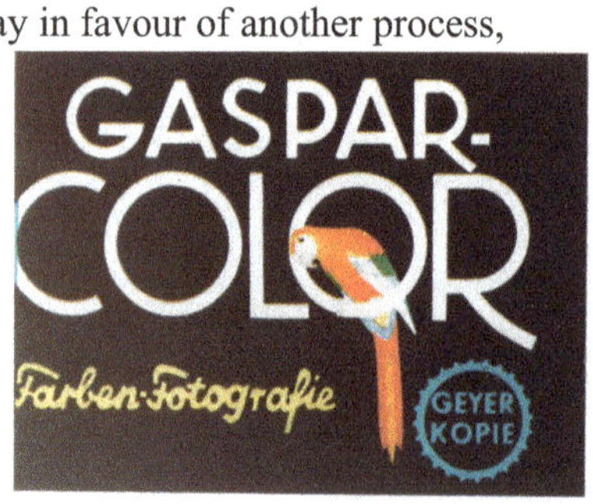

Germany. In 1934, he set up business in Britain. Among his first customers was another Hungarian, George Pal, who made stop-motion puppet advertising films, including one called *On Parade* for Horlicks. He also chose Gasparcolor for his own Puppetoon series of shorts (photo below). Another classic animated film released using the process was Len Lye's *Rainbow Dance* made for the Post Office.

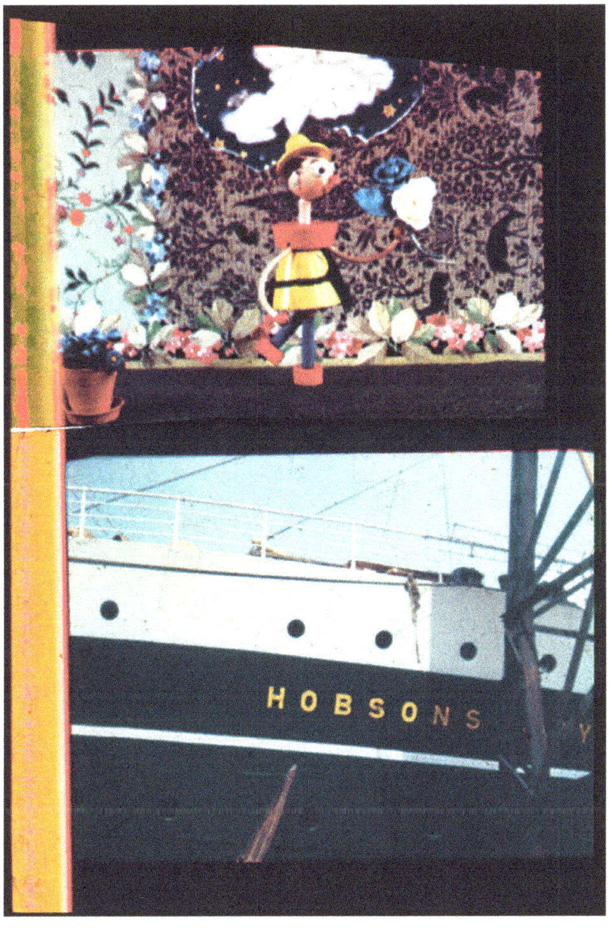

Gasparcolor film stock, made by Gevaert, was unusual in having the colour dyes already included in the emulsion layers during manufacture. It had a blue-sensitive cyan-dyed layer on one side of the base and a blue-sensitive magenta-dyed layer and a red-sensitive yellow-dyed layer on the other. It was a positive- to-positive process requiring three separation positives, which were printed in turn onto their correct layers using appropriate red or blue filters. During processing, the dyes were destroyed in the exposed areas in proportion to the developed silver images, which after being removed left a strong, highly saturated colour print.

Unfortunately, Gasparcolor's dye destruction type film was not sensitive enough to be used as a camera film, so separation negatives were still needed. Without a suitable three-strip camera available, most of Gasparcolor' s footage was animation. Providing separations of static subjects is relatively simple using a normal camera equipped with a filter wheel to photograph the three, red, green and blue filtered black and white images successively along a single film. During the later printing stages a 3:1 step printer is used.

'72' successive film negative for live action Gasparcolor which ran at 72 frames per second

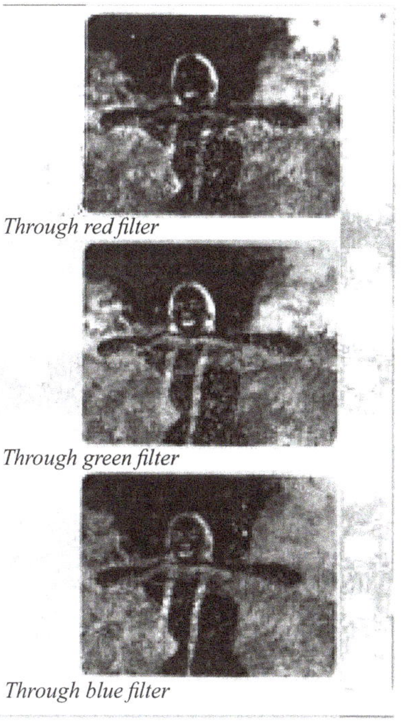

The successive-frame method is not really considered suitable for live action due to objects moving between exposures causing colour fringes on the print. However, Gasparcolor did give it a try using a camera running at three times normal speed (72 frames per second). The results proved to be reasonably successful providing the live action wasn't too alive and didn't move too much.

One short film photographed this way was *Colour on the Thames*, featuring slow-moving river craft. Gasparcolor were obviously so concerned that the risk of colour fringing would spoil their reputation, that they gave the following advice to users of the "72" method.

"This technique of obtaining separation negatives requires discretion. Now and then something moves rapidly enough to give rise to a colour fringe. The flick of a cow's tail or the sudden flight of a seagull across the sky will result in very conspicuous colour fringes. These shots MUST BE CUT OUT."

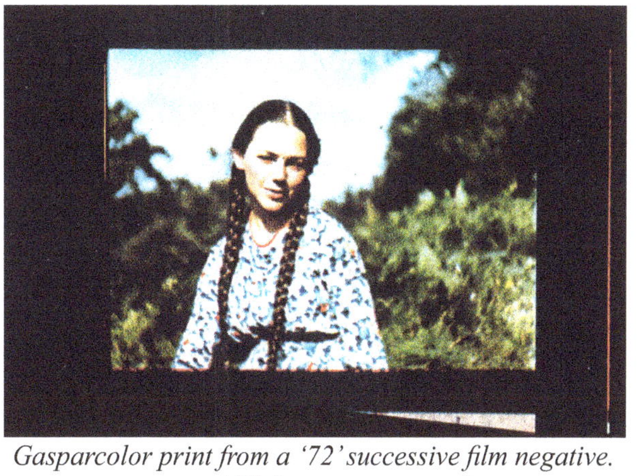

Gasparcolor print from a '72' successive film negative. ran at 72 frames per second

On to Technicolor

Gasparcolor prints were expensive and most of its users turned to Technicolor's dye-transfer prints when its new British plant came into operation during 1937. The plant wasn't ready in time to service Britain's first Technicolor film Wings of the Morning, the processing having to be done in Hollywood with the "rushes" taking four weeks to arrive back at Denham Studios.

A detailed descriptions of Technicolor's dye-transfer process follows immediately after this section, but basically, it was a photo-mechanical procedure akin to colour lithography, but printing its images onto transparent film instead of paper. Its famous 3-strip beam-splitter camera produced the three black and white separation negatives recording the red, green and blue components of the scene. These were used to make "matrices" which carried positive relief images made of hardened gelatine. These were used like printing plates to transfer in turn the yellow, cyan and magenta dye images onto the blank film, creating the final colour print. The receiving film wasn't entirely blank, having previously been printed with a normal black and white sound track and, in the early years, a faint black and white "key" image to improve the results. The transfer of the dyes took several minutes, during which time the matrix and the blank had to be held in close contact and in perfect register. This was achieved using the now famous 240 foot long pin belt. Over the years, the process was speeded up, reducing the transfer time from the original ten minutes to 45 seconds.

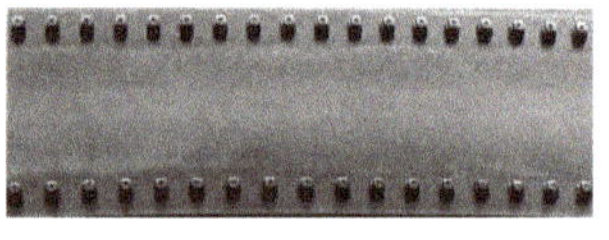

Amateurs steal a march

During 1935, 16mm Kodachrome was introduced. This was a three-colour multi-layer reversal process primarily intended for amateurs, with Kodak processing the camera film directly to a positive for projection. However, during the 1940s, it was to have limited use as an alternative source for obtaining Technicolor's three separation negatives, either by blowing up 16mm, or using a special 35mm lower contrast version (monopack) more suitable for copying. British use of monopack includes the short *English Village* (1943), shots in *Western Approaches* (1944) and *Scott of the Antarctic*.

Two colours are better than none at all?

The news that Technicolor was about to arrive in Britain led many in the industry to believe that there would be a great demand for colour. To steal a march, a number of mostly two-colour processes were marketed. These were either home grown or franchised from abroad. One of the first off the mark in 1935 was **Ondiacolor**, a two-colour process working out of a lab in Wardour Street. Among the films to reach the screen was a series

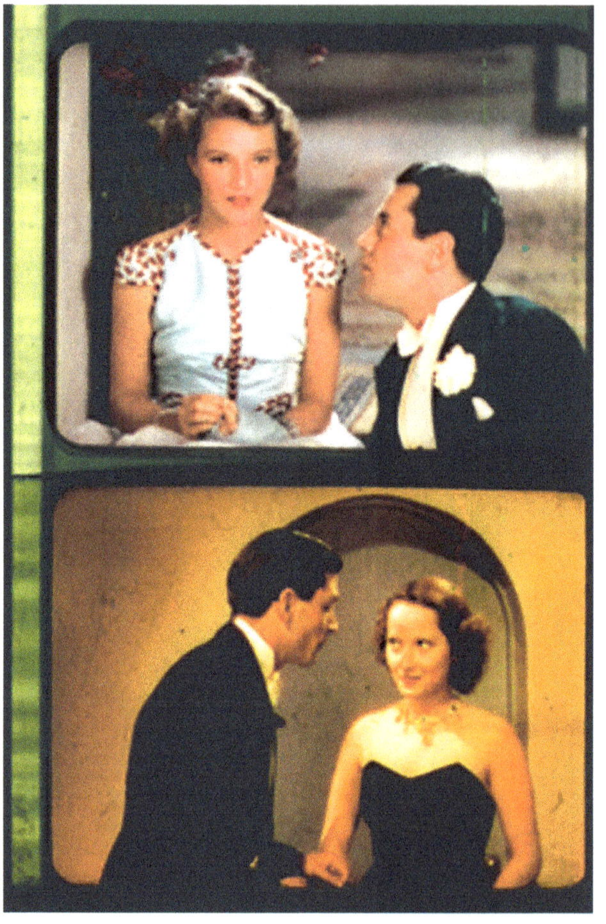

Britain's first Technicolor film Wings of the Morning (top frame) had to be processed in Hollywood. The lower frame shows another 1937 Technicolor dye-transfer print, this time processed in Britain - Divorce of Lady X

of travel shorts called *Beautiful Britain*. Also on offer was **Brewster-Color**, which was demonstrated using a specially shot short, *Let's Look at London* featuring both exterior and interior scenes including sights of the city and a trip to the ballet. Although the colour was considered perfectly acceptable, it was mostly used for animated advertising films.

New too in 1935, was **Dunningcolor**, noteworthy for being chosen by animator Anson Dyer, who set up Britain's first dedicated cartoon studio. Among the characters he created was a hapless soldier called Sam, and one of his cartoons, *Sam and his Musket*, has been quoted as being Britain's first colour cartoon (1935).

The only system which was used for features, albeit short ones, was **Chemicolor**, a British version of a German 2-colour process called **UfaColor**. Using Agfa stock, the processing was undertaken by Humphries Laboratories in London who produced a colour reel for the four reel (40 min) featurette *Pagliacci* starring the opera singer Richard Tauber. The same process was called **Spectracolor**, when it was used for two more four-reel films, *Faust* and *Railroad Rhythm*.

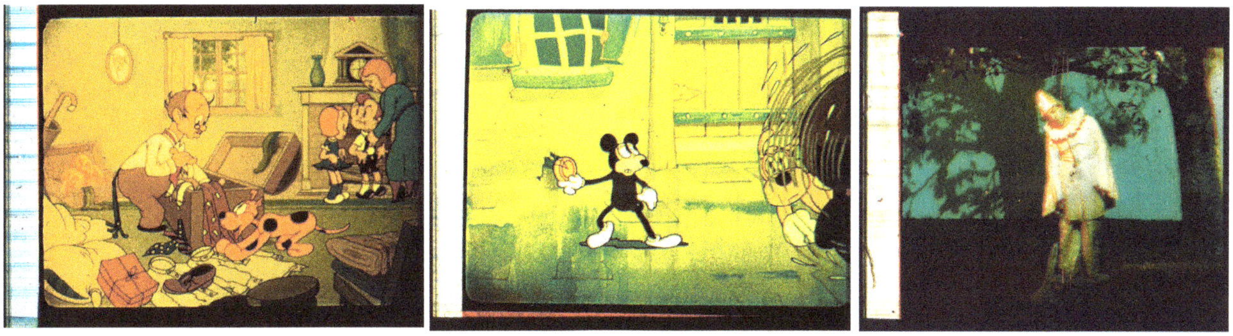

L-R: Frames of Dunningcolor, Brewstercolor and Chemicolor (Pagliacci)

Also competing for customers was **Harmonicolor**, used for a 20 minute short *Talking Hands* and **Polychromide**, also known as **Veracolor**.

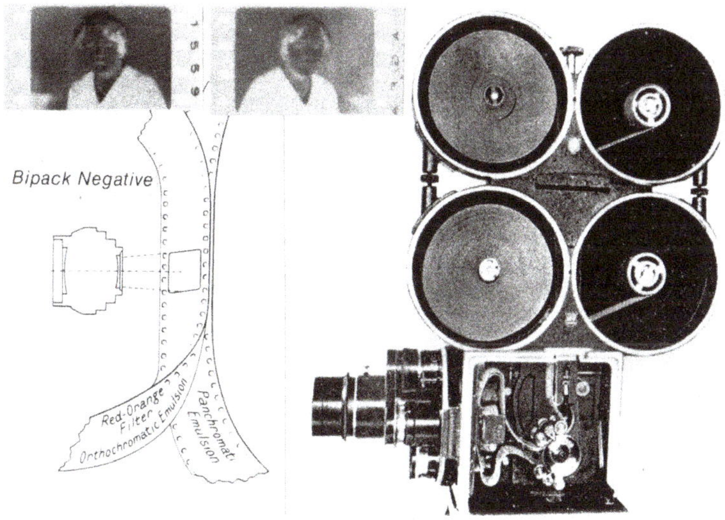

Bell & Howell bi-pack two-colour camera with 'piggy-back' twin magazine. Allowed you to shoot colour, but not recommended for filming in fast cars or locations with low ceilings!

Plenty of choice

Creating a two-colour process wasn't too difficult. The required stock and chemicals were available on a non-proprietary basis from Kodak, Agfa and Gevaert. For cartoons and other static subjects, the single film successive frame method could be used to provide the pair of separation negatives. For live-action, the most popular choice was a bi-pack camera running two B&W films emulsion to emulsion together through the gate. The front orthochromatic film was exposed through its base recording the blue-green image. On its surface was a red filter layer which stopped all but red light passing through to the rear panchromatic film to create the red negative. The companion double-coated print stock had a B&W blue-sensitive emulsion on both sides of the film with a yellow filter layer in between to allow each side to be printed simultaneously from the two separation negatives. The filter layer was normally removed during processing, although some users left some of the yellow behind, thinking it improved the look of the final print. The principal difference between the individual processes was the way the silver black and white images printed on the two sides of the film were coloured. The image from the red negative was usually turned into the complementary blue-green colour by iron toning, which also provided a satisfactory soundtrack. The side from the blue-green negative was normally changed to red by bleaching and dying the image with a basic dye. This gave a brighter and more transparent image than the red from metallic-toning using uranium or copper. Many of the processes preferred to dye both sides, which gave greater control of the colours. Using basic dyes meant that the mixtures could be altered to match the subject matter and help overcome some of the deficiencies of only a two-colour system, which can never reproduce all the hues of nature accurately.

Sound matters

As we have learned, a dye only soundtrack will not reproduce very well using a traditional sound head, so some means had to be employed to keep the silver in the track. **Chemicolor** and **Spectracolor** kept theirs by coating it with a ribbon of varnish to stop it being bleached and dyed along with the images. Another method was to re-develop the bleached track area and turn it back to a dense silver compound. It was difficult to restrict the re-development solution to only the soundtrack area, so some of the cheaper colour processes made do with a dye only track and audiences had to suffer awful sound as well as often awful colour. Gasparcolor used a re-developed track on its three-colour prints, and the method was still used until we eventually saw the return of pure dye cyan tracks.

The ways to treat each side of double coated stock individually with chemicals also varied. The **Cinecolor** method was to float the strands of film on the surface of the solutions and hope they didn't sink too often. The film could also be run over special capillary rollers which picked up the chemical or dye and transferred it to its surface. These methods required special equipment, but a laboratory's normal deep tanks could be used by coating each side of the film with varnish or

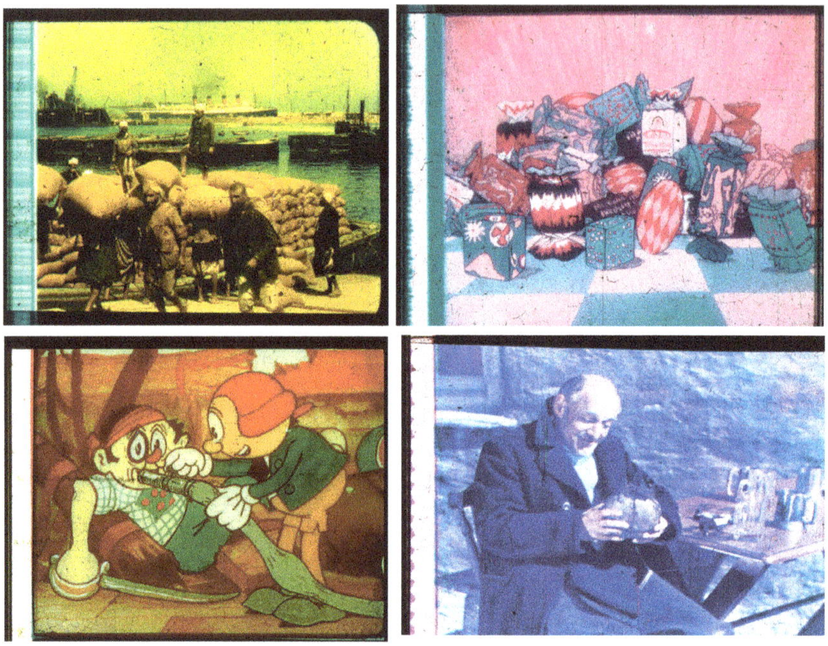

Colour Prints from the 1930s
Cinecolor Harmancolor
Spectracolor Polychromide

lacquer in turn to protect the side not being treated. The fact that Cinecolor was without a laboratory of its own in Britain, didn't mean that audiences here missed out on seeing Cinecolor subjects. Apart from imported prints, a few cartoons were printed locally using one of the British processes. These copies often retained the original Cinecolor credit, but sometimes the colours looked quite different compared with the US originals. Although the accuracy of the colour was not considered important, particularly in cartoons, today it can cause confusion for we technical historians and archivists trying to identify individual colour processes of the period.

Stand easy

In the event, the expected rush to colour by British producers never happened. When Technicolor Limited started making prints in 1937, most of them were British and European copies of Hollywood films. Their first 'British job' was one of George Pal's *Puppetoons*, followed by colour sequences for *Victoria the Great*. During the rest of the 1930s only seven British feature-length films were photographed in Technicolor, most of these by producer Alexander Korda, who had shares in the Company. The titles were: *The Divorce of Lady X, The Drum, The Four Feathers, Over the Moon* and *The Thief of Baghdad* (completed in America). The only others were to be a follow up to *Victoria the Great, Sixty Glorious Years (in glorious Technicolor!) and The Mikado.*

Casualties of war

None of the British colour systems of the 1930s survived World War II, either due to the lack of demand or, like Gasparcolor, hostilities disrupting the supply of the special stock required. On the other hand, Technicolor had a good war. Its single pin belt dye transfer printer never stopped, producing over 50 million feet of colour film per year. Subjects ranged from glossy Hollywood musicals to help keep up morale, to military training films including *Camouflage and Plastic Surgery in Wartime.* British features continued to be made in Technicolor during the war years, including: *Life and Death of Colonel Blimp* and *Henry V.*

Germany's secret weapon

A significant event in the history of colour processes was the discovery at the end of the war, that Germany had been making films using an Agfa 35mm negative-positive system incorporating the principles of what we now call 'modern' colour film. The new **Agfacolor** negative stock, which could be exposed in a normal camera, had the three red, green and blue sensitive emulsion layers coated on the same side of the film, known as an integral tri-pack. Included in the layers were substances called colour couplers which during a single development stage, generated the complementary cyan, magenta and yellow dyes along with (coupled to) the appropriate silver image in each layer. The subsequent removal of the silver left a dye only image with both the tones and colour reversed. This colour negative could then be printed onto similar multilayer film to produce the final positive colour print.

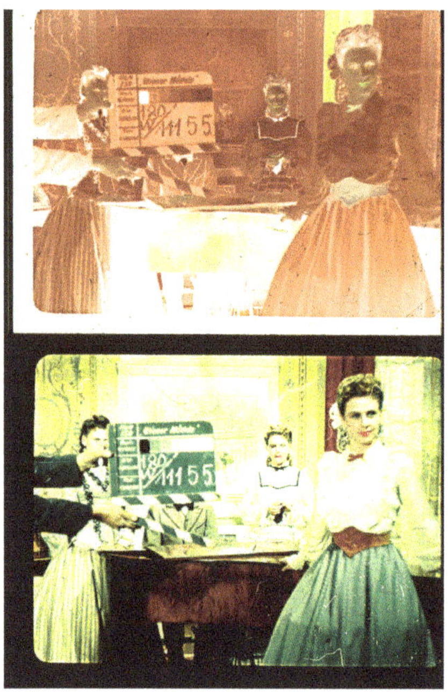

Agfacolor negative and positive, 1945

As part of the spoils of war, all of Agfa's manufacturing details and formulas were disclosed to photographic manufacturers around the world, most of which set to work developing their own versions of Agfacolor.

Kodak was to produce its own colour negative / positive process using similar principles and based on its still **Kodacolor** roll film. In the meantime, Technicolor was establishing its dominant position, becoming a virtual monopoly. However, there were still to be a couple more British processes to at least offer an alternative. The last Dufaycolor film appeared in 1946. After this, Dufay recognising the drawbacks of its additive system and planned to introduce a subtractive process by taking over the development of another British system called British Tricolour, which it renamed **Dufaychrome**.

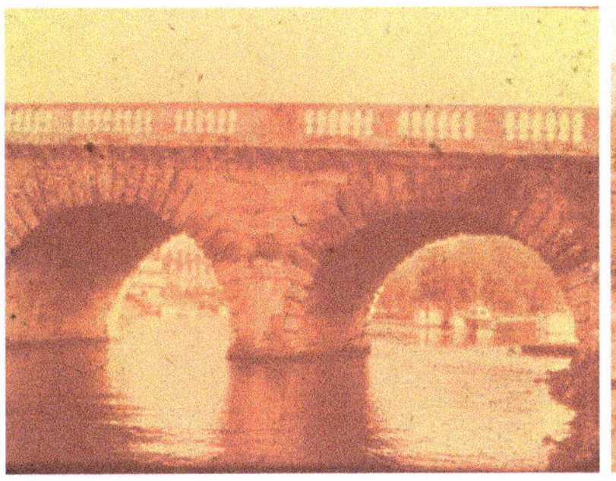
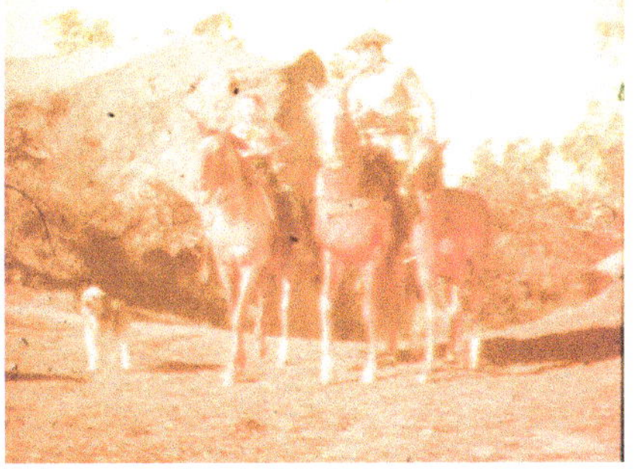

Faded early coupler prints from Dufaychrome (L) and Alfacolor (R)

The heart of the Dufaychrome system was a 3-strip camera similar to that of Technicolor. The prints were made using a rather complicated procedure.
The print film had initially a single layer containing a magenta dye-forming coupler, onto which the green separation negative was printed. The film wasn't processed, but a new emulsion with a cyan colour former was transferred on top and printed with the red negative.
Finally the third layer with a yellow coupler was applied and exposed using the blue negative.
After all this, the complete, new multi-layer film was processed in a colour developer to produce the final colour print.
To add to the complexity, the clear soundtrack area was to be coated with a stripe of positive emulsion to provide a normal silver track. The only evidence of its use I have found so far, are a few stills-on-film film strips marked 'Dufaychrome' and short cinema flashes and announcements.

Also in operation was the Gevaert **Chromart** process. This was basically a two-colour version of the Agfacolor negative-positive system with only two layers incorporating colour forming substances chosen to give the compromise colours blue-green and red-orange. Again, there is little evidence of its widespread use, and I have yet to see a print with a Chromart credit.

Sometimes two colours were enough

At first sight, the decision to try to introduce a new two-colour process was a backward step. However, during the late 1940s there was an unexpected high demand, particularly in the USA, for two-colour processes. They were considered adequate for 'B' features, mostly westerns, and could be shot more cheaply with readily available bi-pack cameras rather than use Technicolor with its restrictions and controls.

At its peak, Cinecolor labs in Hollywood was producing 130 million feet of two-colour prints a year, and when added to the other process available, such as **Magnacolor**, the total output equalled that of Technicolor.
For a brief period, Technicolor in London introduced its own two-colour process, **Technichrome**. This was not to compete, but was specially created to film the 1948 Olympic Games. To overcome the shortage of 3-strip cameras, everything but the opening and closing ceremonies (where at least they got the colours of the flags right) was filmed using bi-pack cameras. The prints were made using the normal three-colour dye-transfer method, the yellow and magenta matrices being made from the same blue-green camera negative. This gave greater control of the colour balance, which led to it being called a two and a half colour system.

Cinecolor's rearguard action

In 1948, Cinecolor announced its plans to expand into Britain and set up Cinecolor (Great Britain) Ltd. To avoid the post war building and import restrictions, a contract was secured with Radiant Films Ltd to start making prints at their laboratories in Slough.

At this time, another lab, **Alfacolor** was also making two-colour prints on double coated stock but producing the colours on each side by colour couplers. Cinecolor was by now able to offer the option of three-colour prints. Alan Gundelfinger had devised a way of adding the third colour to their existing double-coated prints. The new 3-colour Cinecolor prints had the same iron-toned blue-green (Cyan) image plus the track on one side. On the other, the red-orange dye was replaced with magenta. The third yellow component was added to the magenta side by chemically re-sensitising the emulsion, then printing and dying it again. As three separation negatives were now needed, the first three colour Cinecolor prints were cartoons, or live action from Kodachrome.

In 1950, the arrival of Kodak's new Eastman Color negative provided a source for obtaining the three separations, and soon features began to appear photographed in **Super Cinecolor**. At the start of the 1950s, the Cinecolor plant at Slough was employing 100 staff turning out both two and three-colour prints (on either side of the road!). Super Cinecolor never replaced the original process, in fact, most of the output was still two-colour.

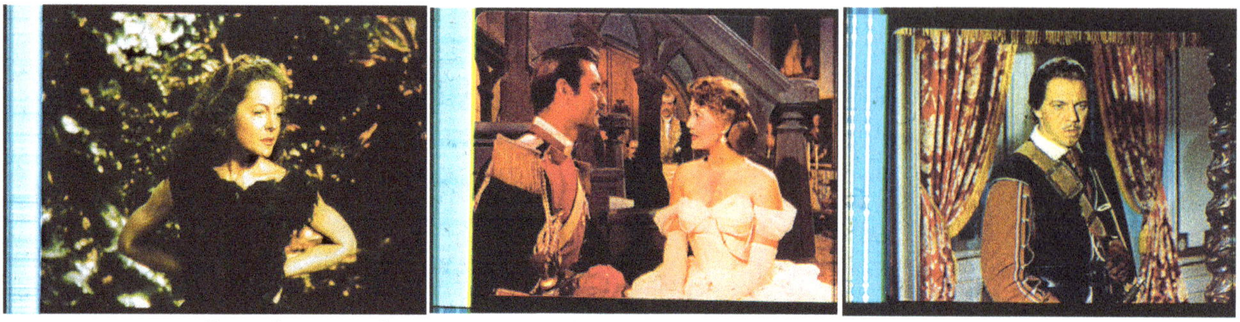

Cinecolor two-colour print (L) with Cinecolor three colour prints (Centre & R)

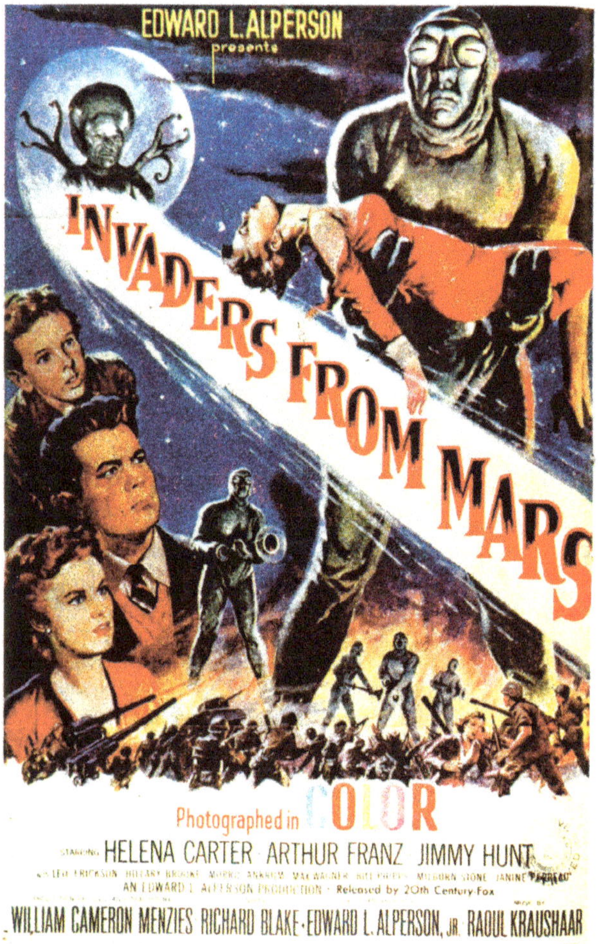

They were also quite happy to produce two-colour prints from Eastman Color, for producers who wanted the cheapest possible copies and thought that audiences couldn't tell the difference anyway. A notable example was *Invaders from Mars* (1953).

By 1954, Eastman Color and colour negative and print stock from other manufacturers became generally available, together with all the necessary duplicating films. This was the beginning of the end for the specific individual processes like Cinecolor, which closed down in 1954. Even Technicolor retired its 3-strip camera during 1955, although they continued making dye-transfer prints from colour negatives until 1977. For the record, the last Technicolor 3-strip films made in Britain were from Ealing Studios, *The Lady Killers, Touch and Go* and finally, *The Feminine Touch* (completed Sept. 1955).

Major Adrian Corwel-Clyne MBE (note the wartime, less Germanic, spelling change) is best remembered today as the author of 'Colour Cinematography', the 'Bible' for those interested in the history of earlier colour processes, particularly British. The book does contain a few inaccuracies due to the Major speculating about the workings of systems of which the details were "secret" at the time. He was also somewhat biased in favour of processes, like Gasparcolor and Dufaycolor, which he was personally involved with. The last edition was published in 1951, just as Eastman Color was being introduced, which he thought might have a significant effect on the future of colour cinematography.... he was right about that.

All the frame illustrations used here are from original contemporary prints. All have retained their original colour, being as good, or poor, as new. The only exceptions are Dufaychrome and Alfacolor which, like other early dye-coupling colour prints, have now sadly faded.

Technicolor 3-Strip System

- how the camera worked

Technicolor® was and is the trade name for a whole series of motion picture colour processes going back as far as 1916 which were continuously developed and improved over the decades. Although various two-colour processes were originally used, with differing degrees of success, it was the Technicolor 3-Colour subtractive 3-Strip system, used from the early 1930s, with its associated 'imbibition' dye-transfer process, that produced the rich (not entirely 'natural') colours that were so much loved by cinemagoers that 'Technicolor' became for many synonymous with 'Colour Cinema Films' rather like 'Hoover' became the generic name for vacuum cleaners.

The various parts of the system included the camera, the blank films on to which the dye images were transferred, the 'matrix' step-projection printer, the special dyes, and the 'imbibition' dye-transfer process.

The camera

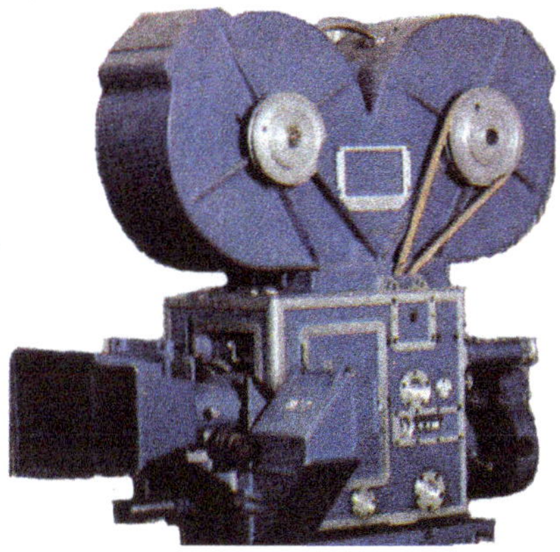

Technicolor 3-strip camera 1934

The Technicolor camera, originally manufactured by Mitchell Camera Corporation to Technicolor's specifications, contained color filters, a beam splitter consisting of a partially reflecting surface inside a split-cube prism, and three separate rolls of black-and-white film. The three black and white separation negatives were exposed simultaneously to light from the beam-splitting prism. The film recording the green record ran through a gate facing the lens, with the blue and red negatives exposed as a bi-pack running through a second gate positioned at 90 degrees.

The beam splitter allowed about ⅓ of the light coming through the camera lens to pass through the reflector and green filter and form an image on one of the strips.

The remaining light was reflected by the mirror and passed through a magenta filter, allowing only the red and blue components to pass to the two strips of film of the bi-pack.

The front film of the pair was red-blind orthochromatic that recorded only the blue light. On the surface of its emulsion was a red-orange coating that prevented blue light from continuing on to the red-sensitive panchromatic emulsion of the film behind, which therefore recorded only the red part of the spectrum.

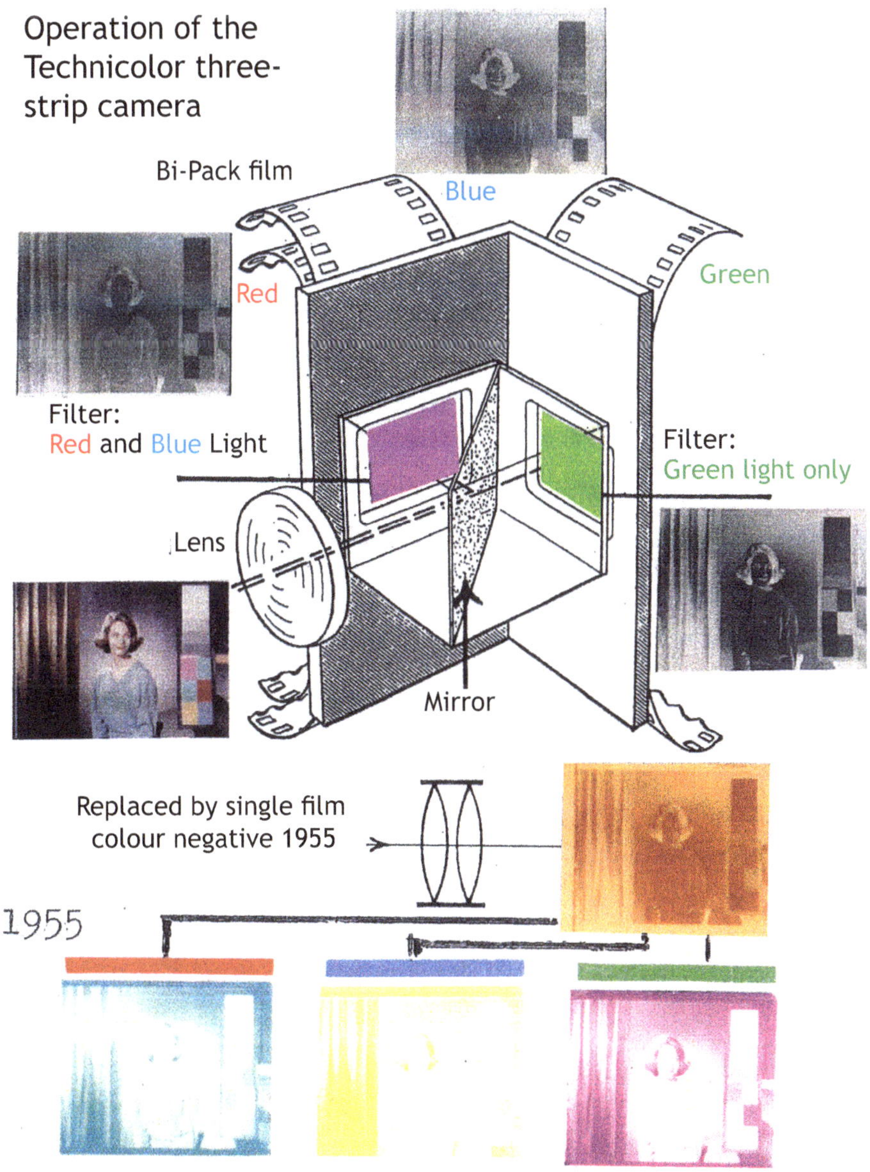

Technicolor 3-Strip

- the dye-transfer process in detail

Technicolor's 3-strip camera and dye transfer printing process held a virtual monopoly of colour filming during the 1930s and 1940s and was still in regular use until the 1970s. In 1997, Technicolor actually reintroduced an updated version of the dye transfer process which was used for the restoration of several classic movies, but it was discontinued in 2002.

Not quite perfection

Although much loved, early Technicolor prints did have their flaws. By today's standards, and even compared with black and white films of the time, they had poor definition and sometimes showed signs of being a little out of register. However, these failings were more than compensated for by their higher contrast and vivid saturated colours, which made 'Glorious Technicolor' look good, particularly on the modest sized screens used in cinemas during the 1930s and 1940s.

Making a dye-transfer print - As much an art as a science

Dye-transfer printing, also known as the imbibition (IB) process, first involves the preparation of three intermediate matrix films representing the red, green and blue components of the picture. These can be derived from the original 3-strip camera separation negatives, multi-layer colour positives and negatives, or electronic images. They are printed and processed in such a way to produce positive relief images, with the different tones represented as varying thickness of hardened gelatine. The printing has to be done optically through the base to retain the image when the unexposed areas ore washed away during processing. Known as matrices, they are used like printing blocks, first to absorb the appropriate complementary yellow, cyan and magenta dyes and then transfer them in turn, on top of each other, onto clear film to build up the final full colour image. While this is taking place, the matrices and the receiving blank film have to be held in close contact and perfect register on a continuously moving metal belt fitted with register pins. The complete transfer process con be repeated, with the same set of matrices being re-dyed to produce multiple copies.

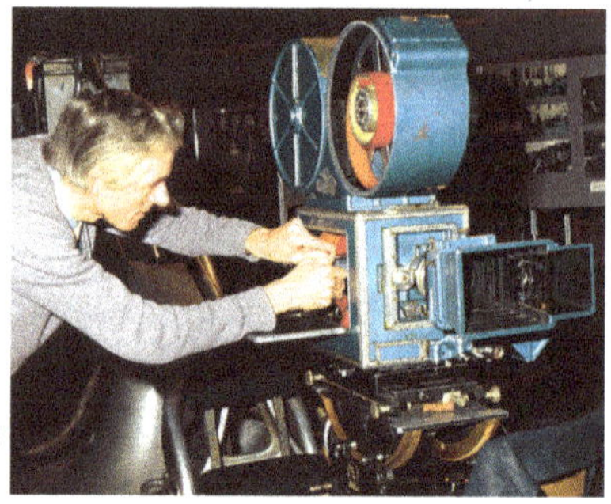

Grant Lobban 'hands-on' with a 3-strip camera

The Blank Film

At first the blank film was ordinary black and white print stock, which was first printed with optical sound track leaving the picture area clear ready to receive the dye image. The blank film was first passed through a water bath to soften the gelatine. This had to be soft enough to absorb the required amount of dye in a reasonable amount of time, but sufficiently hard to stop the dyes spreading too much and spoiling the definition. Also, the second and third transfers tended to smudge the one below. To make this less noticeable, the yellow image was transferred first, this being the least critical in terms of definition in the final print, followed by the cyan and the most important magenta on top. Early prints also included a faint black and white silver image, printed along with the track, to help improve the definition and to give greater density to the darker areas. Throughout the 1940s, the dye-transfer process was improved and speeded up. The additional 'key' silver image was gradually discontinued, the dyes alone now producing excellent blacks, in fact often too good and lacking shadow detail. The classic example being men's dress suits, which reproduced as solid black, even though the negative(s) showed some detail. This characteristic led to much frustration for many cameramen who had carefully lit the scene to include shadow detail, which never appeared on the final print.

Technicolor matrix processing: *Prints from the negative were exposed through the base and developed to produce a relief image*

Technicolor Dye Transfer *The dye in the matrix relief was transferred to the blank gelatine layer of another film, producing a dye-transfer print*

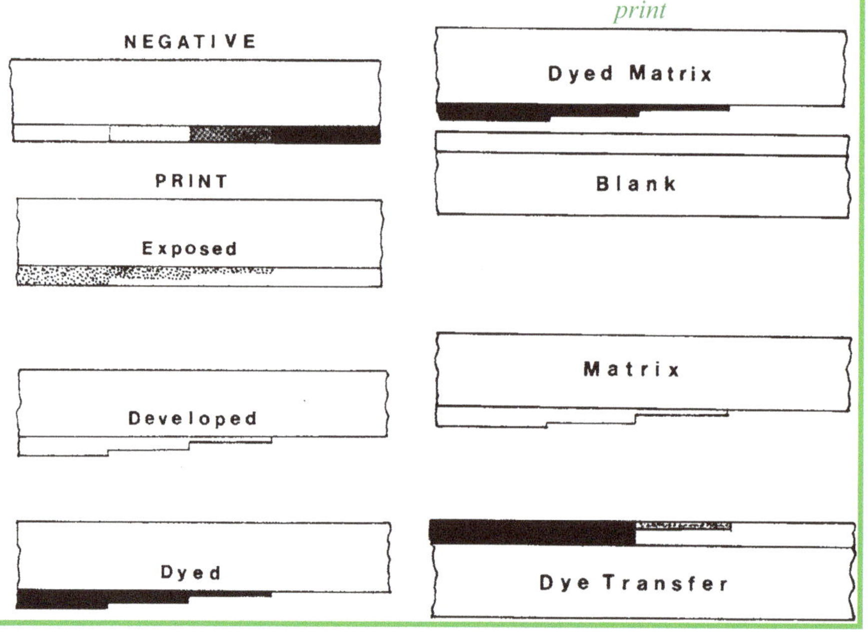

Original Technicolor 3-strip dye-transfer process

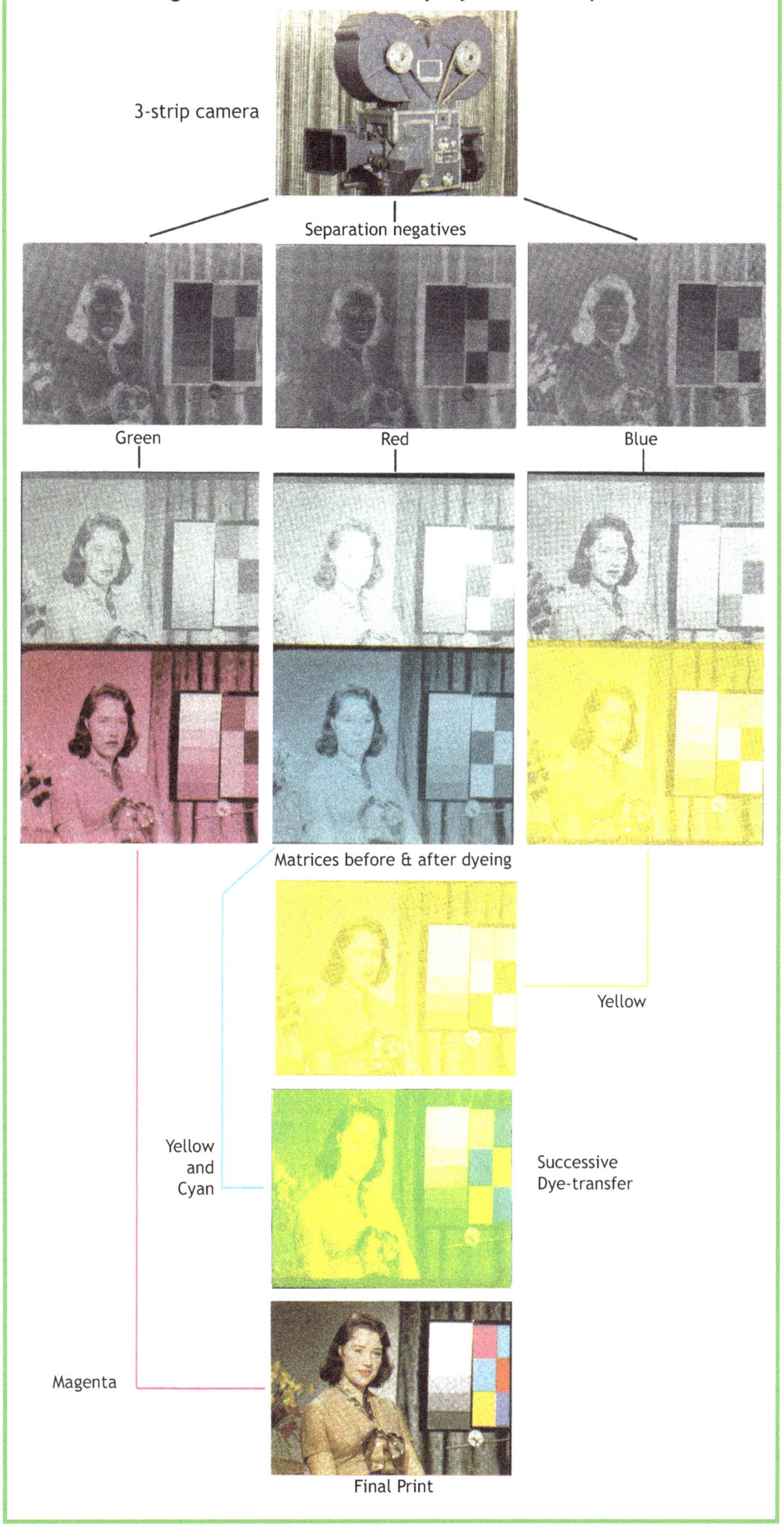

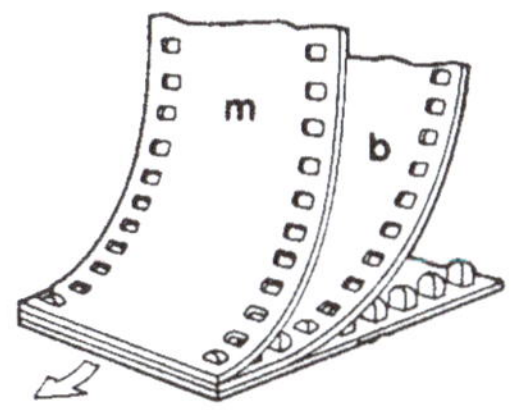

Dye-Transfer Registration: *Whilst the dye-transfer is occurring, the blank film and the dyed matrix were carried together on a moving belt, with registration pins engaging every perforation*

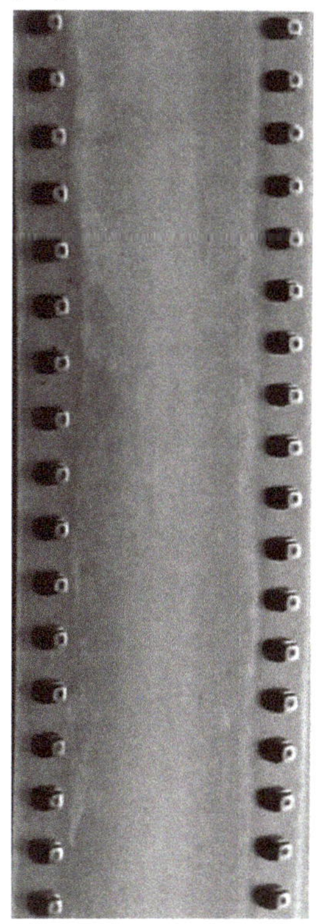

The correct colour balance was achieved through the relative exposure of the matrices, with the final adjustments made during the transfer by dyeing the matrices with an excess amount of dye which was washed off by the required amount before coming into contact with the blank. The few slightly 'off target' prints, in terms of colour balance, were not wasted. They were distributed, but kept away from the West End and other important first run cinemas, becoming examples of the notorious 'north of Watford Technicolor'.

Behold a Pale Competitor

The first threat to the dye-transfer process came at the start of the 1950s, with the Eastman Color single-strip multi-layer colour film. This could be used in a normal camera and then processed and printed by any laboratory equipped to do so. The new stock also made it possible to introduce the various widescreen systems for showing on much larger screens. Technicolor soon adapted its process to allow the matrices to be made from the new colour negatives. Although the colour was often superior, the dye-transfer prints were less sharp than those made on Eastman Color print film. They compared unfavourably when subjected to the greeter magnification needed when the image was either cropped and enlarged onto a wider screen, or stretched out sideways, as in CinemaScope.

Technicolor started an urgent development programme to improve the sharpness of their prints. They asked Kodak, who traditionally supplied all their film materials, to provide better quality matrix stock. At first, Kodak was reluctant to do so, suggesting that Technicolor, like other laboratories, such as Consolidated, Deluxe and Metrocolor, adopt the Eastman Color process. However, although Technicolor began to phase out its original 3-strip camera, in favour of colour negative, they were determined to improve their unique printing system and continue to offer the industry the option of using dye-transfer prints. For a while, Technicolor obtained higher quality stocks from other manufacturers, including DuPont in the USA and Ferrania in Europe, but then, Kodak, realising that Technicolor meant business, and not wishing to lose one of its biggest customers, came up with higher definition matrix films.

By 1954, dye-transfer prints were not only able to record all the detail from the original colour negative, but could also benefit from reduction printing. This procedure produces finer grained and higher definition prints by exploiting the fact that print film has higher resolution than camera film, so can record all the extra detail obtained by using a larger negative in the camera.

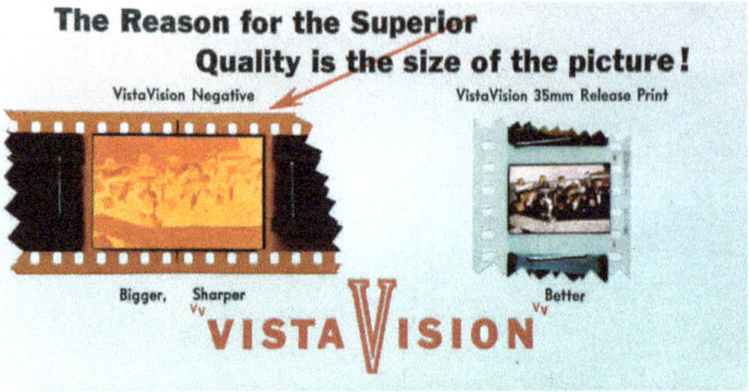

Vistavision & Technirama

To put this into practice, Paramount and Technicolor jointly developed the VistaVision process. The larger negative area was obtained by running standard 35mm film horizontally through the camera, exposing an 8-perforation frame with an image over twice the normal size. This was then optically reduced onto the matrices to produce a normal 4-perforation vertical pull-down dye-transfer print, but with a much higher quality image for showing on larger and wider screens. Technicolor was to produce some beautiful VistaVision reduction prints, together with those from other large-area negative systems which followed, such as the various 65mm processes and its own Technirama (a combination of the VistaVision format and anamorphic lenses).

Even for normal 35mm photography, Technicolor suggested that the full silent frame should be exposed in the camera, as the subsequent reduction down to the Academy sound aperture produced a worthwhile gain in quality. Technicolor's faith in their dye-transfer printing method paid off. From 1952 to 1958 alone, their labs produced a total of four and a half billion feet, 50% greater than the total amount sold since the process was introduced back in the 1930s. (Dye-transfer began as a two-colour process in 1928, the third colour added in 1932.)

Technicolor keeps its good looks

For audiences, "Color by Technicolor" still meant richer and more vibrant colours when compared with the new processes, mostly using Eastman Color, which many regarded as just pale imitations. Sometimes, rivals like Warnercolor and Color by Deluxe did actually look as good. This was usually because Technicolor had been contracted to manufacture the British and European

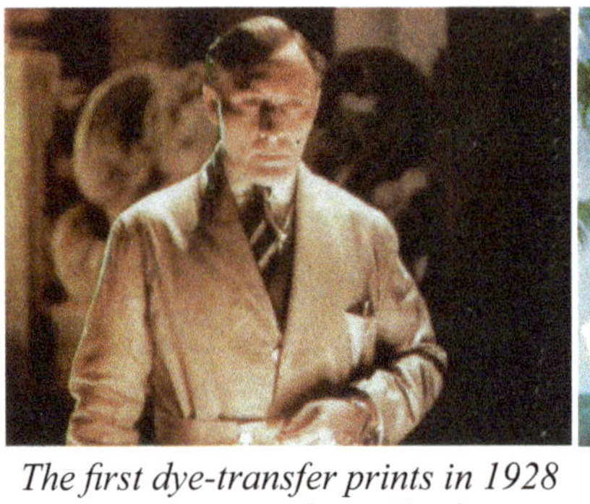

The first dye-transfer prints in 1928 were only two-colour. The frame above from Doctor X (1932) is an example.

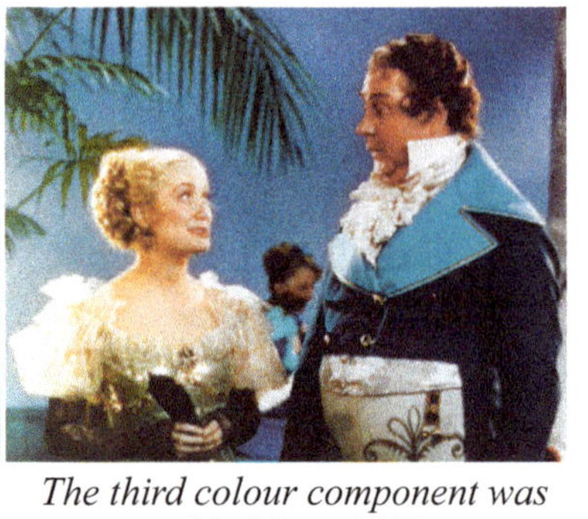

The third colour component was added from 1932. The first live-action feature was Becky Sharp (1935)

prints of colour films serviced by other labs in the USA and still had their original credit. Today, these copies are highly prized by collectors, libraries and archives. Not fully appreciated at the time was the greater permanence of dye-transfer prints. The dyes employed, similar to textile dyes, are colour-fast and don't fade, unlike those in Eastman Color and other dye-coupling multi-layer films. These are created in the film itself by chemical reaction during the development. Sadly, these have proved to be unstable and liable to fade over time, particularly the cyan layer, resulting in pink prints. Even pre-1950 Technicolor nitrate prints have suffered less decay than contemporary black and white prints, possibly due to less destructive chemicals remaining in the print after dye-transfer. A less noticeable advantage of watching a Technicolor print was the seamless first generation optical effects printed directly onto the matrices. Most other colour films had to make do with duped fades and dissolves joined into the original negative, which resulted in a disconcerting drop in quality and a colour change as the effect took place.

Still Glorious

Throughout the 1950s and 1960s, improvements to conventional colour negative and print stocks were matched by advances in the dye-transfer process. The blank film now incorporated a mordant. This is a substance with a greater affinity to the dyes, speeding up the transfer and greatly reducing the image spread, resulting in a higher output of even sharper prints. The transfer order was changed to start with the all-important magenta, then the cyan and yellow, as the mordant was at its most effective on the first colour transferred. Technicolor was an early adopter of polyester based stock to give its matrices greater stability and strength, ensuring perfect registration and a longer life. Despite all the improvements, Technicolor prints retained their distinctive look. The rich, yet transparent colours, together with the deep blacks and clear highlights, made the picture look brighter. The image was a little grainier with higher contrast, perhaps due to the optical printing of the matrices, and the "crushed" blacks were still evident. However these "failings" were not noticed by the average viewer, and in fact made the picture look sharper.

All Shapes and Sizes

Apart from theatrical release prints, Technicolor produced a large number of 16mm dye-transfer prints, from 1941 to satisfy wartime requirements, up to the 1970s. During the 1960s they also made 8mm and Super-8 copies. These narrow gauge prints were made on the same transfer machine, 16mm either as a single copy down the middle of 35mm, or a pair side-by-side on 35mm perforated stock. Standard 8mm prints were arranged double-rank, head-to-tail, in the 16mm areas, and Super-8 as three rows on 35mm. Some of the dye transfer Super-8 copies were complete with a very narrow silver optical soundtrack, not to be mistaken for a scratch! To add to the range of formats, there were also a few dye-transfer 35mm "still" film strips. Unfortunately, due to the small number of prints required, the dye-transfer principle was never extended to the 70mm format. All Technicolor's

Technicolor narrow-gauge dye-transfer prints

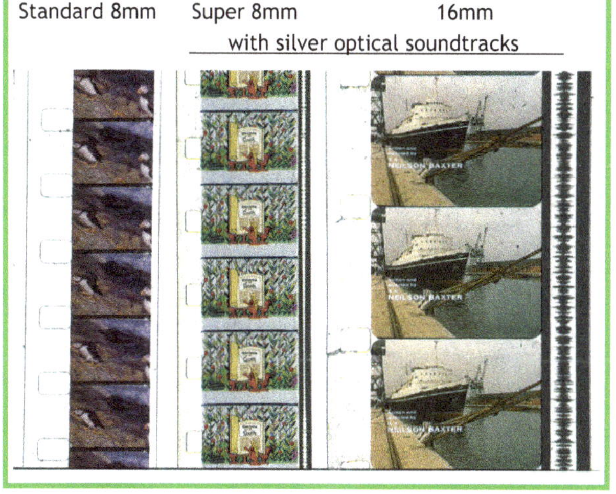

Revised Technicolor transfer sequence from the1960s

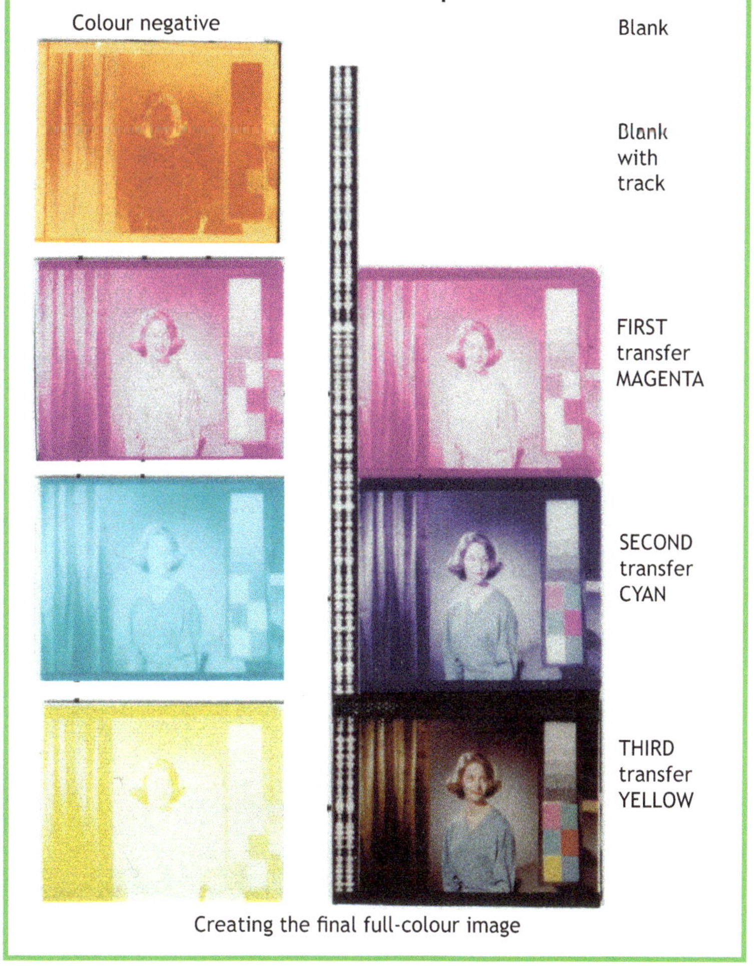

Creating the final full-colour image

70mm prints were made on Eastman Color print film, many of which have now faded.

One of the last innovations, a precursor to today's electronic developments, was **Vidtronics**, Technicolor's video tape to dye- transfer print process. It was used mostly by TV companies to make 16mm and 35mm colour tele-recordings for foreign distribution. Among the few results which reached the big cinema screen was *The Best of Benny Hill*, which included items from his TV shows.

Could this be the end for endless pin belts?

The output of dye-transfer prints peaked in the late 1960s, but by the mid-1970s a slump in cinema business reduced the number of prints required. The process became increasingly uneconomic and found it difficult to compete with colour print manufacturers, who themselves were competing with each other both in cost and quality. To continue to be viable, it was necessary to make a large number of copies from each set of matrices.

In 1975, Technicolor in Hollywood took the reluctant decision to cease dye-transfer and switch to colour print film. The Rome and London plants followed in 1977 and "Color by Technicolor" no longer meant an individual specific process. Among the last dye-transfer prints were copies of the first Star Wars adventure. Technicolor had always been able to process and print conventional colour film, which operated alongside dye-transfer release printing and was used for its original photography, rushes and for limited print runs, including TV movies.

Confucius says "Keep DyeTransfer"

Before the final shut down, Technicolor in London had designed and built a dye-transfer machine for China, who wanted to make large numbers of prints without being dependent on foreign film stocks. They were able to manufacture their own materials for the dye-transfer process, and when London's machinery stopped for the last time, this too was shipped out to Beijing.

In hindsight, Technicolor's decision may have been premature, as shortly afterwards the cinema business bounced back, and with the trend to multi-screen conversions, followed by purpose-built multiplexes, the demand for prints rose again until the average blockbuster required many thousands.

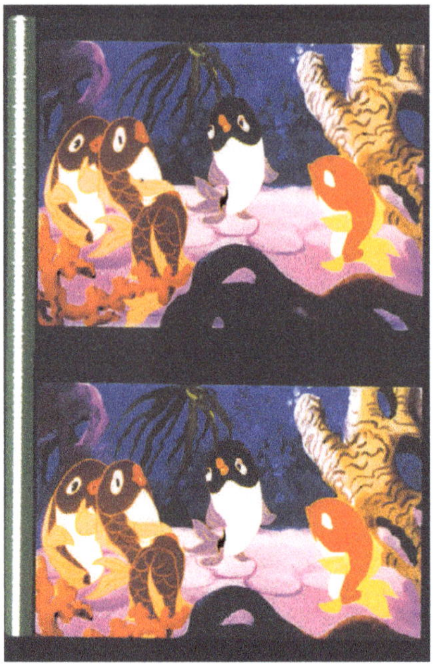

Chinese animation film made using the dye-transfer process

Made to last
Comparison of the state of preservation of a 35mm dye-transfer print and a 70mm Eastman Color print made from the same negative in the early 1960s. Pictures enlarged - not to scale

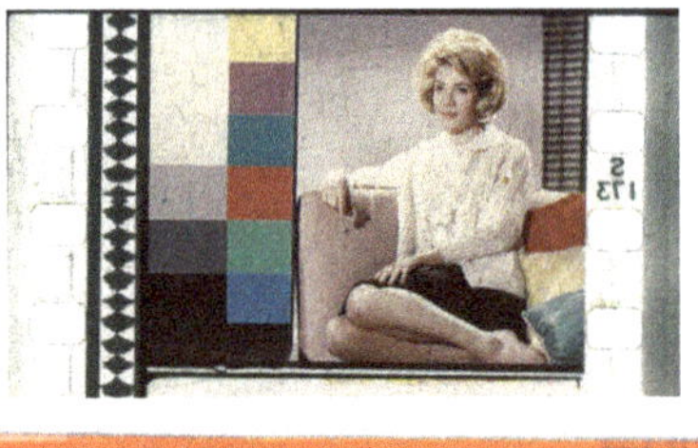

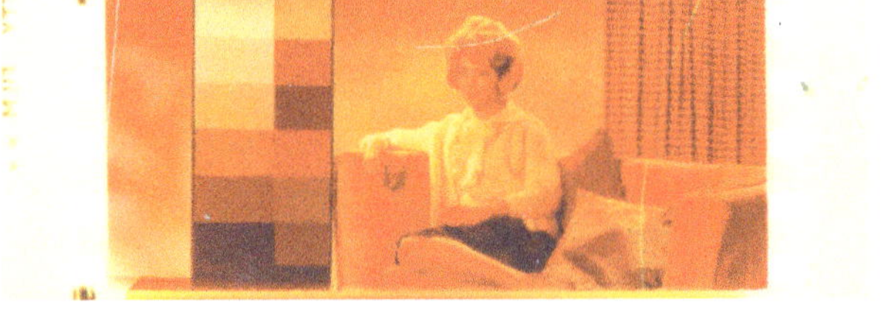

Dye-transfer's extended life in China eventually came to an end in 1994, and the process seemed destined to become part of the cinema's technological history. However, shortly after, Technicolor in Hollywood made the surprise announcement that it planned to revive an up-dated version. The news was given the full publicity treatment, with items appearing in the press and on TV. It was suggested that the advantages of the Dye-transfer process, together with the enhanced picture quality on the screen, would help to ensure the continued use of film projection in cinemas in the face of competition from the emerging electronic cinema.

A strange 'relaunch'

Technicolor fans eagerly awaited seeing the first "Super Technicolor" dye-transfer releases, but it was to be a long wait. Some thought that Technicolor was having second thoughts, but four years later the first prints saw the light of projectors in the US. These were re-issues of Technicolor classics, including *Gone With The Wind* and *The Wizard of Oz*, each using around 50 new dye-transfer prints. The numbers increased for the release of *Godzilla*, with 1000 of the total of over 6000 printed in the US being dye-transfer. Others since then have included some of the prints of *Pearl Harbor* and the re-issue of *Apocalypse Now*.

Surprisingly, Technicolor didn't actively promote its new product, to the extent of asking producers not to refer to it in the film's credits or publicity material. Perhaps they were being cautious about their capacity to satisfy the demand for dye-transfer prints in full and in sufficient time or they might have been waiting to see the effects of the forthcoming introduction of digital cinema before making further investment. This policy of non-disclosure extended to the technical details of the new version.

However, having seen the prints, the procedure appeared to basically the same as that abandoned in the 1970s, but with the prints being made on polyester stock. The optical soundtrack(s) were still pre-printed in black and white, so the silver track remains as the traditional way of identifying a dye-transfer print. Even the digital tracks on the latest prints had the neutral grey look.

Not many prints found their way across the Atlantic, too few to make a fair assessment of their image quality compared with the same conventional prints. Technically, there were no reports of any serious problems, except that some of the early prints shed emulsion in the projector gate. This defect was soon rectified with improved lubrication of the Estar polyester base.

Still a superb system in the digital age

The fact that dye-transfer prints have been around since 1928 didn't mean that Technicolor re-introduced an old and outdated process.

Dye-transfer prints are more than a match for those made on multi-layer colour print film, in terms of colour rendition, dynamic range and greater permanence. Even today's low-fade print stocks will not outlast "no-fade" dye-transfer.

Using externally mixed dyes, the mixture and combination can be altered to offer unique control of the colour reproduction that is not possible with the fixed yellow, cyan and magenta dyes generated by dye-coupling. For example, this advantage could be exploited in the field of special effects and animation.

Current digital processing can be equally applied to the dye-transfer process. Laser film recorders are ideal for exposing the matrices from both film and electronically originated images. Digital imaging techniques can be used to control the colour rendition, including judging the effect of using different dye combinations. The tonal balance can be adjusted, to the point of possibly correcting the deviation from the theoretical norm, inherent in the dye-transfer process, although, hopefully, not to the extent of losing the distinctive look which has helped the prints gain such a high reputation.

'Spotter's Guide' to Technicolor dye-transfer prints

Over the years the prints have had various black and white silver components, and it is possible for the knowledgeable enthusiast spot different versions of dye-transfer prints.

1. Optical soundtrack 'Key' grey image Frame lines. The key image was progressively phased out during the 1940s.
2. The frame lines, with many different aspect ratios, continued into the widescreen period of the mid-1950s before being replaced by frame lines double-printed on the matrices.
3. Apart from a few experimental dye/toned tracks, the silver optical soundtrack was used until the dye-transfer process ceased in the 1970s.
4. The 1990s re-introduced dye-transfer prints still use silver analogue, and now digital tracks.

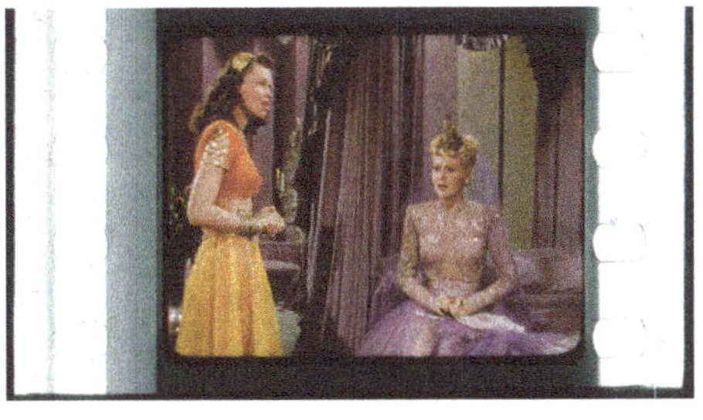

1. Pre-1950 nitrate prints were made on stock with Bell & Howell (negative-type) perforations.

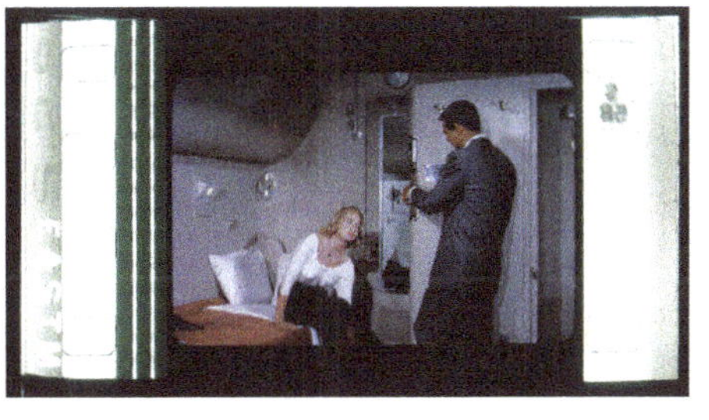

3. VistaVision reduction print.

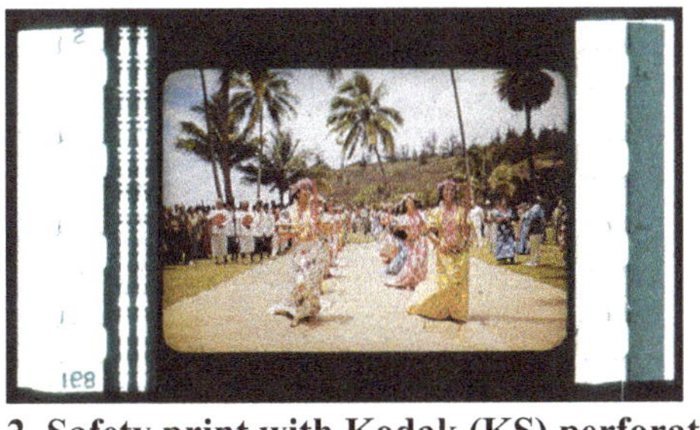

2. Safety print with Kodak (KS) perforations.

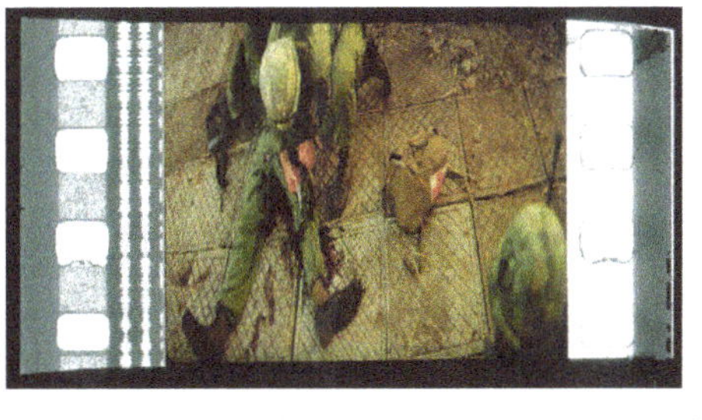

4. 1990s print with silver analogue and digital tracks

Technirama - the birth of another widescreen process

Technirama - The Birth of a Process

Although Technicolor was producing beautiful VistaVision prints for Paramount, the process was only being used occasionally by other studios. Most producers thought that their audiences would be more impressed by CinemaScope's wider screen, rather than better picture quality.

Technicolor decided to introduce its own proprietary widescreen process combining the benefits of both. Their aim was to bring VistaVision quality to CinemaScope-type anamorphic squeezed prints and at the same time, help to ensure the future of its dye-transfer matrix printing system. Development work began at their London plant under the supervision of engineer George Gunn. The new system was to be based on using a large-area camera negative, which could be used to produce every kind of 35mm and 16mm print then in current use. This would need extensive use of optical printing. This had always been part of the normal Technicolor process, needed to produce the printing matrices, so it was going be, according to Technicolor, "right up our street". Known during its development work as the "Technicolor Universal Frame Process", the negative was to be the same as VistaVision's 35mm horizontal double-frame format, but with the aspect ratio of the image increased to that of CinemaScope's 2.35:1, by using an anamorphic lens on the camera. As the VistaVision frame was already a little wider, a lateral compression factor of 1.5x was to be employed, which was only half that of CinemaScope's 2x. This large compressed negative image could then be squeezed further (x1.33) during the reduction to make prints compatible with CinemaScope, or unsqueezed for 'flat' prints, mostly in the 1.85:1 ratio.

The Camera

Technicolor had already converted several of its now redundant 3-strip cameras to the VistaVision format, replacing the triple film beam-splitting system with single horizontal 8-perf movement. With new purpose-built VistaVision cameras now coming off the Mitchell Camera Company's production line, these became available for Technicolor's own system.

The first major problem was to obtain a high quality anamorphic camera lens to match the overall quality of the system. First tests using a lens designed and made up for Technicolor in France were disappointing. It had many of the optical problems associated with early cylindrical refracting anamorphic lenses, including variation of the compression factor across the frame and at different focusing distances. After unsuccessful attempts to find other lenses via the Hollywood plant, Frank Durban, General Manager of J.Frank Brockless Ltd. suggested trying the Dutch Delrama system, of which they were the British distributors. (The company also handled the Philips range of projection equipment

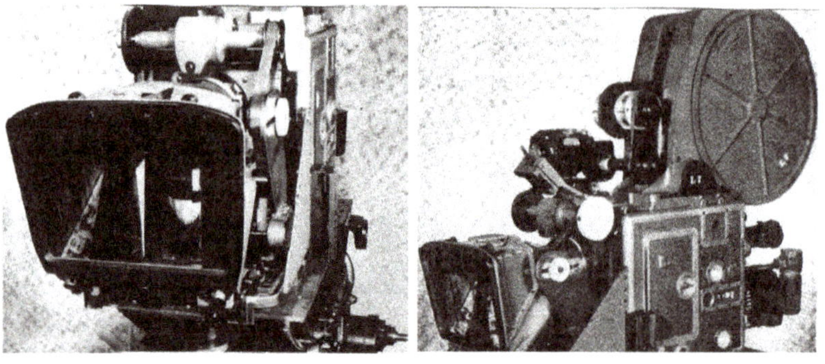

Original 3-strip camera converted to Technirama including its Delrama anamorphic attachment.

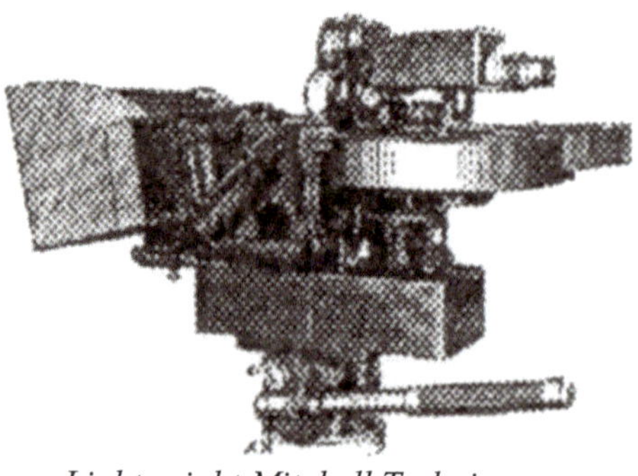

Lightweight Mitchell Technirama camera

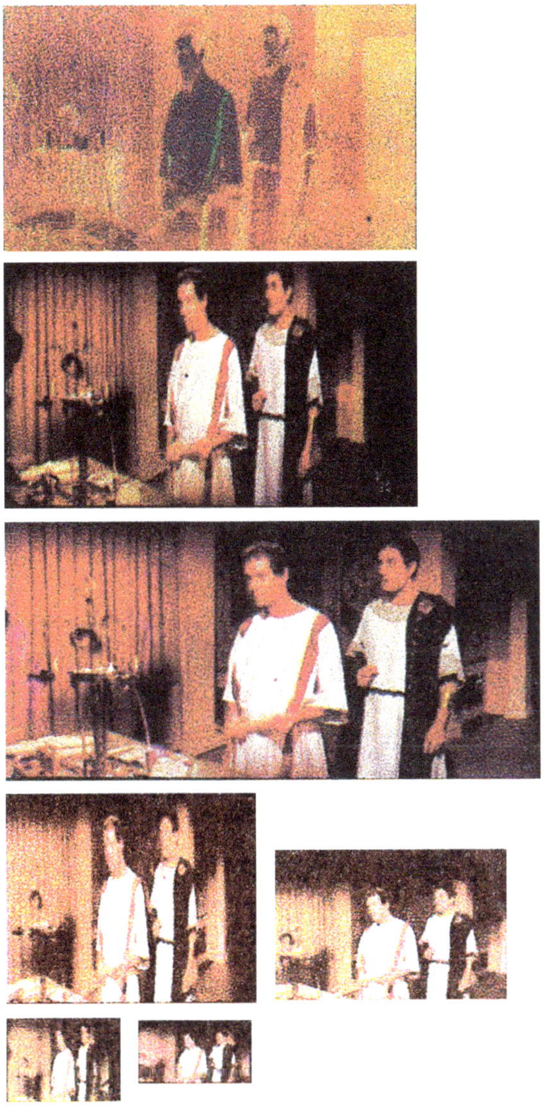

Illustrating the wide range of prints that could be made from a Technirama negative (not actual size)

in the UK, which later was to include the DP70.) The Delrama anamorphic reflecting system used curved mirrors arranged in the form of a periscope, instead of the more usual lenses or prisms, and was free of many of their defects. Tests using a modified projection unit were encouraging, so Frank Durban and representatives from Technicolor travelled to the Netherlands to meet its creator Dr. A Bouwers of NV Optishce Industrie De Oude Delft. He seized upon the problem and came up with a design more suitable for camera use. This employed specially computed curved surface reflecting prisms, rather than cylindrical lenses or refracting prisms. It was an auxiliary attachment big enough to cover the larger diameter of the lenses needed to cover the double-frame negative and allowed for a maximum angle of view of about 60-degrees, equal to that of CinemaScope and the other systems then in use for general film making. The prototype was tested by being sent to the winter sports resort at Sestriere, with instructions to shoot a wide variety of scenes in all kinds of lighting conditions, particularly with the sun glaring off the snow, to make sure that the prime lens and Delrama combination produced

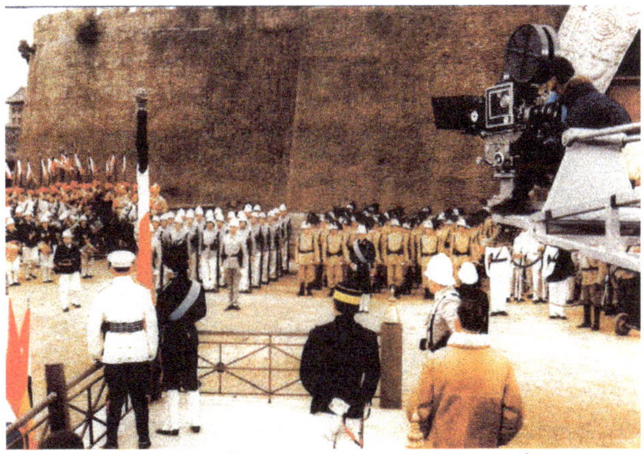

Technirama Camera capturing a scene from '55 Days in Peking'.

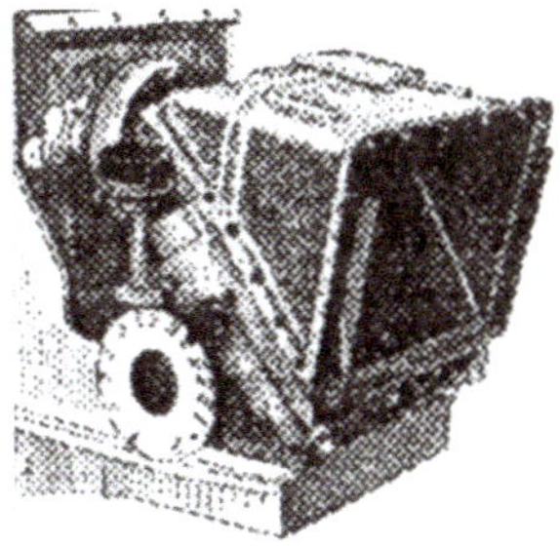

no internal reflections. The results were superb, even at wide apertures, so Technicolor obtained exclusive rights throughout the world to use the Delrama, so it would only be used as part of its own widescreen system. The name Technirama was finally chosen for the system, said to be coined from the words Technicolor and Delrama. (Delrama anamorphic attachments, using the same principle, were made available for 8mm and 16mm users and marketed under the name Vistascope in the USA.).

The Curtain Rises on Technirama

The Sestriere footage was incorporated into a promotional short Technirama demonstration film called 'The Curtain Rises On Technirama', which was used to help introduce the process to the industry in 1956. The principal release format was to be 35mm anamorphic dye-transfer prints, with the option of unsqueezed 1.85:1 prints if required. Apparently Technicolor made a lot of these at the time for German cinemas. At first, it was suggested that horizontal 8-perf contact prints (on Eastman Color print film) be used for special first-run road show engagements. These would be available with a single optical, or multiple magnetic sound tracks. The idea of horizontal prints had already been tried out with VistaVision. Technicolor had actually made a few prints, but they only had limited use, due mainly to the fact that they required additional special projectors, which couldn't run normal prints. It was thought that the arrival of Technirama horizontal prints would revive the format. The British projector manufacturer Gaumont-British Kalee produced a fine horizontal machine for showing VistaVision or Technirama films. For the latter, Taylor-Hobson made a prismatic 1.5x anamorphic attachment, which restored the squeezed image by compressing it vertically, rather than expanding it horizontally, which was said to give better results. Unfortunately, events would show that they had 'backed the wrong horse' and it would have been better to make a 70mm projector.

What About 70mm?

Even when first announced, the possibility of adding 70mm to the range of prints available from the versatile Technirama negative was discussed. However, at the time, although Todd-AO and 70mm projection was making news in America, it had yet to make any impact elsewhere. For example, it couldn't be seen in Britain for another two years. For the moment, horizontal 35mm prints were being promoted in the UK as Technirama's prestige format. The first Technirama feature, *The Monte Carlo Story*, starring Marlene Dietrich, was premiered this way at the Reposi Cinema in Turin in December 1956, using an Italian Micronlamda VistaVision horizontal format projector with a 1.5x anamorphic lens.

The initial option of making horizontal prints led to different practices regarding the camera apertures and printed areas in use on either side of the Atlantic. Cameras supplied by Technicolor's European plants used an aperture of I.480inches x 0.915 inches, leaving a clear area above the image for the soundtrack. Hollywood's view was that, with the failure of VistaVision horizontal prints to catch on, Technirama horizontal prints wouldn't be needed, so their cameras had an aperture of 1.496in. x 0.992in. This meant that the first American prints were reduced from a slightly larger negative area. Also, the Hollywood plant was already gearing up to handle the 65mm/70mm systems. They would soon be making 35mm dye-transfer reduction prints from Todd-AO and MGM Camera-65 65mm negatives, alongside those made from their own Technirama large-area system. The first Hollywood Technirama feature was Universal-international's *Night Passage* in 1957, often quoted as the first ever Technirama film. The first British production was Ealing Studio's *Davy* (1957). The process proved to be reasonably successful in its original form, but later in 1959, the option of 70mm prints was finally added to its list of available formats and 'Super Technirama 70' was born.

Super Technirama 70

By 1958, 70mm was becoming well established, helped by the availability of multi-purpose 70mm/35mm dual gauge projectors. 65mm/70mm processing and printing facilities were now being installed in Technicolor's London and Rome laboratories. The dye-transfer system was never adopted to make 70mm prints, with all Technicolor's 70mm prints being made directly on to Eastman Color positive print film. The first Technirama 70mm print was made for Walt Disney. Always closely associated with Technicolor, they had made their cartoon feature Sleeping Beauty (1959) in Technirama and wanted to give it the added status of a 70mm release. It was photographed in the Technirama format using a cartoon camera which photographed each of the cells three times through red, green and blue filters in sequence along a single black and white negative. The squeeze was incorporated by a lens supplied by Panavision and this was to form the basis of the printer lens needed to make the 70mm print. Similar lenses were also obtained from Cooke Taylor-Hobson.

The first live action customer to get the 70mm blockbuster treatment was Solomon and Sheba also in 1959. In both cases the decision to make 70mm prints was made shortly before release, so both films only carried the normal Technirama credit in their titles, although much was made of the 'new' Super Technirama 70 process on the posters and other promotional material. The process was given a further boost with the success of Spartacus (1960), with the full credit now appearing in Saul Bass's wonderful opening credits. Incidentally, on this particular film, Panavision also received a credit. This only refers to its printer lens; the camera still used the Delrama anamorphic system. (Apparently, some later Delramas were also assembled for Technicolor in the USA by Bausch & Lomb.)

Super Technirama 70 prints were fully compatible with Todd-AO and the other systems using a spherical 65mm negative. Although technically a blow-up, this was only needed in one direction. The height of the Technirama negative already matched that of a 5-perf 70mm print, so it was only necessary to un-squeeze the image to fill the frame. Coming from a negative less than two thirds the size, the image admittedly appeared a little grainier than contact prints from 65mm originals. However, the results on the screen were still often stunning, fine examples being El Cid and Zulu. Technicolor took great care when making their 70mm prints. The negatives were specially processed (zircotan bleach) to give them an image with the grain and contrast characteristics more suitable for optical printing. As the numbers of prints were relatively small, the original negative was always used, after making black and white separation protection masters. A liquid gate printer helped to hide any blemishes. In this technique, pioneered by Technicolor, the negative was immersed in a chemical solution having the same refractive index as the film's base. This had the

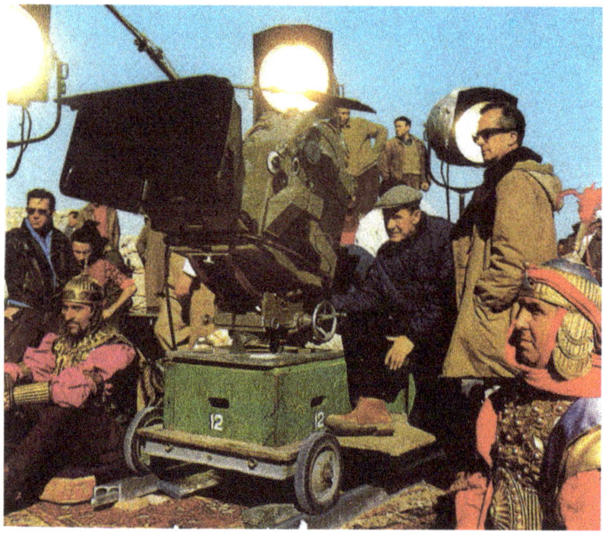

The Technirama camera in its lightweight blimp, shown filming 'El Cid'.

effect of 'filling in' any scratches on the base side of the film so they wouldn't show up on the print. Sometimes, the only clue that a Technirama 70mm print was being shown was the rare sight of a negative emulsion scratch running horizontally across the screen and sometimes, if mis-framed in the projector, impressions of the eight negative perforations could show along the bottom frame line. More recent 70mm reprints of Technirama films cannot always recreate the original quality. For example, the recent 70mm restoration of Spartacus wasn't made from the original negative, which was found to have faded, but was contact printed from a new 65mm duplicate colour negative generated from the Technirama format B&W protection colour separations.

Technicolor engineers continued to develop the process. Although they continued to use the old converted 3-strip cameras, these had a state-of-the-art motorised follow-focus system to adjust the prime lens and Delrama simultaneously. At first, the original huge 3-strip blimp, which occupied some sixteen cubic feet of studio space, was used for sound shooting and, with the film running at twice the normal speed, the 1000 foot magazines meant constant reloading. Later a small fibre-glass blimp, only a third of the weight, was engineered, together with special 2000 foot coaxial magazines. Technicolor now boasted that the Technirama camera could be moved around by only two men! A Mitchell lightweight VistaVision camera was also adapted for Technirama and an underwater housing constructed.

One important advantage over the other large-area systems was that Technirama still used standard 35mm film in the camera. This made it particularly popular outside America, where 65mm processing facilities were limited. The negative could be processed by any laboratory and Technicolor could also provide a mobile printer installed in a caravan (trailer) for making 'Scope reductions of the rushes without delay (photo right). Two such vehicles were equipped and sent to locations all over the world, one travelled as far as Japan. The most dedicated European user was producer Samuel Bronston, choosing to make most of his epics in Technirama, including King of Kings, El Cid, 55 Days at Peking and Circus World (G.B. title The Magnificent Showman). The latter was shown in 70mm single-lens Cinerama, who supplied Technicolor with a special printer lens which left the image at the sides of the frame slightly squeezed. This corrected itself when shown on Cinerama's deeply-curved screen. At one time, a printer set-up was even constructed to convert Technirama to 3-strip triple panel Cinerama.

A couple of Technirama films, Michael Powell's Honeymoon (1959) and Black Tights (1960), were converted to ARC-120 (Not done by Technicolor). This curious process unsqueezed the image, divided it down the centre and printed the two halves side-by-side vertically within a normal 35mm frame. The resulting print was shown through a special twin-lens projector attachment which reassembled the image onto a deeply curved screen.

Technirama films continued to be made without having 70mm prints made. Actually the credit 'Filmed in Super Technirama 70' could be described as misleading. The 35mm release prints were no different from 'ordinary' Technirama films, with no 70mm stock involved in the process. Anyway, nobody ever complained and it looked more impressive on the titles. The last Super Technirama 70 film was another Cinerama presentation, Custer of the West in 1967. With constantly improving film stocks, producers no longer felt that the added cost of using double the amount of negative stock was justified. If needed, satisfactory 70mm prints could now be made by blowing up a 35mm anamorphic negative. And at the other end of the picture quality scale, Technicolor was now finding more customers for its 2-perforation pull-down 'half-frame' Techniscope process. Disney revived Technirama in 1985 for its animated feature, The Black Cauldron, before the process was finally put back on the shelf. Fortunately, many notable features were made in Technirama (see list) and with many now to be seen on TV and video, the trademark on the credits will help keep the memory of this fine widescreen process alive.

Some Technirama films presented in 70mm

Sleeping Beauty 1959
Solomon and Sheba 1959
Spartacus 1960
El Cid 1961
King of Kings 1961
Barabbas 1962
55 Days at Peking 1963
Circus World/The Magnificent Showman 1964
Zulu 1964
Custer of the West 1967

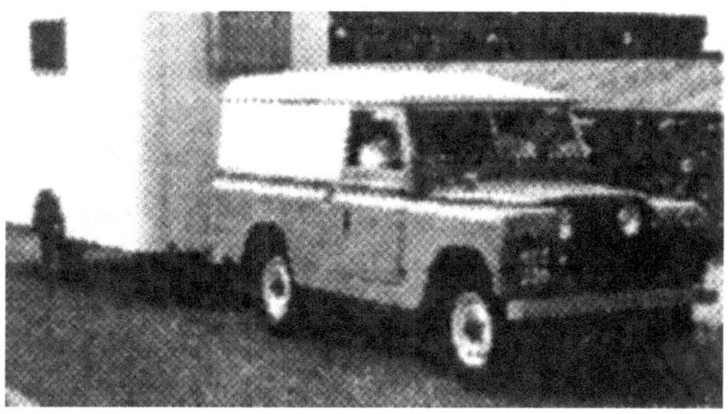

Restoration

No Restoration without conservation

The traditional view

It wasn't so long ago that the term 'film restoration' conjured up an image of dedicated archivists engaged in a race against time to save our cinema heritage by repairing and copying old nitrate films before they literally self-destruct. Also brought to mind are major restorations like Kevin Brownlow's passion, which lasted almost a quarter of a century, for reconstructing Able Gance's silent epic *Napoleon* (1927). He, and other film historians, are continuing their work to bring back to life the classics of the silent screen for other audiences to enjoy and appreciate.

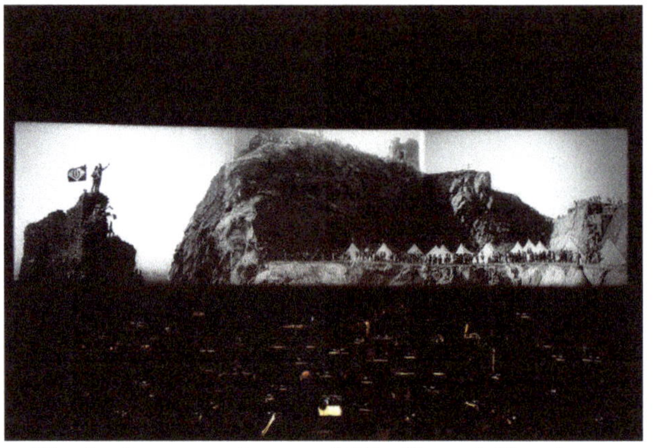

The final twenty minutes of Able Gance's Napoleon, restored by Kevin Brownlow, uses a three panel 'Polyvision' projection system where three film projectors are synched. The curtains are quickly drawn back to reveal the full width of the screen and the three panel 'triptych' images

Not always so old

These days, however, there are few re-issues of even relatively new films, both at the cinema and on video, which don't boast the use of a 'newly restored print', with the latter also digitally re-mastered for good measure. Many potential customers may have been surprised that films like *Lawrence of Arabia, Spartacus* and *My Fair Lady* had to be restored, and wondered why such important and popular films were not looked after properly in the first place.

How permanent?

In a world of ever changing video formats, film is often quoted as the ideal mastering medium, and praised for its permanence and long-term protection. However, those of us who handle and work with film, both old and new, know how fragile and vulnerable it can actually be.

It started on celluloid

It's now a well known fact that for the first 50 years, the professional cinema was in reality a wonderful world of celluloid, using films with a cellulose nitrate base. 'Nitrate' films are not only highly inflammable, but will eventually decompose. The life of nitrate film was estimated to be around 50 years, so its use was not a problem, when in current use and in good condition. Some cheap kinds of stock made using wood cellulose, rather than the usual cotton, broke down first, lasting only ten or twenty years. This stock was often chosen for prints with only a short working life, such as newsreels and topical shorts. Many of these, which are now long gone, would have been of great historical value. Of the other nitrate films, most have already disintegrated, and the life of those which remain is hard to predict. For example, the Imperial War Museum once had over 1000 nitrate based films, dating from the First World War. Today, less than 50 still survive, the rest decomposing during the 1950s and 1960s. When its time comes, nitrate film destroys itself, and once started, the process of decay cannot be halted. Even if previously copied, it is still a heartbreaking experience, as the quality of the images can rarely be replicated. It's also a nasty business. First the film becomes sticky, before rapidly turning into a gluey congealed mess, then finally to brown powder. While this is all happening, the decaying film gives off dangerous and explosive gasses. In the interests of health and safety, if any of the early signs of the film's demise are detected, then it must immediately be put out of its misery and destroyed.

Safety first

When nitrate film was the industry's normal 'stock in trade', it was handled and run without any concern. Cinemas were licensed and inspected by the authorities to ensure that the safety regulations, designed to protect both the staff and the audience, were observed. Projection room rules included a separate rewind area, plus automatic fire-proof safety shutters on the portholes to stop any fire, or sign of it, reaching the audience. The projectors had to have enclosed spool boxes, complete with fire traps. Trip switches in the film path shut down the machines in the event of fire. Projectors continued to be supplied with many of these design features, long after nitrate prints had been discontinued, right up to the long-play revolution in the 1980s. Nowadays, nitrate film has gained such a reputation, that some new projectionists starting work in the few specialized theatres still equipped and licensed to run it, (like the National Film Theatre), often feel nervous during their first show, like being trapped in a room with an unexploded bomb. I can remember my own final 'official' nitrate show at the BBC's last nitrate-equipped preview theatre at Lime Grove studios. The sense of danger was heightened when the film was delivered complete with its own BBC

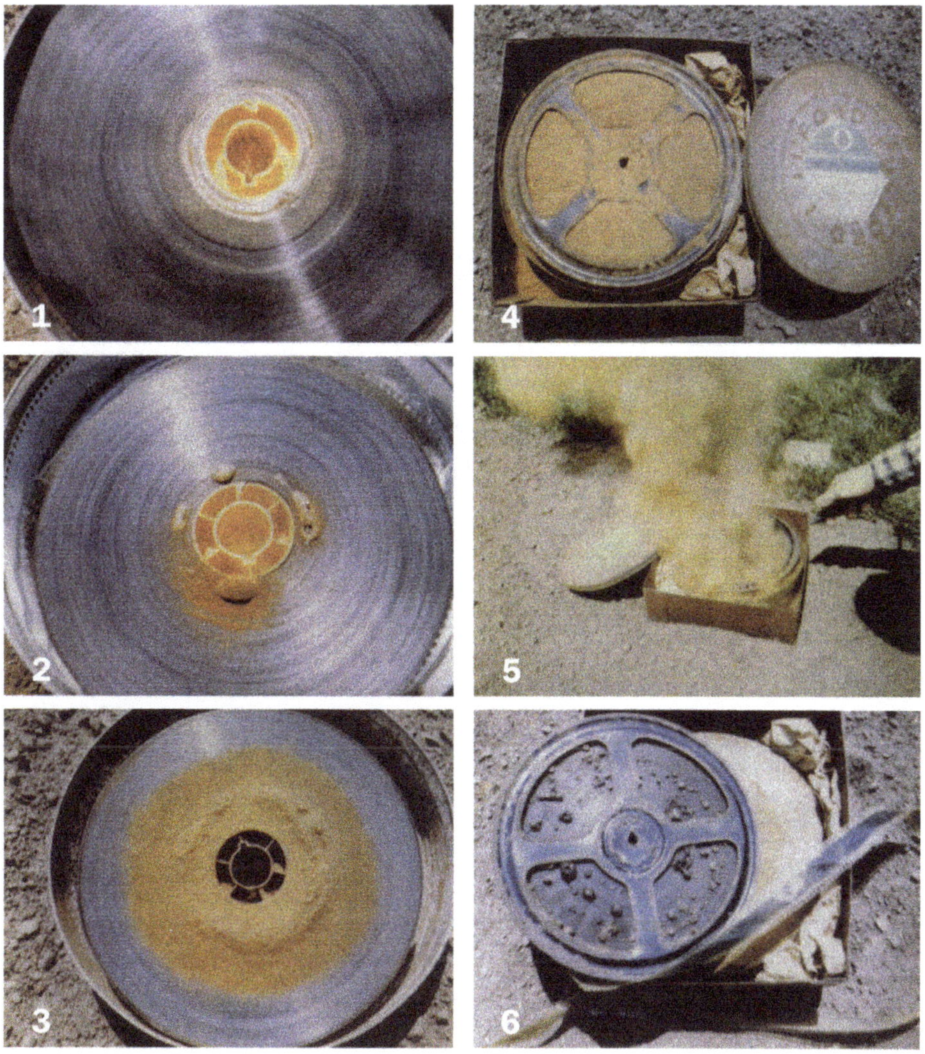

Pictures of nitrate film - going, going, gone!

1. Centre of the roll becoming tacky, with adjacent layers of film often sticking together.

2. Centre of the roll becoming sticky and blistered with brown powder beginning to appear.
In both the above cases, if the unaffected outer parts of the rolls are isolated immediately they can be saved for long enough to be copied.

3. Roll disintegrating to acrid brown powder.

4. Can opened after 35 years.

5. Powder being blown away

6. To reveal a spool full of a solid congealed mass of unsaveable film.

fireman, holding a fire extinguisher in one hand and a bucket of sand in the other. All survived the event and enjoyed the showing of a beautiful Technicolor nitrate print of *Saraband For Dead Lovers* (1948), before the theatre was closed down and eventually demolished, along with the studio.

Why did it take so long?

Why did the industry continue to use such a hazardous substance for so long? A 'Safety' slow-burning cellulose-acetate stock was introduced in 1908 for the Kodak roll film still camera. It was subsequently made available for motion picture work in the 1920s. However, at the time, safety film wasn't as strong, flexible or transparent as nitrate, so it was only adopted for 16mm, 9.5mm, and later 8mm films, in order to make life less hazardous for amateurs. Acetate also cost more, so why pay extra for prints which only lasted half as long? It was not until 1950 that an improved tri-Acetate base was introduced which matched the physical characteristics of nitrate. From 1951, the change to safety film was rapid and since then, most nitrate films, particularly those with any commercial value, have been copied onto acetate stock, most of them long before they came up to the end of their life. The arrival of television helped speed up the re-printing process, as many safety prints were needed for broadcast directly from telecine.

Safe but not permanent

Another advantage of safety film was said to be its longer life, sometimes even described as 'permanent'. Unfortunately, the passage of time has shown that acetate film also has its own process of decay. It is known as the 'vinegar syndrome', named after the smell of the acidic fumes given off by the film during its own road to ruin. This makes the base increasingly brittle, and if left untreated it will eventually crumble to dust. The condition was first noticed during the 1960s, with one of the first complaints to Kodak coming from the Government of India, whose films were stored without any protection from the hot humid climate. By the 1980s, the condition had become a general problem, striking first at magnetic tracks and striped prints. Unlike the decay of nitrate, the vinegar syndrome, if caught early, can be arrested. The search for a cure, or at least a method to slow down the process, has resulted in a number of proprietary procedures. These include chemical treatment to the film itself, or a packet of chemicals stored along with the film in the can. This acts as a sponge to absorb moisture and harmful contaminates released by the film. Plastic 'vented' cans or alkaline-buffered cardboard boxes are also available to get rid of the fumes. Protecting large collections can be a very expensive business. Those of us with smaller collections and who have begun to notice a smell of vinegar coming from under the bed, may like to try one old archivists' wives tale and put a sprig of mint from the garden in each can. I'm told it seems to work!

Nitrate can last 100 years

It now appears that the best surviving nitrate stock, when properly stored in the cool and dry, has a much longer life than was previously expected. Some of the early nitrate based films, which were kept after being copied, have actually outlasted the acetate copies originally made to save them. Some films, dating from the birth of motion pictures and now over 100 years old, are still in reasonable condition, while the camera negative of the last major American feature photographed on nitrate stock, *Sunset Boulevard* (1950), has started to decompose. Another dramatic example of the staying power of early nitrate films, was a collection buried, when the mining town of Dawson City in northern Canada was abandoned in 1928. When the films were dug up out of the permafrost in 1978, they were in excellent condition. One related use of nitrate film was for early cartoon' cells', before they too changed over to acetate sheets. Today, some collectors pay thousands of pounds for early examples, showing great faith in the future condition of their celluloid investment.

Polyester problems?

We are now told that the modern answer to 'permanence' is a change to a polyester base, with a life of between five and ten times longer than acetate, However, in the years to come what currently unknown affliction may also strike this kind of base? The emulsion is already coming unstuck from some of the first polyester films.

Food for fungus

On whatever kind of base, the film's emulsion, with its silver black and white, or coloured dye images, is also at risk. It's very much an organic substance made up largely of gelatine. In the right warm and damp storage conditions (or should it be wrong?), it makes the ideal food for various creepy-crawlies, fungus, mould and bacteria. Although the invaders rarely destroy the film's images completely, their waste products leave spots and blotches, which are often hard to remove or disguise. If the emulsion is discovered to be 'alive', the unwelcome visitors can be dealt with, using a dose of fungicide, or even killed off by being irradiated with gamma rays.

Terrible tales

Films are not always safe, even in the cool and dry of a well protected 'vault'. There are few of these, at studios, libraries and laboratories, which have not at one time or another, suffered a fire, flood, or even an earthquake. Such disasters continue to happen. On a hot summer's day in 1978, a fire at the International Museum of Photography at George Eastman House in Rochester, New York, nearly destroyed the original nitrate negatives of *Gone With the Wind.* It was blamed on spontaneous combustion inside a nitrate store, which didn't have any temperature or humidity control, or even any proper fire detection or control equipment. Unfortunately, The disaster did claim the negatives of another 327 features and short films, plus a number of early cartoons. Nearer to home, on the hottest day of 1993, a similar fire started in the vaults at Hendersons, a south London laboratory specializing in printing old black and white films. After it was all over, we had to say goodbye to the original negatives of such British classics as *Whisky Galore*, *Passport to Pimlico* and *The Belles of St Trinian's*. Of course, in both cases, none of the most important films were at any risk of being lost completely. The first rule of conservation dictates that duplicate negatives and other pre-print materials are always kept at other locations. Also, there are still many good quality prints around of the most popular films. At greater risk from these catastrophes, are the lesser known films, with no back-up material readily available.

Human destruction

Although at risk from acts of God, the greatest danger comes from the decisions and actions of man. It is estimated that, of all the films produced before 1950, only a half are still in existence, with the proportion rising to three-quarters lost from the silent era. When sound arrived in the late 1920s, silent films were considered to be worthless. Millions of feet were destroyed, sold off to junk merchants for the price of their silver content. Even the celluloid was 'melted down' and turned into patent leather shoes and handbags. Apart from deliberate actions, many of the films, particularly the less popular and less well known, have been lost by simple neglect.

After a film's negatives and other pre-print material had served its purpose making the release prints and sometimes 16mm reduction prints for the non-theatrical market, the rolls of film were put on the shelf and forgotten. In the years to come, although the film inside remained in excellent condition, just the sight of the rusted cans with their faded labels was enough to invite the film to be junked, if orders came from the top to make room on the shelves. This was far more likely to happen in the years before the coming of television and later earnings from the release of films on video cassettes and the ever hungry satellite channels. At the other end of the scale, even the successful blockbusters, with many re-issues in cinemas, were in danger of suffering from over work, with the negatives ending up worn out and damaged, by being required to make too many prints.

Conservation counts

Films - a valuable asset

Today, films with any kind of entertainment value are now a sought after asset. In 1986 The Turner Entertainment Co. of Atlanta, Georgia, paid $1.5 billion dollars for the MGM / UA Studio. It was just to get hold of its library of films, with the other assets of the company were soon sold on. The collection of 2,200 features, which also included pre-1950 Warner Bros. films, were needed to help fill the programme hours of Ted Turner's many cable and satellite stations plus possible future films-on-demand channels. At the time of the purchase, the expected cash flow, produced by the library from the films' showings on TV networks around the world, plus their release on video cassettes and laser discs, was expected to top $100 million a year. The films included such classics as *Gone With the Wind, Casablanca, The Wizard of Oz, 2001: A Space Odyssey* and *Ben Hur*. The number of films later grew to 3,300, with the acquisition of the domestic US rights to the old RKO library. The TV rights outside America were purchased outright some years earlier by the BBC. The deal was criticised at the time by some critics, who thought that colour TV licence payers would not like to hear that the Corporation had spent a rumoured sum of over 2 million pounds for a load of old, mostly black and white movies, even if they did include *King Kong* (1933), *Top Hat* and *Citizen Kane*. It has since proved to have been a fantastic bargain, providing many 'no-cost' transmission hours on the BBC's own channels, plus the income from showings on rival networks and satellite channels. Other major collections are now in the hands of international broadcasters. The Fox library is operated by Rupert Murdoch's News International, and Warner Bros. by Time Warner Inc., the largest entertainment company in the world.

Caring for your assets

It has at last been realized that, considering the earning power of these libraries and the millions of dollars spent making and marketing new major features, the actual films themselves have not in the past been properly cared for. In recent years new state of the art storage facilities have been built, which provide conditions that match or even better those found in the best national archives. In 1992, Warner Bros. spent $9 million dollars (still only one-tenth the cost of making and launching some new major features) on a new high-security vault at its studios in Burbank, California. It has an advanced fire detection system, with halon gas fire suppression, just in case. The latest temperature and humidity control, includes cold storage areas for keeping colour negatives. All the rolls of film are kept in vented containers to allow any vinegar syndrome accelerating vapours to be removed using a charcoal filtration system. Samples of air within the vault are systematically drawn off and fed to an automatic gas analysis unit, which warns of any build up of harmful substances.

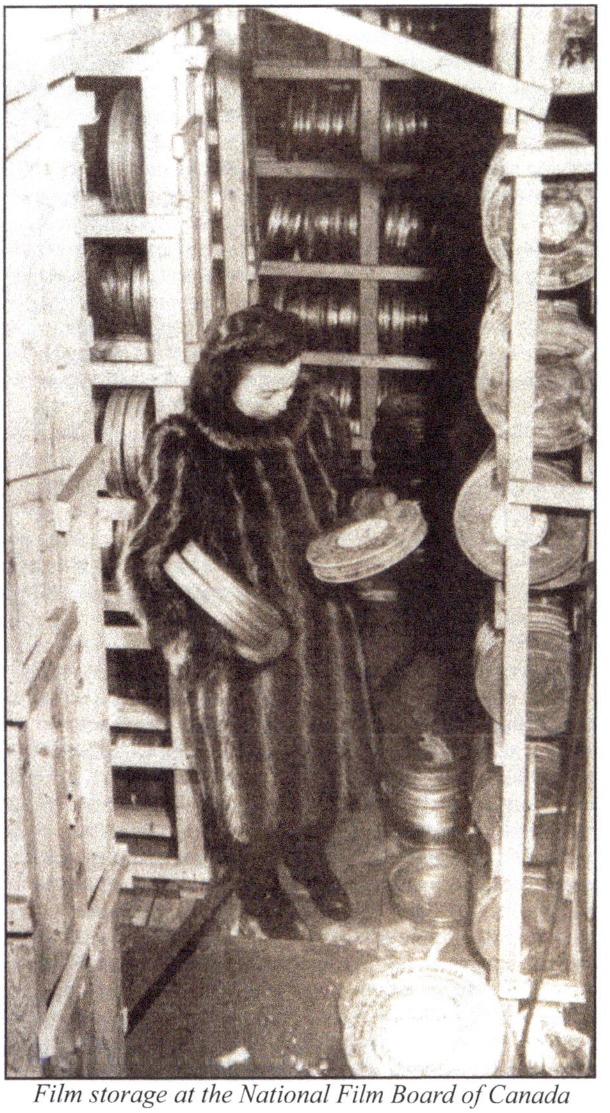

Film storage at the National Film Board of Canada Library in Ottawa, pictured during the 1940s. The combination of the unheated vault and the country's cool climate provided ideal conditions for film storage.

Paramount's vault

Another example of film vault construction is Paramount's facility, built in 1990 to house its own vast library of 270,000 rolls of film. It is situated on its Hollywood lot and cleverly disguised as a New York City street and has been used as a backdrop for many of its movies. Like most of today's archives and libraries, the move to computer records has helped to prevent past 'losses' due to vulnerable card index systems and the reliance on the long memories of staff, who often retire taking their secrets with them. To prevent any possible risk of a catastrophic loss of a complete collection, back-up material is always stored at different locations. As well as its main collection held at its HQ in Los Angeles, Turner Entertainment Co. also uses rented space, along with others like Disney, at the Kansas Record Center, deep underground in an old limestone mine. Paramount uses another underground vault in Pennsylvania. Disused mine shafts, caves, and redundant nuclear bomb shelters, are popular locations for archives. In Britain, one interesting site is the one operated by Security

Archives in a network of underground tunnels, forty metres below London's Tottenham Court Road. It was originally built in secret during the second world war as the wartime HQ of General Eisenhower.

Due to stricter nitrate rules introduced during the 1970s, most of the Hollywood studios, with the exception of Disney, donated their nitrate holdings to national archives, museums or universities. The UCLA film archive has the second largest collection of entertainment films in America. It was started in 1971, when Twentieth Century Fox and Paramount Studios gave all their material on nitrate stock to the University. Most of Britain's nitrate films have ended up at The National Film Archive. A small amount (up to 12 tons!) is kept at the J. Paul Getty Jnr. Conservation Centre at Berkhamsted. The main nitrate store, holding another 160 million feet, is at Gaydon in Warwickshire, on an isolated site once used to keep spare parts for Britain's nuclear arsenal. The film is stored in 216 well separated vaults, laid out like a firework factory, to limit any losses due to a fire or explosion.

The (film) Library of Congress

The largest collection of release prints in the United States is held by the US Library of Congress in Washington DC. They were obtained, without cost, as part of their copyright registration. The library also looks after the American Film Institute collection. There is no such copyright requirement to help swell our own national collection. The National Film Archive relies on the goodwill of the commercial film companies to give them copies. Some, like the Rank Organisation, supplied duplicate master material for making new prints, while others only hand over a 'good' used print, left over after the film's release.

Even so, the Archive has about 50% of Hollywood's total output, and 75% from British studios. Generosity in the past, has saved the day for many film companies, who later needed to replace footage that had been lost or damaged. The NFA also has a budget to purchase prints, enabling them to add important films to their collection. Almost all of the old British features shown on Channel 4 are taped from NFA prints.

Rights & Responsibilities

Rights to most of our favourite British classics are still in British hands. Ealing Studios' films, along with those from ABC and EMI are cared for and exploited by Lumiere Pictures, the principal collection kept in the vaults at Pinewood Studios. Alexander Korda's, London Films, is still very much alive and still controls the use of its films, including *Things to Come, The Four Feathers and The Thief of Baghdad.*

Sometimes the theatrical, TV and video rights for a particular film belong to different organisations. Rank Film Distributors, together with its library of films, was sold to Carlton for £65 million. Many independent films belong to smaller companies and even individuals. Tracing copyright holders and obtaining clearance is a responsible and important job in any TV production company or broadcaster.

The public domain

Not all films in the U.S. are protected by copyright, many of the lesser known are in what is known as 'the public domain', which means they can be owned and exploited for profit by anybody. Over 20,000 U.S. film copyrights were never renewed after the initial 28-year period, either because the holder had gone out of business or didn't think it was worth the time and expense to renew it for the remaining 28 year period. Some important features have lost their protection in America simply because someone forgot to file the application. Some British features like *Evergreen* (Gaumont-Brit. 1934) and *Pygmalion* (1938), which are still copyrighted here, where the time period (50 years) and rules are different, are now in the public domain over in America. In the past, most film companies didn't bother to register their cinema trailers for copyright. In some cases, these can now be used without payment, rather than clips from the actual films, which can cost hundreds of pounds per minute.

Private sources

An important 'alternative' source of supply, and often used to replace films 'lost' from official collections, is the network of private collectors and enthusiasts around the world. Once considered by many in the industry as a bunch of strange obsessive fanatics dealing in stolen property, they are now recognised for their work in saving many films from destruction. Such is today's change of attitude, that many collectors now co-operate with archives and film companies in the search for complete copies or missing parts of films. Indeed, in appreciation, the film companies are prepared to give back the originals, or make new copies of the films, which are returned to the collector, providing they are not commercially exploited. Film prints have always escaped from the system, old stand-by prints being found abandoned in the ruins of derelict cinemas, or priceless classics ending up in Wardour Street skips. Large numbers have also come to light in the estates of former studio bosses, producers and film stars, who started out by keeping copies of their own films, but then went on to catch the collecting bug. Jack L. Warner and stars like John Wayne and Peter Sellers were found to have large and valuable collections. Many of today's collectors have extensive holdings of 16mm, 35mm and even 70mm features, many larger than some of the smaller national archives. Although well known to each other, with a lot of wheeling and dealing in prints going on, they had to keep a low profile officially, with doubts about their rights of ownership and the constant fear of repossession by the copyright holder. Also the keeping of nitrate prints at home would not be approved of by insurance companies.

Celebrity cares

One high-profile example of action taken against a collector was back in 1970, when Bob Monkhouse had to defend the right to keep some of his films. Bob was not only a well known performer, but also an expert film historian, particularly in the field of film comedy, and over the years built up a huge collection of films. With the help of supporters, like the National Film Archive, he eventually won the case, but admits that the legal action took the heart out of his collecting activities.

Even so, he still has the fourth largest private collection in the world, with over forty-thousand individual subjects on various gauges, including hundreds of features. The current largest private collection belongs to a German collector. Some of the major collectors and dealers in films now use computers to monitor the ownership and copyright status of thousands of films. Some private collections have been fully, or partly commercialised. One of the first in America, belonged to the late Raymond Rohauer who, from his college days, found and collected many rare silent and early sound films. Although his methods didn't always endear him to the film establishment, often upsetting laboratories and many official archives around the world, he must be given credit, with others, like our own Philip Jenkinson, for trying to save and popularise silent films, at a time when few others were interested. One well known collection over here was established by film historian John Huntley, and it has often come up with fascinating clips, adding interest to many a TV documentary.

Where are they now?

Sometimes the rights to a company's back catalogue of films is purchased, but not all the actual prints can be found on the shelves. One example was the BBC's acquisition of Butchers Films, a provider in the past of British 'B' movies. The deal didn't include all the actual prints, so they circulated an appeal for copies to fill the gaps, including 35mm or 16mm prints borrowed from private collectors (no questions asked!). In the end, it will probably mean a lot of restoration work to come.

The quest for the definitive version

Blood and thunder

Although a film may have managed to overcome the many natural and man-made obstacles to its survival, it may still be wounded, having suffered cuts. To most movie-goers, the news that a film has been cut is usually associated with censorship, but they are much more likely to have been cut or altered by their own producers or distributors, if this was thought to improve its chances of success at the box office. This may have happened before, during, or after its initial release, often resulting in different versions of a particular film.

Scissor-happy?

Nowadays, many consider that films should be treated as works of art, creations of their directors and not to be interfered with by anyone else. However, back in the days of the all-powerful studios and their bosses, it was not uncommon for directors, however distinguished, to be told to cut great chunks out of their films, if it had been decided that there was any risk of boring the audience. Known as the 'restless bum factor!', it was either based on the movie moguls business acumen, or by studying the comments made by audiences at special sneak previews. Their reactions often led to cuts, or even new sequences being shot, before the film was released. Scenes were lost, regardless of their original cost and the creative effort put into them. If a director didn't co-operate he risked not being paid, or even worse, another director being employed to make the changes.

Compulsory 'Happy endings'

Distributors also had a great influence. After the original road-shows of *Fantasia* (1941), Disney had to cut it down from 126 minutes to 82, before RKO would release it on a double-bill with a western, again fearing audience tedium. Sometimes new 'happy endings' were demanded, to help ensure that audiences left the theatre with a high feelgood factor. Even well-known classic stories were not safe. Unlike the climax of Henryk Sien-

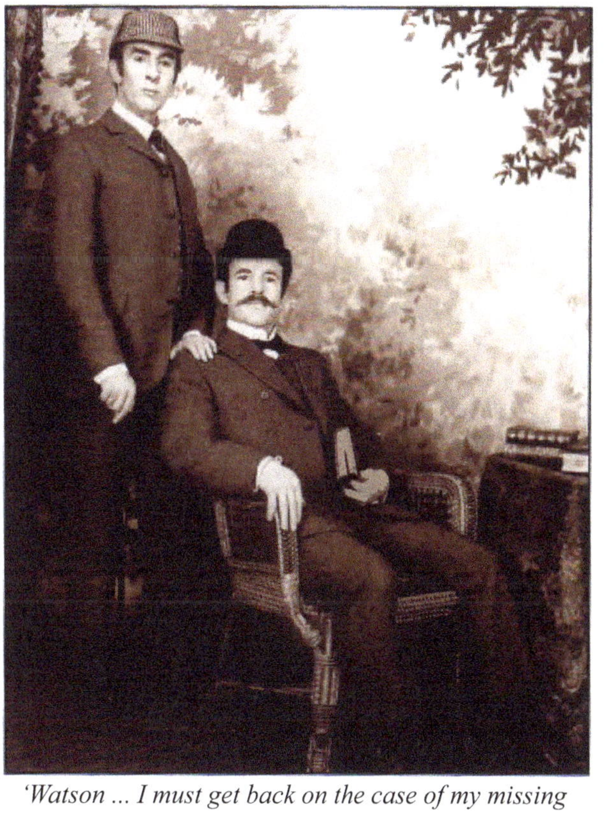

'Watson ... I must get back on the case of my missing film'. Robert Stephens and Colin Blakely in Billy Wilder's 'The Private Life of Sherlock Holmes'.

kiewicz's novel, the character played by Deborah Kerr, in MGM's *Quo Vadis* (1951), didn't perish in the Roman arena, tied to the horns of a bull.

An extra song and dance number was deleted from *The Wizard of Oz* (1939). Although entertaining, it didn't contribute to the progress of the story. The footage was kept safely by MGM and has since been seen in a documentary about the making of the film and used in other musical compilations, including *That's Dancin'* (1985). There has never been any suggestion that this sequence should be put back in the film, as it was never part of the final version and would result in two versions of an otherwise one-off and unique classic.

Similar cuts were made to a later Judy Garland vehicle, *A Star is Born* (1954), when 27 minutes of musical and dramatic scenes were removed. This time, the deed was done in response to audience reaction and critical reviews, after the film had already started its first-run engagements at key cities around America. Before the negative was cut to make the bulk of the release copies, those already in circulation were intercepted and edited on site by studio representatives, sent out with a pair of scissors and a sheet of instructions. All the cut footage was returned to Warner's vault, where it remained separated from the main body of the film and proved hard to find for a later restoration. In this case, as the original version had already been seen by a large number of movie-goers, it can be regarded as a legitimate restoration project. Some other possible restorations, may be considered less justified. Howard Hawks's thriller, *To Have and Have Not* (1945), had a long dialogue sequence taken out before its release. Although important to the understanding of the plot, it was removed in order to get on with the interplay between the film's stars, Humphrey Bogart and Lauren Bacall. Warner executives wanted to reflect the then current public interest in the couple's real-life off screen romance, even if it made the story harder to follow. Again, the original had already been seen outside the studio before the re-think, this time shown to American forces, before the film's release into normal theatres.

The unkindest cut?

A contender for the greatest amount of footage cut from a film, as it was first delivered by its director, but before release, must be Billy Wilder's *The Private Life of Sherlock Holmes* (1970), which was to lose almost 90 minutes! It was originally conceived as a true 3½-hour epic, complete with an intermission and 70mm roadshow engagements. However, its distributors UA, believed that the public was tiring of over-long films, following box office disasters like *Dr. Doolittle* (1967) and *Star* (1968). Even David Lean's *Ryan's Daughter*, which followed, wasn't as successful as expected. They said a two-hour version would do, and they got their way. Originally, the film had four episodes in which Holmes becomes entangled with women. These were cut to two and, as we shall see later, an attempt has recently been made to reconstruct the original, with only limited success.

Getting the timing right - a choice of versions

Equally drastic cuts are sometimes made after a film's release. There were at least three different versions of the notorious *Cleopatra* (1963) in circulation at the same time, as Fox continued to cut and recut their failing epic. Running times ranged from the 4-hour plus of the roadshow prints, down to the 2¾-hours of the last general release version, with Cleopatra's entry into Rome and the Royal Barge sequences severely truncated. Even today, TV stations still have the choice of running times available for broadcast.

Foreign versions

As well as the 'domestic version', there may also be different foreign versions, either longer or shorter and with a new title. The British film, *The Wicker Man* (1973), had extra scenes added to the American prints, to help spell out the reason why Edward Woodward's character, (an adult male virgin), was the ideal candidate for the final pagan sacrifice. In its efforts to show the longest possible version, the BBC borrowed the extra footage from the director's own U-matic tape copy of a 16mm print. In this case, it was for a special showing in its 'Movie Club' slot, aimed at movie buffs. Subsequent showings, including one on Channel Four, reverted to the original version. In the search for lost material, foreign prints can be a disappointment. In the past, it was not unusual to export old refurbished domestic prints which, although still having the original soundtrack, are often found to have been cut and with sub-titles etched into the emulsion.

Another chance to see

Back in the days before TV and video, there were few opportunities to see a film again once it had finished its week's run at the cinema. Apart from the limited 16mm non-theatrical market, only a very small number were ever re-shown in theatres. One chance was the, 'Sunday, for one day only' bookings. For these, cinemas were usually sent one of the few remaining prints left on the shelf after the film's original release. As longserving projectionists can confirm, these were often in poor condition and eventually run to destruction. Sometimes, particularly popular films were given a wider re-release, requiring new prints. Some well-remembered classics, like *Gone with the Wind*, returned intact, but others were often shortened by 20 minutes or more, in keeping with their changed status as second features, or to make them fit into double bills. This fact was often acknowledged, with the advertising and small print in the credits stating that it was now an 'abridged version' or 're-edited re-issue'. If a large number of new prints were required, this usually meant that the original negative or printing masters had to be cut. Occasionally, the major studios sold a film's rights, and handed over the master material to smaller companies specialising in re-issues. They too, often chose to alter the film in some way, including reediting and changing the title. A few Technicolor films were re-issued using cheaper inferior 2-colour processes, or even only in black and white. The copy now seen on TV of *Nothing Sacred* (1937), is only the 2-c:olour (Cinecolor) reissue, with the Technicolor credit removed and replaced with just, 'Photographed in Color'.

Although giving films a new lease of life, they risked further physical damage and loss of original material. Cut footage was often not reinstated and once separated from the main body of the film, was in constant danger of being further separated and eventually lost altogether. Today, when a new copy is required for broadcast or transfer to video, it is sometimes unknowingly made from its last re-issue version. Attempts to obtain a new print of the original, are often thwarted , when only a cut negative or printing master can be traced. A BBC showing of *Joan of Ark* (1949), with Ingrid Bergman , carried the tell-tale 'A Special reedited re-issue' on the credits. If spotted, this may have spoiled the showing for some viewers, who may have wondered what was missing.

Longer restorations

In the past many films 'shrank' with age, in more ways than one. Today, it is now almost obligatory that any new restoration or re-issue must be longer than the original. The publicity people demand a 'newly restored print', complete with extra 'previously unseen footage', plus the film being generally tarted up in one form or another, preferably involving the magic word 'digital'. This has led to the creation of additional versions, variously described as a 'Special Edition', a 'Director's Cut' or their 'Preferred' version, which now exist alongside the originals. These new editions can have another advantage. In some circumstances, if a film is significantly altered, including the colourization of black and white films, they can be copyrighted again as a 'new' film. It's not a new idea to add extra scenes to films. Special longer TV versions were prepared of features, such as *King Kong* (the 1976 remake) and *Airport 77* (1977), increasing their length, to allow for more commercial breaks.

Re-makes

However, special editions have given directors the opportunity to re-work their films. For one of the first, back in 1980, Steven Spielberg was able to both cut and add previously unused scenes to his *Close Encounters of the Third Kind* (1977), including extending the spaceship finale and adding interiors. This new edition, like Ridley Scott's re-cut *Blade Runner*, are now the ones most often shown. With continuing TV and video showings, more people have now seen these new editions than the originals. Other new editions have been considered less successful. Kevin Costner's *Dances with Wolves* , returned to the screen within only a few months with 55 minutes added to a film , which many judged to be rather overlong in the first place. Even the much loved *Cinema Paradiso*, was soon back with a similar amount added, but wasn't universally applauded, even by its devotees. As a result, the film is still available for revivals in its original form. Even low-budget 'alternative' productions are getting in on the act. During a recent light-hearted TV interview, John Walters, helped to push the release on video of his camp *Pink Flamingos*, starring the late Divine, by claiming it included fifteen minutes of previously unseen footage, 'found in the producer's loft!'

What is the definitive version?

All this will make it difficult for scholars of the cinema and historians to decide what should be regarded as the definitive version. Of course, the prime reason for these special re-issues is to encourage people to pay up and see the film again at the cinema and more importantly, buy a new video, even if they already have a copy of the original. For some critics, the results of many of these restorations just go to show that the reasons for the original cuts may still be valid. Is the Director's Cut always the best? They are sometimes too close to their own films and loath to lose sequences they may have taken extra care over and spent (too much?) time on. Producers and editors can be more objective. Most of the extra scenes re-instated by David Lean to his Director's Cut of *Lawrence of Arabia*, are of long lingering shots of the desert. These look magnificent on the big cinema screen, particularly in 70mm, but are in danger of slowing up the pace of the film, when the film is seen on TV or video.

When the 'ethics' of the restoration business are discussed, some restorers still think that every frame is sacred, and aim to arrive at the longest possible print, even at the risk of 'over-restoration' and giving the average viewer a sore bum again. Others are content to keep for posterity an example of the most popular domestic version, as seen by the greatest number of people at the time of release.

The effects of the censors

Censorship has had its effect on surviving material. Films reflect the standards and rules in place at the time they were made. As time has passed, standards have generally become more relaxed, so later cuts were seldom necessary, unless required for a change of category. Exceptions were a few films made in the early 1930s. One of these was *King Kong* (1933). Although the Industry's own 'Hays Office' issued its first Production Code in 1930, it was tightened up in 1934, when the independent and very strict Catholic Legion of Decency was founded and started to issue its own classifications. This meant that the film had to be cut in 1938 for the first of its many re-issues. Twenty-nine cuts were ordered, amounting to a loss of three minutes, and some other scenes were printed darker, to make Kong's violent behaviour less graphic. Most of the cuts were put back for its re-release during the 1950s, but it was

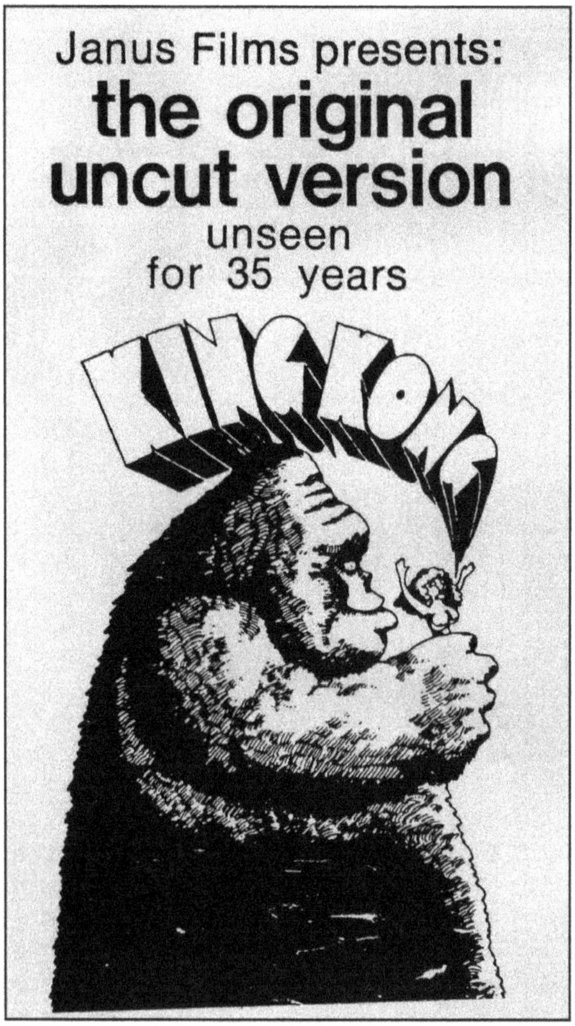

King Kong enjoying getting to grips with Fay Wray again in this advertisement for the film's revival in the 1960s.

not until the late 1960s that the last remaining acts of sex and violence were restored. These included, Kong pulling off Fay Wray's dress, chewing the heads off hapless natives and crushing others under his giant foot. Although 'lost' by the studio, the now legendary cuts were still known to exist, doing the rounds in the world of collectors, mostly on 16mm. Poor quality footage was acquired and incorporated into the 'Complete! Uncut' 1960s cinema revival in the US. Dupe negative from this was later added to the Library of Congress Archive's negative. Later, in 1989, a collector came up with a can of 35mm nitrate film, labelled 'King Kong fragments', and this was found to include much better-quality examples of the censored scenes. These became the basis of a restoration project for the Turner Entertainment Company. The rights to *King Kong* outside America belong to the BBC, who also only had a censored copy. They looked at the newly restored print, but found that the overall picture and sound quality was inferior to its own master copy. This was made up from a number of the best remaining British prints, all made from a less worn and possibly earlier duplicate negative. However, the Corporation did eventually purchase a copy of the American restoration, just to get hold of the missing shots. These have now been incorporated into their existing print, so the BBC now has one of the best existing copies of the complete film.

The publicity for the restoration of *Spartacus* (1960), made much of the inclusion of the bath house scene, with Laurence Olivier telling Tony Curtis of his liking for both 'oysters and snails', indicating his versatile sexual preferences. This was originally removed, not so much because it may have shocked audiences in the 1960s with its daring, but the studio was more worried that movie-goers wouldn't understand what on earth he was on about.

Self-censorship and social mores

Studios themselves occasionally exercise retrospective self-censorship, to match changing social attitudes. Critical viewers may have noticed a marked drop in the picture quality during the Beethoven's 'Pastorale' sequence in Disney's *Fantasia*, featuring the mythical, half-man, half-horse, centaurs. This is because the image was enlarged and re-framed to eliminate the black centaurs. These were drawn in the late 1930s, and conformed to the American Negro "Sambo" stereotype, which is now considered offensive. The last time they appeared, was in the first full-length re-issue, in 1956, although they could still be spotted briefly later in some of the trailers. For *Fantasia's* next outing, Disney may choose to bring the black centaurs back into view, by using today's computer techniques, to make the drawings less demeaning.

Destructive tendencies

Its not unheard of for attempts to be made to deliberately destroy whole films. MGM purchased the rights and the camera negative of the British Victorian thriller, *Gaslight* (Thorold Dickinson 1939), in order to eliminate a possible rival to its own glossy remake of 1943, starring Ingrid Bergman and Charles Boyer. However prints survived, one being used to make copies for a release in the US under the title *Angel Street*. As MGM found, it is easier to lose films by neglect and mistreatment, rather than by wilful destruction. This has not stopped others from trying over the years. They range from repressive governments to rich and famous actors and actresses, attempting to hide their early embarrassing film appearances, by buying up the negative and all the prints they can find. One memorable case being the 1940s Hollywood star, Hedy Lamarr and her millionaire husband's efforts to suppress an earlier European film, *Extase* (1933), in which she appeared nude.

Get It right

It's possible to get into trouble by showing the wrong version. During a consumer rights programme, a company was put in the dock for selling videos of a so-called 'full-length' version of Leni Riefenstahl's account of the Berlin Olympic Games of 1936, *Olympiache Spiele*. It later proved not to be the case, only the longest version available from the supplier of the print. It was admitted that the marketing people often know little about the films they promote, having to rely on others to provide a complete print. The publicity surrounding the more commercial restorations, some actually little more than just cleaning the negative and making a few new prints, has at least raised the profile of the whole business of film restoration. The repair, re-construction and conservation of films, has always been a constant and never-ending task going on behind the scenes at archives, libraries and laboratories around the world, and we now start looking at the technical aspects of restoration, including work carried out on many of the films already mentioned, when using various types and condition of original material.

The business of restoration - technical aspects

Having looked at the continuing need for restoration, to prevent the loss of films by natural decay and human neglect, we move on to the technical aspects of the task. Although digital technology is an important new tool available to restorers, its current high cost restricts it to the more 'commercial' restorations, where the costs can be recovered from re-issues in the cinema or a release on video. Many projects still rely on traditional repair and photographic techniques. Even if computer processing is to be employed, the best possible original material still needs to prepared for the initial digital scanning.

Finding the 'originals'

The detailed accounts of some of the more high-profile restorations describe the search for all the remaining material and its preparation for final printing. They may have been fortunate to find the original camera negatives in good condition to work with, or at the other end of the quality scale, having to make do with a worn projection print. In between there are many forms of "pre-print" elements, described as "dupes", "inter-positives", inter-negatives", "lavenders", "one-light printing masters", etc. In the case of colour, "separation negatives", "master separation positives", "matrices" and "CRIs", are among the terms banded about. To understand what all these descriptions mean, and how they are dealt with by restorers, it is worth looking at a summary of the way motion pictures have been photographed and printed over the last 100 years, starting with black and white.

Black and white

Professional film making has been almost exclusively based on the negative/positive process, in which the negative exposed in the camera, or some form of copy of it, is used to produce all the prints shown in the cinemas. What made it all possible, was the availability of a thin clear flexible base made of cellulose nitrate. Some of the first pioneers obtained raw celluloid, cutting and coating it with light sensitive emulsion themselves, creating their own individual film formats, many with images close to the size of lantern slides.

The Kinetoscope

The first commercially successful moving picture device using photographic film was the Edison Kinetoscope, introduced in 1893. It was an individual "peep-hole" viewing machine loaded with an endless loop of film 13/8th inches wide with perforations along both edges, four on each side of the small 1in x ¾in frames. This "Edison" format was essentially the same as the 35mm format used today. Other pioneers, both in the U.S.A. and abroad, were soon building cameras to produce their own films for showing in the Kinetoscope, or the many illicit copies of it. These same cameras were also being employed to make films for the first projectors, most of them being designed around the Edison format. Projection of moving pictures onto a screen rapidly became the preferred means of presenting films to the public, including many now being liberated from the confines of the Kinetoscope's cabinet and shown on the big screen.

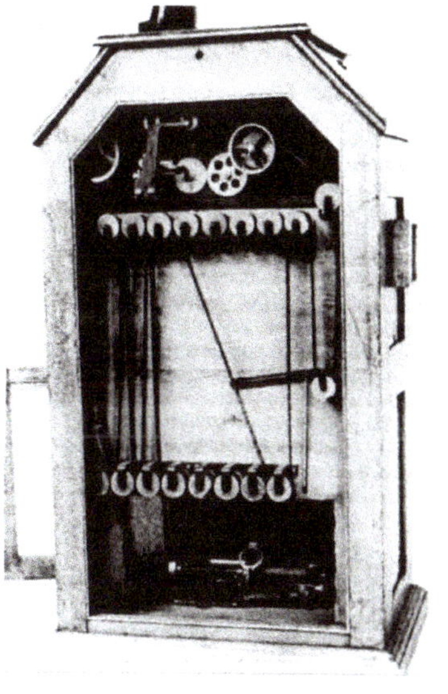

The 35mm standard

By the beginning of the 20th century, 35mm film was the most widely used and had already become the de facto standard gauge. Photographic manufacturers like the Eastman Kodak Company were supplying pre-slit stock coated with emulsion, similar to that used in early roll film still cameras, like the first "Kodak". The same type of film was used for both negatives and prints and the smaller movie frames resulted in less sharp and grainy images. Also some of the first prints were made on a matt or frosted base, making them less suitable for projection.

New and better stocks

In a short time, specific "Motion Picture" negative and print stocks were made available, the latter being on a clear transparent base producing a more contrasty and brighter picture on the screen. It was also slower than the camera film, making it easier to handle during printing. The first black and white emulsions were mo-

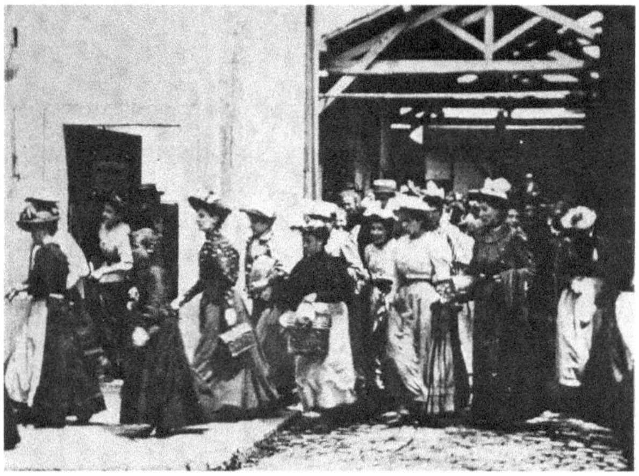

The Lumière's first film subject, workers leaving their factory at Lyon. This famous scene was filmed on three separate occasions. The original version, shot in March 1895, was the last to be discovered and preserved.

no-chromatic, sensitive only to blue light. The camera negative's sensitivity was subsequently increased to include a little green, described as ortho-chromatic. This distorted the tonal scale of the scene somewhat, producing the paler skin tones seen in early silent films. To help compensate, "ortho" make-up was used, which included purple lipstick. The one great advantage of this limited colour sensitivity was that the film could be handled safely under red light during the manufacture, processing and printing.

Seeing the images

Some cameras had gates with cut away back pressure plates, allowing cameramen to compose the picture and judge the exposure required, by observing the image coming through the back of the film. In some cases, this could be done while the film was actually running through a spy-hole or viewing tube covered with a red filter. In later years, a black backing (anti-halation layer) was coated onto the negative's base to reduce light scatter, putting an end to this novel and useful feature.

Varying perforations

Although the Edison 35mm format soon became the accepted standard gauge around the world, the actual dimensions of the perforations and gate apertures varied between producers. Camera outfits often included a perforator to match their sprockets. The American & Biograph Co. perforated the blank stock in the camera, at the time of exposure. In 1911, the British camera maker Newman and Sinclair advertised a perforating service for its customers. To-day, some experienced archivists can help to identify the films of individual producers by studying their sprocket holes and other physical differences. As the movie business grew, a common specification was needed to allow the interchange of films, which could be run on any projector. One particular problem was the different position of the frameline relative to the perforations, which meant constant reframing. In 1917, the first standard issued by the newly formed Society of Motion Picture Engineers, was for 35mm film. This included perforations conforming to those made by the Bell and Howell perforator. Introduced in 1907, This precision machine had already become the most widely used by the industry, including the stock manufacturers providing already perforated stock.

Early processing

Before separate laboratories were set up, around 1900, the camera negative was developed by the cameraman himself and his helpers. They photographed and processed their negatives to provide the type of image favoured at the time. Early primitive projectors de-

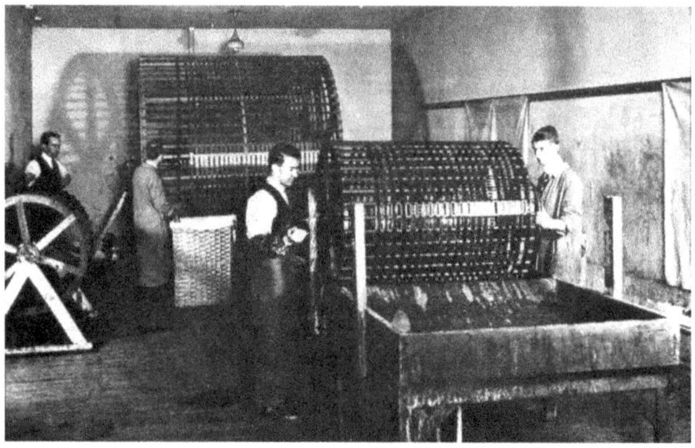

Early processing by hand, with up to 300ft of film wound around a drum

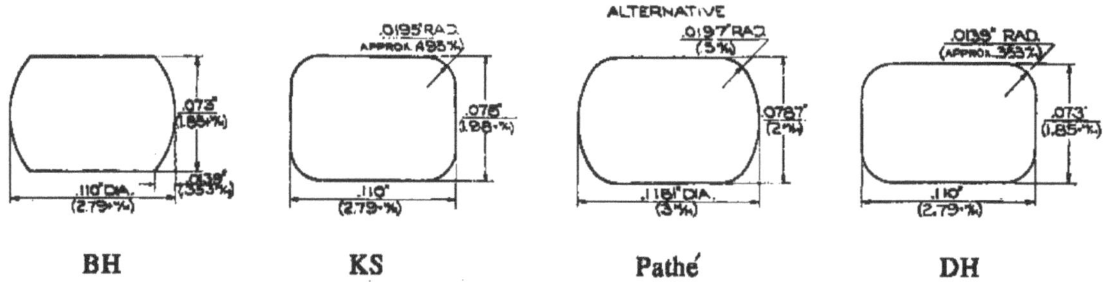

The perforation types that evolved are shown form left to right:
Bell & Howell (BH) for negative and positive, and after 1925, negative only. The Kodak standard (KS), which was also the SMPE standard for positive films. The Pathé, which for two years was also the SMPE Alternative positive perforation. The Dubray-Howell (DH) perforation proposed for positive and negative. Not shown are the BH modified with corner fillets or the CinemaScope (CS) perforation. (Originally appeared in J.SMPE, April 1932)

manded prints with a steady image, plenty of contrast with everything dead sharp. Some exhibitors even asked for no distracting camera movements and to see the performers shown full-length and not cut off at the knees! Some surviving prints now look pale and faded, but these may be examples of the lower density "limelight prints", which were also available for early projectors with poor light output. The processing was done by either winding the film around a drum and rotating it through troughs of chemicals, or on a pin-frame which was immersed in deep vertical or shallow horizontal tanks containing the solutions. Both methods allowed the forming images to be observed and, if necessary, the time in the developer could be altered to compensate for inaccurate exposures in the camera. The film could be "snatched" to prevent an over exposed negative from becoming too dense, or left longer to "stew", if under-exposed. In both cases, the printed image suffered a loss of quality. Many early negatives can vary greatly, in terms of contrast and density, throughout their length, adding to the task of making a satisfactory modern print. As a rule, darker negatives were preferred to help hide the inevitable scratches and other blemishes.

Rudimentary 'editing'

To save expensive stock, it was common practice not to make a print immediately. The cameraman would assemble the negative in slate order and then hand it over to the director and his assistant. They would then subject it to numerous viewings to assess its content, select the chosen scenes and undertake the rudimentary editing of the time. After all this, even the first positive copies could already show signs of considerable wear, printed through from the negative. The final quality of prints also depended on the way they were printed. The most satisfactory, was the step-contact method, in some cases using the camera itself as a printer. The negative and print stock was run emulsion-to-emulsion in close contact through the gate, with the lens replaced by a light source, which could be an electric bulb, or even a gas jet. Another method was the continuous contact printer in which the two films passed over a common sprocket behind a narrow illuminated slot. It was operated by hand at a speed judged to give the correct exposure, after inspecting the negative as it passed over a red light. The latter method, often produced less steady prints with poorer definition, due to loss of contact between the two films.

The projection printer

There was a third option, the projection printer, fore runner of the optical printer. For this procedure, two cameras faced each other, one of them set up as a projector to form an image of the negative in the gate aperture of the other containing the print stock.

Its first use was for creating trick shots, such as reverse action. If their projector mechanisms allowed it, many early projectionists, instead of rewinding the film at the end of the show, ran it back to the start through the projector, much to the amusement of audiences. The entertainment value of this comic effect was soon recognised and incorporated into the films themselves.

Early duplication using normal film stocks

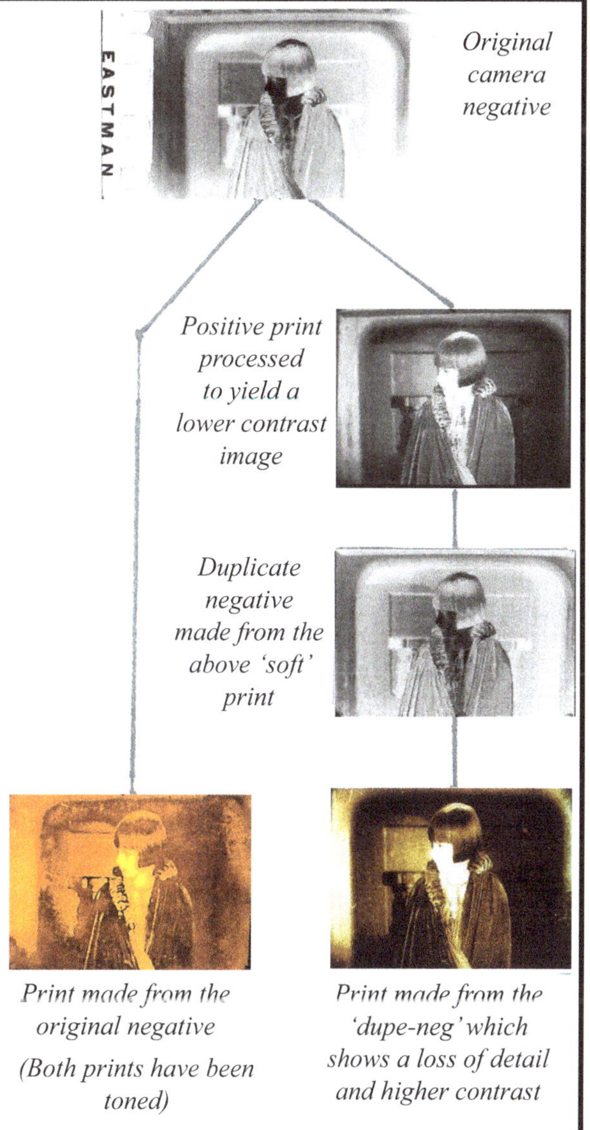

The image quality of the two prints became a closer match with the introduction of proper duplicating stocks, starting at the end of the 1920s

'Mass' production

At first, the showing of moving pictures was just a sideshow novelty, with a relatively small number of prints being shown exclusively by their makers, or sold outright to showmen. If a particular film proved popular many more prints were made for sale, with the original negative in danger of being run to near destruction. If a part was damaged beyond repair, it was sometimes replaced with an alternative take to extend its working life. At a time when films were short, relatively cheap to produce, it was still a practical proposition to obtain a new negative by re-shooting the complete film.

Which version?

This often created a new version of a film, but still having the same title and catalogue number. Perhaps the first example of the confusion this can cause, was Lumière's first film, featuring workers leaving their factory in Lyon. This was first filmed in March 1895, soon after their "Cinematographe", combined camera, printer and projector was patented. After many private showings, the scene was photographed again in June to provide a better print for showing along with other short films to delegates at an important Photographic Congress in Lyon. It was this later version which was included in the programme presented to the first paying audience in Paris on the 28th of December, of the same year. This event has now become accepted by historians as "The birth of the Cinema". Before the existence of the two versions was generally known, it led to controversy during debates about which of the various movie pioneers filmed what first, and when. Some sharp-eyed researchers questioned the Lumière's claim that a film, allegedly shot in March, showed the workers in summer clothes and a branch of a tree, appearing at the edge of the frame, was in full-leaf. In fact the workers were to be filmed a third time, with the original being the last to be discovered and preserved.

Business deals

In the early years, when the showing of motion pictures was still just a sideshow novelty, a relatively small number of prints were either shown exclusively by their makers, or sold outright to showman. Later, the individual films gained a wider audience by being swapped via a network of Film Exchanges. Eventually, it was the owners of the exchanges who bought the prints and then rented them out for a period of time to the exhibitors. In 1903, Edison produced a short narrative film "The Great Train Robbery". This event, together with the move towards the showing of films in permanent cinemas, marked the beginning of the theatrical motion picture business. Longer and more sophisticated films were now being distributed to exhibitors around the world.

More prints

With ever rising production costs, the original camera negatives were becoming increasingly valuable, and without a satisfactory way of making copies, they were still being used to make an ever growing number of prints. It soon became common practice to photograph an extra set of negatives. This was achieved, by either repeating the action, or using two cameras operating simultaneously. In this way it was possible to shoot both a domestic and foreign negative. Today, the search for material sometimes produces more than one copy a particular film, but they may not always have been made from the same negative. When restorers try to make up the best copy from different parts of supposedly identical prints, they find it difficult to match the action, or there may be a noticeable shift of viewpoint, if the joins have to be made in the middle of a scene.

Even if, at the time, more than one negative was originally shot, making copy negatives was sometimes unavoidable, not forgetting the inevitable making of illicit prints.

Quality considerations

Whenever a duplicate or "dupe" is made, there is always a marked drop in image quality, with an increase in the grain and contrast, together with a loss of detail particularly in the shadow and highlight areas. Being a negative/positive process, a duplicate negative cannot be made directly, but has to be made via an "intermediate" positive. If a normal and already contrasty projection print is used (as in most pirate copies), the new dupe-negative will produce prints with excessive grain and contrast, with the image often described as being made of "soot and whitewash" and looking rather like a poor photocopy of a photograph. However, it was possible to improve the results by creating a special inter-positive print, which although not suitable for projection, had an image with less grain and contrast and was more suitable for making duplicate negatives. Although still using ordinary negative and positive stocks, their exposure and development times could be manipulated. For example, the inter-positive could be given more than the normal exposure during its printing. This was compensated for, by spending less time in the developer, before the build up of too much grain and contrast. It was also possible to process the positives using "softer" working negative developer. Another technique is "flashing", in which the stock is given an initial overall exposure of white light, to lower the amount of contrast. Although the prints made from duplicate negatives derived from these "soft prints" were a little better, they were still not good enough to avoid printing from the original camera negatives, which was to remain the accepted practice well into the 1930s and beyond. If early duplicating methods had been more successful, many more original camera negatives might have survived in better condition.

Special effects

Another practical advantage would have been the possibility of incorporating photographic effects, such as fades, dissolves and wipes, during the making of a duplicate negative. Throughout the silent era, almost all these effects were performed "in camera" during the original photography. Lenses with totally closing irises or variable shutters were used to create fades, with the negative being wound back for dissolves and superimpositions. In front of the lens, rudimentary wipes could be made via sliding or swinging mirrors and parts of the scene could be altered using painted glass shots. Matte boxes could be fitted with masks for split-screen effects, or used to obscure portions of the scene, with the unexposed area filled in at a later time and location using a counter-matte to protect the previously photographed part of the image. Although these special effects matched the quality of the rest of the negative, they had to be written into the shooting script. However, some of them, like fades and dissolves could still be added later to the processed camera negative using chemical means. One way to create a fade, in or out, was to suspend the chosen portion of the negative in a column of bleach which was then slowly drained away through a tap, progressively bleaching away the image. Dissolves, along with superimpositions, could be made by overlapping the negatives and running them together through the printer. Negatives are still found prepared for this procedure, with the layers of negatives held in place with spots of cement or tied together with threads of cotton through the perforations. However, many negatives didn't live through the experience. It was risky way of doing things, with the extra thickness of film often ending up ripped to shreds after first riding off, and then wrapping itself around the printer's sprockets. Sometimes, only a few important prints were made this way, the rest using a joined in duped section made from one of the previous direct prints. Again, this means differences between individual prints, with some having better quality effects. Another way, was to make soft prints of the portions of the scenes requiring the fades or dissolves and then double printing them onto a dupe negative using a variable resistance in the lamp circuit to perform the transitions. Despite the difficulties, many silent film directors, like Alfred Hitchcock, exploited elaborate montage and multiple-image sequences. Like other innovations, audiences had to get used to them, before they became accepted as part of "the language of the cinema". Apparently, some patrons thought that the projectionist was having trouble with his equipment, which was producing jumbled up images!

Captions & inter-titles

Silent films are often described as being a truly international medium. However, although there was no dialogue to listen to and understand, there were always the captions and inter-titles to consider. Much research is sometimes needed to ensure that a particular negative or print still has its originals. At the time, the opinion of many exhibitors was that, "the better the film, the fewer the titles". Despite this view, some dramatic films, with a complicated story line could have as much as 30% of its total length made up of titles. After its initial big city release, a plodding drama may have had the number of inter-titles reduced or changed to more "jokey" ones to lighten the mood. Even if still in the original language, some may have been simplified to match the literacy and reading skills of the local audiences. When sent abroad, the foreign negative or print supplied usually had each title reduced in length to only a few frames to save on shipping costs and any import duties based on footage. It was up to the local distributor to either restore them to the correct length using a projection printer, or enlarge a chosen frame to make a new title card. In most countries, they just served as a guide for the translation and position. Some producers included a discrete reference number in the design of their titles, which can be a useful guide to present day researchers.

Filmstock developments

During the period from 1922 to 1924, new black and white stocks were introduced, resulting in changes to both the photographic quality and physical characteristics. There was a changeover to faster and finer grained panchromatic camera negative. Being sensitive to all colours, it reproduced a more accurate tonal range, recording correctly the scale of brightness of the scene. In the studios, it allowed the use of tungsten lighting, with less reliance on blue-rich arc lamps and daylight coming through the roof of "glass house" type stages. The negatives now had to be processed in total darkness or very dim dark green safe lighting. Cameras, like the French Parvo, could no longer offer the option of viewing the image off the film itself while the camera was running. Print film remained monochromatic, sensitive only to blue light, so could still be handled safely in red light. However there was another change made to print stock. The Bell & Howell type perforations, flat at the top and bottom with curved ends, had proved ideal for camera negatives requiring great accuracy, but tended to split at the corners after repeated runs through a projector. These eventually led to rips and breaks, shortening the life of release prints. So just for prints, the B&H design was replaced by a new "Kodak" (KS) type, which was rectangular with round corners, which proved to be more robust for repeated runs. The change of shape is a useful, if only a rough guide, to the date of manufacture.

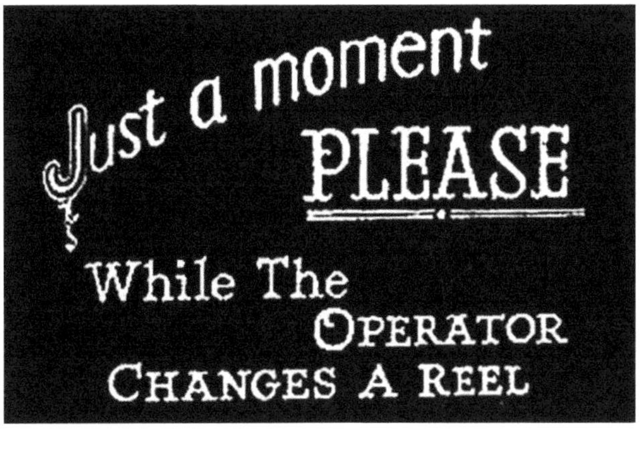

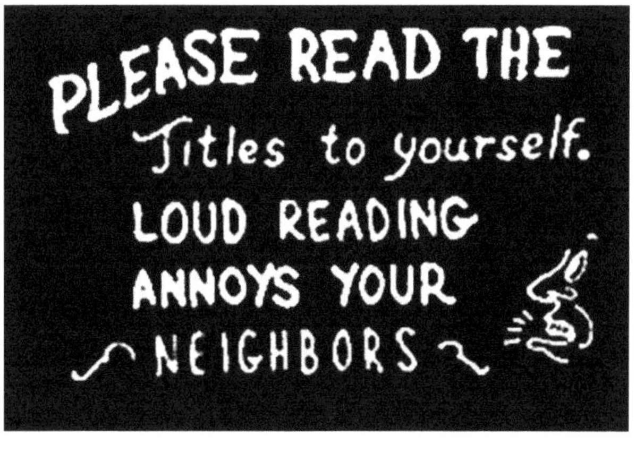

Identifying earlier print types

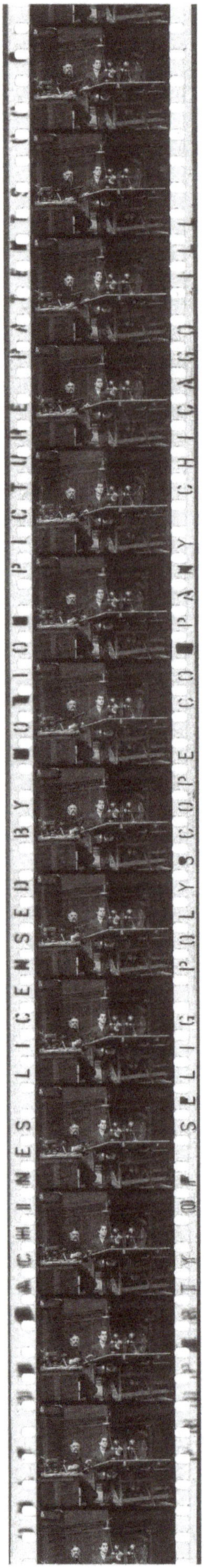

Left:
Early silent print with edge markings giving the producer's name and a copyright warning. The Motion Picture Patents Company was formed in 1908 and attempted to control the industry. It was unsuccessful and ceased in 1915.

The figures along the film edges read MACHINES LICENSED BY MOTION PICTURE PATENTS CO and PROPERTY OF SELIG POLYSCOPE COMPANY CHICAGO ILL.

Below:
'sub-standard' 16mm 'Kodascope' library print reduced from a 35mm original. For hire to home movie enthusiasts. Photo enlarged from 16mm for clarity

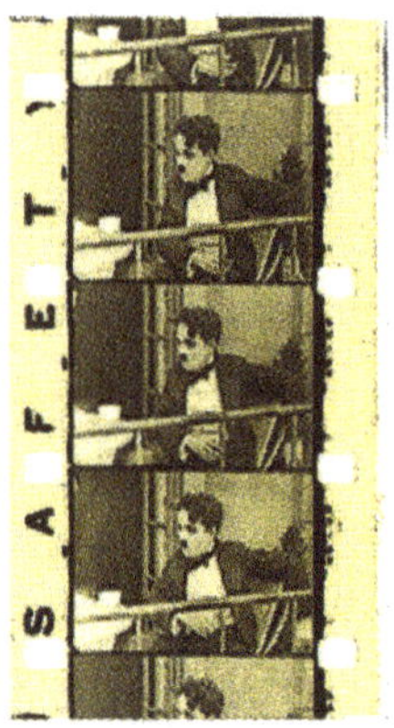

Below:
35mm print from the beginning of the 20th century and before a common standard. The small Edison-type perforations would only run without damage on projectors with the correct sprockets

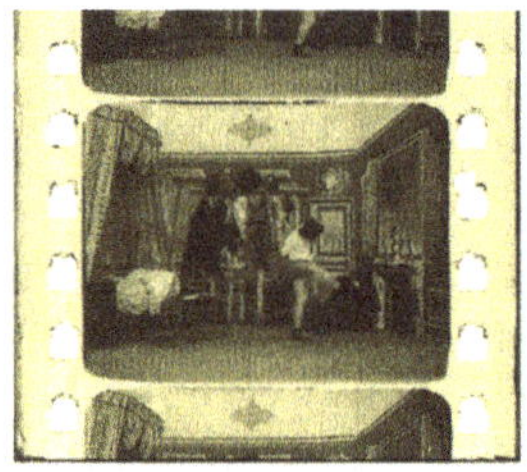

Below:
Standard 35mm film (SMPTE 1917) with Bell and Howell perforations and the frame line midway between the perfs.

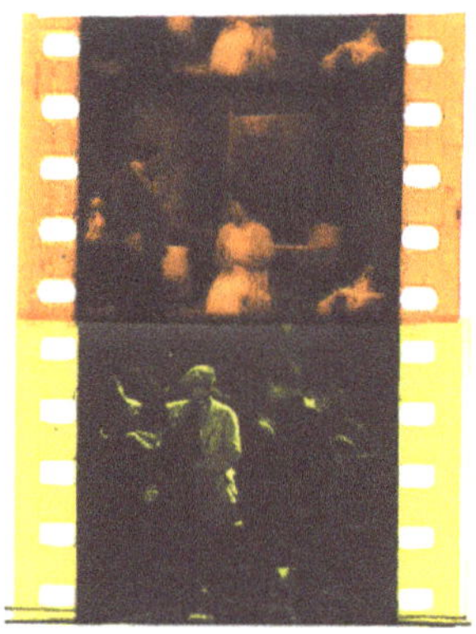

From around 1923 the perforations used on prints were changed to the more robust Kodak-type sprocket holes (KS)

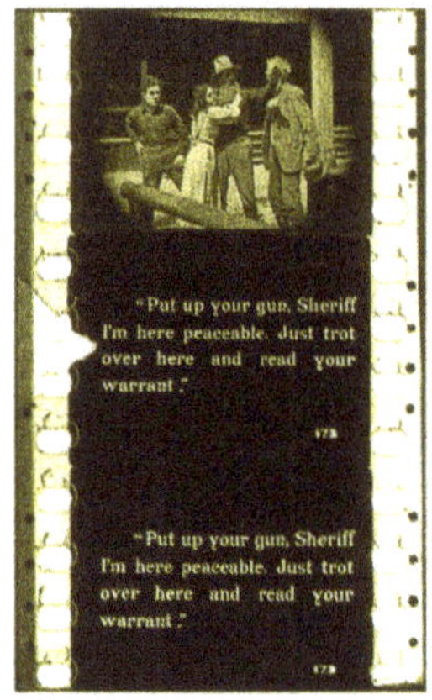

Above:
Silent film inter-titles were sometimes numbered, which can be a useful guide to restoration.

Below:
With no special duplicating films available, some of the early dupes ended up with high contrast 'soot and whitewash' images

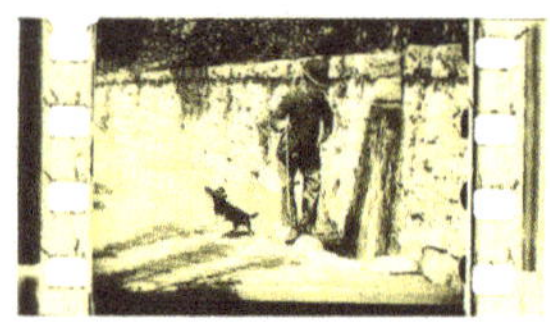

Right:
Kodak films carried code symbols giving the stock's type and date of manufacture. These are often a useful guide to researchers

Print date

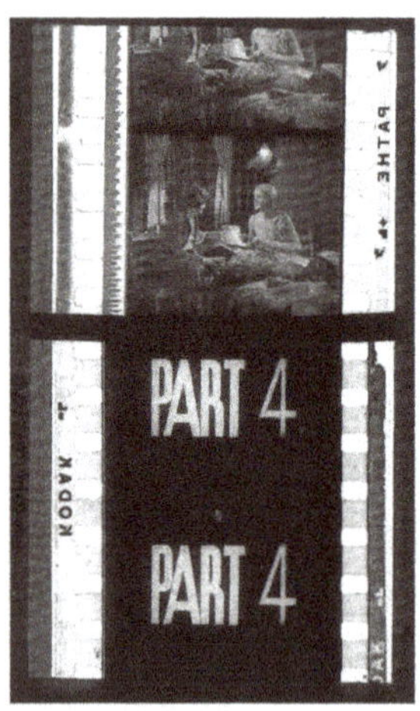

Kodak date code on Pathé print stock

+ L = 1931

Both
+ L = 1942 (British)

From the negative

Gathering information

Information on the print, which can be found away from the image area, can provide a wealth of information to the archivist, often more than the contents of the picture. If still intact, the leaders were sometimes embossed with the film-makers name. Melies did this, as well as punching a star in the first frame of his negatives. For copyright purposes, some producers printed their company name at intervals along the edge of the print. These could be easily lost during the printing of unauthorised copies, so another copyright notice was sometimes placed in the corner of the frame, an early form of today's electronic "DOG" (Digital Optical Graphic). Others could be "hidden", somewhere in the scene, such as a picture on the wall.

Detective work

One of the clues as to a film's origin may be where the raw stock was made. In America and Britain, Eastman Kodak dominated the market, with DuPont also supplying much of the stock in the U.S.. Kodak also manufactured its stocks in Canada and Britain along with Selo (Ilford). Other sources were Pathé in France, Gaevert from Belgium, German Agfa and Ferrania from Italy.

Edge markings

Apart from their name, film stock manufactures began adding extra information at intervals along the margins of their stocks, in the form of a latent image which became visible after development. From 1915, Kodak began adding discrete "runic signs" to indicate the type of stock and where and when it was manufactured. A different set of date symbols was added to Kodak's British made stock in 1917 and to Pathé stock after Kodak's takeover in 1927.

This information is invaluable to archivists, many of whom, know their date code tables off by heart. They don't necessarily indicate the year of production, but no film can pre-date the stock on which it was photographed. The code sequence appears on all kinds of stock, both negative and positive. On a straightforward neg/pos print, the original negative symbols appear clear, while those associated with the print show up in black, They may not always be the same year, but if close, would usually indicate an original print. On a film, which has gone through many duplication processes over the years, the symbols can be much harder to decipher. Some types of printer didn't print them through or obliterated them. Also, at some of the printing stages, stock from a different manufacturer, without date codes, may have been used.

The East Anglian Film Archive made a study of edge codes for different formats right back to 1932 and the The National Film Preservation Foundation, created by the U.S. Congress to save America's film heritage, has much reference work on this topic.

EASTMAN KODAK DATE CODE CHART

1922	1942	1962	●■	1982	●■X
1923	1943	1963	●▲	1983	X▲X
1924	1944	1964	▲■	1984	▲■▲
1925	1945	1965	■●	1985	■●▲
1926	1946	1966	▲●	1986	▲●▲
1927	1947	1967	■▲	1987	■▲▲
1928	1948	1968*	●●●	1988	++▲
1929	1949	1969	+	1989	X+▲
1930	1950	1970	▲+	1990	▲+▲
1931	1951	1971	●+	1991	X+X
1932	1952	1972	■+	1992	■+▲
1933	1953	1973	+▲	1993	+▲▲
1934	1954	1974	+●	1994	+●▲
1935	1955	1975	+■	1995	+■▲
1936	1956	1976	●	1996	X●▲
1937	1957	1977	■	1997	X■▲
1938	1958	1978	▲	1998	X▲▲

There are also other manufacturer codes that tell the determined investigator in which plant a particular Kodak film was made - note how the position of the dot between the letters of the word SAFETY indicates the origin. .

S•AFETY - ROCHESTER
SA•FETY - CANADA
SAF•ETY - ENGLAND
SAFE•TY - FRANCE
SAFET•Y - AUSTRALIA

Key numbers

In 1923, Kodak added reference or "key" numbers to camera stock to be reproduced on rush prints to help film editors cut the camera negative to match the cutting copy or work print. Before this, it had to be done frame-for-frame by eye, which could be difficult on long shots or scenes with little action.

Other clues

Sometimes blemishes proved useful as distinguishing marks. Also to be found on the films edges were the words "nitrate" or "safety". The former appeared on almost all 35mm stock, to distinguish it from the non-inflammable or "non-flam" stock introduced along with the new amateur 16mm and 9.5mm gauges. These less than the standard width 35mm, "sub-standard" formats, led to the development of more elaborate projection printers, now becoming known as optical printers, and needed to make reduction prints of professional films for home viewing.

Many of these, like early 16mm Kodascope Library prints, were made directly from original 35mm negatives and were of excellent quality. Being on safety stock, some have since been enlarged back up to 35mm, as the only way of preserving subjects lost on 35mm nitrate through decomposition.

Effects of restoration

With the arrival of sound in 1927, the role of the optical printer grew in importance. The restrictions imposed by early sound filming saw an end of most of the in-camera effects, particularly scene transitions like fades and dissolves. For a short while, they almost disappeared altogether. When the French feature "L' Atalante" was restored, researchers found that, although dissolves were indicated in the shooting script they never appeared in the prints shown at the time of its original release in 1934. For the new preservation copy, it was decided to include them this time, an act which many purists may consider to be a case of "over- restoration".

Optical effects

Chemical fades were still being employed, but laboratories were now creating them on their newly installed optical printers. They were executed while making a duplicate negative of the scenes requiring the effects. These duped "opticals" were then cut back into the original negative. Unlike their in-camera equivalents, they showed a marked drop in quality. If the scenes on either side of the optical were short, they were usually duped in their entirety. If over about 10 feet, they were cut back to the original negative as soon as possible, whenever practical, using movement to cover the cut. Experienced viewers began to notice the sudden change in quality and register and knew that some form of optical effect was coming up. To help improve the quality, stock manufacturers made available special intermediate duplicating films. They all had a very fine grain structure, and in some types, the emulsion also contained a yellow dye to allow contrast control by placing yellow or violet filters in the printer light.

Lavender prints

They could be used for making both negatives and positives, the latter being known variously as a Dupe-Pos, Master-Pos, Fine-Grain, or a Lavender Print. The last term was due to some being on a pale blue tinted base. The copy negatives made from them didn't always look like the original, usually having a higher overall density. Proper duplicating films led to better quality prints for

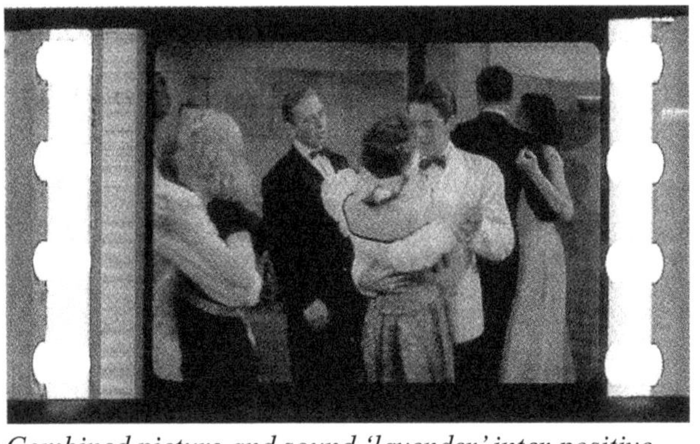

Combined picture and sound 'lavender' inter-positive print. Although looking like a rather dense release print, its purpose was for making duplicate negatives. Note the Bell & Howell negative perforations.

foreign release. The practice of shooting a separate negative had already been largely abandoned, with the overseas distributor now having to make do with a "good print" or a duplicate negative made on ordinary stock. Domestic prints continued to be made from the camera original.

Sound synchronisation

The coming of sound, both on disc and sound-on-film, meant that the negatives could no longer be arbitrarily cut, or frames lost while making repairs, without losing synchronisation. Many sound-on-disc picture negatives are found to contain blank frames to maintain the sync, as do some sound-on-film negatives, the result of not wishing to mutilate the sound negative to match. Modern prints of early "Laurel & Hardy" sound films, which were originally available for showing using both sound systems, still have the occasional blank frames.

Special purpose stocks

New special stocks also started to be introduced for recording optical sound tracks. Some of the early sound systems, like Fox's Movietone, exposed its variable density track along side the picture in the same camera on the normal negative stock. This was to continue for Newsreels, but for features a second synchronised "sound camera" was used for exposing the track. Although normal picture negative was acceptable for density tracks, it was less suitable for use with the higher contrast needed for the variable area types. Some early recordings were sometimes made on positive film.

Soundtrack processing

Soundtrack processing was far more critical than for the picture, requiring sensitometric tests and development using the fixed time and temperature methods. This suited machine processing, in which the film passed continuously through a series of deep tanks or pipes containing the solutions. Continuous processing machines were already in use during the 1920s, but were rather erratic in operation, so were only used for replaceable release prints. Studios usually insisted that the camera negatives still be processed by hand, due to the fear of damage. During the 1930s, improvements lead to greater confidence in the machines and the close processing controls were extended to the picture, requiring cameramen to be more consistent with their exposures, helped with the growing use of light meters.

Duplicating films

Also during the 1930s, improved black & white film stocks continued to be introduced, including better duplicating types. The prints made from a duplicate negative moved closer in quality to those made from the original camera negative. It became sensible to make all prints from duplicates and preserve the originals from the danger of damage. In Britain and most of Europe, this became common practice. The bulk printing from a duplicate negative was easier and safer, as it had no joins to fail and offered the option of incorporating all the scene-to-scene light changes while making the inter-positive. The negative made from this now had the same density throughout and is known as a "one-light" printing negative. In the interest of quality, most of the Hollywood studios continued to print from the camera negative, which despite the risks, produced the finest prints possible, complementing the much admired black & white photography of the 1930s and 1940s. Duplicate positives and negatives were still made for sending to laboratories abroad and to act as "protection masters", which, as the name suggests, were kept aside in case the original suffered damage.

Printing complications

Although the prints from the original cut negative were of enhanced quality, their printing was more involved, as all the light changes had to be repeated for each pass through the printer. This was automated, with notches cut out of the edge of the film, or metal foil or clips placed between the perforations, these used to trigger the mechanism for varying the lamp voltages or shutter openings.

One system used a 35mm strip of opaque black paper, punched with circular holes of different sizes, to control the light. These, together with other various kinds of punched grading cards or tapes, employed by other control systems, are occasionally found in the film's can along with the negatives. Prints are sometimes found, with evidence that the "timing" or "grading" was a little out of sync, with the light changes missing the scene change by a frame or two. This often happened before automation. Then, highly skilled operators watched the illuminated frame in the printers gate while keeping a finger touching the moving negative to anticipate any change in its density and then make any subsequent light adjustments manually using their "snap judgement".

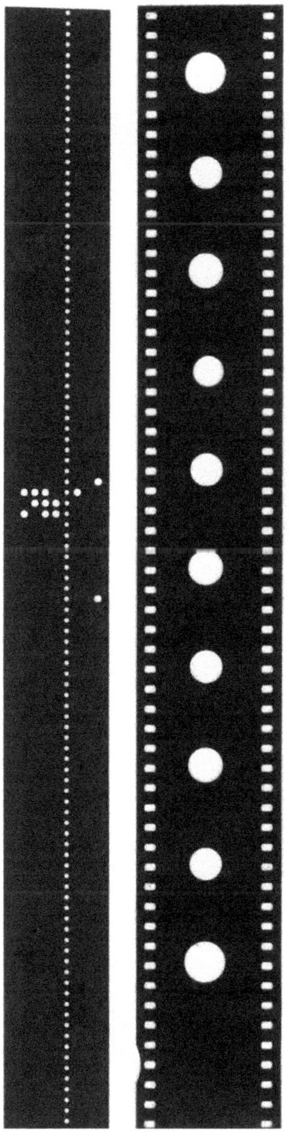

Sometimes found in the can along with the negative are paper film strips of punched tapes, used as part of the mechanism for controlling the printer's scene-to-scene light changes

Different versions

The coming of sound and the making of release prints via duplicates resulted in an increase of the "pre-print" material deposited in film vaults. Along with the cut negative, was selected unused footage held for future uses such as stock shots. Also kept, were the duplicate negatives and positives and a couple of studio show prints for future viewings. The separate sound negatives, not only included the "final mix", but also separate dialogue and music tracks, together with a "music and effects" track (M&E), needed to produce foreign language dubbed versions. Sometimes all the original music recordings were retained and it's not unknown for it to be heard again in later films. To cut down on the total footage, it was common for each roll of sound negative to have two different recordings running in opposite directions down both sides of the film.

Sometimes, the film was actually slit down the middle, creating individual 17.5mm tracks. With no picture to accommodate, original studio recordings were often double-width to improve the quality and background noise.

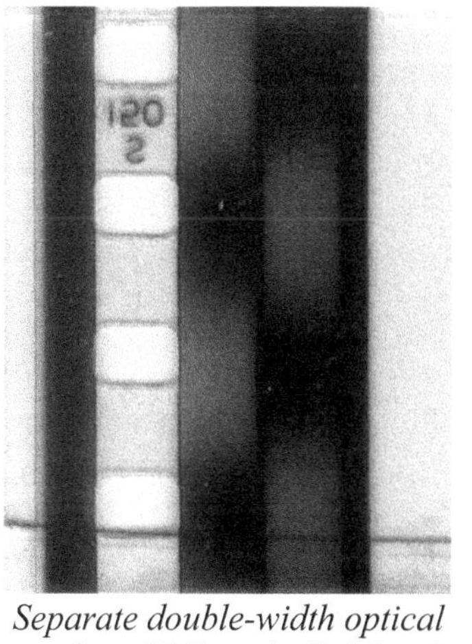

Separate double-width optical track on 17.5mm (split 35mm) film. One of the methods used for original studio tracks before the introduction of magnetic recording in the early 1950s

Starting around 1947, original optical photographic tracks began to be replaced by magnetic recordings on coated 35mm film.

1950 saw the rapid switch from nitrate to safety based films. Some productions made during the transition period made use of both types of base. For example the negative may have been shot on nitrate, with all the prints being on safety film.

Storage

It was always good practice to store a master copy of a film at a different location to guard against a total loss due to fire, flood or earthquake. Again to reduce additional storage space, a "combined" sound and picture fine-grain positive was made to make new negatives if necessary. At first sight, these can be mistaken for a rather dense release print but like all intermediate films, they have Bell & Howell "negative"- type perforations, providing a clue to its original purpose.

Getting the best copies

All this shows what a variety of material can be used to generate new copies. The aim is to produce a print as close as possible to that made from the original negative, even if this is no longer available. As well as following the normal duplicating routes, laboratories specialising in archive work have become skilled in modifying the grading, printing and processing procedures to deal with the particular needs of archive work. More often, the only surviving copies of early black and white films in danger of being lost are well worn projection prints.

Additional techniques have been devised or adapted to improve the results. An example is the post-treatment of the original or final print using image reduction and intensification processes normally associated with still photography. One snag with combined sound prints is the change in density of the sound track, causing distortion or an increase in noise level. However, if the primary purpose is only to provide a print for video transfer, the sound can be re-recorded onto magnetic film before the treatment takes place.

Preparation

For many restoration projects, the greater part of the effort, and ultimately the final cost, is the pre-printing tasks of tracing all the available material and its physical preparation. Cut camera negatives will have the potential of producing the best results, but need the most preparation. Hundreds of individual joins may have to be inspected and if necessary, re-made without the loss of frames. Obsolete grading clips or foil tabs may have to be removed before regrading. As a rule, the original negative is always the first choice but if for example, a largely join free one-light printing master is available it may not only be more economic, but produce a print with picture quality closer to that seen by its original audiences. For example, in recent years, only relatively poor copies of Universal's ever popular "Flash Gordon" serials from the 1930s and 1940s were available. However, there was a dramatic improvement in both the picture and sound quality when they were last broadcast on TV. This was because a set of the British printing masters was discovered deep in the vaults of the Rank Laboratories (later De Luxe). Last used to provide prints for kids Saturday morning shows in the 1950s and 1960s, they were still in good condition and used again to make excellent new prints and perhaps avert the need for a future and more costly restoration using less suitable material.

Cleaning

Whatever kind of original, the film is sure to need cleaning. Both well tried hand and machine methods have in some cases been made less effective by the loss of certain chemicals through legislation to protect workers and the environment from hazardous chemicals. The greener alternatives have been found to be less effective, requiring longer treatment times. Cleaning processes range from simple re-washing, to the use solvents, with or without ultra-sonic agitation. Mechanical dry methods include the use of brushes and tacky rollers. Still one of the most effective methods for old films, with deeply ingrained dirt, is by hand, pulling the film through a pad of cotton cloth soaked in environment-friendly, fume-free cleaning fluid, without the risk in earlier years of involuntary solvent abuse.

Shrinkage correction

Old nitrate films will have inevitably shrunk due to the loss of moisture during many decades of storage. In severe cases, they are now so brittle and warped that they are no longer able to run through a printer. Remedial work can range from re-washing, to proprietary processes like Redimension, in which the rolls of film spend between two days and three weeks in a vacuum chamber, while fluid vapour impregnates the film.

Re-humidification can bring the dimensions back to near that of fresh stock, so they can be run together through a step contact printer, still the first choice for older silent films. With careful pitch adjustment and running slowly, the still somewhat shrunken and buckled film, can be eased, if only once, through the printer's gate and onto its registration pins. There is the option of using an optical printer, without the need for the old and new stock to travel over the same sprockets. A more recent type, without the strains of intermittent transport, is the continuous optical printer. The films run separately, with the image transferred via a relay lens system which, like a conventional optical printer, can be adjusted to restore the image size and position. Separate sound negatives often have to be rejuvenated too. These have to be printed on a continuous contact-type printer. If shrunken, they can end up on the combined print out of alignment and the reproduction marred by flutter and interference from the sprocket holes. Also, the track may go in and out of focus, due to loss of contact when being printed, with a loss of the higher frequencies.

Special film joiners are available with movable pins for shrunken film, although many skilled archive workers still prefer to make hand joins. Missing perforations can be reconstructed using patches made from old scrap film, with the same degree of shrinkage.

Scratch concealment

All but the worst scratches and other abrasions can be removed or disguised. Negative scratches, printed along with the picture, appear white on the screen. Those on positives are usually black, unless deep enough to have reached the base. "Cinch" marks are horizontal scratches caused when a loosely wound film has been pulled tight, most noticeable at the ends of reels. Lighter base, or cell-scratches, can be polished out using spinning glass rollers, after the base has been softened with acetone. Less radical, is to leave the scratches and use wet-gate printing techniques to render them less visible to the printer's light. This works by coating or immersing the film in a fluid having the same refractive index as the base, which fills in the scratch. For scratches in the emulsion, the film can be treated in a caustic solution which swells the gelatine, closing up the scratch.

Infestation

Apart from scratches, the image carrying emulsion can show signs of infestation by bacteria, fungus and even larger creepy-crawlies, with legs on!
These unwanted guests and growths find the largely organic gelatine structure an ideal meal. This is usually due to the films be stored at high temperature and humidity, or have been in a flood. The growth of mould seems sensitive to pressure and on tightly wound film, its effect can be seen mostly in the thinnest parts of the image, such as light sky areas and white titles. Treatment usually involves the film being sterilised in fungicide, or a mild acid solution, and the worst stains and spots removed by hand using swabs of pure alcohol. Any remaining marks are treated in the same way as scratches.

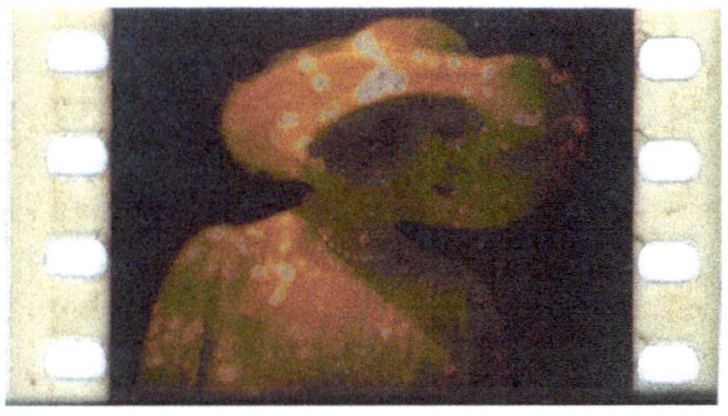

'It's a bug's life'. What remains of a stencil colour image after becoming a meal for bacteria

Digital processing

Digital image processing was originally too costly for most day-to-day restoration work, but as prices have fallen it is increasingly used to alter scene contrast, remove scratches and other signs of damage, and even recover detail lost as a result of decomposition.

All this effort continues as film companies, commercial libraries and collections have to maintain their assets in good condition and deal with new acquisitions. However, many labour intensive and expensive projects involve the saving of non-commercial films. These include historically important documentaries, old silent films and long forgotten and uninspiring features, which are long out of copyright and no longer have an "owner" to help foot the bill.

Archives

The restoration of this kind of material is usually undertaken by National archives, like our own National Film & Television Archive, which receives government funding and now lottery money to help save our film heritage. Not to forget, the contribution made by benefactors like J. Paul Getty Jnr, after whom the NFA's Conservation Centre at Berkhamsted is named. In the U.S.A., funding often comes from Educational Foundations, business corporations and sometimes individuals, with a particular interest in a specific film or subject.

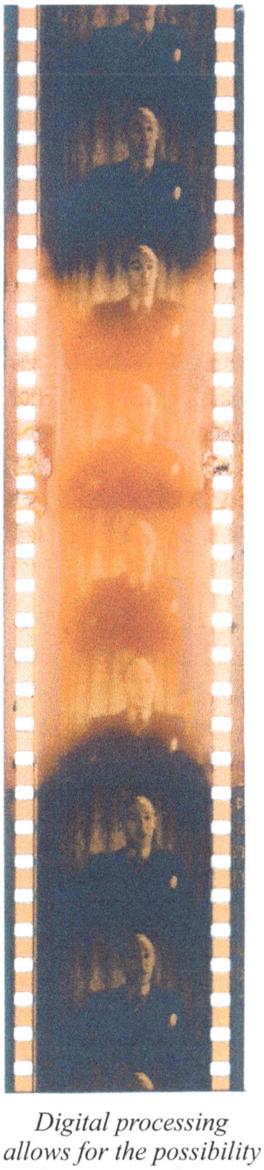

Digital processing allows for the possibility of re-creating frames lost through decay.

The Lost World

To illustrate how all these aspects of conservation work come together, its worth looking at a particular restoration project. While computer generated dinosaurs were being created for Steven Spielberg's *Jurassic Park: The Lost World*, another much earlier creature-feature was being restored, the 1925 silent version of Conan Doyle's *The Lost World.*
Five years in production, the film featured prehistoric monsters animated by pioneer stop-motion model animator, Willis O'Brien and was to be a forerunner to his later triumph, *King Kong* (1932). To bring his dinosaurs to life, he used up to seven cameras at one time, with the single frames triggered simultaneously. This arrangement provided for a choice of camera angles and the extra footage needed for the foreign negative, with the additional live-action footage for this being made up of second camera, or alternative takes. The domestic version was ten reels (9209 feet) long, lasting nearly two hours at around 20 frames per second, which was the average projection rate at the time, although the film itself was photographed nearer to 16 fps.

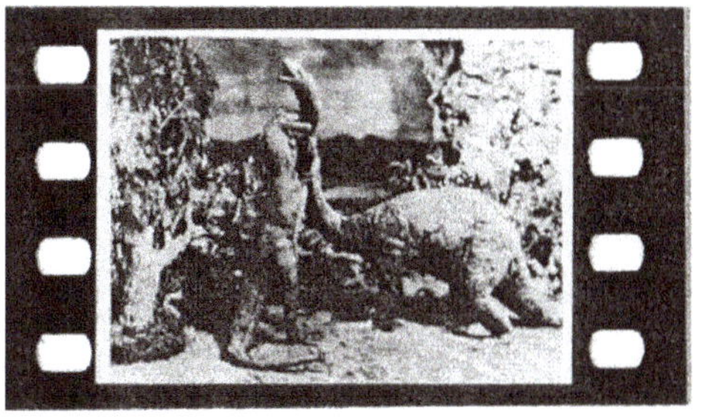

After a successful worldwide release, the Kodascope library bought up the non-theatrical 16mm rights and cut down the domestic version from ten reels to five, with the discarded negative eventually becoming lost. The all-action monster footage was retained, with the losses coming from the less exciting plot development and the inevitable romantic situations. Later, the story rights were renegotiated, with a view to making a sound remake. But in 1932, RKO purchased *The Lost World*, to make sure it stayed lost to prevent any possible copyright difficulties killing off their own King Kong prematurely. Orders went out to destroy any remaining prints and the foreign negative.

For sixty years, the only version available for re-prints was the Kodascope five reel version. The original 16mm prints were of excellent quality, but over the years this dropped, as dupe negatives of these were used to generate subsequent 16mm, 8mm, and eventually Super-8 prints for home movie collectors. Back in 1948, Kodak's 5-reel nitrate 35mm negative was preserved at George Eastman House in Rochester, together with a new 16mm master positive. By the 1970s, the 35mm negative was beginning to decompose, with three of the five reels "going sticky", the first stage of the decay. Just in time, funding from The National Endowment for the Arts allowed a 35mm fine-grain master positive to be made on acetate safety film.

Unlike many old silent films, *The Lost World* was not entirely forgotten, and in 1991, it was released on laserdisc, for the benefit of fantasy film buffs and collectors. The source was Eastman's 5-reel version and although only being half its original length, it proved successful. To help compensate for the lost footage, the disc included an added music score and the original 1925

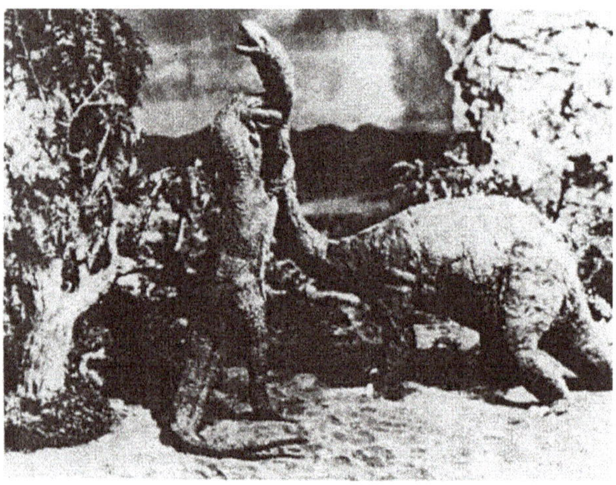

The Lost World discovered - again

theatrical and promotional trailers, these being provided by the UCLA and Pacific Film Archives. Included too, were production stills from the missing footage. Some of these showed scenes which although actually shot, were never used in the original release. They were for protection, in case Willis O'Brien didn't come up with convincing monsters, and could be used to turn the film into a conventional jungle melodrama.

A complete version

The appearance of the laser disc inspired the Eastman House Archives to attempt a 35mm restoration of the full-length version. An international appeal was mounted for both any additional material and the all-important funding, now with the help of the ubiquitous website. The film was out of copyright and no longer has a corporate owner, so patrons and benefactors were needed to adopt *The Lost World* and to help subsidise its restoration and continued existence. Fortunately, in this case, major funding came from Hugh Hefner, whose interests not only include the Playboy empire, but he is also a great Conan Doyle fan. He had previously helped save

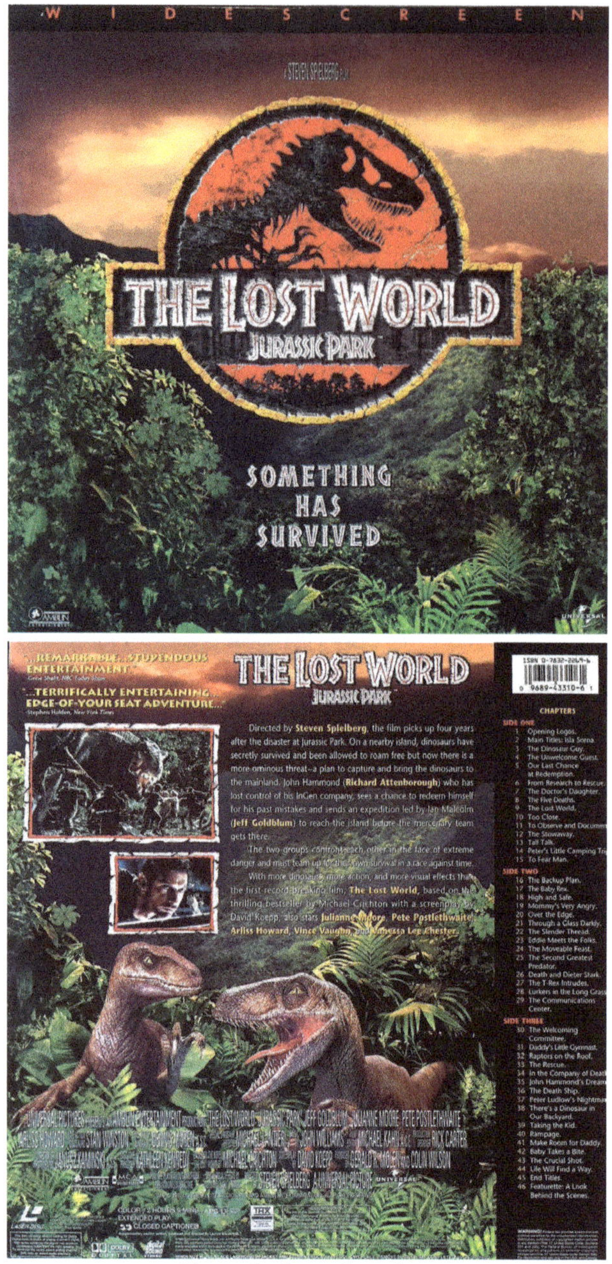

From the laserdisc sleeve

the original nitrate negatives of twelve Basil Rathbone Sherlock Holmes films. These had been abandoned by their copyright owner, not wishing to continue the responsibility of storing them.

News of the first additional footage came from a U.S. stock-shot company, who found a reel of positive animation out-takes left over from *The Lost World*. These showed the common mishaps of stop-motion work, including fogged frames, animators caught in shot and the miniatures falling over. Another find came from Thee Library of Congress Archive, who discovered in their collection, a roll of nitrate tinted print fragments from the film. Although only 150 feet long, it contained several unique shots. In both cases, preservation negatives were made and deposited at George Eastman House. However, the restoration became a reality, when word came from the Filmovy Archiv in Czechoslovakia, that they had a full-length copy of *The Lost World*. This was not the first time that the Czech Republic has come up trumps in the search for films lost in the West. Before the First World War, Prague was the last stop for film distribution in Eastern Europe, with well-worn copies being abandoned, rather than being shipped back to the distributors. Many of the films eventually found their way into the National Archive, which has become a treasure trove for lost films. More recent discoveries include, John Ford's first film as a director, *Straight Shooting* (1917), and the Technicolor sequences from the silent *Ben Hur* (1925).

Their written description of the *The Lost World* print stated that it was made from the original foreign camera negative. This was required to make literally hundreds of prints for all over Europe and Asia, and their surviving copy must have been among the last to be printed, with many repairs and scratches printed in. The local inter-titles were joined in later, and did not show so much damage. Apparently, the print itself was also physically well-worn, being badly scratched, with missing footage at the beginning and ends of the reels. The country's censors had also demanded cuts to the scenes which included the violent deaths of both the humans and model monsters. Fortunately, these scenes remained intact in the Kodascope version and between the two of them, around 90 to 95 per cent of the narrative and action could be reconstructed.

As it turned out, the Czech's nitrate print had in fact decomposed. A previously made copy negative, although the best possible, was unfortunately done without the aid of a liquid gate printer.

Truly international efforts

This restoration project was to show the international nature of Archive work. After all the negotiations for the use of the material was completed, the actual reconstruction and printing work was undertaken at the Haghefilm Laboratory in the Netherlands, in collaboration with George Eastman House. The final result is not an exact match to the original US domestic version. The foreign prints were always slightly different, having different camera angles and shot lengths. Without an original shot list, the only guidance for the final cut was the scenario and the logic of the remaining footage. Without knowing for certain what the original looked like, the aim was to produce the most entertaining and watchable version possible, from all the available sources, to the extent of adding 800 extra feet from the animation out-takes, which never appeared in either the domestic or foreign versions. Whether, a true replica or not, another silent classic has been saved from extinction, returning in a new 35mm tinted print.

Although only photographed in black and white, *The Lost World*, like the great majority of silent films, had colour tints added. Among the scenes tinted, was a volcanic eruption highlighted in red. Building on this work, subsequent discoveries of new and better quality replacement footage have been incorporated into a Lobster digital restoration for the latest extended 103 minute (16 fps) Blu-ray release. This now includes a flaming torch in a dinosaur's mouth, originally coloured by the Handschiegl process.

The BFI National Archive

The BFI National Archive holds a magnificent collection of film and television material. Holding one of the largest film and television collections in the world, dating from the earliest days of film to the live capture of current television content, the collection contains nearly a million titles.

Using the latest preservation methods, teams of specialists in all areas of conservation and preservation care for a variety of obsolete formats so that future generations can enjoy the UK's film heritage. As early as 1940 the BFI opened its first, state-of-the-art film archive at Aston Clinton in Buckinghamshire. In 1968 new premises were acquired at Berkhamsted, Hertfordshire, which became home to the acetate (safety film) collections.

In 1978 another site at Gaydon opened with the facilities to house nitrate film, and the BFI has an ongoing programme to transfer unstable nitrate material to more stable acetate stock. 1987 saw the opening of the new, purpose-built Conservation Centre on an 11-acre site at Berkhamsted, named after its sponsor, John Paul Getty, whose generous donation also enabled the BFI to move to new headquarters at Stephen Street, London,
In 2010 the BFI secured funds from Government to build a new state-of-the-art, environmentally sustainable and architecturally pioneering film storage facility at

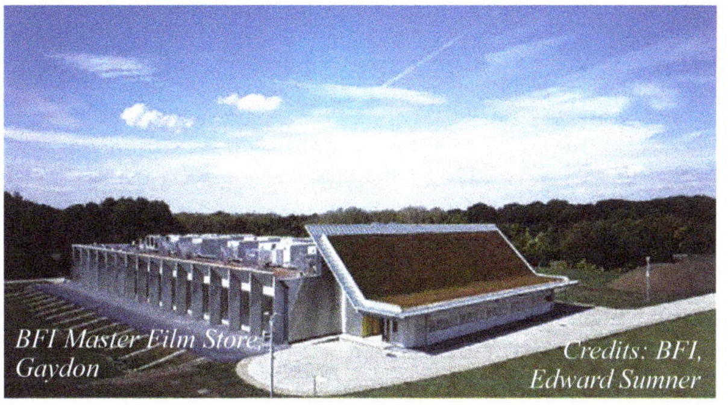

BFI Master Film Store, Gaydon *Credits: BFI, Edward Sumner*

Gaydon, allowing the long-term preservation of all the master film collection, both nitrate and safety. Material is held at minus five degrees Celsius at 35% relative humidity.

As part of the BFI's five-year Unlocking Film Heritage programme the BFI National Archive is developing a digital infrastructure to reflect the changes in film production technology. This infrastructure will preserve digital titles, both film and TV, as well as the thousands of titles due to be digitised as part of that same programme.

For details of how to access the various collections and to purchase material, go to:
https://www.bfi.org.uk/archive-collections/searching-access-collections

Colour Film Restoration and Preservation

The procedures for the physical repair and restoration of colour films are much the same as those employed for black and white, but in most cases they require even more work and care when preparing them for reprinting and preservation.

The danger of losing the colour with the bathwater!

The water and spirit based colour dyes used for tinting and both the hand and mechanical colouring of black and white prints may be at risk from the more vigorous forms of cleaning and washing. One way to test their effect on the dyes is to pull a length of sample film through a pad soaked in the proposed cleaning fluid to see if any colour comes off the print along with the dirt. Tests should also be made before using any of the scratch removal systems or the 're-dimension' of shrunken film by the impregnation of chemical vapour in a vacuum chamber.

A lost frame can ruin a film

Natural colour films, which recorded their colour information in the form of separate filtered black and white images, need particular care during inspection. If on separate strips of film, a multi-sprocket synchroniser is required to ensure that they still match and are in sync at each scene change. Single-film negatives or prints must be checked to make sure that the regular sequence of the colour records along the length of the film has not been disrupted by previous, less careful repairs. For example, a Kinemacolor film which jumps out of sync with its alternating filters ends up with surreal reversed colours.

Bringing back rose-tinted images from the past - plus other colours too

For preserving original nitrate tinted and toned black and white prints, archives usually start by producing a new safety duplicate negative on panchromatic stock and keeping a record of the colours chosen for each scene. Any loss of contrast when making a new black and white duplicate negative from an original tinted print can be restored by using filters of a complementary colour. When having to copy from a positive projection print, the build up of excessive contrast can be controlled by reducing development times or temperature, or by 'flashing' the duplicating stock. This involves giving it an extra overall exposure to light before or after the actual image is printed, which has the effect of reducing the contrast. The traditional way of producing a colour version is to print the black and white negative onto colour print film, manipulating the colour of the printing light to give the required tint. This tends to give a look more like toning. For a more accurate overall tinted effect, the print stock can first be flashed by running it through a continuous contact printer giving it an overall exposure to coloured light which is complementary to the final tint. The black and white negative is then printed, with its image graded to give a neutral image or in a different colour to simulate a combined tinted and toned print. This method is offered commercially as the Desmet process for restoring tinted and toned prints.

Old recipes for new colour

In recent years, efforts have been directed at recreating the often more vivid colours of the original prints by reviving the same tinting and toning methods which were used to produce them. Much research was required to establish the type of dyes used and the chemical formulas needed to produce them. Unfortunately, some of the most effective treatments cannot be used again today on health and safety grounds, now being considered too toxic or inflammable. The extra work involved is considerable as all the scenes of the same colour have to be tinted or toned separately and then assembled in the correct order (pos-matched) to make up the final print, which like an original, now has a join at each change of colour. In practice, this has not proved to be a problem, particularly when printed on polyester stock with secure welded joins. An example of all this effort can be seen in the latest prints of Hitchcock's THE LODGER (1926).

The original negatives of early black and white films, which were intended to be tinted or toned, are sometimes found with scenes out of sequence, with those to be in the same colour next to each other in separate rolls to be treated together.

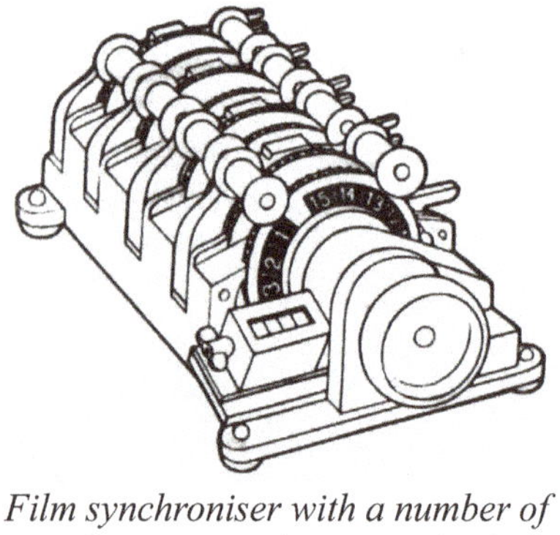

Film synchroniser with a number of sprockets mounted on a single shaft. Needed to check that colour separations are still in step

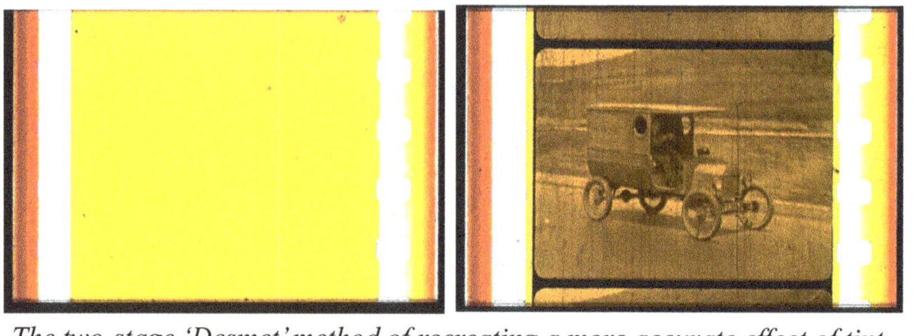

The two-stage 'Desmet' method of recreating a more accurate effect of tinting on modern colour film by first 'flashing' the stock in the required colour (left), followed by a second run through a printer to add the image (right)

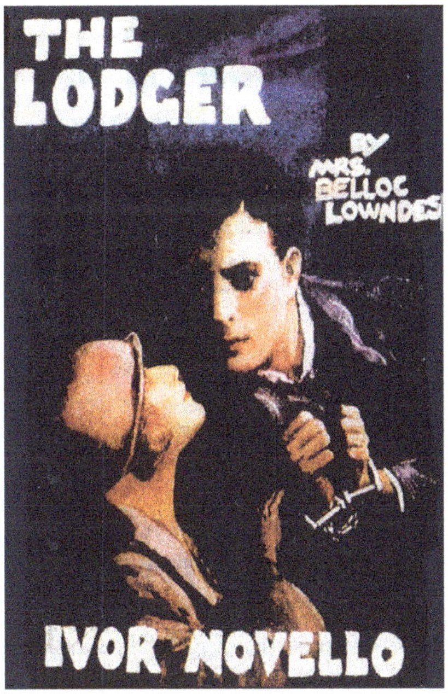

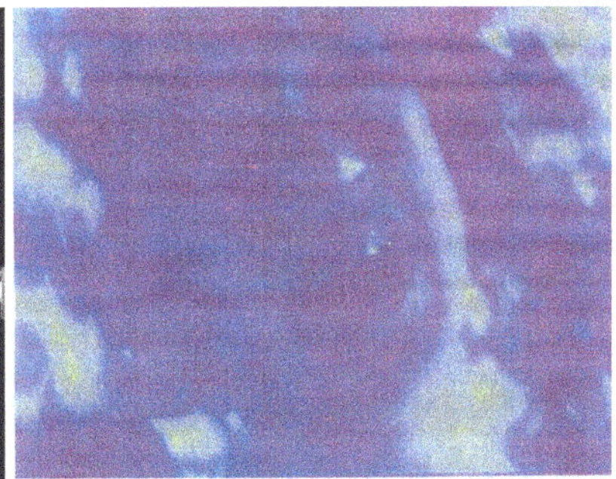

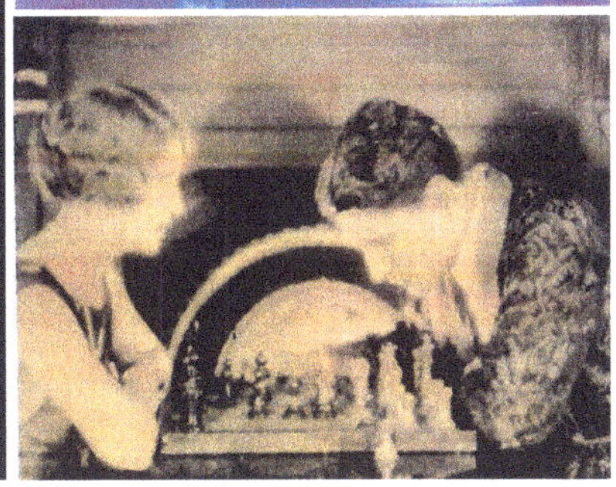

Some of the later black and white prints of Hitchcock's early silent film 'The Lodger' (1926) used the original methods of tinting and toning (right)..

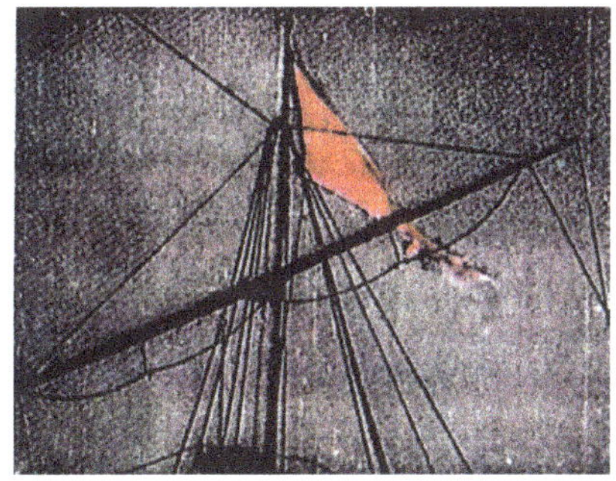

Hand-coloured red flag (originally white on the B&W image) raised during 'Battleship Potemkin'(1925)

Blue movies for after dark

This complication was one of the reasons why the practice fell out of favour after the arrival of sound. If used for sound films, the number of different colour effects was often limited, or the film tinted or toned the same colour throughout. At the time when colouring black and white films was popular, it was used mostly for its artistic effect to complement the subject matter, which in most cases, could still be enjoyed if left uncoloured. However, for some, the colour is important to the understanding of the film.

Among the most often quoted examples are the blue tinted day for night sequences in *Nosferatu* (1921), which if left uncoloured appear to show Dracula carrying out his nocturnal activities in broad daylight, without suffering the same fate as many nitrate films and crumbling to dust (legend according to later Hammer versions).

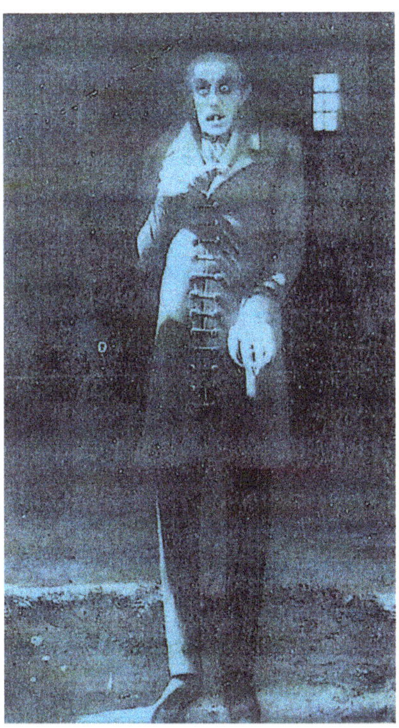

In 'Nosferatu' (1921)a blue tint meant that it was night time and safe for Dracula to be up and about, but yellow daylight was bad for his health!

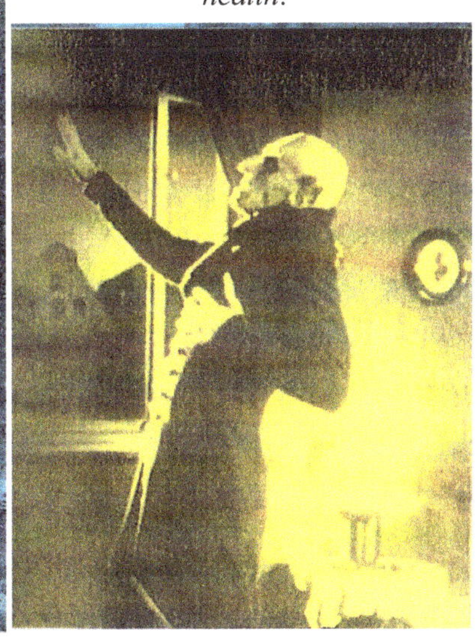

At the time of filming, a white flag was raised on *The Battleship Potemkin* (1925), not in surrender, but later to be coloured red on the prints to change it to a sign of victory by mutineers during the abortive Russian revolution of 1905. (Picture above).

Every frame a miniature artwork

Duplicating hand and stencilled coloured films presents the same potential problems as when having to make the copy from any high contrast colour projection print not intended for the purpose. For long term preservation, black and white separations can be produced, which, if necessary, can then be printed directly onto colour print stock, or used to provide a colour negative via an inter-positive. An alternative is to make the colour negative straight from the original coloured print, but the results are likely to be inferior in terms of colour and contrast. Unlike black and white, colour intermediate duplicating stock is far less tolerant to being underdeveloped to reduce its contrast, as it upsets the integral masking and the inter-image effect between the layers. A ten per cent variation of the development time or temperature is about the maximum possible before errors in the balance between the layers begin to show in the final prints, usually as a magenta cast in the shadows, together with green highlights. Flashing the stock can be more successful, giving it an initial exposure to white light, or coloured light for some forms of colour correction. Some types of special duplicating stocks, which proved to be

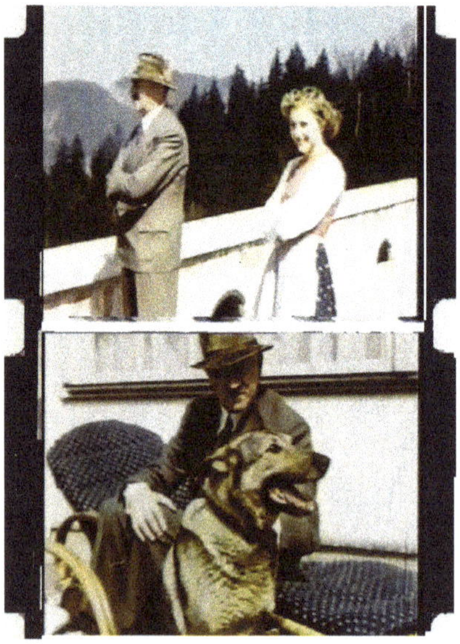

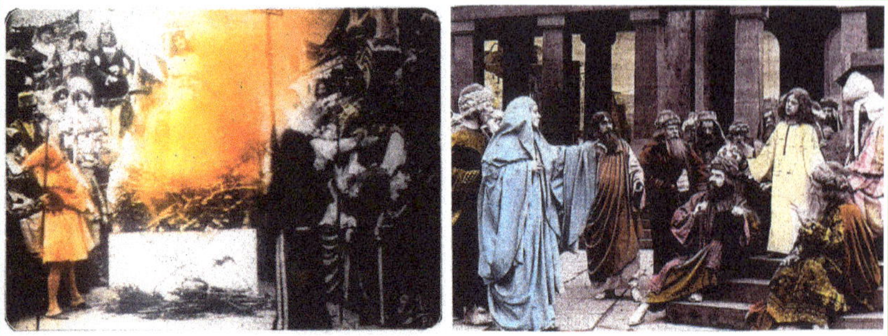

Producing preservation colour negatives or B&W separations from higher contrast projection prints is not ideal, but is the only option when copying original hand or mechanically coloured prints.
Above left: Hand-coloured frame from 'Joan of Arc' - Georges Méliès 1900
Above right: Pathecolor stencilled frame from 'La Vie de Notre Seigneur Jesus Christ' (1914)

useful in the past, are no longer readily available, including those, both reversal and negative, for making copies of amateur and professional films shot on Kodachrome, Ektachrome and other colour reversal camera stock. An example was the lower contrast inter-negative film for copying reversal news film. It supplemented the normal reversal duplicates when greater numbers of copies were needed for the wider distribution of newsworthy items. On rare occasions, amateur cameramen captured the only colour record of important historical events. Perhaps the most famous, and copied, were the Zapruder 8mm Kodachrome film of the assassination of President Kennedy in 1963 and Eva Braun's Kodachrome home movies of Hitler enjoying time off at Berchtesgaden during WWII. (Pictures above)

Since the 1940s, many thousands of industrial, educational and other non-theatrical colour films have been photographed and printed on 16mm reversal film. Kodak provided a special lower contrast (commercial) version of Kodachrome, which was more suitable for making copies. It was used in the 1950s to film the *Cisco Kid*, one of the first American TV series to be shot on 16mm colour film. Even after Eastman Color negative became available in 16mm, many professionals continued to use reversal film, preferring the finer grain inherent in the reversal process compared to the coarser grain structure of the early 16mm colour negative films. (Reversal emulsions were the first to have a mix of both fast and slow grains. The larger and faster grains react to light first and form the negative image exposed in the camera. This is subsequently removed during processing, leaving the remaining less sensitive smaller grains to be re-exposed to create the final positive image.)
When the Beatles TV movie *Magical Mystery Tour* was revived, (it had been shot in 1967 on 16mm Ektachrome reversal colour film), it proved to have much better definition and finer grain than, for example, the 16mm Eastman Color film inserts still to be seen in the often repeated early TV shows like *Dad's Army* and *The Good Life*.

Also shot on 16mm lower contrast Ektachrome Commercial reversal colour film was the notorious *The Texas Chainsaw Massacre*, which was blown up to 35mm via an enlarged inter-negative for cinema release. This low-budget horror film from 1974 has become a cult classic, so, in keeping with its new status, the camera original has been rescued from its less than ideal storage conditions. After thirty years at room temperature, the film showed the effects of shrinkage and fading, so a new inter-negative has been made using the latest and more stable duplicating stock. This will ensure that even if the film's power to shock fades over time, the colour of the image won't.

With the switch to electronic news gathering and the introduction of constantly improving colour negative stocks, reversal colour film returned to being used mostly by amateur film makers. Special reversal duplicating stock continued to be available for copying home movies. Similar film was also used occasionally by professionals in both 16mm and 35mm gauges. An example being during post production, when an extra join-free copy of the editor's cutting copy (work print) is required for use in the dubbing theatre. Today, many colour restorations, which involve the copying of projection prints and other higher contrast originals, now use camera negative as the duplicating stock. The latest camera films have extremely fine grain and the definition is more than adequate for copying older colour films. They also have wide exposure latitude and are more controllable during processing to help compensate when having to print from less than ideal originals.

Restoring Kinemacolour and Biocolor

Restoring original nitrate Kinemacolor sequential-frame additive colour films is the same as dealing with other early black and white films. In fact, on some occasions, Kinemacolor has been mistaken for an ordinary black and white print and shown as such. The clues to its true origin include a noticeable pulsating effect visible in areas of the image representing the most saturated

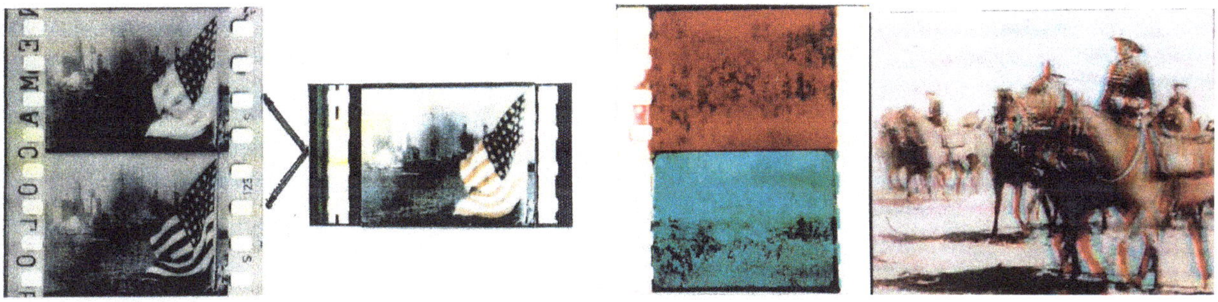

When working on restoration projects involving Kinemacolor or Biocolor film, for easier access each pair of alternating frames can be superimposed, with the appropriate filtering, onto a single frame of modern colour film. But as the picture on the right shows, however well re-printed, the inevitable colour fringes caused by the subject moving between the separate red and blue/green exposures cannot be eliminated. (Perhaps today's digital processing could help?)

colours, together with a slowing down of the action. Like most other additive processes, the prints can only be seen in colour when they are projected through the correct colour filters. For 'authentic' showings, they can be shown using a projector modified to run at 32 frames per second and fitted with a rotating filter wheel with alternating red and blue/green filters.

For easier access, the pair of B&W colour records can be used to produce a normal colour print. This can be done using two runs through a skip-printer, exposing alternate frames of a print or negative with the appropriate filtering, in register onto a single frame of colour negative or print film. Some archives prefer to use the skip-printer to produce a pair of separation negatives for making colour versions of their Kinemacolor films. Another successful method made use of both an original print and a surviving filter disc. The optical printer was set up to advance two frames of the original for every one of the print stock. In a single pass, the alternate frames were printed in turn through the appropriate sector of the filter and superimposed on each frame of the new colour negative.

However produced, the new colour prints can be shown normally, providing the projector will run at 16 frames per second. The rival Biocolor, and other similar systems which dyed the frames their correct colour to act as built in filters, can be reprinted in much the same way as Kinemacolor. In fact, if available, a Biocolor camera negative is identical. Back in 1913 the high cost of battles with its competitors in the law courts over patent infringements was one of the factors leading to Kinemacolor's demise in 1916. If having to work from an original Biocolor print with its alternating red and green stained frames, the new black and white negative would have to be made on panchromatic stock with filtering to control the contrast. Trying to combine them onto colour negative directly from the print has proved to be less successful.

If a replica of the original is required, the frames can be coloured in the printer and left adjacent on the print. Again, for an authentic showing, the print, can be run at 32 frames per second with the images superimposed in the brain of the viewer by persistence of vision. Films shot using other early additive processes have also had their colour revealed, with their ready-made black and white separation images printed onto modern colour film. Among them was some rare three-colour **Chronochrome** footage, made somewhat more complex due to its triple non-standard 3 perf. high frames.

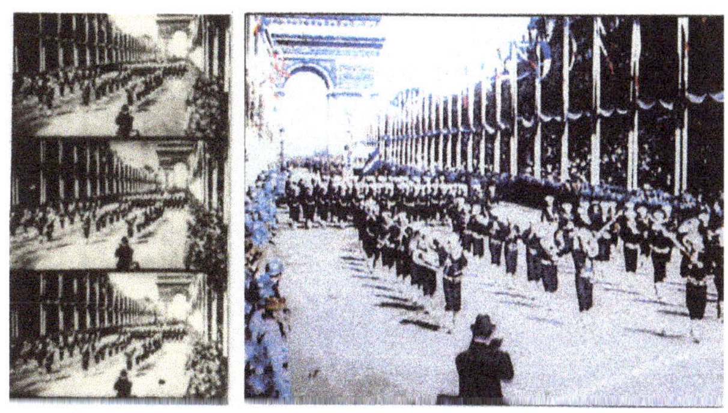

To make access easier when carrying out restoration, old additive processes can be converted to subtractive prints on colour print stock. This shows a clip of the Victory parade in Paris (1919) in Gaumont Chronochrome on the left and as transferred to colour print stock (right)

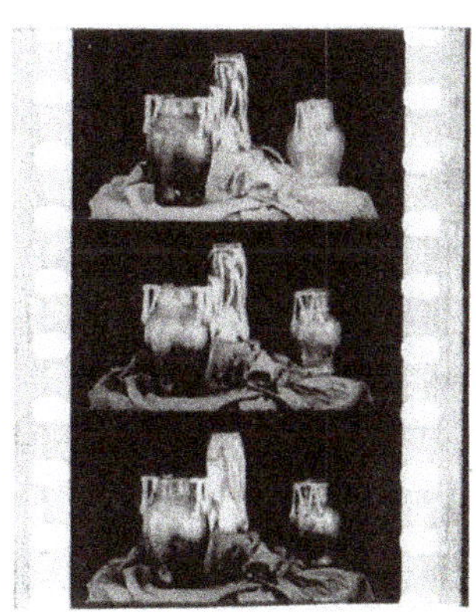

Original Gaumont Chronochrome print with its triple three-perf RGB filtered frames for showing simultaneously using a 9-perf pull-down projector equipped with three lenses and filters.

Below is shown a modern example of a restoration of a Chronochrome print made on modern colour film, showing Deauville beach in 1912

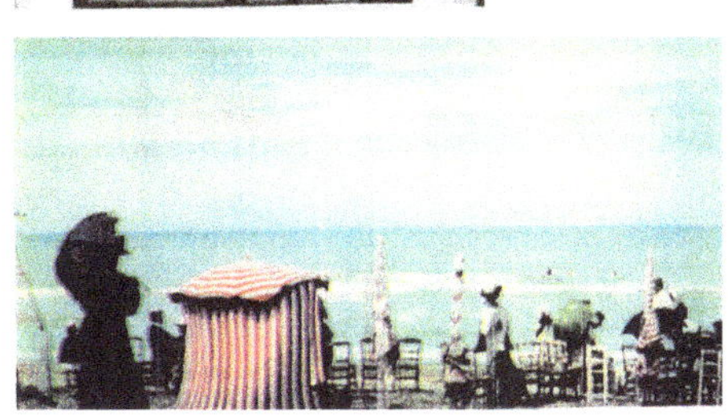

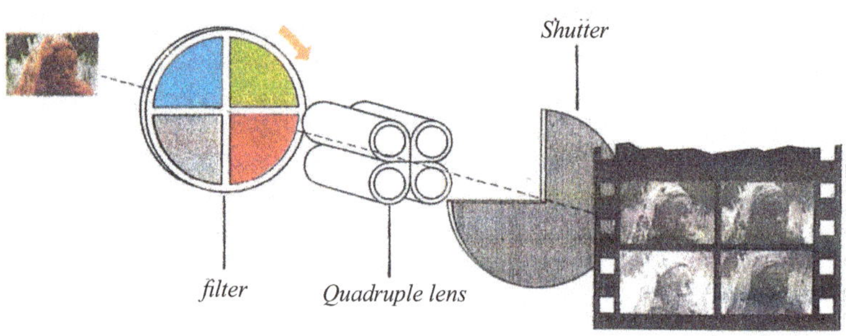

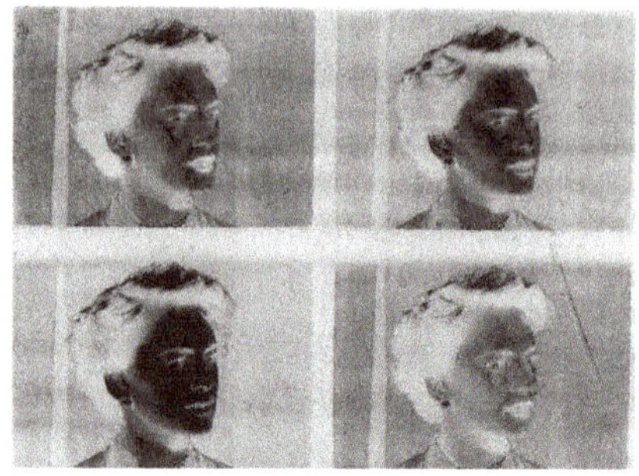

***Rouxcolor**, like other similar additive systems which reduced the size of their colour records to fit within the normal 35mm picture area, can be reprinted by enlarging the ready-made black and white separation negatives via the appropriate colour filters and superimposing them in register on colour negative or positive film. This can be made easier by adapting their original multi-lens camera or projection optics for use on the printer.*

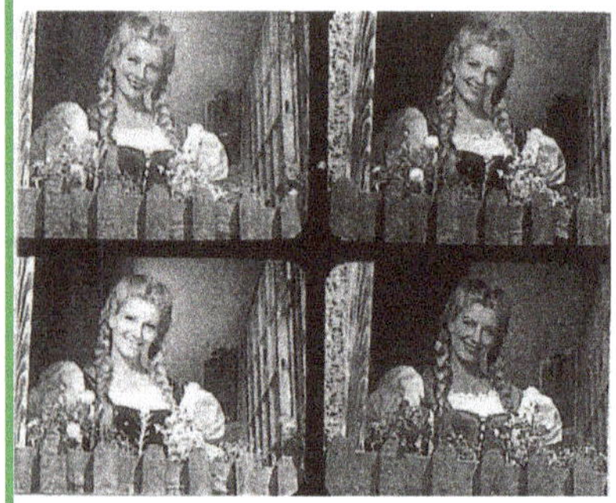

Clips from La Belle Meuniére (1948) - The Miller's Daughter, using Rouxcolour. Left shows the original additive print and Right shows the good results obtained from another clip transferred to colour print film

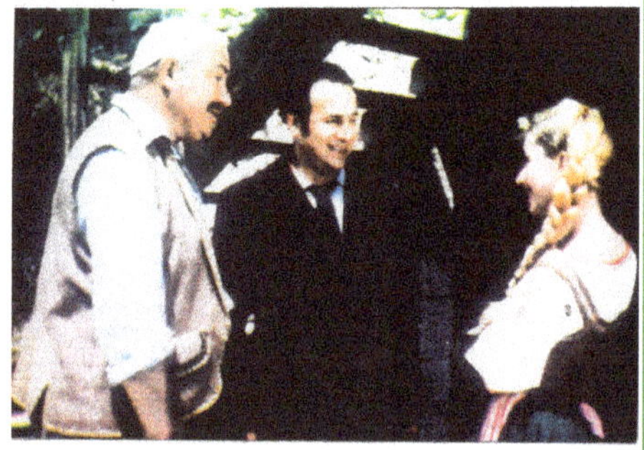

Other systems employing sets of images reduced in size to fit within the space of a normal 35mm frame have also been successfully restored in colour. Most were made possible by the availability of their original multi-lens camera or projector attachments which were adapted for use on the optical printers.

This was the case for *The Miller's Daughter*, which was produced in France using **Rouxcolor**, one of the last attempts to introduce an additive system, in 1948. The negative and prints had four quarter size images photographed and projected simultaneously through red, green, blue and yellow filters. Like many of the other restorations, the new colour prints allow audiences to see colour images often better than could be achieved when originally shown by additive projection. Unfortunately, the colour fringes inherent in most of the systems are still accurately reproduced.
A showcase for seeing examples of some of these restorations is the first instalment of the award winning TV documentary series *The British Empire in Colour*, which is now available on DVD. It includes clips from one of Kinemacolor's most popular films, *Delhi Durbar* (1912), a brief Gaumont Chronochrome shot of a victory parade in Paris during 1919, and Biocolor scenes filmed around Britain showing everyday life in the towns and countryside in the 1920s. (Pictures right).

Not to be left out, **Dufaycolor** makes an appearance later in the series with Movietone's colour newsreel of King George V's Silver Jubilee celebrations. Apart from this, many travel films and general interest shorts were made throughout the 1930s in Dufaycolor. These were always printed on safety film, so the original prints, if still in good condition, can be shown today. However, for long term preservation, many have been reprinted on colour print stock, including the only surviving parts found so far of the colour sequences included in *Radio Parade of 1934*, and the only feature filmed entirely in Dufaycolor, *Sons of the Sea* (1939).

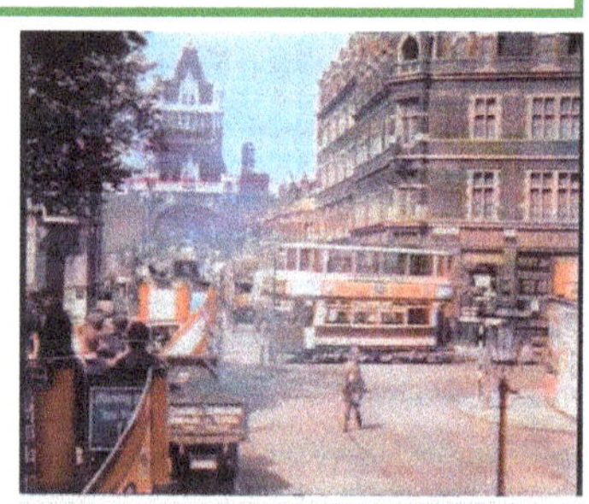

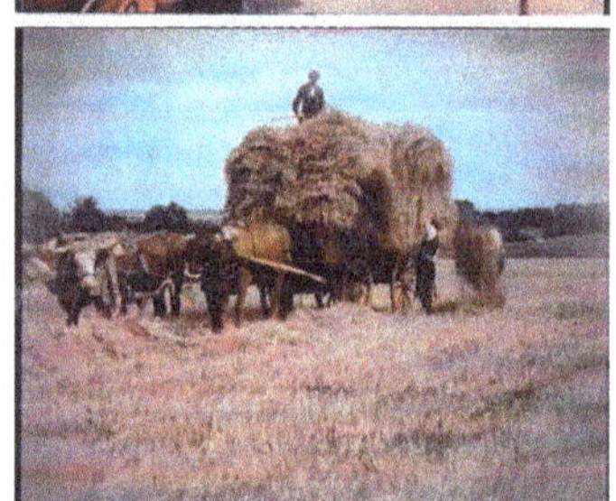

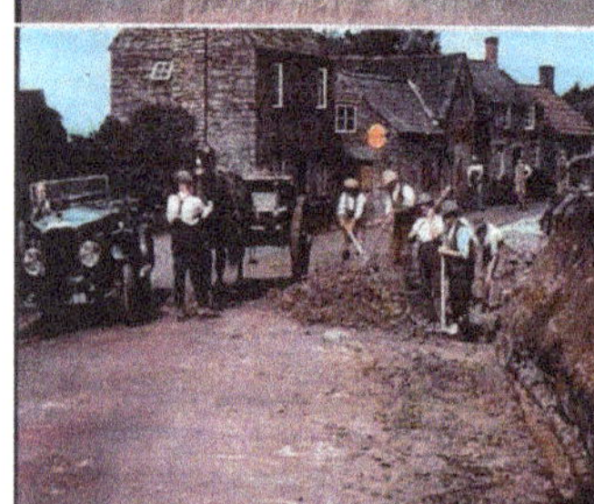

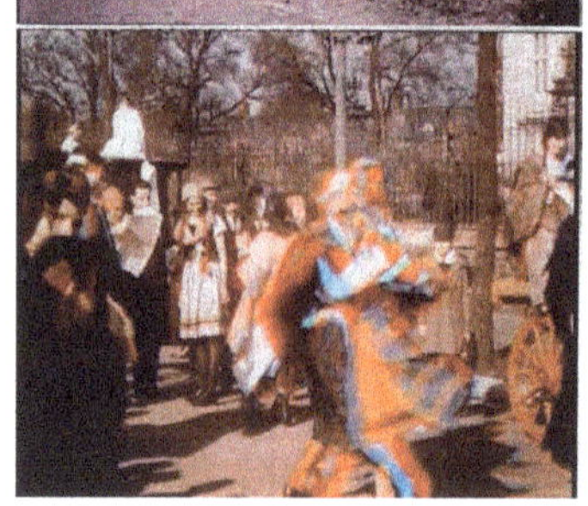

Right: Images from a restored Biocolor film 'Open Road' showing everyday life in towns and the countryside during the mid 1920s.
The sequential frame system suited the slower pace of life at the time, but, as the bottom picture shows, when the camera caught the couple dancing in the street the result was just a multi-coloured blur.

When first introduced in 1932, Dufaycolor was only available as a reversal process and remained so in the 9.5mm and 16mm sizes but by 1937 the 35mm version was changed to negative/positive along with special developing and printing techniques to improve the quality of the copies. It was used by Pathe News to film King George VI's Coronation procession. Although still additive, the built in screen of tiny red, green and blue filters on the base allow it to be viewed and copied like a subtractive negative or print. When printed, the image is often slightly de-focused to help obscure the mosaic of filter elements which, although not visible if viewed from a distance, can cause moiré interference patterns when run on a telecine or scanner.

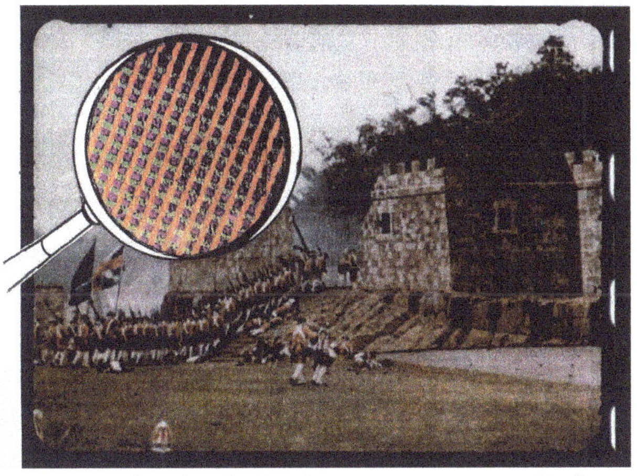

Compared with today's colour prints, surviving Dufaycolor copies have a higher overall density, even in the clear highlight areas, due to the high absorption of the transmitted light by the pattern of tri-colour filters on its base. The picture shows an original Dufaycolor print with a magnified area showing the microscopic pattern of filter elements on its base (reseau).

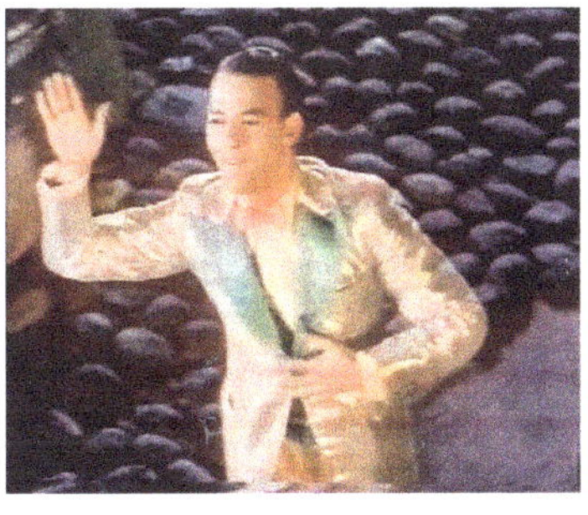

A frame from a restored Dufaycolor sequence in 'Radio Parade of 1935'. A modern reprint on colour print film may be considered as an improvement on the original

Better than before

Again, a modern re-print can look better than the darker and muted colours of a Dufaycolor print, with its filter screen (reseau) absorbing two-thirds of the transmitted light. This led to a dilemma for the National Film and Television Archive when making new prints of Len Lye's abstract animation film *Colour Box* (1935). Although originally shown using Dufaycolor prints, the 'negative' was in fact a positive with coloured inks hand painted onto clear film. The first new print, via a colour inter-negative, looked nothing like Dufaycolor. It can be argued that Len Lye was obliged to use Dufaycolor, being the only readily available system at the time, and would probably prefer the new print with its brighter colours. However, to please everybody, the archive made an alternative print graded to simulate the look of an original print.

Breaking the colour code

Copying a lenticular original is far more difficult, which is why this additive method was largely restricted to amateur film makers. Kodak launched Kodacolor 16mm reversal lenticular film in 1928 and this remained the only practical means of making home movies in colour until the arrival of first, Dufaycolor, and in 1935, Kodachrome, after which time Kodacolor rapidly fell out of favour and was withdrawn in 1938.

Filming on lenticular film was less convenient, with a banded colour filter over the lens, which had to be set at full aperture, the exposure controlled with neutral density filters. Like all other 16mm films, intended for showing in the home, surviving lenticular prints are on safety stock and can be preserved in their original form. When current, most 16mm camera and projector manufacturers included Kodacolor filter attachments among their accessories. Examples can still be found, to enable these films to be seen in colour again.

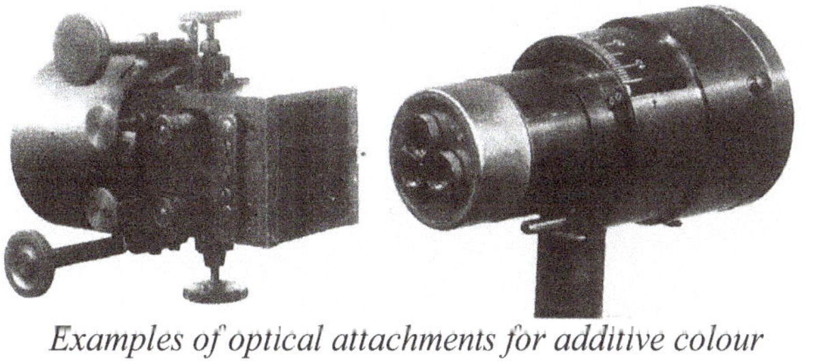

Examples of optical attachments for additive colour processes. L - Gaumont Chromochrome, R - Lumicolor

Early Home Movies

The value of early home movies as social history is becoming more appreciated and many are now donated to national or regional archives. Those in colour are particularly sought after and may be of commercial value to producers of the various 'IN COLOUR' documentaries.

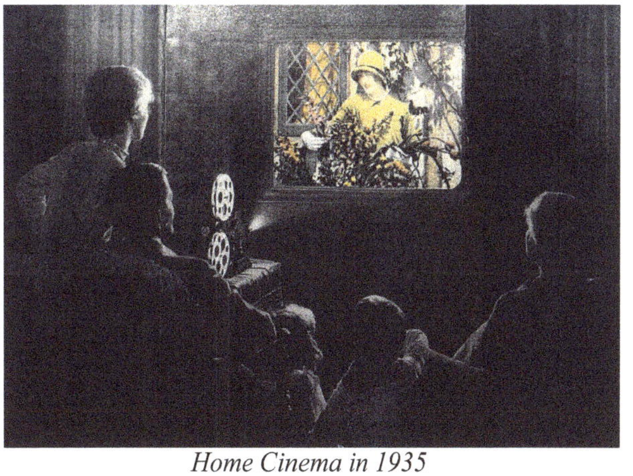

Home Cinema in 1935
From a Kodacolor brochure

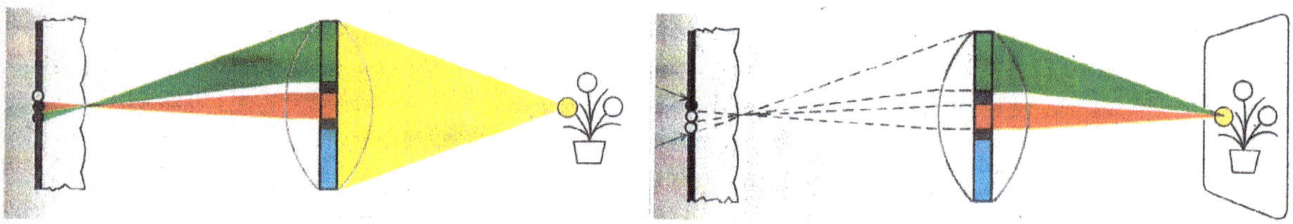

The basic principle of the ***additive lenticular colour process*** *was relatively simple (shown here recording and reproducing the colour yellow) particularly when using the special embossed black and white reversal film and projecting the same processed positive film back through a matching optical system and tri-colour banded filter onto a screen. However, using this original as a source for making extra lenticular copies or ordinary subtractive colour prints proved far more difficult.*

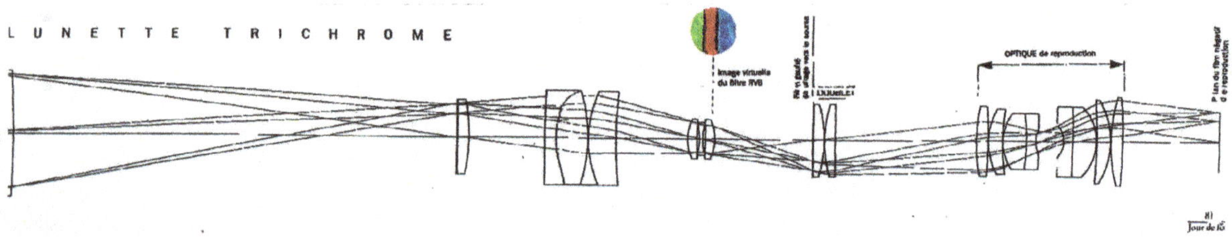

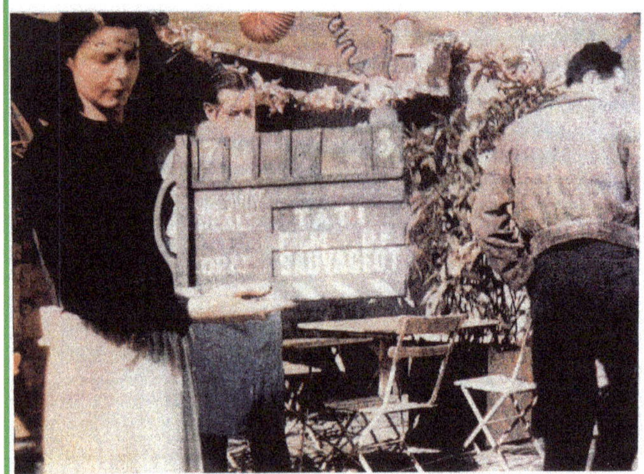

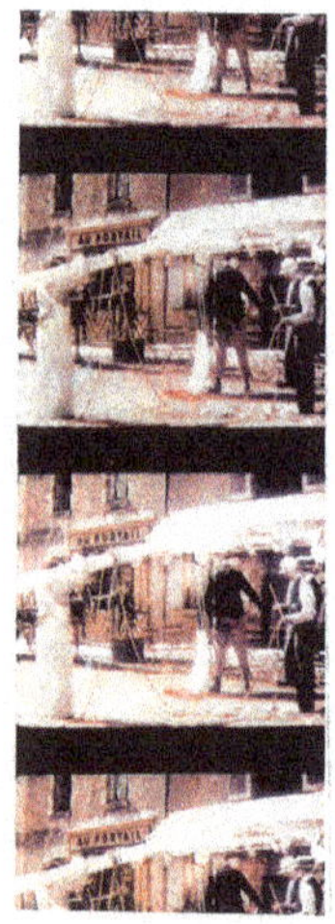

This was the case for the abortive attempt to make a colour version of Jacques Tati's 'Jour de Fete' in 'Thompson Color', which used a reversal lenticular film in the camera. At the time, in 1947, no way was found to make satisfactory colour release prints, so only the simultaneously shot black and white version was shown. In 1994 a computer designed printer lens was constructed and used to finally produce the colour version, almost 50 years late.

The pictures show one of the first images from the lenticular camera original to have its hidden colour revealed, and frames from the final colour print

During the 1920s and 1930s, amateur film making was mostly a rich man's hobby, so gives us the opportunity to see the social elite of the time at play, unguarded moments in the private lives of the rich and famous, and historical figures from the past. To this end, The National Film Archive did manage to devise a way to copy some lenticular films onto colour print stock to make the viewing in colour more convenient and to preserve the originals. A banded filter was used, but the operation was complicated by the fact that it was intended for a wide aperture lens with a focal length inter-related to that of the lenticles on the film's base, and all calculated for projection at a distance onto a screen, and not focused closer on an optical printer. After modifications to the light source and additional lenses, satisfactory copies were produced. Among the subjects chosen, was unique colour footage of Ascot races from the 1920s.

One of the few professional colour processes to employ lenticular film was the French **Thompson Color**, which was used to film a simultaneously shot colour version of Jacques Tati's *Jour de fete.* A reversal lenticular film was exposed in the camera to be used as a source for making subtractive colour prints via separation negatives.
The prints were to be made on double coated stock, the red record from the lenticular original printed on one side and dye-toned cyan, with the blue on the other side toned yellow. One of the sides was then to be recoated with emulsion in order to print the green image, which was toned magenta.

Due to insurmountable registration and processing problems, no satisfactory prints were ever produced.
After a final try using Agfacolor multilayer print film, the colour version was abandoned and the film had to be released in 1949 using the back-up black and white version.

For a reissue in the 1960s, Jacques Tati re-filmed some scenes of the black and white version. He was still frustrated at the loss of the colour version, so he had 'splashes' of colour added to some of the scenes in the black and white prints. Hand painted (rotoscope) cels were used to colour flags, lanterns and lighted windows, which were combined with the black and white image using an aerial image rostrum camera. After Jacques Tati's death, the original uncut lenticular camera film was discovered to still exist and in 1987 yet another attempt began to produce the colour version. The struggle to restore it took seven years, much of this time trying to devise a successful way to copy the lenticular original.

At times, it looked like history would repeat itself and all attempts would fail, but after months of trial and error and eighty hours of computer calculations, an optical system was constructed to accurately decrypt the hidden colours. The rushes were then edited to match as near as possible to the 1960s picture and soundtrack. The few scenes which were never shot in colour were colourised, guided by the natural colours of the rest of the film, and in 1994 the colour version was finally delivered, after a delay of nearly fifty years.

Kodachrome - a safe place for keeping colourful memories

When first introduced in 1935 the dyes formed in the layers of Kodachrome were very unstable, with the colour image fading to a pale pink after only a few years. In 1938 the processing procedure was changed, after which the dyes gained a high degree of permanence equal to dye-transfer, and became the amateur's 'Technicolor'.

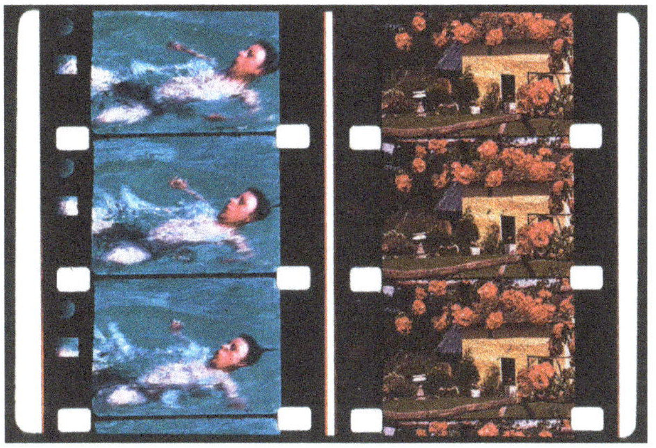

Kodachrome 16mm from 1938 - and still looking as good as new

An early splash of colour in 16mm

When Kodak introduced its 16mm gauge in 1923, it soon set up the Kodascope library so that its early users could hire 16mm copies of original cinema films. These were of excellent quality, usually reduced directly from the 35mm negatives and printed on distinctive amber tinted stock. Almost all were black and white, but in the early 1930s a few rare colour prints were produced of films shot in or containing sequences in two-colour Technicolor.

At the time, Technicolor could not provide 16mm colour prints, so the job was given to another lab, Dunning-color. They used an unusual type of print stock which had a single layer of emulsion with a mixture of red and blue sensitive grains. One of the separation negatives was printed on its own set of grains using coloured light and then processed and toned the correct colour, leaving the remaining material unfixed and the still sensitive emulsion ready to be exposed to the other negative, which was similarly treated to produce the second colour of the final two-colour image. This idea was not generally pursued for later colour films, where the multi-layer approach was preferred, including Kodak's own Kodachrome, which was soon to follow.

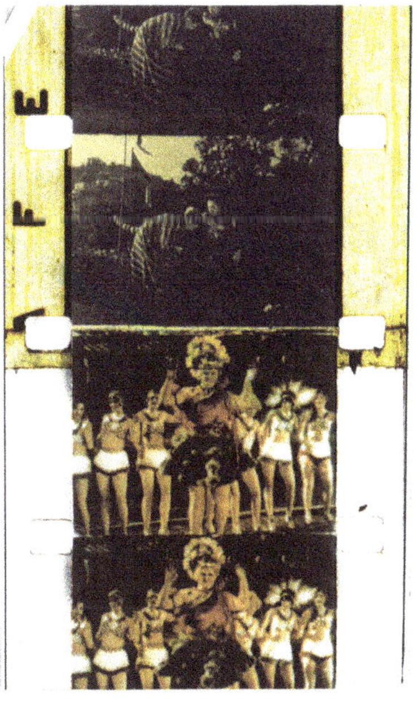

The illustration shows a colour sequence joined into a black and white film on amber film stock.

Preserving and restoring Technicolor and others - understand the history

Those involved with restoration need to understand the history and development of the film material which they are working with so as to be able to make the best possible decisions as to how to carry out their vital work of preserving the cinema's colourful history most effectively.

If it's in colour, it is probably Technicolor

During the 1930s and 1940s, Technicolor rapidly became the most popular and commercially successful colour process, evolving from a two to a full three-colour system. After toying with a two colour additive process whose images were described as needing 'a cross between a college professor and an acrobat' to keep in register on the screen, Technicolor was among the first to admit that the subtractive principle was the way to go, with colour prints that could be shown on a normal projector by a normal projectionist. Their first subtractive two-colour process was introduced in 1922, using a single strip double-frame negative with the pair of simultaneously shot filtered B&W images positioned toe-to-toe along the length of the film. The images were printed onto two thin based films which were processed to give positive images in the form of differentially hardened gelatine. These were cemented together back to back in register and then individually coloured the appropriate red or blue/green by floating each side on the surface of the baths of dye.

When YCM Labs in the U.S.A. restored Technicolor's first feature to use the process, *Toll of the Sea* (1922), they were fortunate to have access not only to the original negative, but the beam-splitter colour camera that had shot it complete with its filters. This enabled them to gain much information about the registration and nature of the chosen combination of colours. To check the accuracy of the two colours reproduced on modern print film, test scenes were also printed first as separate positives in each colour to compare them with the original filters before superimposing them on the final print. This gave a potentially better colour balance than faithfully recreating the look of a surviving contemporary print, which often varied from print to print. When our own National Film and Television Archive made a new copy of Douglas Fairbank's *The Black Pirate* (1926), their original Technicolor two-colour cemented print was considered too green, so again they chose to adjust the balance when making the new print.

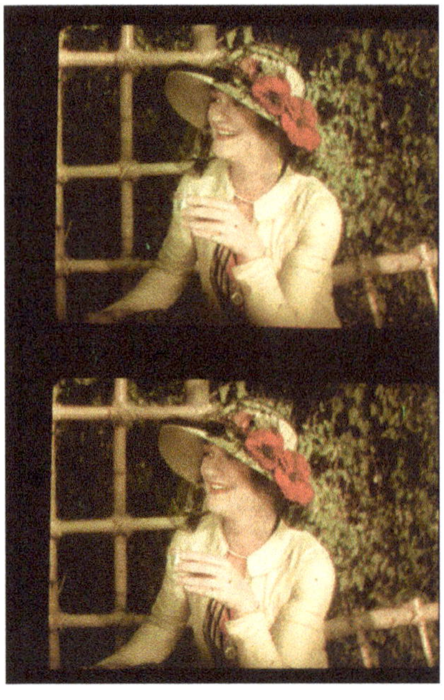

Restored print from 'The Toll of the Sea' (1922). Restored in 1985 from the original two-colour camera negative it is one of the great technical achievements of film preservation. This earliest surviving feature in the two-colour Technicolor process was restored by UCLA Film & Television Archive.

The change to dye-transfer

Problems with the cemented prints buckling in the heat of the projector led to the change to dye-transfer. Again two films were printed with the positive images represented as varying thicknesses of hardened gelatine. Now known as matrices, they were used to first absorb the dyes and then transfer them in turn to the same side of a third clear blank film. The same pair of matrices could be used repeatedly like printing plates to produce up to about fifty copies before having to be replaced. Although around one hundred films employed two colour Technicolor between 1922 and 1933, less than half were complete features. Many studios preferred to exploit the novelty of colour as shorter inserts in their black and white

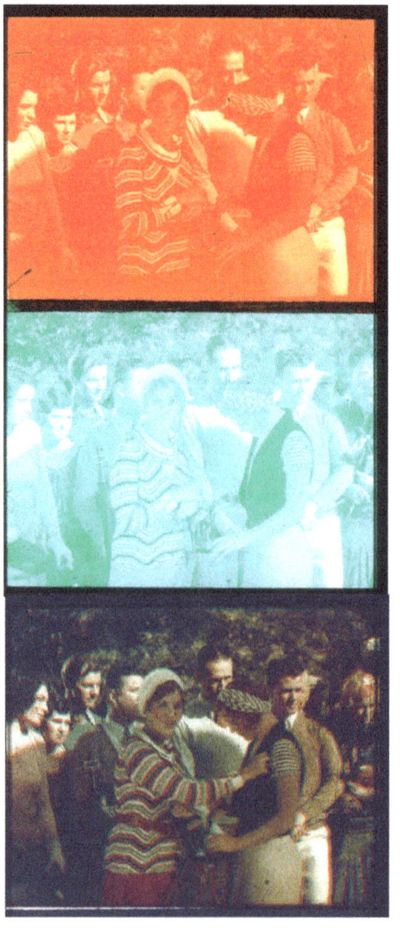

'Follow Thru' (1930), was also restored from the original two-colour Technicolor camera negative, , with the separate colours first printed individually to match the colour with the original filters used in the camera (top two pics) before being superimposed on the final print (bottom pic)

films, before audiences tired of the often poor colour and definition. Many of these have been lost, but early silent and sound films which have had their colour sequences restored include, *The Ten Commandments*: (1923), *Ben Hur* (1926) and *King Of Kings* (1927). Moments of colour enhanced the horror of *The Phantom of the Opera* (1925), the rest of the film tinted yellow, blue and eerie green. The first all-talking, all-singing, all-dancing and now all-Technicolor feature was On With The Show in 1929, followed by *Broadway Melody, Show Of Shows, Gold Diggers Of Broadway* and *King Of Jazz*.

The demands on Technicolor during this rush to colour meant the quality of the prints varied greatly. Critics praised 'the lovely colour work' in *Rio Rita*, but considered the colour sequences in *No No Nanette* to be 'the poorest yet seen with tiresome and badly blurred colour'. As the popularity of these stage review type musicals waned, so did Technicolor and the first boom was over. With the pressure off, the last two features *Doctor X* (1932) and *The Mystery Of The Wax Museum*

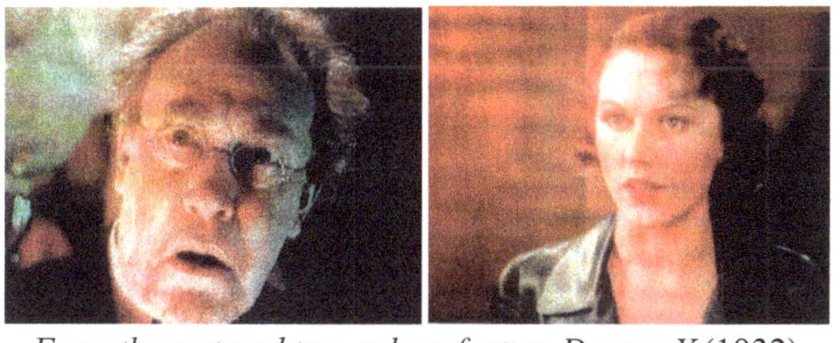

From the restored two-colour feature Doctor X (1932)

(1933), were judged to have the best colour that could be achieved using only two colour components. Like surviving Technicolor prints from this period, the more recent restorations also vary in quality, particularly those having to be made from original prints in poor condition. Over time, it has been possible to improve on some of them, due to the later discovery of better source material in archives around the world, or provided by private collectors, following appeals made using one of the most successful restoration tools, internet websites.

One restoration project, stalled while awaiting such a find, is *Gold Diggers Of Broadway* (1929), which remains on the list of 'lost' Technicolor films. Only two reels in two-colour Technicolor are known to exist and have been restored. If any of the other eight ever turn up, a complete set of the accompanying Vitaphone discs has survived to join them.

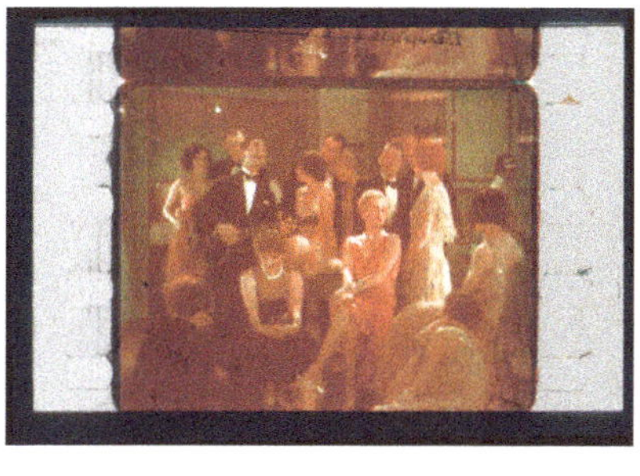

FOUND! Only a single frame from one of the missing reels of the two-colour Technicolor 'Gold Diggers of Broadway' (1929)

Technicolor added the third component, turning it into a full-colour process, in 1932, following the construction of its renowned three-strip camera and adding another run through the transfer machine, which now transferred yellow, cyan and magenta dye images onto the blank. After the coming of sound, this had a normal black and white emulsion to allow an optical track to be printed and processed before the colour picture was transferred. The sight of the neutral grey or black silver track remained the principal way of identifying a Technicolor dye-transfer colour print throughout the life of the process.

Colour given another chance

Past experiences when using colour made producers reluctant to try the new improved Technicolor. In exchange for a three year exclusive contract for making three-colour cartoons, Walt Disney used one of the first 3-strip cameras for *Flowers And Trees* (1932), followed by *Santa's Workshop, Funny Bunnies* and *Three Little Pigs*. These proved so popular that Micky Mouse soon appeared in colour too. Disney agreed to reduce the contract to two years, to enable other animators, who had been obliged to continue to use the old Technicolor and other inferior 2-colour processes, such as Cinecolor, to switch over to full-colour.

By the early 1940s, black and white cartoons were a rarity, with almost all now in Technicolor. The sequential-frame method of photography was used, which Disney had also adopted in time for their first feature-length cartoon, *Snow White and The Seven Dwarfs*. To help encourage its use for live-action, Technicolor helped finance an experimental short, *La Cucuracha*. The excellent colour led to sequences being added to black and white films already in production including the closing scenes in *The House of Rothschild, Kid Millions* and *The Little Colonel*. But after the critical success of the first full-length 3-strip Technicolor feature, *Becky Sharp* in 1935, the demand rapidly grew and the rest is history.

During the next forty years, many thousands of features, shorts, advertising films and trailers were printed in dye-transfer derived from 3-strip and successive frame separation negatives, together with Eastman Color and other multi-layer single strip originals. Prints were sometimes made from l6mm and 35mm Kodachrome or Ansco Color reversal camera films. Notable blow-ups from Kodachrome include the original wartime documentary *The Memphis Belle* (1944), Disney's *True Life Adventure* nature films and *Conquest of Everest* (1953). Complete films shot using 35mm reversal stock include *Son of Lassie* (1945) on Kodachrome (Monopack) and *The Man On The Eiffel Tower* (1949) using Ansco Color. Although the 3-strip camera was retired in 1955 in favour of Eastman Color and other colour negative films, the dye-transfer method of making the prints continued for another twenty years. During the late 1960s, 'Vidtronic' dye-transfer prints were also made from video tape.

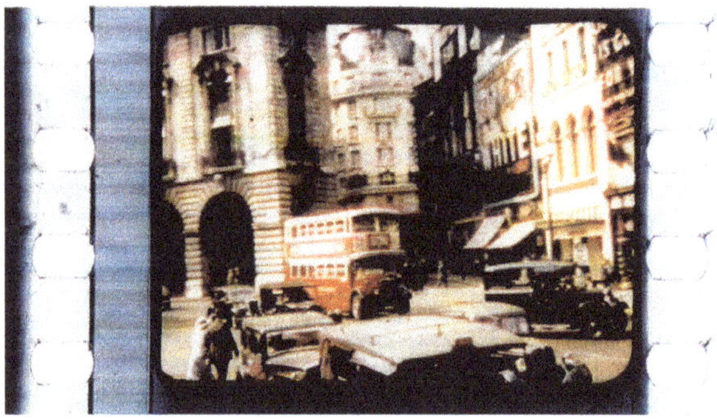

Some of the first Technicolor 3-strip films include interesting exterior colour footage, such as Piccadilly Circus as it was in the mid-1930s, which appeared in Britain's first Technicolor feature 'Wings of the Morning' (1937)

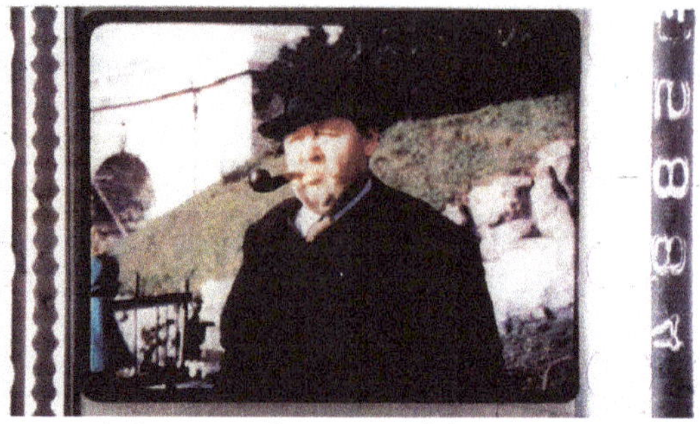

Along with 3-strip and sequential-frame cartoon negatives, a few Technicolor dye-transfer prints were made from single-strip colour reversal camera originals, mostly Kodachrome, both 16mm and a special 35mm version (Monopack). An exception was 'The Man on the Eiffel Tower' (1948) shot on Ansco Color 35mm reversal film, starring Charles Laughton as Inspector Maigret.

Behind the doors at Technicolor

Although the details of the dye-transfer process are now better-known, and explained in a previous section of this book, during the time it was operating, Technicolor made great efforts to keep its secrets from possible competitors. Even its customers knew little about what happened to their film as it passed through the lab. The resulting dye-transfer prints are also referred to as IB or imbibition prints. The added cost of filming in Technicolor included the extra shelf space needed in the vaults to store the large amount of pre-print material which accumulated when using the process. After the three camera negatives were developed, the blue record was used to provide black and white rushes. This negative was chosen as any signs of the extra handling would be less visible in the yellow image it produces on the final print. The last few frames of each chosen take, which included a colour test chart, were joined together and matrices made to print colour 'pilot' strips to help the cameraman to judge the final colour. Before the matrices were printed, protection master positives were made from the cut camera negatives and kept aside in case they were needed to make replacements if any parts of the originals suffered a mishap during their journey through the lab.

Often never needed for this purpose at the time, they were to save the day in later years. The negatives were then used to make the matrices, with extra sets being sent to Technicolor's overseas plants to print the foreign release copies of equal quality. The matrices could be regarded as just a means to an end and discarded after all the required number of release prints had been transferred. However, many were kept for some time in case a re-print was anticipated. In the event, relatively few 3-strip films were shown again in cinemas using new prints. Limited re-issues, including the 'Sunday for one day only' revivals, used existing-off-the-shelf library copies. Technicolor were quite astute when assessing the possible need for re-prints. If they thought a film was likely to become a popular classic, they would keep the transfer machine running and produce extra prints which

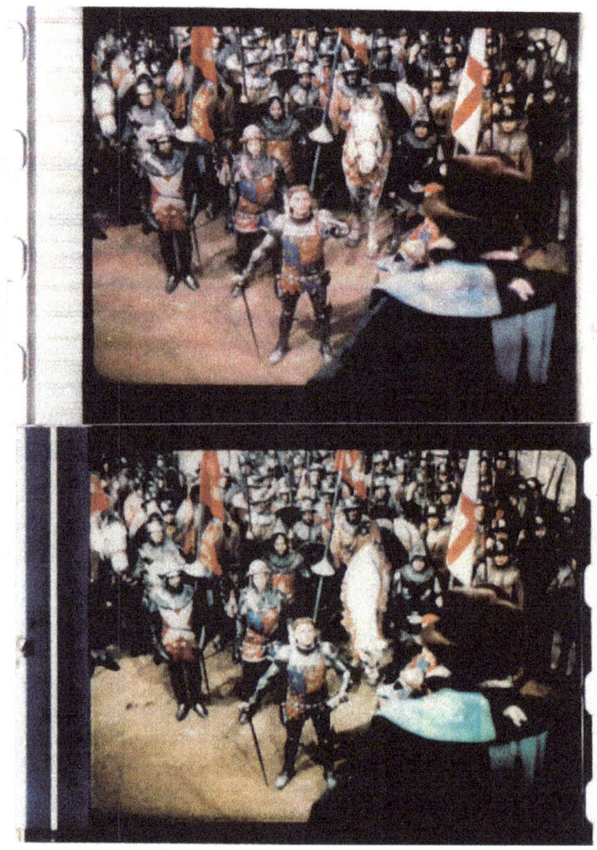

Technicolor dye-transfer print of 'Henry V' (1944) and a reprint made from the original 3-strip negatives onto colour print film. This gives you extra image for your money! This is because the original involved the optical printing of the matrices, resulting in a slight enlargement of the picture (about 5%). The later copy was made using a contact registration step printer, and shows the complete picture area as photographed by the camera, with more image at the edges of the frame.

were spirited away to fulfil any future order without the need for further work. Of the around eight hundred 3-strip Technicolor features made between 1935 and 1955, only about forty were re-printed in dye-transfer for showing again in theatres.

It isn't only feature films that are of interest to archivists - it is equally important to preserve short subjects. Jack Cardiff photographed many rarely seen 3-strip documentaries and travel films, including the 'World Window' series. These clips (L-R) are from the wartime series *This is colour* (1942), *Colour in clay* (1942) and *Steel* (1945)

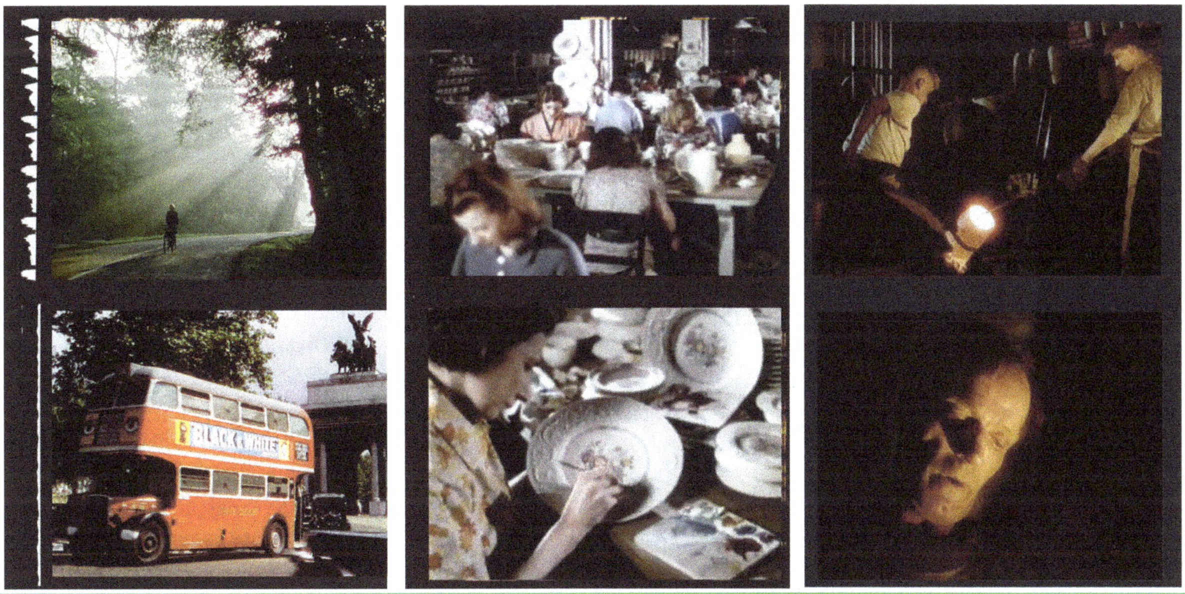

Two-Colour lives on

While Technicolor ruled the world of colour in the cinema, the only practical alternative was to use one of the various two-colour processes, which had managed to survive in the shadow of the literally mighty 3-strip camera. As we have seen in earlier chapters they used simpler bi-pack cameras and double-coated prints, with an orange/red dyed image on one side of the base, and a chemically toned blue/green image and track on the other.

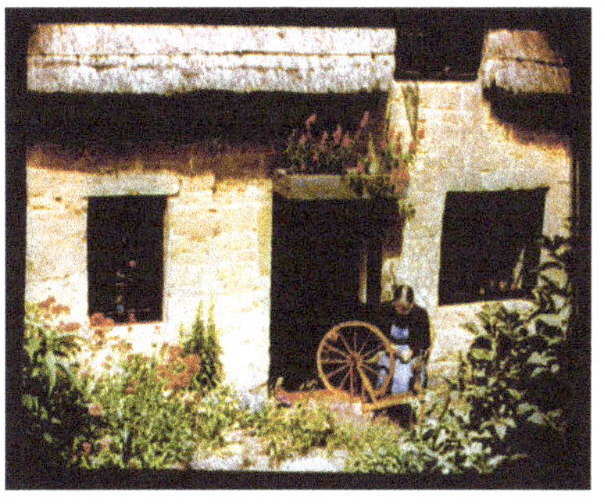

Also shot during the wartime period (by Frank North) was English Village (1943) an experimental film in Monopack, made by Technicolor.

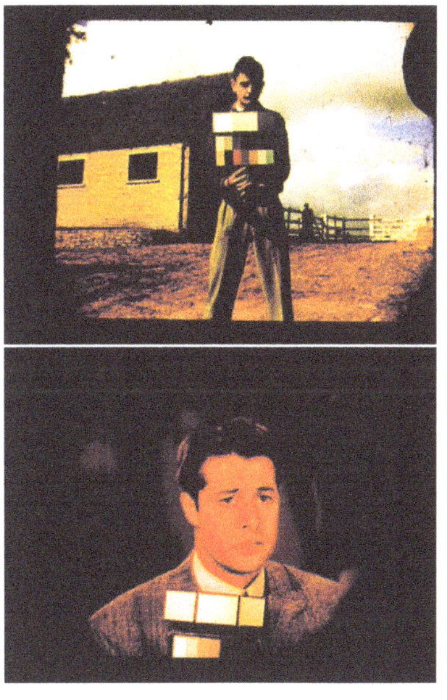

Example of the pilot strips provided to cameramen to judge the colour. The rest of the rushes were only in black and white. They include a test chart called a 'lily' which was displayed at the end of each take.

To those working on restoration projects the bright blue track, and occasional orange and blue scratches or blemishes, are the giveaway that you may be handling an original two-colour print. The most popular, operating in the U.S.A., were Magnacolor, Cinecolor and the first Trucolor process. Trucolor differed, in that it used special Eastman double-coated print stock incorporating colour couplers for processing in a colour developer. The emulsion layer on one side included a mixture of magenta and yellow couplers to form the red/orange image, and a cyan coupler in the other to create the blue/green; image. Trucolor was used mostly by Republic studios and a couple of two-colour Roy Rogers westerns have been aired on TV over here. The most popular and widely used two-colour process was Cinecolor, giving the chance for the producers of lower budget films to film in colour, without the restrictions of Technicolor. It freed them from having to use the cumbersome 3-strip camera, supplied complete with its own crew, and the ever present colour consultant who watched over the production to make sure that Technicolor's recommendations were followed, even though they could stifle the creative use of the colour. Cinecolor also provided a consultant who helped ensure that the restricted colour range was handled carefully and not noticed by the audience. Fortunately, the tanned faces in B-westerns photographed quite well, including Randolph Scott's in one of the best, *Canadian Pacific* (1949). Also worth looking out for, when shown on TV, is *Slaughter Trail* (1951), which praises Cinecolor in its title song.

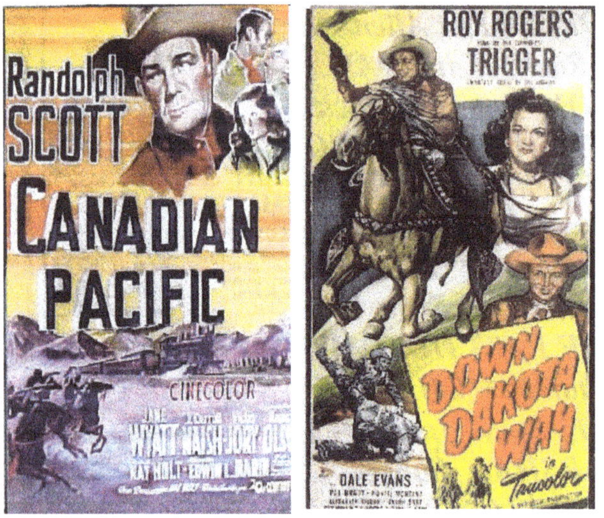

Posters showing Cinecolor branding for 'Canadian Pacific' and Trucolor branding for 'Down Dakota Way' - both 1949

With the ever-growing number of TV channels to fill, other old two-colour B-Westerns found their way into daytime schedules. Amongst these are *Bells of San Angelo* (1947) and *The Plunderers* (1948) in Trucolor, and *Coroner Creek* (1948) and *Cariboo Trail* (1950) in Cinecolor.

If carefully balanced during the transfer into the full three-colour video domain, most viewers will be unaware of the limited range of colours, although some may notice that the ladies often end up with orange lips.

During the 1930s, a number of two-colour processes were operating in Britain. They were used mostly for advertising films and cartoons, including Anson Dyer's *Sam and his Musket*, produced in Dunningcolor and claimed to be Britain's first sound cartoon in colour. Chemicolor, a version of the German Ufa-Color two-colour process using Agfa stock, was chosen for the fantasy scenes in *Pagliacci* (1936) starring the opera singer

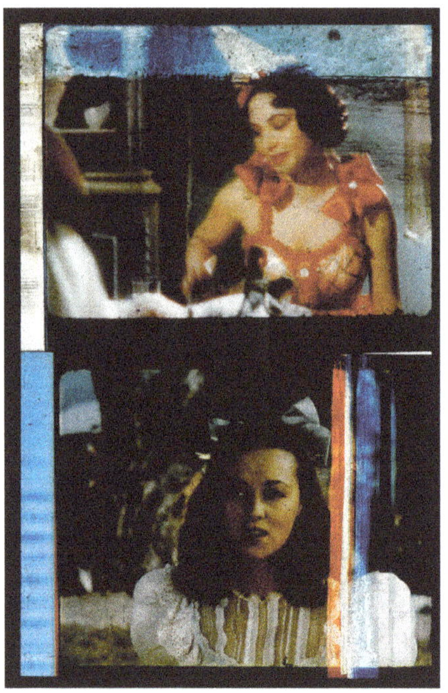

Damaged two-colour films on duplitized stock clearly show the nature of the colours on either side of the base. Upper: 'Pagliacci' (1936) in Chemicolor. Lower: Song of Old Wyoming' (1945) in Cinecolor.

Richard Tauber. The same process was called Spectracolor when used to film a four reel (40min) featurette *Faust* (1936). Both have been restored and reprinted by The National Film and Television Archive, working from original prints. All the British processes came under pressure when Technicolor set up their London labs, and none survived WWII.

Back in Hollywood, the first major studio to release a feature in Cinecolor was MGM with *Gallant Bess* in 1946. Others also used it alongside their Technicolor features for some of their shorts and travelogues, such as Twentieth Century-Fox's *Magic Carpet* travel films. Some, usually Technicolor, cartoon series, like Paramount's *Popeye* and Warner's *Merrie Melodies*, had to temporarily switch to Cinecolor during a period of industrial unrest and strikes at Technicolor, returning to dye-transfer prints after the troubles were over. Cinecolor had found a way to offer three-colour versions of their basic double-coated prints by re-sensitising one of the sides to add the third colour in a separate operation. Without ready access to a 3-strip camera, the process was limited to cartoons and blow-ups from l6mm Kodachrome. The service expanded, when Eastman Color negative became available in 1950 and could be used in a normal studio camera. First used for *The Lady In The Iron Mask*, which carried the credit Natural Color, the three-colour process was to become better known as SuperCinecolor. It never replaced the original two-colour process, in fact, Cinecolor were happy to provide two-colour prints of features shot on Eastman Color for producers who wanted the cheapest possible prints and thought that audiences couldn't tell the difference anyway. An example was *Invaders From Mars* (1953), an original two-colour print is still shown on TV today, with no ill effect on the alien's green complexion. The current video masters of the SuperCinecolor features, *Abbott And Costello Meet Captain Kid* (1952), *Jack And The Beanstalk* (1952) and *The Diamond Queen* (1953), all appear to have been made from original prints. In theory, these could have been made using new prints from the original Eastman Color negatives, but perhaps these are now either lost, or can no longer be printed.

Seen again, but off-colour

A number of 3-strip Technicolor features from the 1930s were later cut and re-issued in the cheaper two-colour Cinecolor process, with the prints made using only the red and green camera negatives. They included *Dancing Pirate, Nothing Sacred, A Star is Born,* and *Becky Sharp*. In the case of the latter, although reduced to two-colour, Becky returned with a fairly healthy complexion, but her dress turned from a brilliant yellow to a demure pink. Despite a worldwide search of archives (including our own NFTA, who only had a worn Cinecolor copy), not all of the discarded footage could be found for UCLA's restoration of Becky Sharp, back in 1985. As a result, the initial prints had to be made from a patchwork of two and three-colour material. When one

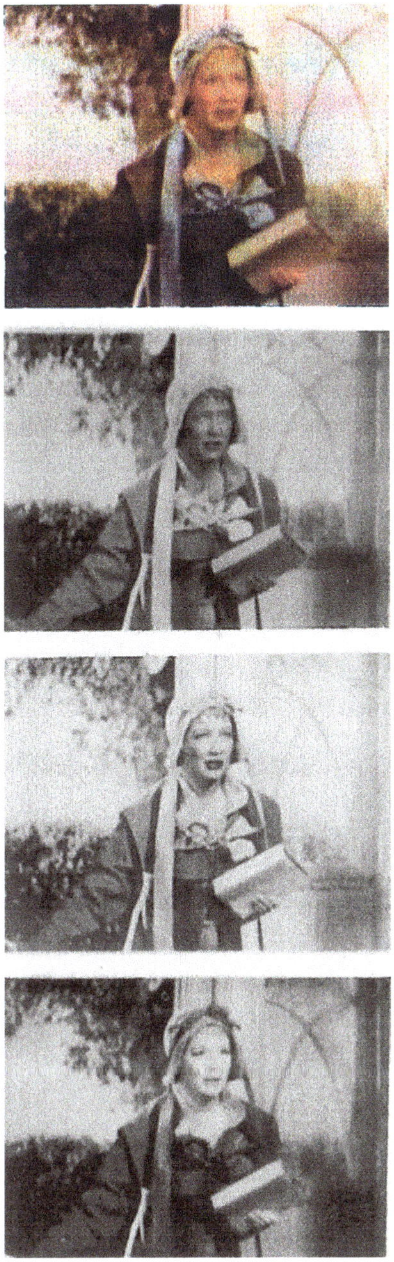

The restoration of 'Becky Sharp' (1935), Technicolor's first 3-strip film, included providing new black and white separation master positives for its future protection

The arrival of Eastman Color made it easier to film in colour using the various wide and large screen processes which employed 'non-standard' film widths and image areas. Although many of these are no longer current, they may now be an added complication when restoring films using the original camera negatives.

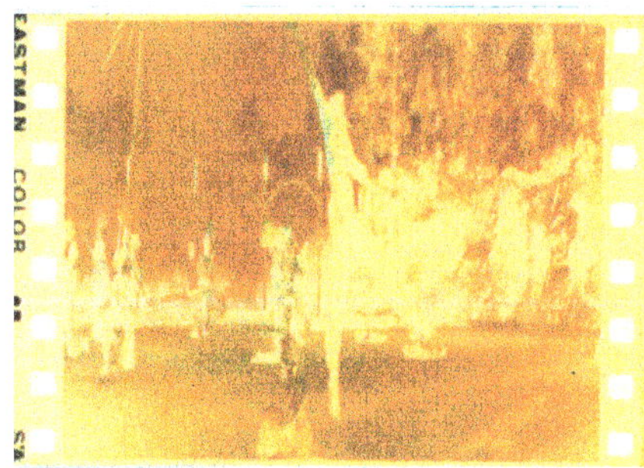

TCF's CinemaScope-55 55mm 8-perf negative with a four times larger squeezed image for producing higher quality standard 35mm CinemaScope reduction prints. Only two features, *Carousel* and *The King and I*, were made in this way in 1956, before the process was abandoned in favour of TODD-AO with its 65mm 5-perf camera negative with a non-anamorphic wide image, as shown in the costume test clip for *Cleopatra*.

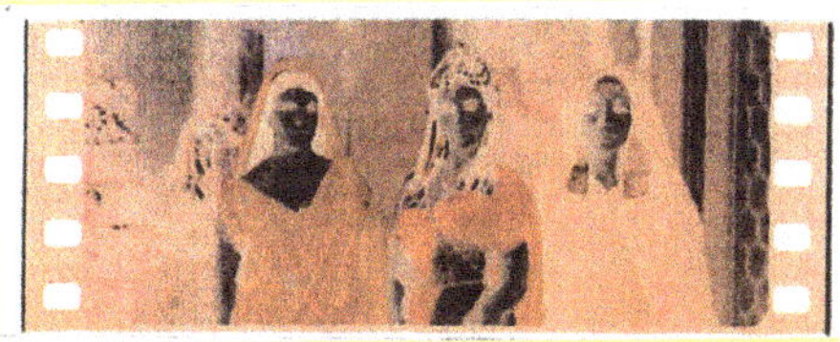

of the 3-strip elements was missing, a replacement was created by printing one of the remaining others twice, green for a missing blue, and blue for a missing green. This ploy has been used for other three-strip films with lost or badly damaged master material, and the results can be surprisingly successful. Fortunately, since its original restoration, later discoveries of extra three-colour footage have allowed Becky Sharp to be updated in full colour.

More two-colour stuff

By the end of the 1940s, two-colour processes were again being offered in Britain. The choice included Radiant Color, Chromart and Alfacolor. Even Technicolor reintroduced a two-colour system. Known as Technichrome, it was specifically devised to film a colour record of the 1948 Olympic Games held in London. All of the few available 3-strip cameras were rounded up to photograph the opening and closing ceremonies, to get the colours of the national flags right, but all the other events were shot using more readily available bi-pack cameras. The pair of negatives was printed using the normal three-colour dye-transfer method. The cyan matrix was printed from the red negative, with both the yellow and magenta made from the same blue/green negative. Although the balance was adjusted from scene to scene, the overall colour was noticeably inferior to the original three-colour footage. Apart from a couple of Technichrome shorts filmed in Spain, the process was never offered again commercially. Cinecolor opened a plant in Slough at the beginning of the 1950s which turned out both two and three-colour prints, until closing down along with its American counterpart in 1955. At their peak demand, the total footage of the various two-colour processes equalled that from Technicolor. Even so, little is seen of it today, probably due to its use for mostly unremarkable and missable programme fillers.

With double-coated print stock no longer available, or the means to treat each side separately, modern copies are made on colour print film. The most commonly used processes were printed from bi-pack or sequential frame animation negatives. If these are still available, they can be printed via red and cyan filters directly onto the print film, or a new colour negative produced through an inter-positive. More likely, an original print will have to be the source for a new colour negative and print. This has the advantage of being able to use it as a guide to the final colour.

Actual examples of the various processes are useful as a reference to the original look, if this is required and only the negatives are available, but have a credit indicating the print process employed when first released. However, even within a particular process, the balance or nature of the pair of colours were sometimes modified to suit the subject matter, to help compensate for the shortcomings of only a two-colour system. During the last days of two-colour, a few films had their pair of negatives printed onto Eastman Color and other early three-colour print film. Examples include, the delayed release of *Montana Belle* in Trucolor, and *Babes In Bagdad* (1952), filmed in Exotic Color, promoted as being 'almost' a three-colour process! In the past, both Cinecolor and Trucolor films worth a re-issue were later reprinted on ordinary Eastman Color print stock, and could be an improvement on the first double-coated prints and not always recognised as being only two-colour.

Today any new colour inter-positive or negative should be clearly identified as being only two-colour. In the future, a commercial laboratory may try and analyse them thinking they are three-color. They should not be treated in terms of yellow, cyan and magenta, but only cyan and red (yellow plus magenta).

Changes to make room for Eastman Color

When first introduced in 1950, the Eastman Color system did not include colour intermediate duplicating films. This suited laboratories like Technicolor and Cinecolor, who adopted the camera negative and the print stock for providing colour rushes, but made all the release prints using their established printing processes. Although only a single negative was now exposed in a normal camera, the amount of vault space actually increased. At first, Technicolor had to produce three black and white separation negatives from a set of master positives made from the original colour negative by printing them in turn through red, green and blue filters onto panchromatic stock. The quality of the final dye-transfer prints did not match those derived from negatives produced directly from the subject in the 3-strip camera. The quality gap soon closed, when new improved panchromatic matrix stock allowed the matrices to be printed directly from the colour negative, and the days of the 3-strip camera were numbered. Some early prints carry the credit `Print by Technicolor'.

After a year or so, Eastman Color duplicating films were added in the form of a fine grain black and white separation stock and a colour duplicate negative film. Many other laboratories were now able to offer a colour service. At first, they too had to produce their duplicate colour negatives via separations, but by 1953 the system was completed with a masked colour duplicating film which could be used to produce either a master positive or duplicate negative. When making a duplicate negative, it is possible to incorporate fades, dissolves and other optical effects, like superimposed titles. These are then joined into the original cut camera negative, with the extra printing generation showing as a noticeable drop in quality as the 'optical' takes place.

To avoid further losses, many laboratories chose to make all their domestic release prints from the original cut camera negative, despite the risks. Others, like most in Britain, preferred to make just a few prestige copies from the original and the rest from duplicates, which were also exchanged to allow foreign versions to be printed locally. As the quality of duplicating films improved, the printing from duplicate negatives became standard practice. With colour duplicating stock available, black and white separations were no longer strictly necessary, it was up to the individual studios to decide if they wanted them to protect their investment. Sometimes, only the most important features were backed up with separations. They were always recommended by Kodak to guard against the loss or damage to the original negative, and possible fading of the dye images. This latter statement in the small print was not always taken seriously at the time, but in later years, it proved to be a problem in waiting.

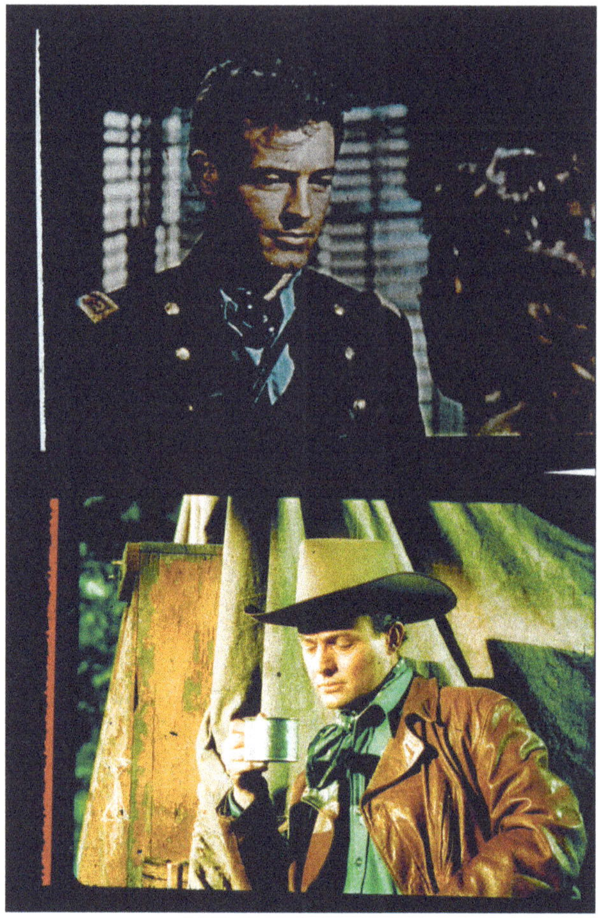

Prints from prints
Top: A poor, high-contrast copy of Drums in the Deep South (1951) in SuperCinecolour. Below: a rather better copy of Down Dakota Way (1949) in two-colour Trucolor

More colour than ever

For audiences there was more colour than ever, with films now to be seen in WarnerColor, Color by DeLuxe, Color by Pathe and Movielab, which were all in reality Eastman Color by another name. MGM's Metrocolor labs began by using new negative / positive colour stocks from Ansco, but after a couple of years, switched to Eastman Color. Trucolor turned into a three-colour process, again using Eastman Color negative, but first printing onto colour print film from DuPont, before they too adopted Eastman Color throughout. The final three-colour version of Trucolor was credited as 'Trucolor by Consolidated', the laboratory which processed it.

After Technicolor retired its 3-strip camera, and both DuPont and Ansco withdrew their colour film stocks for theatrical use, Eastman Color became virtually the standard for 35mm colour cinematography in the USA.

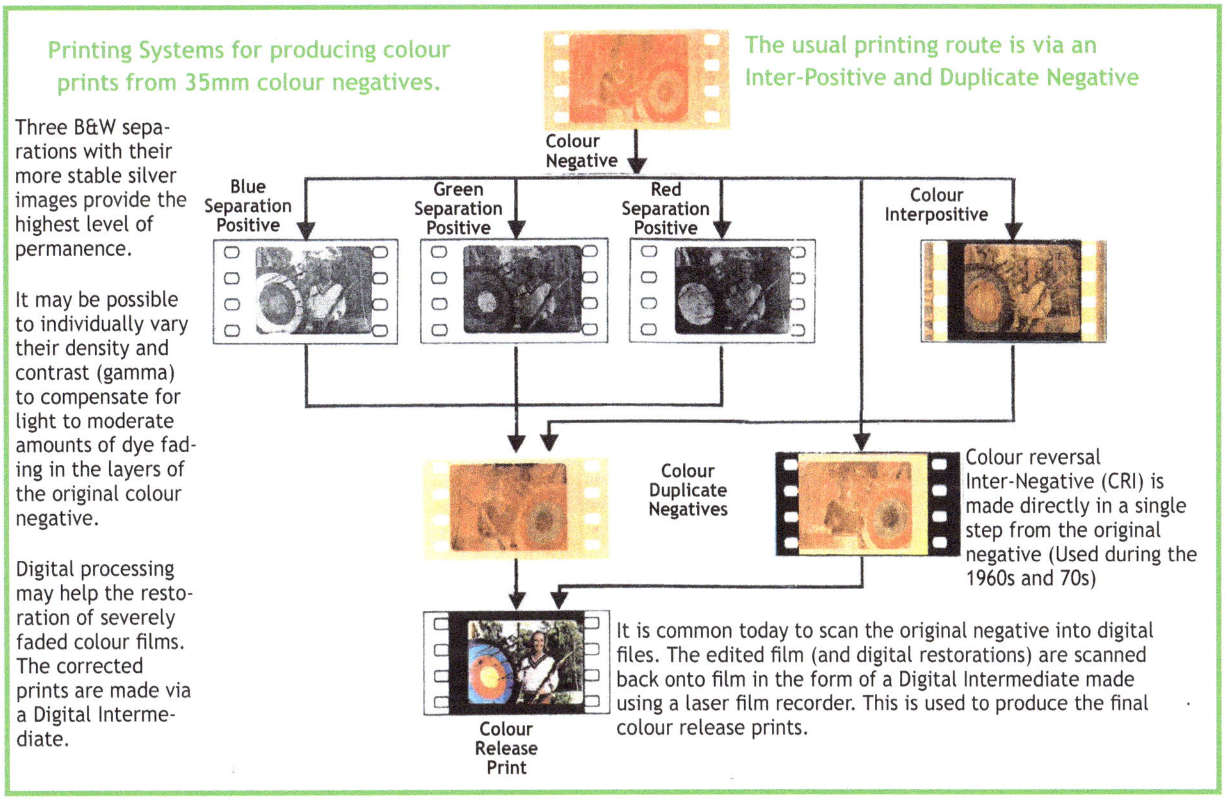

In Britain, and the rest of Europe and Asia, the choice was greater, with both colour negative and print stocks also available from Gevaert, Agfa, Ferrania and Fuji. Many productions printed on Eastman Color print film in the USA were printed on different stocks abroad. Their negative films proved to be less popular and didn't gain wide acceptance until the 1970s, when they could employ Eastman Color's integral masking system which, till then, was an exclusive patented feature. Technicolor continued to offer the industry the option of using dye-transfer prints. Continuous improvements kept pace with those made to conventional print stocks and allowed the dye-transfer method to successfully compete until the late 1970s, when economic factors led to its demise and after fifty years, Technicolor ceased to be a specific unique process. At the end of the 1990s, Technicolor in Hollywood re-introduced dye-transfer to test its viability alongside its normal output on print film. With the transfer machine operating again, the opportunity was taken to reprint a few 3-strip classics in dye-transfer, including *Gone With The Wind* and *The Wizard of Oz*. The process has since been suspended, with Technicolor now concentrating its efforts on becoming a leading light in the world of digital cinema.

TV hungry for old films and new prints

Back in the early 1950s, electronic images were already giving the film industry something to think about, when the growing popularity of television was taking the blame for a drop in audience numbers. Eastman Color was to play an important role in the fight back. It allowed colour films to be made in new screen processes like Cinerama, 3D, CinemaScope and all the various non-standard negative widescreen formats. Anamorphic lenses were not compatible with the beam-splitting optics used in Technicolor's 3-strip camera. Also, prints using the existing dye-transfer process didn't stand up well to the extra enlargement needed to fill the bigger screens until improvements let them join the cinema's widescreen revolution. These innovations did help for a while in the battle with television, but by the mid-1950s, one by one, the studios broke ranks and decided to fraternise with the enemy and make money out of the new medium. They formed subsidiaries to make their own TV series and sold or leased the TV rights to their libraries of old pre-1950 movies. Many of these were in colour, mostly 3-strip Technicolor. Soon, the TV releasing companies required new 35mm and 16mm prints, the latter for syndication to the smaller local U.S. TV stations. Large numbers of copies were needed when, at first, all films were transmitted 'live' directly from a telecine machine and then often retained for possible repeat showings.

The Arrilaser Film Recorder

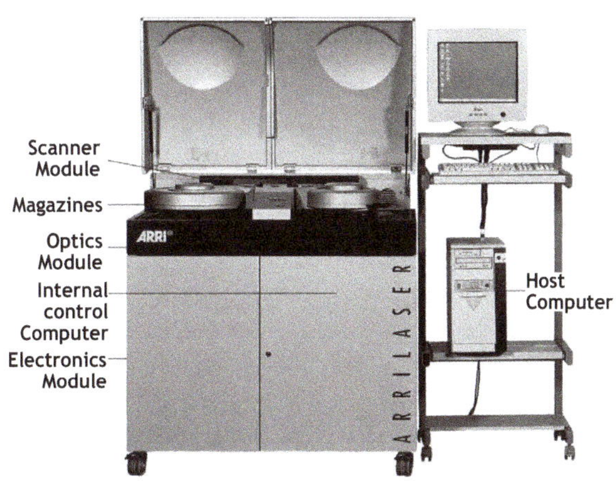

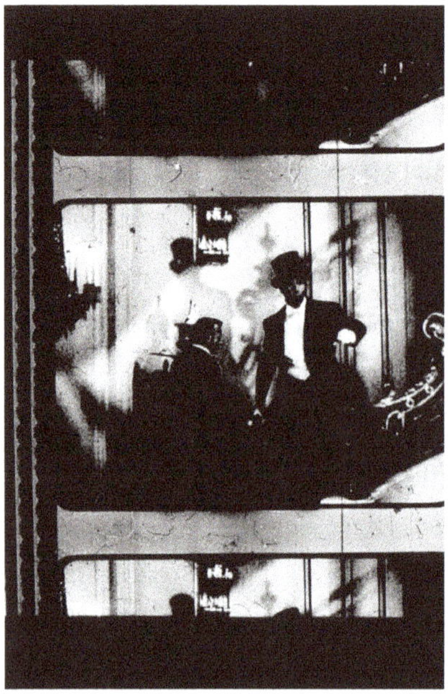

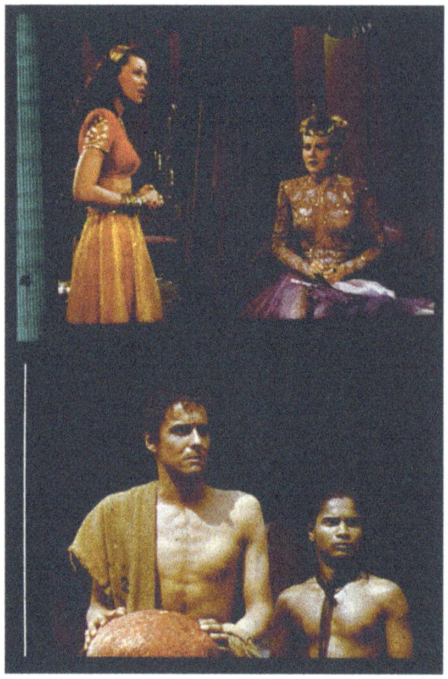

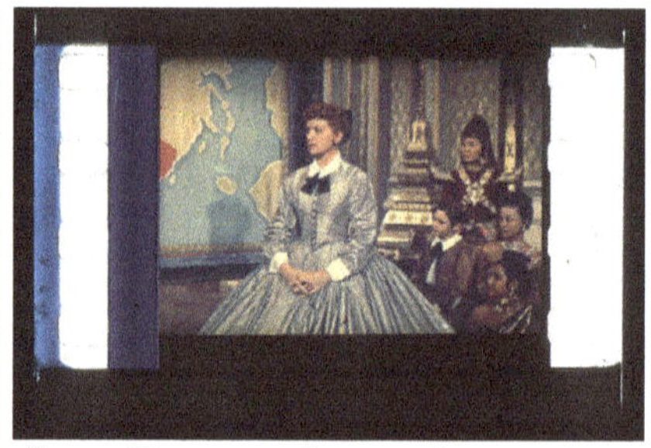

Above: Un-squeezed pan and scan print from 'The King and I'.

Centre: A comparison between a typical Technicolor release print (top)and a lower-contrast desaturated dye-transfer print for TV. Bottom frame is from 'Thief of Bagdad'

Left: Black and White copy of a Technicolor print on panchromatic stock for showing on TV before the arrival of colour.

To cut costs, Technicolor films were often only printed in black and white, either from the original green negative, or a new negative from the master positive. The green element was chosen as it was the sharpest and had the most important visual information. An alternative to a 'green print' was one made via a combined (picture and track) dupe negative made on panchromatic stock from a colour release print. The quality was considered sufficient for the small screen and had the advantage of a more accurate representation of the original colour tones. Many of these black and white copies had any reference to Technicolor removed from the film's titles, either by cutting the credits, or blotting it out with a black patch.

Colour TV

After a slow start in 1954, colour TV in America eventually caught on in the 1960s with the need for many more colour prints, with the numbers increasing as colour TV spread worldwide. Technicolor could make new dye-transfer prints, provided a batch of no less than 25 was ordered to justify the making of new matrices. Usually, like other laboratories, the triple negatives were combined onto colour duplicating stock for printing on colour print film. Post 3-strip Technicolor films, shot on colour negative, were printed like any other Eastman Color production.

TV prints of later CinemaScope and other anamorphic films were also available as un-squeezed full-frame versions, with the image re-framed using an optical pan and scan printer. Any movement, or a cut to a new position across the wider picture, took place during the closed shutter period. Early rudimentary setups only had a limited choice of positions and pan speeds. Sometimes the first frame or two at the start of a scene was blurred, when the printer was unable to jump between extreme positions before the shutter opened. Titles were either left squeezed up, or shown letterbox, sometimes with a nice patterned boarder inserted at the top and bottom. Black bars on TV screens were frowned on in those days. Not satisfied with many of these conversion prints, many broadcasters later preferred to use original anamorphic copies, which were un-squeezed and scanned electronically on the telecine machine.

Archivists have to work with what they are given Un-squeezed TV prints, both full-frame and masked, were available in both 35mm and l6mm and also proved useful to non-theatrical film libraries for loan to users without an anamorphic lens. At first sight, a converted print would be of little interest to an archivist for preservation. However, it may be the only record of the original version of the film. Today, a revival in the cinema, and on DVD or video, is often in the form of a special edition or directors cut, and includes extra footage to encourage us to see it again or buy a new copy. In the past, when only re-issued in theatres, the reverse took place. Features were often cut to become part of a double-bill, or long epics shortened to fit in an extra performance. As an example, for many years, before its restoration for a widescreen release on video, the longest available version of *Cleopatra* (1963) was the TV pan and scan print.

Actual 35mm prints are now rarely sent to broadcasters, the films now being distributed on digital tape. 'Scope films are still available as full-frame pan and scan versions, but more often with an anamorphic image allowing a choice of final screen shape using a format converter.

Colour Reversal Intermediate - The restorer's film stock from hell

In 1967, Technicolor was one of the first laboratories to trial a new duplicating stock from Kodak. Known as Colour Reversal Intermediate (CRI), it allowed a duplicate negative to be made in a single step, without the extra generation loss of having to go through an interpositive. If properly handled, CRI could produce excellent results, with a quality closely matching the original. It was designed to be optically printed and to incorporate all the opticals and grading changes for one-light high speed release printing.

It won an Academy technical award and many production companies were so impressed, they took the opportunity to clear the vault shelves of all their old Technicolor nitrate negatives. These were combined onto CRI, after which many were destroyed, although fortunately for some, not before also being used to produce new safety master positive separations. Even then, the more responsible couldn't bring themselves to destroy the original negatives of their most important features, which were either kept, or donated to museums, or national and university archives, with the UCLA in America giving sanctuary to many. CRI was to have a life of ten years, in more ways than one. It was withdrawn in 1979, after an improved colour intermediate film was introduced which could be used to make either interpositives or internegatives in the traditional two step method. The loss of CRI was not mourned by most laboratories, as it required to be optically printed to maintain the same emulsion position as the original negative, and separate processing machines with more complex reversal processing. It was not unknown for CRIs to be produced on a contact printer, the original negative printed through its base.

The present day recommended printing routes for making copies of earlier Technicolor 3-strip films vary according to the availability of the surviving printing elements and the number and use of the prints required. When reprinted commercially, previously made single-strip colour interpositives or internegatives are usually available for most 3-strip films, a restoration using separations is only required if these are now considered to be unsatisfactory.

Going back to the original nitrate 3-strip camera negatives or the protection master positives is not always possible, as they have either been lost due to self-destruction or with human help. The useful life of those which have survived so far may well be longer than previously thought. The latest research, including accelerated incubation tests, has shown that in some circumstances properly stored nitrate based films can have a predicted life of up to 400 years, compared to only 40 for some less fortunate acetate safety films.

Here in Britain, the responsibility of keeping the original nitrate material in the face of the strict fire and safety regulations has led many libraries and film companies to hand it over to the National Film and Television Archive. Large quantities of original Technicolor negatives and prints, together with other early colour processes, are now at the Archive's nitrate vaults at Gaydon in Warwickshire and can be recovered if needed for restoration projects.

Too good to use?

Archives and specialist laboratories may only wish to make a few of the highest possible quality prints for preservation and perhaps for a few restricted showings and digital mastering. If the original set of Technicolor camera negatives is still available and in good enough condition to be run through a printer a number of times, they can be re-combined through tri-colour RGB filtering directly onto colour print film. Like all printing from separations, this is a slow, skilled and costly operation. This is particularly so, if only one or two prints are needed, with any scene-to-scene variations in the density and colour balance compensated for without too many trial answer prints. If also available, the positive protection masters offer a more secure join-free source for making a new colour negative, which if necessary can then be used to make a greater number of prints for wider access. The National Film Archive has used this procedure on large numbers of Technicolor 3-strip films, choosing to use camera colour negative stocks, which match the contrast levels of Technicolor protection master positives better than colour intermediate films.

If only the master positives survive, then these can also

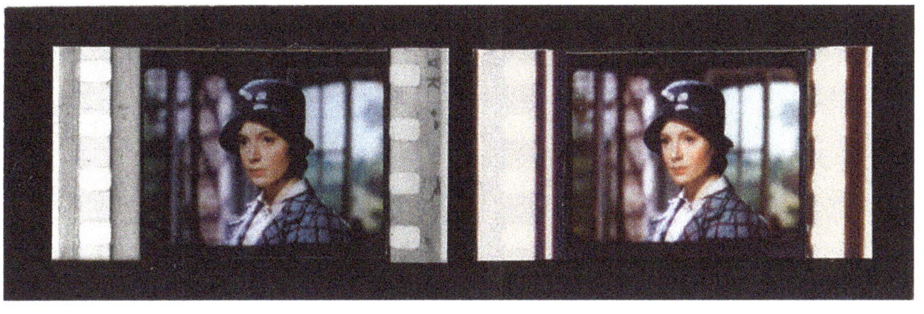

Comparison showing original Technicolor dye-transfer print (left) and a close match on colour print stock (right).

be used to produce safety separation negatives which, like the originals, can be printed directly onto colour print stock. These direct prints are generally superior to those made via a colour negative, having a sharper and more brilliant image, with greater colour separation and saturation. However, all this extra skilled work may make the prints too valuable to risk damage by being loaned out to theatres for repeated showings. Whichever way the original nitrate material is used, it is always recommended that, if not done previously, new safety versions are made first. Sometimes this is delayed until an acceptable print has been produced, to enable all the light changes to be incorporated.

One of the added complications when printing from Technicolor separation camera negatives is that they are not equally sharp and don't have the same emulsion position. The sharpest is the visually important green record which was directly behind the lens and had the normal emulsion position. The other blue and red negatives were exposed via the beam-splitter's reflected image as a bi-pack running together through a second gate with their emulsions in contact. The front blue record was exposed through its base so also ended up with the correct emulsion position. The odd one out, with the reversed emulsion position, was the rear red negative which faced the reflected image. If using a step contact printer, the red negative has to be printed through its base, compromising the overall definition. In practice, the red negative was always the least sharp anyway, having been exposed through both the base and emulsion of the front blue film. Optical printing may be preferred, which can be re-focused for the red record, and becomes the only option if control of the registration is also needed.

Keeping it all in register

Essential when making or printing from separations, is to maintain perfect registration, to within 1/2000th of an inch, to avoid the risk of colour fringes. Whether produced in a camera or an optical or contact intermittent printer, the film movement includes register pins which engage a pair of perforations, one on either side of the gate, as the image is exposed. One of the pins, known as the pilot or big pin, is a close fit and to ensure the best registration, needs to engage the same perforation during subsequent runs through the printer to maintain the same image position relative to the perforations.

Care is needed, as the various colour processes used different perforations for registration. Earlier colour systems, which made their release prints directly from separations, like Cinecolor or Technicolor, used print stock with Bell & Howell 'negative' type perforations (flat at the top and bottom with curved ends) to give the best registration. With the change to safety based film in 1950, Cinecolor continued to use B&H perforations, but Technicolor changed over to the normal and more robust print 'KS' (Kodak Standard) rectangular sprocket holes.

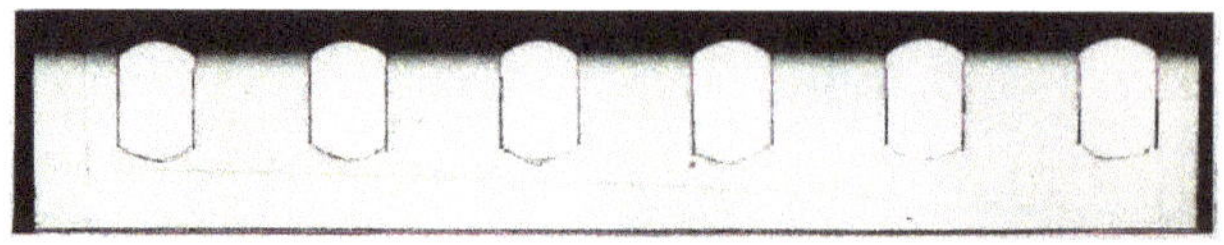

Technicolor prints with Bell and Howell (negative) type perforations (flat top and bottom with rounded ends) are on a nitrate base and can only be shown with the appropriate strict fire precautions.

This is a useful feature, when identifying earlier nitrate Technicolor dye-transfer prints, which can no longer be shown to the public unless in a theatre, like the NFT, which is licensed and equipped to meet the strict fire regulations.

For modern prints made directly from separations, colour print stock can still be ordered with negative-type B&H perforations and can be used as an option for the best registration. It is most commonly used today to ensure a steady picture when the prints are run on studio special process front or back projection projectors, which employ a camera-type claw plus register pins film movement, rather than the intermittent sprocket found in normal cinema projectors.

Difficulty in registering the images during printing, particularly from older nitrate sets of separations, was usually put down to differential shrinkage. This was often exacerbated by being left wound at different tensions, most noticeable at the centre of the rolls near the bobbin. They should also have been stored with the same in or out emulsion position, and all either head or end out.

Beautiful Technicolor 3-strip camera ..but not without sin

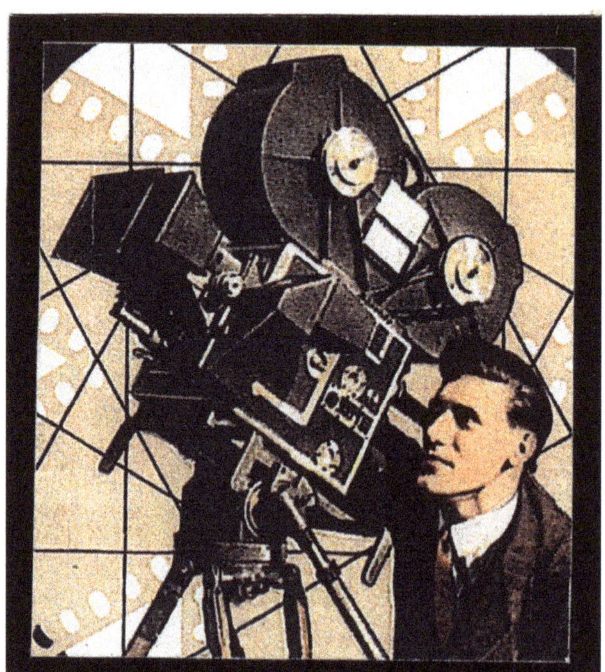

Technicolor 3-strip negatives are sometimes discovered to be out of register. This too can be blamed on shrinkage, but did not explain why, on some occasions, only individual scenes within the roll were at fault. It is now known that their renowned 3-strip camera, a beautiful example of camera engineering, was still capable of actually photographing 'out of register' images. This was usually due to slight mis-alignment of the beam-splitting prism after its removal and replacement in order to clear the occasional, but inevitable, film break or camera jam. This resulted in mis-registration between the green negative in one gate and the blue and red in the other. At the time, the customer was never aware of any problems, as all Technicolor's optical printers had micrometer adjustment to restore the correct registration when making the matrices. The original fault subsequently came to light when Technicolor films were re-printed by other laboratories using a step contact printer. Again, a switch to optical printing is the only way to solve the problem. An example was MGM's Metrocolor laboratories, who routinely re-printed their Technicolor 3-strip films onto Eastman Color print film, together with those from other studios. Whenever possible they used the camera negative as the original source. To this end, they set up a triple-head optical printer with its 'exclusive' Metro-Movement to allow the images to be re-aligned by eye if found to be out of register due to shrinkage or camera problems. Later, liquid gate printing was added to reduce the appearance of base scratches and blemishes.

'Gone With The Wind' back again, and again...

All this proved its worth when, in 1967, MGM decided to re-issue its often reprinted money-maker *Gone With The Wind*. This time, the well run camera negatives were to be used to make Metrocolor (Eastman Color) prints, including the notorious 70mm vertically panned and scanned wide screen version. The titles were also redesigned to fit wider screens. The release prints looked nothing like those made previously by Technicolor in dye-transfer. They were claimed to have richer and brighter colours than the more muted tones of the first copies made in 1939. After the nitrate camera negatives had been used to make the colour inter-positive, new protection master-positive separations and duplicate negatives were produced on safety film. The originals were then retired and donated to the International Museum of Photography at George Eastman House in Rochester, New York.

When Ted Turner bought MGM in 1986, principally to acquire its film library, *Gone With The Wind*, one of the 'jewels in the crown', was among the first films to be re-printed. This time the original opening title sweeping across the screen was to be restored and the colour graded to match as near as possible an original dye-transfer print, using a release print from 1954 as a guide. It was planned to use MGM's 1966 duplicate separations, but the results didn't come up to expectations. Fortunately, the original fifty year old nitrate camera negatives were still found to be in satisfactory condition and were temporarily donated back so that a complete new set of preservation and printing elements could be produced, more suited to the latest types of improved colour duplicating and print stocks. For its most recent theatrical release, *Gone With The Wind* was printed again using Technicolor's original dye-transfer process during its trial re-introduction at the end of the 1990s. Other classics, including *The Wizard of Oz* and *Giant* were also printed this way, before the dye-transfer method was suspended in 2002. Unfortunately, *Gone With The Wind*, like other modern prints of older 1.37:1 academy format films, was printed with a reduced sized image to prevent the loss of picture information when cropped for widescreen projection. Despite this, these new prints will no doubt become sought after collectors items, like other surviving dye-transfer prints from the past.

The look of love ... of Technicolor

The 'original' Technicolor still has its admirers, with many special events and film festivals being organized, showing only dye-transfer prints to enthusiasts reliving the glorious days of Technicolor. Its look, particularly during the 3-strip era, was a combination of the production's colour design, which was more or less influenced by Technicolor's own colour consultants, and the characteristics of the dye-transfer process itself. These gradually changed over the years as improvements were

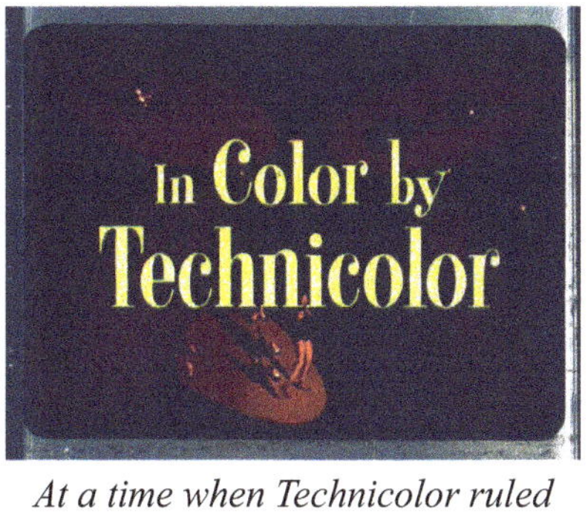

At a time when Technicolor ruled the world of colour in the cinema, audiences were left in no doubt about who to thank for being able to see their favourite stars in colour

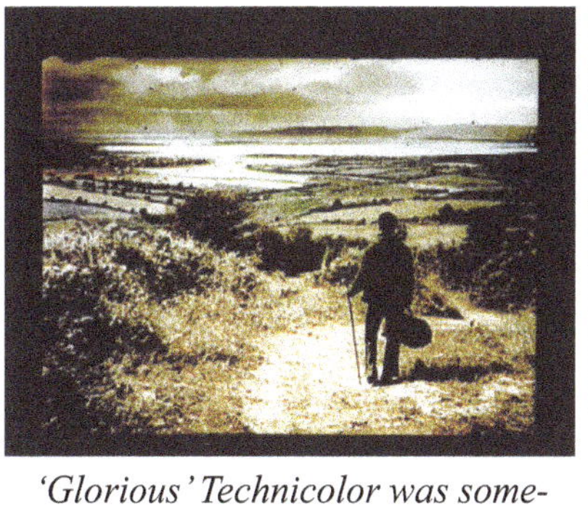

'Glorious' Technicolor was sometimes toned down for particular films like 'Moby Dick' (1956)

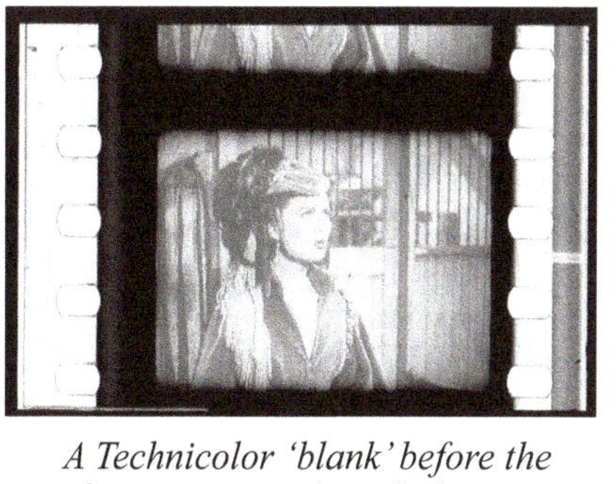

A Technicolor 'blank' before the dyes were transferred, showing its silver sound track, 'Academy' frame and faint key image, which was phased out during the 1940s

made. For example, better dyes allowed the additional black and white key image to be phased out during the 1940s. This happened at a time when producers, particularly in Hollywood, wanted as much colour for their bucks as possible. This, together with the resulting brighter and more transparent colours, led to the process gaining its 'glorious' reputation and the name Technicolor being used to describe anything which was brightly coloured.

Some users did prefer to find ways to keep the overly vivid hues under control, such as the more subtle 'British Technicolor' which was much admired. Technicolor initially objected to the use of diffusing and coloured filters when shooting John Huston's *Moulin Rouge*, but later helped him give *Moby Dick* the look of an old coloured etching by superimposing a black and white image, similar to the earlier silver 'key', to subdue the colour. Chances to see the changing look of the actual process, are the re-issues of Technicolor classics from the 1930s and early 1940s, which required new prints. These include, *The Adventures of Robin Hood*, *The Wizard of Oz* and *Gone With The Wind*, together with British successes like *The Four Feathers* and *The Thief of Bagdad*, which were also re-printed more then once in dye-transfer, up to the 1960s.

The best possible copies

Unless specifically requested, Technicolor did not attempt to keep the precise look of the earlier prints, but made the best possible copies incorporating all the subsequent improvements. The later prints often show 'fresher' brighter colours, than the more muted warmer amber tones of the original copies with their extra black and white silver component. The mechanical transfer of the dyes was always an art as much as a science, with the results monitored by experienced eyes. The colour balance did vary a little from print to print. Almost all the copies leaving the laboratory would be considered perfect, with the very best shown in the West-End and other first-run theatres, together with those to be kept as studio prints and library copies.

At the end of the print run, the remaining slightly 'off-target' reels were not wasted, but sorted to assemble complete copies with the same off-balance colour shift. These were then banished to local cinemas 'up north', where audiences were presumably less critical! Unfortunately, a few of these 'north of Watford' Technicolor prints have since found their way into archives and are not the best examples of a particular film. If possible, a number of different copies should be viewed when assessing the colour as a guide for a modern re-print. Even then, the customer paying for the prints may prefer their film to look like a modern one. It may be possible to produce two versions, with one having a colour balance and image contrast that is a closer match to an existing contemporary print. This can be used for preservation and special showings to appreciative audiences. Among

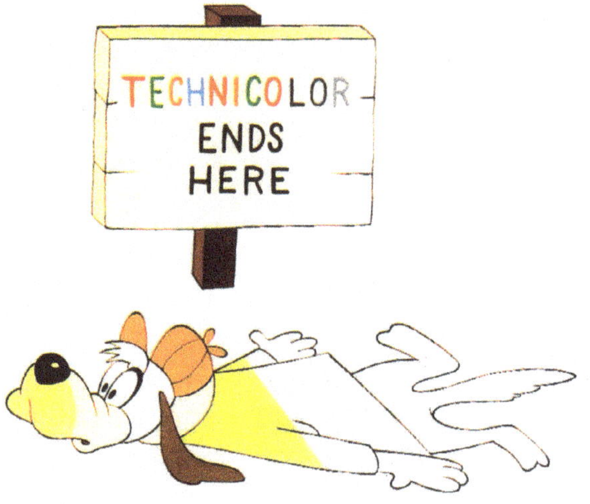

From 'Lucky Ducky' (1948) . Fortunately, Technicolor's dye-transfer process didn't actually end until 30 years later, in 1978

the printing and processing modifications now available are the various bleach bypass techniques, which could be tried to simulate the black and white silver key image.

Even the later dye-transfer prints made from colour negatives are greatly valued for their permanence and unique image quality, which is still difficult to replicate. Like some other recent cinema revivals, *The Railway Children* boasted the use of 'sparkling new prints' superior to those originally shown back in 1970. Many who can still remember the glowing colours of the first dye-transfer prints may disagree. Dye-transfer printing operated at Technicolor for 50 years. At their best, the prints had saturated yet transparent colours, plus a wide dynamic range with clear highlights and deep blacks, although these could become too 'solid' with crushed and missing shadow detail. The optical printing of the matrices increased the apparent grain, and the resolution, particularly during the 3-strip camera era, was poor, but the compensating vivid colours and high contrast made the prints look sharper when projected on the modest sized screens used in cinemas during the 1930s and 1940s.

Technical developments

At first, Technicolor prints couldn't match the resolution of its new rival, Eastman Color. An urgent development programme to reduce the spreading of the dyes during transfer and new improved matrix and blank stocks dramatically increased the definition and allowed the process to join the cinema's bigger and wider screen revolution at the beginning of the 1950s. The improvement was such that the prints could also show the benefit of reduction printing. Many of the prints reduced from larger-area VistaVision, Technirama, Todd-AO and the various other 65mm camera negative systems, were some of the finest ever produced. Dye-transfer release prints continued to be available for another 25 years, successfully competing with Eastman Color and other colour print films, only being abandoned on economic grounds during a period of shorter print-runs in the mid-1970s. From then on, Technicolor made all their prints on colour print film, and was no longer a specific process.

Technicolor and the video image

When colour television arrived, filmed colour TV series and feature films provided ready-made programme material, with the quality of the received picture often better than those produced by early colour TV cameras. Unfortunately, this was not always the case for Technicolor films. Their more vivid colours and higher contrast made them less suitable, with some European broadcasters rejecting them altogether, as being below broadcast quality (a term not commonly used today). This was particularly so in Germany, where they said that the prints did not meet the European Broadcasting Union's guidelines for telecine use, and wanted lower-contrast copies on print film. Stock manufacturers added low-contrast colour positive print films to their ranges as an option for TV prints. However, when dye-transfer was still a current process the prints were sometimes the only ones readily available for transmission. When used, the vibrant colours of a Technicolor print were often reduced to a pale, blue-biased image, by telecine operators who were slaves to producing the 'correct' waveforms on their oscilloscopes regardless of the poorer colour image appearing on the monitor. In their defence, they could be forgiven, as they were unlikely to have been given the opportunity to see the same print projected optically on a screen for comparison. Also, the operator who assessed the necessary colour corrections during a rehearsal was not on duty for the film's actual transmission and able to refine the colour balance and saturation decisions. The results could vary with different showings, and when the 'live' transmissions, direct from film, gave way to video tape copies, it was hit or miss if the best possible colour was achieved during the transfer.

Enter the colourist

The performance of both man and machine has advanced over the years, with the science of colour grading now considered an 'art', with telecine operators turning into 'colourists'. If handled with care, dye-transfer prints can now produce excellent video images. It was a sad day when many beautiful dye-transfer prints had to be replaced with new copies on colour print film, after doing the rounds of TV companies and ending up with ever increasing numbers of cuts, lost frames, joins and peppered with obtrusive visual cue marks to give warning of upcoming commercial breaks.
Although a film may be credited as being in Eastman Color, or another of the trade names given to it, such as Warnercolor or Color by DeLuxe, a dye-transfer version may also exist. Many of the US studios, who printed their domestic copies on Eastman Color, contracted Technicolor in London or Rome to make the foreign release in dye-transfer, without a change of credit. Once their value was appreciated, many of these prints have been rounded up and returned to the company vaults. If available in good condition, a dye-transfer print would have retained its original colour and may produce a better video master, at less cost, than a new print from a possibly faded original negative or colour intermediate.

A double life on16mm film

Along with surviving amateur footage on smaller gauges, almost all cinema colour features, cartoons and shorts were also made available on 16mm film, used at the time for Television and for hire by non-theatrical film libraries. Interesting sponsored shorts could also be loaned, often free, from groups like The Post office, British Transport Films, oil companies, and other organisations with their own film units.

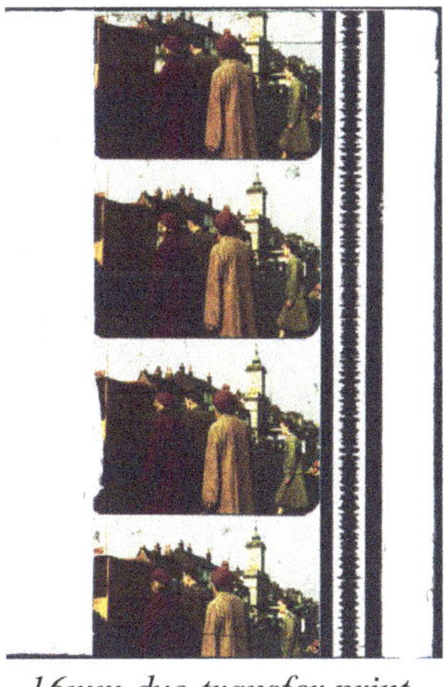

16mm dye-transfer print

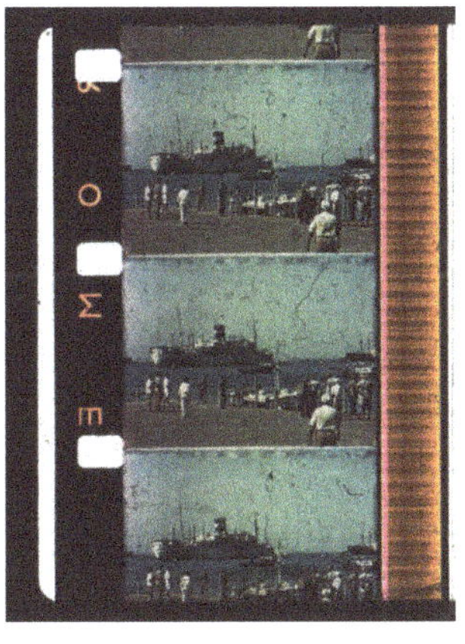

16mm
Kodachrome print with optical sound track

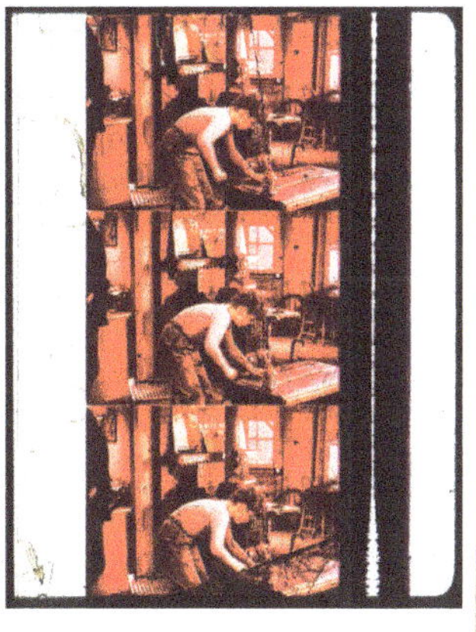

16mm
Colour print film showing signs of fading

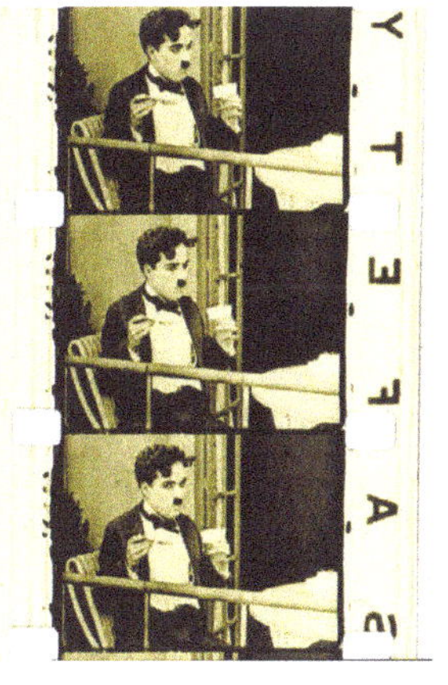

16mm early 'amber' or 'sunshine' tinted print from Kodak's Kodascope library (1925). Excellent quality was achieved by direct reduction from a 35mm negative. (Chaplin's 'The Adventurer').

Apart from the black and white TV versions, colour copies were made using various printing systems. Many thousands of 16mm dye-transfer prints came out of Technicolor's laboratories, starting during WWII to provide the forces with instructional and entertainment films. Cinecolor in the U.S. also made 16mm copies in their two-colour process, complete with the familiar bright blue track. Reversal Kodachrome prints were also common, this time identified by a yellow/amber coloured optical sound track and black sprocket hole area. From the end of the 1950s an increasing number of copies were being made on the far less stable Eastman Color print stock.

The most-prized 16mm colour prints today are those in Technicolor dye-transfer, with most of the contemporary prints on Eastman Color or other makes of colour print film likely to be found faded. Even if not faded, it is sometimes difficult to find prints in good condition. Library prints had a hard life in the hands of inexperienced projectionists at home, or in schools and village halls.

Like 35mm, the most vulnerable part of the film was at the beginning of the reels, due to poor handling and mishaps during threading and starting the projector. To help extend the life of frequently borrowed prints, including those in Technicolor, an Eastman Color reprint of just the start of the reel was replaced. As a result, the film may now begin with a disappointingly pink image, but after a couple of minutes burst into unfaded Technicolor.

The making of 16mm prints dramatically reduced after the coming of video cassettes, DVDs and video projectors. Many labs, like Technicolor in London, withdrew their 16mm services in the face of falling demand.

Curiously, one of the last customers was the British Prison Service. 16mm prints are still available from the British Film Institute for film groups whose members still prefer the experience of watching a 'real' film, without being sent to prison!

Super 16, the ultimate 16mm format?

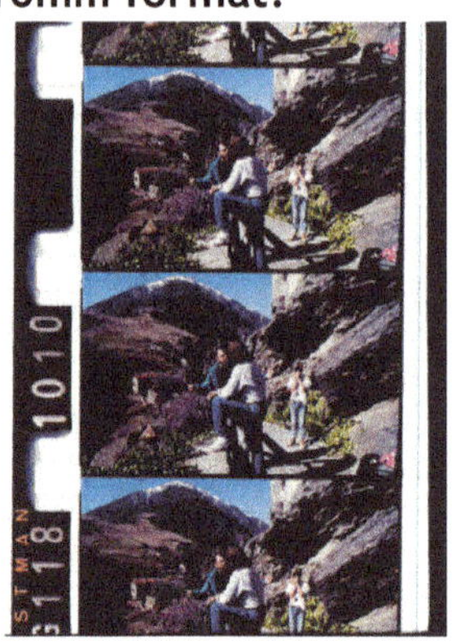

The Super-16 format uses 16mm single perforated negative with the image extended into the normal soundtrack area. Devised in 1970, it was originally intended to provide a wider picture more suitable for enlargement to 35mm and shown on cinema wide screens. The release prints from Super-16 negatives had a reduced height image with an aspect ratio of 1.66 to 1.

For TV use, the negative was usually scanned into and stays in the digital domain, so few positive film prints will find their way into archives. Before the general switch to all-digital production, many TV dramas and series were photographed on film with Suuper-16 cameras for the new 16x9 screens.

Other formats also provide a hidden archive

Although home movie makers have moved on to using camcorders or even mobile phones, there are still millions of feet of historically interesting 16mm, 9.5mm, 8mm and Super-8 amateur colour films waiting to be liberated from cupboards and lofts around the world. For these narrow gauges, digital preservation may be more convenient than copying onto film, particularly in the same format.

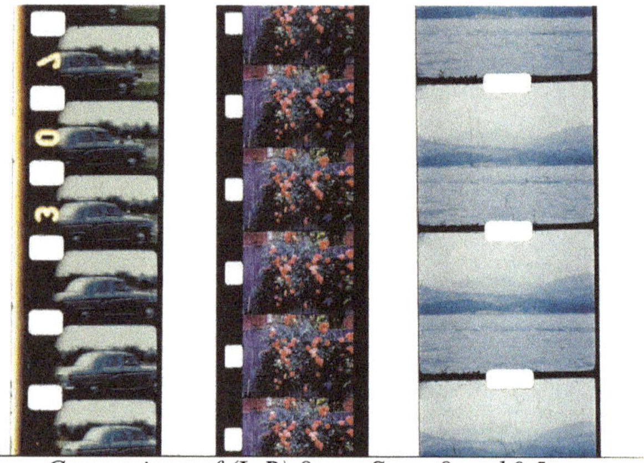

Comparison of (L-R) 8mm, Super8 and 9.5mm (not actual size)

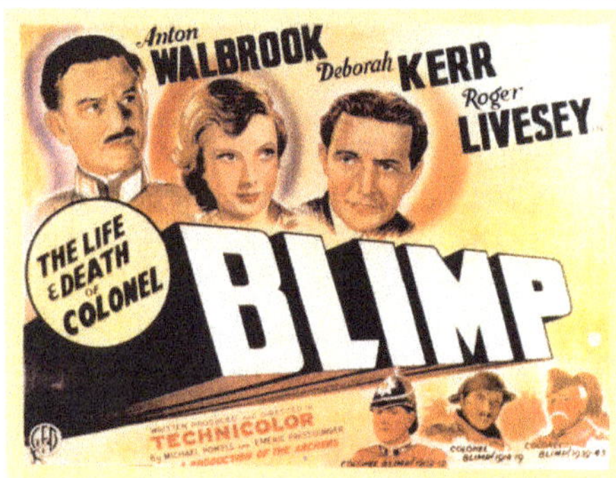

The National Film and Television Archive's restoration of *The Life and Death of Colonel Blimp* (1943) in the 1980s helped to spark renewed interest and appreciation of the work of Powell and Pressburger. This led to other reprints of their Technicolor films. Among them were *The Red Shoes* (1948) and *The Tales of Hoffmann* (1951) - below.

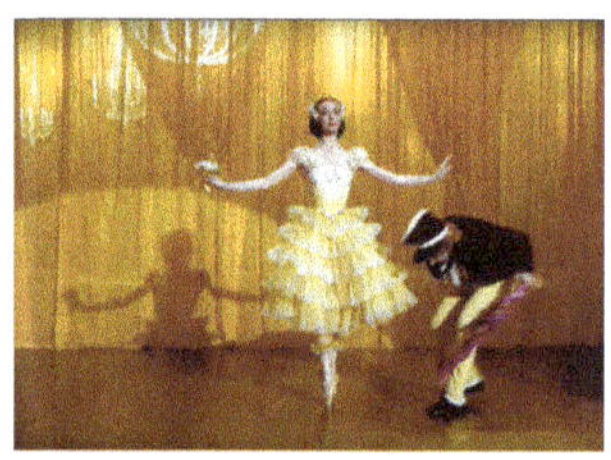

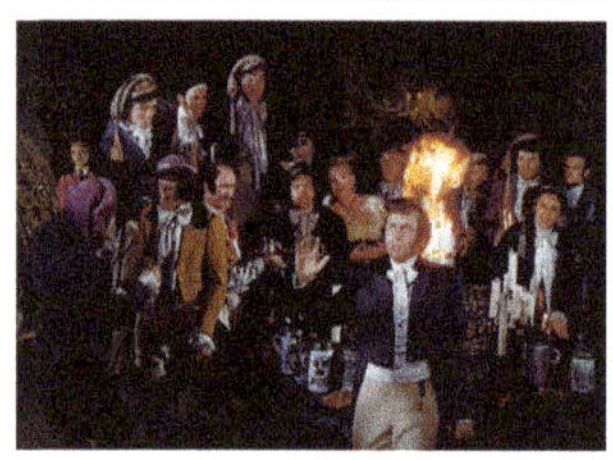

These films, with their vibrant, sometimes garish colour were among the few exceptions to the generally more restrained and often admired examples of 'British Technicolor'.

The original colour design and 'look' of a film may be altered to some extent by the balance chosen for the new copy, and tastes may change.

For a new print of *Gone to Earth* (1950) Michael Powell actually preferred the modern copy with its brighter colours than the original dye-transfer prints, which were given a more muted 'period' look.

Old pix don't die, they fade away...

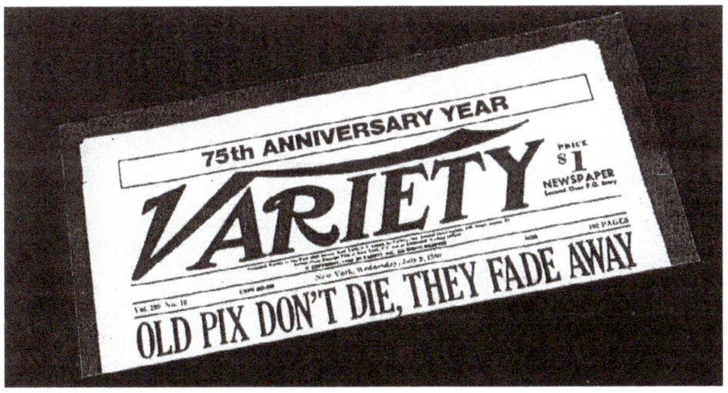

This 'Variety' headline appeared in 1980, as a result of a campaign, initiated by director Martin Scorsese, drawing attention to the danger of losing colour films due to fading. He wrote to over two-hundred stars, directors and other luminaries of the industry, warning them that, 'All our agonizing labor and creative effort is for nothing because our films are vanishing'. Many went on to add their names to a petition presented to Kodak and the other stock manufacturers demanding that they not only produce more permanent stocks, but also be more open about the dye stability of both their current and past colour negative and print stocks, in order to help work out strategies to preserve the films made using them. Up to this time, Kodak considered this information to be too commercially sensitive to be published and that it might have led to a fading war breaking out between manufacturers.

All dyes will eventually fade, but not all are in equal danger. The rate of fading depends on the way they were originally produced and subsequent storage conditions. Dyes will start to fade when exposed to light, but in case of those used in colour films, even the intense light of the projector has little effect, as each frame is only subjected to it for a fraction of a second. The most serious type of fading threatening colour films is 'dark-fading' which occurs over time due to the chemical breakdown of the dyes, even when kept out of the light in a container.

Some films start out with healthier colours

Not all colour films will suffer this fate. Those using externally manufactured dyes, including the early black and white films which were tinted or toned, or had their colour added by hand or through stencils, appear to have retained their original colours, and have a life as long as the nitrate print itself, which is more likely to be lost due to physical decay. Colours formed by chemical and metallic toning have also proved to be relatively stable, including those used on some of the later two-colour processes.

Along with the renewed interest in reviving the original methods of tinting and toning, the analysis of the dyes has shown that, in fact, some examples have lost much of their original brilliance, or changed colour over time. As an example, some forms of red toning have turned brown, now looking more like sepia. When preparing to produce a new colour print from a Pathecolor stencilled original, Soho Images in London noticed that some uncoloured areas showed traces of a dye, which had either faded or been lost from the print in some other way. The budget didn't allow for any attempt to replace the missing colour. One way this could have been done, was to produce a hand drawn matte, the equivalent of the original stencil, and flash the appropriate coloured light through it during an additional run through the printer.

The Technicolor dye-transfer process employed modified textile dyes, which were virtually fade-free, and surviving prints have colour images which have remained the same since first transferred. Even pre-1950 nitrate based prints seem to have better overall keeping qualities than contemporary black and white films, possibly due to the less destructive chemicals remaining in the print after dye-transfer. The types of dyes most likely to fade are those generated in the emulsion layers during chromogenic (dye-coupling) colour processing.

Back in the 1920s, this process was proposed as an alternative means for toning black and white prints, but was not widely adopted, due to its lack of permanence. However, the principle of dye-coupling went on to become the basis of modern colour film. For some earlier multi-layer films of this type, dating from their general introduction, at the beginning of the 1950s, through to the start of the 1980s, the rate of fading has been rapid if not kept in cool and dry conditions. Although a temperature of 21degrees C and up to 40% relative humidity is considered acceptable for black and white films, a much lower 2 degrees C and 15% RH has been recommended for colour. **An increase of 5 degrees C can halve the useful life of the colour image**.

In practice, the rate of deterioration is unpredictable, with films processed at around the same time and stored in similar conditions having faded at different rates. Suggestions as to why this should happen include the different tightness of the film wind and the type of

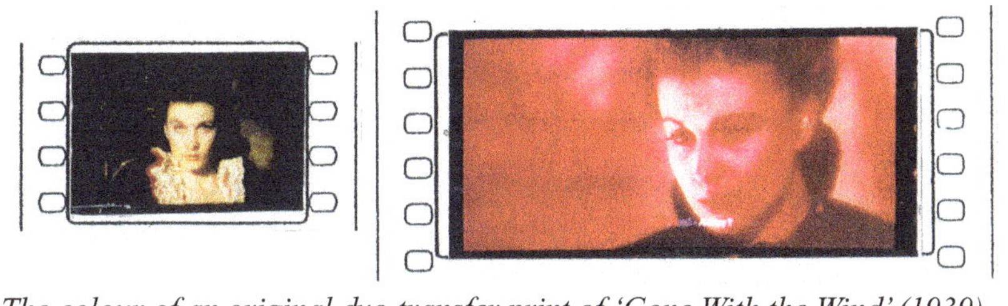

The colour of an original dye-transfer print of 'Gone With the Wind' (1939) (left) has outlived a 70mm print made during the 1960s on Eastman Colour, which has self-destructed to pink

wrapping and/or container used. Experience has shown that fading is greater if kept in a sealed can, compared to a ventilated cardboard box. More likely was the effect of the care taken during the original processing, particularly the final stabilizing bath, which was designed to leave traces of formalin in the emulsion layers after processing, to help preserve the dyes. In some early processing machines this bath was non-circulating and, as it had no visual effect on the image, it was sometimes used to the point of exhaustion before being replenished. This was most likely to happen when processing colour release prints, which were only considered to have a limited life anyway.

Colour negatives, with their more critical and closely monitored processing, are less likely to have suffered from this problem. Some laboratories routinely re-wash and clean the negatives before making mew prints. This can reduce the effect of the stabilizer step and it has been recommended that the negative be re-treated before being put back into the vault.

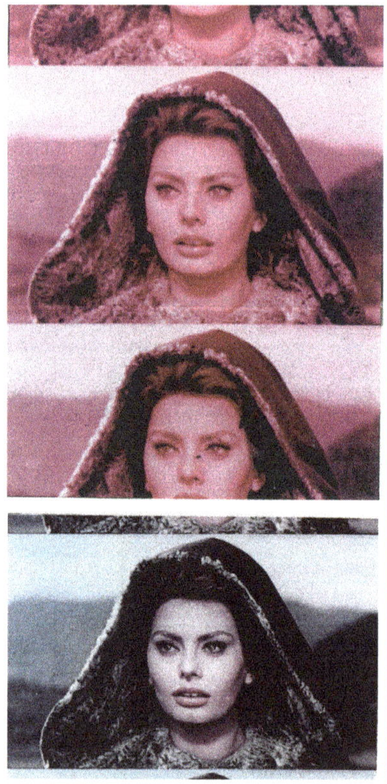

Typical look of a badly faded print. If this is all that is available to make a new copy, a re-graded (timed) 'dupe' may still be far from perfect, but its colour could be acceptable to the average viewer.

A better result may be possible by combining the faded original with a separately printed compensating colour masking film, or digital processing.

Some colour negatives have a better chance of remaining printable than others. During the 1950s and 1960s, most negatives were fully exposed and developed, giving them a reserve of density to help cope with possible future fading. The fashion in the 1970s for the 'available light' style of photography left much thinner camera negatives which soon show the effect of even light fading. An added problem is that the amount of fading differs in each layer, resulting in a shift of the colour balance. The effect is most often seen in colour prints, with the least stable cyan layer fading the most, leaving the familiar pale pink image.

First Aid during projection

It is not unknown for projectionists to take matters into their own hands and show severely faded prints through a green filter in the hope of giving the audience a better picture. Of course, a faded print is no indication of the condition of the negative, which may well be able to produce perfect new prints. However, if this too has faded, the problem is more serious. In the case of negatives, it is usually the yellow layer which is most likely to fade and lose contrast. The orange colour mask makes this less noticeable to the naked eye, and only becomes apparent when making new prints. A relative loss of about ten per cent can be corrected during printing, with any defects only being noticeable to a trained eye. It is this degree of loss which is considered the limit when assessing the predicted life of the various film stocks. Further loss of density of up to 50% is still within the printer's range, but the associated loss of contrast in the different layers results in the crossed contrast effect. If re-balanced (graded) to give neutral mid-tones, the highlights still have a yellow cast and the darker areas remain predominantly blue. Although time consuming, a skilled grader (colourist), familiar with printing from faded negatives, can produce results more pleasing to the average audience by balancing each scene individually, taking into account the colour of the subject. This usually means aiming for the best flesh tones and hoping that the colours in the rest of the picture appear acceptable.

In practice, most feature films shot on colour negative, and that have been re-printed at different times over the years, are likely to have an alternative source for making a new print. Apart from the camera negative, there is likely to be an additional colour inter-positive and a duplicate negative, and for major productions, a set of three black and white separations. Made from the original colour negative using red, green and blue filters, they are either known as protection master positives or YCMs, referring to the colour layers in the negative they represent. However well produced and printed, separations cannot normally produce a replacement colour negative to match the quality of the original. Prints from the new negative are usually a little less sharp, with

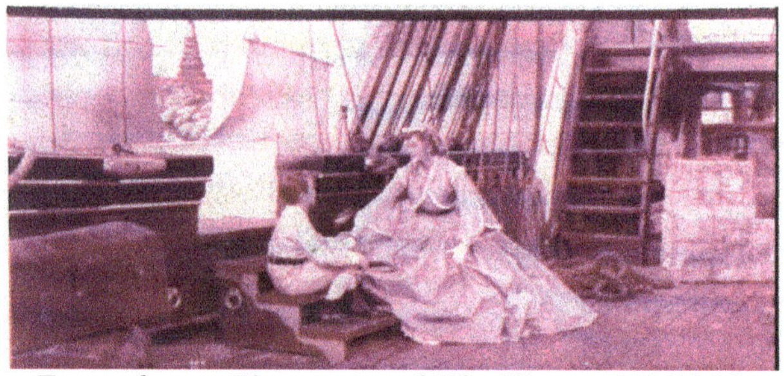

Frame from a 70mm print of 'The King and I' (1956) which, although in otherwise good condition, is now too faded to ever again show to the public. Like other faded 70mm or 35mm prints with magnetic tracks, it may still be of value as an extra source for the stereo sound if the master recording has been lost or deteriorated.

higher contrast and some loss of shadow detail. However, separations, on more stable black and white film, have always been recommended as protection against the risk of fading in the original negative.

When preparing the 1991 re-issue of Stanley Kubrick's *Spartacus* (1960), the original camera negative was discovered to have faded past the point of being able to produce satisfactory prints. Fortunately, Technicolor's separation B&W protection master positives were still available and were used to make a new duplicate colour negative. Both the new 35mm and 70mm prints were excellent, but in the case of the 70mm, didn't quite match those produced for its original release, which were all individually printed from the camera negative. Like most 70mm prints dating from the 1950s to the start of the 1980s, all of the existing copies of *Spartacus* had turned pink and could no longer be shown to a paying audience. Even with faded images, 35mm and 70mm magnetically striped prints may still be of great value as they may be the only source of the original stereo sound if the magnetic masters have been lost, or can no longer be replayed due to deterioration. However severely faded, some films are still worth seeing. During a Widescreen Weekend held at the Pictureville Cinema in Bradford, a surviving but 'monochrome' pink copy of the Cinemiracle production *Windjammer* was shown free of charge using the theatre's triple-panel Cinerama set-up to an appreciative audience of enthusiasts.

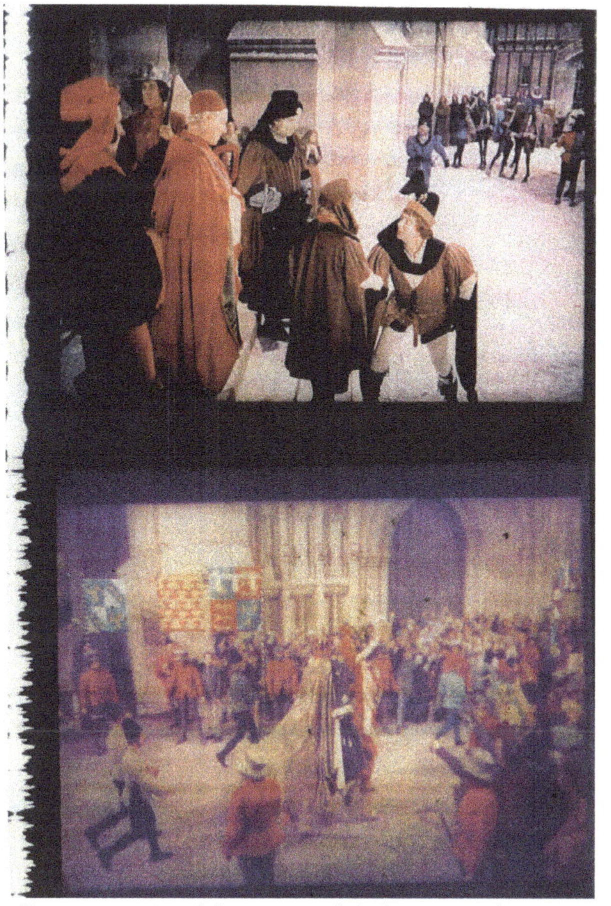

Top scene printed from an un-faded portion of a negative, with, below, another showing signs that it has faded (a blue cast in the shadow areas and yellow highlights). Sometimes this is a duplicated section of the negative containing an optical effect.

Different techniques

What can be done if a film only exists in the form of a faded negative or print? Apart from 'creative' grading, other purely photo-chemical methods have been tried. Perhaps the most 'scary' is to chemically reduce the density of the less faded layers to match that of the lowest and then make high contrast separations from the now balanced, but very pale and low contrast original.

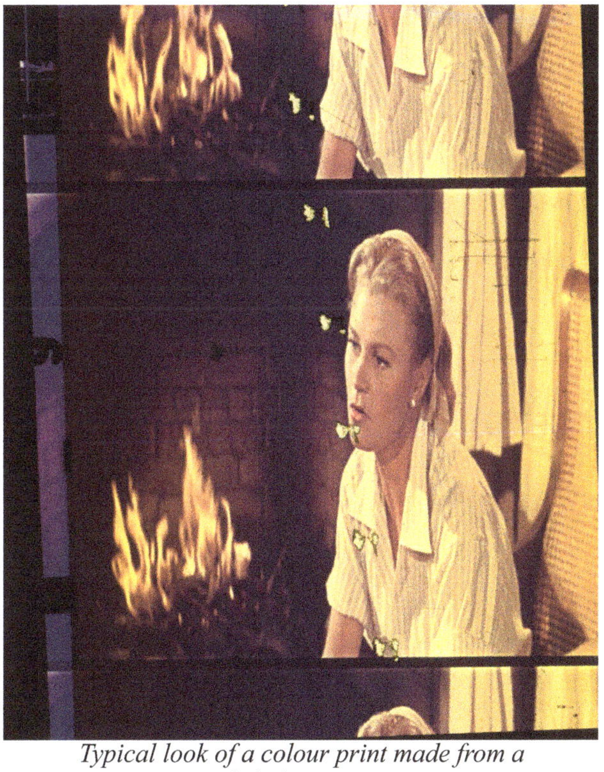

Typical look of a colour print made from a faded negative

A more practical and less risky solution was the flash-dupe mask method for restoring the lost colour from a faded print. A reversal copy is made with filtered light calculated to produce a colour-correcting positive masking image in a colour equal to that missing from the original. Both prints are then run together in register through a printer to produce a new colour negative. The need to make the masking film on colour reversal stock largely limited its use for restoring 16mm news film or documentaries shot on reversal camera film, or from faded prints without the original negatives available.

The use of a separate colour mask to replace the lost colour is also the principle behind the Academy Award winning Restored Colour Image Process (RCI) for saving the images on badly faded colour negatives. The technique is more complex. The faded negative is first used to produce a pair of intermediate elements, an uncorrected colour inter-positive and a faint reversal

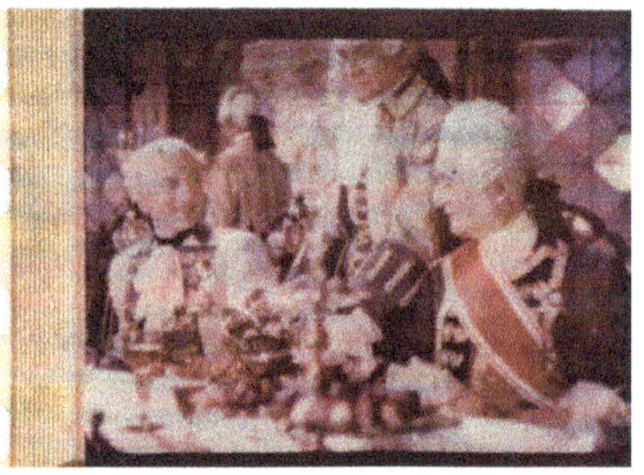

An over 70 year old Agfacolor print of 'Munchausen' (1943). Although now badly faded, the film's existing printing elements are still able to produce new satisfactory prints.

black and white negative mask. This is combined with the original negative to restore its contrast when it is used again to print a registered yellowish positive mask on colour print film with BH negative-type perforations. Finally, this colour mask, which represents the lost colour, is combined on a double-head optical printer with the inter-positive to produce a corrected duplicate colour negative.

The most common form of film based colour correction is to make black and white separations, increasing the relative density and contrast (gamma) to compensate for the loss of dye density in the faded negative. This is not always successful in the worst cases. Ideally, the three separations should be treated identically, with the only difference showing in the final images being the different colour records. If any one of the elements is 'forced' developed to the extent of producing a more grainy image, it can show up in the final print as a colour dependent grain structure. In the worst cases, certain highly saturated colours, like blue skies, have a 'boiling grain' effect.

'Flashed-dupe' masking method of restoring the lost colour from a reversal original or other faded print without a negative

Original 'pink' faded print

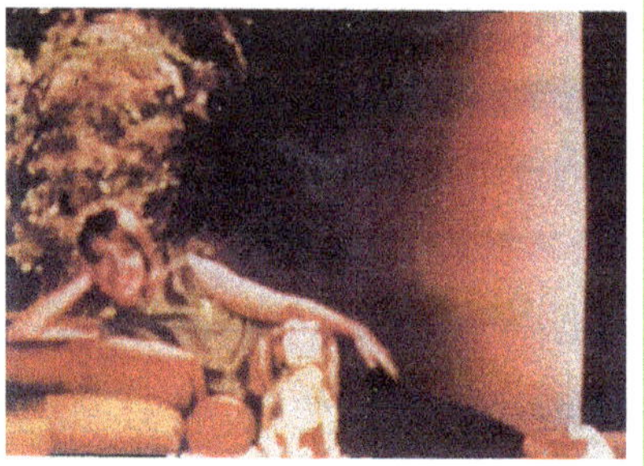

Flashed-dupe reversal positive mask representing the lost colour

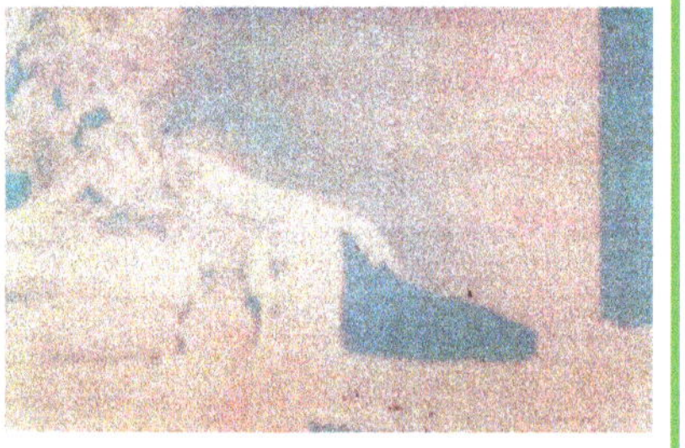

Combined with the original during printing to produce a new restored reversal print or duplicate negative.

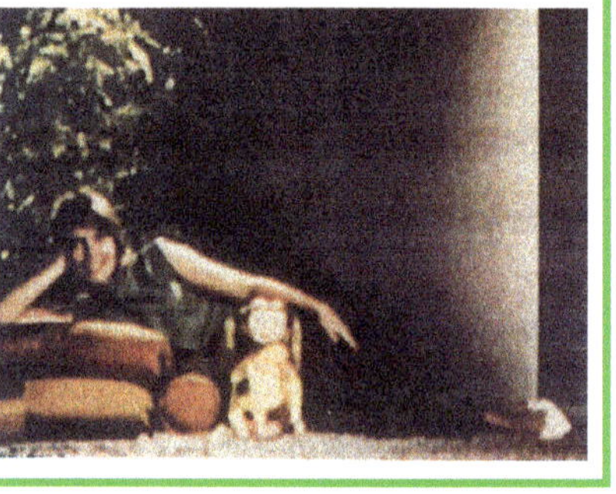

The Good news - Low-Fade stocks arrive

After the campaign against fading in the early 1980s, Kodak and the other manufacturers soon responded by introducing stocks with much greater dye stability. The new ranges of LF and LPP type films were now expected to have a useful life of over 100 years, even at room temperature. In fact, Kodak had already been offering an alternative low-fade print stock for some time previously. Being more expensive, it was generally used only for making special studio, library and archive copies. Using an analogy to book publishing, Kodak described the low fade copies as the more valued hardbacks and those on ordinary print film as disposable paperbacks. In the event, it was mostly supplied in the smaller gauges, such as for the making of the 16mm prints loaned by non-theatrical film libraries, which were expected to have a longer life of up to 10 years, compared to the 10 months of a typical cinema release print. The slower fading print stock was also chosen by some distributors of Super-8 movies sold to collectors, who would not appreciate their investment turning pink after only a few years on the shelf. By 1983, the improved dye stability qualities were incorporated into replacement print films for general use. In an American ad for Kodak's new low-fade print stock, they assured users that their prints would now enjoy longer runs and wider audiences, and decades from now, will still have the crisp, bright colours of its world premiere.

And now the Bad news

Along with the good news for the future, came the bad, with the final publication of the expected life of older colour stocks. The predicted rate of loss beyond the 'acceptable' 10% varied greatly between stocks, ranging from as little as 6 years to up to 50 at room temperature. Particularly disturbing was that, in many cases, the stability of a new stock was less than the one it replaced. The very first Eastman Color negative, introduced in 1950, had better keeping qualities than subsequent 'improved' versions, not being matched until 1968. Among the intermediate films listed, the greatest shock was the high rate of fading of the once universally praised CRI (Colour Reversal Intermediate), which was likely to have faded past the point of being difficult to print after only 7 years. Perhaps the most public consequence of this was the planned re-issue of the original *Star Wars* trilogy. All the special effects for the first film had been composited onto CRI and were found to be unprintable without digital help. To make the most of the situation, these were digitally corrected and up-dated to match current expectations. It is claimed, that this CRI near disaster was one of the reasons why all future *Star Wars* episodes were to be shot using digital cameras.

Storage temperatures

Also subsequently published were the results of tests made by Kodak to establish the effect on the fading when the film is stored at temperatures lower than the normal room or warehouse temperature of 75 degrees F (24 degrees C). The improvement was dramatic, with a drop to 55 degrees F (13 degrees C) slowing the rate of loss by a factor of 4 times, a drop to 35 degrees F (1.7 degrees C) by 20 times, and at Zero degrees F (-18 degrees C) the rate of loss was reduced by a factor of 400, which in practice meant that fading had effectively ceased. Unfortunately this research came too late for many older colour negatives and intermediate films which have already faded.

To play their part in helping to save these, Kodak can now provide a new improved polyester based black and white separation stock, with ultra fine grain and wider exposure latitude for manipulating the gamma to restore an even greater degree of fading. Adjusting the gamma was used for the revival of Alfred Hitchcock's *Vertigo* (1958). The well exposed camera negative, in the large-area VistaVision format, showed light to moderate fading which could successfully be corrected. Unfortunately, like many other films, the duplicate negative sections, including the opticals and special effects, were more severely faded and could not be fully corrected. However, the 1.5 million dollar all-film restoration was considered to be an 80% success, compared with the original Technicolor dye-transfer prints.

For most restoration projects, the first choice, as an original source, is whenever possible the camera negative, before turning to alternative intermediate pre-print material. For a cinema re-release of another Hitchcock VistaVision feature, *North by NorthWest*, the camera negative was discovered to be too faded to produce satisfactory prints. Corrective separations and gamma adjustment would have cost up to 300,000 Dollars. Although this was far less than the two million needed for a digital restoration at full film (VistaVision) resolution, the tight budget meant that only the existing protection separations could be used. In the event, test footage showed that a newly printed duplicate colour negative made from them was no better than one made 10 years earlier, which was used again to make the new prints. Although audiences could enjoy seeing the film again on the big screen, they could not experience the quality of the first Technicolor VistaVision reduction prints shown back in 1959.

Images frozen in time

With what we know today about storage conditions, it is interesting to speculate that the price of a large chest freezer, plus the cost of maintaining and running it for 30 years, would still only be a fraction of the money spent restoring films like *Spartacus* and *Vertigo*, which, if their negatives had been kept refrigerated, may not have been necessary. For today's movies it has been suggested that the more stable low fade stocks, together with cold storage, has made costly separations unnecessary, particularly for lower budget and independently produced films. Making and working from separations is a more difficult and skilled operation and can never quite match the potential quality of printing from the original negative, or intermediates derived from it. However, the additional security of separations is a small price to pay to protect a 150 Million dollar blockbuster, and for major studios wishing to safeguard their investment in past productions.

Film for archiving digital pictures

Even films shot with digital cameras can have their colour images protected on film, with three black and white separations exposed using a laser film recorder. For perfect registration these are now made on dimensionally stable polyester black and white stock, but an alternative arrangement is to record the RGB images in sequence along a single film, like an old cartoon negative. For negatives and positives on colour stock Kodak and others in the US have opened state-of-the-art preservation vaults which offer film-makers cost effective cold storage facilities. For the same price as protecting a film with separations, storage space can be rented for up to 200 years. Another advantage of cold storage is the reduced risk of the acetate base decomposing (the vinegar syndrome), the onset of which is also known to accelerate the rate of fading.

Although colour negatives and inter-positives have been chosen as the original source, most video transfers are still made from positive prints. Cold storage of a low-fade 'master' reference print will ensure it retains its original colour. Treated with care, it can be run on a telecine to produce a video master. It is also a record of the original grading decisions for future film prints.

Maintaining 'the look'

For colour design reasons, the image may not have been printed with a neutral colour balance, but shifted to give the film a certain 'look', which can change throughout the film. Audiences have learned to associate warmer 'nostalgia-vision' tones with period dramas and scenes set in the past, and a bluer balance with the cold light of the present day. Without an unfaded original colour print as a guide, new prints or video copies made in years to come, may look completely different from the picture seen on screens when the film was first released. As an example, for a couple of more recent westerns, the colours in the normally exposed negative have been reduced on the release prints to nearer the look of a sepia toned photograph from the old west. This decision by the production designers and directors may be overruled in the future, when tastes could change, and the negative be printed again in glowing 'full colour'.

Digits to the rescue

Providing the original will run through a scanner or telecine, almost all the problems encountered when restoring colour films can be dealt with digitally. Although the cost has fallen since 1993, when Disney spent seven million dollars using Kodak's newly introduced Cineon system to give *Snow White and the Seven Dwarfs* an electronic wash and brush up, it is still high enough to restrict its use to the more commercial digital restorations, which can recover the cost from a theatrical re-release and sales of videos and DVDs. Also for archival and preservation work, there is a reluctance to compromise on quality, with some archivists accepting nothing less than full film resolution 4K processing to maintain maximum transparency of the digital contribution.

At this level, particularly with uncompressed and component imaging, the original scanning, downloading and the final transfer back onto film can take literally days for a feature length film, even before adding any hands-on work by the digital restoration artist at their workstation. Most of the savings have come from the development of more sophisticated, faster, and largely automated programmes working at ever higher resolutions. All the proprietary digital intermediate systems have specific restoration software in their electronic tool-kits. These can remove or reduce the appearance of scratches, replace lost image information, including reconstructing missing frames, and stabilisation programmes to improve unsteadiness resulting from worn or damaged perforations. It is also possible to reduce, or even eliminate grain. This may be considered undesirable, as, apart from the build up of excessive grain due to over duplication, **the aim should always be to return the image, including the grain, to as near as possible to its original appearance** before suffering from years of wear and tear and natural decay. Some processing procedures, including temporarily reducing the file size and resolution to speed up the image manipulation, can result in the 'digital look', including the artificial and stationary grain effect, which can be very noticeable when working with older colour films with their inherently grainier images.

To bring the cost of digital help within reach, some restorers believe that 2K resolution is more than adequate, particularly for most early colour films. For example, Technicolor dye-transfer prints from the 1930s and 1940s have poor definition due to the dyes spreading during the transfer process. However, the image on the screen still looked good due to the compensating high contrast and colour saturation, a phenomenon exploited by today's digital cinema projectors. Even so, many commercial digital facilities remain beyond the budget for most of an archive's day-to-day restoration work, without funding help from outside sponsors. However, the computer programmes, which are constantly being developed and improved for the CGI special effects seen in today's blockbusters, may also prove useful for helping to save films from the past. The cutting edge 360 degree camera move around the partly computer generated Colosseum in Ridley Scott's *Gladiator*, involved many weeks of work hand-tracing electronic mattes around the moving gladiators as they entered the arena. This has led to efforts to produce software which will automatically follow the outline of constantly moving image areas. A perfected automated rotoscoping programme could be used to save a stencil coloured print which can no longer be run through a printer or telecine. If the film is also found to exist as an untinted print or negative in better condition, then the complete black and white image could be digitized and the chosen areas coloured to match the damaged colour version, or the rotoscope software used only to generate a set of film mattes for adding the colour using normal printing techniques.

Colourisation - love it or hate it

The, modern equivalent of stencil colouring is the controversial process of electronic 'colourisation'. Many film historians and critics, who admire the artistry of early hand and stencil coloured films, condemn the present day practice of colourising films originally shot in black and white as the worst case of over-restoration. Others make the point that the world around us is in colour and in the eyes of the present generation, it is black and white that is 'unnatural'. Despite the continued debate, and in some cases legal action to try and prevent it, over 200 films have been colourised and offered as an alternative to broadcasters who fear that today's younger viewers will zap past their channels at the sight of an old black and white movie. Only a few have been shown on terrestrial TV in this country, including the rather crudely coloured *Scrooge* (1951) and *Tom Brown's Schooldays* (1951), together with a getting better pan and scan version of *The Longest Day* (1962), and perhaps the best examples of the art so far, *Red River* (1948) and Disney's original *The Absent-Minded Professor* (1960). Many of the first films to burst into colour are now being re-colourised to improve the result. Almost

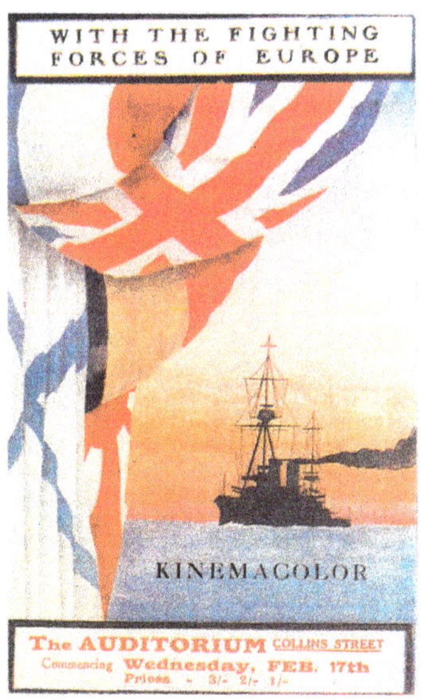

Footage from the First World War was colourised using the latest techniques for a well-publicised TV series, but this Kinemacolor ad from 1915 suggests that there may be some versions to be found in more 'natural' colours.

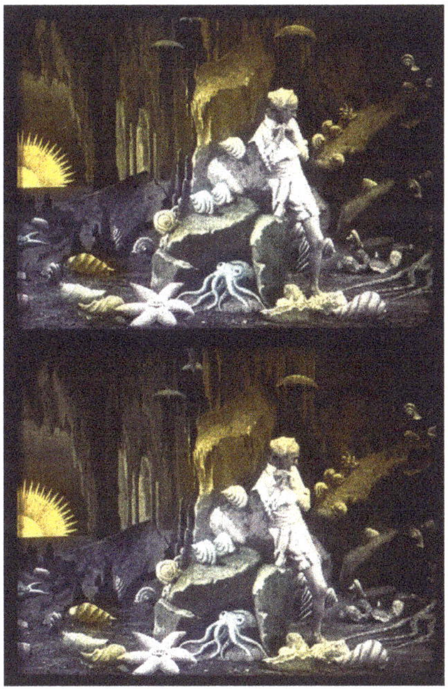

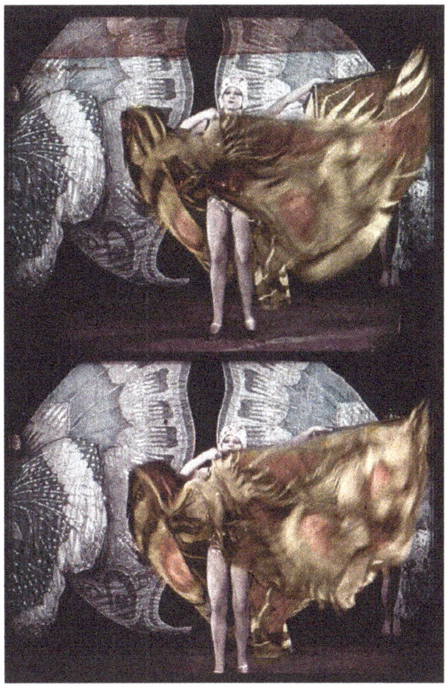

Left: Colourisation from the past: Examples of Pathecolor Stencil Colour

Below: 'Topper' (1937) was one of the first black and white features to be colourised back in 1985. Since then nearly 200 others have, in the eyes of many objectors, been similarly mistreated.

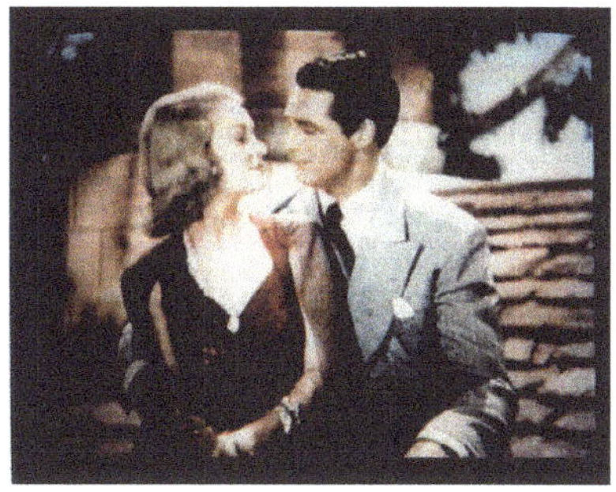

all this colourisation is done at broadcast resolution and distributed on tape, so poses little threat to the black and white originals.

Some colourisation has been done onto film. A number of *Betty Bloop* black and white cartoons from the 1930s were coloured for TV by more traditional means. The process was made more competitive with electronic colourisation, by employing workers in the Far East, who enlarged and traced each frame to make new sets of cels, which were re-painted in colour and re-photographed on film. Alfred Hitchcock's original black and white introductions to his TV series *Alfred Hitchcock Presents* were colourised and used again at the start of the more recent colour re-makes.

Colouring newsreels may compromise their historical accuracy, but even so, footage has been colourised to make it blend into all-colour documentaries like *The Attack on Pearl Harbour*. To reassure customers, companies which offer a colourisation service say it is carried out with great integrity with researchers verifying the colours. Although computer assisted, the process is still very labour intensive, so the original black and white material for *The first World War in Colour* followed in the footsteps of *Betty Boop* and was sent off to the Far East to be coloured, together with an adviser and reference books to ensure that the all-important uniforms came back in the correct colours. *The Russian Revolution in Colour* also colourised contemporary footage to match its newly shot 'natural' colour dramatised reconstructions.

One of the greatest advantages of going digital, is the recovery of faded colour negatives and prints, which are beyond help using all-film photo-chemical means. Even if the dye image in any of the layers has virtually disappeared, it can in effect be colourised using information from any remaining dye density and that from the less faded layers. After assessing the degree of loss, this can be corrected at the time of scanning, reducing the cost by freeing up computer power for any additional digital restoration work.

A recent example has been a digital restoration of the musical *Carousel* (1956). A previous attempt using the original camera negative was thwarted due to its severely faded images. Only digital processing could bring back the colour, and the scanning was done at 4K resolution to help capture all the extra detail on the four times larger than normal Cinemascope-55mm negative. The final prints were made via a 35mm digital intermediate.

Straight to Video

Restoration to video, without returning the results back to film is now commonplace. Some years ago, the BBC experimented by using the original B&W separation master positives of one of its RKO Technicolor features, *Cattle Queen of Montana* (1954) to make a new video copy. The three separations were run in turn through the same telecine, with care taken to synchronise fields etc, to produce separate tapes representing the red, green and blue images. These were then combined and graded onto a third tape. The final full colour image was judged superior to a previously used film copy. More recently, film-resolution digital copies of *The Adventures of Robin Hood* (1939) and *Singin' In The Rain* (1952) have been made directly from the original Technicolor 3-strip negatives. After this, they became 'no-film' restorations, being intended for showing using digital cinema projectors. *Gone With The Wind* has also been 'restored' yet again, this time in an all-digital version direct from its overworked negatives, with any registration problems now easier to correct by digitally manipulating the geometry of the three colour separation images.

Copying film onto video has made it easier to preserve and make available colour films shot in the sometimes more difficult to handle formats like amateur home movies. Although it is still possible, this procedure may now be preferable to attempting to make satisfactory film duplicates either in the original 8mm, 9.5mm, or 16mm gauges, or as enlarged prints. At the same time, digital processing can also improve the often well worn and less than perfectly photographed images. Although archives are sometimes able to keep the original single reversal copies, others have to be returned to their owners. The constant search for unique colour material, particularly by the makers of the various 'in colour' documentaries, has shown the value of colour home movies to archives and commercial stock shot libraries.

Wartime footage is always in demand. Most amateurs who were able to keep filming, recorded life on the home front, but although film stock was in short supply, some ordinary soldiers on both sides took their cameras, loaded with Kodachrome or Agfacolor, on active service with them. They shot their own unofficial account of the human consequences of the conflict, which being free of censorship, was often even more chilling.
A recent discovery, which featured in *Japan's War*, was the personal film record, taken by the Emperor's brother, of the events in Japan leading up to and including the war years. The colour footage was shot using different systems as they became available, starting with lenticular in 1931, moving on to Dufaycolor during the rest of the 1930s and ending the war on colour reversal film.

In happier times, and of particular interest to film fans, are the goings-on behind the 35mm cameras captured by members of the public on 8mm when film makers and stars come to town. Professionals setting off on location sometimes took their own 8mm or 16mm movie cameras along with them, producing interesting colour footage of work on films which were only being made in black and white. Examples now reaching a wider audience include Chaplin's *The Great Dictator* (1940), Marilyn Monroe at work on *Some Like It Hot* (1959) and John Mills' personal record of shooting *Dunkirk* (1958) and *Ice Cold In Alex* (1958).

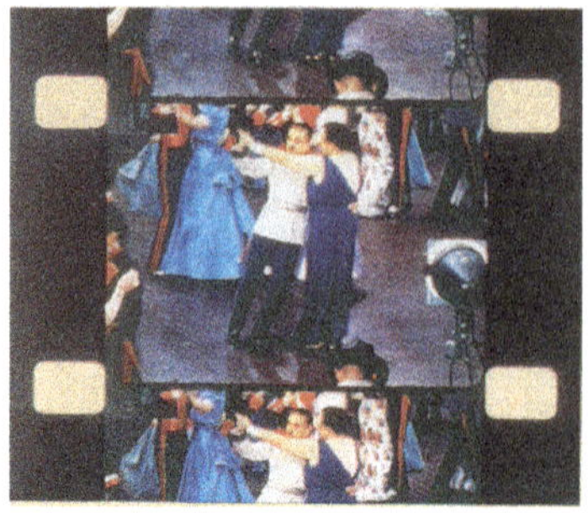

Behind-the-scenes 16mm Kodachrome footage shot by Sydney Chaplin of his younger brother, Charlie, during the filming (in black and white) of the ballroom sequence in The Great Dictator (1940)

For railway enthusiasts, Ivor Peter's beautifully shot 16mm Kodachrome footage of trains steaming out of stations and through the countryside, during the 1950s and 1960s, has appeared in many documentaries since. Most home movie-makers have now switched to using video cameras. The availability of camera stock into the future is uncertain, but, for the moment, Super-8 film and its processing can still be obtained and has found a use by professionals who sometimes include newly shot Super-8 sequences in their films to vary the visual 'texture' of the image. The current fashion for giving images the Super-8 look, has led to the use of a digitally generated simulation of the effect.

The best of both worlds

Digital help can come to the aid of an otherwise all-film restoration. Most of the work restoring *My Fair Lady* (1964) in 1994, was the physical repair and preparation of the original 65mm negative before making the new 35mm and 70mm re-issue release prints and long term preservation material. One damaged section, which couldn't be disguised, was a tear in the opening credits. This was successfully dealt with digitally, producing a better result than copying earlier intermediate duplicating material made before the rip occurred.

For the restored 'special edition' of Disney's *Bedknobs and Broomsticks* (1971), the obligatory 'extras' included the return of 22 minutes of scenes removed to shorten the film at the request of the distributor. In keeping with Disney's high reputation for preservation, the original negative for 21 minutes of the cut footage had been safely kept in excellent condition and was reinstated.

Much of the sought-after colour footage of the Second World War was shot by both amateur and professional cameramen on early Agfacolor and Kodachrome.

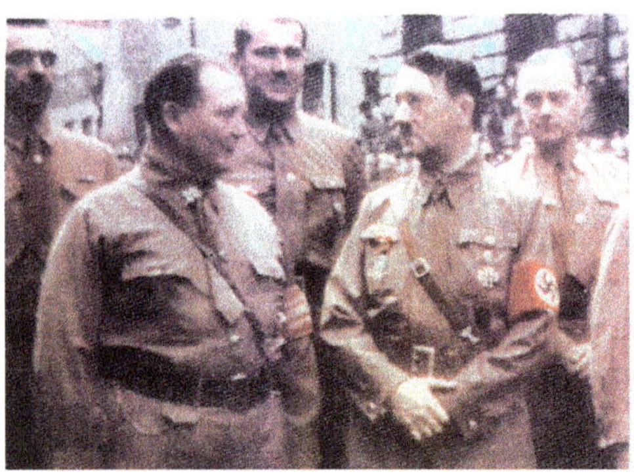

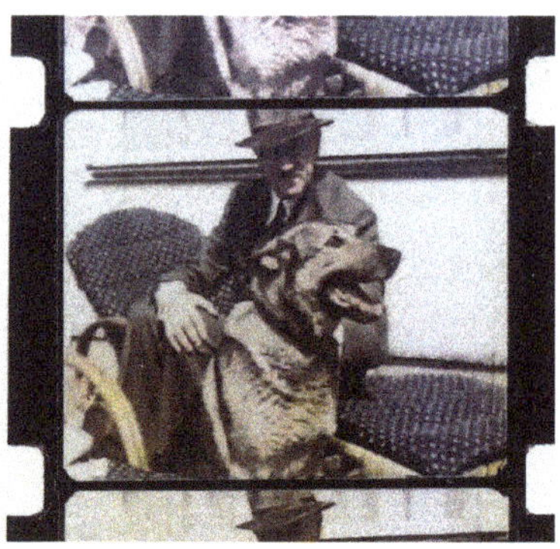

Early Kodachrome colour footage shot by amateurs around the world, beginning in the 1930s, is now highly valued, and even the boxes are worth preserving.

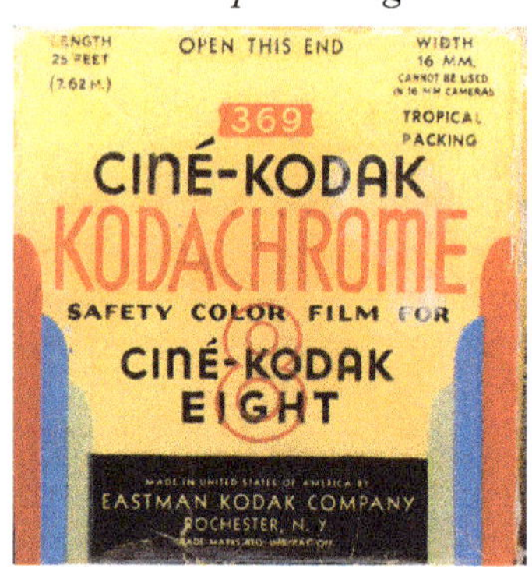

This left a missing minute from the 'Portobello Road' sequence, which had not been finally edited before the deletions were made. The original negative could not be found, possibly discarded along with unwanted trims and unselected takes. The only surviving version existed as part of the editor's work print (cutting copy). This was a positive, badly faded print, with the image further marred by scratches, tape joins and wax pencil marks. To make it useable, as much work as possible was done by traditional means. The film was cleaned, both by hand and ultrasonically, and then liquid gate printed onto camera negative film, graded to correct as far as possible the faded colour. The task was then completed digitally, with the adjacent scenes used as a guide for matching the colour balance. Doing as much of the work as possible in the film domain meant that less processing power was needed, reducing the risk of added artefacts. Although the final result was a little softer, with higher contrast and slightly desaturated colours, the appearance of the once missing minute was no more noticeable than any other of the production's opticals used elsewhere in the film. If new funding becomes available, a previous all-film photographic restoration may be improved with additional digital help.

A possible example was to be Claude Friese-Greene's *OPEN ROAD* travelogue film showing Britain as it was in the 1920s. This rare colour footage was chosen as a suitable subject for a follow-up to the BFI/BBC's successful Mitchell and Kenyon series. Originally shot in two-colour Biocolor, its red and green images were shown alternately on the screen during additive projection at twice the normal speed. It was hoped that digital processing could be used to help reduce the appearance of the inevitable colour fringing due to the difference in time between the separate red and green filtered exposures. Although progress was being made, it was not in time to meet the programme's schedule, so the BFI's archival film restoration which they made about ten

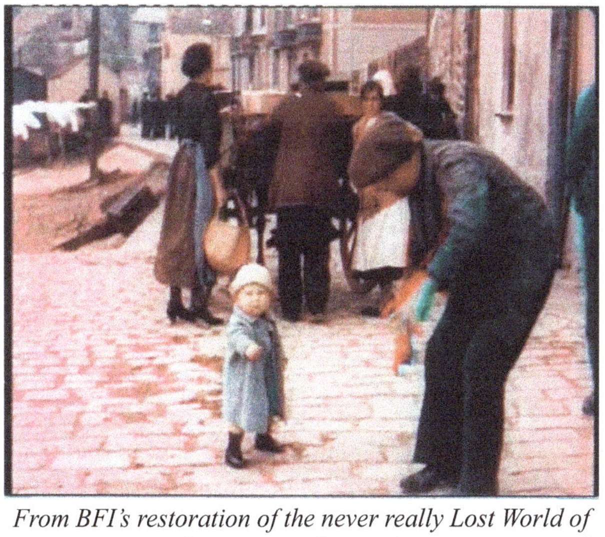

From BFI's restoration of the never really Lost World of Friese-Greene, but now in a better than new version of his original Biocolor system.

years ago was used again. The 'genuine' colour fringes did help to give it an old colour process look, which was otherwise nothing like the flickering images seen by the first audiences, as their brains desperately tried to fuse together the alternating red and green coloured frames by persistence of vision. To give the programme makers credit, they did try to demonstrate the original effect for a few seconds, before there was a risk of giving susceptible viewers an epileptic fit.

The digital threat

Although digital restoration is becoming a valuable new tool available to archivists and restorers, it can be a two-edged sword. In many cases, it may be the only way left to save a badly damaged or faded colour film. For others, it has proved to be life threatening to their original film elements. For just a tenth of the cost of a full photographic film restoration, a possibly already fading print, negative, or colour intermediate can be run through a telecine and, using proprietary software to remove the defects, produce a remarkably good DVD version. The resulting electronically cleaned up image, with its rich and brilliant colours, would be difficult to replicate when printing the same original directly onto colour print film. Unfortunately, after making the video transfer, the original film is usually returned to the vault in danger of further deterioration. As a result, the term 'restoration' is also in danger of becoming de-valued and misleading, joining descriptions like 'dazzling' or 'sparkling new print', often seen included in the advertising hype for the re-issue of older colour films on video and DVD.

Future thoughts on archiving

Many archives and film libraries, like our own National Film and Television Archive, have their own black and white film printing and processing facilities, but make use of commercial laboratories and post production houses for completing their colour film and high resolution digital work. For the latter, it has been mooted that a number of archives could pool their resources and set up a high resolution digital restoration centre to undertake projects which, although vital, do not attract outside funding. These could be subsidised by also accepting commercial work, but they would have to compete with other laboratories which already have a high reputation for their restoration skills and experience. These include YCM Labs and Cinetech in the U.S.A., Soho Images here in the UK, and Haghefilm in the Netherlands. For some projects, they sometimes co-operate to make the most of their particular expertise.

Kodak and others offer bursaries and fellowships to encourage students to specialise in film restoration, both traditional and digital. Most archives now have some form of in-house film-to-tape transfer capability for making viewing copies for easier access to their collections. These have largely replaced the need for and cost of producing extra film prints and the risk of them being damaged when run on viewing machines or projectors.

The new electronic restoration tools are beginning to find their way into smaller and regional archives. An example is the East Anglian Film Archive, which has now added a Bosch 35mm/16mm broadcast telecine and a Diamant digital restoration system to its existing 8mm, 9.5mm and 16mm film printing and processing machines. All this is used, and partly financed, by the sale of a series of videos and DVDs featuring both professional end amateur material showing images from the past and present, reflecting everyday life in the South East of England.

The traditional tasks of physically preparing films for duplication will always be needed, but digital restoration and preservation will increasingly become commonplace, as the cost falls to meet the rising price of film stock. By then, there may also emerge a common recognised format for storing the final digital masters, be it on tape, optical or hard disc, or solid state. In the meantime, and perhaps for ever, the only sure way of making them always readily accessible is to scan their digital images back onto 35mm film to join other surviving colour films dating back over 100 years.

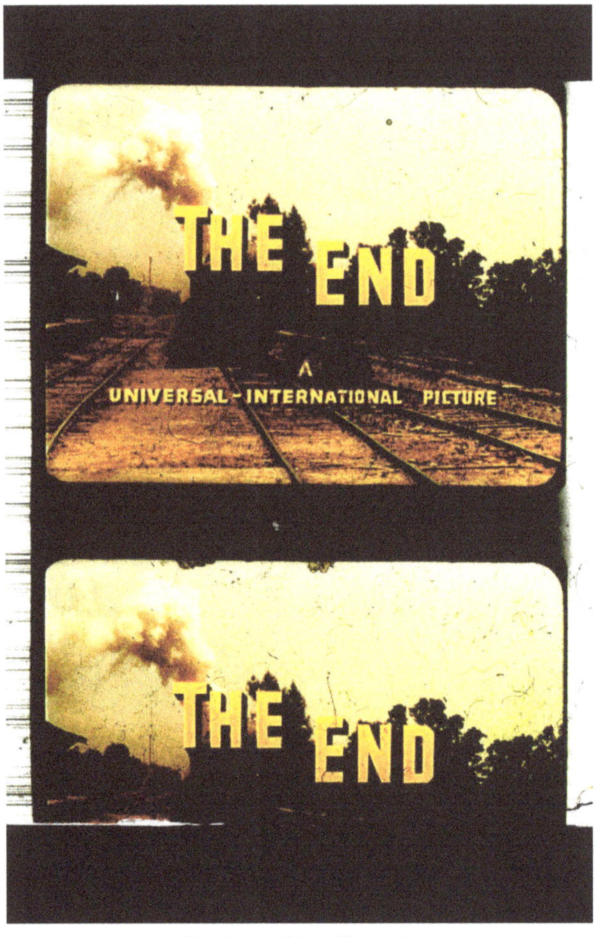

It is never really the end for film, of course - in spite of digital competition the longest lasting archives are likely to be on black and white film separations for generations to come

Sold for 32,000 dollars a frame!

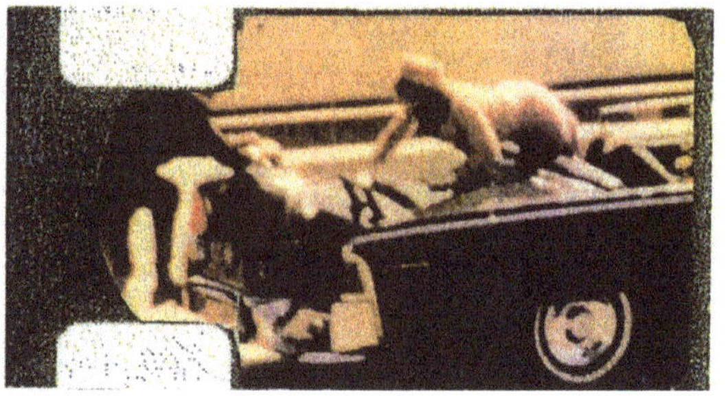

The most valuable home movie ever, in monetary terms at least, is the Zapruder 8mm Kodachrome footage of the assassination of President Kennedy. The original camera film has now finally been purchased from the Zapruder family by the U.S. Government for 16 million dollars. Even at this price the deal didn't include the copyright, which has been transferred to the Sixth Floor Museum in Dallas, Texas.

Having filmed the shooting in 1963, the film was processed by Kodak, and Mr Zapruder had three reversal 8mm copies made by an independent lab. He kept one of them, handing over the other two to the Secret Service. The first commercial exploitation was by 'Life' magazine, who used the original to make frame enlargements for publication in their magazine, unfortunately, not before cutting the film and losing six of the original 500 frames in the process.

Over forty years later the primary preservation format chosen by the National Archives for keeping the wounded original's images safe in the future was the making of three 35mm black and white separations. The 8mm frames were enlarged showing the full width of the film, including the inter-sprocket hole area which has extra spill-over image not normally seen when projected, and which also never appeared on any of the subsequent copies. To preserve the film's 'forensic evidence' status, no form of restoration was allowed, including replacing the lost frames, which are still intact in the first-generation copies.

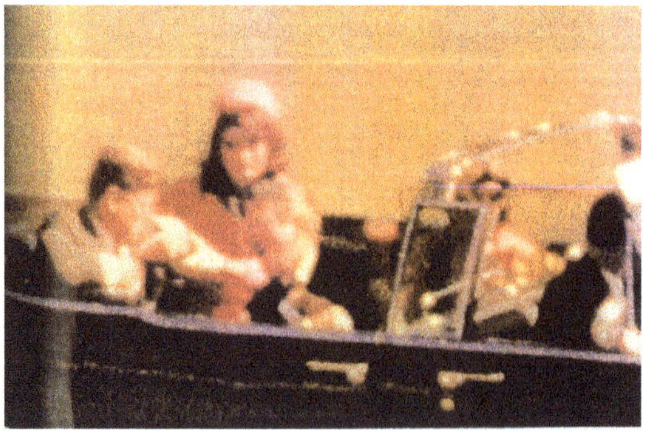

Aspect ratios - An increasingly important aspect of film restoration

Why haven't we settled on a single optimum screen shape for the cinema?

Of all the possible problems encountered during a film's restoration, keeping its original picture shape would seem to be a relatively simple task, compared to that of trying to produce the best possible image quality from sometimes damaged and deteriorating originals.

I'm sure that, for most cinemagoers and TV viewers, the shape of the picture they are watching plays a far less important contribution to their overall enjoyment of a film than its narrative and the action on the screen. If any technical errors should occur, troubles with the focus or sound are usually far more distracting than the more subtle loss of picture information or spoilt composition due to it being shown in the wrong aspect ratio. Unless, of course, the missing part of the image, like subtitles or other text, is vital to the understanding of the plot. However, for those more aware of the pictorial aspects of the presentation, including the growing number of better informed home cinema enthusiasts, if the film is being shown in what they consider to be the incorrect ratio or mis-framed in the projector, it can ruin their complete viewing experience.

At events, like BFI Members Forums, which discuss the technical details of film presentation, the subject of dealing correctly, or more specifically not, with all the different screen shapes which have been introduced over the years, often results in heated debate and recriminations when things are judged to have gone wrong.
At repertory theatres, like the NFT, it's reasonable to expect that they should be able to cope with not only the squarer pictures of the silent era and earlier sound films, but also with at least the most common of the myriad of wider formats which followed in the wake of the cinema's widescreen revolution, beginning in the 1950s.

In theatres and multiplexes only set-up for today's current pair of widescreen formats, even the most conscientious projectionist wouldn't be able to properly show an unexpected revival of an earlier classic. Unfortunately, even in fully equipped theatres with a range of projector apertures, lenses and matching screen masking options, errors still occur. As an example, one of London's specialist theatres put on a season of German silents. Although the organisers provided excellent appropriate musical accompaniment, the presentation was let down when all the silent prints, in their original format, were projected using a smaller sound aperture and at the wrong speed. As a comparison, at a regional venue, with supposedly less resources, a similar programme was shown correctly and the screen even had round corners, like many in use during the silent days.

In their defence, the projectionists and management are not always to blame. The print provided may be the result of some form of optical conversion, with missing image compared to the original.
In some cases, a new reprint may now actually include more picture information from the negative, which was never intended to be shown and didn't appear on the first release prints.

Some widescreen methods only had a recommended aspect ratio, but could be shown in others. The ideal ratio may no longer be stated or indicated on the print and that chosen may not satisfy the more critical in the audience, who may have their own ideas. The framing of films with more picture included on the print than is actually being projected needs extra care, with an eye for composition to try and match the vertical framing intentions of the camera operator. For cinema showings still running film any errors may only effect a particular performance, but in the case of film printing or video transfers they will be built into the new, sometimes master, copy.

4:3, The classic shape of moving pictures

Along with the worldwide adoption of Edison's 35mm film format as the professional standard came its 4:3 aspect ratio, which was to remain the familiar shape of motion pictures for over 60 years, before being pushed to one side by the coming of wider screens in the early 1950s. When the narrower 'sub-standard' gauges, like16mm, 9.5mm and 8mm, were subsequently introduced, they too kept to the same, or close to the same, frame shape, as they not only made it easier for amateurs to make their own movies, but also to show reduced versions of professional 35mm films at home and other non-theatrical venues. When film's electronic rival, Television, arrived, it also eventually settled on a 4:3 display, one of the principal reasons being to be compatible with film, a major programme source and independent of the many different broadcast standards in use around the world. For many years, tele-recordings on film allowed programme exchange before satisfactory electronic standards converters and video tape took over. TV has now caught up with wider screens, but the original 4:3 shape will always remain familiar with audiences as the vast pre-widescreen archive is plundered to help feed today's programme-hungry multi-channel environment.

Aspects of Aspect Ratios

When telling a story of formats, the shape of the image can be expressed as a ratio, generally preferred by the film industry, resulting in descriptions like 1.85:1 and

2.35:1, the higher the figure, the wider the picture. In the world of TV and video displays, proportions in units are more common, giving us screens of 14:9 and 16:9. Like aspect ratio's fixed height, '9' is usually kept the same, to help make comparisons and visualise the different proportions.

For the long established 4:3, or 1.33:1, shape, both terms are commonly used across both the film and TV mediums, rolling off the tongue easier than 12:9. It is also sometimes referred to as the 'Academy' format, which was adopted, back in 1932, after the introduction of sound-on-film reduced the space available for the picture on 35mm film. Originally proposed by the Academy of Motion Picture Arts and Sciences, the final dimensions of the smaller projection aperture (0.825in. x 0.600in.) actually gave an aspect ratio of 1.37:1. Even to the eyes of the most pedantic, the difference on the screen is indistinguishable from 1.33: 1, and when projected at any angle other from strictly head-on, is often modified to a greater or lesser extent during the correction of the keystone distortion effect. It takes only a downward angle of 14 degrees to bring Academy back to 1.33:1.

Not forgetting our Imperial Past

As most of the technical changes and presentation innovations, which have left us with so many different formats to deal with, originally sprung from America,

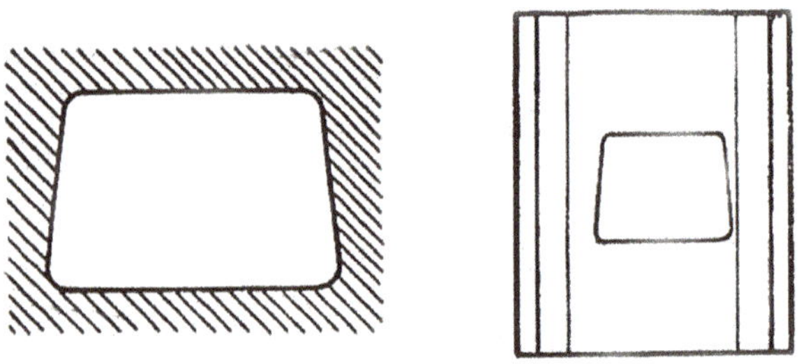

Keystone correction can effectively result in a change in aspect ratio

a country never in a great rush to embrace the metric system, most of the first standards, like aperture dimensions, were stated in inches. Before 1900, film widths too were in inches, Edison's being 13/8 inches. Here in Britain, the camera maker Prestwich advertised models for ½ in., 13/8in and 23/8 inch film widths. When the Lumières in France chose to use the same width as Edison, the nearest metric equivalent of 35mm also began to become familiar. In the pioneering days, the high demand for movie making equipment led many American producers to obtain cameras from Europe. A notable example was the wooden Pathe '35mm' Studio Camera, which was a popular choice in Hollywood, before being displaced by the all-metal Bell & Howell and Mitchell models, by then also described as 35mm cameras. However, film gauges in millimetres seemed to be the only concession, other dimensions staying imperial, such as the film's 'footage'. Today's international standards often include both. Whether in inches or millimetres, film has always been praised for its enduring acceptance and common standards, now extending over two centuries. After all this time, it's surprising that we have not finally settled on a single screen shape, which is both pleasing to the eye, and would simplify both production and presentation.

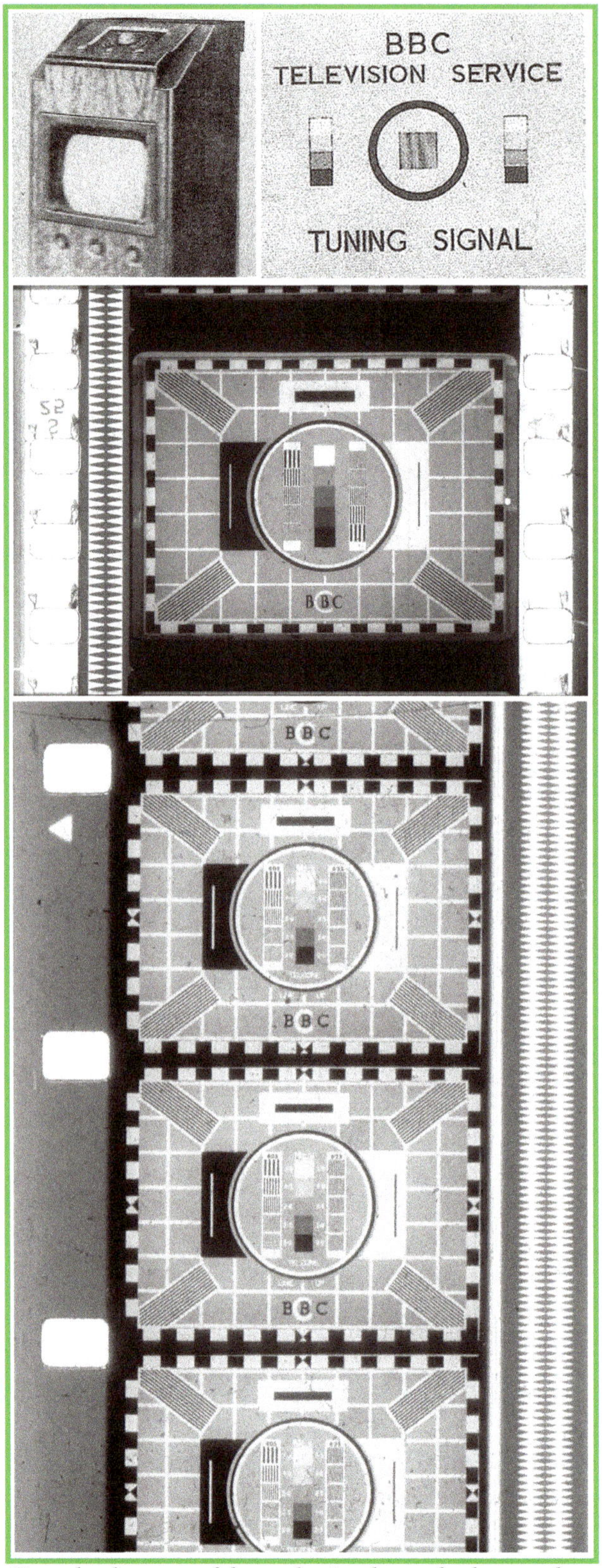

To make the most of the early circular cathode ray tubes British TV began with a 5:4 aspect ratio picture, but with the coming of rectangular faced tubes in the 1950s it was quietly changed to 4:3. One of the principal reasons was in order to be compatible with film.

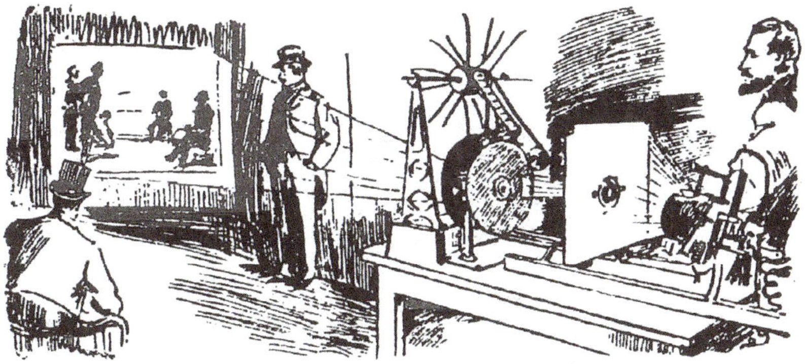

First demonstration of Latham's Pantoptikon, later known as the Eidoloscope projector, in 1895

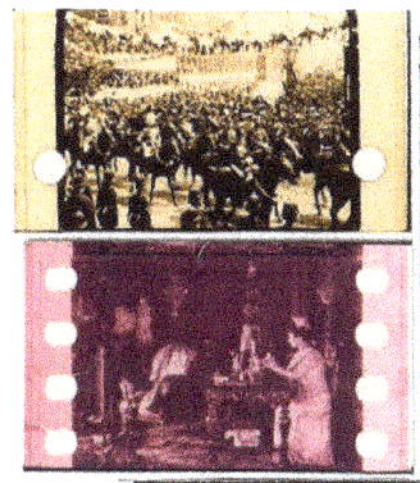

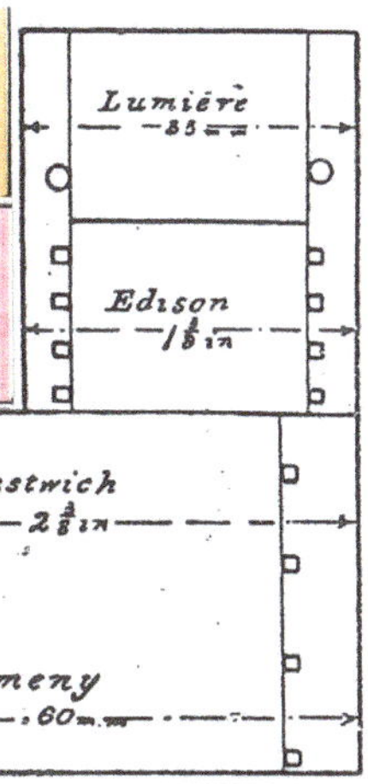

Right: Current film formats in 1889 Lumiére Edison Prestwich Demeny

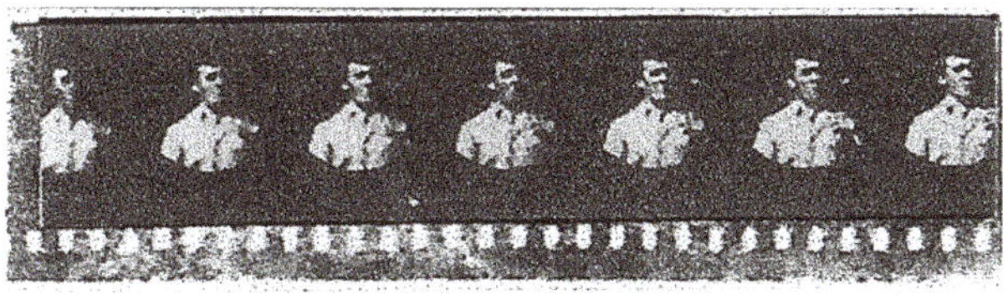

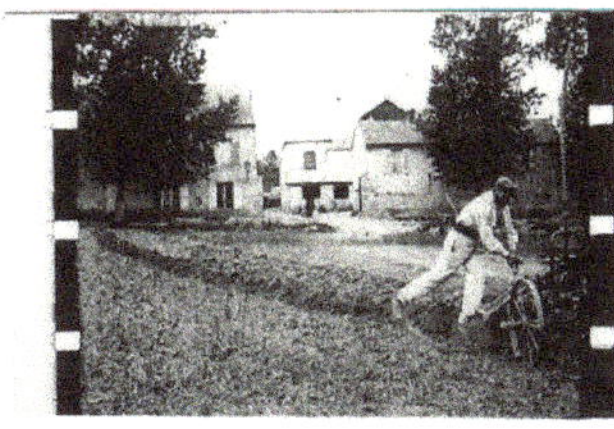

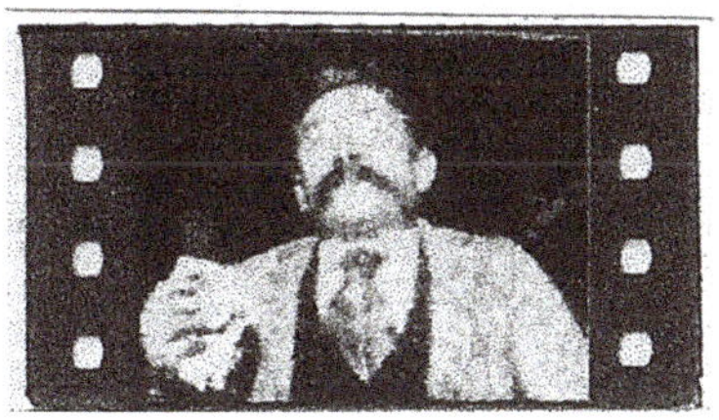

The prototype of the Kinetoscope used narrower horizontal-running film with circular images before settling on the final 'Edison' format with its 4:3 rectangular pictures (1893)

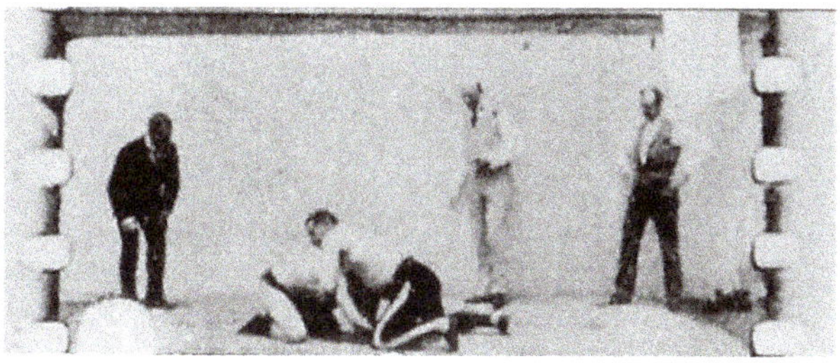

Above: A frame of Eidoloscope 51mm wide film

Who gave us 4:3?

Looking back at the accounts of the origin of the 35mm film format, particularly by its creator, William Dickson, would suggest that the choice of its 4:3 aspect ratio was rather arbitrary, with no mention of any artistic or psychological considerations. However, it did evolve, with the first prototype of its original home, Edison's Kinetoscope, using narrower horizontal running film with circular pictures. Even after the final width and perforation lay-out was arrived at, there was still a choice of picture shape available depending on the number of perforations used for each of the now vertically-running frames. Dickson would have been well able to appreciate the merits of different frame proportions. As well as being, a clever inventor and engineer, he was also a keen photographer, with his work exhibited at the Orange Camera Club, and later, after leaving Edison, he would join a rival as a cameraman.

His choice of four perforations for each frame gave us 4:3. Five would give an almost square shape, but use more film. Three would have resulted in a more 'dynamic', wider picture, but would look smaller through the peep-show machine's eyepiece and its subjects were unlikely to include less animated landscapes. Later writers have suggested that if he had known that his film would soon escape from the confines of the Kinetoscope and be projected on large cinema screens, he might have preferred a wider format like a theatre stage.

Rival formats take shape

Even Dickson wasn't wedded to 4:3. While still working for Edison, he was helping his friend and fellow inventor, Eugene Lauste, to build a camera and projector for Woodville Latham and his sons. Together with their partner, boxing promoter Enoch J. Rector, they were already exploiting the Kinetoscope by using rows of special higher capacity versions (150ft instead of 50ft) each showing a round of specially staged prizefights. However, like other early pioneers in the movie business, they thought projection was a better and more profitable idea. Their first projector, the Pantoptikon, later known as the Eidoloscope, used the same continuously moving film with brief flashes of light to arrest each frame as the Kinetoscope, so was very inefficient compared to those with proper intermittent movements. To help increase the light output and possibly to avoid patent infringement, the width of the basic Edison format was increased 50% to 2in (51mm), with a corresponding wider picture. No mention was made about the 'widescreen' shape of the picture when it was first demonstrated to the press, and even the artist's impression of the event shows a normal squarer shaped screen being used. Perhaps their first model used Edison's gauge.

An example of the Latham's Eidoloscope projector is currently in the photographic collection at The Smithsonian Institute in Washington D.C., and a request to measure the gate established it at 20mm x 37mm. The machine is among the contenders claiming to be the first to project films to a paying audience in 1895. It was the first widescreen format, and its 1.85:1 aspect ratio is still being shown to paying cinemagoers today.

An even bigger and taller challenger

Behind Edison's back, Dickson also guided another friend, Herman Casler, to design a camera to take animated pictures for a rival peep-show device, the Mutoscope, which used the already familiar flicker-book principle. The camera also used wider film, this time 211/16 in (68mm). Also, to avoid patent trouble, it was made to be as different as possible from Edison's machines. The unperforated stock was moved intermittently through the camera using partly cut away rubber rollers which momentarily lost their grip, stopping the film for each exposure, at which moment a pair of circular

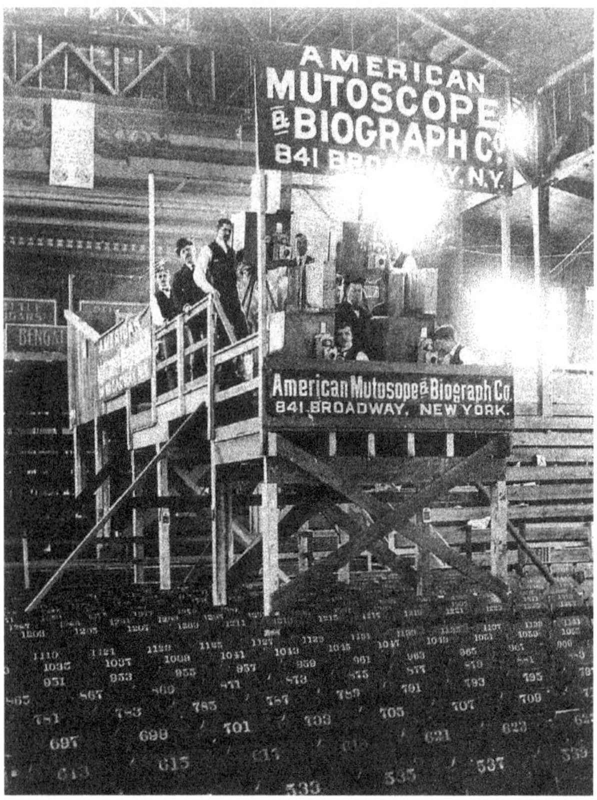

perforations were punched between the inevitable irregularly spaced frames, and all happening at 40 frames per second. The perforations were only used to register the images during the printing onto the flip-cards for the Mutoscope.

By 1896, with many others working on constructing projectors, the negatives were also printed onto transparent film for a design of their own. Their wide gauge projector, known as the Biograph, soon took priority. Its 68mm prints (also quoted as being 70mm) didn't have any perforations and were also transported at 40 frames per second by the gripping action of mutilated cylinders which made contact with the film for only a fourth of a revolution. Not offering the best registration, the operator had to keep hold of the framing knob to stop the picture from wandering up or down on the screen. Apart from this, the images from its 2 x 2½ inch projection aperture were far superior to its, mostly 35mm competitors.

When the Mutoscope & Biograph Company opened up in Britain, in 1897, its London showcase was The Palace Theatre of Varieties, where it was said the screen occupied the entire proscenium opening. The Biograph was the Imax of its day and when booked into other theatres their management had to pay more than charged for 35mm showings. It offered big screen quality entertainment to discerning audiences at a time when moving pictures didn't always have a good reputation, like many of the music halls, in which they were just another 'turn'.

When the Company's other enterprise, the Mutoscope, first appeared in 1897, it too provided edifying and wholesome entertainment, but soon went down-market, showing more risqué 'What the Butler Saw' subjects. After all his collaboration with the enemy, Edison dismissed Dickson, who then joined Biograph to run their European operations. He travelled widely as a cameraman bringing back wide-film footage of wars, royalty and news-worthy events from around the world. Like the original Imax, although big screen, Biograph wasn't widescreen, with its 1.25:1 aspect ratio narrower than Edison's 1.33:1.

The combination of wide film and a wider picture hit the screen again in 1897, as the result of another contest. Enoch J. Rector continued in the fight, game by securing the exclusive film rights for the return boxing match between 'gentleman' Jim Corbett and British fighter Bob Fitzsimmons to be staged on March 17th, 1897 at Carson City, Nevada. His Veriscope Company in New York built cameras using Eastman film 2½ inch (63mm) wide with a 50mm x 30mm frame. Its 1.66:1 widescreen image was probably chosen to allow the static cameras to cover the whole ring in one shot. The fight was staged outdoors in daylight with the cameras in mind. In order not to miss any of the action, three were set up side by side, each being able to film for six minutes before reloading. Rector also had a copyright notice displayed in shot on the side of the ring to help protect his investment. At the end of the contest, Fitzsimmons had won by a knockout, the last time a British fighter would hold the world heavyweight title.

The Veriscope camera would also set a new motion picture record of the time, having exposed over two miles of film, the longest amount devoted to a single event. The final film, said to have lasted I½ hours, opened at

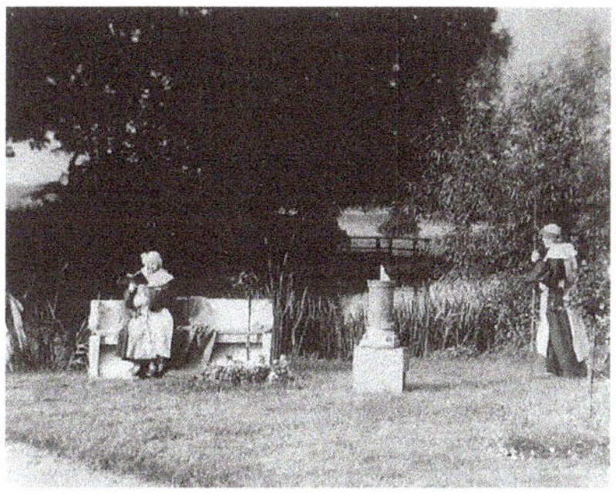

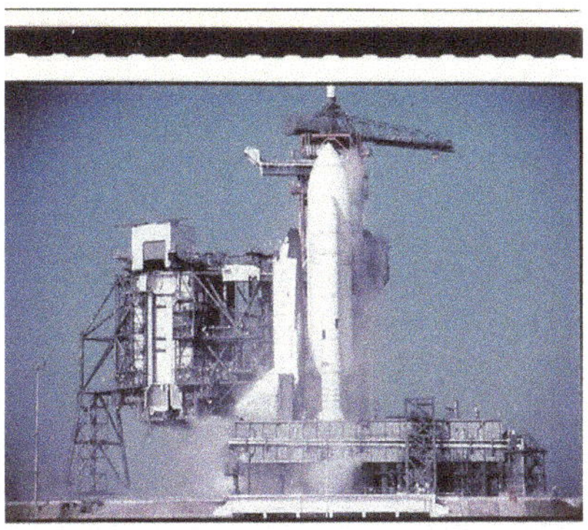

Biograph's wide film format of 1896 (left) was the of its day

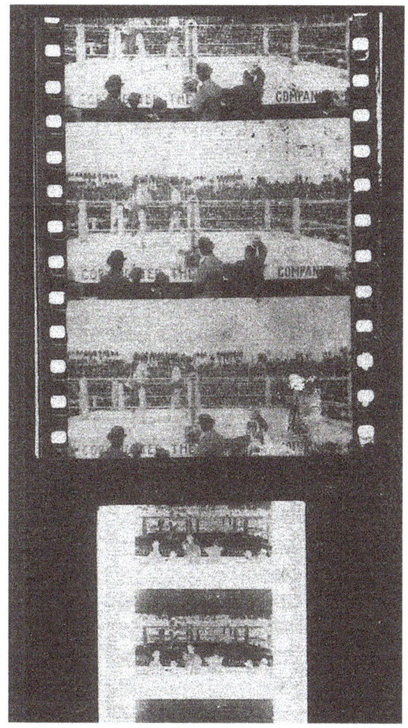

Right: The Corbett-Fitzsimons prizefight on Veriscope 63mm film, and the 35mm copy negatives made by Karl Malkames

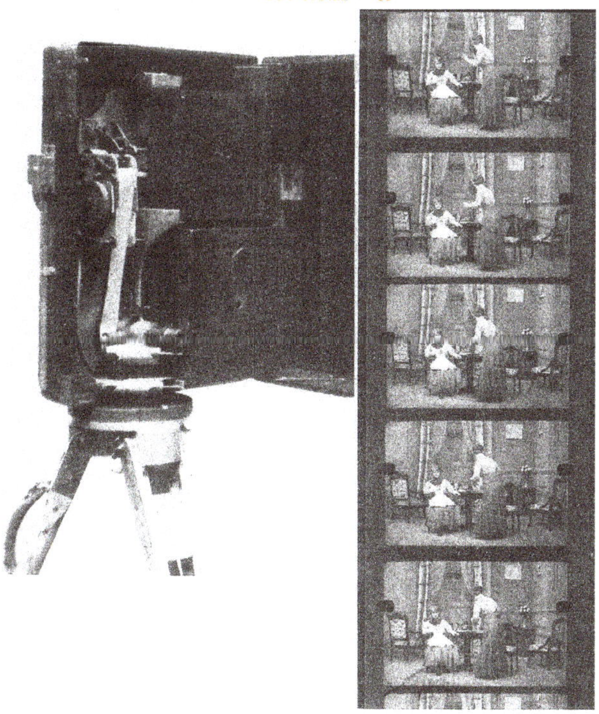

The 35mm Biograph camera with a paper print of its in-camera perforated negative - notice the random spacing of its frames

the Academy of Music in New York, and then, using twenty projectors, it was shown all over America making over three-quarters of a million dollars for the company. The Veriscope boxing film came to Britain during September 1897, opening at the Aquarium Theatre in Westminster. According to contemporary press reports, the audience, who paid up to a guinea for tickets, could 'see the figures projected life-size with every line of their faces clearly traceable'.

Biograph also ringside

Another boxing match was recorded on wide film, when the American Mutoscope & Biograph Co. had exclusive rights to film the bout between Jim Jeffries and Tom Sharkey in 1899. This time, using artificial light, inside the arena on Coney Island, four of their 68mm cameras were trained on the ring lit by four-hundred arc lights. To escape the heat, the boxers had to take cover under umbrellas between the thirty-three rounds. Boxing was a popular movie subject, particularly with lady fans in America, who were not normally allowed in to watch prize-fights, which in some states were banned altogether.

Can we see these early fights again today?

In the case of the Corbett-Fitzsimmons fight film, a number of reels of an original 63mm print ended up in our own National Film Archive and back in 1983 they undertook the task of copying them onto 35mm film. Like most restorations these days, funding was required, and this, together with extra footage, came from Jim Jacobs, American boxing promoter and archivist with the largest collection of films on the subject.

Harold Brown enters the ring

The actual copying work fell to Harold Brown, the archive's doyen, back in the pre-digital days when it came to dealing with unusual formats. This was a job for his, now famous in the world of archiving, Mark IV printer. Its construction began back in 1954, following a request from the French Cinèmathéque to copy some early Lumière 35mm film. This only had a single round perforation on either side of the 20mm x 25mm (1.25:1) frames. These were adequate, then, to move the short films only by the intermittent claws of the sprocketless Cinematographe combined camera/printer/projector transport mechanism. Harold set-to building the printer, at almost no cost, using bits of sheet metal, wood, Meccano and, the now notorious knicker elastic.

The first results were disappointing, with vertical jumping images. This proved to be due to the irregular pitch between the Lumière's perforations, and using the same claw to gate separation of their original machine cancelled out the inaccuracies to give a steady picture, The printer was soon being employed to copy Edison-type 35mm films, particularly badly shrunken examples which their normal printers couldn't cope with. Each frame was pressed into contact with the copying stock by the overall pressure of an opal glass plate at ten pounds per square inch, enough for the most severely buckled originals.

For optical enlargement or reduction to 35mm more Meccano based parts were added to the projection end and at the other a Newman Sinclair 35mm camera 'borrowed' from a Spottiswood stereoscopic set-up, now in the hands of the BFI. Before losing one of its eyes, it had been used to photograph some of the Festival of Britain's 3-D films in 1951. Harold's printer was subsequently adapted to copy many non-standard gauges, including the Corbett-Fitzsimmons wide film. This was also copied onto 35mm film by one of Harold's counterparts in America, Karl Malkames. He too, specialised in the building of special equipment to solve specific photographic problems, including dealing with unusual film formats, for customers like The Museum of Modern Art, The American Film Institute and George Eastman House. He was aided by having a collection of fully working vintage cameras of various gauges, which could provide information about the methods of transport and registration, and in some cases used as part of the actual printing processes. For the Veriscope fight-film, his multi-purpose variable pitch printer produced a reduced masked down image across the full width of the new 35mm negative, keeping its original 1.66:1 aspect ratio. Harold Brown's BFI version differed in having a slightly smaller image with a space left for a possible sound track.

Knowing these new copies had been made, I always expected to see at least a clip in documentaries, particularly during the build up to more recent important fights involving British contenders, to show one of them landing an historic knock-out blow. I have been told that a few seconds did once appear on TV, but I missed this opportunity. My chance came while down in Cornwall watching TV, when unexpectedly, Bob Fitzsimmons hit the screen, and Jim Corbett, again during the BBC's 'Spotlight' local news programme. At the time of the Millennium, it highlighted some of the West Country's greatest figures, who included Fitzsimmons, born in Helston, Cornwall. In a local press story, the programme's correspondent, Stephen Hall, told how he tracked down and was able to show this rare footage. The BFI couldn't let him use any of their print. The rights now belong to ESPN in New York, and, knowing that such footage might cost as much as 10,000 dollars a minute, it would be far beyond his budget. But luckily, the negotiator was British, which helped him to do a deal for two showings of a minute's worth at a fraction of the normal price. This example of gaining access shows that saving images from the past doesn't always make it any easier for the rest of us to see them again today.

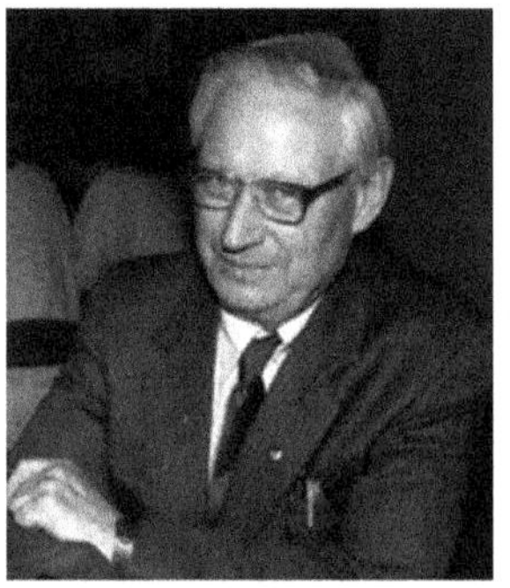
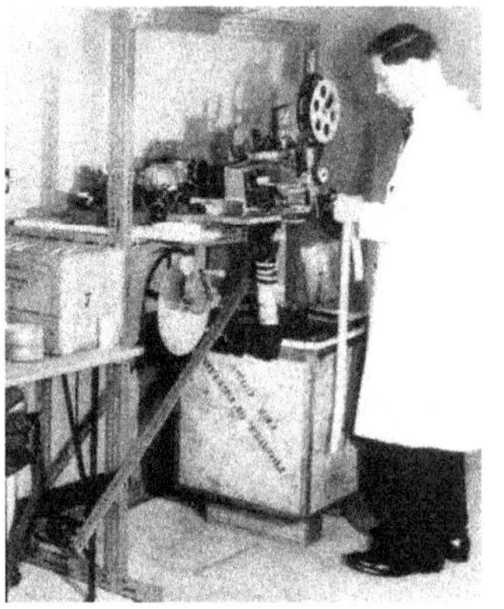

Harold Brown and his famous Mark IV printer, now in the National Film and Television Archive

Both the Biograph and Veriscope wide gauge films were exclusive to their respective companies. The only other wide-film which had a fair degree of usage was the Demeny-Gaumont 60mm Chronophotographe, which was generally available for sale in 1896. An almost identical 23/8in. (60mm) camera was on offer from Prestwich. Although using larger film, Gaumont' s 60mm outfit was far cheaper than many of the rival Edison gauge machines. This, together with its better image quality and potentially brighter pictures, made it popular with

Bob Fitzsimmons hit the screen, and Jim Corbett again during the BBC's 'Spotlight' local news programme

Archive footage gives Spotlight feature plenty of punch

Bob Fitzsimmons (left) battles against 'Gentleman' Jim Corbett, in Carson City, Nevada in 1897.

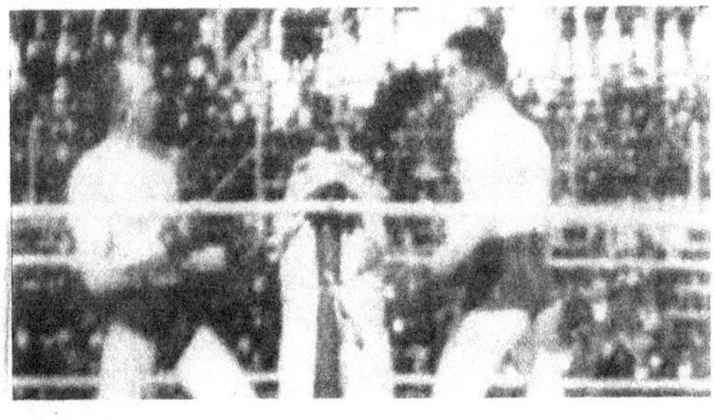

Cornishman Fitzsimmons remains the only Briton ever to have held the World Heavyweight Championship outright.

BBC South West's Millennium correspondent Stephen Hall tracked down this rare footage – thought to be the first ever film of a major boxing match – for a series of five-minute profiles called *People of the Millennium*, which highlights some of the West Country's greatest figures.

The ten films are being shown once a week as inserts into the regional news programme *Spotlight*.

'We felt very privileged to obtain and broadcast this extremely rare film footage,' Hall said. 'The British Film Institute has a copy, but only a few seconds have previously been shown on British television.'

Hall tracked down the American company that own the rights to it – ESPN in New York – and negotiated a special deal for a minute's worth of the footage, which was shown twice last week.

'Normally such footage might cost $10,000 a minute, way beyond my budget, but luckily the man I dealt with turned out to be British and I got it for a fraction of the price,' Hall said.

Originally from Helston, Fitzsimmons emigrated to New Zealand and then America where he not only won the World Heavyweight, but the World Light Heavweight and Middleweight crowns as well. His boxing career spanned 31 years.

Despite its age, the original film was an incredible 90 minutes long and shot in 63mm widescreen using three cameras.

Boxing had only just been legalised in the USA and moving pictures were in their infancy – so when it was shown in cinemas audiences were spellbound.

The ten subjects chosen for *People of the Millennium* were selected from viewers' and listeners' nominations. The other subjects are computer pioneer Charles Babbage; author Thomas Hardy; polar explorer Robert Scott; politician Nancy Astor; naturalist Gerald Durrell; steam pioneer Richard Trevithick; Sir Humphry Davy, who developed the miners' lamp to which he gave his name, and, of course, Sir Francis Drake.

November 9 1999

ARIEL•9

some early fairground operators and lecturers, who were beginning to add moving pictures to their lantern slide shows.

One notable example was the American traveller and explorer, Burton Holmes. He started his globe-trotting in 1883 and helped finance his trips by giving illustrated talks to large paying audiences, for which he first coined the term 'travelogue'. Burton Holmes' photographer and lanternist, Oscar B. Dupue, described how, on a trip to Europe in 1897, he purchased a 60mm Demeny camera in Paris, using it first to film scenes in Rome. On returning to America, George Eastman agreed to supply negative and positive film pre-cut to 60mm, but like other early film-makers, he had to perforate it himself. Among their first subjects was what they claimed to be the first moving pictures of the somewhat static Grand Canyon. Although their views of the world looked better using wide film, by 1901 Dupue had to accept that, "60mm was more difficult to handle than 35mm, which was becoming, the standard, and we could not always obtain film when we needed it, nor could we sell our wide film to the trade; in short, 60mm was passé." It was replaced with a 35mm camera. Between the years 1908 and 1922 Burton Holmes produced weekly travelogues for Paramount, and continued to travel and lecture up to his death in 1958.

End of the first wide film era

By 1902, Biograph too began the switch to 35mm, using a camera of their own design using the same in-camera punched perforation system as its 68mm big brother. During printing the single holes on each side of its unevenly spaced frames were sought out by spring-loaded pins to register them on normal 4-perf. prints. For more recent copies, Karl Malkames employed a surviving Biograph camera from his collection to form one end of his printer. On both the old and later prints, traces of the original in-camera perforations can sometimes be seen jumping up and down at the edges of the frame. This is because those next to each frame are not the ones used to register it during printing. Like the negatives from their earlier 68mm camera, knowing its punch to gate separation is essential for steady pictures.

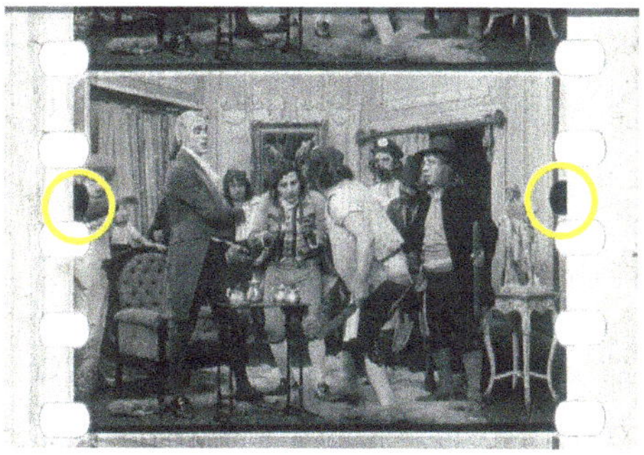

A Biograph 35mm print in which traces of the negative's perforations can be seen (circled) at the edges of the screen.

Even back in the 1900s, following the demise of these odd formats, ways were found to still profit from their images by re-photographing them onto 35mm film. In the case of the Biograph films, frames had to be eliminated to bring down their speed from 40 to around 16 frames per second. When watching these, and later reduction prints, viewers would normally be unaware of their wide-film ancestry. Although best kept intact, their squarer 5:4 images were usually cropped slightly to 4:3, in order to provide the customer with a compatible 35mm print.

Moving pictures from the 1890s are always fascinating. The fact that some of them were photographed on wider film may be of interest to the more technically minded film historians and 'gauges through the ages' spotters, they usually only become an issue, or a complication, if their subject matter attracts funding and archives are given the opportunity to make new, better prints and transfers. They can now call on digital assistance, with computer programmes available, useful for more effective speed changes and making it easier to produce steadier pictures, particularly from the Biograph wide-film prints with no perforations to help register them.

The last time I spotted some results was a scene from Dickson's 68mm Biograph footage of troop manoeuvres, taken during the Boer War in South Africa in 1899, and now included in a TV documentary about the history of war films.

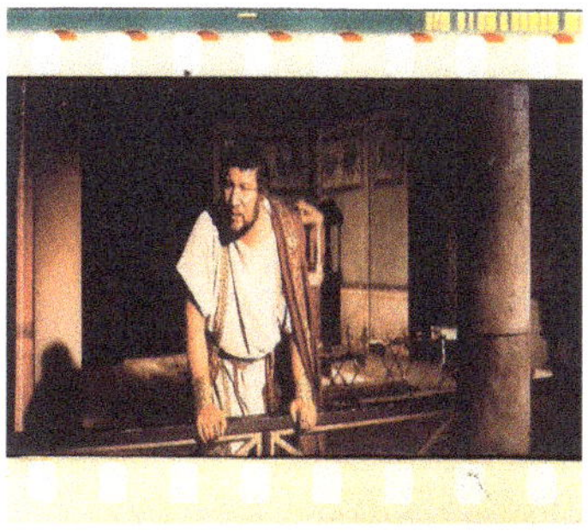

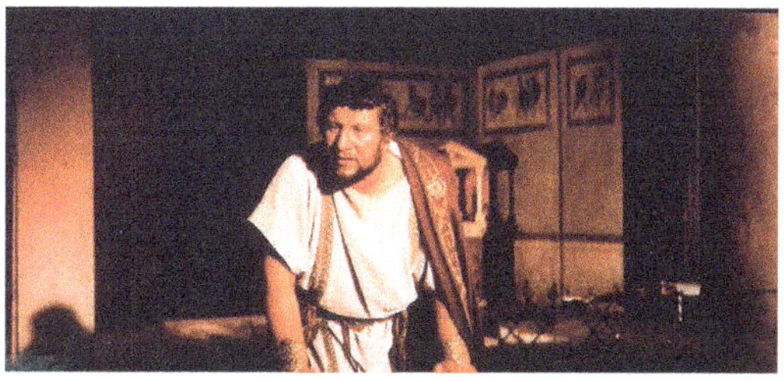

Helping future archivists. Spartacus (1960) was shot in the old Technirama process - 35mm horizontal 8-perf frames with a 1.5x squeezed picture. To make life easier for the future, the new master preservation film elements are now on 65mm with an un-squeezed image.

All shapes and sizes - The quest to find the perfect shape for the movies

Looking at how the industry decided that it was time for a change of shape

We have seen how the 35mm film format's early success at becoming the worldwide 'standard' for professional film-making and exhibition meant that its nominal 1x¾ inch frames resulted in cinema screens having the same proportions of 4:3, also described as having an aspect ratio of 1.33:1. In 1917, the newly formed American Society of Motion Picture Engineers established this 1.33:1 picture shape, with a projection aperture of 0.906 x 0.680 inches. This shape and 35mm's other dimensions were closely followed internationally, the metric equivalent being 23.11 x 17.25mm. When later 16mm and other narrower 'sub-standard' gauges were introduced, these too we designed to be compatible with or close to the same 1.33:1 frames.

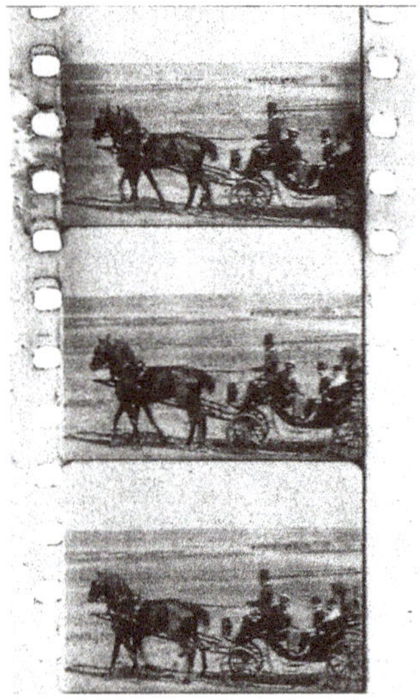

An old 35mm film clip, showing its 1.33:1 aspect ratio

Time for a change?

The first serious possibility of a change to the shape of cinema screens came at the end of the 1920s, along with the coming of sound and a brief flurry of interest in introducing widescreen cinema. It was even being suggested that it was time to abandon 35mm in favour of a new wider gauge, providing the extra space needed to make room for the sound-on-film optical tracks and offering an opportunity to present audiences with a wider, more 'dynamic' picture.

Looking to both science and art for a more shapely alternative

Unlike 35mm, which had emerged, back in 1893, from Edison's Research Laboratory without a wider prior debate about the choice of its 4:3 picture shape, this time many more eyes and minds were recruited onto various committees and viewing panels to consider any artistic, engineering and psychological evidence to support any future change of shape. Researchers were sent off to museums and art galleries to see if the great master painters could offer any guidance. The Kodak Research Department published a report in 1930, after studying 250 works of art. Although restricted to only those painted in the wider than tall landscape format, the results would disappoint those in favour of wider screens. The final graph peaked at the existing 1.33:1, with an average only a little wider at 1.4:1. There was to be much talk of 'whirling squares', 'dynamic symmetry' and the 'golden mean'.

Beware Greeks bearing Aspect Ratios

No discussion of aspect ratios would be complete without the infamous 'Golden Section' raising its perfectly proportioned rectangle. A creation of the ancient Greek mathematician Pythagoras, it can, apparently, if you look hard enough, be seen to have influenced the design of classical architecture and a number sequence linked to its calculation is also found in the beauties of nature like flower petals and snowflakes. We will not dwell on all the maths involved, but it ends up giving us a 'perfect' ratio of 1.618:1. An entertaining source of information on this fascinating aspect ratio was Disney's Oscar-nominated cartoon *Donald in Mathmagic Land.* Released in cinemas in 1959, it went on to become one of the studio's most popular educational subjects. Ironically, after spending much of the film extolling the virtues of this perfectly shaped rectangle, the film itself was seen mostly in classrooms using l6mm prints projected onto a 1.33:1 screen, and this is still the ratio of the current DVD version.

Although, according to the theory, we should all instinctively prefer to watch moving pictures in the golden ratio of 1.618:1, we don't always cooperate. A much later study by Philips, preceding the move to widescreen TV, offered a panel of viewers a choice of formats, which included the golden section. Although most liked the idea of a wider picture there was no particular preference and choices sometimes changed depending on the screen size and viewing distance. Although the world of moving pictures didn't seem to be particularly enamoured by the golden section, the 'card' industry was, using its shape to make the first credit cards even more appealing.

1930s graph showing the choice of aspect ratio for the 'top 250' works of art

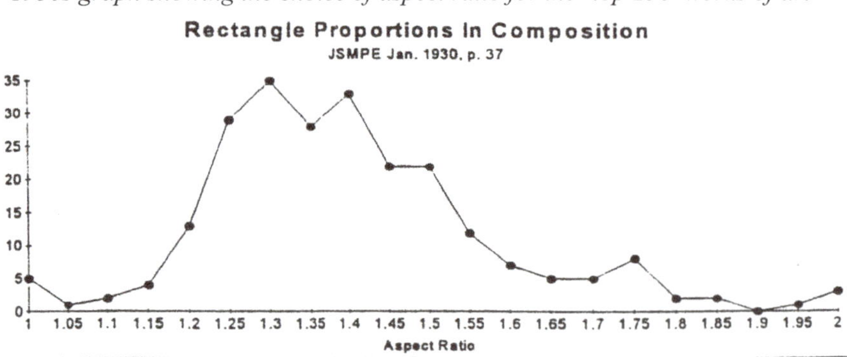

Creating the classical 'Golden Section' rectangle

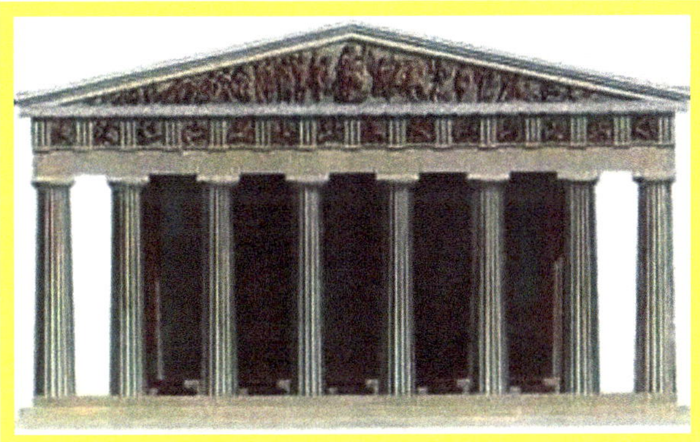

If the length of a straight line is divided into two parts, one short and one long, in such a way that the ratio of its full length to the larger part is the same as that of the larger to the smaller part, then if the smaller part becomes the height and the larger the width, then 'hey presto!' you have the most artistic and perfect 1:1.618 shape for a credit card!

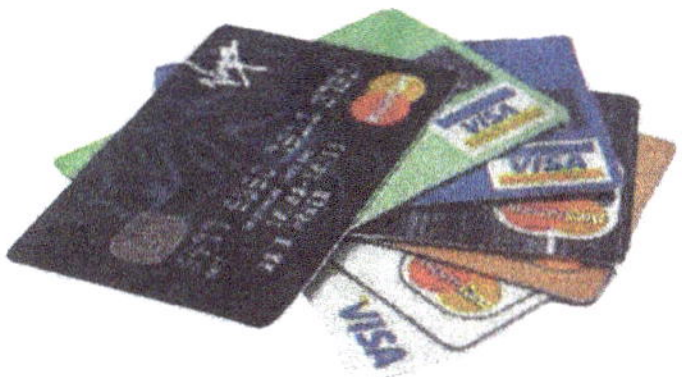

Still looking at different views

Back during the 1930s debate, it was also argued that the art of moving pictures is a completely different medium to that of displaying still images which can be individually framed knowing the subject matter will stay put. It was suggested that a constantly changing aspect ratio would offer the ideal solution. In the silent era, the iris effect was popular, and directors like D.W. Griffith often masked off part of the image to highlight the action. Bell & Howell could supply 52 differently shaped mattes for the gate of their 35mm camera, and another vignetting device had moving blades which could also change the shape of the picture, even when the camera was running.

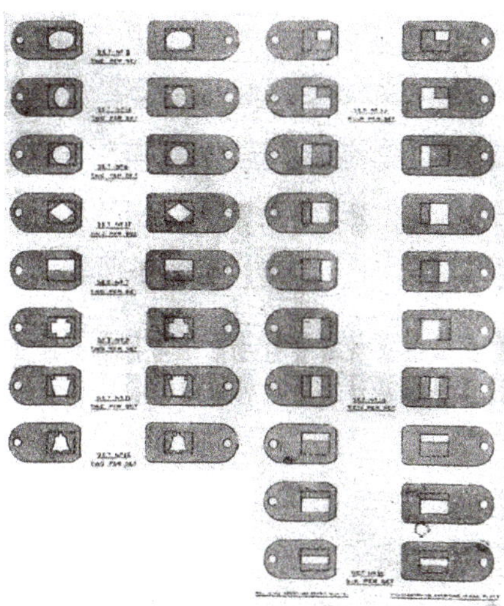

A few of the gate masks available to change the shape of the picture during the silent era

The Russian director, Sergei Eisenstein, in Hollywood at the time, proposed that any new film format should have a 'dynamic square' frame which could accommodate any required aspect ratio, horizontal or vertical. Experiments, over the coming years, which employed a constantly

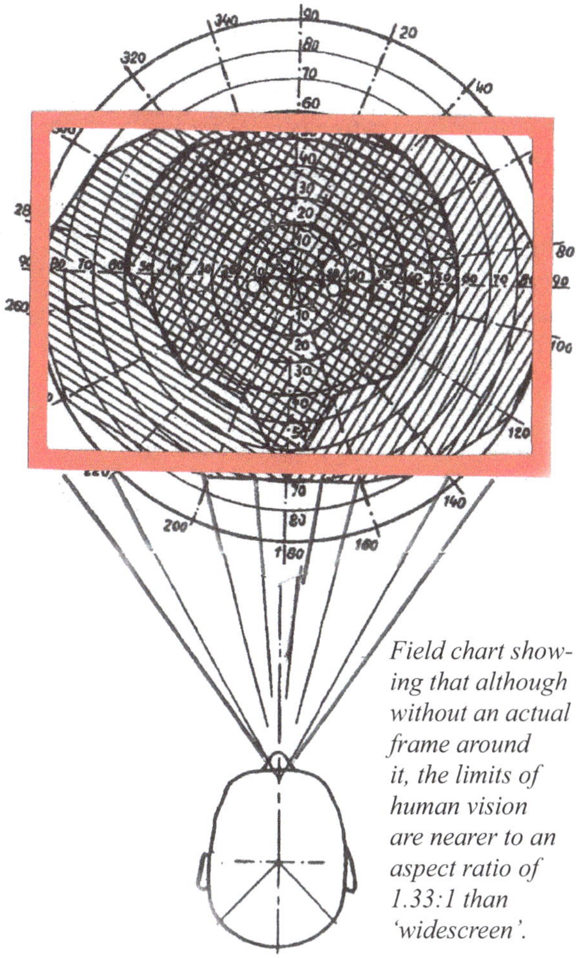

Field chart showing that although without an actual frame around it, the limits of human vision are nearer to an aspect ratio of 1.33:1 than 'widescreen'.

changing screen shape have shown that for certain types of film-making this idea can be quite effective, but for normal story telling it can become distracting (like some say 3D is). Of course, a fixed frame does have help from the camera, which, like our own view of a moving world, has the added facility of being able to constantly pan and tilt to capture and re-frame the images.

Are wider screens more natural?

The knowledge of the limits of human vision also provides conflicting evidence. Field charts of the binocular coverage, both including peripheral vision, or just the much narrower central area of acuity, where we can see and concentrate on a sharp image, are again near to 1.33:1, although without a frame around it. This led to inventors coming up with new kinds of screens which eliminated the familiar hard-edged black masking, letting the picture gradually disappear into a dark, or illuminated surround.

Despite there being no overwhelming evidence to support a move to wider screens, many still thought that they enhanced the viewing experience. In practice, most human activity takes place in the horizontal plane and evolution has provided us with easier and greater eye and head movement horizontally than vertically. If this factor is taken into account, perhaps psychologically, given a choice, we prefer wider screens.

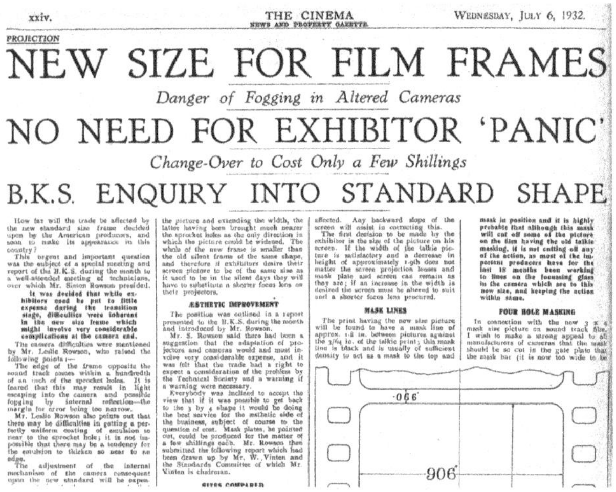
xxiv. THE CINEMA NEWS AND PROPERTY GAZETTE WEDNESDAY, JULY 6, 1932.

PROJECTION

NEW SIZE FOR FILM FRAMES

Danger of Fogging in Altered Cameras

NO NEED FOR EXHIBITOR 'PANIC'

Change-Over to Cost Only a Few Shillings

B.K.S. ENQUIRY INTO STANDARD SHAPE

How far will the trade be affected by the new standard size frame decided upon by the American producers, and soon to make its appearance in this country?

This urgent and important question was the subject of a special meeting and report of the B.K.S. during the month to a well-attended meeting of technicians, over which Mr. Simon Rowson presided.

It was decided that while exhibitors need be put to little expense during the transition stage, difficulties were inherent in the new size frame which might involve very considerable complications at the camera end.

The camera difficulties were mentioned by Mr. Leslie Rowson, who raised the following points:—

The edge of the frame opposite the sound track comes within a hundredth of an inch of the sprocket holes. It is feared that this may result in light escaping into the camera and possible fogging by internal reflection—the margin for error being too narrow.

Mr. Leslie Rowson also points out that there may be difficulties in getting a perfectly uniform coating of emulsion so near to the sprocket hole; it is not impossible that there may be a tendency for the emulsion to thicken so near to an edge.

The adjustment of the internal mechanism of the camera consequent upon the new standard will be expen- the picture and extending the width, the latter having been brought much nearer the sprocket holes as the only direction in which the picture could be widened. The whole of the new frame is smaller than the old silent frame of the same shape, and therefore if exhibitors desire their screen picture to be of the same size as it used to be in the silent days they will have to substitute a shorter focus lens on their projectors.

ÆSTHETIC IMPROVEMENT

The position was outlined in a report presented to the B.K.S. during the month and introduced by Mr. Rowson.

Mr. S. Rowson said there had been a suggestion that the adaptation of projectors and cameras would and must involve very considerable expense, and it was felt that the trade had a right to expect a consideration of the problem by the Technical Society and a warning if a warning were necessary.

Everybody was inclined to accept the view that if it was possible to get back to the 3 by 4 shape it would be doing the best service for the æsthetic side of the business, subject of course to the question of cost. Mask plates, he pointed out, could be produced for the matter of a few shillings each. Mr. Rowson then submitted the following report which had been drawn up by Mr. W. Vinten and the Standards Committee of which Mr. Vinten is chairman.

SIZES COMPARED

affected. Any backward slope of the screen will assist in correcting this.

The first decision to be made by the exhibitor is the size of the picture on his screen. If the width of the talkie picture is satisfactory and a decrease in height of approximately 1-9th does not matter the screen projection lenses and mask plate and screen can remain as they are; if an increase in the width is desired the screen must be altered to suit and a shorter focus lens procured.

MASK LINES

The print having the new size picture will be found to have a mask line of approx. 1-8 in. between pictures against the 3/64 in. of the talkie print; this mask line is black and is usually of sufficient density to act as a mask to the top and

mask in position and it is highly probable that although this mask will cut off some of the picture on the film having the old talkie masking, it is not cutting off any of the action, as most of the important producers have for the last 18 months been working to lines on the focussing glass in the camera which are to this new size, and keeping the action within same.

FOUR HOLE MASKING

In connection with the new 3 x 4 mask size picture on sound track film, I wish to make a strong appeal to all manufacturers of cameras that the mask should be so cut in the gate plate that the mask bar (it is now too wide to be

·066"

906"

Don't panic! Not a prediction of the end of 35mm film prints in 80 years time, but just the introduction of the Academy aperture in 1932

False start for wider screens

While all this discussion was going on, a few privileged American audiences were already being treated to widescreen movies. These were being tried out by the major studios, photographed and projected using various wide-film formats ranging from 56mm to 70mm with aspect ratios from 1.66:1 to 2.15:1. This experiment was short-lived, as its promoters failed to convince the industry that the added cost of widescreen was necessary to attract cinemagoers who, despite the economic depression, were already flocking into theatres to see and hear the new talkies. In case there was a change of minds in the future, the SMPE did have a common wide film format ready. This was 50mm wide with a 1.8:1 aspect ratio.

With the idea of introducing widescreen cinema put on hold, at least for the next 20 years, the search for a new aspect ratio lost much of its impetus and in 1931 the various committees were disbanded without declaring a winner.

Making room for sound

Even without the adoption of a wider film format, the coming of sound was already changing the shape of cinema screens. The separate sound-on-disc systems initially left the full 35mm silent aperture, with its 1.33:1 aspect ratio, untouched, but the rival sound-on-film optical tracks stole some of the picture area down the left hand side.

The space given up depended on the overall width of the different types of optical track, which varied from 0.100 in. to 0.125 in. During the transitional period, many of the last silent films were hastily given a soundtrack by lopping a strip off the side of the original picture. The same fate befell later sound-on-film versions (and dual-purpose prints) of some sound-on-disc films, which had originally used the full silent frame.

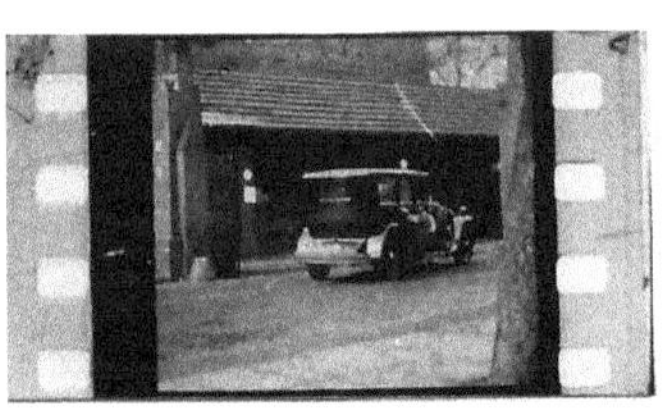

35 mm format

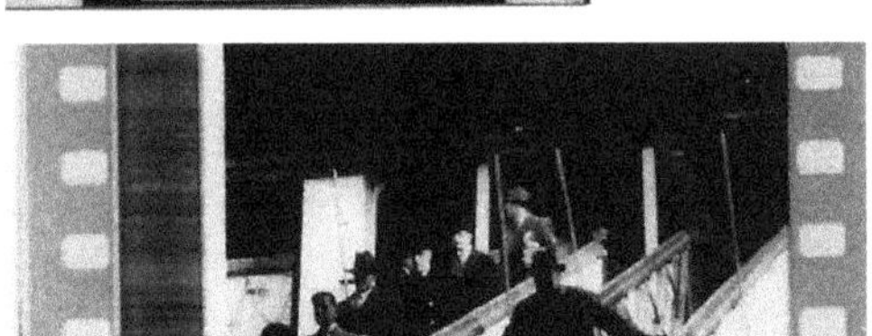

SMPE 50mm wide format

In 1931 SMPE had its new 50mm format ready, but it was never called upon to replace 35mm. It had an 'ideal' aspect ratio of 1.8:1, very close to today's 16x9, 1.78:1

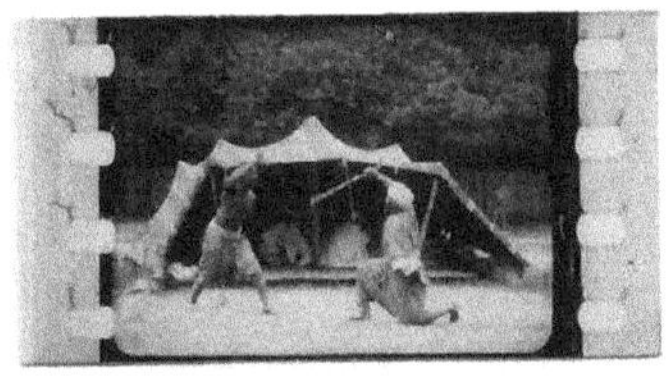

Examples of the different shapes of 35mm frames being shown during the early 1930s

Top: Silent (Disc)

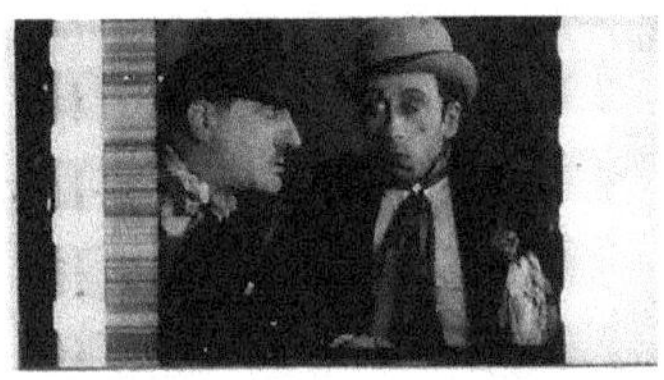

Centre: Early Sound

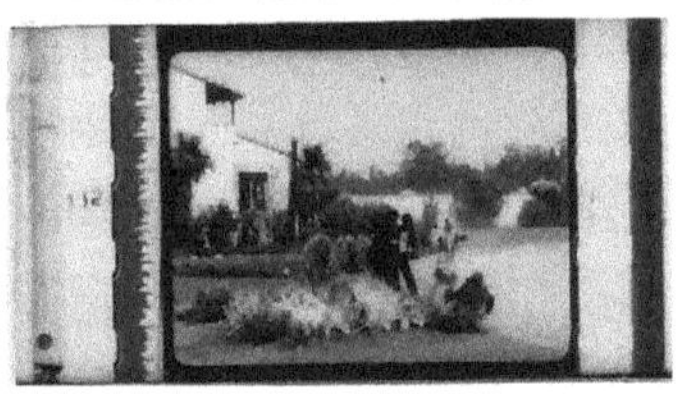

Bottom: Reduced Academy

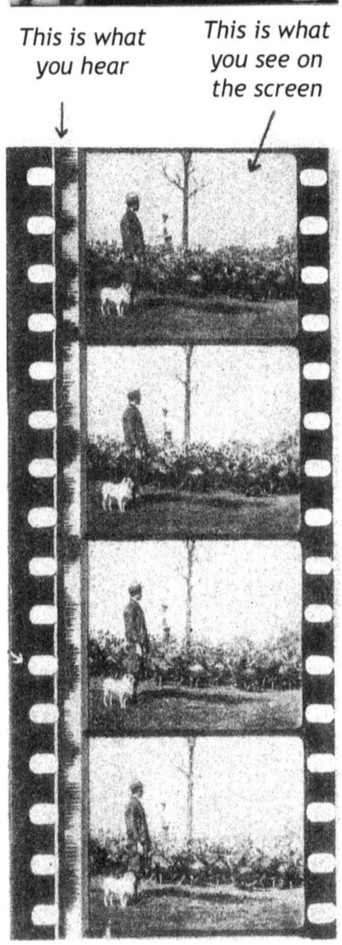

Contemporary illustration from 1928 showing how you can now hear as well as see 35mm film, albeit at the cost of a squarer picture

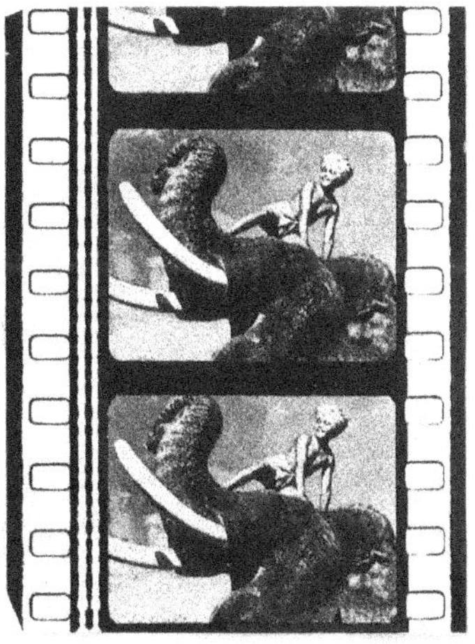

An Academy sound print with its familiar wider frame lines

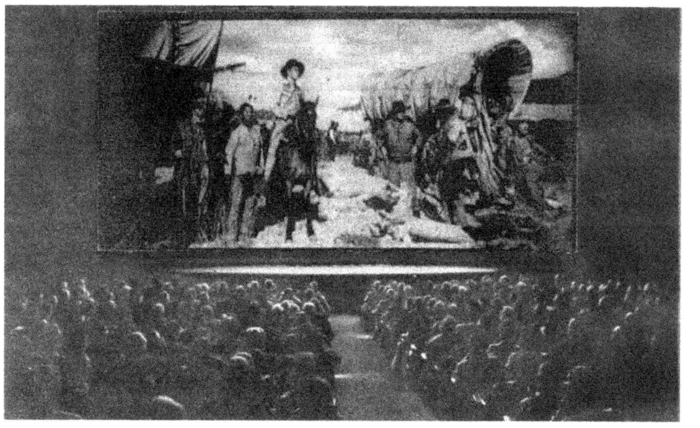

At the end of the 1920s and early 1930s a few lucky American audiences had the chance to see the shape of the cinema screen to come. Others had to wait for another 20 years. (The Big Trail 1930)

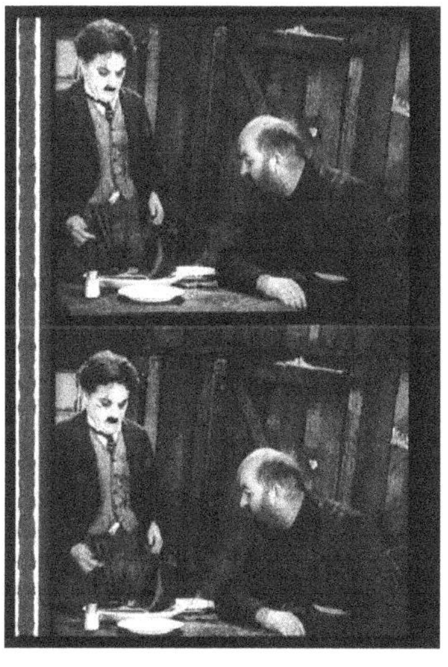

An optical sound track added to Chaplin's 'The Gold Rush' (1924). In this case resulting in the loss of part of the silent frame down the left hand side, which will be further cropped vertically if shown or copied through an Academy gate

Unwelcome change of shape

The new optical soundtracks had to be masked off in the projector's gate, creating an additional aperture. Sometimes called the 'Movietone' aperture, after the first widely used optical sound system, it wasn't fully standardized, but the most often quoted dimensions, including for the pre-cut plates supplied by projector manufacturers at the time, was 0.800 x 0.680in. The vertical centre line of the picture was moved over from the centre of the film to the right and its aspect ratio reduced to an almost square 1.18:1. Many theatres also fitted early forms of variable screen masking, like a sliding mask or hinged flap, which was moved into position when a sound film was being shown.

By common consent, the resulting 'early sound' squarer picture was considered aesthetically less pleasing. It was also leading to production problems, with group shots needing the less sensitive microphones of the time to be positioned further away above the actors, who now couldn't be properly back-lit, without the risk of the lights intruding into the taller frames.

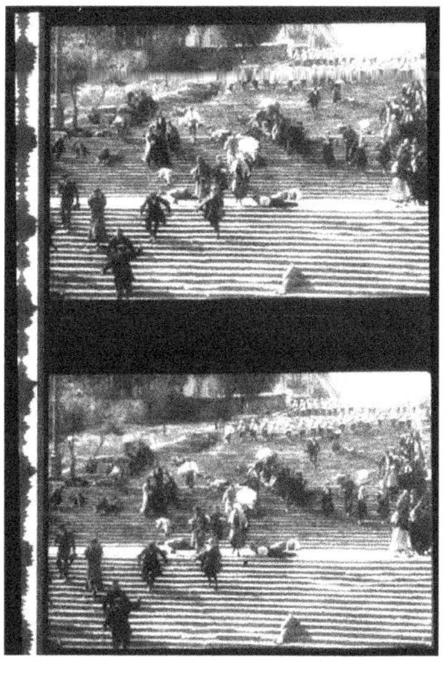

The Battleship Potemkin' (1925) Correctly re-printed, with no loss of picture, by reducing the full silent frame to produce a compatible Academy sound print

Bring back 4x3

At first, all the sound films with an optical track were composed and projected using this 'early sound' format. However, it wasn't long before its disliked taller frames were being masked down in the projector's gate in order to return to the original 1.33:1 aspect ratio. This practice required another 'reduced' or 'proportional' aperture.

Again, no standard, but a popular choice was 0.800 x 0.600 inch. Ideally, a shorter focal length projection lens was also used to maintain the same height of the screen. The Exhibitors showing films through this smaller aperture showed little regard for the cameramen's carefully composed images.

The best the projectionist could do was to adjust the framing, or racking, control to effectively re-compose the cropped picture, and try to prevent the loss of any important part of the image, including the titles.

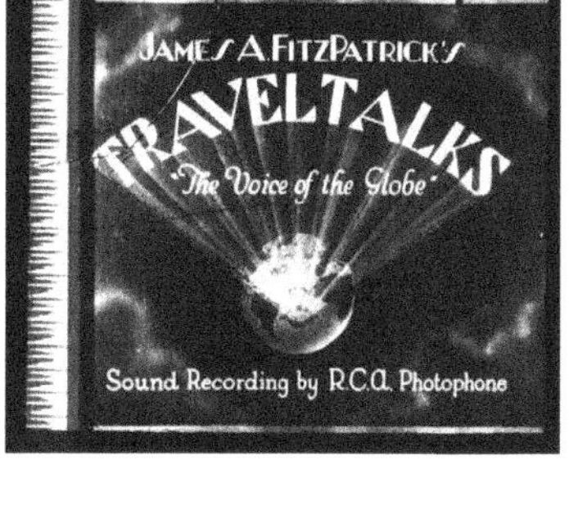

Care is needed when showing the almost square early sound format to avoid cropping any of the image, including titles, which often occupied the full height of the frame

The studios began to complain that their pictures were being compromised by being projected through different apertures. Although the earlier silent and sound-on-disk films were on the way out, cameramen were still obliged to compose for the proportional aperture, but 'protect' the, still exposed, taller frames. With the proportional projection aperture becoming the de facto standard, in 1932, the Academy of Motion Picture Arts and Sciences moved to make it official. An earlier agreement, that the tracks on 35mm release prints should not exceed 0.100 in. in overall width, allowed for a slightly larger 0.820 x 0.615in. aperture. It was also stated, that only the 'Academy' frame be exposed in the camera, which would result in wider black frame lines on the print. These would ensure the correct framing in the projector, with the added advantage of making joins less visible. All this was circulated to interested parties, including the BKS in Britain.

Despite concerns about the picture being too close to the perforations, the proposals were accepted. In the event, the size of the frame was revised again before the SMPE published the final 35mm Sound Film Standard in 1934. Still to be known as the Academy projection aperture, it was established at 0.825 x 0.600 in. This actually produced a slightly wider aspect ratio of 1.375:1, but, as pointed out at the time, if projected at the average rake of 14 degrees, the downward stretch effect presented a picture of about 1.33:1 on the screen. All American and British films were now being composed and projected using the Academy aperture, but its adoption in Europe was more gradual, with the original sound format still being used well into the 1930s. These too, can suffer some loss of picture if shown, or copied, with an Academy aperture.

Other aspects to look out for

From 1932, most studio 35mm cameras were fitted with the new Academy gate aperture, theirs being 0.868 x 0.631 in. However, many others, including some 'mute' newsreel and documentary cameras only altered the viewfinder markings, continuing to expose the old silent frame. When printed, the picture occupying the soundtrack area was lost, but the full height still contained an image. For those trying to ascertain the date of footage, these have the look of much earlier sound films, but were always intended to be shown through the later Academy gate. It is worth noting that the silent aperture was never assigned to cinema history, as it continued to be used within studios to provide the maximum image area for back projection, and other applications where the need for accommodating a soundtrack was not required.

Although silent films were soon forgotten, some of the most popular were later revived, usually with some form of added sound track. These could be properly re-printed, with their full silent frames optically reduced and re-centered within an Academy frame, but others just added a soundtrack to a cheaper contact print, resulting in an off-centre cropped picture on the screen.

Usually the most noticeable effect is on the lopsided titles which, if the designers made the full use of the silent frame, have parts of them missing. Unfortunately these poorer prints are sometimes the only source available for present transfers. Sometimes alternative 16mm copies can be found with a reduced full silent frame, but these too can suffer from being made from the later poorly produced 35mm originals.

Today, with the much greater respect for original aspect ratios, and if the availability of suitable source material allows, even the earlier squarer 1.18:1 sound format has been preserved on the most recent digital transfers. It is good to see this happening, even with the risk of complaints from the less informed viewers who think there is something wrong with the shape of the picture.

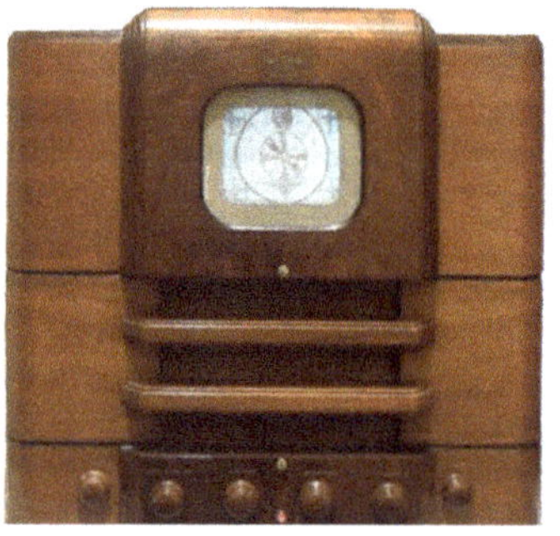

In the 1930s, with cinemas content with their 4:3 screens, alternative 'small screen' pictures began to appear.

Cinema stays special

It is interesting, with the benefit of hindsight, to see how cinema has survived and thrived throughout the decades, in spite of the growing competition from Televison, even at a time when it is possible to buy Ultra High Definition 4K resolution television receivers with superbly bright and high contrast displays and screen sizes of anything up to 65 inches for a few hundred pounds. The real secret of cinema's success over the years, as we discuss in our later sections of showmanship, is that a visit to the cinema is a special event, a social occasion to be enjoyed and an experience to be shared with others.

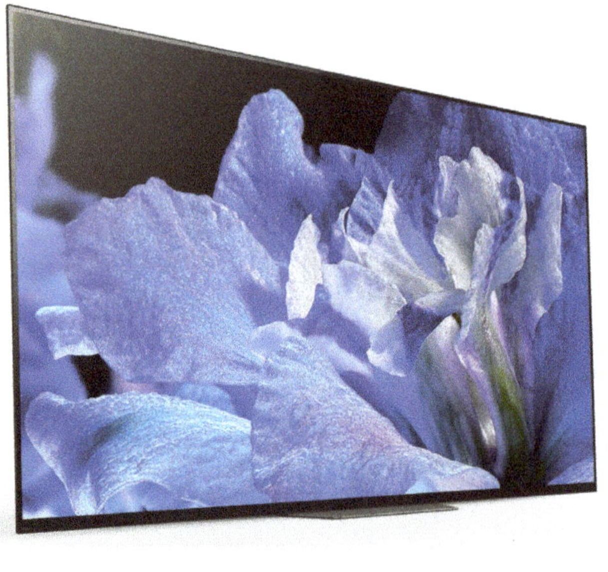

All shapes and sizes - Smaller formats for everyone

Film archivists and restorers have to be able to deal with a wide range of different film formats and as well as understanding the technology and the history of 35mm and larger formats it is important that they also have a good knowledge of the many different smaller formats that have played an important part in cinema history.

By the early 1900s, the first era of the wider and unusual film formats was over in the face of the trade's general acceptance of the basic Edison gauge as the de facto standard. It would still take a few more years before international agreement about 35mm's finer dimensions, particularly its sprocket holes, ensured its wider compatibility. For example, film stock could now be supplied already perforated, knowing it would run through all the different film making apparatus being manufactured around the world.

Home cinema takes shape

In the coming years, most new gauges and formats would be smaller, to help tempt amateurs to be in at the start of the new hobby of movie making and home cinema shows. As early as 1899, British pioneer Birt Acres designed the 'Birtac'. This lower-cost (still 10 guineas) combined camera and projector produced images a quarter the size of 35mm by simply splitting normal film down the middle with two of its original perforations at one side of each frame. The idea of slicing up an existing gauge as a starting point for new more economic formats would be used again in the coming years. Many of the makers of professional equipment also entered the narrow gauge market. Prestwich advertised their 'Junior' camera using daylight loading half-inch (13mm) film but few, if any, were ever sold. Gaumont joined in with its 'Pocket Chrono' taking 15mm film with centre perforations, a popular ploy to leave the maximum area available for the picture. It was also notable, in 1900, for being the first amateur cine camera driven by a clockwork motor. Centre perforations were also a feature of the 17.5mm Ernemann Kino camera which, with various attachments, also allowed it to be used for printing and projection.

One of the more successful amateur outfits was the Biokam sold by The Warwick Trading Company, which received the backing of a couple of British pioneer film makers. It was first promoted and demonstrated by T. C. Hepworth, father of Cecil, in 1899. For six guineas you got a 'Combined Cinematograph & Snapshot Camera, Printer, Projector, Reverser and Enlarger'. It too used 17.5mm film, but this time by splitting unperforated 35mm stock and punching special shallow space-saving perforations between the frames. The 25 feet of film could take 45 seconds of movies or 700 stills using its single frame release option. You could also buy versions of 'Public Entertainment Films' available at ten shillings each. Most of these were provided by G.A. Smith, who produced both individual Biokam subjects and versions of his professional films using a17.5mm Biokam camera alongside the 35mm. Smith's wife ran the Biokam side of the business, as his attention turned to developing the first commercially successful motion picture colour process, Kinemacolor. The Biokam continued to be advertised until around 1906.

Some of G. A. Smith's Biokam films have since found their way onto Harold Brown's printer to preserve examples of his work which have not survived on 35mm. Despite this early choice of narrow gauge equipment, none managed to popularise home movie making. The emulsions at the time meant that their smaller frames, together with the poorly lit projection, didn't produce very good pictures. Most of the few early enthusiasts

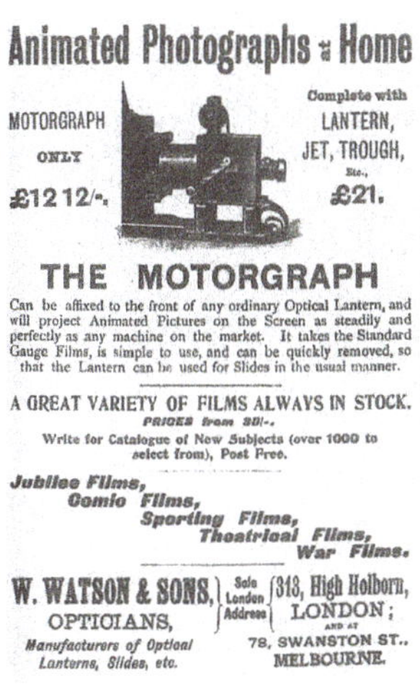

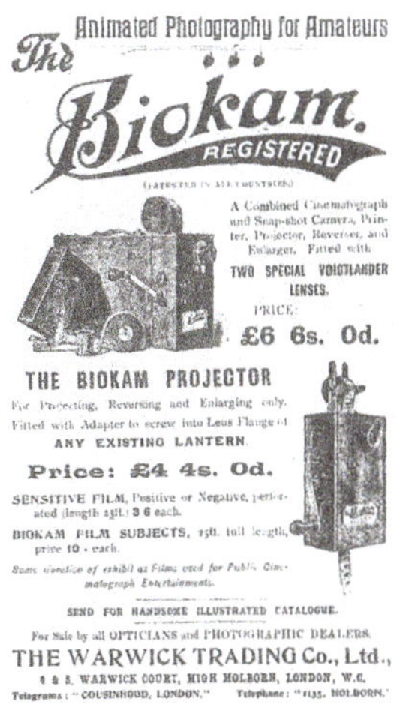

There was a choice of big or small cine formats for amateurs as early as 1899

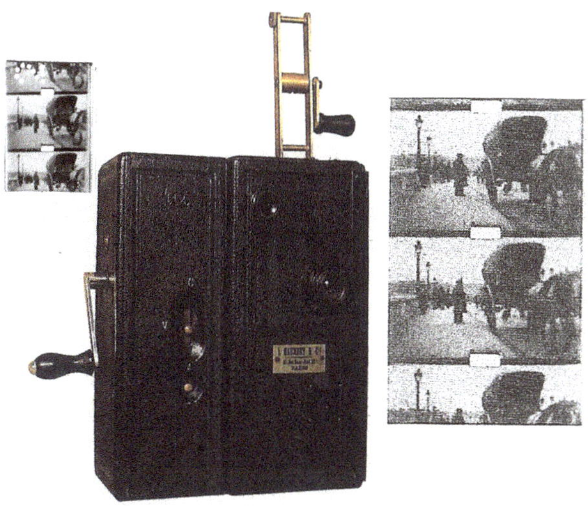

15mm centre-perf Gaumont Chrono-de-Poche camera / projector 1900

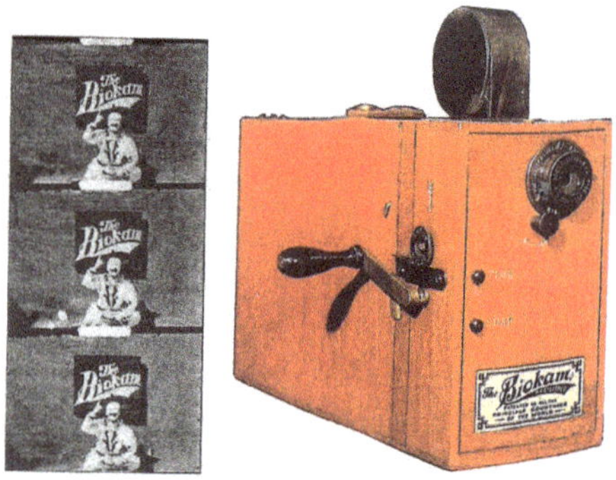

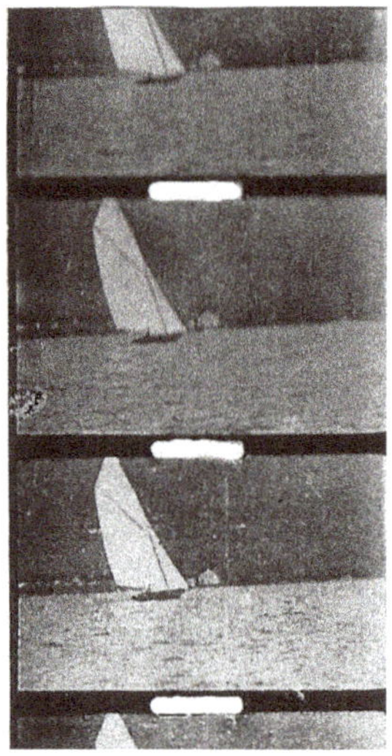

Above: 7.5mm Biokam film and camera. Right: Enlarged Biokam clip shows that as the 1.61:1 images were a little wider than the normal 1.33:1 they could be described as an early widescreen format.

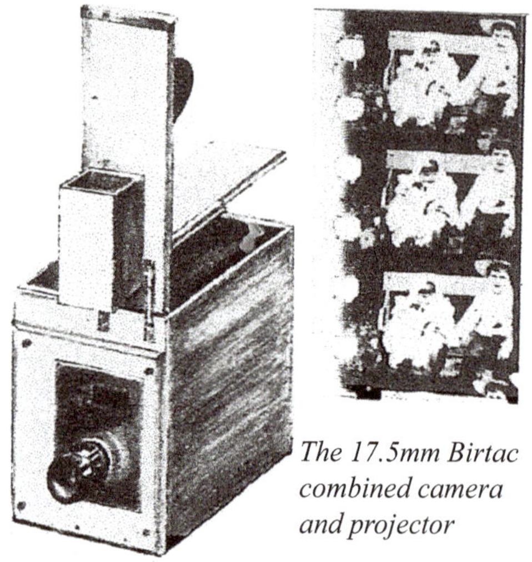

The 17.5mm Birtac combined camera and projector

preferred to use cheaper and lighter weight amateur versions of 35mm equipment. Even so, they still had to pay professional prices for their negative and positive film stock which, after processing and printing, cost around six pence a foot. This was a tidy sum in the early 1900s, remembering that 35mm at sixteen frames a second runs at 60 feet a minute. Most 35mm film finding its way into the home was in the form of short lengths or loops for toy projectors. As a popular choice of light source was an oil lamp or gas mantle, this, together with the highly inflammable nitrate films, often, unknowingly, let a dangerous combination cross the threshold.

Making life safer

Safety, or 'non-flam' film became available in 1912, but it could not match the strength and clarity of nitrate, which remained the industry's choice until the 1950s. This remained so, even after disastrous fires and loss of life had, by 1909, resulted in public showings being highly regulated and licensed, along with strict safety measures, including fireproof projection rooms or 'boxes', and in case of emergencies, adequate fire exits and toilets. However, the new safetyfilm was soon adopted for showings away from licensed cinemas, such as in schools, churches, and the home. The danger of nitrate in the home had become a particular concern. There were stories of children, after discovering how inflammable their films were, gaining more entertainment value from setting them on fire than actually viewing them.

One of the first users of safety film was Edison for his Home Kinetoscope. Its 22mm prints carried three rows of small pictures, about 6mm x 4mm, separated by two rows of perforations, one for each frame. After the first column of pictures was projected, the machine went into reverse to show the middle row, and then reversed again for the third row. If its designers had included a fourth row the need for rewinding would have been avoided! Only sold as a projection format, the prints were made on a special printer by optical reduction from 35mm. To copy them today, an original projector may help, but, like other strange formats, they are now an ideal candidate for digital help.

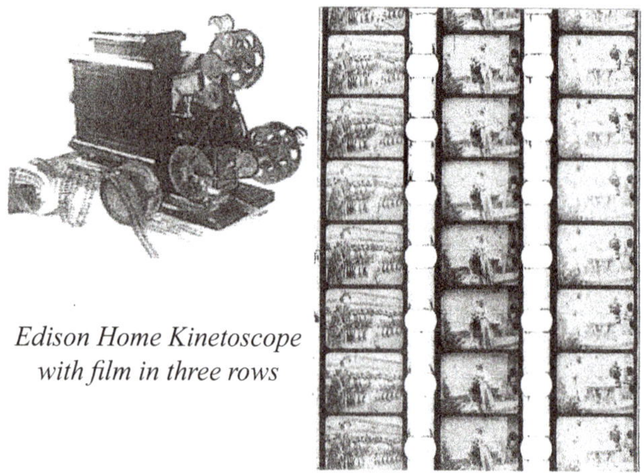

Edison Home Kinetoscope with film in three rows

Where there is a will, there is a way

One of the laboratories making the most of digital film restoration techniques is Haghefilm in Amsterdam, which has attracted work from archives around the world facing challenging restorations. Apart from the more familiar formats, they were also able to cope with an example of Edison' s 22mm Home Kinetoscope, when George Eastman House sent a print of possibly the earliest adaptation of Dickens' *A Christmas Carol* to be enlarged back to 35mm. This was done in stages. First, using their Oxberry Cinescan scanner's universal gate, the full width of the 22mm film with its three columns of images was scanned in blocks of nine. Next, the individual frames were extracted and put in the right order and then digitally stabilised using the perforations as a reference. As when dealing with other forms of reduction printing, it was noticed that visual traces of the original 35mm perforations could just be seen at the extreme edges of the picture. Using these as a second reference produced an even steadier image for the Arrilaser film recorder.

Welcome Pathescope

Another early safety film format, also introduced in 1912, was Pathe's 28mm. Again, it was primarily intended for showing prints made from 35mm films, which only required a small reduction to fit its 19mm x 14mm'frames. It also had a novel perforation layout,

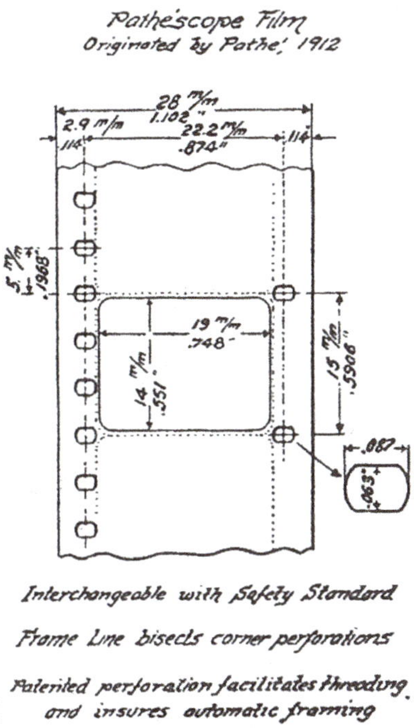

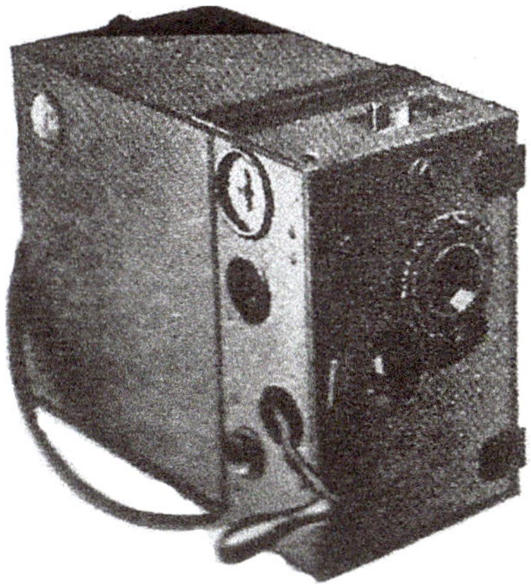

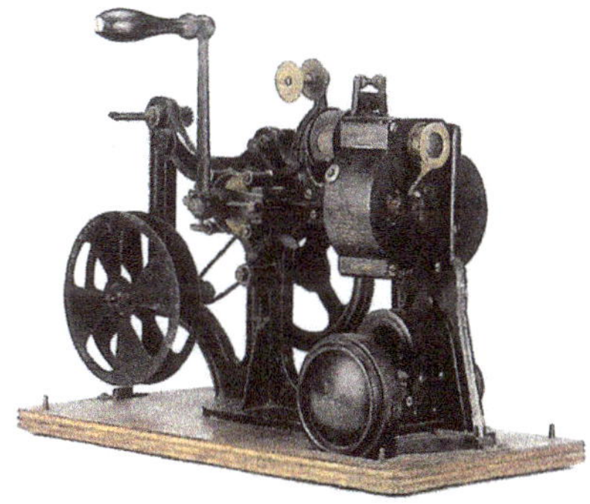

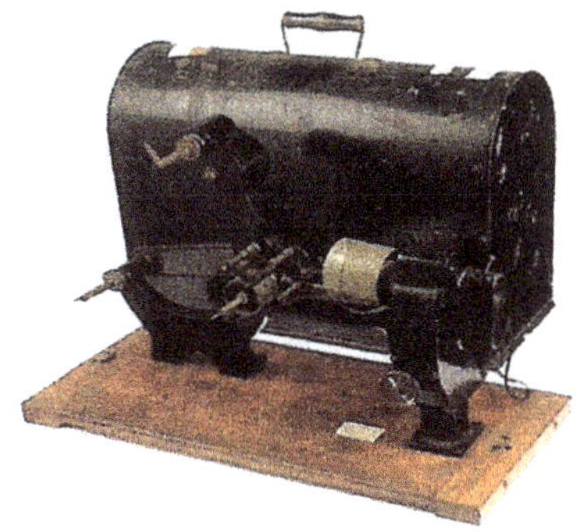

Left: Layout of Pathescope 28mm film from 1912

Above: Pathescope 28mm camera

Right: Pathescope Hand-wound go-anywhere 'sewing machine' projector.

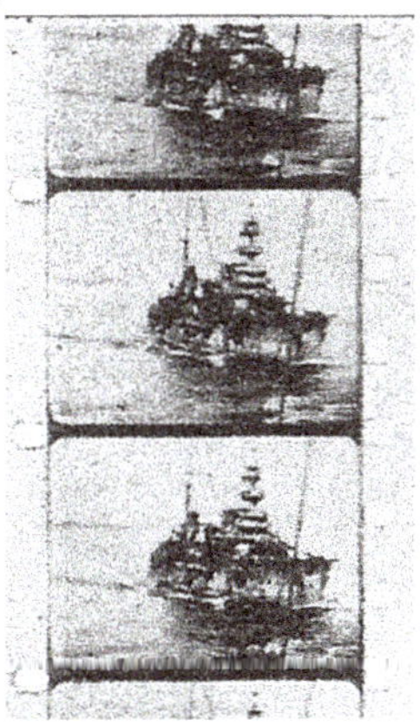

with three perforations per frame on one side to be driven by the sprockets, but only one on the other side for the projector's intermittent claw. This helped the less experienced operators to ensure the correct framing in the projector. 35mm, with its four perfs per frame, can readily go as much as half a picture out of frame, or 'rack', due to incorrect lacing up or faulty joins.

Pathe's first KOK 28mm projector, named after the company's trademark, a crowing cockerel, looked like an old sewing machine, and could put on a show anywhere. It was hand-turned and completely independent of gas or oil lamps, having a built-in generator to power its bulb. Many of its shows at the time would have been without mains electricity.

28mm's heyday

28mm was marketed as Pathescope, a name which would become as familiar as Kodak to an earlier generation of home movie makers and showmen. The 28mm gauge was not only to become popular in Britain and Europe, but was one of the few non-Eastman Kodak inspired gauges to be equally successful in America and Canada. Pathe's projector was built under licence and backed up by a huge library of films for rent. Many of these were educational and religious subjects; but also available were theatrical entertainment films cut down to fit the machines' 400ft spools. A few full-length deluxe specials were printed and most silent stars could be seen on 28mm. At one time, there were over 10,000 machines in use in the USA, many in the field of education. For example, 100 schools in New York City had 28mm projectors.

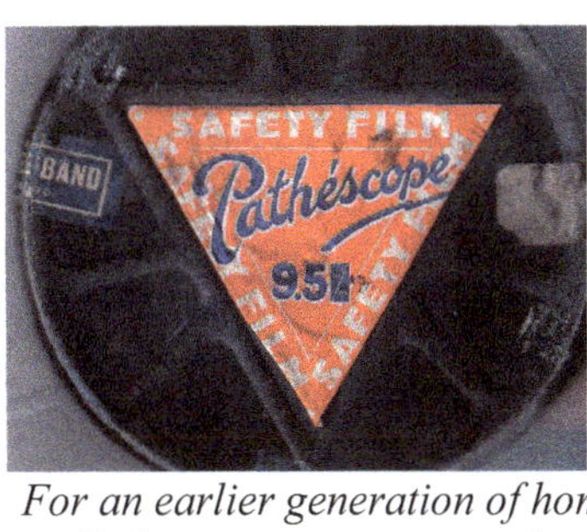

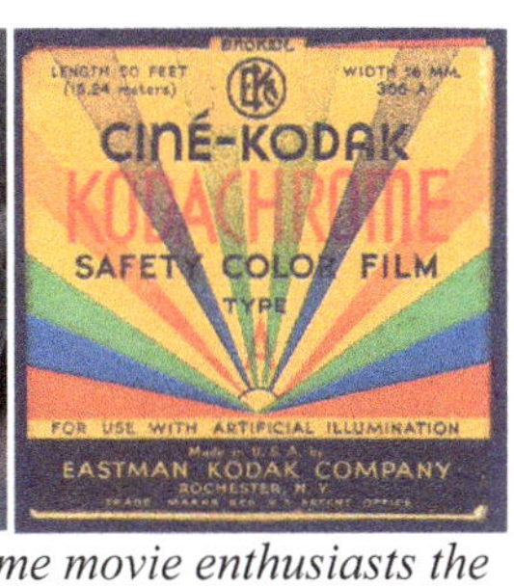

For an earlier generation of home movie enthusiasts the Pathescope name was as familiar as that of Kodak

Perhaps due to their French connections, 28mm was particularly popular in Canada. The Ontario Motion Picture Bureau had over 2500 films available. The progress of 28mm was halted by the First World War, which cut off supplies of film and projectors from Europe. Also the materials needed for its non-flam base were now required for coating aeroplane wings.

To help keep 28mm going in America and Canada, the Victor Company introduced the Victor Safety Cinema which used-the same basic format, but had three perforations on both sides of the frame, not being able to use Pathe's patented arrangement. This period of wide use, together with its longer lasting safety base, has left us with large numbers of 28mm prints, with most archives having at least a few in their vaults. Most of Canada's copies are now in their National Film, Television and Sound Archives, after thousands of prints were discovered stored in an old barn by a French-Canadian Catholic priest and avid film collector.

A project to copy the entire collection onto 35mm film justified the construction of a 28mm pin-registered wet-gate for their Oxberry optical step printer. A similar device is also available on Haghefilm's Oxberry scanner,

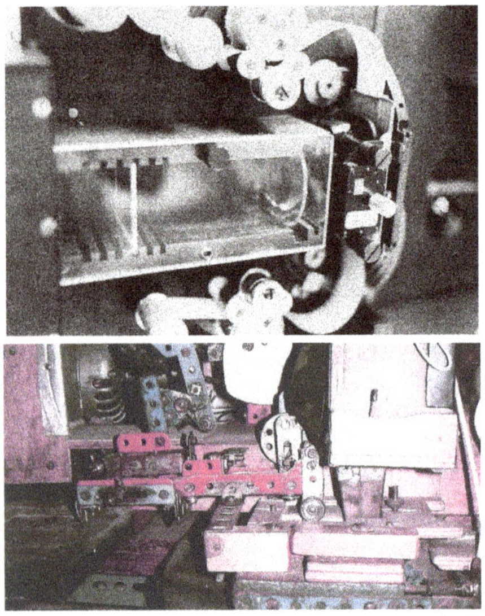

Top: 28mm pin-registered gate on an Oxberry film printer, and below, Harold Brown's Meccano and wood version

which was used more recently to digitally copy onto 35mm a 28mm print about the benefit of fire insurance, for the Library of Congress. In the UK, at the BFI National Film and Television Archive, 28mm took its turn on Harold's printer, an example being silent star Pearl White in 'The Perils of Pauline', a pioneer movie serial once considered lost but now back again on 35mm.

Although mostly remembered as a projection format, Pathe also produced a camera with 400 foot daylight loading magazines, unusually containing nitrate 28mm stock with three perfs per frame on both sides. The gauge did receive a boost, when Victor in the USA lobbied the SMPE to recognise their version as the Safety Non-theatrical Standard in 1918. However its role in this field would increasingly be challenged with the arrival of Eastman Kodak's 16mm gauge in 1923. Pathe's American library closed soon after, but others were still distributing 28mm prints up to the early 1930s, after which they became sought after treasures for collectors.

Movie making for all, available in sizes to suit your budget

Unlike earlier attempts to popularize home movie making, 16mm cameras were loaded with new reversal-type film, which after processing produced a print ready for projection without the extra need and cost of a negative. Although more compact and easier to use than 35mm, the first equipment was still too expensive for most budding amateurs. Looking at 16mm home movies from the 1920s and 1930s, they usually show the better off enjoying themselves at home and abroad.

Pathe tempted those with less to spend, with its rival 9.5mm format, which launched just ahead of 16mm in 1922. It was designed to be as economical as possible. The projector was on the market first to show short 30 foot prints prepared from 35mm professional films. Known as the Pathe Baby, the hand-turned machine, with low-voltage lamp, was specifically aimed at the unskilled operator, with cassette loading and auto-threading. To save film, it had a notched-title device. The film's titles

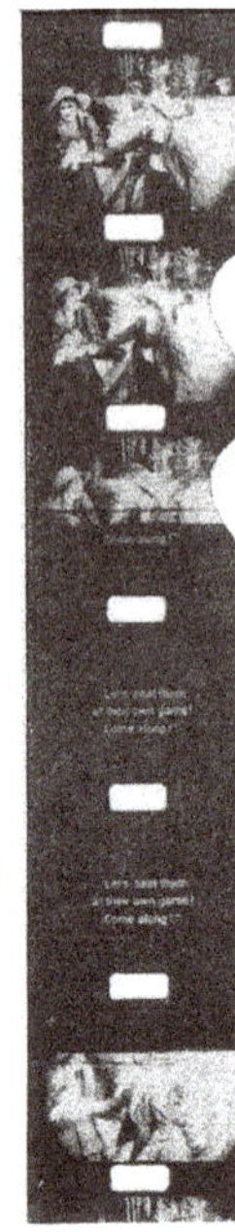

Right: 9.5mm film with notches cut into one edge. The notched-title device enabled the film's titles to be reduced in length to only a couple of frames.

were reduced in length to only a couple of frames. A preceding notch, cut into the picture's edge, triggered a still picture device which held a stationary frame long enough (about 4 seconds) to read it before the intermittent movement was re-engaged. It took a year or so before a camera was added to the outfit so you could include your own films in the show. It too, used easy to load cassettes, known as 'chargers', containing 30 feet of reversal film. To make the most of it, the first models ran at 14 frames per second. A notch cutter was available for your own titles and static scenes, which allowed the opportunity to also make use of Pathe's early form of a 'compression' system to make your own footage last as long as possible.

Battle of the gauges

Although much narrower than 16mm, Pathe claimed that its centre perforations left a projected picture area (approx. 9.2mm x 6.3mm) close to 16mm's 9.76mm x 7.26mm. They did cheat a bit. The Pathe Baby's pressure runners were cut away at the gate to project the full width of the film. After a few showings this left a rainstorm of scratches down both sides of the picture, to join the inevitable signs of damage left when the claw missed the sprocket hole and landed on the picture.

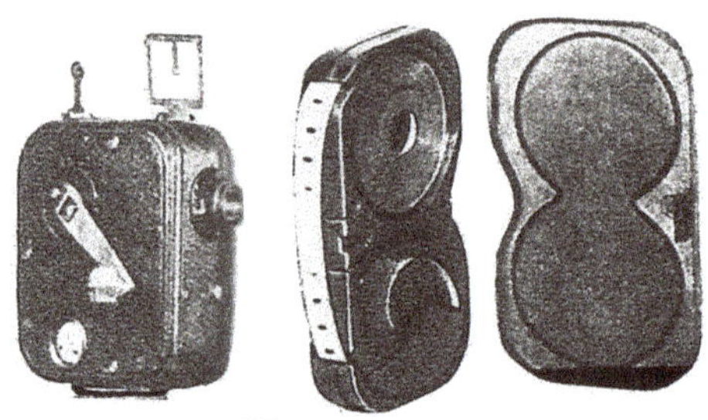

Left: Pathe-Baby 9mm camera with film in charger.

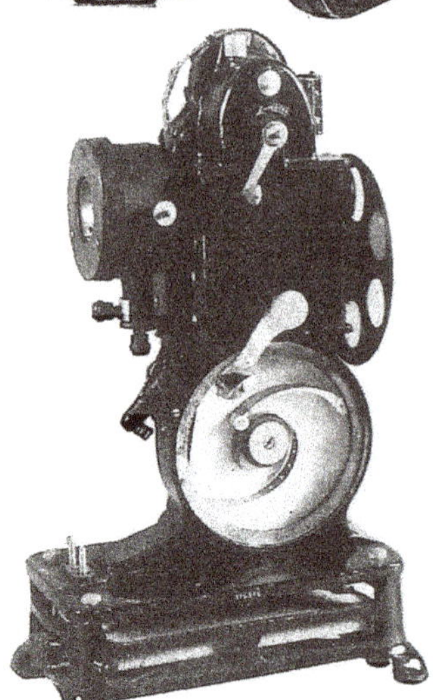

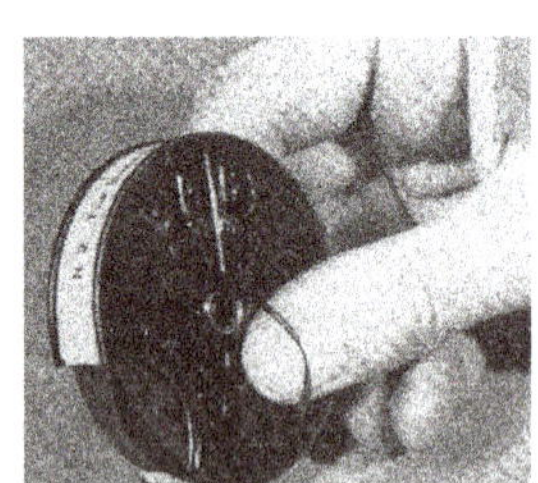

Left: Pathe-Baby 9mm projector and (below) film in its enclosed container

If the worst happened, you could actually buy spare sprocket holes! They looked like a little box of sequins. The small circular patch of film, with a new sprocket hole in the middle, was stuck over the torn one with film cement. Later models of 9.5mm projectors restricted the aperture to within the runners (8.2mm x 6.2mm A.R. 1.32:1). They could also run longer films on conventional spools and without the notched titles, which may have suffered under their brighter and hotter lamps.

Making room for sound

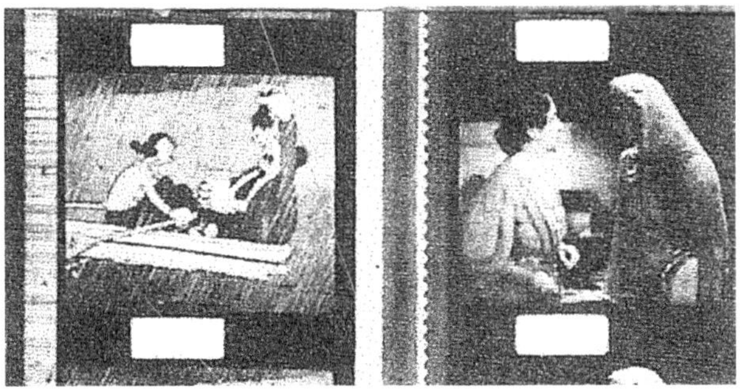

9.5mm sound prints with density and area optical sound tracks

When optical soundtracks were added, 9.5mm, like 35mm, had to give up some of its picture width, leaving a nearly square image (6.2mm x 7.3mm A.R. 1.18:1), with reductions from 35mm now having to be cropped at the sides. 16mm simply sacrificed one of its rows of perforations, leaving the picture intact. Although only driven by one set of perforations, this didn't seem to affect the stability, and even silent projectors in the future only had single-perf sprockets and claws, so, if desired, could cope with a sound print. Apart from special professional combined sound systems, most camera stock remained double-perf until, in more recent times, the Super-16 format took over the extra space for its wider picture, (12.05mm x 7.26mm A.R. 1.66:1).

16mm cameras, likely to be used by amateurs, also became available for single-perf stock in case they wished to add sound, usually recorded on a magnetic stripe applied to their reversal films. One early complication was that the SMPE standard chose to give up the right hand row of perforations, relative to a correctly orientated picture, for the new track. Unfortunately, the German DIN standard selected the left, due, it is said, to misreading the SMPE drawings. From then on, the word 'IMAGE' was always added to film specification diagrams to show which way round it was supposed to be. For a few years, before a revision adopted the SMPE arrangement as the common standard, both coexisted, with some of the first European sound projector manufacturers choosing to go with DIN. Prints with the different geometry could usually be run on the other's projectors but you either had to develop the skill of reading any titles backwards, or buy a 'DIN mirror' or prism attachment to correct the now laterally reversed image. For those not in the know, a DIN print was often dismissed as a faulty copy.

An unkind cut

One feature shared by both 16mm and 9.5mm was that their perforation pitch was very close and they both had 40 frames to the foot. This helped to simplify the design of dual-gauge projectors. If you didn't have one of these, it also offered another conversion opportunity. If you had a 16mm print, but wished it was 9.5mm, a service was available to physically change it by slicing off the 16mm's perforations, leaving a width of 9.5mm, and then punching the centre perforations on the original frame lines. Even sound films could be converted by shifting the process off-centre to include a portion of the 16mm's soundtrack at the expense of some of the picture on the left, which, as proper 9.5mm sound used the DIN position, was now also back to front. It would have been a way to recycle old 16mm DIN sound prints, which, when born again as 9.5mm, would project correctly. If spotted, many collectors of 9.5mm films try to avoid these inferior conversions.

A new gauge from the country

As Kodak's 16mm soon began to attract the more professional non-theatrical, industrial, and educational markets, Pathe didn't try to promote 9.5mm into these fields, but fought back in 1925 with its 17.5mm 'Rural' format aimed at providing portable shows in country areas without permanent cinemas. At first sight, it could be mistaken for 16mm. This time to claim the maximum frame area, (165 sq.mm, compared to 16mm's 80.5 sq.mm), its smaller square perforations actually encroached into the picture, to be hidden by the very rounded corners of the projector's gate, which produced a screen shape like an old TV.

At first, not seen much outside France, it was supported with a library of excellent quality full-length reductions of mostly French and Italian silents. These included the original four and three-quarter hour version of Abel Gance's epic 'Napoleon' from 1927. Some of this 17.5mm footage later also found its way onto Harold Brown's BFI printer to enlarge it back to 35mm, helping Kevin Brownlow's reconstruction of the film.

In 1934, it was relaunched more widely as a sound format, with an optical track added in the same manner

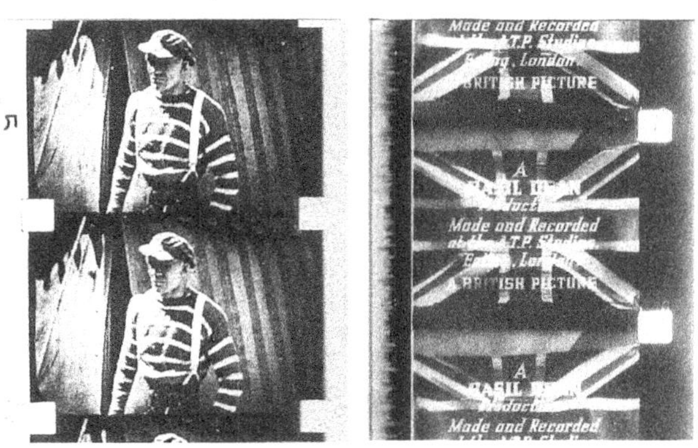

Left: 17.5mm Pathe 'Rural' silent format, 1926
Right: Sound version from 1934

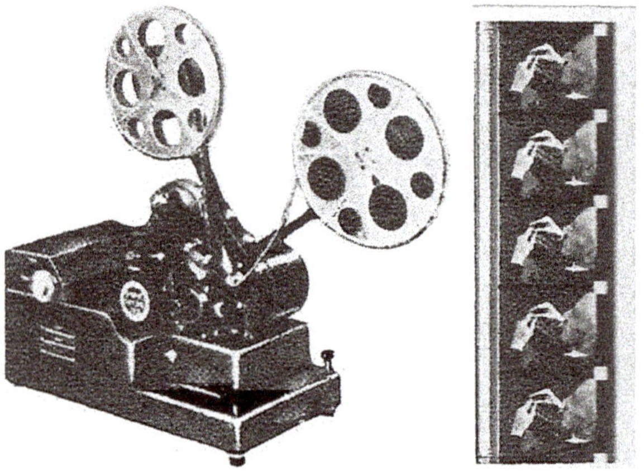

Pathescope Home Talkie - last of the 17.5mm machines

as 16mm with single-perf prints (DIN position) and the image now kept inside the sprocket hole area. To help promote Pathe's own Home Talkie 17.5mm projector when it arrived in Britain, an outfit was used in 'The Pathe Cinema Van', which, for a few months during 1935, provided film shows to over 16,000 travellers on express trains between Kings Cross and Leeds. The format didn't make tracks to capture a wider usage, as it soon became obvious that 16mm was gaining the international market. Before losing out, quite a few British features from the 1930s, mostly from BIP and Ealing Studios, appeared on 17.5mm before the ill-fated gauge finally disappeared during WWII.

Another gauge-related war story tells how, to keep them safe, British Lion stored many of their original negatives under cover in the tank at Beaconsfield Studios, only to lose them when it flooded after hostilities ended. As a result, some of their features can now only be found on 17.5mm or 9.5mm. Although it can be provocative to declare a film as 'lost', it can sometimes prompt a new search. Worth looking out for on 35mm are *The Flying Squad*, an Edgar Wallace thriller from 1932, which at the moment can only be seen on 17.5mm, and *It's a Grand Old World*, a Sandy Powell comedy from 1937, now only available in a somewhat abridged 9.5mm version. For many, not fine examples of classic British cinema, but still worth preserving.

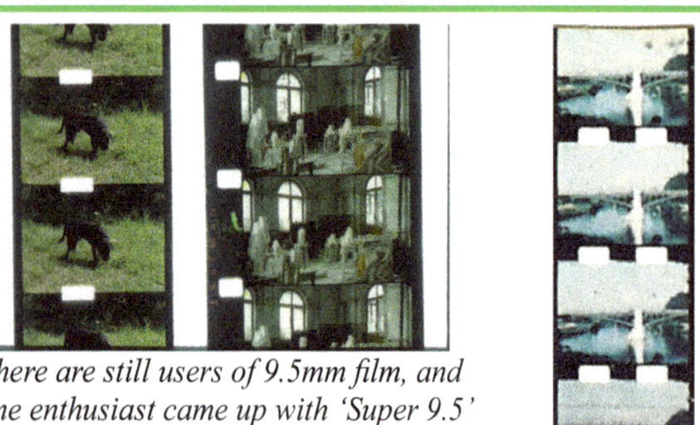

There are still users of 9.5mm film, and one enthusiast came up with 'Super 9.5' film with its width increased to near 12mm to provide a wider picture and offer an alternative to Super-16, which has its wider image extending into the normal soundtrack area. Another development was duplex 9.5mm which had a pair of perforations between the frames.

The fortunes of war helped in the progress of 16mm, being recruited by both sides during WWII to provide training and entertainment films for troops on active service. In the U.S., the 16mm projectors used by the forces were awarded with more rugged 'JAN' specifications (Joint Army and Navy) which included many common spare parts to help them keep running during the conflict.

Bootlace movies

9.5mm and 16mm continued to have their own loyal band of amateur enthusiasts, but home movies for the masses really arrived in 1932, with Kodak's 'bootlace' 8mm. This used the old idea of splitting an existing gauge in half. Although described as 8mm cameras, they were actually loaded with spools of 25 feet of special double-perf 16mm stock with twice the number of perforations. This was run once through the camera exposing quarter sized pictures, one per perf, down one half of the film. It was then reloaded and run back to expose the other half. After processing, on normal 16mm machinery, the film was slit in half and joined together to end up with 50 feet of 8mm film ready for projection.

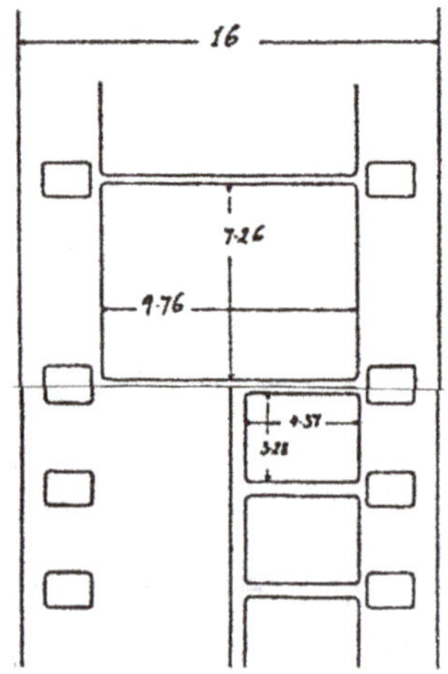

Double-run 8mm on special 16mm film

8mm was not entirely trouble-free. Although an extra foot or so was added to the solid-sided daylight loading spools for threading, many users, wishing to make their 8mm movie making even more economical, often tried to film on it, particularly not stopping before the camera ran out. This resulted in 8mm's familiar progressive fogging, either side of the laboratory's halfway join, which was left in by amateurs whose interest in their hobby didn't extend to buying a splicer.

In later years, innovations like flip-over film chambers and pre-loaded cartridges were tried, but the original 'double-run' spool loading system remained the most popular with camera makers, if not with the less skilled users who had to fumble with them. This didn't worry the growing number of serious amateurs, the most critical of which soon learned that 8mm's perforation tolerances were not always as good as professional stock, and advice from the experts always recommended that cameras and projectors be chosen with the same claw-to-gate separation, to avoid possible unsteadiness. Eventually, a magnetic sound track could be added to 8mm films, using a narrow stripe outside the perforations.

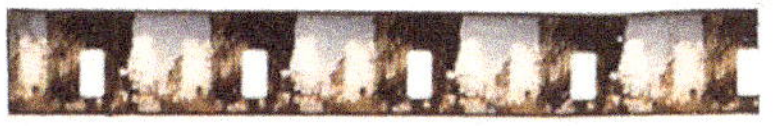

Pathe's 4.75mm format (top) was not the smallest gauge.
The prize for this goes to Eric Berndt's centre perforated 3mm film (left) employed by NASA for instrumentation use in early spacecraft

Goodbye Pathescope

By 1960, the rise of 8mm had taken its toll on the market for 9.5mm, and its principal supplier, Pathescope (GB) Ltd. closed its doors. Its demise wasn't helped by its last ditch attempt to compete with 8mm, by introducing its even narrower 4.75mm horizontal-running format. Special 'Duplex' 9.5mm stock, now with a pair of perforations between the frames, offered a choice of single-run or running it double-run style with the camera held on its side and half the aperture masked off. After slitting, you got twice the running time in, what was described as, 'the vivid realism of wide screen cinematography'. In its 'Monoplex' horizontal mode, the 1.5:1 picture failed to attract many more customers, but the diehards continued to film on the original 'Classic' 9.5mm format, which Popular Photography called 'the living corpse'. 8mm lived on and thrived, with the sale of ever more sophisticated equipment, reaching its peak in 1963. However, its owners began to hear, for many disturbing, rumours that Kodak was hatching a cunning plan to render all this investment obsolete.

Super-8

Easier fogging-free loading came in 1965 with Kodak's Super-8 cartridges containing a single run of new improved 8mm film. Although robust, the 16mm size perforations of the original 'standard' 8mm are rather large for the small (4.37 x 3.28mm A.R. 1.33:1) projected frames. The re-designed Super-8 had smaller more delicate sprocket holes, which, combined with a greater pitch, provided a 50% larger (5.36mm x 4.01mm A.R. 1.33:1) projected image, with its frame lines better positioned and no longer cutting across the perforations. Other improvements included a proper space allocated for a soundtrack on the opposite edge away from the perforations, and a specified claw to gate distance.

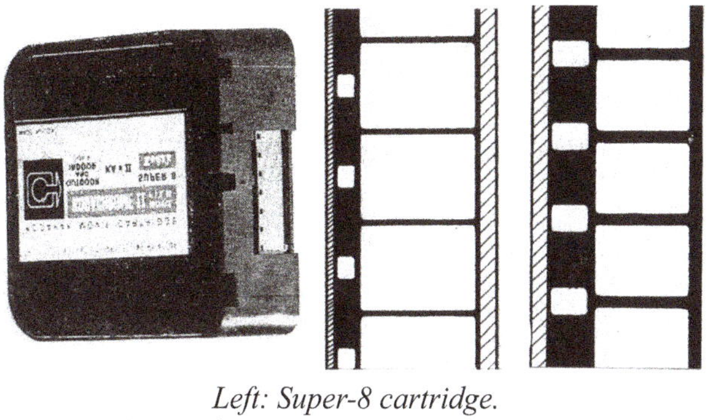

Left: Super-8 cartridge.
Super-8 provides a 50% larger picture area than the original 'Standard' 8mm.

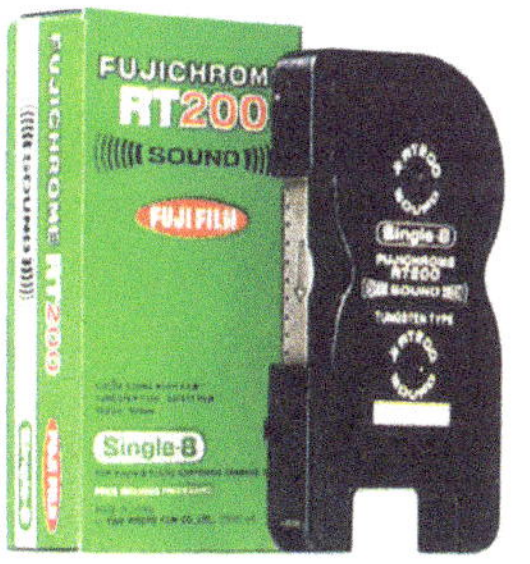

Hot on its heels, from a new rival, was Fuji's 'Single-8' using the same film format, but replacing Kodak's small but chunky coaxial cartridge with a slim-line easy loading design with in-line rolls of thinner polyester based stock needing a smaller space for the same 50 feet. Although using different camera systems, once ready for projection, Super-8 and Single-8 are fully compatible. Both soon introduced slightly larger versions of their cartridges, loaded with pre-striped stock, for sound-on-film cameras. Most tracks on Super-8 are magnetic, but some optical sound prints were made, mostly for use in audio-visual daylight viewing machines and earlier in-flight movie systems. The quality of the sound was surprisingly good from an optical track so narrow it could be mistaken for a scratch!

Like 16mm, Super-8 was initially aimed at amateurs, but its plastic 'Instamatic'- type cartridges also found their way into more semi-professional cameras popular with film school students and experimental film makers. The Super-8 'look' is still sometimes used in documentaries to temporarily change the visual character and texture of the image. Sometimes you have to search for it, but you can still obtain stock for both the 8mm formats, and even 9.5mm is still available. As the process of applying the magnetic coating to pre-striped stock has now been declared eco-unfriendly, this is the hardest type to find, and has effectively silenced the combined sound-on-film cameras.

Home movies take their place in history

In the past, the need to copy all these narrower gauges was mostly limited to amateurs wishing to save their memories onto more convenient video and DVD. For those engaged in copying them, most of the work is in the preparation, joining up the small rolls straight from the camera and removing as much as possible of any fogging, without losing any of the treasured images. Today, home movies are regularly seen in documentaries and complete programmes built around them. Behind-the-scenes and unguarded moments of off-duty film stars and other celebrities are particularly sought after by researchers.

Transfer facilities are now readily available, for example, the BBC added a 9.5mm telecine gate to their long standing Standard and Super 8rnm capabilities, available to both in-house and outside users. Most finds are on 16mm or 8mm, but memorable 9.5mm examples include the dancer Anna Pavlova in Egypt, which Harold Brown enlarged to 16mm for preservation at the NFTA, and

Laurel and Hardy in their theatre dressing room, shot on 9.5mm by Stan's cousin Nancy Wardell during a tour of' Britain.

Today, with cameraphones and CCTV everywhere, few news-worthy incidents go unrecorded, but in the past amateur movie cameras did manage to bring back a few scoops. Still often seen is the 8mm footage of a car stranded on the twisting and rocking roadway of the Tacoma Narrows 'Galloping' suspension bridge shortly before the high winds finally caused it to collapse in 1940.

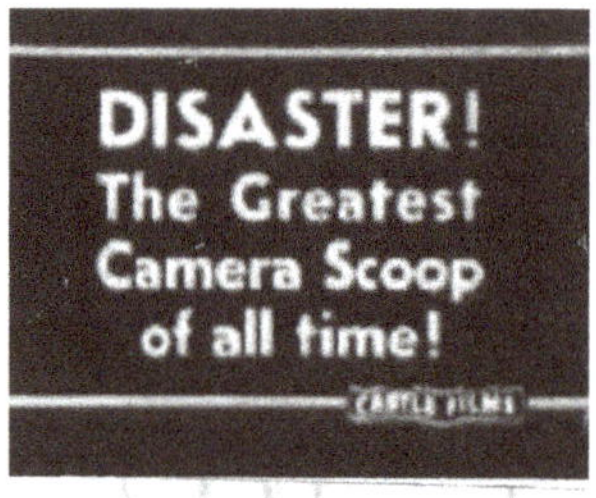

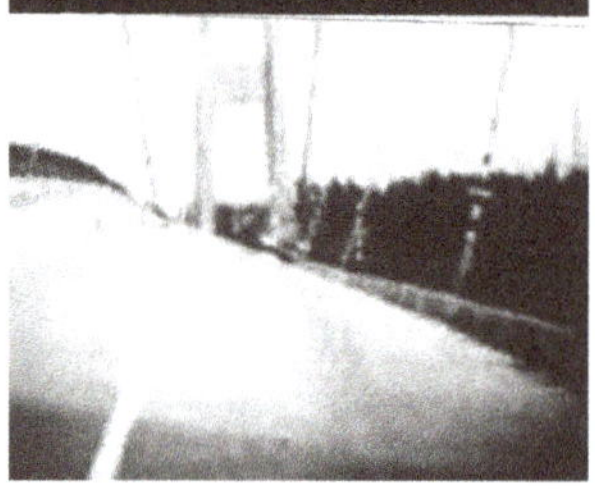

The most valuable piece of 8mm is the 500 frames of the Zapruder film of the assassination of President Kennedy, which was purchased from the Zapruder family by the US Government for 16 million dollars.

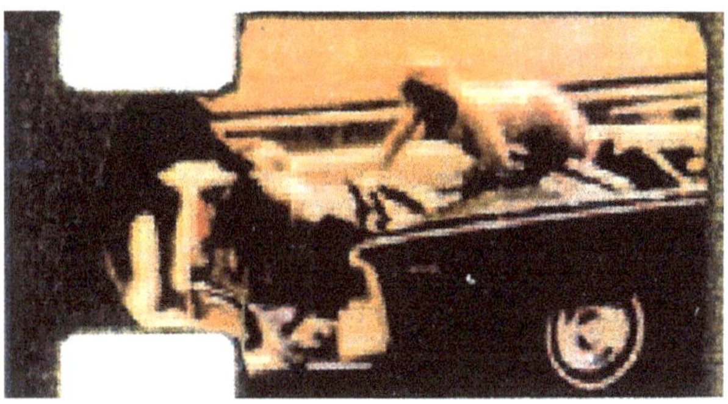

Transfer to 35mm

For long term archival preservation, smaller formats are often enlarged onto 35mm film. Even for digital restoration, the trend is now to produce at least one copy reproducing the full width of the original, as the sprocket hole area can include extra information. 35mm films, particularly those in danger of being lost by decay, are also being copied this way as the extra area can include producer information and date codes, which would be lost if only the picture is recorded. In the case of the Zapruder Standard 8mm footage, the perforation area showed extra spill-over image not normally seen when projected or conventionally printed or copied digitally.

A digital conclusion

An advantage of taking the digital route is the various stabilization programmes available, particularly useful for formats, like the Biograph wide-film prints, which have no perforations.

On a smaller scale, when a 'lost' Buster Keaton film, 'Hard Luck' (1921), was found in the 1980s, its final gag, one of Buster's favourites, was missing. It showed him jumping off a diving board, missing the pool and crashing through its cement surround. After the title, 'Years later', and after presumably reaching China, he climbs back out of hole together with a new Chinese wife and children. More recently, Serge Bromberg at Lobster Films, in France, located another copy of the film complete with the gag. A new problem was that it was on an unusual French home movie format called the 'Cinelux' which used thin ozaphane safety based 24mm film with no perforations. Its almost 35mm size frames were captured beneath a digital camera and, after being digitally steadied, the scene was added to the earlier restoration. The quality of this final scene was noticeably poorer, but worth the effort to have the last laugh!

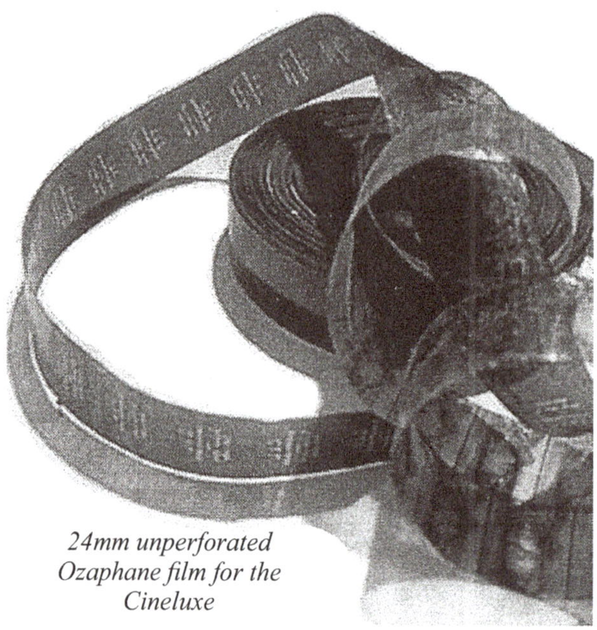

24mm unperforated Ozaphane film for the Cineluxe

Principal sub-standard (smaller than 35mm) film gauges

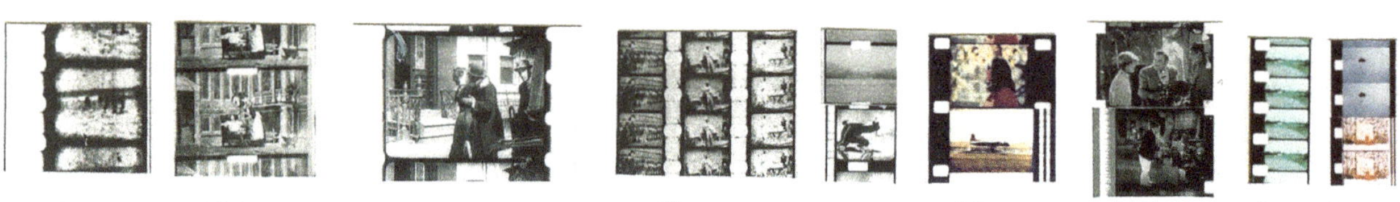

Birtac · Biokam · Pathe 28mm · Home Kinetoscope · 9.5mm · 16mm · 17.5mm Pathe Rural · 8mm · Super 8

All shapes and sizes - Remembering earlier 'alternative' movie formats

One of the most significant contributions to the birth of motion pictures was the availability, in 1889, of long lengths of tough and flexible transparent film. It is interesting to recall that before this (and well before video!) not all moving pictures came on reels of film. In this continuing look at the history of the development of moving picture formats we look at some of the alternatives to film, where pioneers had to make do with much less suitable glass or paper, and it is interesting to learn that even after the breakthrough of celluloid, some would still manage to record and display their moving images without the aid of film. We also look at how in the cinema, 35mm was challenged from some new wider gauges.

Worth more than the paper it is printed on!

Sometimes, we can only read about lost films from the early days of the cinema, but, in some cases, their actual moving images have ended up on paper. Until 1912, the copyright law in America didn't apply to the new medium of motion pictures on film, but only to still photographs and the printed word. As early as 1894 Edison placed together eighty-one frames of his Kinetoscope subject 'The Sneeze' (below) on a single paper print and entered it for copyright as a series of photographs.

Other producers tried to protect their films by pinning representative frames from each scene onto cards. This was the method chosen by many British pioneers who sent plot descriptions, still photographs and frame clippings to The Stationery Office for protection. In the 1990s, a large number were found in the National Archives at Kew and handed over to the BFI, becoming a valuable resource for researchers of early British cinema. An example was the Welsh pioneer William Haggar. He and his family were fairground exhibitors who expanded into producing films, with perhaps the most famous being among the first British 'story' films, *The Life of Charles Peace* based on the life and death of a real notorious criminal. This is only one of the four known to still exist. The Haggars produced at least thirty others, which were popular both here and abroad, including a number reaching America. The surviving clips of those now lost films help historians to appreciate the full extent of their work.

Edison's 'The Sneeze' from 1894. Restored from a paper print.

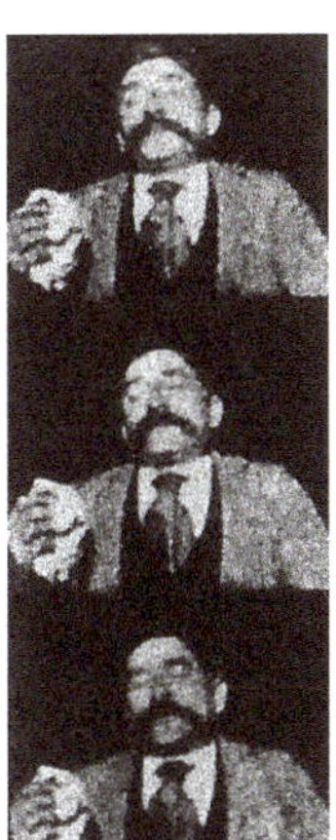

Metal film from the 1930s for projection by reflection. Not a success then, but the principle returned with the light bouncing off the modulated oil surface in earlier Eidophor video projectors, and now in the micromirror DLP® chips and SXRD (reflective crystals) found in many of today's digital projectors.

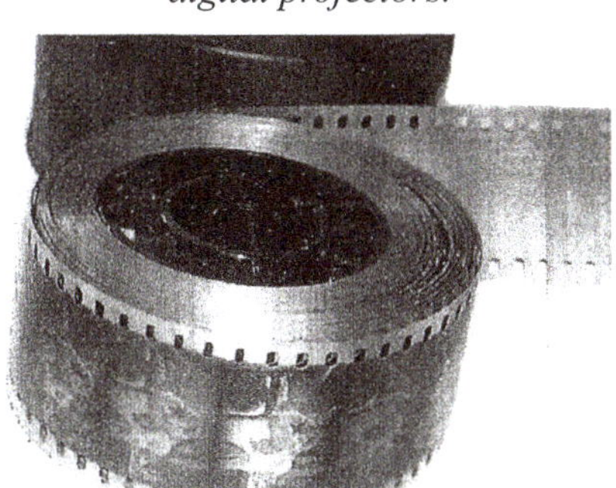

Back in America, the final acceptable copyright procedure was to print the complete film on 35mm perforated photographic paper. This continued to about 1915 and the Library of Congress ended up holding aver 3500 examples of these 'photo collections', and starting in the 1950s, a project began to copy them onto 16mm film. As a result of this work, many early films were saved, although their original celluloid counterparts were lost by decay or neglect.

The idea of actually projecting paper prints was tried in 1917 for an economical home projector. The 'cheaper than celluloid' 35mm prints were shown using the reflecting Episcope principle, also used at the time for what were called post-card projectors. Ten years later, the Campro did the same by fitting a pair of lamps onto the front of a 35mm camera to use it as a projector for showing the paper prints. A future proposal for a big screen professional version used 'indestructible' aluminium metal prints to stand up to the greater heat from an arc lamp.

Flip-books - real 'flicks'

Perhaps the most familiar paper movies are flip-books, needing only the digital technology of fingers and thumbs to view them. They also played their part in helping the first movies to reach the screen. The German pioneer, Max Skladanowsky, financed his projection experiments from the production and sale of such books showing brief animated items like folk dancing, music hall turns and the ever-popular boxing kangaroos. Even more stimulating subject matter was soon appearing through the eyepiece of the 'What the Butler Saw' Mutoscope, which used the same basic principle. To encourage its customers to put more coins into the machine, the shows were made longer by attaching hundreds of picture cards onto a bobbin to form a reel. When turned by a handle, a metal finger, resting on their edges, permitted only one at a time to flip over. As the Mutoscopes had a large peep-hole opening and viewing lens, some modern copies of this early form of 'exploitation movie' have been made, and given a suitably furtive look, by pointing a camera down its eyepiece. There was

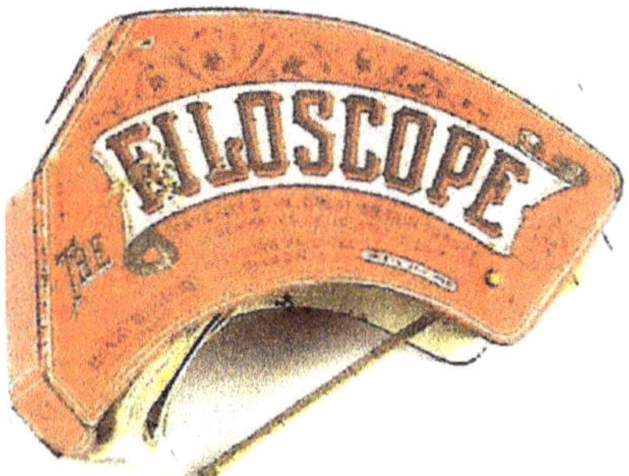

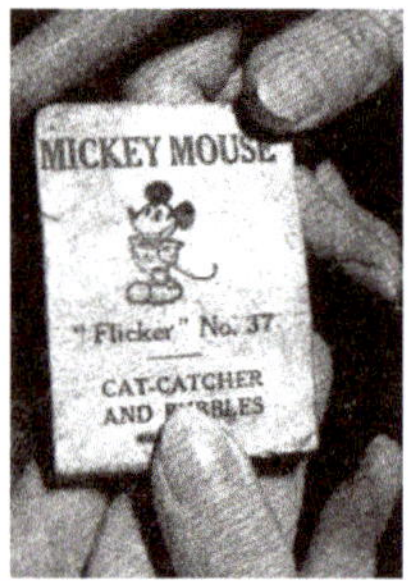

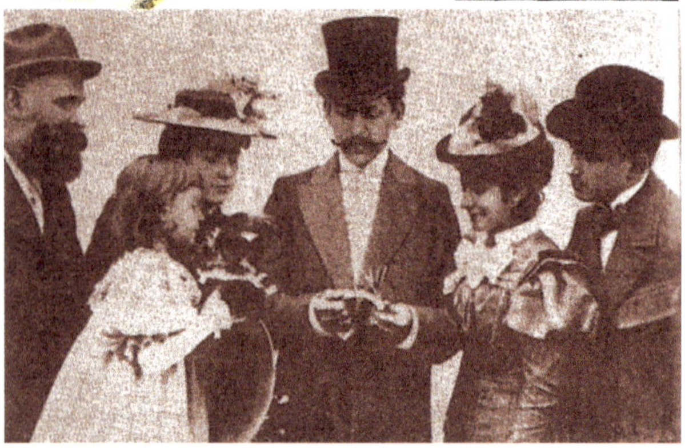

Clockwise from top left: The Filoscope from 1897, a mechanised flip book with lever device to flip the pages - from British film pioneer R.W. Paul. A Mickey Mouse 'Flicker' from the 1930s. Max Skladanowsky shows off one of his flip-books.

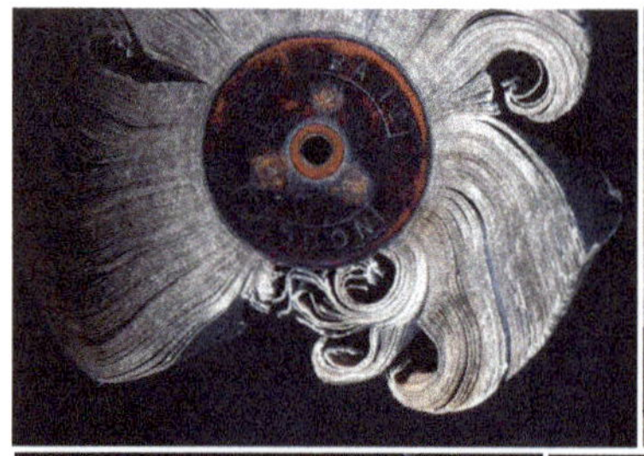

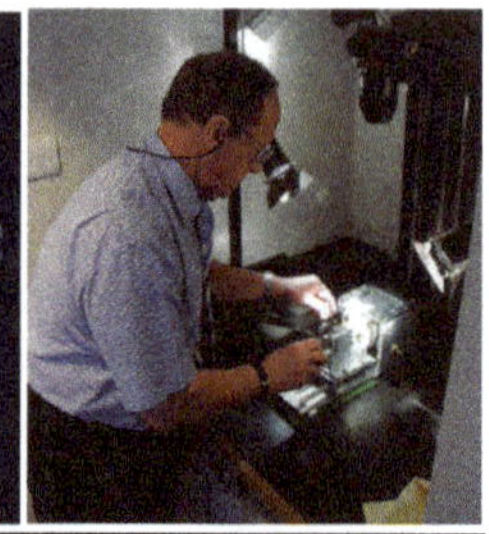

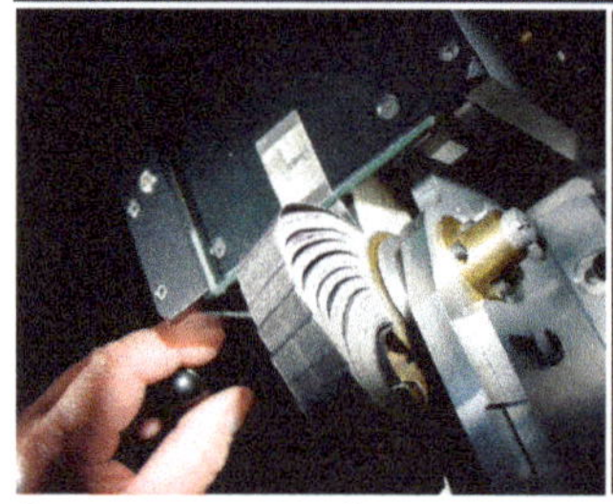

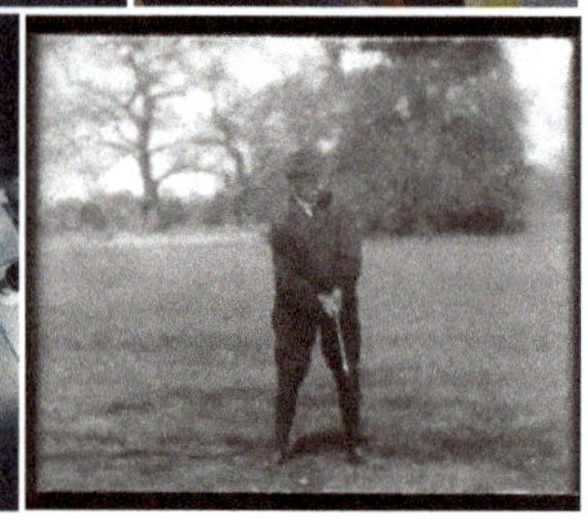

Restoration work on the well-worn Kinora reel showing golfer Harry Vardon, six times winner of 'The Open'. His first win came in 1896.

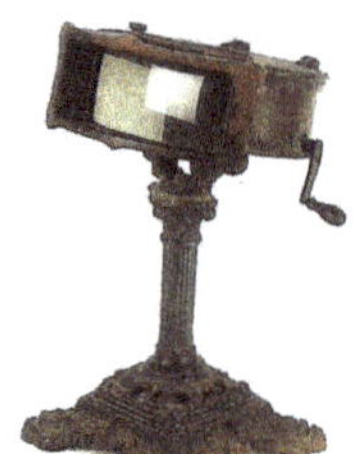

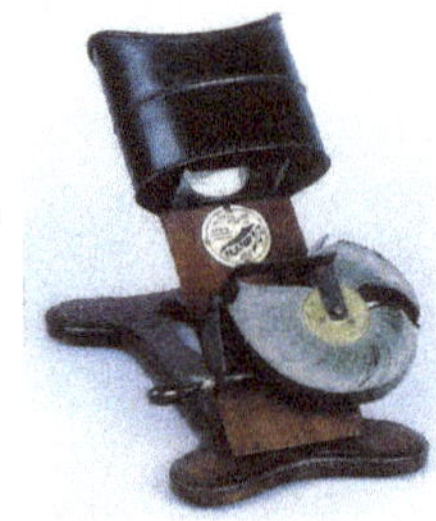

Two models of the original viewer

sometimes also the need to increase the cards illumination, normally provided by a frosted glass window on top of the machine.

A home version of the Mutoscope was the Kinora, which could also be used for making your own home movies. The negative material, one inch wide and unperforated, could be either celluloid or cheaper paper. It came in a light-tight box and passed through the hand turned camera to another using the mutilated rubber roller type intermittent movement. The full take-up box was returned to Kinora, where it was processed and used to make a series of paper prints, with any inaccuracy of register being corrected when mounting them onto reels for the Kinora viewer. These ranged from cheap hand-turned models to ornate pedestal versions driven by clockwork.

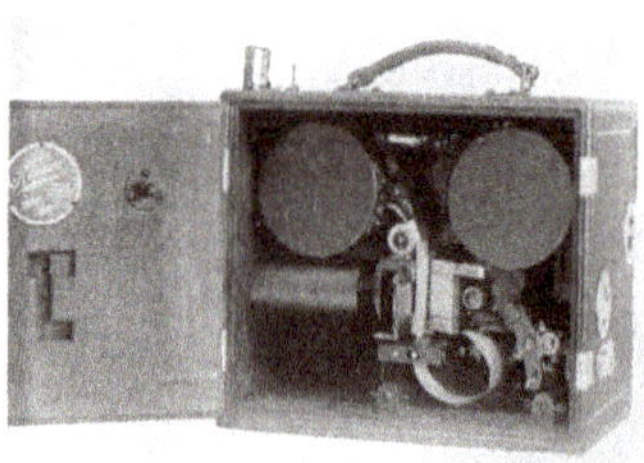

Kinora home movie camera loaded with its paper negative 1908

One notable feat of restoration from these earliest times was carried out by TMP, part of the VTR Media Group, who went to enormous trouble to design and build a special rig to save images from Kinora reels. It was used to copy 'footage' of a famous golfer, Harry Vardon, demonstrating his skills, back in the early 1900s. The original negatives were believed to have been lost when the Kinora factory burnt down in 1914. The specially built restoration device successfully held each picture flat under a digital camera, without harming or having to remove the deteriorating and curling paper pictures from their bobbin. The 600 plus frames were digitally cleaned-up and stabilised, before being transferred onto 35mm negative to become part of The Royal and Ancient Golf Club Archive.

Mutoscope 'What the butler saw' coin in the slot viewing machines were launched in 1897. Later versions (right) were to be found in amusement arcades and piers up to the 1960s

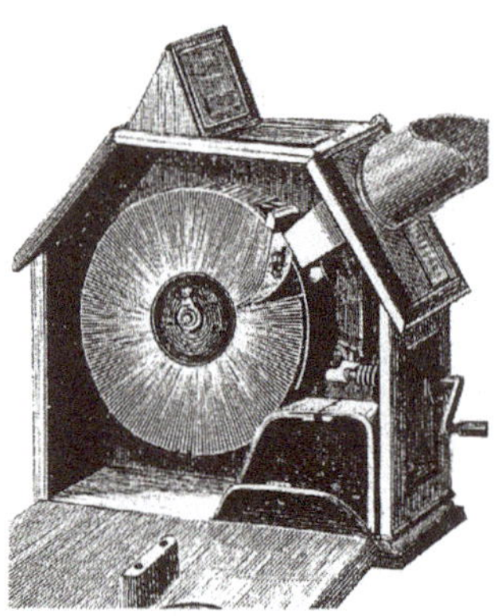

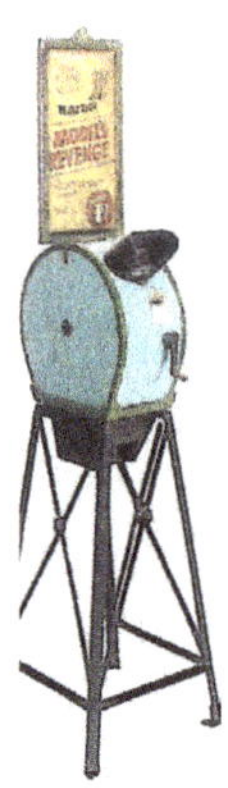

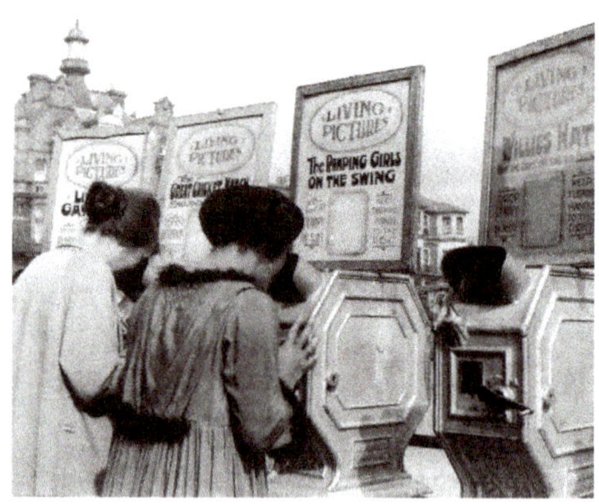

Flicker books were still a popular toy in the 1930s, costing six old pence from Woolworths and stationers, bringing to life excerpts of Disney and 'Flip the Frog' cartoons or sports subjects. Many of these were made by Flicker Productions, run by Scottish businessman Norman Loudon, who did so well out of it that he was able to buy an estate in Surrey and, when his ambitions turned to cinema film production, it became Shepperton Studios. Flicker books are still produced today, sold or given away as novelty items and their images are sometimes included in the corners of the pages of ordinary books.

Victoria the Great, on a grander film

Some of the first moving pictures of Queen Victoria were shot, in 1896, on wide-film when Royal photographer Mr. Downey was summoned to Balmoral during October to take still photographs of a private visit by Russia's Nicholas and Alexandra. He also took along a newly completed Grand Kinomatograph movie camera, and the Queen gave permission to film some scenes of the occasion. The film in the camera was about 60mm wide with four round perforations on each side of the frame. The results were shown a month later to her Majesty and members of the court at Windsor Castle. The wide-film footage shared the bill with some 35rnm subjects run on a Paul Theatrograph, together with a lantern slide show given during the change-over. Sadly, unless still to be found in a palace basement somewhere, no copies are believed to exist, but some of their images also ended up on paper. Fifteen strips of the print, complete with its perforations, were reproduced across three pages of a special supplement to the Lady's Pictorial magazine, published in December 1896. These have since been animated and although the quality is very poor, it gives us some idea what the presentation looked like.

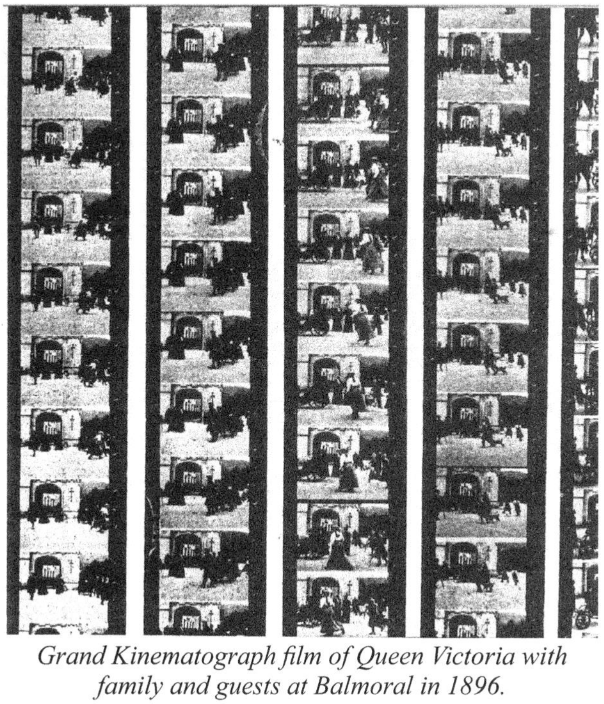

Grand Kinematograph film of Queen Victoria with family and guests at Balmoral in 1896.

Movies on glass

Before the coming of flexible celluloid film, which made workable cine cameras possible, some earlier inventors had tried using rapidly changing lantern slides, with a series of hand painted pictures or posed photographs to create the illusion of movement. However, images on glass were sometimes given another chance to help cut the cost for amateurs. This time, each slide or plate, which could be bought and processed quite cheaply, ended up with hundreds of miniature pictures in vertical or horizontal rows.

In the early 1900s, a system from France fitted 1200 frames, equal to 75 feet of standard film, in horizontal rows on a normal 5x7 inch photographic plate. This was attached to a metal holder which engaged with the camera and projector's intermittent mechanism to expose and show each row in turn. A magazine held up to 12 plates, which changed automatically to keep everything going without a halt.

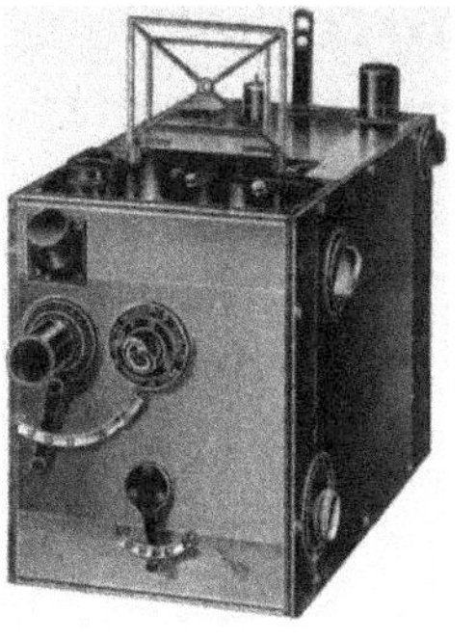

The basic idea was also applied to more convenient and less vulnerable film. In 1914 Kasimir Proszynski, the inventor of the compressed air driven Aeroscope 35mm camera (right), replaced his own earlier glass plate system with a 120mm wide film with rows of 15 small 7x5 mm pictures running back and forth across its width. Perforations down both sides transported it through its combined camera/projector in the same manner as a typewriter. Running costs were kept to a minimum by reducing its speed to 10 fps, with 30 feet of film lasting almost an hour. Known as the OKO, it was manufactured by the Warwick Trading Company in London, and in the early 1920s about 100 were made in Warsaw.

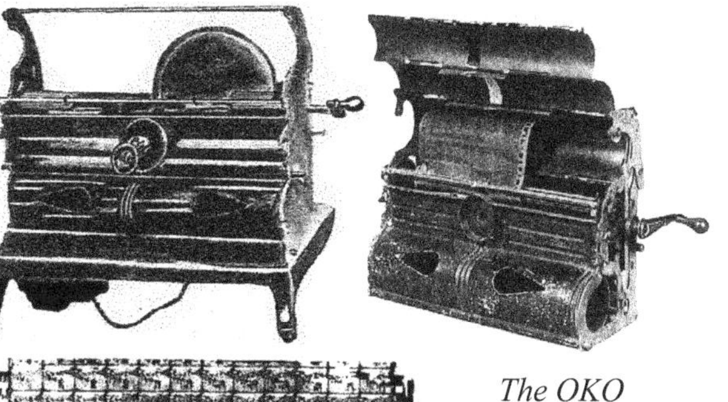

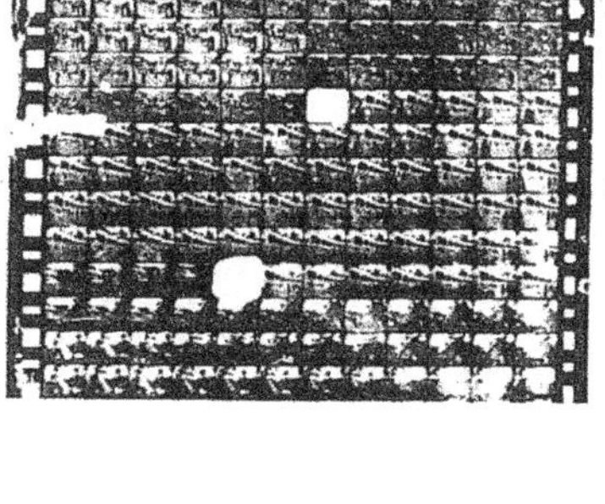

The OKO 'typewriter-style' machine from 1914, shown in its camera and projector modes, used 120mm wide film with rows of tiny pictures

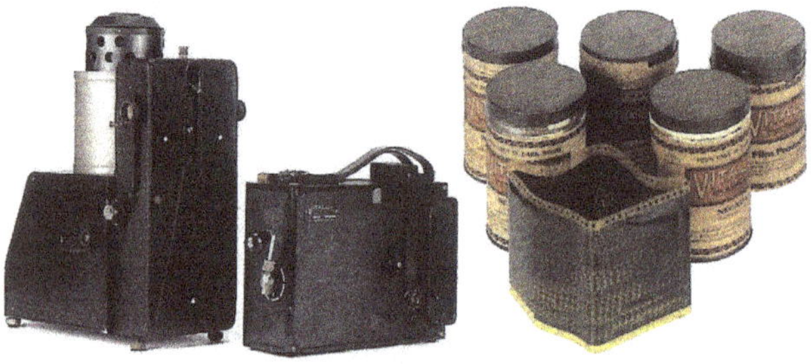

Vitalux projector and camera, with packs of its endless-loop film

Also around this time, the Vitalux Cinema Co. in America launched their camera and projector taking a loop of Eastman safety film 5x17½ inches with a slow helix thread of around 1600 frames. Some commercially produced films were available, but its short 2 minute running time and no chance of editing led to its quick demise.

Fifty years later, in the early 1970s, Dr. Leon W. Wells, inventor of other odd-ball film formats, (e.g. the ARC-120 / Wonderama 35mm split-frame twin-lens projection system for deep curvature screens), came up with the Pik-A-Movie rear projection viewer for providing hotel movies. It was loaded with a cartridge containing 300 feet of specially perforated horizontally running 70mm film with 12 rows of Super-8 size images, together with another 12 of optical sound tracks. After showing the first row of pictures, an inaudible tone superimposed on its track caused the mechanism to step to the next row and change direction. It took two hours to complete all the passes, enough for most features. Again, its stay was cut short, having to make room for cable and satellite TV.

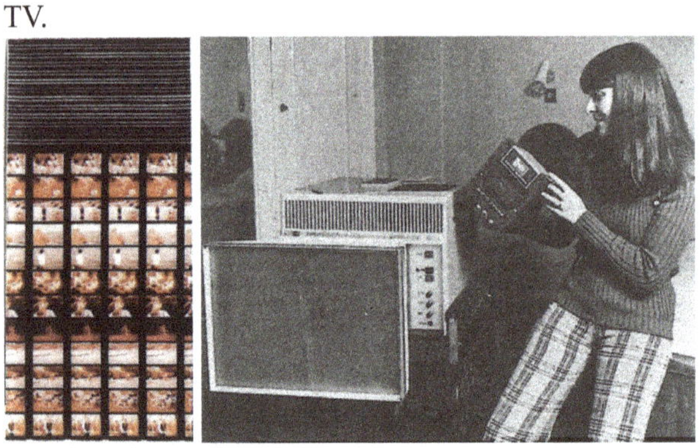

A Pik-A-Movie 70mm film and rear projection viewer

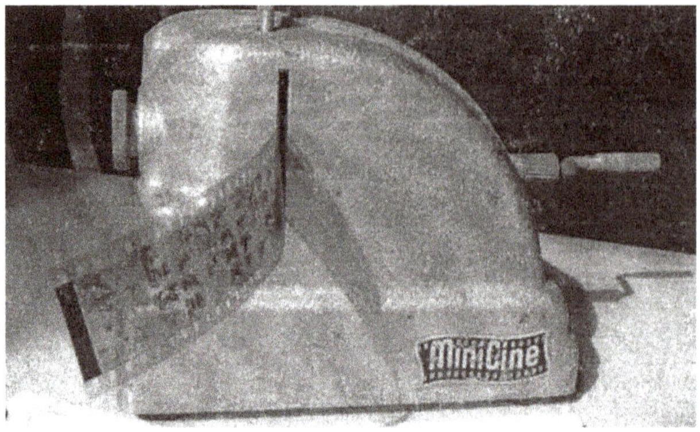

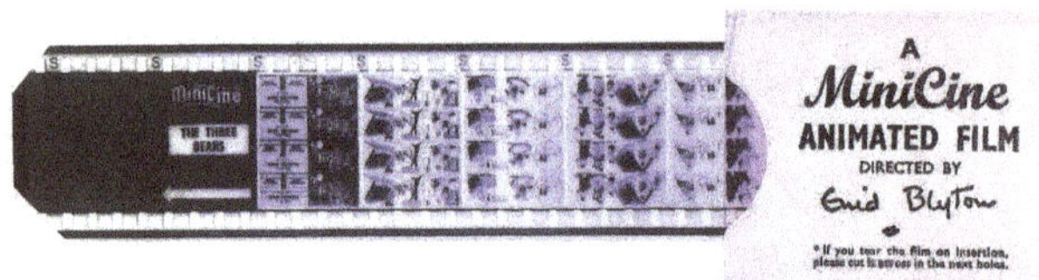

For this writer, of a certain age, all this brings back memories of his much loved Mini-Cine hand-turned toy projector. It too, ran a horizontal 35mm film strip with rows of tiny pictures, and my first projectionist job was using it to show 'animated' (just about) films to my school mates in the 1950s.

Movies on disc

Long before the DVD, you could still record and replay moving pictures on discs. Back in 1900, the Kamm Kammatograph combined camera and projector used a 12½ inch glass disc with a spiral of 600 images. It was rotated intermittently as it slowly traversed behind the lens. For a special event at the late lamented MOMI, early cinema specialist Stephen Herbert managed to bring back to life an original Kammatograph borrowed from the Pollock Toy Museum. Its thin glass disc had already broken into two many decades ago, but, with the help of some sticky tape the demonstration went ahead regardless and showed a small child playing with her dog, way back around 1900.

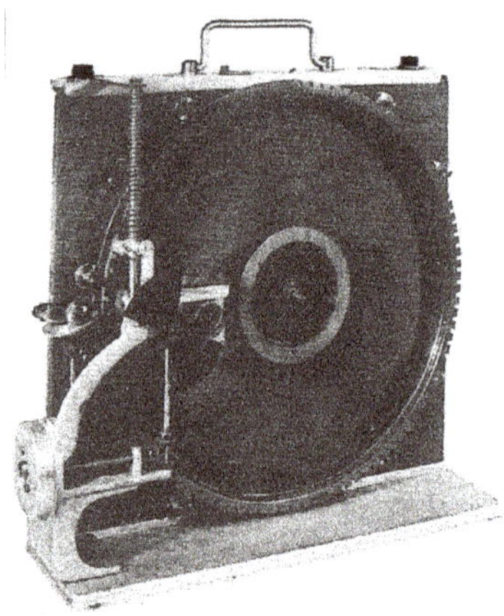

No, not another multi-image projection format, but three 9.5mm copies printed together on specially perforated 35mm film which escaped from the laboratory before being split into three separate prints.

Most narrow-gauge printed films were made this way on 35mm, 8mm and Super-8 four at a time and 17.5mm and 16mm in pairs on special 35mm or 32mm stock.

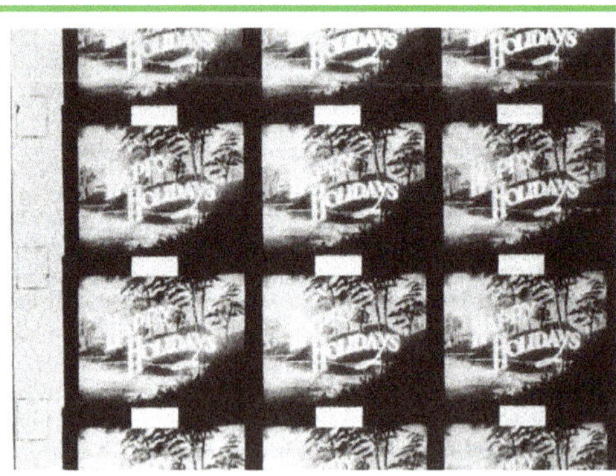

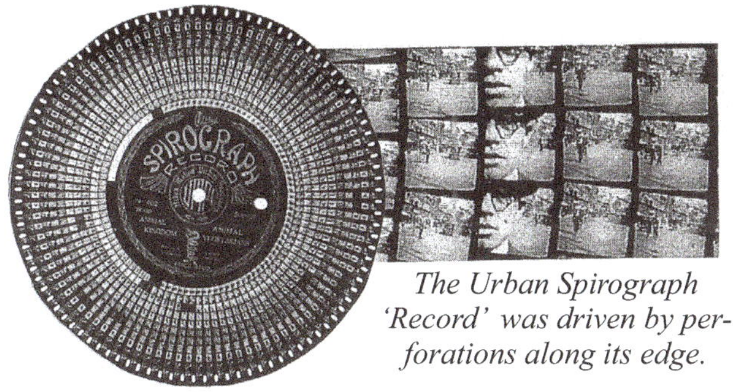

The Urban Spirograph 'Record' was driven by perforations along its edge.

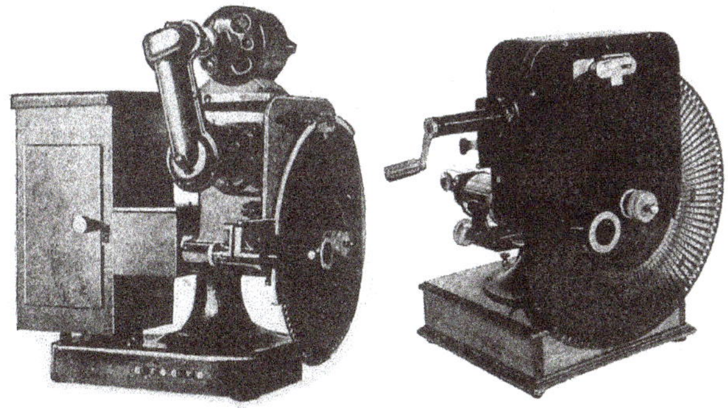

Spirograph projectors from 1914 and 1923

An up-dated version of a disc machine, the Urban Spirograph 'Motion Picture Record' managed to fit 1200 frames (0.22in x 0.16in) on a 10½ inch disc of Kodak safety film. Printed from a glass disc negative, it was only designed for showing professional films in the home and no camera was available. It remained available into the 1920s but, like the Vitalux, it was soon over-shadowed by the arrival of 16mm and 9.5mm film, which really got amateur home movies moving. Quite a few Spirograph discs have survived and some subjects have been successfully scanned back to 35mm film using the digital skills of Haghefilm.

For the ARC-120 system a wide picture was printed and shown in two halves. The projector attachment blended them back together on the screen, with each lens having to cope with only half of its deep curve. The sound was on magnetic stripes outside the perfs.

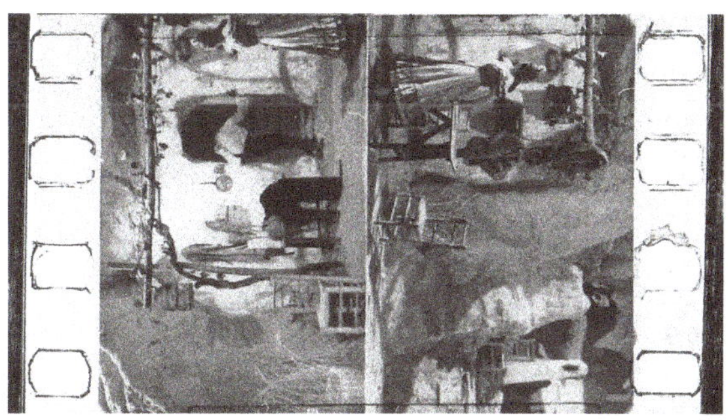

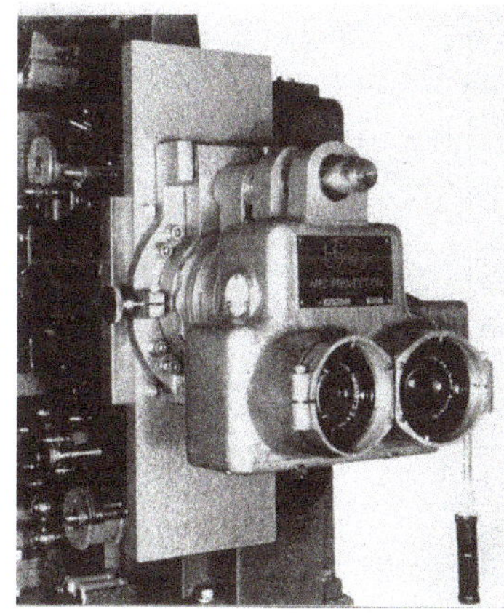

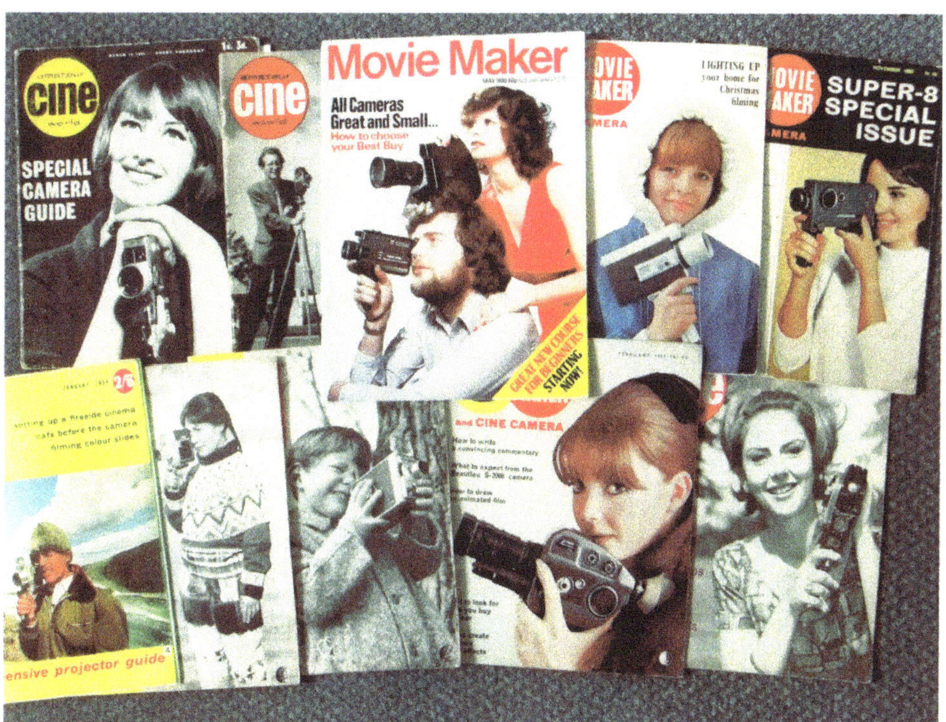

Long before video camcorders and camera phones, the 1960s and 70s would become the most popular years for 8mm and Super-8 movie making, with many magazines offering advice.

All shapes and sizes - Back to the big and even bigger screen

We have seen how the archivist and restorer needs to recognise and understand a whole range of sometimes unusual film formats, but although the various narrow gauges and other devices vied for their share of the home movie and other non-theatrical markets, 35mm film generally remained unchallenged for both production and cinema exhibition

Although 35mm was originally only intended for the Kinetoscope peep-show viewer, its small frames proved equally suitable for projection on ever increasing screen sizes as film shows soon graduated from converted shops and fairground tents to larger theatres and purpose-built 'picture palaces'. However, compared with today's viewing experience, even in the largest of these, screens remained relatively small. As an example, when New York's new 'Cathedral of the Motion Picture', the Roxy, first opened in 1927, its 'acre' of 6000 seats (plus room for 500 standing!) auditorium only boasted an 18 x 24 foot screen, a width which would seem quite modest in a present 400 seater. Back then, a desire to increase screen sizes was somewhat limited by the resolution of earlier film stocks. At first, seat prices followed that of live theatres, with the best nearest the stage, but after patrons began to appreciate that the picture looked steadier and less grainy the further back one sat, the prices were changed over.

Back over here in Britain, there was a British Standard for screen sizes, which ranged from 8 feet, to a maximum 30. The recommended choice of width was between one-fifth and one-sixth the distance to the rear seats. It is interesting that following improved film, and now digital, technology, it's now not unusual to find the back row only one and a half times the width away from today's bigger and wider screens.

For a while during the 1920s and 30s, some theatres found room for a larger screen, typically up to 30 x 50ft, for **'Magnascope'** presentations. For this, much of its area was normally kept covered by variable masking which opened out on cue to expand the picture during certain, usually spectacular, scenes, when the action on the screen diverted attention away from the effects of over magnification. First exploited in larger theatres, with a spare projector to show the enlarged sequences, the later availability of variable focus zoom projection lenses allowed many more cinemas to join in. When used appropriately as an artistic device, it could be very effective, but like any new toy it soon lost its novelty, particularly when used too often at the whim of the projectionist. Distributors soon objected to their films being messed about with, and this particular aid to showmanship ended up being employed for less important films, like newsreels and bouncing-ball musical shorts, before being abandoned when the screen needed to be replaced, usually with a less costly smaller one just for the normal size picture.

More recently, the old Magnascope idea of surprising the audience with an expanding picture was used again during the Imax showings of 'The Dark Knight'. There have been attempts to bring back Magnascope for special showings of early films known to have employed the process, like the naval battles in *Old Ironsides* (1926) and the aerial dog fights in *Wings* (1927). Some years ago, the NFT managed it, but during a Merian C. Cooper season, I waited with great expectations to see the screen open out for the elephant stampede in *Chang* (1927), but no luck this time. The technical challenges would be even greater for a revival of MGM's *Trail of 98* which was originally shown in 1928 using a variation called the 'Fantom Screen'. This time, the expanding screen physically moved forward towards the audience, which even today, would make those in the front rows nervous.

Zoom projection lenses soon disappeared, returning in the 1960s as a common feature on narrow gauge portable machines, for adjusting the screen size. They

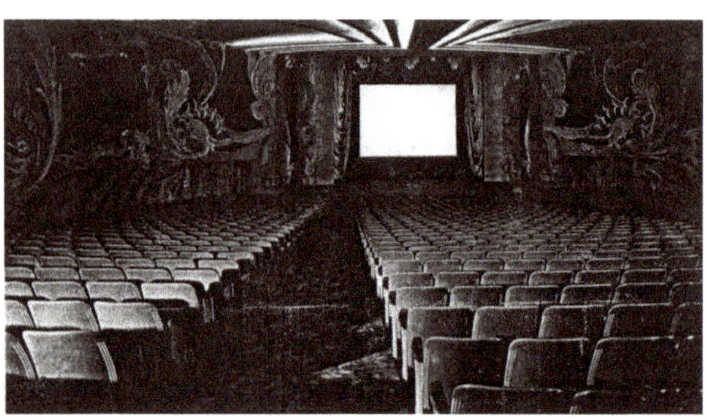

The cinema viewing experience in the 1920s & 30s was often a case of 'an acre' of seats looking at a postage stamp screen

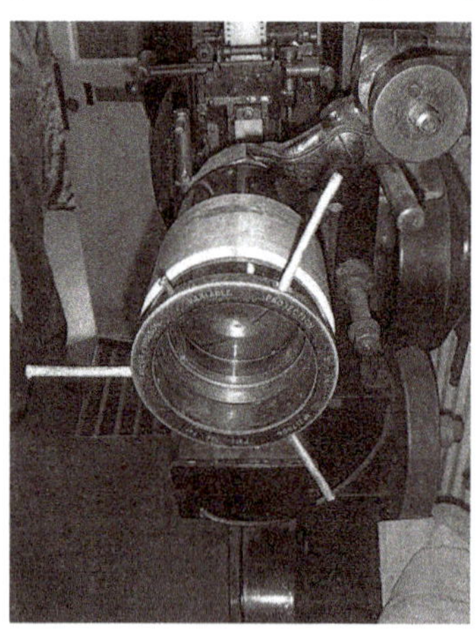

Taylor Hobson variable focus projection lens (3 to 5¼ in.). It was used during the early 1930s to produce the expanding screen Magnascope effect. The prongs on the zooming ring were an aid to its smooth application. This example was spotted at The Cinema Museum, Kennington, South London.

are now back in cinemas, with many of today's digital projectors having 'auto' motor-driven variable focus lenses to help accommodate their different chip areas and aspect ratios.

Magnascope was, sometimes referred to as being 'widescreen', possibly because, in some theatres, architectural features, like balconies, cut off some of the larger picture which now looked wider. For the public this was only an occasional treat, but behind the scenes ways were being devised to enable complete films to be shown on much larger screens. By the end of the 1920s, all the methods which would eventually bring us bigger and wider pictures had already been worked out and demonstrated. These included, forming a single panoramic image from separate film strips, running the film sideways or using anamorphic lenses to squeeze a wider picture into a normal frame and restore it back during projection. Even without any desire to introduce larger screens, the need to sacrifice part of the picture area on the 35mm print for the new optical sound-on-film tracks was already compromising image quality. Looking for a solution to both problems, the studios began to take an interest in a possible change to a larger film format.

One of the first on offer was the result of several years of development by film business pioneer, George K. Spoor of Essanay Studios, and his partner, John Berggren. Their **'Natural Vision'** process used film 63.5mm wide (2½ in.) with a six perforation 2.06 x 1.12 inch frame, which they said could fill a screen with a 1.85:1 aspect ratio up to 70 feet wide.

When the Roxy in New York opened in 1927, its first night souvenir book included the news that Spoor Natural Vision would have its world premiere installation at the Roxy and the first film in the process was already in production in Hollywood. Like other wide screen systems, it was suggested that it gave a greater sense of depth and its particular 'third dimension achievement' was enhanced by a special screen which instead of the using the usual black masking, was arranged so that the edges of the picture softly diffused into a delicate gauze surround. Although two of its six projector positions were promised to Natural Vision,

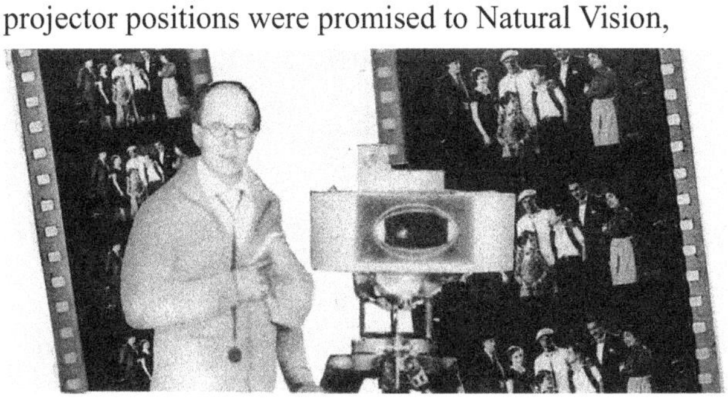

The first Spoor Natural Vision 63.5mm feature would have been J.Stuart Blackton's 'The American' in 1927, but it was never shown.

within a week of its opening, the theatre was sold to William Fox who was working on his own wide-film process.

Grandeur Pictures
....the entertainment of the future

William Fox's wide film contender was **'Grandeur'**. It was very much a personal enterprise, which he hoped would advance his empire-building ambitions by persuading the rest of the industry to adopt it and then charge royalties. Grandeur used 70mm film, but differed from present day 70mm by having larger perforations set at a greater pitch. There were four to each frame, with a projector aperture similar to todays, at 1.810 x 0.880 inch, and an aspect ratio of 2.1:1. This still left room for an extra wide Movietone variable density optical soundtrack.

The Simplex Grandeur 70/35mm projector (1930-31) was well ahead of its time, with a triple lens turret and dual gauge rollers and sprockets, recessed for 35mm. (Carey Williams Collection)

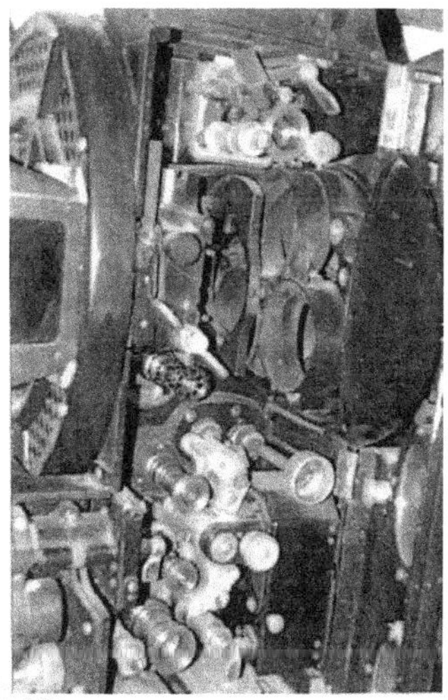

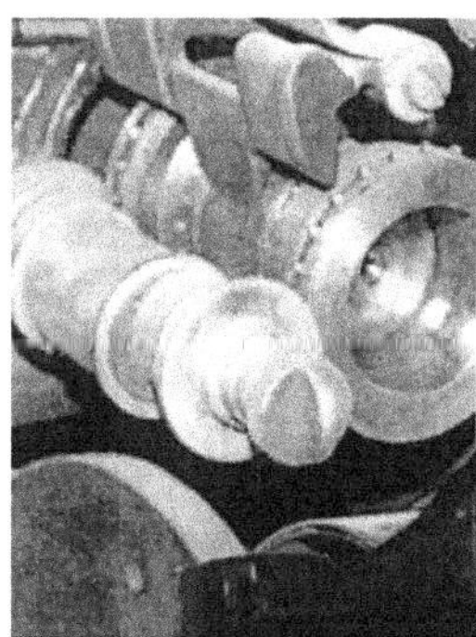

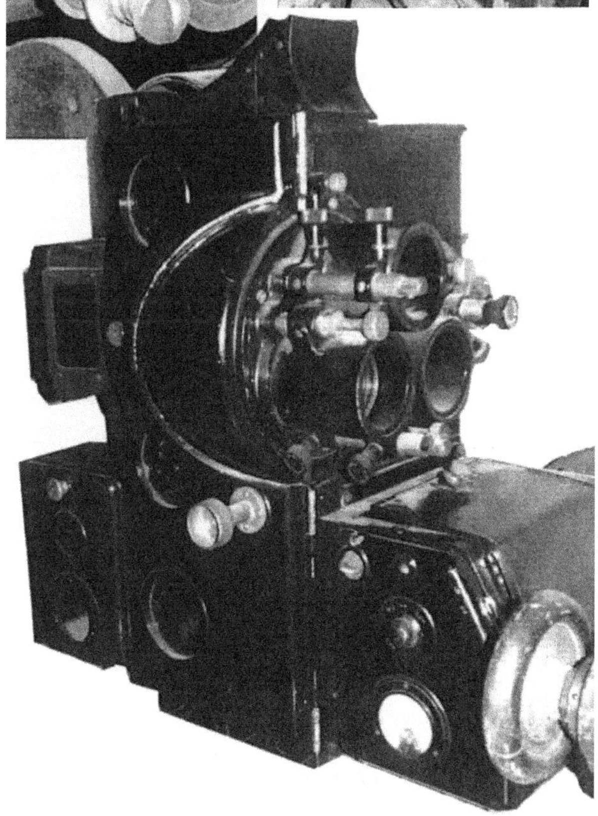

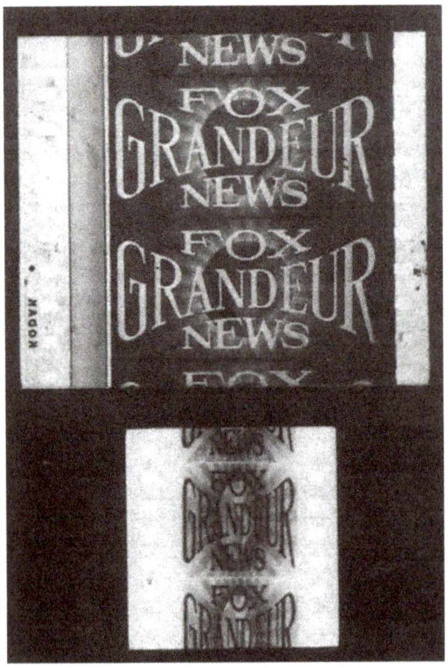

Original 70mm Grandeur images now preserved as 35mm anamorphic reductions.

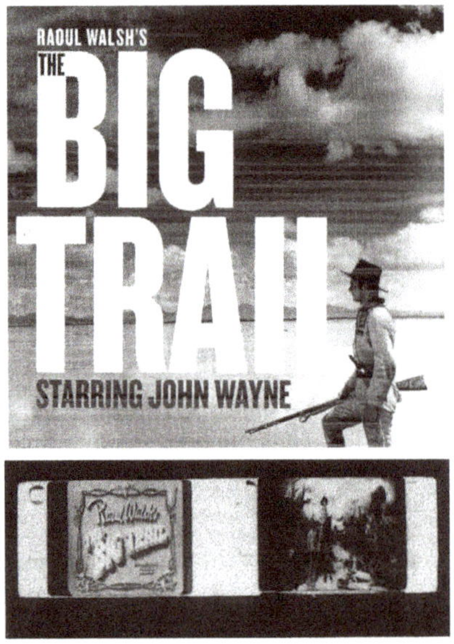

Examples from The Big Trail

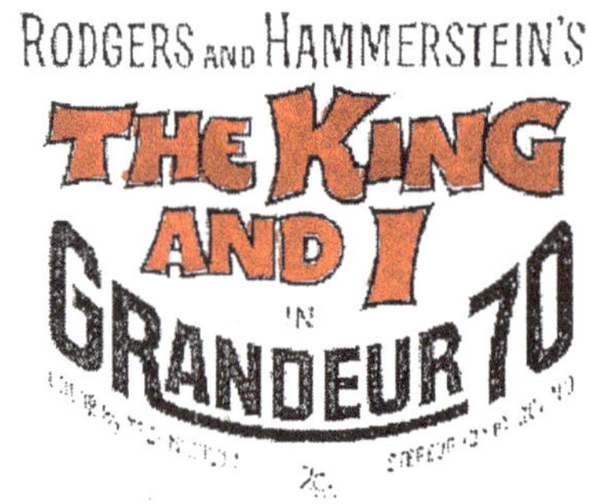

The name Grandeur was revived for the 70mm reissue of The King and I (1956), which was shot in another short-lived wide film process, CinemaScope 55 (below)

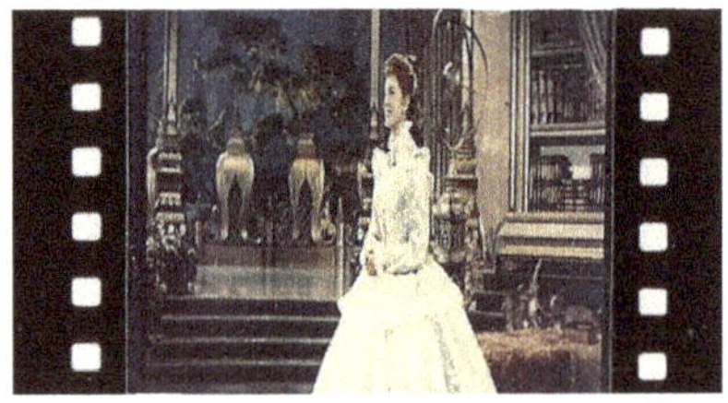

CinemaScope 55 , a 55mm wide format

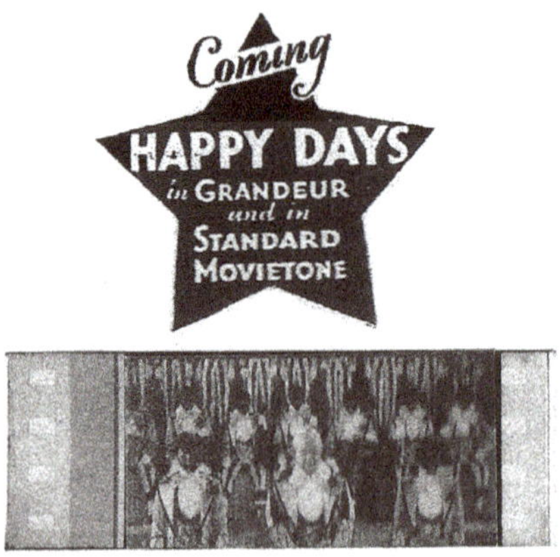

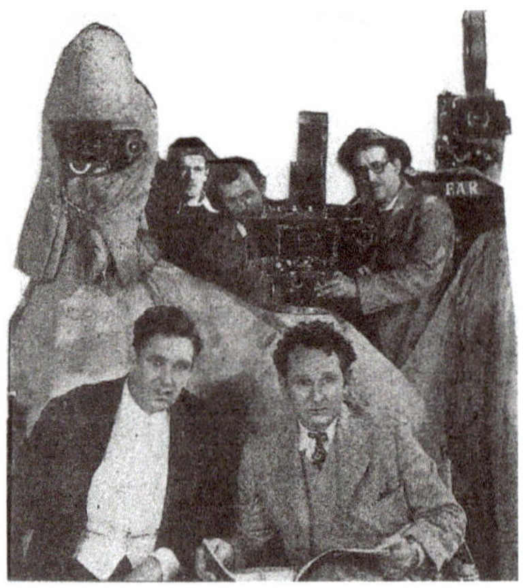

Left: One Grandeur feature that was never shown in 70mm was 'Song o' My Heart' (1930). The strange hooded creature looming over its star, John McCormack (left) is one of the 35mm cameras in its sound-deadening 'horse blanket' cover

The pictures

Fox Studios began filming a series of 70mm Grandeur pictures, most shot simultaneously with the 35mm versions. First of these was a special newsreel which included suitably spectacular shots of Niagara Falls and speeding locomotives. This, together with a Grandeur version of *Fox Movietone Follies of 1929* was premiered at the Gaiety in New York, with the theatre's proscenium only having room for a 35 x 17 foot screen. Next came another musical, *Happy Days*, followed in 1930 by the most famous of the Grandeur films, the Raoul Walsh epic western, *The Big Trail*, which gave John Wayne his first starring role. It opened at the Roxy using a larger 42 x 20 foot glass-beaded screen. Although impressed, the New York audiences never became as excited as some in the industry, who thought that the days of 35mm film were numbered. This enthusiasm soon spread to equipment manufacturers who started work producing wide-film apparatus. The Mitchell Camera Company supplied Fox with ten of their new Grandeur-FC 70mm cameras and began building fifty others ready for the expected wide film revolution. Other cameras were built by Debrie and the Fearless Camera Company were fearless enough to produce a convertible standard/wide film model. Simplex projectors were used to show the Grandeur prints and Ernemann also made a similar convertible multi-gauge model.

Although Grandeur was to be the most prominent, in terms of investment and publicity, the other major studios followed and introduced their own variations. Some did so reluctantly, only feeling they had to compete after their bosses failed to persuade Fox that this was not the time, so soon after the transition to sound, to introduce another innovation. Some, preferring a more modest commitment, purchased or leased wide film cameras but didn't always equip their theatres with wide gauge projectors. An example was MGM who borrowed Grandeur cameras from Fox for their own **'Realife'** process, but reduced the 70mm negatives onto 35mm. The prints provided a finer grain 2:1 aspect ratio picture across the full width of the film between the perforations for showing using existing Magnascope lenses and screens. The sound would be available on a separate film or disc. MGM filmed two westerns in Realife, alongside the normal 35mm cameras, the first *Billy the Kid*, directed by King Vidor in 1930, followed by *The Great Meadow* in 1931.

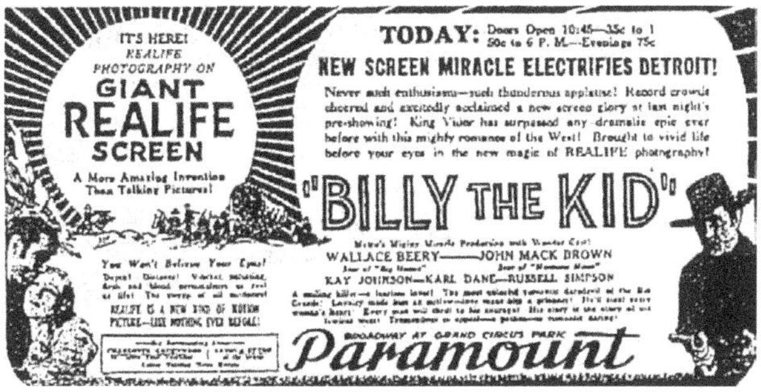

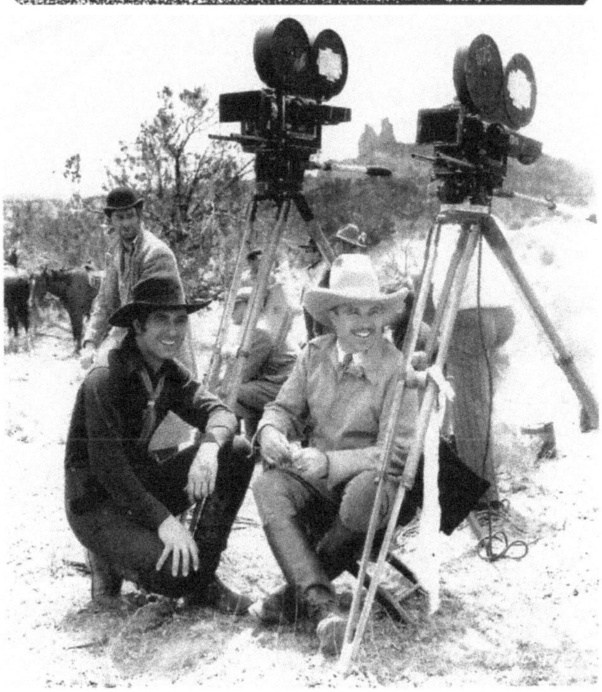

Taking a break during the Realife filming of 'Billy the Kid'. On the right, below the 35mm camera is director King Vidor and left, near the 70mm, is the film's star John Mack Brown, who was also in MGM's other Realife western 'The Great Meadow' in 1931.*

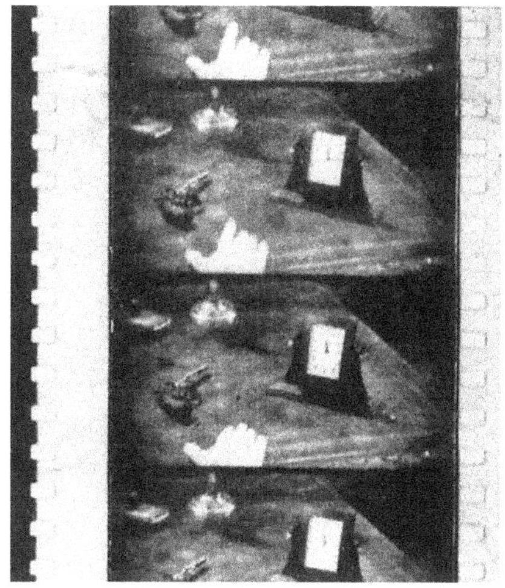

The wide film version of 'The Bat Whispers' was shown in Magnifilm format, advertised as 'Twice the size, twice the thrills'.

RKO tried out the **Spoor Natural Vision** process, using it to film a railroad drama, *Danger Lights*, in 1930. Being conceived as a silent format, the sound had to be added using a separate 35mm optical track. This ran at the normal 24 fps, but the 63.5mm picture was shot at 20 fps, which may have caused synchronisation problems if either broke during the show. Paramount came up with their own **'Magnafilm'**, which was basically 35mm with the width increased until the picture had an aspect ratio of two to one, ending up at 56mm. They only made a musical featurette called, *You're in the Army Now* in 1929. It was shown briefly at the Rivoli in New York. Unfortunately, both the film and its new 20 x 40 foot screen image received indifferent reviews, with the latter's illumination and focus falling off at the sides. This was possibly due to using camera lenses with insufficient covering power, or inadequately converted 35mm projectors used to show the 56mm prints.

After this, Paramount decided to join most of the other studios and adopt a 65mm format, which was becoming the chief rival to Fox's Grandeur. It had a similar frame area and aspect ratio, but used standard perforations, five to each frame. Warner Bros named it **'Vitascope'** to complement its Vitaphone sound for widescreen versions of *Kismet* and *The Lash* in 1930. United Artists used it for their **'Magnifilm'** presentation of *The Bat Whispers'* also in 1930. Warner Bros also called it **'Magnaframe'** when planning to use it for *Life of the Party*, but decided to film it in two-colour Technicolor instead, which was another, more successful, novelty at that time. There were other films which were announced as being, or going to be, shot on wide film, but which subsequently only appeared on 35mm.

The curtain closes on wide film

Suddenly, all this wide film activity came to a halt. News was coming back from exhibitors that having just converted to sound, they were not prepared to find any more money for even more new equipment. Some independent theatre owners took the cynical view that, the film companies, seeing millions of dollars being spent on sound gear from radio and phonograph manufacturers, now wanted them to buy new projectors and screens from companies in which they had a financial interest. William Fox, for example, was all set to profit by purchasing the Mitchell Camera Corp. and a major share of The International Projector Corp., whose Simplex and Powers machines had an 85% share of the USA market. Most producers were not too disappointed with this show of resistance, having got off the wide film hook. The Producers and Distributors Association of America met at the Hays Office, more famous for its moral code, and, in effect, censored wide film, agreeing not to 'by word and gesture to cause the public's curiosity to be aroused about any new invention for at least two years'. Its president, Adolph Zukor, put the exhibitors' minds at rest by assuring them that the introduction of wide film has been delayed until 'it is necessary again to provide an added attraction to the public'. All were still free to continue with their wide film research and development and it was agreed that a common format was needed.

Although 65mm was already being referred to as 'standard', the SMPE was charged with arriving at a final choice. To cater for most concerns, they came up with an 'economy' 50mm format. Like Paramount's earlier 56mm Magnafilm, it was just 35mm widened out with room for a more modest 1.85:1 picture, and space for a wider track. To make it more attractive to exhibitors, it could be shown on existing projectors using a 'simple' conversion kit. Fox cooperated by converting a Grandeur camera and projector to run SMPE's proposed 50mm format and produced a demonstration film which was shown on a 23 x 41 foot screen, its 16 x 9 proportions showing the shape of things to come.

However, even after the embargo was over, wide-film, whatever its gauge, remained on the shelf. Although once thought immune, the depression had finally caught up with the film industry, which couldn't afford any additional burdens. One of its chief champions, William Fox, had suffered personal and financial problems and was no longer in a position to revive Grandeur. Perhaps the most upset was George Spoor, who still had faith in his Natural Vision process and considered the whole situation to be 'commercial murder'. His 63.5mm film was last seen in the Spoor Spec-tac-culum at the Century of Progress exhibition in Chicago in 1933. From the birth of the movies, world fairs and exhibitions would offer a more willing home for unusual film formats and some, like IMAX® (Expo 70 in Japan), would live on to become successful in the later alternative 'special venue' market.

Typifying this sudden loss of interest was the ASC's 'Cinematographic Annual'. The 1930 edition had devoted two chapters to wide-film developments and the photographic challenges associated with the new wider screens. Looking at the following 1931 edition there was hardly a mention and, like many flirtations, best forgotten.

Wide film legacy

What can be seen today of this brief early flurry of activity in wider film formats? In the 1980s, Fox gave all its nitrate Grandeur material to the Museum of Modern Art's film archive, and, to celebrate its 50th anniversary in 1985, funding was found to restore the Grandeur version of *The Big Trail*. A printer was built to reduce the 70mm negative to a 35mm 'scope anamorphic print. The film's original 2.1:1 aspect ratio was retained by leaving a small area blank at the sides of the image placed within the normal 2.35:1 frame. The new safety preservation fine grain master positive and negative also used the same format. The decision not to make use of modern 65/70mm stock was said to be due to having to deal with the unusual perforation layout of the old 70mm (still known as type-I) negative, and the lack of current black and white 70mm (type-II) print film. The first specification of Grandeur stated that its thirteen frames to the foot ran at 20 fps giving the same 90 feet per minute as 35mm at 24 fps. As no frame rate problems were reported during its restoration, *The Big Trail* must have been shot at 24 fps. The new 35mm prints have allowed easier access, and the film has been regularly shown again on a wide screen at festivals and other special events, including at the NFT, with the BFI retaining a copy in their archives.

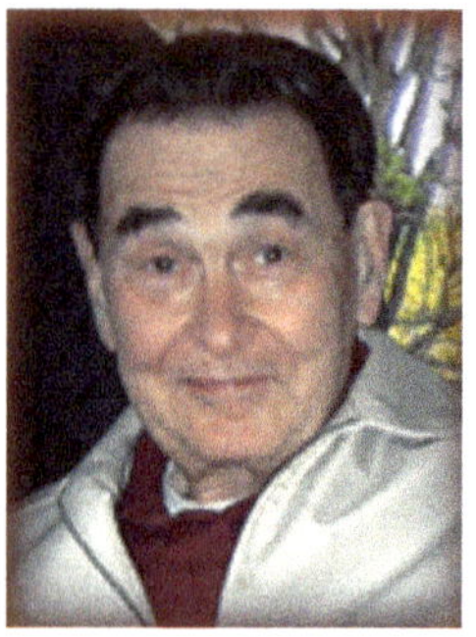

We should here pay tribute to Karl Malkames ASC (1926-2010). Karl was a noted cinematographer and constructor of special cine equipment which, over the years, has helped to save many films that were, at the time, considered to be too difficult for conventional methods. One of his triumphs was the 70mm Grandeur to 35mm printer that was used to restore *The Big Trail*.

Save the bats

Not long after, *The Bat Whispers* returned to wider screens following a restoration for the UCLA Film Archive by Robert Gitt and the YCM Labs in Burbank. The same 35mm anamorphic format was chosen for the final prints but, this time, the preservation safety masters could be made on 65mm.

It was discovered that the 1930 65mm film conformed to current stock. This was because the Fearless Superfilm 65mm camera, which photographed *The Bat Whispers*, would later become the first Todd-AO camera, the process which would successfully re-launch wide film in the 1950s. Also among the surviving material was evidence that 35mm reduction prints had also been made back in 1930. *The Bat Whispers* was the only American wide screen feature from this 1929-1930 period, to be shown on a wide screen in Britain. Some years ago, speaking to Richard Floyed, a projectionist who worked at the old Regal Marble Arch during the

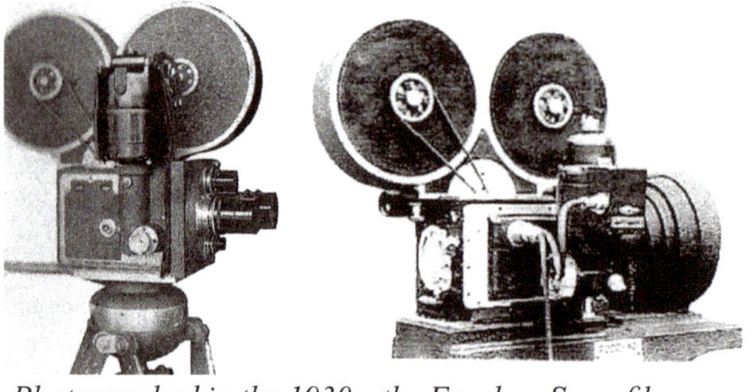

Photographed in the 1930s, the Fearless Superfilm camera (left) returned in the 1950s, together with its 65mm film, when it became the first Todd-AO camera (right)

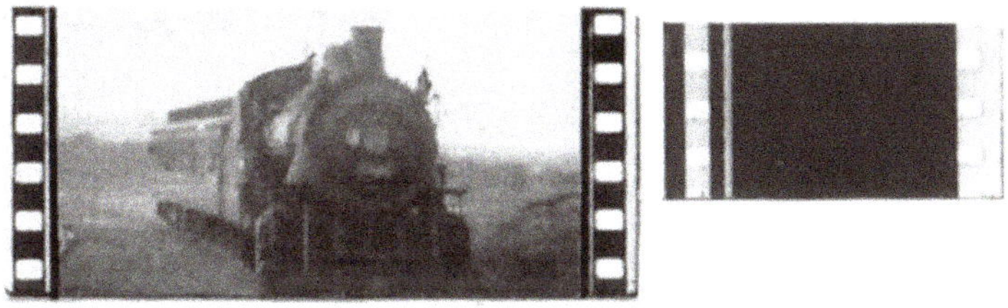

Spoor Natural Vision 63.5mm with separate 35mm soundtrack (Danger Lights)

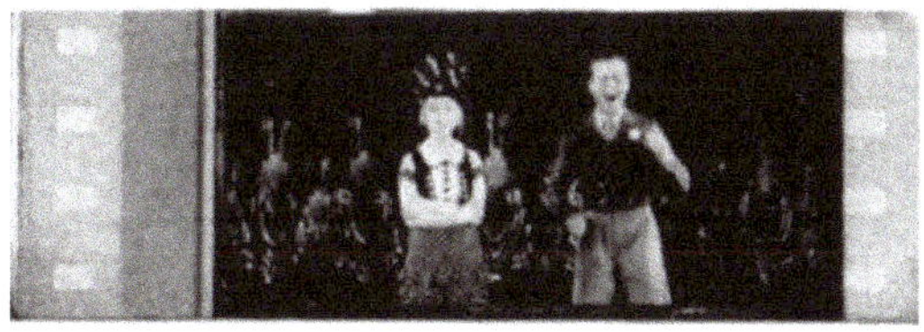

Fox Grandeur 70mm (Happy Days)

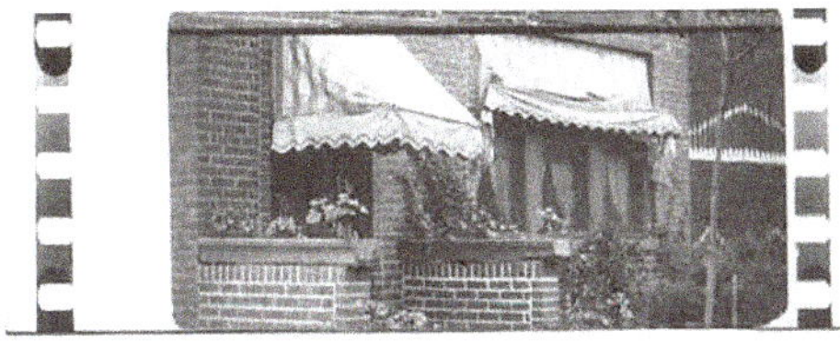

65mm (Paramount test)

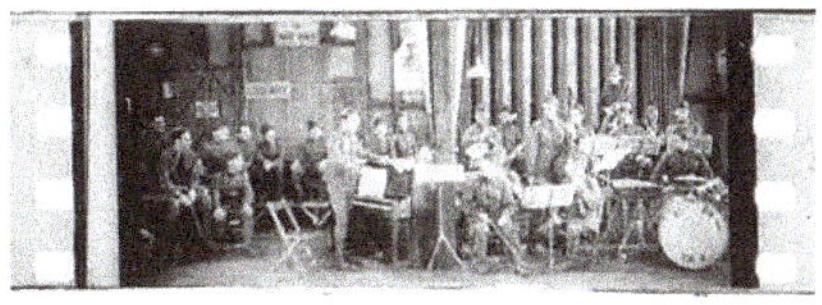

Paramount Magnafilm 56mm (You're in the Army Now)

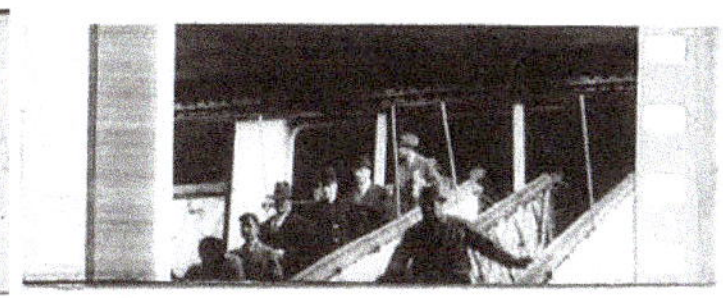

SMPE 50mm standard (Fox demonstration film)

Wide screen format comparisons (not exact size)

1930s, he said the film was projected using a 35mm reduction print made from the 65mm negative. The combined sound print had the finer grained 2:1 aspect ratio picture printed across the middle of the frame and United Artists supplied the necessary aperture plates and lenses to show the film on the theatre's own 'Giant Expanding Pictures' Magnascope-style screen. The Regal had separate big and small screens which could be flown into position when required. Richard remembered the occasion as much for the fact that Mary Pickford and Douglas Fairbanks, who were in London at the time, came along to see the results.

Now on video

Both films can now be seen again in widescreen on video, mastered from the new 35mm 'scope copies. The 'Magnifilm' version of *The Bat Whispers* was available for a while on a BFI VHS and more recently a special edition DVD 2-disk set of *The Big Trail* offers the choice of viewing either the normal 35mm or Grandeur version, with the extras including an interesting account of the Grandeur process. Watching their wide screen images today certainly gives them a modern look, but the audio quality, particularly *The Big Trail*, betrays their early sound era ancestry.

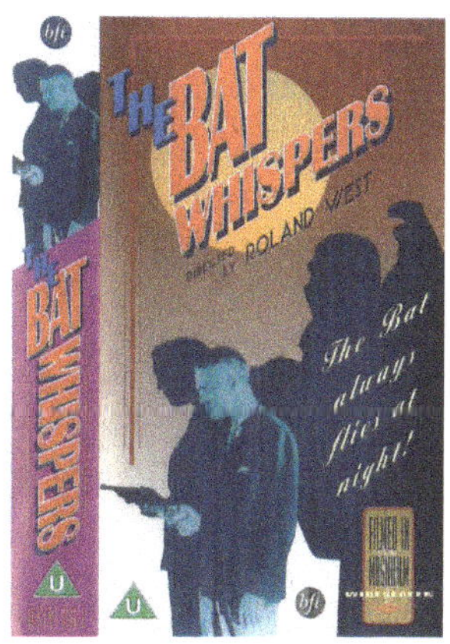

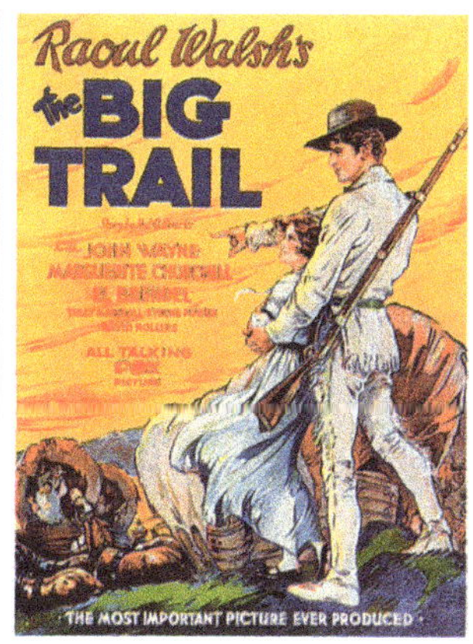

Small format equipment in the PPT museum

The Projected Picture Trust aims to Educate, Preserve and Restore cinema equipment. It has one of the largest technical archives anywhere which is available to members (by appointment). The Trust has locations throughout the United Kingdom with local co-ordinators for members to get involved. Run by an eclectic mix of respected industry professionals and cinema enthusiasts, the trust boasts a world-class collection of cinema technology artifacts and a growing digital archive acting as a hub of knowledge for just about anyone interested in finding out more about this side of the cinema business. Details: *www.ppttrust.org* email: *contact@ppttrust.org*

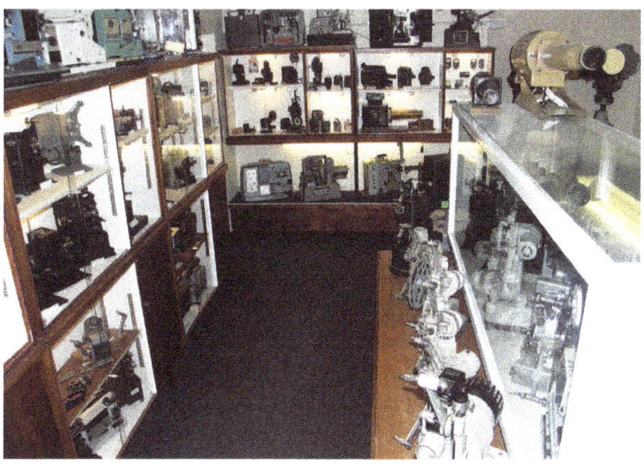

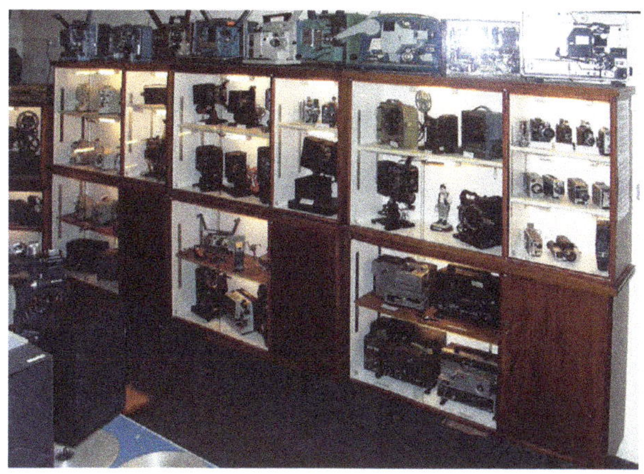

Frame rates - See and hear how they run

We take a closer look at 35mm film, relating to archives and restoration, and examine the importance of understanding about frame rates of original and restored versions if optimum restorations are to be achieved.

35mm is the oldest gauge, and was in constant use for theatrical motion pictures for well over a hundred and twenty years before beginning to step aside in favour of digital cinema technology. Even so, origination on film is still a popular choice, although inevitably the results are soon scanned for digital post production. In the end, along with the digital copies, in many cases the results are also transferred back to film in the form of a digital intermediate needed to produce a negative and projection prints for those screens around the world yet to go digital, and sometimes for archival purposes. For many producers, physical strips of 35mm film, at best in the form of long-life polyester black and white silver colour separations, remain the chosen way to archive and protect their investment rather than hoping that a current hard drive and its file format will still be playable after another hundred years. The digital preservation master copy will probably have to be regularly re-mastered to keep pace with the latest means of digital storage.

Die Hard 35mm

Even after the last roll of 35mm photographic film has been manufactured, its long history of use will have left us with a vast amount to deal with. Fortunately, whatever happens in the future, film viewing technology will remain relatively simple and it will be easy to build the necessary machinery. 35mm film has already out-lived many much younger video formats. Even today, it is sometimes difficult to find and maintain the equipment needed to replay and transfer some of the earlier, and now considered obsolete video tape formats.

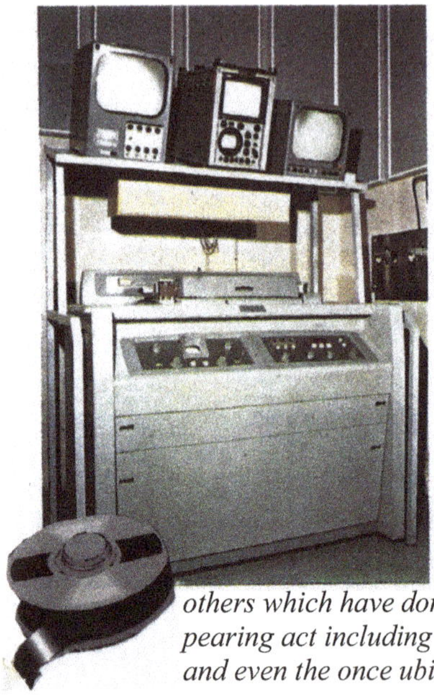

35mm film has already seen off the first of its electronic rivals, the 2 inch quadruplex video tape. Launched by Ampex in 1956, and widely used by broadcasters in the 1960s. Today it can be difficult to find a working machine able to play this obsolete format, and the same applies to others which have done a similar disappearing act including 1-inch, half-inch and even the once ubiquitous U-Matic.

The Human Touch

As is already the case for 'film' editors, new entrants into the field of cinema projection may never be required to touch a piece of 'real' film. Hopefully some may choose to gain the extra knowledge about handling this important legacy format and add what may become a new category of archival projection and presentation, to their range of skills.

The secret of 35mm's success

The success of 35mm becoming the world standard was due to the early agreement on its physical dimensions, which have remained virtually unchanged since it first rushed past beneath the peep-hole of Edison's Kinetoscope, way back in 1893. During the following years, the reluctance to change it, particularly by cost conscious exhibitors, meant that innovations, like the coming of sound and the widescreen, have all been accommodated without the need for radical changes to the basic design. The film has just been modified, creating the various formats.

Off to a flying start

One aspect, which remained variable for many years, was the taking and projection speeds. The first 35mm films did literally rush through the Kinetoscope at the rate of 46 frames per second. To simplify its design, the film ran continuously with each frame frozen for an instant by the stroboscopic effect of brief flashes of light (1/1000 sec) provided by a spinning slit shutter. This high frame rate, although over-generous in terms of reproducing movement, was needed to reduce the flicker. Our brains need at least about 48 interruptions to the light before it appears to be continuous. When projectors arrived, shortly after, most used true intermittent mechanisms which actually stopped each frame to be projected, giving the opportunity to show it more than once, so increasing the required flicker rate without using so much film. Despite this advantage, another early fast runner was the 68mm Biograph camera and projector which was remarkable in being able to move intermittently its IMAX size frames at 40fps without the aid of perforations. When shown today, the few surviving original Kinetoscope and early Biograph films, if not specially copied, appear to have been shot in slow motion.

The simple idea of using a strobe lamp to view continuously moving film is still with us. Past BKSTS trips to Technicolor let us see their strobe projectors used to immediately check the continuously moving film prints emerging from the high speed processors, now so fast there's only time to give a flash every few frames. The idea has also been applied to special telecines, particularly those suitable for running sometimes shrunken

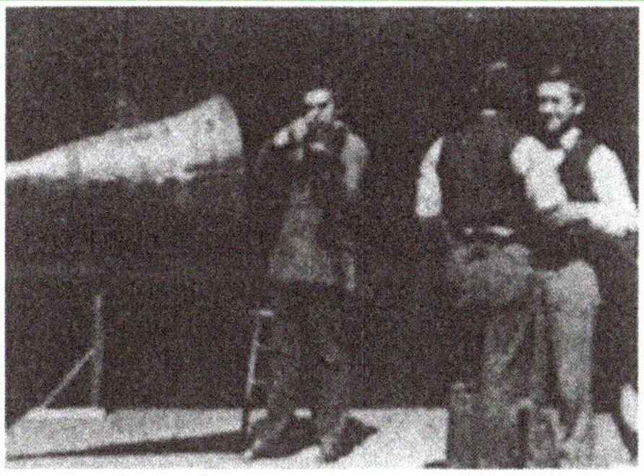

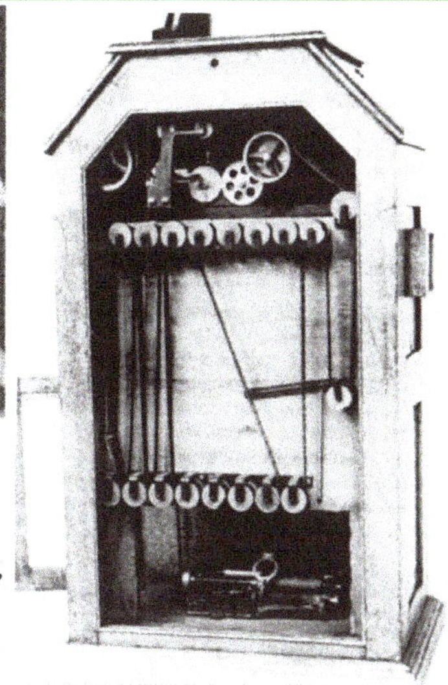

A test for Edison's Kinetophone, the sound version of the Kinetoscope. In both machines the 35mm film ran at 46fps. The photo above shows a violinist, believed to be the inventor W.K.L. Dickson, playing into the horn of an acoustic cylinder recorder. The last time I saw a clip of just the picture, it wasn't being used to illustrate the first ever sound film, but, as it features two of Edison's male workers dancing together (now in slow motion at 24fps) the suggestion instead was that this was the first gay film! Only in 1997 was the picture reunited with its sound on cylinder soundtrack, originally heard via stethoscope-style ear tubes connected to a player at the bottom of the cabinet. However, it took digital help and advice from a violin playing expert with perfect pitch to help judge the correct running speeds, before this 17 seconds of film history could be restored.

and brittle archival film. Such machines made practical a project in the mid-1990s to transfer to video the entire Fox Movietone cinema newsreel library. After six decades (1919-1963), the American collection alone amounted to over 40 million feet, not counting the British and European collections. The process operated 24 hours a day using a gentle on the film continuous transport with a xenon strobe lamp flashing (10 millisecond) each frame into a CCD video camera, the timing triggered by the position of the perforations. Everything was copied at real time (24fps), with the early silent footage slowed down during subsequent tape to tape transfers. For previewing the often vulnerable film, an equally kind "Strobiola" was built, using the same up-dated Kinetoscope principle.

Time To Slow Down

The Lumieres decided that 16 fps was adequate for reproducing movement and chose this for their Cinematographe in 1895. The inevitable flicker produced by its single blade shutter was tolerated in exchange for the magic of seeing moving pictures projected on a screen. Soon extra 'flicker' blades were added, with a three bladed shutter increasing the frequency to 48, in effect showing each frame three times before moving on to the next, or refreshed as described today. Even after this made watching films easier on the eyes, the term, 'going to the flicks' continued to be used to describe a trip to the cinema.

Speed of the Silents?

16 fps soon became regarded as the 'normal' speed. Most cameras conformed to the convention, set by the Lumieres, that two turns of the handle moved one foot of film, equivalent to 16fps, or 60 feet per minute. Cameramen prided themselves in being able to maintain this regular uniform rate; only changing it to increase or slow down the action for comic or dramatic effect. To help, some cameramen could be heard counting or humming a waltz as they cranked. Even so, the frame rate did vary, even the growing weight of the film in the take-up magazine could slow things down a bit.

The same applied to projectionists, but as film shows grew longer they had to keep turning, usually once per foot, hour in and hour out during a working day. To help even out any variations, some projectors had centrifugal governors fitted and before long, electric motors were being bolted on. Initially, some in authority, including some states in America, banned motors, fearing a greater fire risk from projectors which may

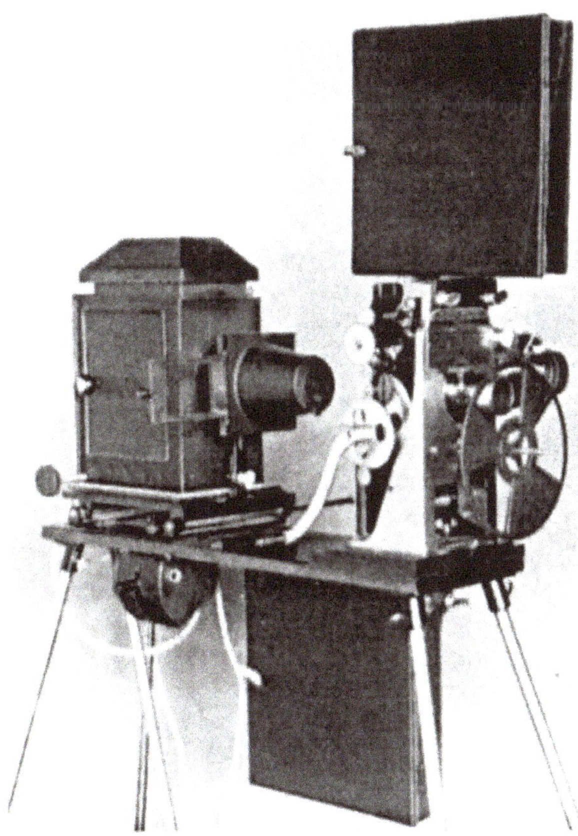

A hand-turned 35mm projector from the early years of the 1900s, already fitted with a three-blade shutter for easier on the eyes flicker-free pictures

now be left unattended. Many motor driven projectors kept their cranking handle, now made to disengage, as an aid to lacing, before replaced with an inching knob.

Motors and the art of projection

Although motors freed the operator of the tiresome task of cranking, some said it took away one of his important skills. A projectionist manual from 1915 declares, "There is no such thing as a standard camera speed and it needs a practiced and intelligent hand to tell the approximate speed at which the picture was taken and to adjust his speed to a far nicety than is possible by a mechanical agency which maintains a constant speed." In response, equipment manufacturers put the operator back in control with variable speed drives, in the early days mostly mechanical variable friction drives. The art of projection was also under threat from another outside agency, the theatre's management. They would often ask for the film to be speeded up or slowed down to make those of different lengths fit a set programme time. Often a faster rate was ordered to try and increase business by fitting in more showings in a day, particularly at the weekends.

Producers were soon complaining that "Our fine productions are being outraged by the manager compelling the projectionist to over-speed the projector in order to keep within a given schedule." The renters tried to help them by indicating the running time on the cans and in some cases stating the total running time on the posters, in the hope that the public would also complain if the film finished too early. These ploys usually failed, with the former ignored and the latter covered up. It should be said that, back at the studios, cameramen also sometimes came under pressure to do the opposite with directors wanting the camera slowed down to fit more of their story into a given number of reels.

D.W.Griffith's 'The Birth of the Nation' (1915) was shot between 12fps and 15fps, but invariably shown much faster. Audiences didn't seem to mind and actually appreciated the added pace when watching some plodding dramas.

Keeping in time with the music

Also found in the instructions, among the advice on offer to early hand-turning projectionists was this warning, "Keeping pace with the musical accompaniment may also induce the inexperienced operator to inadvertently accelerate or retard the speed of projection." From the very first shows, 'silent' films were rarely projected in silence. Apart from the familiar piano, they were also accompanied by live narration, sound effects performed from behind the screen, sometimes with the help of ingenious mechanical effects machines, and in the larger picture palaces, a full orchestra. If they could afford them, many smaller local cinemas employed groups of musicians. To guide them as to the choice and mood of the music throughout the film, the studios began to issue cue sheets. Many of the most important productions had specially composed scores and the sheet music supplied often included instructions to the operator about the required running speed of the projector. To help cooperate, a useful accessory was a speedometer and some models of projector, like those from Kalee and Ernemann, had them built-in, calibrated in frames per second and/or feet per minute.

In the face of this running speed anarchy, The Society of Motion Picture Engineers made an effort to arbitrate. Formed in 1916, it had already produced accepted standards for 35mm film, including frame dimensions and the size and shape of its perforations, all with close tolerances. However, the frame rate was far less specific, again, only suggesting that 16fps be regarded as normal. In 1923, they also attempted to standardise its running speed. Observers with stopwatches were sent off to studios to undertake time and crank motion studies and theatres were surveyed about their current running speed practices.

The results showed that cameramen were indeed keeping to near 16fps, sometimes even less, whereas projectionists were well ahead in the race, ranging from 18 to 27fps. For the best chance of a reconciliation, the SMPE took a pragmatic view and compromised by proposing a

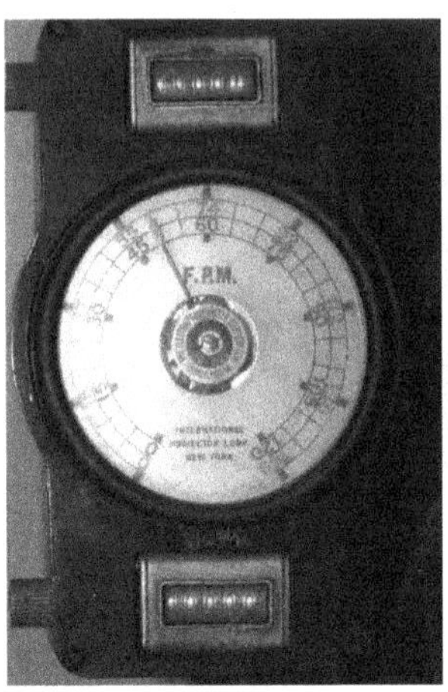

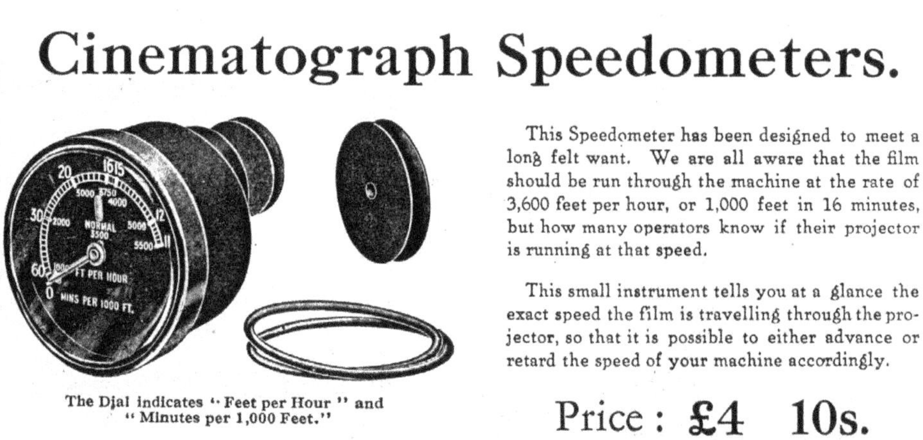

Left - As late as 1930 the Simplex Grandeur projector had a speedometer calibrated in feet per minute for both 35mm and 70mm film. Right: An ad for an add-on projector speedometer.

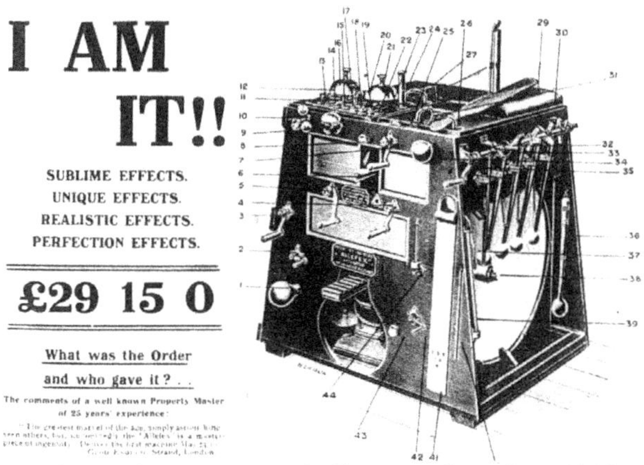

Mechanical cinema sound effects machine from 1910. Fifty different sounds without the aid of microprocessors, and you didn't even need to plug it in!

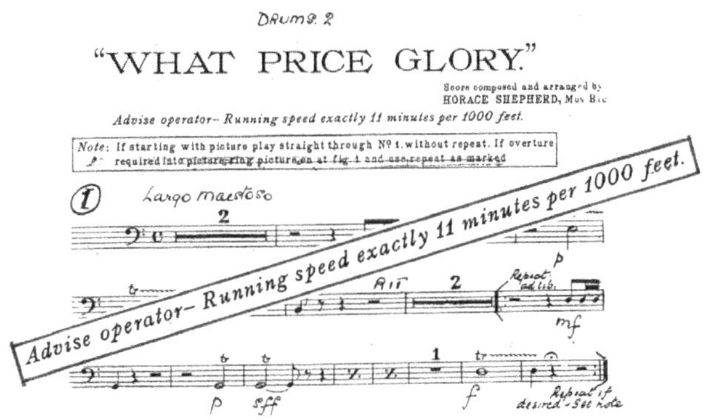

Music scores included running speed instructions. In this case 11 minutes per 1000 feet, which is 24fps, although Kevin Brownlow judged the camera speed to be nearer 22fps in 1926.

different standard for the taking and projection speeds, 16fps (60 feet per minute) and 21fps (80 feet per minute) respectively. Even at the time many of its members thought that an organisation dedicated to high standards should actually recommend a practice which would result in a form of distortion, even if audiences had already been conditioned to it. However, the practice did benefit the viewer, with less flicker and smoother, albeit faster, motion on the screen.

In the event, the exhibitors took little notice and not wishing to give up their flexibility, they literally put their foot down and the gap continued to grow. In response, the studios finally instructed cameramen to increase their speed, and, by the end of the 1920s, most of Hollywood's silent films were being shot at 20 to 24fps. British studios generally followed suit, but others abroad continued at 16fps. Hand-turned cameras were used throughout the silent era. Motors were available as an accessory, and sometimes fitted to free the cameraman to concentrate on the more elaborate and fluid camera moves seen in many of the later silents. Occasionally, hand-cranking 'mute' cameramen could still be spotted among the banks of newsreel cameras covering special events and ceremonies right up to the 1940s war years.

Sound brings harmony

The coming of sound finally ended the running speed conflict and brought forth a common fixed filming and projection speed. The ear is far less forgiving of discrepancies, with only a slight difference changing the pitch of familiar sounds. One early believer in sound films was Lee de Forest who adopted the SMPE' s recommended projection speed of 21fps for his Phonofilm sound-on-film system. A number of shorts were shown in selected theatres which were wired for sound, beginning in 1923, but sound was still regarded as a novelty and no threat yet to the art of the silent cinema. However, when the sound revolution did begin in 1927, it was 24fps which was to become the new speed of the motion pictures. Warner Bros, in partnership with Western Electric, selected it as part of the specification for its sound-on-disc 'Vitaphone' system, one factor-being that a survey of its theatres showed that this was the average speed at the time. It would be Fox's 'Movietone' which would set the pattern for the competing sound-on-film systems. This included the established 20 frame offset on the print between the intermittent picture and the continuously smooth running optical sound track. They also adopted the same 24fps. Not entirely an independent choice, as there was a fair degree of co-operation between those developing the different systems. Western Electric, also working on their own sound-on-film system, was the main supplier of amplifiers. RCA also adopted 24fps for their 'Photophone' optical tracks. They could also share the same speed-controlled motors fitted to many of the early universal disc and optical sound projectors, which were in use for a while before sound-on-film finally won the day. The linear speed of the film at 24fps, was the minimum needed to allow the early optical tracks to match the same 5KHz frequency range as discs.

During the transition to sound, many of the last silents were turned into sound films by adding recorded music, often that originally composed for the theatre musicians, together with synchronised effects and tacked-on 'talkie' sequences. Early sound films, like the landmark 'The Jazz Singer' (1927), were basically silent films, complete with inter-titles, with only an occasional dialogue scene. For an early British effort, film maker George Pearson revamped his otherwise silent 'Auld Lang Syne' (1929) into sound by marrying old footage of its singing music hall star, Harry Lauder, to one of his existing commercial gramophone records. This was re-recorded onto an optical track at sound speed of 24fps. The picture had been shot at 16fps, so had to be 'stretched' to fit by printing every other frame twice. The two were then kept, more or less in sync with the help of some additional cut and patch editing. This technique of stretch printing would continue to be used in the years to come when including old silent footage in documentaries, compilation films, and some re-issues with added sound. This method is now regarded as unsatisfactory, resulting in a noticeable judder to the action and reinforcing modern audiences' view that old silent films were jerky. Some film discoveries are found to have been previously stretch printed and archivists often now choose to put the film back on an optical printer to eliminate the repeated frames.

There was an attempt to offer a reverse process to shrink 24fps sound films down to 16fps. It was thought that it could be useful when making silent versions of professional sound films for showing on home movie projectors. Little use was made of the service, relying on amateur showmen to rev-up their variable speed projectors if they wanted more natural movement. Home movie making was to play its part in the enduring view that 16fps was the speed of silent cinema. When introduced in 1922 and 1923, the first hand-turned 9.5mm and 16mm cameras soon gave way to spring-wound motors governed at 16fps. 8mm followed suit in 1932, and the sound/silent switch on narrow gauge sound projectors set them running at either 24 or 16fps. However, around the start of the 1960s, in the interest of smoother action, and perhaps to sell more film, the speed was quietly changed to 18fps, and when Super-8 was introduced in 1965, this was its standard speed for amateur filming. The last 16mm machines also upped their 'silent' speed to 18fps.

Lights, camera, and now natural action

With the coming of sound, cinema projectors around the world were now all running at a fixed 24fps and audiences could settle back and enjoy everything moving at the correct speed. Strangely, at first, many who had become psychologically conditioned to the speeded-up silents, thought the new sound films 'dragged', until their brains slowed down to match. The more static and stilted production techniques of the first sound films didn't help either.

Silent films still sell tickets

With the end of the silents, most cinema musicians lost their jobs. One instrument harder to get through the exit door was the cinema organ. From the 1920s it was built-in feature in many of the larger theatres. These one-man orchestras, which could also provide a range of sound effects, continued to entertain audiences between the new sound films for another 30 years or so, the last only silenced by the multi-screen conversions, beginning in the 1970s. A few have survived, a notable example at the Odeon Leicester Square, can still make an impressive appearance, when its illuminated console, and regular organist, Donald Mackenzie rise from the orchestra pit at premieres and other special occasions. These include Donald's special morning concerts, which usually include an item accompanying a silent comedy short, complete with bells and whistles, giving his audience a chance to re-live the experience of the cinema's not so 'silent' days.

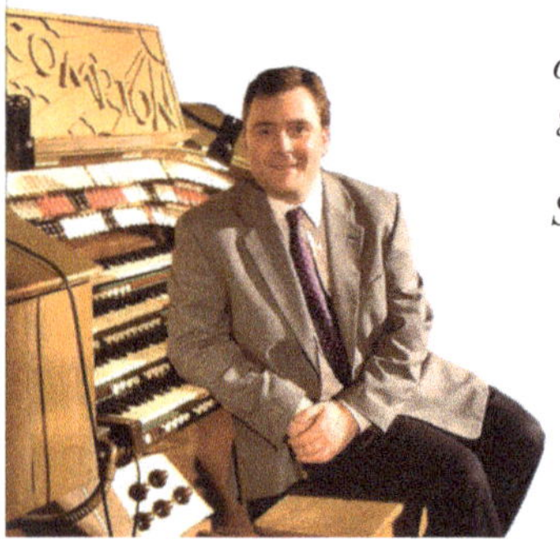

Donald Mackenzie is one of Europe's finest organists. He has presided at the Odeon Leicester Square organ for over 25 years. He has a reputation for being the finest exponent of silent film accompaniment on the organ.

www.donaldmackenzie.org.uk

Let us now enjoy a film

Silent films have also offered an alternative programming opportunity for churches, and a chance for their organists to extend their repertoire. For a short fund raising season, Truro Cathedral hosted, an appropriate choice, *The Hunchback of Notre Dame* (1923), featuring Lon Chaney. The layout meant that organist, David Briggs, couldn't see the screen, so had to follow the action via a TV monitor, in this case laterally reversed, coming from a video camera looking at the images on the back of the screen. Like many of today's showings at venues new to film, life was made easier by using a video projector. The DVD copy used had also been transferred with regard to the film's original running speed.

Video can help

Among those who have strived over the years to popularise silent cinema and present the films in the best possible way, is Kevin Brownlow, and running speeds became an issue during the pre-production for his Thames Television 'Hollywood' series, which celebrated the silent era. It was thought that, although the first audiences became conditioned to accepting the accelerated motion, modern viewers, more used to a natural portrayal, might now blame it on poor presentation. Back in the pre-digital 1980s, he, and his co-producer, David Gill, hoped to produce the programmes on film, but stretch-printing the many clips proved to be disappointing. It was decided to master the series on video tape, which allowed the use of a variable speed telecine. In this case, the only one readily available at the time was an old Mechau polygon mirror-drum machine borrowed from the BBC.

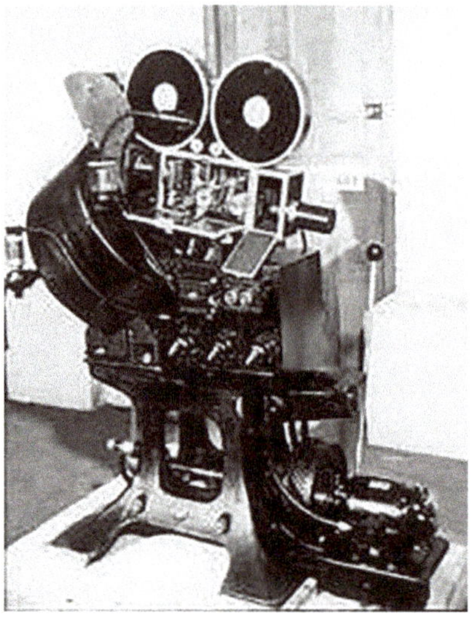

This was also used for previewing the clips and to determine, as far as possible, their original filming speed. As everyone has a slightly different sense of rhythm, it was thought wise to base the decisions on more than one opinion. As a guide for others, Kevin shared his research by going on to publish a list of 25 of the most often shown silent classics, together with their average original filming frame rates compared to the actual projection speeds, usually faster, based on evidence provided by studying surviving cue-sheets and music scores. The success of the series helped to revive an interest in silent cinema and restored prints of many classics returned to the big screen. Particularly popular are the special event showings with live music, with the earlier 'Thames Silents' proving that once forgotten silent films could still draw an appreciative audience.

Similar events are still being regularly staged, not only at festivals in conventional theatres, but at other public spaces, like concert halls, civic centres and other venues, including outdoors, which have room for a full orchestra. The chosen music is sometimes the same as written or suggested for the original showings, but to attract a modern audience, new scores are often commissioned and conducted by celebrity composers. They are not always to the taste of all silent film buffs, remembering record producer George Moroder's pop 'disco' version of 'Metropolis', appealing to an even wider audience back in the 1980s. The film has been subject to many restorations, the latest, with an extra 20 minutes found in Argentina, is being presented with the original 1927 score by Gottfried Huppertz.

It can be difficult to state a specific running time for silent films, without also giving the projection speed. When given in film guides, this is usually now the present 24fps. Looking at contemporary silent film catalogues, back in the hand-cranking days, only the footage is given.

Projection choices

Increasingly, digital projection is being used, but 35mm film prints are still often preferred, particularly for the largest screens. Specialist archival projection teams can provide high light output projectors, sometimes water-cooled, together with three bladed shutters and variable speed motors to match the original filming speeds.

As an example, Bell Theatre Services supplied the projection for a presentation of the 1925 version of 'Ben Hur' at London's Royal Festival Hall, with Carl Davis conducting the Royal Philharmonic Orchestra (see panel). This time, the original filming speed was examined even more closely and was judged to have been shot at five different frame rates and involved seventeen changes to the projector's speed during the performance.

Carl Davis was back at the podium for 'The Gold Rush' (1925) using a score created by Chaplin for its 1942 sound reissue. This was shown at 24fps, but the screening this time was to be at 22fps, so the music had to be extended to fit the now longer sequences.

		Camera fps	Projector fps
Blind Husbands	1919	16	?
Foolish Wives	1921	16	18
Four Horsemen of the Apocalypse	1921	20	21
Monsieur Beaucaire	1924	18	24
Robin Hood	1922	19	22
Scaramouche	1923	19	22
Merry Widow	1925	19	24
Ben Hur	1925	19	22
The Crowd	1928	20	24
Show People	1928	20	24
Flesh & The Devil	1926	20	23
Mysterious Lady	1928	20	24
The Black Pirate	1926	20	24
Lilac Time	1928	20	24
Love	1927	20	24
The Eagle	1925	22	24
Wedding March	1928	22	24
The Strong Man	1926	22	24
What Price Glory?	1926	22	24
Trail of 98	1928	22	24
Woman of Affairs	1928	24	24
The General	1926	24	24
Docks of New York	1928	24	24
Queen Kelly	1928	24	24

Kevin Brownlow's fascinating filming speed and projection list. Courtesy Kevin Brownlow

The process of selecting the best frame rate has been made easier with the more readily available calibrated multi-speed viewing and transfer facilities, both film and digital. However, forward planning is essential, as its not unknown that all this effort to be thwarted on the eve of the show when it's discovered that the music has been written or arranged using a previously supplied video copy of the film running at a different speed.

Not forgetting a few fast runners

Although 24fps was to become the cinema's standard frame rate, a few proprietary projection systems chose a higher rate. One, in the silent days, was the additive Kinemacolor process, which photographed and projected black and white 35mm film through alternating red and green filters at 32fps. This was just fast enough for the viewer's brain to blend the image s on the screen together to create a limited range of colours.(1907)
In the interest of a smoother and flicker-free image on the biggest screens, the original, 3-strip Cinerama ran at 26fps, and 70mm Todd-AO at 30fps, although both were subsequently reduced to the normal 24fps to facilitate the printing of various forms of compatible reduction prints. In the special venue market, Showscan went higher at 60fps, and other enhanced 35mm and. 70mm systems selected 48fps, which if necessary could provide 24fps copies by printing every other frame.

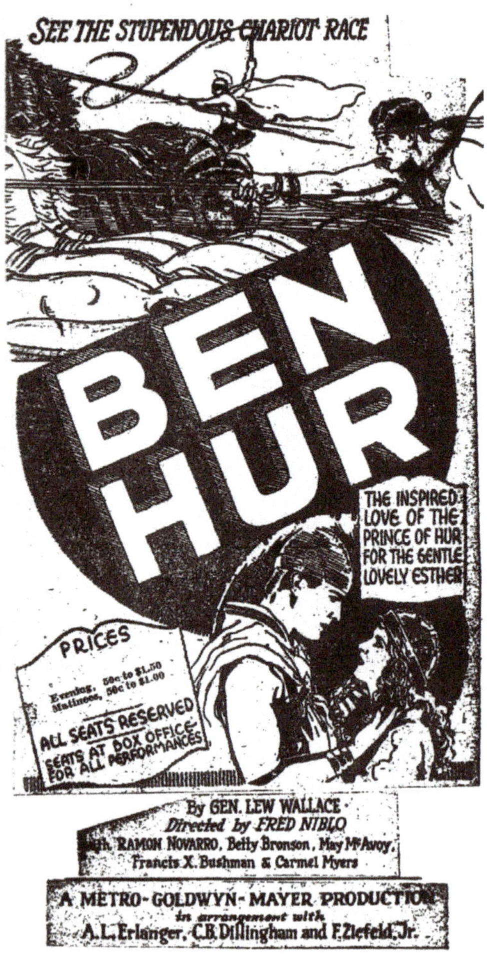

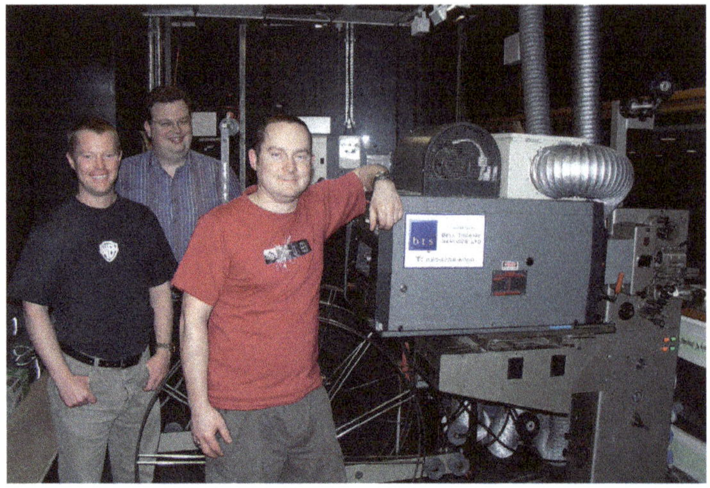

One movie, 17 speed changes!
Steff, Ian and Barry formed Bell Theatre Services 'archive team' for the projection of the 1925 version of Ben Hur - 17 speed changes were needed during the performance. The speed changes were carried out on the Kinoton FP20 by means of a pre-programmed inverter. The projector speed was calibrated back at the BTS office using a stroboscope, and the inverter frequency noted for a given film speed. The frequency of the inverter for a desired frame rate was then calculated. All required inverter frequencies were programmed to the inverter to correspond with the required frame rates. The film speed was then selected by means of a rotary switch controlled by the operator, who followed a running script or attempted to sync the scene changes to a DVD which had been mastered at the correct frame rates for each shot.

BFI restoration of Napoleon on Blu-ray

Elsewhere in this book we explain why Abel Gance's heroic depiction of the rise of Napoleon Bonaparte is an undisputed cinema landmark. Famed for its ground-breaking technical innovations – including its famous triptych finale – and a running time of 5 ½ hours, the story's chapters play out in exhilarating fashion, tied together by an incredible feat of editing and technical ingenuity.

In 2016 The BFI announced a new chapter in the epic history of this film. As the culmination of a 50-year project, film historian Kevin Brownlow and the BFI National Archive completed a new digitally restored version of Gance's cinematic triumph. Audiences across the UK were able to experience this extraordinary cinematic masterpiece, with Carl Davis' magnificent score, and it is available on BFI DVD/Blu-ray and BFI Player.
This new version of Napoleon shows the film's original tinting and toning, including colour combinations which could not be achieved in the existing 35mm print. Integration of sections sourced from a wide range of elements were also been improved by detailed digital image repair and alignment. The film was entirely re-graded and digitally cleaned-up, providing the most complete version of the film available.

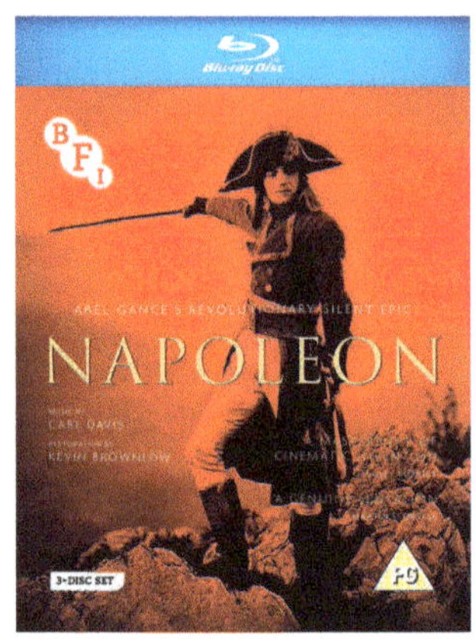

Kevin Brownlow spent over 50 years tracking down surviving prints from archives around the world since he first saw a 9.5mm version as a schoolboy in 1954. Brownlow and his colleagues at Photoplay worked with the BFI National Archive on the restorations.

Running at over 5½ hours,
the film demands a huge investment of resources, from projectionists, musicians, conductor and audiences. Napoleon offers one of the most richly rewarding and thrilling experiences in the history of cinema, this version offering a brilliant pairing of film and music, the score composed and conducted by Carl Davis and newly re-corded in 7.1, this definitive digital restoration presents this silent masterpiece in all its grandiose glory.

https://shop.bfi.org.uk/dvd-blu-ray/early-cinema/napoleon.html

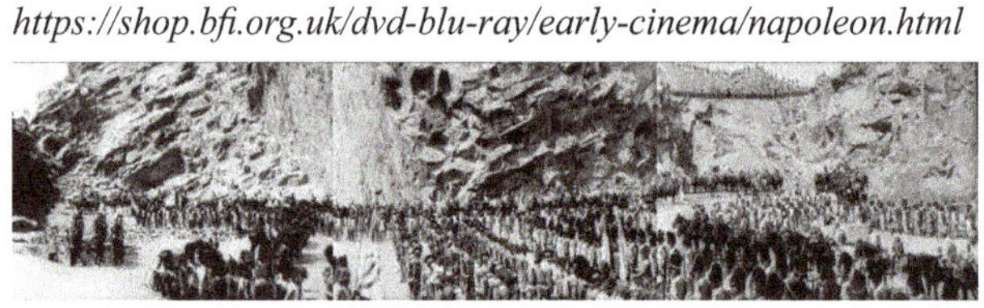

More on Aspect Ratios - Windows on the world & marketing tools for cinema

Film restorers need a historical perspective on how different aspect ratios were used if they are to understand how to save the images from the more unusual film formats and other moving picture devices which have appeared since the birth of cinema. Back in the 1890s, the sight of the first motion pictures would have been just as amazing whatever the shape of the image. Even for many of today's viewers the proportions of the screen are far less important to them than what is being shown on it. However, at times during the history of the cinema, changes to the shape of its pictures, along with the names given to the various methods used to bring them about, have been promoted as an added attraction and sometimes given even greater publicity than the stars themselves.

We continue our history of the changing shape of cinema and TV screens with a look at some of the early pioneers who tried to give cinemagoers a broader horizon and a reminder of how things developed.

The traditional view

It would be the early commercial success of the 35mm film format which would determine the shape of the cinema screen for the first 60 years. This was to have the proportions of 4 by 3, also described as having an aspect ratio of 1.33:1. It first emerged, fully formed, from Edison's research laboratory in 1893, the result of the film's 1 inch by ¾ inch frames.

The reasons for the choice were never fully explained by its inventor, W. Laurie Dickson, particularly any artistic factors influencing the shape of the frames. Apart from his inventive mechanical skills, he was already an accomplished 'still' photographer.

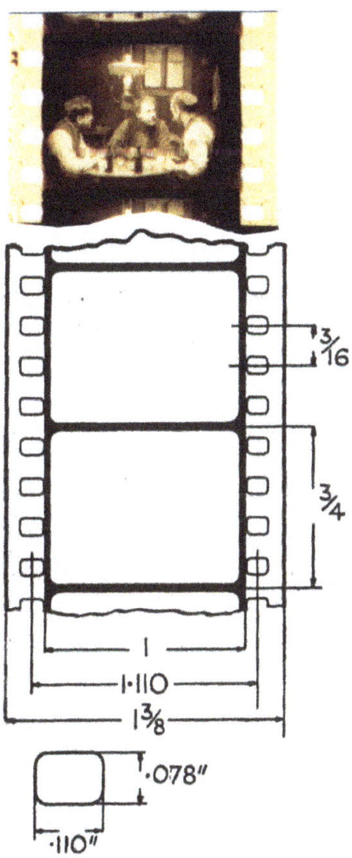

The worldwide acceptance of the Edison gauge included its 1.33:1 aspect ratio

At the time, photographic prints and lantern slides were presented in many different shapes. If rectangular, like paintings, they could either be in the higher than wide 'portrait' format, or described as 'landscape' with a greater width than height. Oval and round images were also popular, and the first easy to use amateur 'Kodak' camera from 1888 produced circular pictures on a roll of new flexible celluloid film, the material which would soon be seized upon by inventors and finally make movies possible. Dickson's first experiments also produced circular images on narrower horizontally running film before he finally settled on the 4 by 3 landscape shape for his own moving pictures, now on vertically running 13/8 inch film, half that of the Kodak 2¾ inch width.

Technically, the proportions of the frames made efficient use of the space between the perforations and not being too far from a square made it a good match to both the circular coverage of lenses and light sources. Whatever the reasons, the now 'classic' 1.33:1 aspect ratio would soon become familiar to audiences and is still very much with us, having to be accommodated among today's many different display shapes.

In 1907, 4 by 3, together with the 35mm film format, became the international standard for professional film making. Artistically, as the art of cinematography advanced, cameramen embraced the 4 by 3 format, successfully using it creatively to convey both intimate scenes and wide open spaces, with few of them expressing any need for a change.

Taking a different, wider view

Although to be outnumbered by those working on bringing colour and sound to the screen, there were to be a few persistent innovators who wished to escape the confines of the 4 by 3 frame and add even more to the realism by making it wider to include a greater, more natural, field of view. Between them, working up to the end of the 1920s, they would demonstrate every conceivable means of achieving it.

Sharing a wider view

The method of assembling a single continuous panoramic image from separate strips of film dates back to 1897. For a moving picture version of the painted and lantern slide Panorama exhibitions of the time, Frenchman Raoul Grimoin Sanson mounted ten movie cameras facing outwards to cover the entire horizon. The films were shown using ten mechanically linked projectors onto the inside surface of a cylindrical screen, up to 100 metres in circumference, surrounding the audience. His 'Cineorama' system was chosen as an exhibit at the 1900 Paris Exhibition. For this show, the camera rig, which took the strength of three men to crank it, was fitted into the

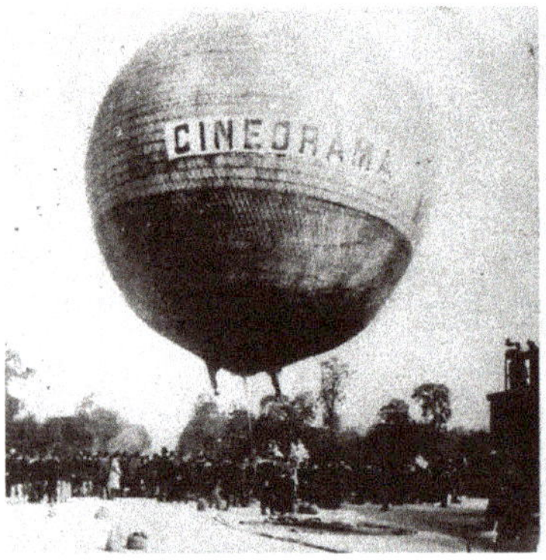

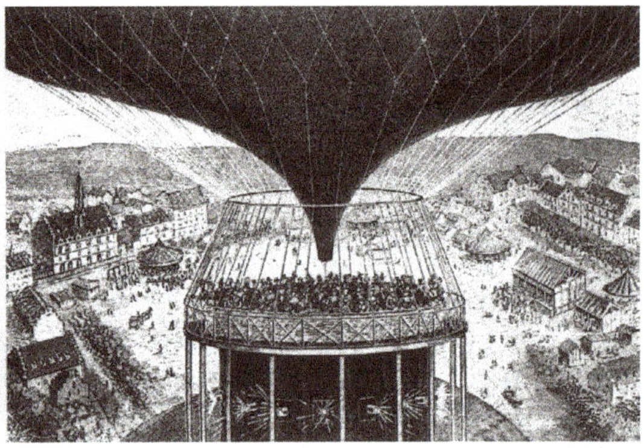

Cineorama takes to the skies, and an artist's impression of its presentation in 1900

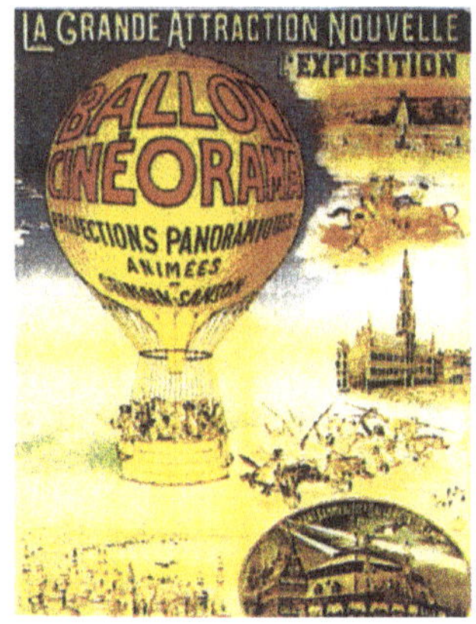

basket of a balloon and taken for a trip over Paris and Brussels. Back on the ground, visitors to the show could share the experience by standing in a simulated balloon basket, mounted on top of the projection box, to watch the hand coloured films all around them.

Sadly it wasn't long before the police rushed into the hall to cancel any future flights, fearing that the heat from the ten inadequately ventilated 40 amp arc lamps would cause a fire, turning the basket and its passengers into an equally spectacular flaming 'Wickerman' demonstration. I'm not sure if Cineorama's multiple images, if successfully blended together into a single endless picture, had an aspect ratio. Perhaps you could call it 1 to infinity?

Later, much safer full-circle processes, like Disney's Circarama and Russia's Circlorama, left narrow gaps between their individual 9, 11, or 22 (two tier) 1.33:1 screens. These not only made matching their edges less of a challenge but also provided a convenient position for the synchronised projectors to throw their images through the gaps to the screen opposite. This arrangement requires an odd number of screens, which were usually raised above a standing audience to stop them getting in the way of the beams.

Although none of the earlier Cineorama footage is known to have survived, Disney's current version of Circarama and other similar 360 degree systems are still a feature in many of today's theme parks. Like other film based 'rides', most are now following the commercial cinema and going digital.

Back in 1922, American John D. Elms presented his much simpler 'Widescope' process, which could be shown as part of the programme in ordinary cinemas. His twin lens camera (pictured right) photographed a wider field of view on a pair of normal 35mm films. These were shown side by side on a double width screen using interlocked projectors linked together with a connecting rod and universal joint, hoping that not too many viewers noticed the seam down the middle of the picture.

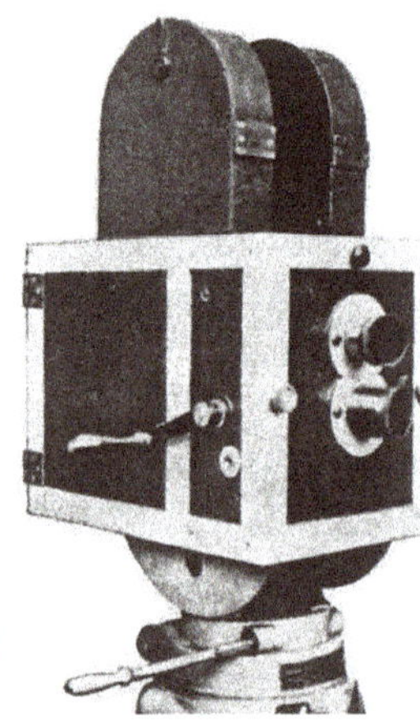

After one trade demonstration of Widescope, one prophetic industry expert and spoilsport suggested that, "If double width pictures are desired, it seems hardly necessary to go to the great trouble and expense involved, when it would be quite possible to get the same results by using standard film and masking off a portion of the top or bottom, or both, and then using the proper focus objective lens to project the picture to the size required."

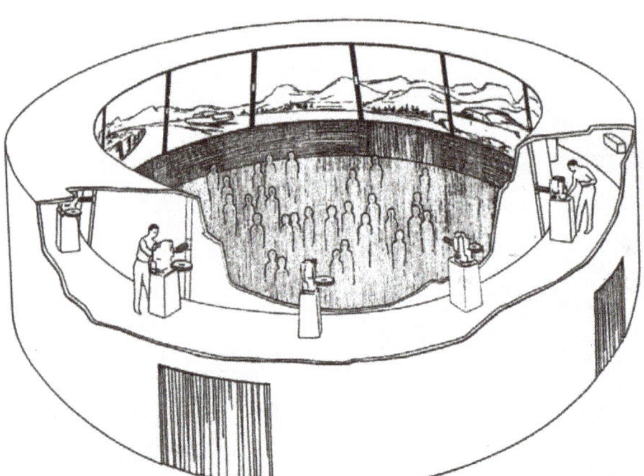

Layout of Disney's first 360 degree Circarama, with 11 16mm projectors placed between segments of the screen

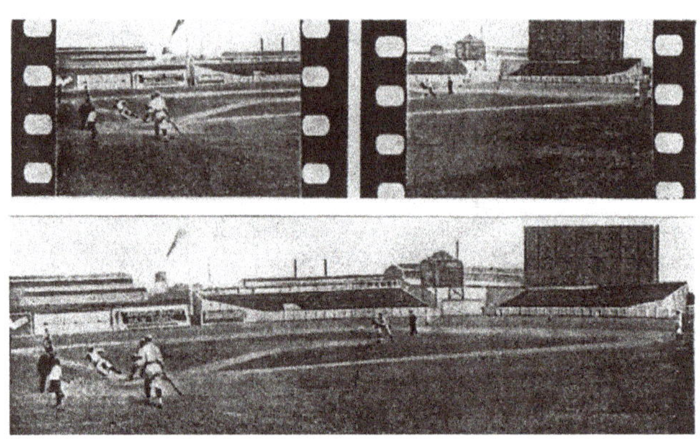

A pair of Widescope 35mm film prints and the final screen image

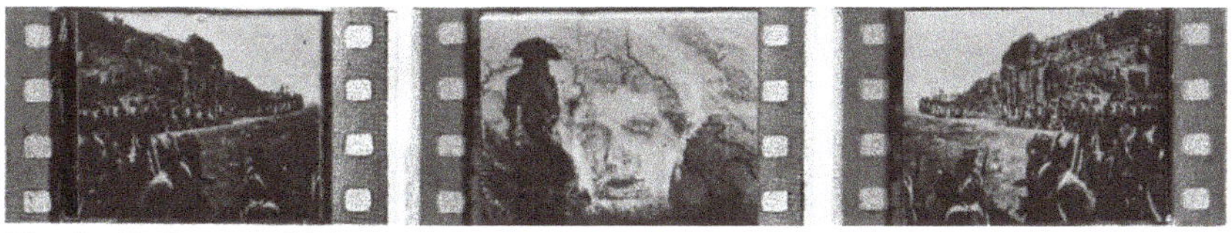

Triple 'Polyvision' 35mm prints

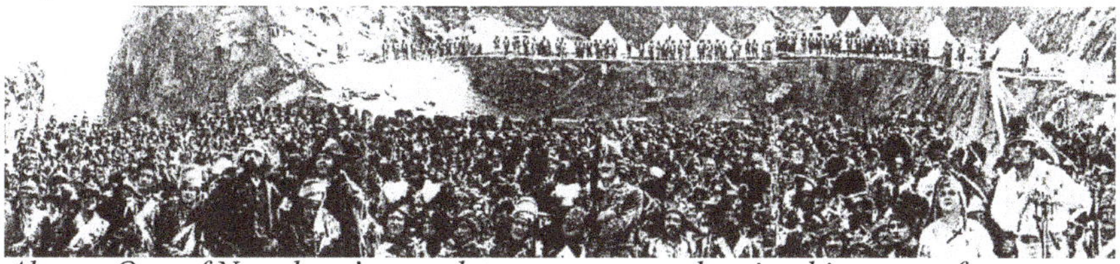

Above: One of Napoleon's complete panoramas showing his army of extras invading Italy.

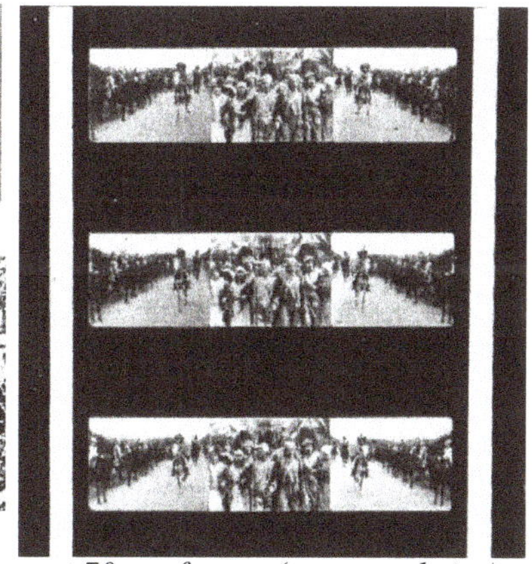

Right - triptych printed across a current 70mm frame. (not actual size)

Napoleon invades the auditorium

Now to France, when in 1927, Abel Gance added a third panel to Widescope for sequences in his more influential 'Napoleon'. Three stacked electrically driven Debrie 35mm cameras were angled to record a panorama of almost 4:1. Only a couple of these complete panoramic shots made it into the final film. Most of the story was played out on the centre of the screen, with the other two projectors only started up at its climax, and then mostly to create a multi-image triptych, typically with the main action in the centre flanked on either side by contrasting or complementary images.

The film's premiere at L'Opera in Paris was a great success, accompanied by a full orchestra and three projectors installed to show the triple panel sequences on a 100 foot wide screen. Repeated in other European cities, Napoleon was well received by the more sophisticated opera type audiences, but didn't fare well when shown in ordinary cinemas. A shorter general release version was still considered too long and disjointed. Cinemagoers at the time were also not ready for all the film's cinematic innovations like rapid cutting, hand held camera work, double exposures, and 'Polyvision' multiple images.

These included the triptychs, now losing all their original wide screen impact by being reduced in size to three tiny pictures across the frame of a single film. American audiences never had the chance to see Gance's 'Triple Ecran' system in all its glory. Some studio bosses feared that repeating the experience might have caused Napoleon to inspire a widescreen revolution, "needing the added expense of three cameras and projectors every time we shoot." Even so, soon after, Hollywood did start experimenting with widescreen pictures and even considered changing to a wider film.

In the years following the defeat of Napoleon's wide screen ambitions, the triptychs were exiled to become jumbled up shots in future copies of the film, including the Pathé 17.5mm and 9.5mm versions. It was these, discovered during his school days, that began Kevin Brownlow's passion to restore both the film and the reputation of its director. It took him 30 years, working with the National Film Archive, before his first reconstruction was ready. One of its first showings was at the 1979 Telluride Film Festival in Colorado. It was seen by Francis Ford Coppola, who thought it was time for America to experience the film properly, this time accompanied by an orchestral score written by his father Carmine.

As an alternative to the need for three synchronised 35mm projectors, the triptychs were printed across the frame of a current 70mm print. In 1980, Napoleon became the first 'Thames Silent', with a score prepared by Carl Davis and launched with a triple projector premiere at the Empire Leicester Square. Similar special event showings are still being regularly staged to sell-out audiences around the world, with the film's 'before their time' production techniques no longer a problem for today's pop video generation.

Perhaps one remaining criticism, like other showings of silent films with live music, is they can become more like a concert, with a film included. Technically, the investment in the orchestra often means that, understandably, greater prominence is given to the musicians, particularly their lighting, which can spill onto the screen, degrading the picture.

You can have too much screen illumination - especially if some of it is coming from the orchestra!

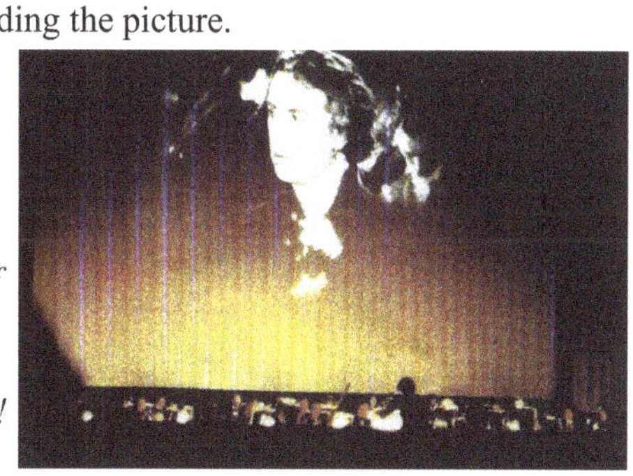

Napoleon has been restored again a couple more times, growing in length to over five hours, meaning an even longer wait for its spectacular wide screen climax, and a welcome rest for the orchestra. As a treat for some of us with less staying power, the optional 70mm finale became a popular item during past BKSTS "Fantastic Film Formats" presentations. I wonder if possible digital versions in the future will be such fun, without an envelope of film clippings to take home.

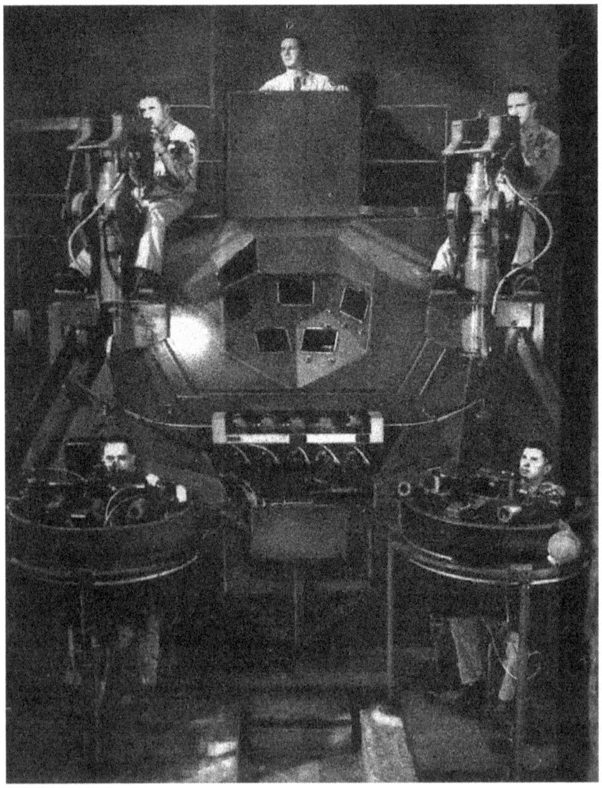

Left: Waller's anti-aircraft gunnery training simulator from WW II.
Right: Fred Waller and his original eleven-eyed camera rig.
Below: How five projectors can be used to fill a domed screen

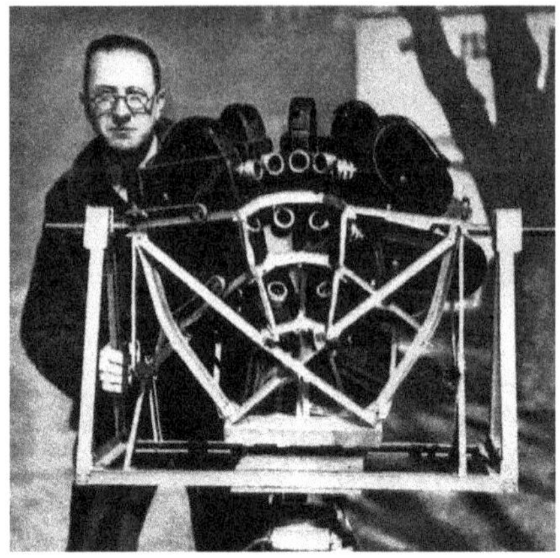

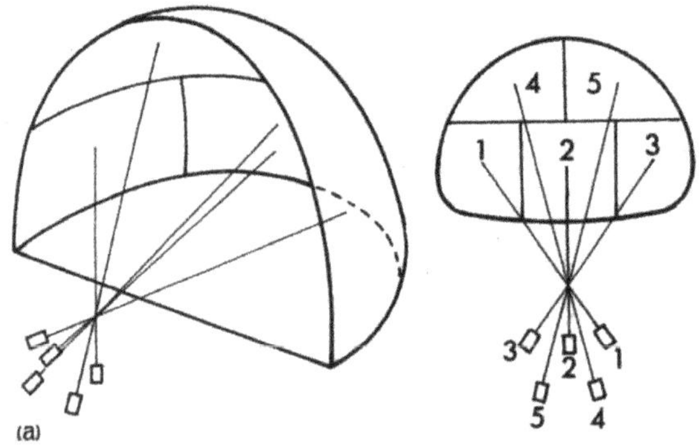

The Cinema's bow windows on the wider world

Although considered too complicated and costly for normal cinemas, multiple film strip systems would occasionally be seen again at other non-theatrical situations like trade exhibitions and world fairs, which would become a proving ground for new screen techniques. Building up the complete picture from separately angled projectors made it easier to keep it sharp on very deeply curved or domed screens. These attracted the attention of special effects expert, Fred Waller, who believed that including the viewer's peripheral vision was the key to providing the sensation of 'being in the picture'. This would normally need the space to accommodate a huge screen to fill their complete field of view, but bending it around them made it easier to fit.

In 1937, Waller was asked to help produce a display for the petroleum industry at the New York World's Fair. For economy sake, his first experiments used 16mm film. His friends at Eastman Kodak provided him with eleven cameras equipped with perfectly matched lenses. The resulting mosaic of 16mm Kodachrome films was projected on to a large hemispherical screen which also formed most of the auditorium. Although impressed, the system proved far too complicated and radical for the oil men who chose to make do with a normal single film and a slide show. Others were more enthusiastic and joined Waller to form the Vitarama Corp. New investors allowed the switch to 35mm, with only five films now needed to cover the same screen.

With the coming of World War II, Vitarama became the basis of the Waller Flexible Gunnery Trainer, with five synchronised Century 35mm projectors building up the complete image (pictured above left). This was fired at by the trainees, a hit being recorded when, at the time of firing, the dummy gun's position matched that of the target on the screen. His five lens camera rig provided different battle scenarios for the 75 trainers in use across America and Hawaii by the Navy and Air force during the war. Some of Waller's trainers were said to be destined for Britain, but whether they ever made it across the Atlantic or not, over here, as part of their war work, Technicolor constructed a similar device for our own forces. After the war the US Navy commissioned a single film version using a new type of 'fish eye' ultra wide angle lens to cover the domed screen. This too would be given a try by future developers of new widescreen methods.

Although not intended for entertainment, thousands of servicemen saw this new kind of moving picture experience and Waller began to hear, 'When are we going to see regular pictures like this?' With the war over, he began working on a simpler theatrical version of Vitarama. The projectors were reduced to three and now only covered the curved cylindrical section of the screen directly in front of the viewers, eliminating the previous domed area jutting out above. The remaining screen was made up of hundreds of venetian blind style vertical strips, angled to make it appear solid to the audience, but allowing cross reflections to pass through, preventing them from spoiling the contrast of the picture. This solved a problem common to all deeply curved and domed screens. To add to the visual realism, a fourth film was added carrying multi-channel high fidelity magnetic sound.

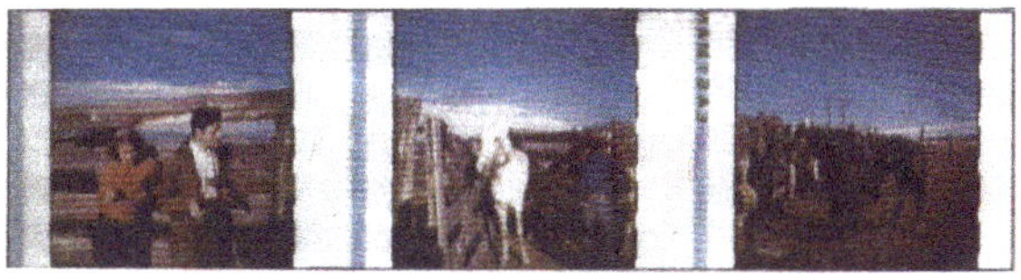

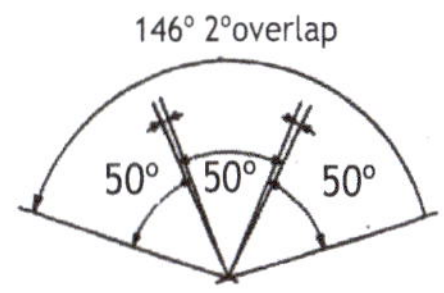

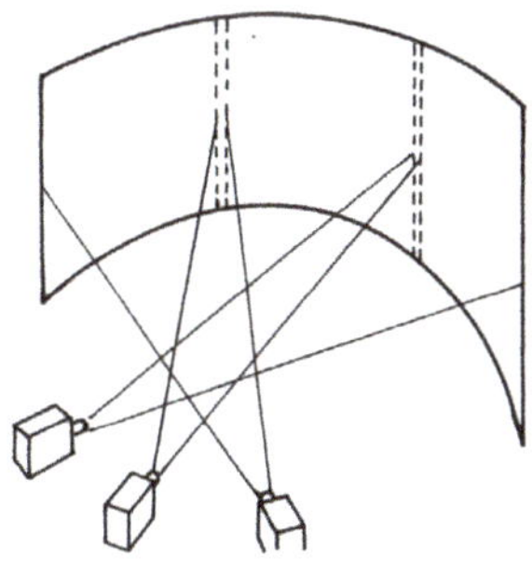

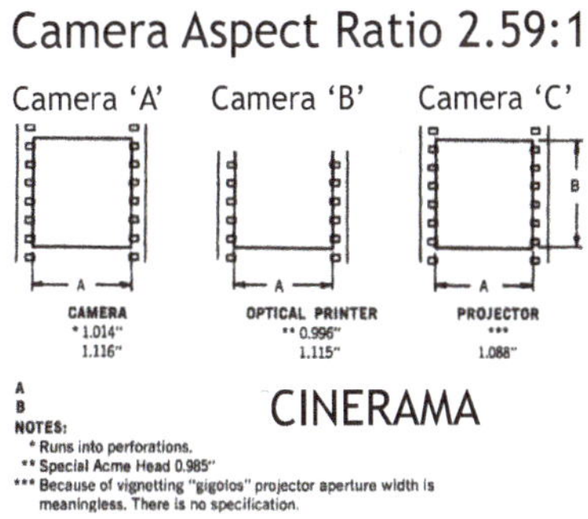

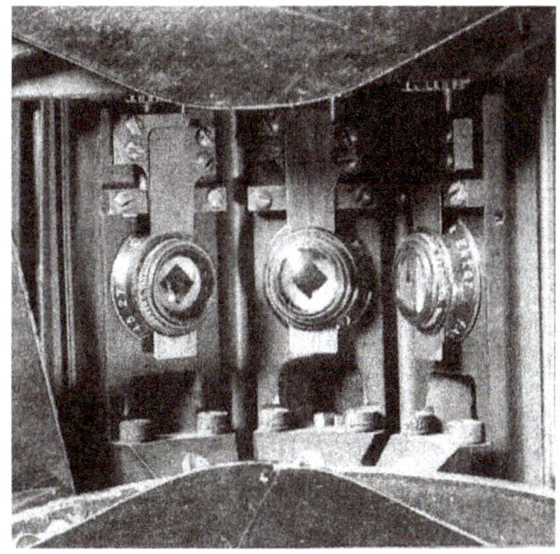

Right: The Cinerama camera's triple lenses had to point in different directions to cover the complete 146 degree angle of view.

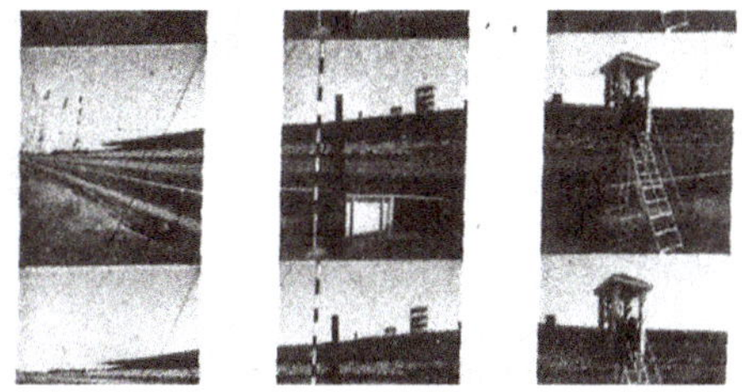

With the new name 'Cinerama', it would go on to become the most famous and commercially successful multiple camera and projector system.

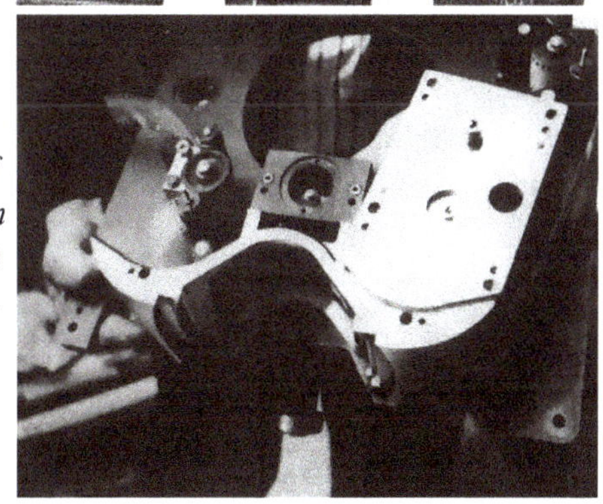

Cinerama's experimental 35mm 16 perf horizontal film transport with a curved gate, to be used as source for its 3-strip prints.

Can you see the join?

Common to all multiple film systems was the visibility of the junctions between the panels. These have to be perfectly matched in terms of density and colour balance, and shown using steady projectors with equal illumination. Cinerama blended them together with the help of its soft edge vibrating saw tooth 'jigolos' which blurred the frame edges in the projector gates. Even so, Cinerama, using the technology available in the 1950s, never completely solved the problem of the joins. Although also perfectly matched, Cinerama's three individual camera lenses had to point at different angles to cover its complete panoramic picture. As a result, each of the three parts of the image had its own perspective, converging to different vanishing points. This introduced a kink or fold at the junctions, which was exaggerated by Cinerama's three already very wide angle lenses needed to cover its total ultra-wide 146 degree field of view. This flaw was most noticeable when the joins passed through closer subjects filling most of the screen, or objects moved between the panels. Cinerama cameramen and directors, knowing the system's shortcomings, would try and avoid inter-panel movement and, whenever possible, hide the joins up vertical objects like trees, telegraph poles and corners of buildings. They were harder to lose during the flying sequences. A popular shot was flying under a bridge which appeared to bend at the seams as the camera passed under it. The joins could still be spotted in the various forms of single film reduction prints made on an optical printer of some of the Cinerama 3-strip films for general release in ordinary cinemas. These included 'How the West was Won', among the last filmed in the original 3-strip process in 1962.

Ironing out the problems

After 50 years, the latest DVD release of How the West was Won was scanned from the original negatives and used a digital stitching programme to virtually eliminate the visibility of the joins and also straighten out the kinks. You can't please everyone, as for many Cinerama devotees the joins are all part of the original process and also worthy of preservation. The new copy now looks more like an ordinary film, with perhaps the only remaining clues to its origin being the Cinerama credit and its constant very wide angle picture, which tends to bulge in the middle when viewed on a flat screen.

To help make amends, the restorers, also Cinerama enthusiasts, have provided a special 'Smile Box' version. Although still seamless, the image curves in at the top and bottom and is slightly distorted to give the impression that you are sitting directly in front of a deeply curved screen. From this position in actual Cinerama theatres the apparent aspect ratio was 2.06:1, but varied from other viewing angles. When flattened out, the official figure was 2.59:1, much less than Napoleon's almost 4:1 triptychs because Cinerama's three 35mm side by side frames were 50% taller, six perforations high instead of the normal four. In the 1960s, before digital help, Cinerama eventually turned to 70mm to fill its screens, its new single lens process sacrificing its original ultra wide view realism for a more convenient seamless picture and greater choice of product to show.

Back on the big screen

Fortunately, the public can still see the first 3-strip system, as it is now a working exhibit in The National Media Museum at its Pictureville cinema in Bradford. Just to see what it looked like, scenes from the latest digital transfer were screen tested on the theatre's actual deeply curved louvred Cinerama screen. Although this exercise was never considered as a replacement, it would be interesting to see if a proper digital three camera / projector updated 'D-Cinerama' format could ever be tried out in the future, and if the same electronic version of the gigolos would be able to seamlessly stitch the triple digital images together 'on the fly' in real time as they are being projected.

Wider film for wider pictures

As Cinerama finally decided, if you wanted a join free widescreen picture, one answer was to use a wider film. As described earlier, back at the birth of the movies, there were a number of different film sizes sharing screen time, before soon losing out to the dominance of the 13/8 in. Edison standard. Lumière's similar 35mm format, with its pair of round perforations per frame, (20mm x 25mm) had a 1.25:1 aspect ratio as did its other much larger rivals, like Demeny-Gaumont's 60mm gauge, Biograph's 68mm and Lumière's 75mm, intended for big screen shows at the Paris Exposition in 1900. Like Cineorama at the same event, not all went well. Footage was shot on the opening day, but was never shown publicly as the projector wasn't constructed in time, the 60 foot screen having to be filled with their normal 35mm.

All these early larger formats offered the chance of brighter and bigger screens, but not with a wider shape. The first 'widescreen' film was the short lived 'Eioldoscope' in 1895. Its 2in (51mm) film had an 2:1 aspect ratio, but it appears that the full width of the frame was not projected. This

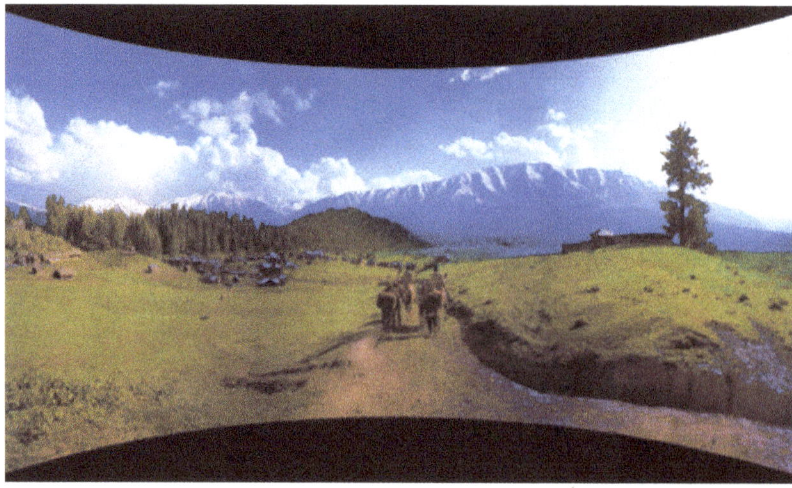

How the West was Won *... the latest 3-strip Cinerama digital restoration actually involved eliminating one of its original features, the joins. Shown here in its 'smile box' version*

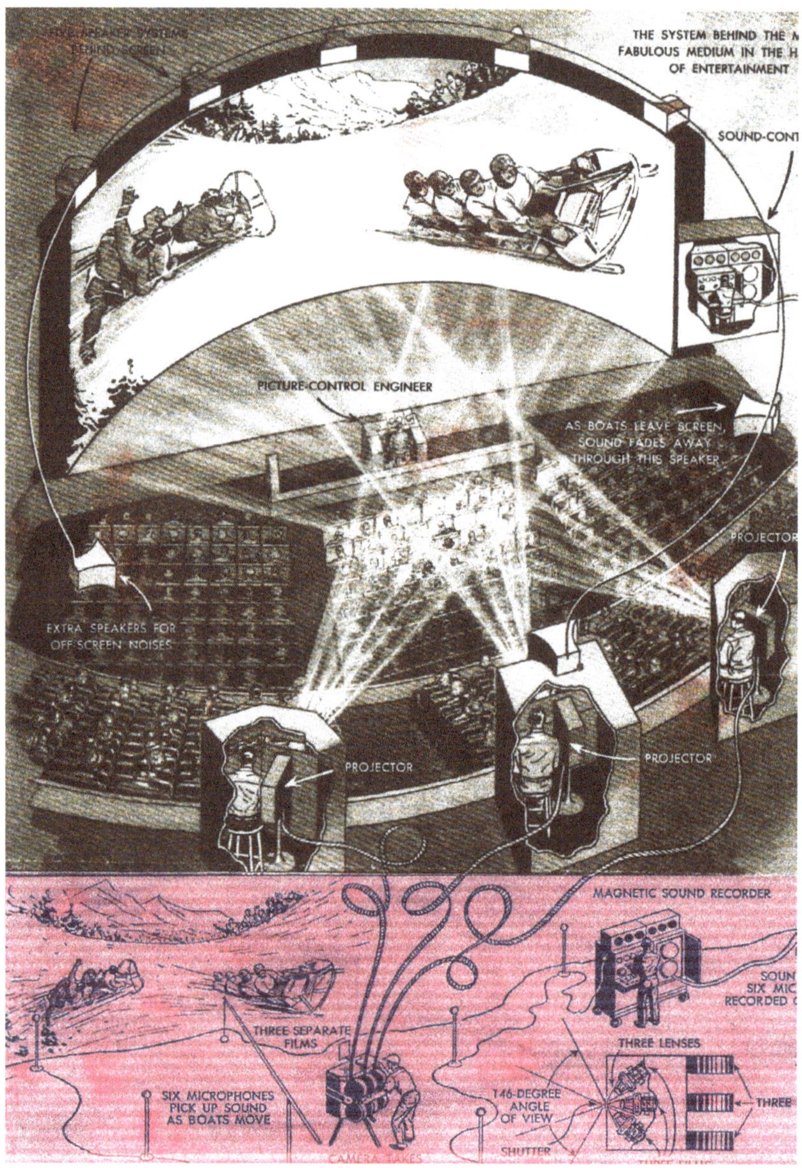

The often seen Popular Mechanics Magazine's schematic of producing and showing a Cinerama 3-strip film. They were kind enough to leave out any trace of the 'joins'. Seeing this drawing in his schooldays led to the author's enduring interest in all things technical to do with the cinema

was followed in 1897, by the more successful 63mm 'Veriscope', again created for a special event, its 1.66:1 frames chosen as the best shape to cover the ring of the Fitzsimmons-Corbett prize fight, in Carson City. Copies of the original 63mm prints survived and, now safely transferred onto current formats, reside in the archives of the ESPN sports channel in New York.

A swinging way to a wider view

Little more was heard of efforts to break free of the now well-established 1.33:1 screen until our next hero of early widescreen, Italian, Filoteo Alberini, began working on his 'Panoramica' process in 1914. It used 70mm film with a 23mm x 58mm, 2.52: 1 frame. He too wanted to fill it with a much wider field of view.

However, he didn't like the deeper perspective and the distortions affecting the picture when using very wide angle lenses. His aim was to retain the intimacy of a normal lens, but put the actors against a fuller wider background. To this end, he adopted a rotating lens system borrowed from special panoramic still cameras. As it turned around its optical centre, a narrow strip of its image swept across the film running through a laterally curved gate, to capture a 70 degree view. The movie camera's pull-down took place as the lens continued to revolve back to its starting position ready to expose the next frame. It would be interesting to see the results again today.

Panoramica was said to have been used for a special sequence in an Italian film, 'Il Sacco di Roma' in 1923. Apart from showing the full width 70mm prints, the negative could also be printed down to 35mm, the height of the image reduced from 18mm to 14mm, sacrificing some of the original picture's width.

The advantage of reduction printing from larger area negatives to provide higher quality images on the less sensitive, but inherently finer grain print stock was already appreciated and allowed them to stand up to the greater magnification needed when projected onto bigger screens. An example, for smaller screens, were the new 9.5mm and 16mm reduction prints from 35mm cinema films for home showings, which produced much better pictures than expected from their small frames.

Taking them laying down

One way of achieving a larger negative without changing to a wider film was to run normal 35mm sideways, the usual width of the frame now becoming the height and the new width determined by the number of perforations advanced for each frame. An 8 perforation horizontal system was patented in 1918. Apart from a more pleasing shape to the picture, the idea was to use the same normal 2 inch focal length lens, which now covered more of the scene. Its promoters claimed that the added cost of using twice the amount of film stock could be compensated for, by being able to save just as much by fitting more of the action in each of its new bigger frames and so avoiding unnecessary cutting back and forth between actors. At the

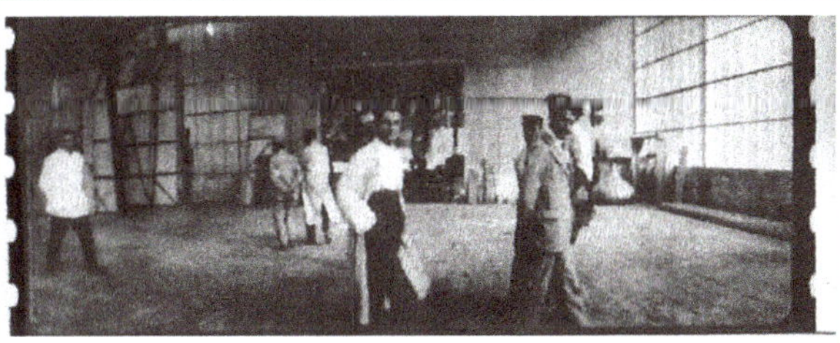

Alberini's Panoramica swinging lens system.
Above, first with 2.52:1 frames on 70mm film. Below, his later version, with the rotating lens sweeping across a 35mm 10 perforation horizontal 1.66:1 frame, captured a quiet moment in London's Piccadilly Circus during 1924.

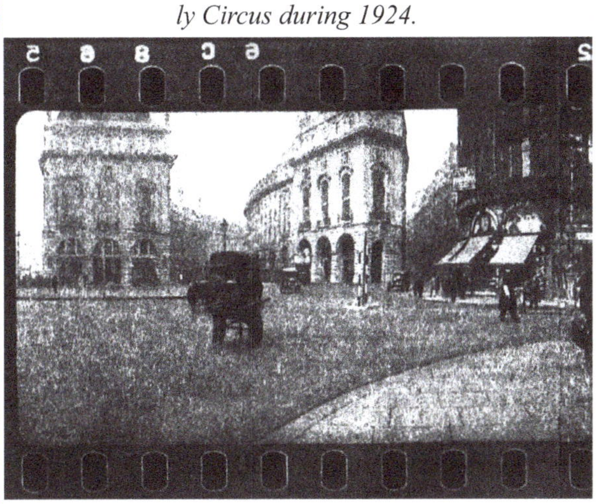

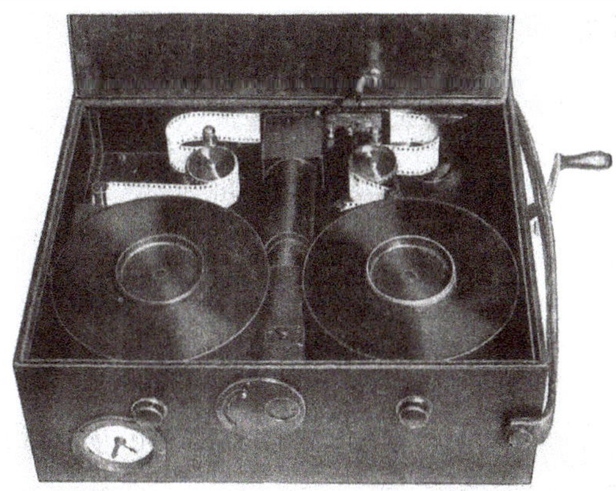

35mm horizontal 8 perf camera from 1918

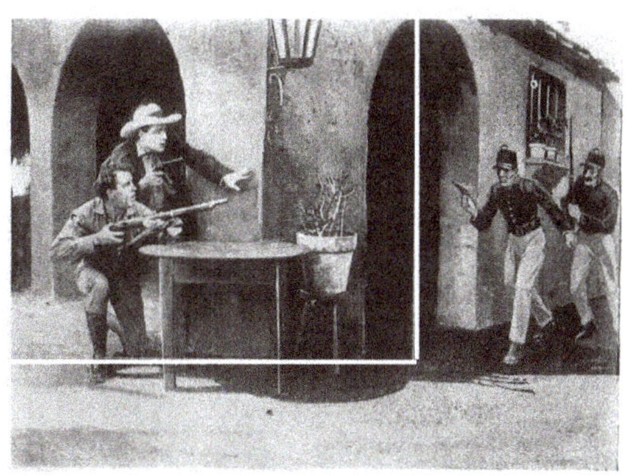

Comparison between the standard and its new larger frames which can include more of the action

time, no producer could be persuaded to try out its claimed advantages and as one industry observer remarked, "It is difficult indeed to upset the standardized state of the motion picture."

Around this time, 35mm motion picture film repaid its debt to Kodak's roll film for its existence, by offering itself for still photography. Early prototypes of these new 'miniature' 35mm still cameras were soon being employed by cinematographers as a quicker and lower-cost way of taking test shots on the same perforated stock which they were running through their cine cameras.

In Germany, Oskar Barnak chose the 8 perf horizontal format for his Leica 35mm still camera. Barnak considered the 1.5:1 aspect ratio of the new 'Leica format', 24mm x 36mm, to be "the most beautiful and convenient ever produced."

Still swinging

For sharp images across the full width of the wider frames, swinging and rotating lenses need to be combined with a curved gate with a radius equal to the focal length of the lens. This is easier to achieve with horizontally running film, and in 1924, Alberini collaborated with British camera engineer George Hill to replace his original 70mm panoramic system with a new rotating lens camera which recorded a 60 degree view on a horizontal ten perforation 35mm negative. Like before, its larger 24mm x 40mm frames were to be reduced onto a standard 35mm positive for projection onto a wider 1.66:1 screen. At a time when frame rates were beginning to rise, efforts had to be made to speed up the lens in its rotating drum. To avoid vibration, his original camera was limited to around 8 frames per second, which restricted it to fairly static scenes. Test shots with the new system were taken in London, including Piccadilly Circus, but they didn't generate enough interest to take the project further. However, George Hill was still designing special cine equipment for laboratories and studios up to the 1950s, when the success of Cinerama spurred the industry to, at last, introduce cinemagoers to some new screen techniques. Out of his Soho workshop came various forms of 3D and widescreen attachments, including Hammer Films first 'Hammerscope'.

Returning to 1924, John D. Elms also chose a swinging lens to improve his dual film Widescope process to help satisfy its need for a pair of perfectly synchronised prints with the same density. His new camera had an oscillating lens sweeping back and forth across a single 2¼ in (57mm) film. This was basically 35mm with the width increased to accommodate the double width negative between its perforations. This was optically split down the middle and each half printed onto the two separate 35mm films for projection.

This may seem like a strange way of going about things, but years later, Cinerama considered the same idea to simplify the production of their 3-strip prints. An experimental 35mm horizontal 16 perforation film transport was constructed with a curved gate. No suggestion, this time, of combining it with a swinging or rotating lens, but the curve helped to counter balance the distortion of an ultra-wide 150 degree 'fish eye' lens. This was to keep the total 146 degrees provided by the 3-strip camera's triple 50 degree (27mm) lenses. Four degrees were lost due to the slight overlap at the seams.

Although this particular project was abandoned, Cinerama did go on to make a more limited use of the splitting idea. A few scenes, which would have been problematic for the 3-strip camera, like the back projection shots in 'How the West was Won' were photographed on a single 65mm negative and then optically divided up to join the original 3-strip camera shot footage. It also made it possible to recycle footage from a couple of previous big screen westerns shot on 65mm, *Raintree County* and *The Alamo*. These split scenes have a noticeably different look to dedicated 3-strip viewers. Although the joins were actually less visible, they were grainier, with a restricted field of view. Also, as the proper 3-strip Cinerama was being phased out in favour of filling their screens with ordinary 70mm

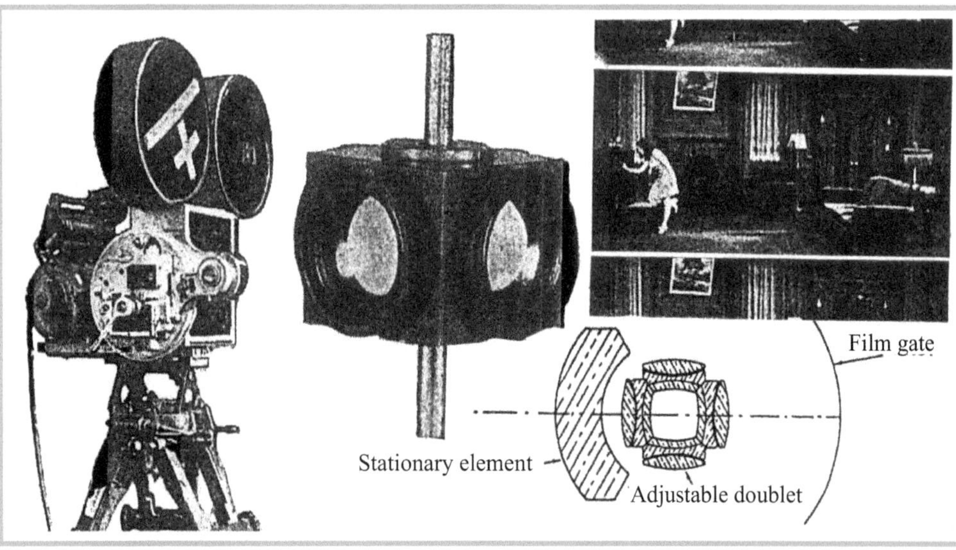

Left: The Elms Widescope 2½ inch (57mm) camera with an oscillating wide angle lens.

Centre: The later four direction revolving lens.

Top right: A test shot on Grandeur's 23mm x 46mm frames.

productions, a few of these were also split up for showing in the last remaining 3 projector theatres.

Final spin

Before this, back in the late 1920s,some of the Hollywood studios did briefly consider introducing wider screens, but soon received the thumbs-down from exhibitors, already trying to cope with all the technical turmoil and expense involved with the coming of sound.

We previously followed the fortunes of the various competing processes on offer at the time. One of the most prominent was Fox's 70mm Grandeur wide film system. Knowing of his widescreen experience, Elms was recruited onto its development team. They were having difficulty finding suitable wide angle lenses with sufficient aperture that could cover Grandeur's larger and wider frames with equal illumination and sharpness across the full field of view.

Elms still had faith in the swinging lens principle to do the job, but he too had to make it operate at higher frame rates. He designed a symmetrical revolving lens which worked equally well in both directions and which was able to expose two frames during each rotation. He took its construction problems to the optical experts at Kodak's appropriately named, Hawk Eye lens factory. They came up with an even better solution in the form of a light weight, well balanced four direction spinning lens which worked successfully up to 24fps. Although tested, and thought suitable for at least certain scenes, there were no reports of it ever being used in the production of the few Grandeur films completed before both the lens and the process itself ended up on the shelf.

The Grandeur wide film cameras did roll again following the more successful second coming of widescreen cinema in the 1950s. However, although the revolving lens remained in use for panoramic still photography, this was one innovation which was never pursued for later movie widescreen systems. Apart from mechanical difficulties, with the risk of noise and vibration, another drawback was that they tended to distort the shape of rapidly moving objects passing in front of the camera, stretching them if followed by the moving lens, or compressed if caught going in the opposite direction. The continuing progress in lens design during the 1930s and 40s, meant that wider views could be taken with a normal fixed lens with far less trouble.

Widescreen before 1900

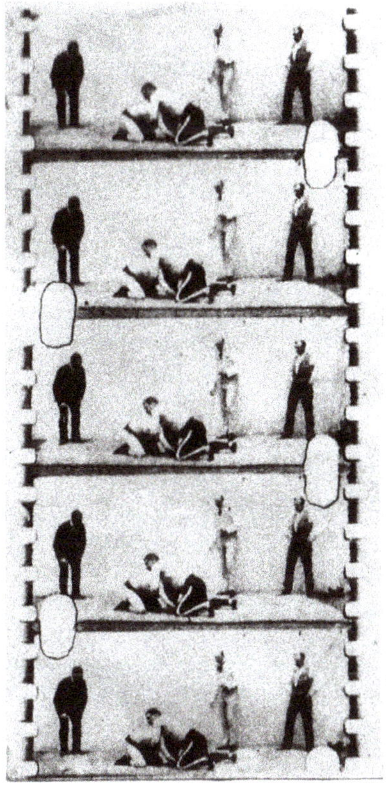

The Eioldoscope 2 inch (51mm) wide film from 1895. Its 20mm x 37mm wide gate didn't show the full width of the picture, possibly to avoid showing the holes in the frame lines. These were not damage, but allowed electrical contacts to be made through the film to trigger a sparking arc lamp. This was an early form of pulse light shutterless projection.

Below: 1.66:1 frames on the Veriscope 63mm wide film format in 1897.

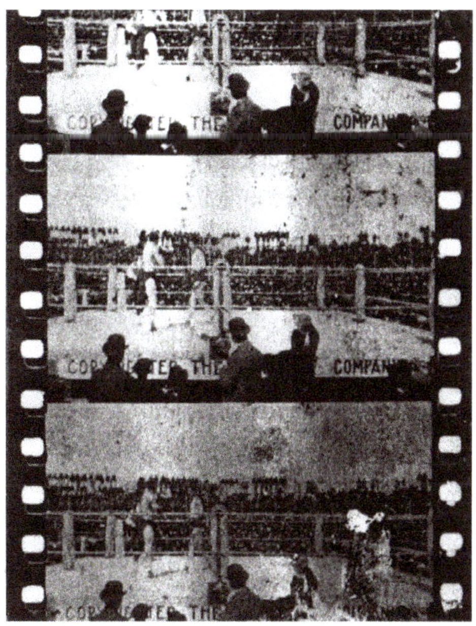

Anamorphosis
- squeezing and stretching those aspect ratios

With the ongoing aim of helping film restorers to produce the optimum results from the different types of film material which they come across, we take a look at some of the early methods of anamorphosis used by film makers/

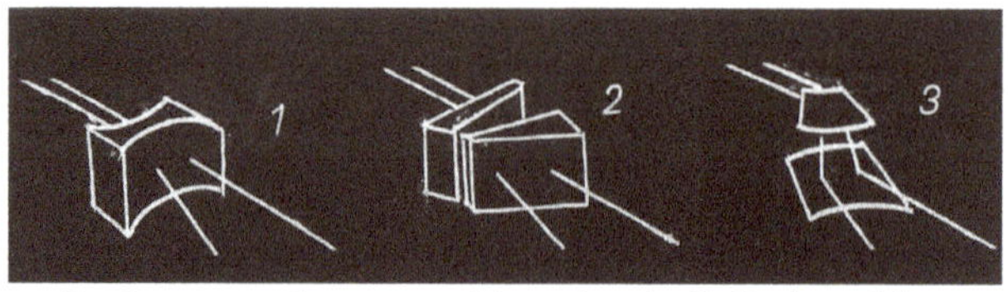

Basic types of anamorphic units. 1. Cylindrical lens elements 2. Pair of prisms 3. Curved mirrors

Although the makers of camera and projector lenses normally strive to eliminate optical aberrations, sometimes designing a lens which actually distorts the image can offer another way of changing its aspect ratio. It is usually the case that the aspect ratio of the magnified image on the cinema screen matches that of the image area bounded by the film projector's gate aperture, or that created by today's digital projector chips. However, there is one screen changing shape method which separates this relationship by exploiting the principle of anamorphosis which deliberately distorts the image to make it fit into a frame with a different shape and then restores It back again for its final presentation in its original proportions.

Anamorphosis: B.C. (Before the Cinema)

The theory of anamorphosis dates back many centuries. Five hundred years ago, artists such as Leonardo da Vinci would purposely create distorted paintings and sketches knowing that they would only be looked at from a position way off-centre. Holbein's picture 'The Ambassadors', painted in 1533, includes a curious stretched out shape in the foreground which, when viewed from an acute angle or through a glass rod, is revealed to be the image of a skull. Using the same idea today, although far less artistic, are the elongated signs painted on road surfaces which appear correct from the approaching driver's point of view.

Later, in the 18th Century, the popular 'Anamorphoscope' used a vertical cylindrical mirror to reflect a recognisable image of an otherwise grossly distorted and meaningless looking painting placed on a horizontal plane around its base. Apart from being a harmless novelty, and long before digital encryption, it allowed various forms of "forbidden" images to be restricted only to those in possession of the 'key', a correctly curved mirror. As an example, Scottish loyalists used the principle to keep illicit pictures of their hero Bonnie Prince Charlie after he fled to France in 1745. These were viewed via the polished surface of the goblets used to drink his health. Less risky fun, but this time leaving the anamorphosis uncorrected, was to see yourself in fairground distorting mirrors. A more subtle version, although perhaps only a retail urban myth, was the suggestion that some of the full-length mirrors in clothes shops fitting rooms were very slightly curved to flatter their customers and encourage sales.

an″a-mor′pho-scope, 1 an′ə-mēr′fo-skōp; 2 ăn″a-môr′fo-scōp, *n.* A vertical cylindrical mirror so placed as to produce a correct image of an object from a purposely distorted representation of it on a horizontal plane at the mirror's base. ANAMORPHOSIS + -SCOPE.]

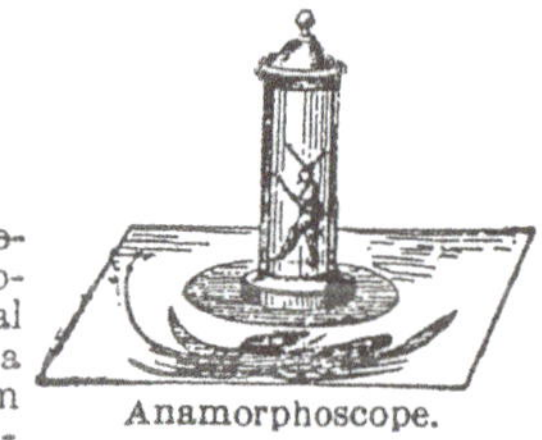
Anamorphoscope.

Early Cinema flirts with Anamorphosis

With the invention of photography and moving pictures, some thought that anamorphosis might prove useful if incorporated into a proper lens system. Ordinary lenses use 'spherical' elements to magnify or reduce images in equal proportions in all directions. Their elements have the familiar 'lens' shape with the profile of a sphere. However, special lenses began to be described using 'cylindrical' elements which, like a cylinder, only curve in one direction. If used in conjunction with a normal lens they have the effect of adding an extra power of magnification or reduction in one plane only. They became known as anamorphotic lenses or anamorphosers. If correctly orientated in front of a camera lens they produce compressed images on the film which can be restored by reversing the process by projecting them back through the same lens. It had also been observed that the same optical effect could be obtained by using a pair of angled prisms and, as early as 1862, such a system was patented in Britain by Sir David Brewster. A later alternative would make use of a pair of curved mirrors arranged like a periscope to compress or expand the image. However, cylindrical types would receive the most attention and an early design was the subject of a Zeiss patent in 1898, but there is no evidence that any practical use was found for it.

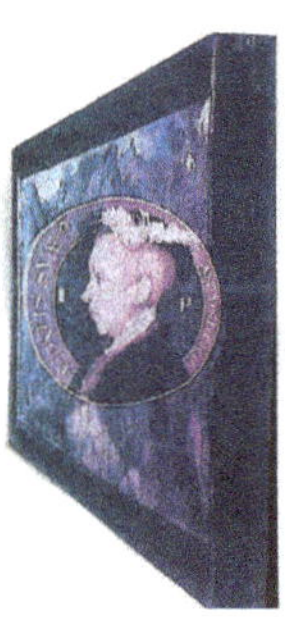
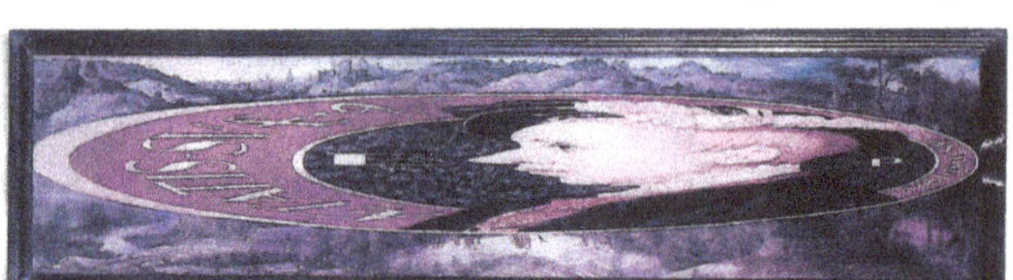
William Scrots 'anamorphosis' painting of a stretched Prince Edward VI (1546), who appears correctly proportioned when viewed from the right hand edge of the frame.

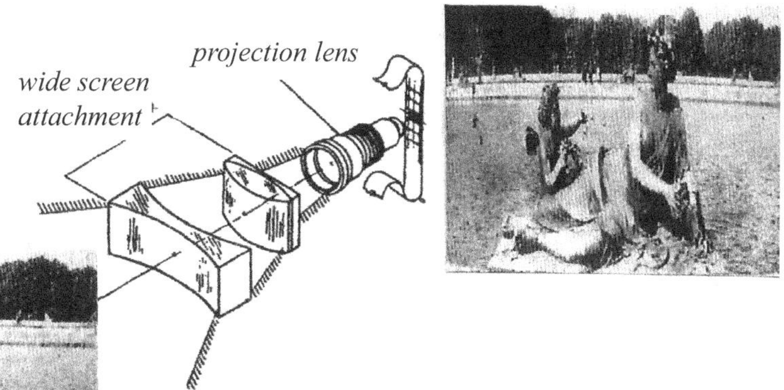

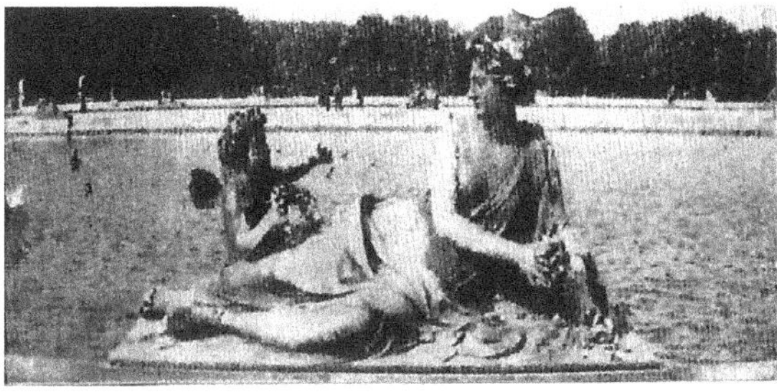

An early illustration showing how an anamorphic attachment spreads out the compressed image after it passes through the normal projection lens.

Finding a role

One of the first applications of the idea to motion pictures came in 1912, when an Italian, Ernesto Zollinger was granted a patent for a 'process for reducing the size of pictures on kinematograph films and of projecting such pictures to their normal proportions'. His scheme was to use anamorphosing optics to vertically compress a normal 1.33:1 frame to half its height. One possible use described was for a two colour additive system, in which the pair of filtered images were made to fit within the same space as a normal frame. During projection, they were expanded by de-anamorphosing optics and each directed through their appropriate red or green filter and superimposed on the screen.

Another suggestion was to halve the required footage by interlacing two separate subjects on one film. In this case, only alternate images were expanded and projected, the others for the second run being masked off. Not on the list of uses was any desire to use the system to change the shape of the cinema screen. In the event, none of these ideas could be put into practice at the time because of the difficulties encountered when actually trying to construct a well corrected anamorphotic lens capable of producing high quality pictures.

Despite degrading the definition, simple anamorphotic devices were still being manufactured and could be found in many cameramens' lens accessory kits. They became a popular means of deliberately distorting the picture for its dramatic or comic effect, with no intention of correcting the distortion in the projector. It could be set with the axis in any direction, or twisted during the shot, to provide all kinds of 'drunken' effects. Around 1918, British film producer, Julius Hagen exploited the effect by using a mirror distorting device in a series of 'Kineture' comedies. The French seemed to be the most willing to give anamorphosis a try, often seen in their avant-garde and surreal films of the 1920s.

Also, in the 1920s, Taylor-Hobson made a cylindrical modifier for the Bell & Howell Company, who offered it as an accessory for its new Filmo 16mm camera. This also enabled amateur film makers to have a go, and according to the instructions, add 'laugh producing effects or grotesque scenes as seen in dreams and nightmares' to their own films.

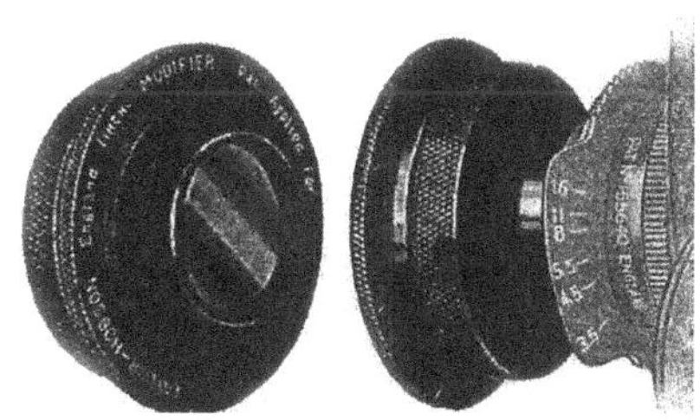

The Filmo cylindrical lens modifier. Made in the 1920s for deliberately distorting the image for its comic or dramatic effect.

The Professor shows off his Hypergonars

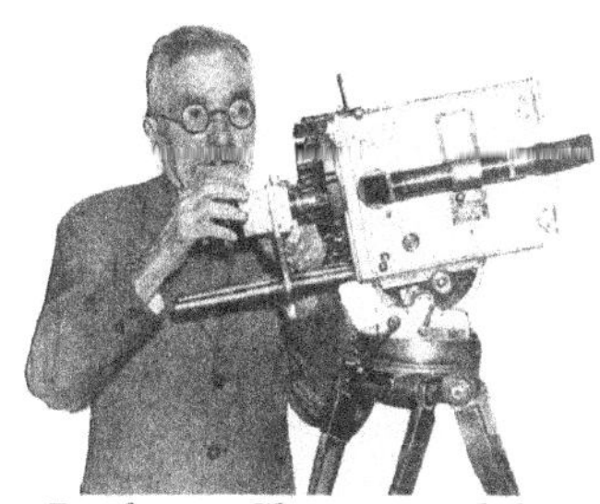

Professor Chretien with his Hypergonar lens

In 1927, Louis Lumière presented a communication to the French Academy of Sciences, describing a cylindrical anamorphosing attachment called the 'Hypergonar'. It was the invention of Henri Chretien, an eminent astronomer, optical scientist and a Professor at the Sorbonne and the Institut d'Optique in Paris. The Hypergonar turned out to be the first practical design suitable for photography. When placed in front

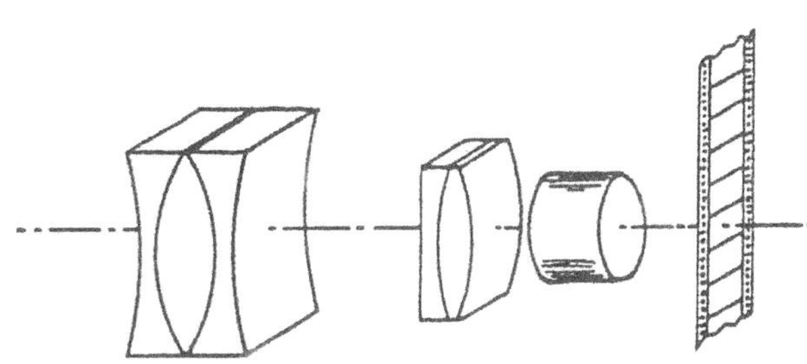

The 'Hypergonar'. From Henri Chretien's original patent showing the cylindrical lens elements arranged to compress and expand the image vertically. A use described was to squeeze two frames into the space of one. (x2 compression ratio)

of a normal lens, it doubled the amount of information recorded on the film. As before, the first suggested use for motion pictures was for squeezing up multiple images for colour or stereoscopic photography.

The same optical principle also interested the French military and Professor Chretien developed a tank periscope, which allowed the crew to keep their heads down while still having a wide angle view of the battlefield. Later, he also used his lens to squeeze more pictures into an aerial reconnaissance camera. However, after Henri Chretien saw the impressive panoramic triple-screen sequence in Abel Gance's Napoleon, the emphasis was then given to its possible use for extending the cinema screen. It was this aspect which was stressed during subsequent presentations, including one given to the Optical Society of America in 1928. Over twenty years later, he wrote to Abel Gance to tell him that he had dedicated his original lens to him, stating that: "It was your film 'Napoleon' which gave me the idea of applying this panoramic technique, after suitable conversions, to a camera which I made for military purposes."

First to exploit its cinematic possibilities was Claude Autant-Lara, using an early Hypergonar for his 'Pour Constuire en Feu', a short film based on a Jack London story about gold prospectors in the frozen north of Canada. He used the lens in a novel way to expand the screen in both directions, vertically for scenes of pine forests and horizontally for the snowy wastes. Sometimes multi-images were shown, such as a man waiting in his tent, while another flounders in the snow. The film ran for several months at a Paris cinema during 1929, but unfortunately the negative was destroyed in a studio fire in 1932, so this unique presentation cannot be recreated again today. A company, with Henri Chretien as its technical director, was formed to manufacture and promote the Hypergonar commercially. Although offered first to the French film industry, there were few takers. One was Marco de Gastogne, who used the lens in 1929 for the battle scenes in his film about Joan of Arc, *La Merveilleuse Vie de Jeanne D'Arc*. The wider screen was only used occasionally as a novelty, rather like the Magnascope process described earlier.

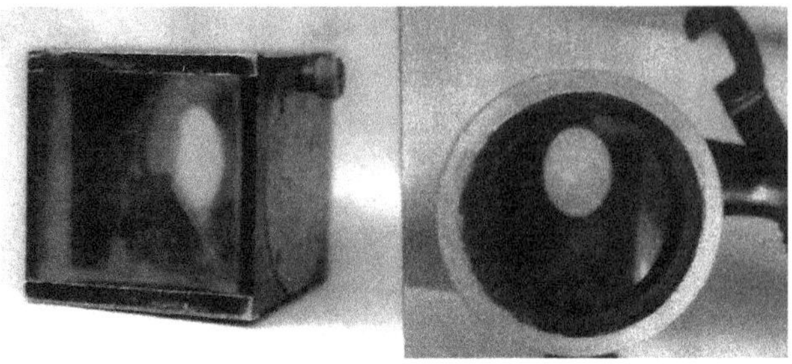

Although anamorphotic lenses would eventually play an important role in changing the shape of the screen during the cinema's wide screen revolution in the 1950s, both Chretien's Hypergonar and Ford's Fulvue were largely ignored when demonstrated during the 1920s and 1930s.

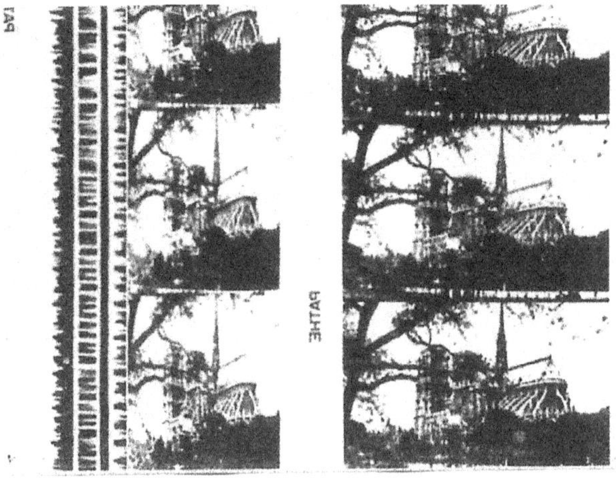

A suggestion, in the 1930s, was to use the Hypergonar to make space for three individual sound tracks and a wider picture.

Anamorphosis vs wide film

Earlier, in 1928, an American, Dr H. Sidney Newcomer, M.D. was in Paris studying optics and became interested in the possibilities of anamorphotic lenses and discussed the subject with Professor Chretien. He tried to persuade him to complete the production version of his lens in time to compete with the wide film systems, which were under development in the United States. Most of the Hollywood studios had rival systems including Fox (70mm), Paramount (56mm), Warner Brothers (65mm) and R.K.O. (63.5mm), and they all had plans to introduce the wide screen along with their new sound films. As Henri Chretien was still busy with his military and other projects, no arrangements could be made, so Dr Newcomer returned to America and began working on the design and construction of his own cylindrical lens. Called an 'Anamorphosa', it was similar to Chretien's, but his formula produced a lesser compression factor of x1.5, providing a final screen shape with an aspect ratio of 2:1, nearer to that produced by the various wide film formats. Unfortunately, by the time he had overcome the problems of actually constructing his lens and demonstrations were being held in New York, at the beginning of 1930, work on the wide film systems was well advanced. They were already being used to film a number of features, including a 70mm version of the Raoul Walsh epic western *The Big Trail* (1930), which introduced John Wayne in his first starring role. After investing large amounts of money, the wide film promoters were already competing with each other for industry acceptance and didn't want to hear of simpler methods using existing 35mm film.

Not only did the studios plan to recover their development costs, but to go on and take their share of the fortune still to be made selling new wide gauge projectors to the exhibitors. On their side and helping to fight off the threat of anamorphosis, were the many optical experts who still maintained that cylindrical lens systems could not be made to match the quality of normal spherical lenses.

After demonstrations proved that anamorphosers were more than adequate, the experts changed tack and declared that although individual prototypes could be made to produce satisfactory results, the grinding of cylindrical deforming elements was far too laborious and costly for mass production. This was countered with the fact that prisms could also do the job just as well, if only for the narrow angles used in projection.

Battling on

Meanwhile, Britain had its own contender, the 'Fulvue'. Announced in 1930, it was developed by George Ford and F.W. Baker of Watson & Sons in London. This too was a cylindrical attachment with a x1.75 compression factor. After a trade demonstration in 1931, a reviewer reported it as being, "striking, novel and eloquent and at a cost of only £20, would do everything that the American wide films could do".

Back in America, Henri Chretien finally arrived to join the fight on the side of the anamorphoser supporters. Unfortunately, by now, the battle was all but over, with the exhibitors giving the whole wide screen idea the thumbs down. They were already caught up in the frantic rush to equip their theatres for sound and were not prepared to spend the estimated extra 40 million dollars needed to replace all the country's existing projectors and screens. Towards the end of the fight, the studios suggested that perhaps the wide films could be reserved for the larger big city theatres and the smaller houses use 35mm squeezed reduction prints. However, the producers finally bowed to the inevitable and promised to put this particular technical development on the shelf, "until the industry needs a fresh stimulant". Although a practical and less costly alternative to wider film, the anamorphotic system was never seriously considered. Even the Royal Photographic Society in London stated, at the end of a symposium on wide screen photography held in 1931, that: "owing to its inferior optical performance, the advantage of anamorphosers in cinematography is illusory and nothing further could be anticipated from them".

More on lenses

Although abandoned for professional use, a version of Sidney Newcomer's lens was manufactured by the Goerz American Optical Company in New York and sold for a short time for 16mm users. Henri Chretien's Hypergonar may have been passed over for the moment by Hollywood, but his optical skills were still appreciated in America by others outside the film industry and in 1932 he designed the telescope at the U.S. Naval Observatory in Washington D.C. He continued to demonstrate the advantages of the Hypergonar, including a trade show at the Regal, Marble Arch in London. Only one Hollywood studio ever took an early interest in his device. In 1935, Paramount Pictures optioned the lens and shot some tests, but decided not to make use of the system commercially. In order not to miss an opportunity to explain his ideas, the professor travelled around with a special double-sided 16mm projector. This ran two films at once, one shot with the normal 1.33: 1 shaped picture and the other showing the same scenes in wide screen using the Hypergonar. At any time during his talk, he could impress his audience by switching over to the double-width panoramic picture.

Public showings

The public was to have a chance to see the results produced by the Hypergonar at the Paris International Exhibition of 1937. Among the attractions was a nightly open-air film show presented on a huge curved screen, 197 feet wide and 33 feet high, on the facade of the Palace of Light, the pavilion built to celebrate the wonders of electricity. The ultra wide screen was filled using two interlocked 35mm projectors fitted with Hypergonars. The two already wide pictures were projected side by side with the images blended together in the centre to produce one continuous panoramic picture with an aspect ratio of almost 6:1.

To help hide the join, saw-tooth masks were placed in the beams three feet in front of the projectors. To provide enough light, the Simplex projectors had Peerless arcs running at 240 amps and burning carbons normally used in naval searchlights. The concrete screen was also sprayed with powdered glass to improve illumination. This historic presentation also has a British connection. The show featured multi-image and panoramic films of power stations and hydro-electric plants. These were photographed in black and white using two linked 35mm cameras equipped with Hypergonar attachments. Also in the programme was a short animated film, 'Phenomenes Electriques', produced by Lens Gameaux. This was in colour, and early in 1937 the negatives were sent to Technicolor's newly opened laboratory in London for printing.

In the archives

After the Exhibition closed, nobody showed any interest in the material and many years later, the late Bernard Happé, Technicolor's former technical manager, found the nitrate negatives in their vault. Realising their significance, he saved them from destruction and presented them to The National Film Archive. There they are still waiting for a sponsor with an interest in big screen cinema, to help fund a restoration and then provide a screen wide enough to show it on. Although the film was not actually photographed using an anamorphotic lens, the cartoon images having been drawn already compressed, it is probably the first ever 35mm colour film intended for this kind of projection.

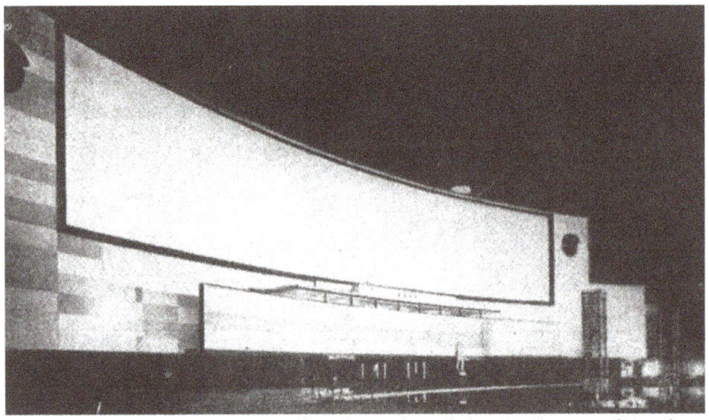

Panoramic screen on the facade of the Palace of Light at the Paris International Exhibition 1937

Throughout the 1930s and 1940s, anamorphosers could still be spotted being used to produce special optical effects, the distorted images often illustrating the effect of drink or drugs. A 1940s Joe McDoakes comedy short (Warner's answer to MGM's 'Pete' Smith Specialities'), *So You Think You Need Glasses,* which can be seen again today on DVD, featured the principal character visiting an optician. The trying on of different spectacles provided an opportunity to show off the full range of multi-image prisms and other special effects lenses, including anamorphosers.

The final push

Henri Chretien's final effort to sell his wide screen ideas to the film industry was at the 1951 Congress Technique International in Turin, Italy. Again little interest was shown, but his 20 year wait was almost over. With the decline in cinema-going and the growing threat from television, the search for the now much needed stimulant would send representatives from more than one Hollywood studio to his door, clamouring to get their hands on his Hypergonars. They were disappointed to learn that the British had got there first, reporting back that, "the Professor, a pleasant old fellow about 75 - beard and all" had already given the Rank Organisation an option, which still had a couple of weeks to run. Rank must have decided not to gamble on this particular new screen technique, but already waiting to step in was Twentieth Century Fox. After test footage, shot by their Paris Movietone News office, proved its potential, a deal was struck to acquire Chretien's entire stock of Hypergonars. These were soon in Hollywood, and after further evaluation, the best performing examples were mounted on the cameras shooting the first films in the new modern miracle, 'CinemaScope'. After being used to make an early start on the first three CinemaScope productions, the original Hypergonars were retired. As all the basic anamorphoser patents had by now expired, including Chretien's, other lens makers were free to manufacture the now easier to pronounce, 'anamorphic' lenses, which would play their part in launching the cinema's this time successful, widescreen revolution.

More about earlier formats

From the BKSTS Guide to Release Prints

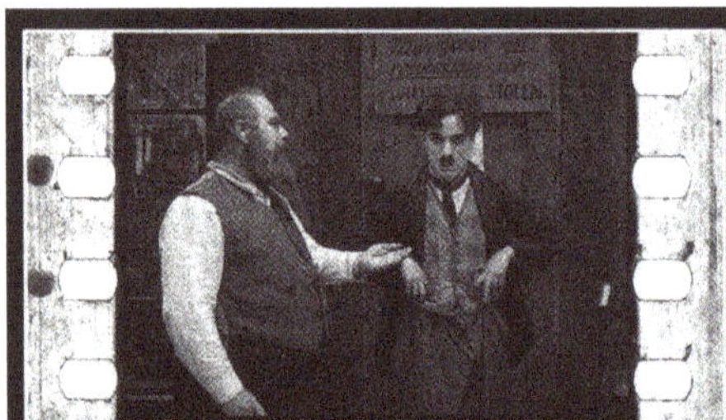

'Edison' format with the frame line positioned between the perforations. Adopted as the international standard in 1909.

SILENT FORMAT
Projector aperture
0.906″ × 0.6795″
Aspect Ratio 1.33:1

Vertical centre line of the image corresponds to that of the film

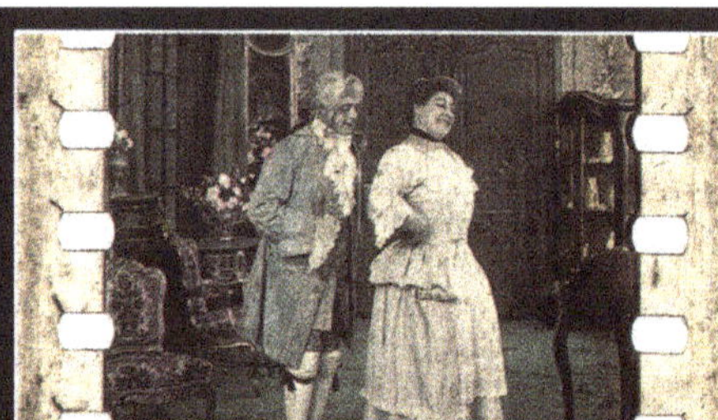

Early French variant with the frame line coincident with the perforations

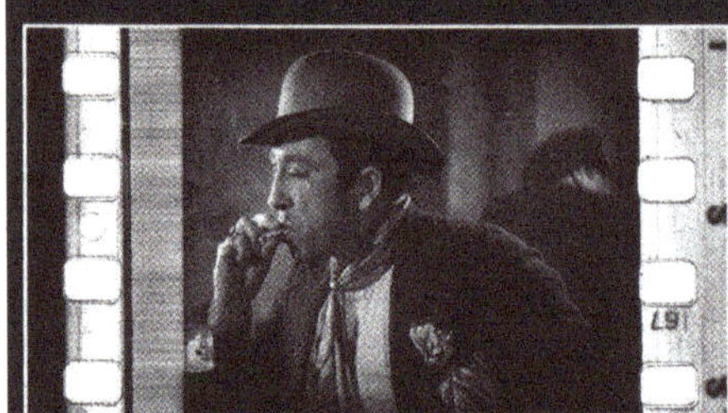

Soundtrack added to an originally 'silent' film

EARLY SOUND FORMAT (from 1927)
Original Sound projection
Aperture 0.800″ × 0.6795″
Aspect Ratio 1.18:1
Vertical centre line of the projected image moved to the right
Soundtrack width
0.100″ to 1.125″

Also projected using the 'Proportional' or 'Reduced' Aperture 0.800″ × 0.607″, Aspect Ratio 1.32:1

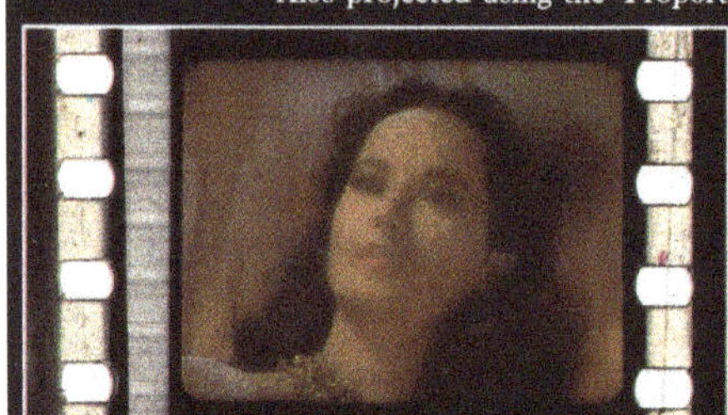

Frame with Bell and Howell perforations (nitrate)

ACADEMY SOUND APERTURE (From 1932)
0.825″ × 0.600″
20.95mm × 15.25mm
Aspect Ratio 1.37:1
Academy offset centre line
Soundtrack width 0.100″, synchronisation 20 frames ahead of picture

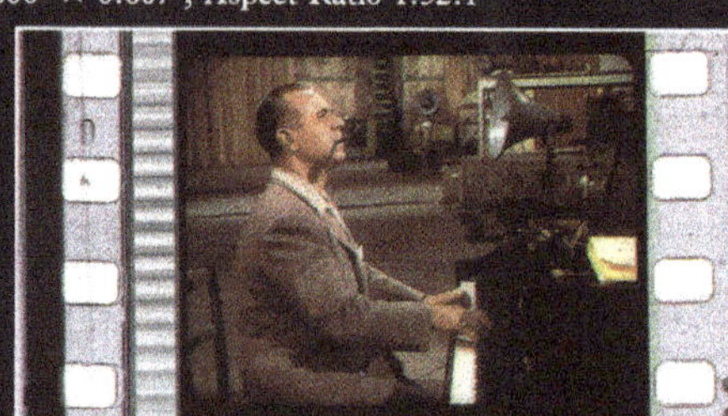

Frame with Kodak standard perforations

From 1923 the damage-prone Bell and Howell (BH) perforations began to be replaced for use on prints by the Kodak standard (KS) perforations (except for Technicolor and some other colour processes which continued to use the Bell and Howell perforations until the early 1950s).

Presenting a broader view - a closer look at the rise, fall and rise again of cinema's most successful and longest -lasting spectacle, the 2.35:1 format

For the present generation, the most familiar shape of moving pictures is now television's 16:9 (1.78:1) ratio, leaving the squarer 4:3 (1.33:1) to add old world charm to films from the past. At the cinema, the wider, 2.35:1 is still currently the most popular screen shape, a survivor from the days of film which has lived on into the digital age. The Telekinema, the 1951 Festival of Britain's cinema of tomorrow, led the way with 3-D, stereo sound and 'electronic' pictures, but missed the chance to be in at the start of the widescreen revolution. The third dimension would come and go, but the other two were about to change for ever.

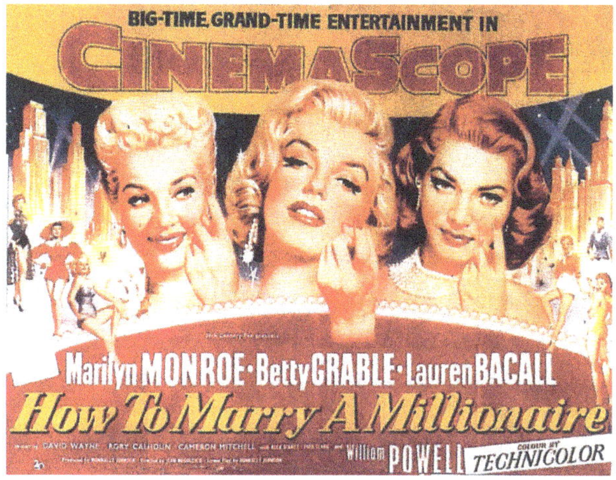

The desire for a bigger and wider screen, dates back to the birth of the cinema, but there was always a reluctance to stray too far from normal practice, particularly the standard 35mm film format. This was pushed to its limits and beyond, when, in the 1920s, the Magnascope process surprised audiences by zooming up the size of the picture to give extra impact to spectacular scenes. Using it too often lost the novelty value and the disappointment when the screen shrunk back to normal led to finding a way to show the complete film on a larger screen. As those seated under the balcony couldn't see the top of it, attention turned to simply making it wider.

Widescreen's false start

At the end of the 1920s, Hollywood took the idea seriously, shooting a few films on wider stock. With each studio choosing a different width and exhibitors' panic at the thought of having to buy new projectors, this advance in presentation was put on hold. No need yet for a new attraction, as the public was already flocking to theatres to see, and hear, the latest "talkie", which could be shown using far less disruptive bolt-on sound equipment.

Don't give up

Although the Depression and later wartime restrictions kept wide-film on the shelf, widescreen also had its own less costly add-on alternative in the form of 'anamorphosis'. This optical trick could squeeze the wider picture onto normal 35mm film and expand it back during the film's projection. The most persistent early promoter of this method was the French professor of optics, Henri Chretien, who first demonstrated his 'Hypergonar' distorting lens in 1927. His first suggested application was to compress two frames into the space of one, perhaps finding a use for those devising new two-colour or 3-D systems. However, after seeing impressive triptych sequences at the climax of Napoleon, his attention turned to using it to expand the screen. Chretien took every opportunity to demonstrate his lens which could help the industry to break free of the 4:3 screen without the need for wider films.

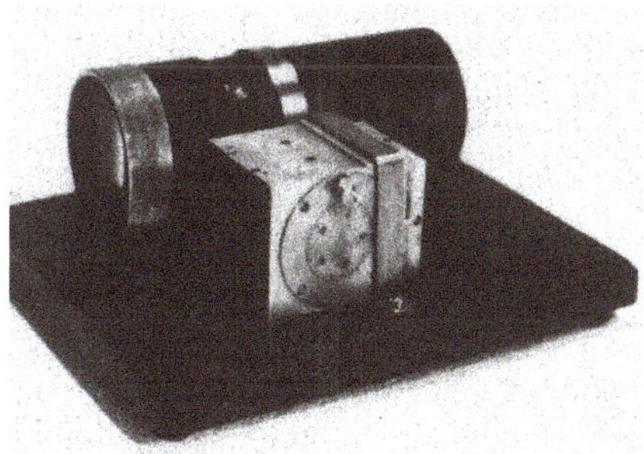

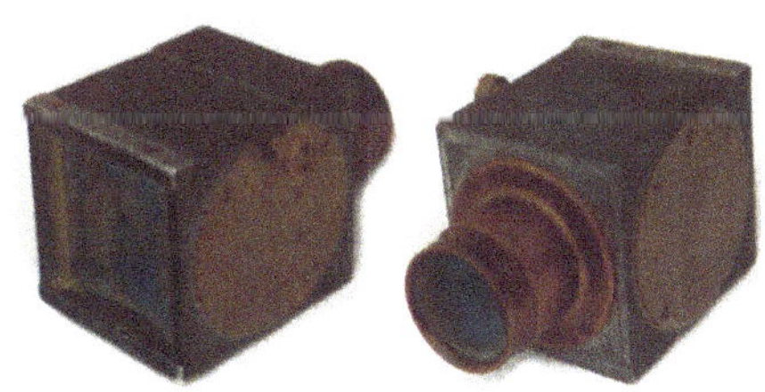

Left: Henri Chretien's original camera and projector lenses, and below, an original Chretien Hypergonar lens which the late David Samuelson kept on his mantlepiece.

Apart from those quite happy with 4:3, many experts dismissed this particular idea with doubts about maintaining the optical quality when mass-producing the more difficult to manufacture cylindrical lenses and other types of anamorphotic devices. The professor proved his attachment could produce good quality images when he projected two, side-by-side stretched out pictures on a huge outdoor panoramic screen on the facade of a pavilion at the Paris World Fair in, 1937.

The Hypergonar wasn't completely ignored, as both Paramount in the US and Pathé in France tried it out behind the scenes, but didn't go on to exploit it commercially. Following its last big push at the 1951 Congress Technique International in Italy, the Rank Organisation took out an option, but they too sat on the idea.

For Hollywood's first go at widescreen during 1929-31, Fox had chosen 70mm film, but for its revival in 1953 they stuck with 35mm and an anamorphic lens, having re-assessed this system after reviewing reports of the giant screen on the Palace of Light in Paris.

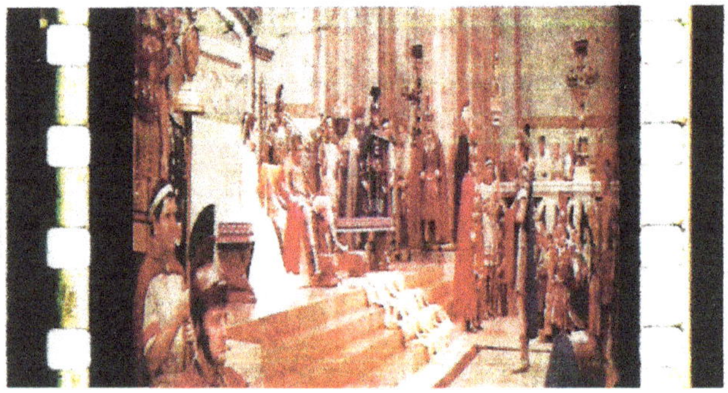

Original CinemaScope prints with their four magnetic stripes had an aspect ratio of 2.55:1

The right time arrives

All would change after the sensational debut of the triple projector Cinerama in New York during 1952. Waiting in the wings for Rank's option to expire was 20th Century Fox looking for a more practical way to bring a similar eye-filling curved screen panoramic picture into ordinary cinemas. Perhaps Rank was wise to let Fox do all the work as, in the coming months, their quest for a wider screen would become the biggest gamble in the studio's history. They were about to spend over $10 million (in 1950s money) developing their new process and commit a further $24 million-worth of productions to a system which no cinema in the world could show. The cost would include another $25,000 to purchase their chosen name for the process, CinemaScope, which was already the registered trademark for a television-to-film transfer system.

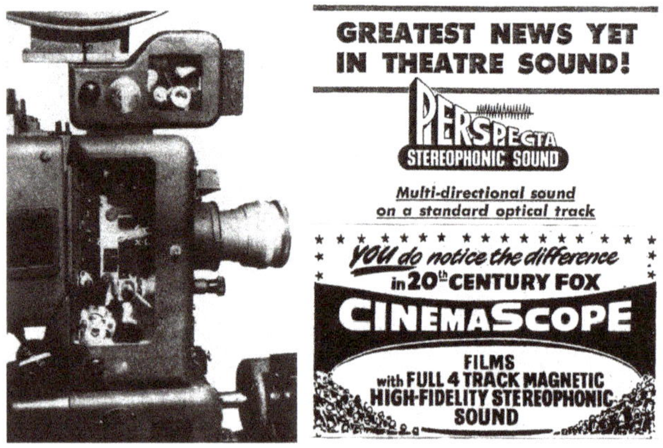

Ready to show CinemaScope prints with mag sound: the 35mm projector had a bolt-on magnetic head above the gate, and an anamorphic lens.

OK for snakes and funerals

Given their first sight, some critics thought this was a little too wide, prompting the well-known comment from one eminent director that its ribbon-like picture was only good for photographing snakes and funeral processions. Others were more positive, seeing a new visual tool, particularly useful for drawing the viewer into sprawling adventures set in the great outdoors, perhaps leaving the old small screen to tell the more intimate stories. Fox hoped the choice of its first productions would prove that all kinds of subjects could benefit from going wide.

Squeezing Marilyn

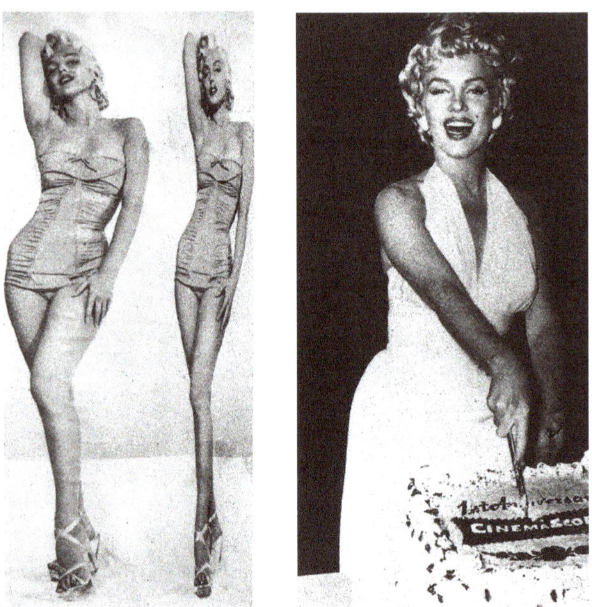

Squeezing Marilyn and then back to her normal proportions helped to celebrate CinemaScope's first birthday

Fox had purchased Chretien's complete stock of lenses, including a couple snatched back from Paramount and Rank, but only three were considered good enough for actual photography. One was soon in front of a normal camera lens filming *The Robe*, a biblical epic which had been halted to start again in CinemaScope (the 4:3 version was also completed). Another was put to work, both above and below the waves, for *Beneath the Twelve Mile Reef*. The third, despite being confined mostly to a New York flat, would improve the prospects of *How To Marry A Millionaire* with the sight of its leading ladies draped across the wide expanse of the screen also seducing the audience. One of the film's glamorous stars, Marilyn Monroe, could already be seen in CinemaScope's show reel performing her 'Diamonds Are a Girl's Best Friend' number from the still 4:3 *Gentlemen Prefer Blondes*. As 3D was beginning to lose its appeal, she was playing her part in persuading the rest of the industry to make a new best friend of a process which could be admired without the need for special glasses.

Never mind the quality, look at the width

Casting a more critical eye on more recent higher-definition DVD and Blu-ray copies of these early films shows that even the best examples of Chretien's original hand-made Hypergonars had noticeable flaws. The nominal x2 compression factor varied across the frame, with the actors gaining and losing weight as they moved across the screen. The compression factor also changed at different distances, more (2.5x) further away, and less (x1.8) clos-

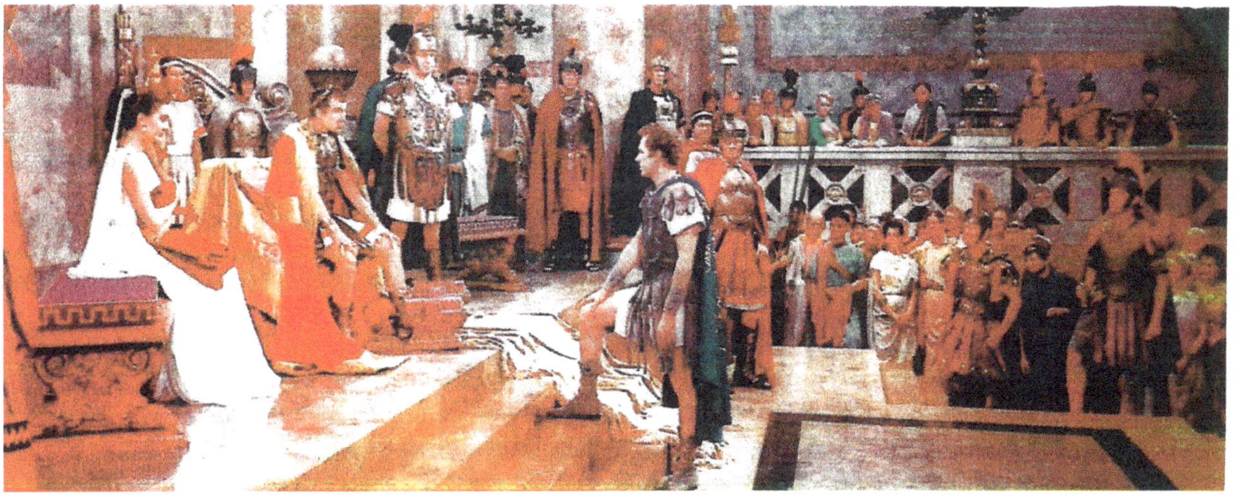

er to the camera. The first films avoided big close-ups to prevent the actors now appearing to have the 'mumps'. Today's wonder of digital restoration could even this all out, as it has done to eliminate the distortions and often visible joins between Cinerama's triple side-by-side images. All very clever, but spotting the joins, and the efforts made to hide them within the complete picture, was all part of the fun of watching a Cinerama film.

Fox would contract the optical company Bausch & Lomb Inc. to supply an improving series of anamorphic lenses, and encourage other manufacturers, in the US and other countries, to produce their own versions, particularly the thousands needed for projection if, as hoped, CinemaScope became a global success. Some of Fox's new camera attachments were set aside for other studios, but most hesitated, waiting for the public's reaction. One of the more confident was MGM which began shooting its first, *Knights of the Round Table* in England, although they did film a 4:3 version, just in case. Another, started before CinemaScope reached cinemas, was Errol Flynn's *William Tell*, but the troubled production never reached the screen.

Back at Fox, *How To Marry A Millionaire* was now finished and ready for release. There would be no trouble grabbing the audience's attention with its new panoramic picture, but to help them appreciate the stereophonic sound, a specially filmed overture was added featuring the full Fox Studio Orchestra playing 'Street Scene' composed by their resident composer, Alfred Newman. He also extended Fox's trademark opening fanfare for its longer 'Presents a CinemaScope Production' logo. A delay in constructing the laboratory magnetic striping and recording machines, meant *The Robe* was also completed, and chosen as a more spectacular launch for the process. It opened in September 1953, just 10 months after the first tests through the Hypergonar. Their faith in it was about to pay off, as both the film and CinemaScope became a big hit both with the public and press which said it "Will bring the missing millions back into the cinema".

This advance in cinema sound stumbles

Like all new presentation techniques, it's always the exhibitors who have the final say. Big city theatres, able to show CinemaScope, both its 2.55:1 picture and stereo sound, to its best advantage, welcomed the boost in ticket sales. Although many of the smaller local cinemas were willing to install its wider screen, even if fitting it in reduced its height to a 'letterbox', they questioned the value for money of the stereo sound. It was suggested that if they turned up the volume of their normal mono optical track, and perhaps added a couple of extra speakers to spread it out, most of their less informed patrons wouldn't be able to tell the difference. Taking the idea a step further, the 'multi-directional' **Perspecta** sound system which could also move the mono around became available. A standard optical track now included three 'hidden' low-frequency control tones which were detected by an additional 'integrator' and used to change the relative volume of the speakers, shifting the apparent source of the sound across the screen.

"You do notice the difference"

Fox stood its ground, still insisting that CinemaScope, including its 4-track magnetic sound, was a complete package and cinemas couldn't pick and choose. Even the Rank circuit was deprived of Fox films, when it stopped short of equipping all its theatres with magnetic sound. Apart from the initial outlay, there were on-going care costs to maintain its superior quality.

Except for the odd blown exciter lamp, and keeping the optics clean, a normal optical track was trouble-free, running largely untouched through its sound-head. The more expensive 4-track mag print had to be kept pressed against its own head, which eventually wore out. Like the rest of the film path, it had to be de-magnetized to prevent a build-up of background noise and partial erasure of the higher frequencies. Joiners too, could add clicks and plops to the track. The rival Perspecta system wasn't foolproof. In less stable pre-microchip valve days, with projectors sometimes straying from 24fps depending on the weather, its decoder could lose control of the sound, leaving it to wander about on its own.

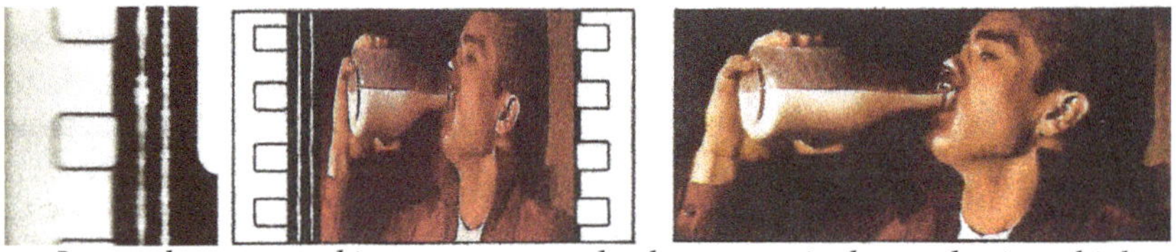

It was the squeezed image on a standard mono optical sound print which secured the 2.35:1 format's future. Most cinemas had to wait for the coming of Dolby's first stereo optical tracks to bring full hi-fi stereo. The sound track on the left shows Dolby's Stereo Variable Area track.

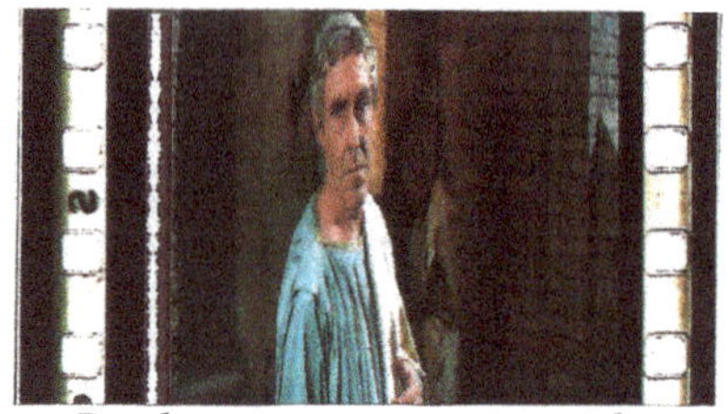

Dual purpose mag print with an additional half-width mono optical track, reducing the aspect ratio to 2.35:1 and bringing the centre line back to normal.

Fox put its foot down, insisting that CinemaScope be shown on its 'Miracle-Mirror' curved screen. A leftover from their earlier 'Eidophor' theatre television project, its brighter, but directional aluminium surface was a mixed blessing for all shapes of auditorium. All changed when MGM announced it would use Perspecta directional sound on its CinemaScope prints. In the interest of the system's future, Fox relented. Cinemas could choose their own flat or curved screen and show on it either a new dual-purpose 4-track mag print with an alternative mono half-width optical track alongside the inner left stripe, or the squeezed image on a standard optical sound print with normal perforations. In both cases, the picture width was reduced a little to give an aspect ratio of 2.35:1.

Perspecta fades away

By the start of the 1960s, Perspecta had gone quietly, and the number of CinemaScope 4-track mag prints had declined, reserved mostly for large scale epics and musicals. A lifeline for magnetic sound would be the re-birth of 70mm, with the original premium large format system, Todd-AO, using it exclusively. Shot on 65mm film, its 70mm prints made room for the stripes, now with six tracks - adding two extra speakers behind the even bigger 2.2:1 screen. Making the system a practical proposition for the larger first-run theatres was its 'multi-purpose' projector, which could also run 35mm magnetic and optical sound prints. With auditoria being split, and the coming of the multiplex, 70mm screens began to shrink, so their additional pair of speakers were sacrificed, their channels now giving directional sound to the surrounds and the shake-it-all-about sub-bass, which had become an essential feature in the new sound of cinema.

Who chose CinemaScope's shape?

The proportions of the CinemaScope screen owe more to engineering than any creative contribution. It would simply be a combination of the shape of the maximum area on the 35mm print available for the picture, doubled in width by the already fixed x2 degree of lateral compression and expansion chosen by Henri Chretien in 1927. As his patents had run out by the 1950s, Fox could have waited and made its own 'anamorphic' lenses with possibly a different squeeze factor and resulting aspect ratio. It wanted Chretien's originals to make an immediate start on its first productions and demonstrations to encourage the industry to join with this latest answer to falling audiences.

CinemaScope would also try and emulate Cinerama with its own 'wonder of stereophonic sound' and accommodating it would also have an effect on the picture's shape. For its early previews, the multi-channel sound would also come from a separate magnetic track, leaving the squeezed image free to use the larger full-aperture (silent) frame, its 1.33:1 aspect ratio stretched to 2.66:1 on the screen. Although common in studios during post-production, and already being used for a few special showings of conventional and 3D films, the 'double-band' method was considered too cumbersome for general use, with twice as much film to deal with and the ever-present risk of it all going out of sync. To make CinemaScope more convenient for cinemas and easier to handle by distributors, it was planned to provide a combined print with four magnetic tracks recorded on narrow oxide stripes placed on either side of the perforations. Although these were made smaller (now square Fox-holes) to gain some extra space, the width of the final picture was reduced a little to 2.55:1.

And the sound?

Although audiences liked greater involvement with the wider picture, there was a mixed reaction to its matching wide-ranging sound. Like many of today's cinemagoers who prefer a quieter life, the temptation to turn up the level of this early immersive sound system left them, as one reviewer said after a demo, "drowning in a cacophony of sound coming at you from all directions". Others loved the clearer and higher-fidelity sound, sparking off the new hobby of hi-fi in the home. At the cinema, Fox enveloped them in true stereo, with even dialogue recorded using three microphones suspended from a special boom. The effects track was used sparingly. The sound sent to the auditorium speakers came from the narrowest of the four stripes, so to avoid a background hiss, they only came to life in the presence of a 12kHz control signal recorded along with the effects. After a few films, Fox followed the later practice of recording the music in stereo, leaving the sound editor to assign the (mono) dialogue to the appropriate track, or the dubbing (re-recording) mixer to 'pan-pot' it between them. Some just left it coming from the centre speaker.

The fate of magnetic sound

Many 35mm films would be 'blown-up' to a 70mm print, principally to gain access to its superior sound

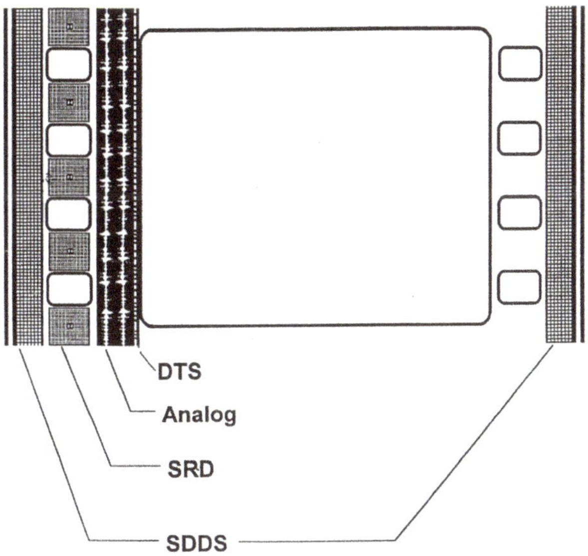

Showing how Panavision lenses could cure the anamorphic 'mumps' which afflicted early CinemaScope's close-ups

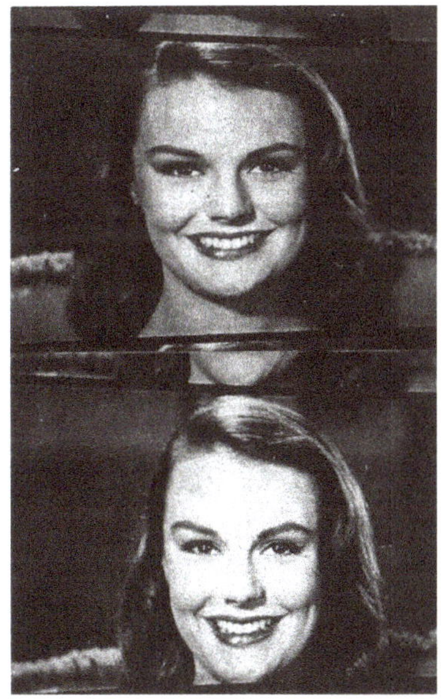

system. Magnetic 35mm prints finally disappeared in the wake of Dolby's stereo optical systems, which brought high-quality stereo to every cinema. In the 1990s, its analogue track would share the 35mm print with the various digital systems, using all the remaining space on the film, including between the perforations, their tracks - read optically - providing either complete sound information or a code linked to a CD. Although 35mm's sound could now match 70mm, this would keep its analogue magnetic stripes until given a fatal blow by health and safety, not to protect our ears, but the planet from chemicals used to produce the oxide paste applied to the film. This didn't kill off 70mm, which kept its voice by adding its own optical code track and a separate digital sound CD.

CinemaScope's more welcome shape

For many, the less wide 2.35:1 version was more pleasing and easier to manage for both production and exhibition. This is sometimes quoted as 2.39:1 following a suggested reduced height projection aperture to hide possible 'flashing' negative joins. Now, helped by the option of the optical sound prints, CinemaScope was here to stay and soon no projection room around the world would be complete without its anamorphic attachments. Some of their manufacturers could also provide camera lenses, leading to a long list of rival, but compatible systems appearing on the credits. These, like CinemaScope itself, would soon be referred to as simply being in 'Scope.

CinemaScope by another name

In Hollywood, MGM, again going its own way, worked with another maker of projection attachments, Panavision Inc., to develop photographic lenses for the studio. Using a different 'mumps-free' focusing method, they soon replaced those from Bausch & Lomb for MGM's 'Scope films, which, for contractual reasons, would still be 'in CinemaScope' up to the 1960s. Although Fox's own later lenses were much better, when Panavision became generally available, they too switched, saying goodbye to their rousing CinemaScope opening. 'Filmed in Panavision' became the most popular process for producers choosing to go anamorphic, with their directors and cinematographers using its 2.35:1 format effectively, not only for glossy spectaculars, but also for more modest intimate stories.

Television takes its toll

The number of 'Scope films took a severe dip in the early·1970s, when the sale to television became an important factor, for many the difference between a profit or loss. The money men decided that widescreen, particularly 'Scope, had no residual value for the then 4:3 TV, and there was the added cost of producing the dreaded 'pan and scan' conversions. Although despised by the film-makers, and those of us more aware of the wider picture, the average viewer preferred them to a letterbox across their smaller screen back home. Even the Bond series dropped anamorphic Panavision for a while (the first Roger Moore ones) but, like others, their 'big picture' look was soon missed, and Bond returned in 2.35:1.

Enter 16:9, the new shape of TV

The prospect of wider TV screens began way back in the 1970s, along with proposed higher or extended definition TV systems. However, 'HD' would be a long time coming, held back by wrangles over international standards, as TV was beginning its own switch to digital, a process which would eventually make the 'HD' idea a practical proposition. At first broadcasters chose to use

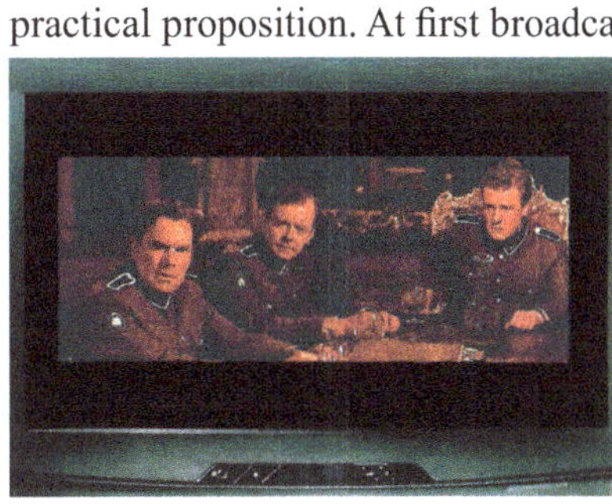

The first 16:9 TVs made the 2.35:1 letterbox option more acceptable to viewers

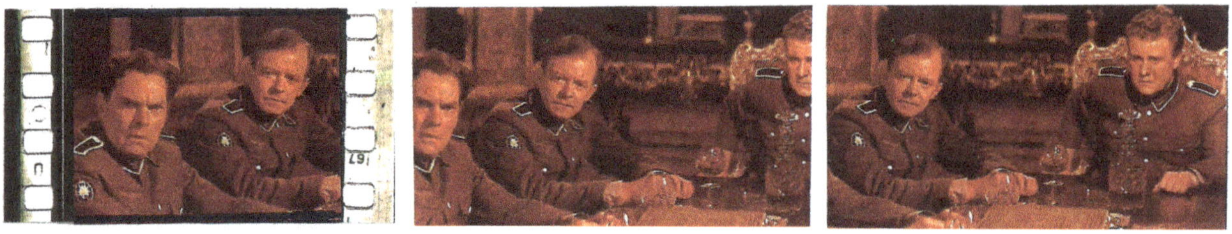

Left: *Earlier 'pan and scan' print for 4:3 TVs. The same result could be achieved during a telecine transfer conversion of an original 2.35:1 squeezed print. Still occasionally shown if this is the only readily available copy.*
Centre: *A centre cut-out for today's 16:9 devices can sometimes produce an unsatisfactory image.*
Right: *A better result using a modern pan and scan technique*

digital's extra capacity to offer more channels rather than fewer higher-definition widescreen ones. However, as the final proportions of the screen were largely independent of the rival HD systems, by the mid-1980s all had agreed that 16:9 was the ideal shape. The rationale behind this choice will be looked at later.

Why wait for widescreen?

With the slow progress of HD, broadcasters and manufacturers asked 'why not cash in and adopt it for standard definition digital TV and DVDs?' The easy way was to copy CinemaScope and squeeze the wider picture information into the normal 4:3 frame. The necessary x1.33 compression could be electronically restored by a set-top box or the DVD player, with their displays including a letterbox for older TV sets, or left squeezed to be stretched out across the screen of a 16:9 TV. Unfortunately, many of their viewers seemed to be quite happy to let the set do the same to older 4:3 films, leading to a further outbreak of 'anamorphic mumps'.

What you don't see, you don't miss?

The pan & scan conversions of 'Scope films only display a 1.33:1 portion of the 2.35:1 picture, but constantly move it across the image to try to keep the most significant action in view. These versions were the mainstay for 4:3 TV and are still occasionally shown today if they are the only readily available copy, particularly of films yet to be mastered in widescreen. Although 16mm and 8mm squeezed prints became available, they were also a useful alternative for film libraries and buyers of packaged home movies for showing without an anamorphic lens.. It would be the original film-based 'home cinema' enthusiasts who would lead the way to e-cinema, with the now familiar DLP and SXRD image forming chips first being used in business and domestic video projectors before invading cinema projection rooms.

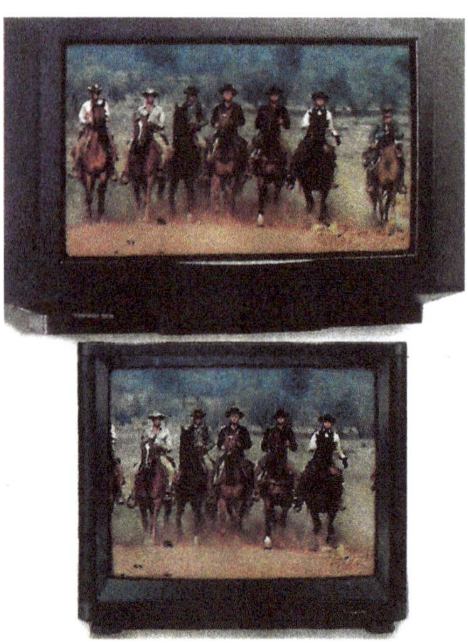

Even when shown at 16:9 (1.78:1) widescreen TVs are much kinder to 2.35:1 films than in the old 4:3 days, when a reluctance to display a letterbox meant that The Magnificent Seven were reduced to five!

Opening the window to a wider world

The first home videos and DVDs also favoured the pan & scan method for their 'Scope films, but as an added sales opportunity, efforts were made to encourage viewers to see and appreciate the complete picture with 'special widescreen editions'. These would look better and be more acceptable, on a new widescreen TV or projector.

When HD TV and the companion Blu-rays finally arrived, they came with an already fixed 'native' picture shape, without a squeeze. 4:3 images sit in the centre with two common options for those in 2.35:1, either complete, with a now less severe letterbox, or enlarged to fill the full height, with the loss of image mitigated by a small degree of pan and scan.

'Scope without an anamorphic lens

Beginning in the 1980s there was a trend to produce this same picture shape without using the larger and heavier anamorphic lenses on the camera. The same squeezed prints could also be made by extracting a corresponding 2.35:1 slice from the middle of a conventionally shot full-frame non-anamorphic negative.

To make the most of it, 'Super 35' extended the image into the area normally reserved for the soundtrack. This wasn't a new idea, as back in 1954, it formed the basis of RKO's SuperScope, RKO being one of the studios which had shunned CinemaScope. The idea would also prove useful for incorporating old 4:3 footage in CinemaScope films. Unlike anamorphic shooting, Super 35 still wastes much of the available negative area, so some productions, still being shot on film, made savings by only advancing the film in the camera by three perforations instead of four.

Fortunately, today, like conventional four perf, after

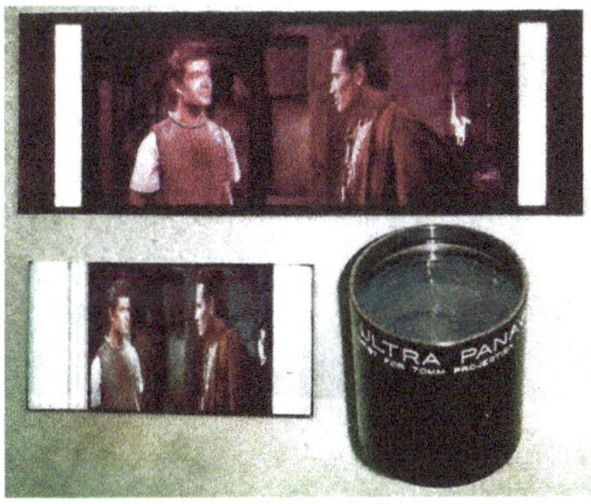

MGM Camera 65 / Ultra Panavision 70mm squeezed print, its anamorphic projector lens attachment and a 35mm 'Scope reduction print

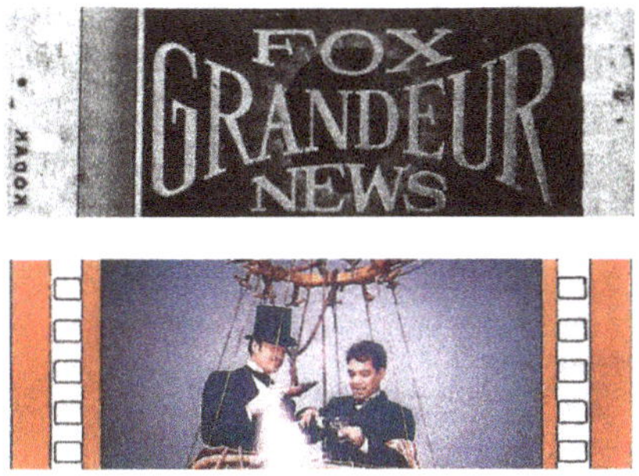

Top: 70mm print from 1929 with optical sound and Below: the later more successful Todd-AO with its magnetic stripes (1956).

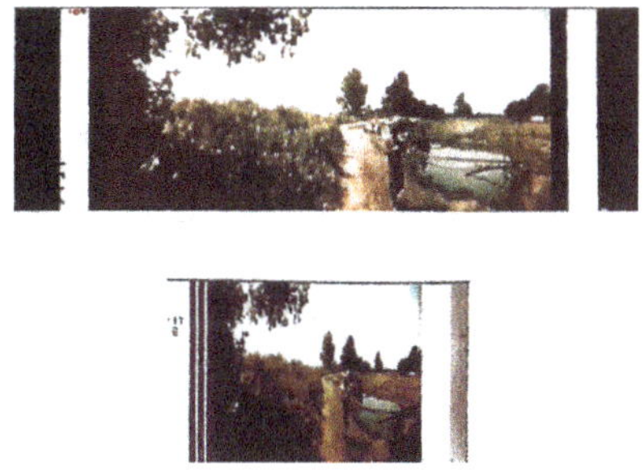

Even a 3-strip Cinerama film could be reduced to a single 70mm or 35mm print (How the West Was Won)

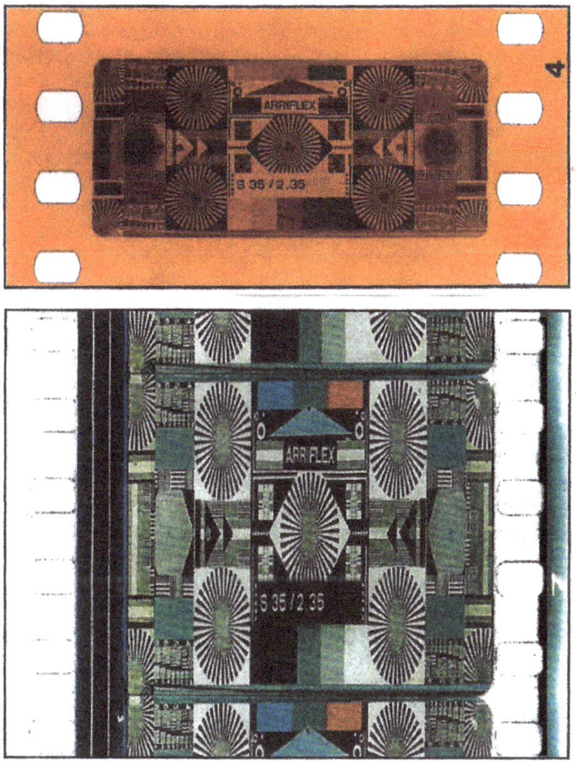

Super 35 area for 2.35:1 'Scope prints. Previously also Superscope 235, MegaScope, WarnerScope and Super Techniscope). The full height is often exposed to allow for other formats, or a 3-perf pull-down can be used to reduce the wasted film area.

leaving the camera and being processed, film can easily be scanned, ready for the rest of the digital route to the screen. Some showing this at 2.35:1 in cinemas use the negative's extra height to provide a 16:9 version for TV and DVD/Blu-ray, usually by adding more image at the bottom of the picture and keeping the same top line. Some home cinema enthusiasts who complained had to be reassured that nothing was missing from the sides.

The same universal format scanners have been used for the more recent digital restoration of films from the golden age of widescreen systems. During the 1950s and 60s there were many individual 'Scopes, 'Ramas and 'Visions, shot with or without anamorphic lenses onto various shapes and sizes of original camera negatives. The general rule was 'the bigger the better' for the best quality prints.

See the film as the Director intended

This popular tag-line promoting wider pictures in the home reminds me of an amusing 'aspect ratio' story from my BBC projectionist days. In preparation for a film review programme interview, we ran the 2.35:1 'Scope feature *Flash Gordon* (1980) to its director and the show's presenter. Hearts sank when parts of the opening titles, based on the original cartoon strip, appeared to be stretched and shouldn't have been projected through an anamorphic lens. Fortunately, once passed, the rest of the film was OK. During a light-hearted after-show chat with its director, Mike Hodges, he admitted that due to some screen shape confusion, the titles had indeed been inadvertently shot without the required anamorphic lens. Unfortunately, no one noticed until much work had already been done fast-cutting them to Queens' rock score. Apart from keeping the planet round, it was decided not to do it all again and any remaining distortion became part of the new overall design. Interestingly, some of the later pan & Scan versions left the titles squeezed, so their viewers saw Flash in his correct proportions.

Giving them names to remember

Still with us is the original **Todd-AO** 70mm format, which, like its **Super Panavision** equivalent, used normal lenses to expose its larger images on a wider 65mm negative with a higher 5 perforation frame. The 70mm prints, making room for their magnetic sound stripes, would become the first Premium Large Format to fill the biggest screens. These became wider when **MGM Camera 65**, later known as **Ultra Panavision**, added a x1.25 anamorphic lens to both the camera and the projector to increase the 2.2:1 aspect ratio to 2.76:1. Cinemas without 70mm projectors didn't miss out, benefiting from the superior 35mm 'Scope reduction prints. Technicolor's contribution, **Technirama**, doubled the size of the negative by running conventional 35mm film sideways through the camera with an 8 perf pull-across movement (like a 35mm still camera). Half of the final

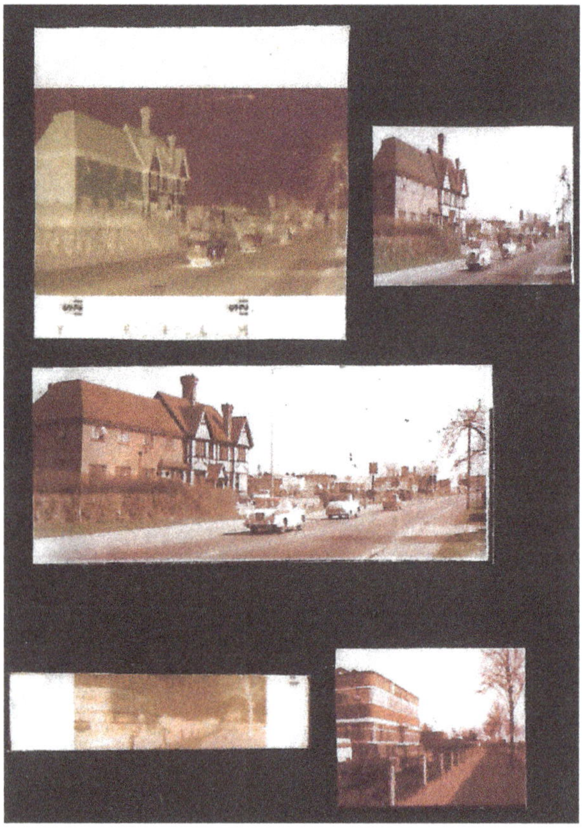

Technicolor's big-budget Super Technirama 70 and their more modest Techniscope

x2 squeeze was achieved by the camera lens (x1.5) and the rest during printing. As well as providing superb (HD) 35mm 'Scope reduction prints, its large-area negative images could be unsqueezed across a **70mm Super Technorama** Todd-AO type print. For a couple of its CinemaScope features, Fox too tried shooting their squeezed images onto a special 8 perf 55mm film with a frame four times the normal size. Again intended to produce better looking 35mm prints, **CinemaScope 55** didn't last long, soon abandoned in favour of Todd-AO.

Something smaller for tighter budgets

With improving finer grain film stocks in the 1960s, Technicolor came up with **Techniscope**, which only advanced the film in the camera by two perforations instead of the usual four. Shot with normal lenses, the resulting half-height, now 2.35:1 images were stretched vertically during printing to produce the compatible four perf squeezed projection print. Although a little grainier, it proved popular for a time, bringing both 'Scope and Technicolor to lower budget films, which would also benefit the most from halving the cost of the negative stock. There would be many other widescreen processes hitting the screen, but fortunately for the producers and exhibitors, such was the laboratories skill at optical printing, almost all could be converted to produce a standard 35mm print for general release. Even the most exotic of the road-show formats, like the process which started it all, 3-strip Cinerama, could continue to make money at your local cinema and eventually on TV and video.

Their memory lingers on

The names of these old processes live on, gracing the credits of past films still being shown and enjoyed today. Future students of the cinema may spot them and wonder what they were all about. Sadly, apart from perhaps the digital reincarnation of IMAX®, there don't yet seem to be any digital equivalents to excite today's audiences, although they are coming in the shape of various 'Premium' formats. Despite HDR, HFR and 4K being available to tempt them, none are exclusive to the cinema, so it took the recent revival of a long-forgotten film process, Ultra Panavision 70, for the release of Quentin Tarantino's western *The Hateful Eight* to again make news and capture the imagination of the public.

You can see the difference?

The photographic decisions for the Bond films have continued to reflect current trends. Although still 2.35;1, from *Casino Royale* (2006) they switched to Super 35 until, after a brief flirtation with digital for *Skyfall*, the later *Spectre* returned to film and anamorphic Panavision.

For today's 2.35:1 digital productions, not just those originated on film, some of their makers still prefer to use anamorphic lenses on the camera. Apart from making better use of the available frame area, for those with an eye for it, they also have their own special, if subtle, anamorphic look, extending the horizontal view without resorting to a shorter focal length lens with its less natural deeper perspective.

However produced, 2.35:1 has survived the transition to digital and is even more popular today, for film-makers and audiences alike, the true shape of the Cinema, compared to the 16:9 on their TVs and other devices. These sometimes share it, giving the cinematic look to many adverts and the occasional drama, now more acceptable on our larger widescreen TVs. A couple of TV manufacturers have tried to tempt cinema lovers with 'Scope (21:9) models, but they haven't caught on yet!

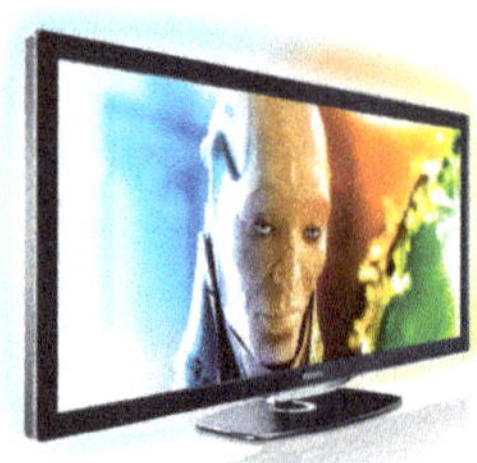

Philips 21:9 TV

Early digital projection

The future of anamorphic lenses is also uncertain. Although some of the first digital cinema projectors, with their earlier squarer 5:4 DLP chips, used a special (x1.9) anamorphic supplementary lens to produce their 2.35:1 pictures, the later wider format (1.9:1) versions could accommodate them without one.

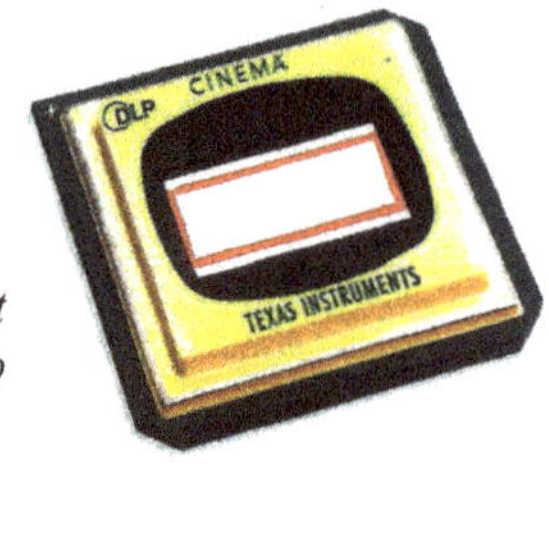

2.35:1 on a current 1.9:1 DLP chip

Digital cameras too

Striving for the genuine look of film, legacy anamorphic lenses are still being used on current digital cameras, recording their still prized images onto their 35mm film frame size sensor. It has led to some of the leading manufacturers of cine lenses introducing new ranges of anamorphic lenses for use on both film and digital cameras, all helping to ensure that the 2.35:1 format will continue to broaden the horizon of cinemagoers.

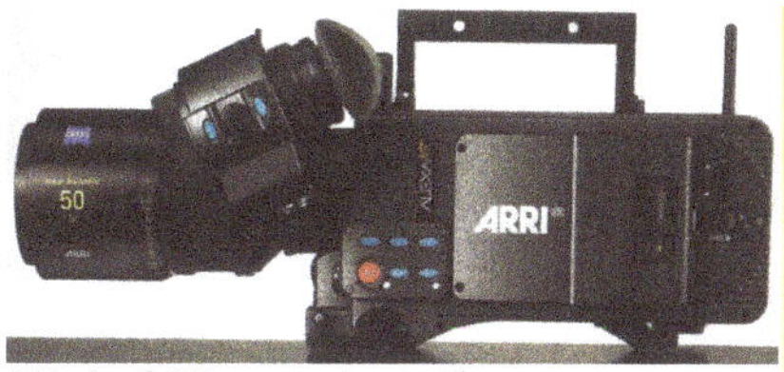

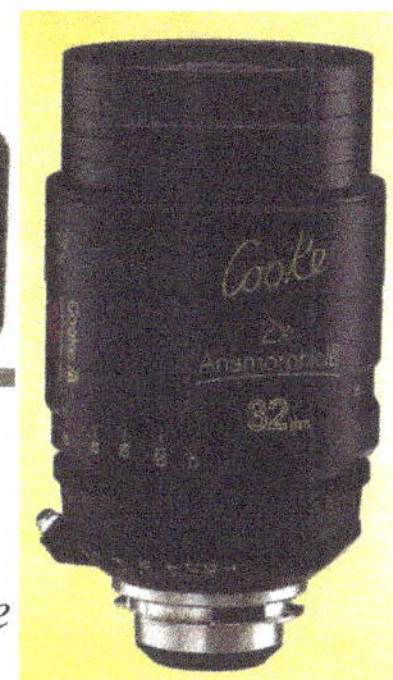

Digital 'Scope: Arri Alexa camera fitted with Zeiss anamorphic lens - others include a new range of British Cooke lenses. Digital cameras like the Arri are often described as having a 'Super 35' film size sensor.

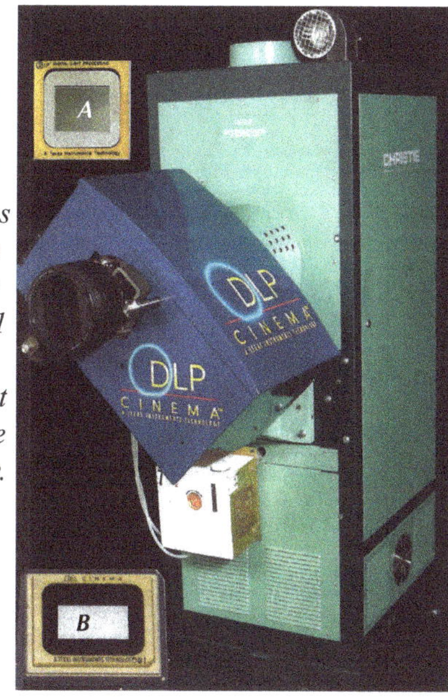

The first digital cinema projectors, which had squarer DLP chips (A) often used an anamorphic lens for the best 2.35:1 pictures. The later wider format versions (B) made them unnecessary.

A wide range of widescreen formats

The names and relative negative areas of the processes most often seen on the credits of films from the golden age of widescreen systems. All the resulting 35mm squeezed prints could be projected through the same x2 'CinemaScope' anamorphic lens. With ever improving film stocks the larger area systems were the first to go.

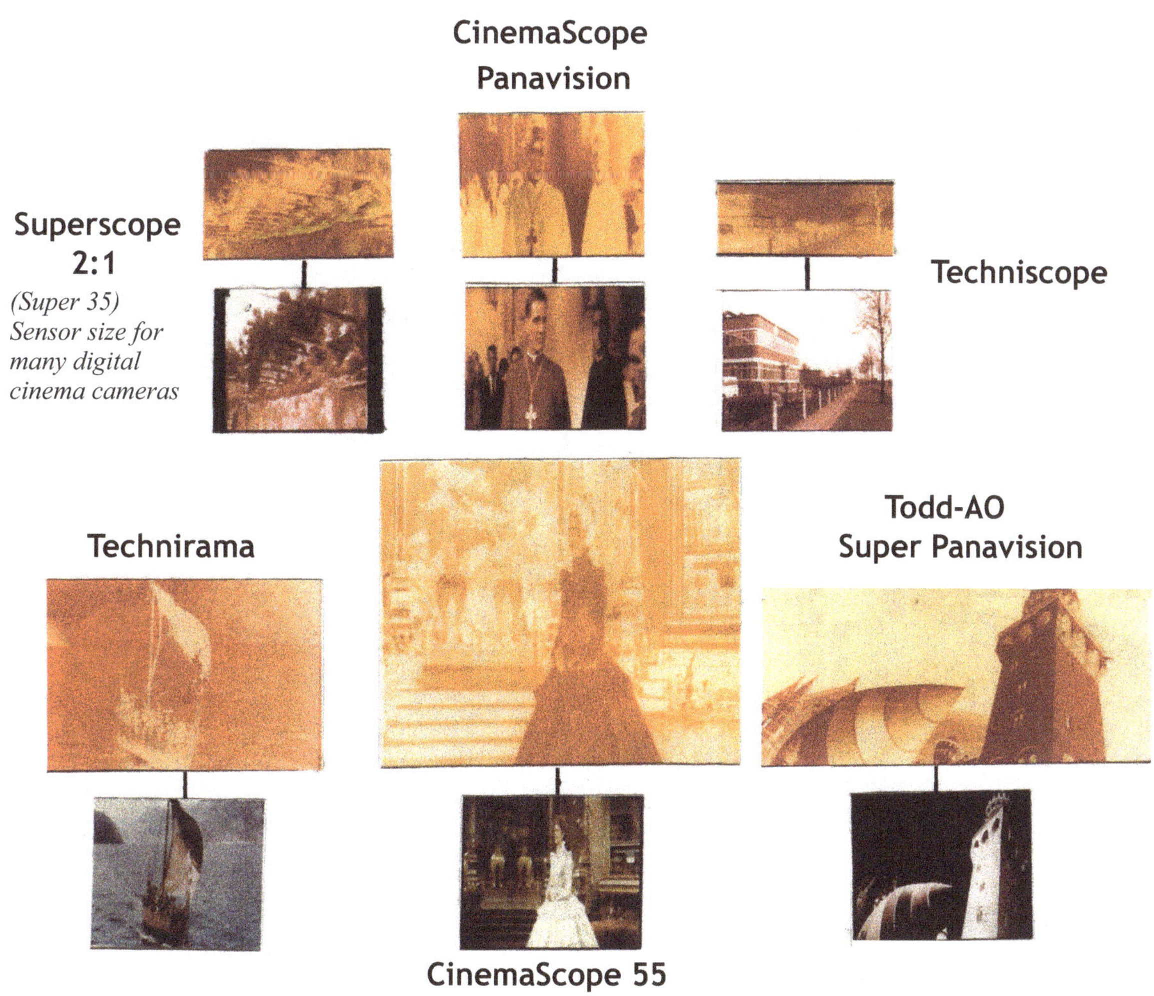

Presenting a broader view - A look at cinema screen's other main shape - the 1.85:1 format, aiming at carrying on with a wider screen but without losing your head!

Having discussed the cinema's popular 2.35:1 picture shape, we will now turn our attention to its slimmer companion, the 1.85:1 format.

The 1950s was an interesting time for projectionists, particularly those wishing to add to their showmanship and presentation skills. On their way to help were the many 'new' screen processes designed to tempt falling audiences back to the cinema. First in the queue were stereoscopic movies and a chance for the picture to break free from its black masking and sit in a pool of light, changing in intensity and colour, to match the image. By the beginning of 1953, 3D was in full swing, and the idea of illuminated surrounds was being given a try. Spurred on by the sensational success of the triple-projector Cinerama, Fox was preparing to give trade demonstrations of its new CinemaScope, an easier way to bring a similar panoramic image into ordinary cinemas. As a taster for the bigger screens to come, Fox revived the old Magnascope idea, enlarging the picture at the climax of *Niagara* as its heroine was snatched from the edge of the falls.

Coming soon, wider screens

Interest in 3D films would soon begin to wane, but fortunately for the cinema owners who showed them, the mini-boom had largely paid for the often makeshift means of projecting 3D. However, its possible replacement, CinemaScope, with its obligatory magnetic stereo sound, would be a much larger investment, and its extra pulling-power would have to last and not be just a passing gimmick. Even though CinemaScope was considered to be a 'poor man's Cinerama', the search was still on to find simpler ways to fill a wider screen.

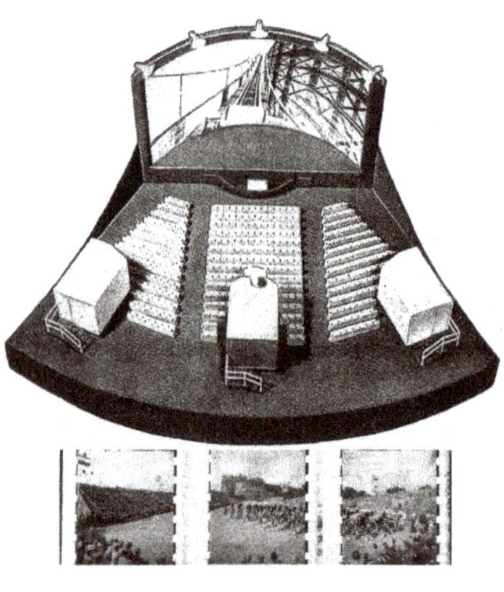

The original triple-projector Cinerama system was far too complicated for the average cinema, so the search was on to find simpler widescreen methods

Less can look like more

Looking in turn for a 'poor man's CinemaScope', there had always been a far less risky and cheaper 'bargain-basement' way to alter the shape of the screen. As early as 1913, an article in the Kinematograph Weekly suggested that, 'if you mask the gate of your projector so that the width remains the same, but the height is decreased; the result is a better shaped picture – more artistic. The portion masked off will never be missed.' There were reports that this was put into practice, such as enhancing the views in early travel films, often accompanying the popular talks by explorers and other globetrotters. Sometimes the bigger Magnascope pictures ended up with a widescreen effect, the top and bottom chopped off by architectural features like balconies and the shape of the maximum size of proscenium openings.

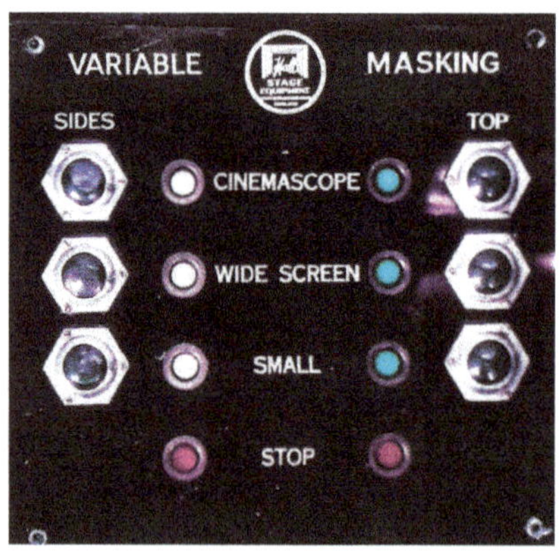

Early control panel for a cinema's 'Magnascope' moveable masking, with its original 4:3 position still labelled as 'small'.

What you don't see, you don't miss

Whether it was going to be missed, or not, images began to be cropped in-early 1953. Hollywood's rush to steal a march on CinemaScope and give screens a new look meant that the frame areas of many up-coming conventionally shot 4:3 films would soon go missing. The idea, of course, was to counter the effect of the projector's masked-down gate, by also changing to a shorter focal-length lens to bring back the height on the screen to at least that of the old 4:3 picture. This was to give audiences the impression that they were seeing more at the sides and not less top and bottom. At first, there was no agreement on how much to crop, with each studio choosing a different screen ratio, ranging from around 1.66: 1 (10% off the top and bottom), to a more severe 2:1.

'Shane' cut down to size

Among the first features to be subjected to this wider-screen treatment was Paramount's classic western *Shane*, which opened at New York's Radio City Music Hall on their new 'Panoramic Screen'. To match its 1.66:1 broader image, it was shown together with a separate magnetic stereo soundtrack. Other already completed 4:3 films, also available with a dubbed-on separate track, included *Julius Caesar* at 1.75:1 and *The War of The Worlds* at 1.66:1. Combining two innovations together, *The House of Wax* was premièred at 1.5:1, giving a slight widescreen look to its 3D. Another, *It Came From Outer Space*, also hit the audience from a wider 1.85:1 screen. Previous favourites like *The Wizard of Oz*, *The Greatest Show on Earth* and *Gone with the Wind* would return on a wider screen. The fact that actors risked losing their heads, or were cut off at the chin didn't seem to bother audiences too much - they were fascinated by the new shape, although there were some complaints when the dancing feet of Fred Astair and Cyd Charisse were cut off during widescreen showings of *The Band Wagon*.

Keeping heads down

Back when projectionists stayed by their machines, the more conscientious could help re-compose the image by keeping a constant eye on the racking. Providing there were no important legs and feet to worry about, or other lower down subject matter vital to the plot, it was found best to lose most of the picture from the bottom of the frame. It also helped that, back in the days of non-reflex viewfinders, and the often undersize keystone compensating projector gates, this had led to a much safer looser framing than today. Some 4:3 films could stand up to being cropped better than others and it was wise to audition them first on a wider screen, before choosing its new aspect ratio.

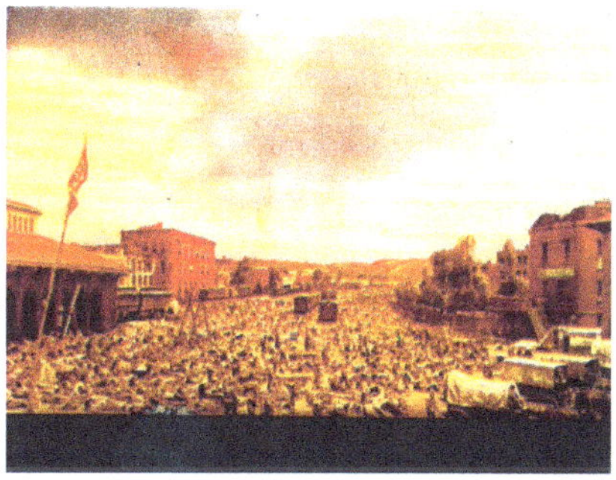

For one widescreen re-issue of Gone With The Wind some scenes had a black bar printed along the bottom of the frame to encourage the projectionist to favour the upper part of the cropped picture. Publicity would use GTWW to mean 'Greater With The Wide-Screen'

New names to conjure with

Although no studio could claim this 'masked-frame' widescreen method as their own unique process, their publicity departments had fun coming up with names for it. As well as Paramount's Panoramic Screen, Columbia had its 'Vistascope' (1.85:1), Republic its 'Vast-Vision', together with 'ScenicScope' from RKO and MGM's 'Variscope' (1.75:1). Warners would be content to call it 'Wide Screen', and this would soon become

Two views of Shane

For many cinema purists any cropping of original 4:3 films shows a disrespect to the visual intentions of their directors and cinematographers. This hasn't stopped an extra on the latest Blu-ray release of *Shane* from offering an alternative masked-down version, justified on the grounds that this was the way many of the first audiences saw it, and was done at the time with the approval of the film's director, George Stevens. No mention if its DoP or camera operator were equally happy to see parts of their work go missing. Like other film-makers, George Stevens would go on to express doubts about the value of widescreen for all types of subjects, but he would eventually begin filming *The Greatest Story Ever Told* in 3-strip Cinerama, before it switched to Ultra Panavision 70, still one of the cinema's widest picture shapes.

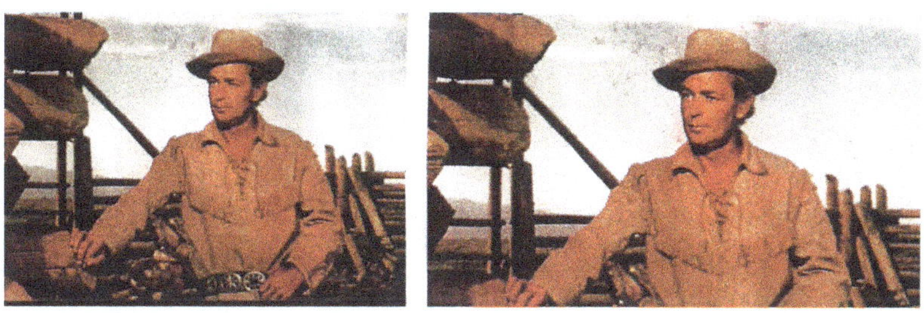

SHANE (1953), like other originally shot 1.37:1 films, was sometimes cropped, in this case 1.66:1, to help kick off the cinema's widescreen aspirations.

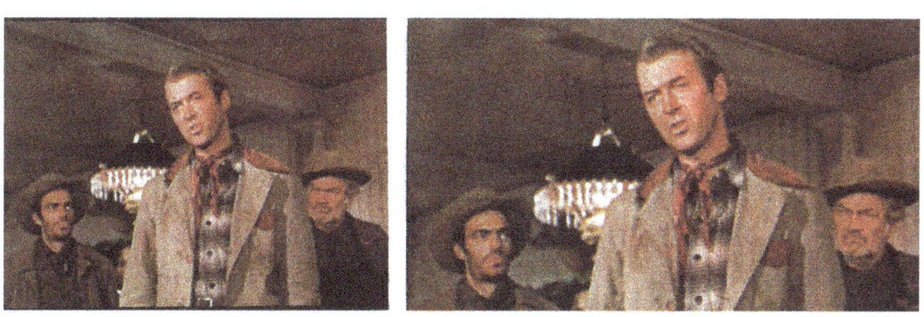

By the mid-1950s all Hollywood features were photographed to allow for cropping, with plenty of 'wasted' space above and below the usually 1.85:1 projected area.

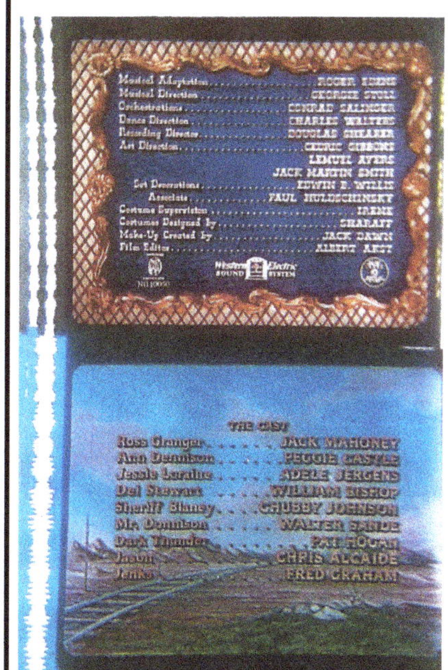

Titles, previously laid out for 4:3 screens, had to be re-designed to prevent the risk of some of the cast and crew losing their credits.

Never mind the film, look at the screen!

The earlier illuminated surrounds were created either by an optical attachment on the projector, which directed some of the light spilling from the gate through a separate lens, or using a much simpler 'Syncro-Screen'. For this, a silver screen was surrounded by a frame of angled panels covered in diffused material , which picked up stray light, mostly from the edges of the projected picture, which, like before, constantly changed in brightness and colour to match the nature of the image. Viewers either loved or hated the effect, but it fell out of favour as there were difficulties in moving it to accommodate different picture shapes.

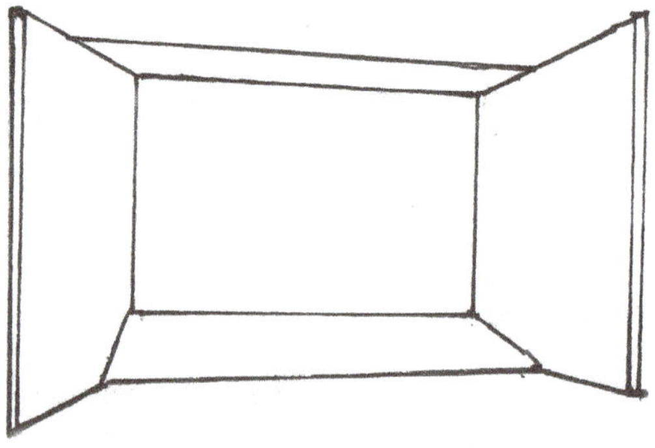

The 'Syncro-Screen' replaced the black masking with angled panels which 'glowed' with light coming from the screen.

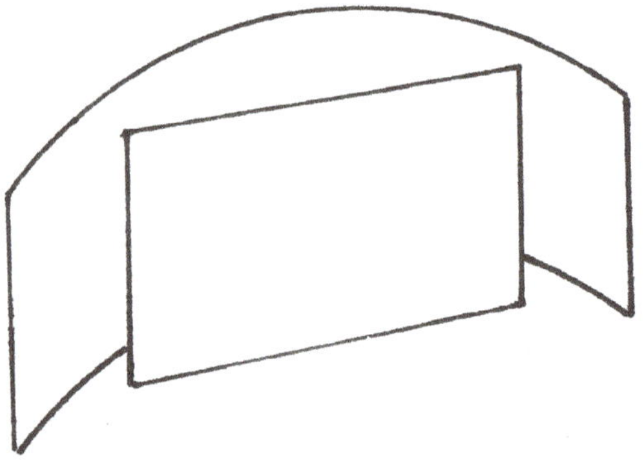

Another 'no masking' idea, which didn't catch on, was the 'Floating Screen'

the common term for this form of presentation. Although occasionally seen on promotional material and posters, these early names didn't find their way on to the credits, which might have caused confusion, thinking they referred to a specific ratio.

Fit for the new screens

Universal's contribution was 'Wide-Vision'. It was introduced with *Thunder Bay*, the first film claimed to have been specially shot for widescreen presentation, with, in this case, all the action kept within an area equivalent to 1.85:1. Other studios followed suit with all their new productions using cameras with guide lines in the viewfinder to mark their chosen aspect ratio. In all cases, the whole frame was still exposed for cinemas waiting to install a wider screen and, although not wishing to make any concessions for its audience stealing arch-enemy television, there was a large 16mm non-theatrical market to consider. Even so, the full frame's 4:3 image did suffer, with the action pushed back and extra unnecessary space above the actors' heads. The wasted image above and below the wide screen projected area was sometimes called losable 'fluff'.

Before the 'depthies' fell out of favour, some of the last 3D films, like *The Creature From The Black Lagoon* and *Dial M For Murder* were composed for 2:1 and 1.85:1 respectively for their mostly 2D showings. Studios would have to re-design their logos and titles layout to prevent members of the cast and crew losing their credits. However, Hollywood's 1953-55 transition period included a backlog of films originally shot for 4:3 screens and although the titles, added later, may appear to be suitable for cropping, the rest of the film looks uncomfortable when shown in widescreen. Directors of Photography had also been reluctant to change their framing part way through a production.

With no fixed aspect ratio, exhibitors too were left to decide the best for their individual theatres, usually dictated by the size and shape of the proscenium opening. Fortunately, many of the big city centre cinemas had large stages to accommodate the popular cine-variety type live shows. The later decline of these and the coming of bigger and wider screens would eventually see the end of decorative theatre-like prosceniums in the designs of new auditoriums, which would become less ornate, with the front wall now dominated by the screen itself.

Looking for guidance

To try and guide exhibitors as to the correct screen shape, the reviews of domestic features appearing, in the U.S. entertainment industry's trade paper 'Daily Variety' stated the studios recommended ratio. However, these were soon dropped when theatre owners who couldn't provide the exact ratio felt somehow excluded from showing the film. To allay their fears, those answering enquiries to distributors were told to say that their films could be shown at any ratio, from the old 1.37:1 up to 2:1, whether they were shot for it or not.

The wide screen storm hits Britain

For our first look at the shape of things to come, it was announced that the premiere of *Young Bess* would be on the Empire Leicester Square's new 'Metroscope' 1.75:1 screen. Not wishing to be beaten, Rank, working secretly at the nearby Odeon, would get in first when, a few days earlier, they surprised the first-night audience for *Tonight We Sing* by, after showing the newsreel and short on its normal 4:3 screen with its familiar black masking, it was flown away to reveal a much larger 1.66:1 screen complete with an illuminated surround.

Here in Britain we tend to soon follow Hollywood's production and presentation methods, and by the time our own cinemas would have to order new gates, lenses and screens, it was expected that a common aspect ratio would have been chosen. It was hoped that it would be a repeat of the similar situation when, back in 1932, the introduction of the various optical sound-on-film systems, each with different apertures, had led to the Academy of Arts and Sciences to come up with a single 'Academy' 1.37:1 sound aperture.

With no widescreen version forthcoming, it was decided to arrive at our own standard. The BKS would play its part with a survey of British cinemas which showed that almost all could accommodate a screen between 1.45:1 and 1.65:1 without having to reduce their present height. Looking ahead to the prospect of fitting in CinemaScope's even wider 2.55:1 picture, they found that only about 15% would be able to keep the same height. Practical tests for the trade were arranged by the Rank Organisation using a special larger screen with variable masking, constructed at their Odeon cinema in Tottenham Court Road, soon to become a popular theatre for trying out new presentation methods. To judge the effect on existing films, they projected samples from current releases at various aspect ratios, and the view was that at 1.6:1, few were visually harmed. Some thought it was actually kind to *The Cruel Sea*, adding greater involvement with the action at sea, without the missing image spoiling the drama below deck too much.

Although the BKS's Theatre Division, forerunner of today's BKSTS Cinema Technology Committee, was describing anything greater than 1.45:1 as widescreen, in practice it was found that it had to be at least 1.65:1 or better 1.75:1 to appear appreciably different to the average cinemagoer. For example, a 35mm still transparency has a 1.5:1 aspect ratio, but was not generally regarded as a widescreen format.

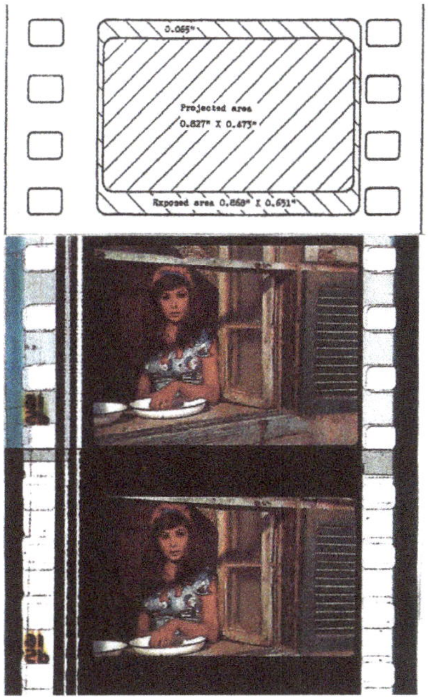

Britain's attempt in 1956 to adopt 1.75:1 as the standard shape for non-anamorphic masked-frame projection. Top image shows the exposed and printed 1.37:1 frame. Lower image shows the area projected for 1.75:1 screens.

Following all this work, The British Film Producers Association recommended that the composition in the studio camera should be standardised at a ratio of 1.75:1; tolerable for both 1.66:1 and 1.85:1. Again, the full Academy aperture would continue to be photographed, but to avoid the excessive headroom, all would use the same 1.66:1 top line. The area for titles would correspond to the possible maximum 1.85:1. This also applied to sub-titles and other inserts, including our familiar censor certificate, which also had to be modified to fit the new screen proportions. Most cinemas using the new 'Magnascopic' motorised variable masking kept their old 'small' 4:3 picture. This could be used for the newsreel and shorts, before, adding to the showmanship, by opening out their new moveable masking in full view of the audience as the widescreen big feature hit the screen.

Hollywood goes for 1.85

Back in America production people were finally having their say, objecting to the compromises needed to accommodate the many different aspect ratios, so, to end the chaos, all the studios agreed that 1.85:1 should now be the accepted format. As before, the whole frame was still to be exposed, but adopting a strict 'shoot and protect' procedure, keeping anything in view above and below acceptable for other ratios, including 1.37:1 showings. Apart from Metroscope, still being used to describe this cropped-frame widescreen method, the other early names were soon forgotten. However there was one proprietary process, intended for providing this kind of print, which would be proudly announced at the start of many films

HD comes to the movies

When Fox's anamorphic CinemaScope arrived, Paramount decided to give it a miss, not willing to accept, in their view, its far too wide and degraded stretched-out images. They would stick to their masked-down prints, but improve the definition of their smaller projected frames by reducing them from a larger negative. This was achieved by running normal 35mm film horizontally through the camera with an 8-perforation frame. All the extra detail recorded on this double-size negative was preserved when printed down to a normal vertical 4-perf print, made on its inherently finer grain stock. Paramount suggested that its new 'VistaVision' could be projected at any ratio between 1.66:1 and 2:1, but recommended 1.8.5:1 as the ideal choice. Its superior image would also stand up to a greater degree of magnification for a much larger screen than normal. Unfortunately, when unveiled in 1954, VistaVision wasn't entirely understood by both critics and cinema-goers, its advantages being far less obvious than the first sight of CinemaScope's panoramic picture. Cinemas didn't help by being content to show it on the same size screen as their other masked-down films. A bigger picture would still need more light through its reduced height gate. Trying to find a way to explain its benefits, one early reviewer compared VistaVision to the then new enthusiasm for Hi-Fi sound, describing it as 'Motion Picture High Fidelity', and this was soon added to the system's logo. Once appreciated, its higher quality image would allow directors, like Alfred Hitchcock, to stage more of the action in long-shot and made it easier to pick out detail in large-scale set-pieces. Although less spectacular than many of its rivals, VistaVision would become one of the finer achievements of the 1950's widescreen revolution, only dropped at the beginning of the 1960s, when much improved colour negative stocks made the difference less noticeable and no longer justified the double cost of the negative running through the camera. However, VistaVision's large-area format would continue within studios for back and front projection, and maintaining the image quality during the multiple printing used to create special effects.

For a bigger and brighter picture a few of the first VistaVision films were shown using horizontal contact prints, needing special dedicated projectors. The idea was not pursued, their role being taken by 70mm prints and their more convenient dual-gauge projectors

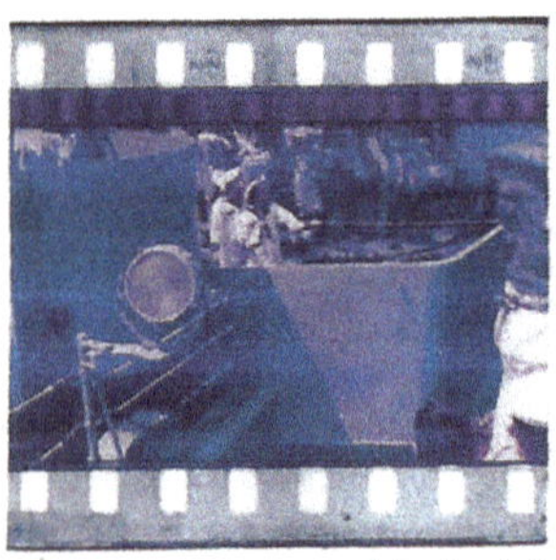

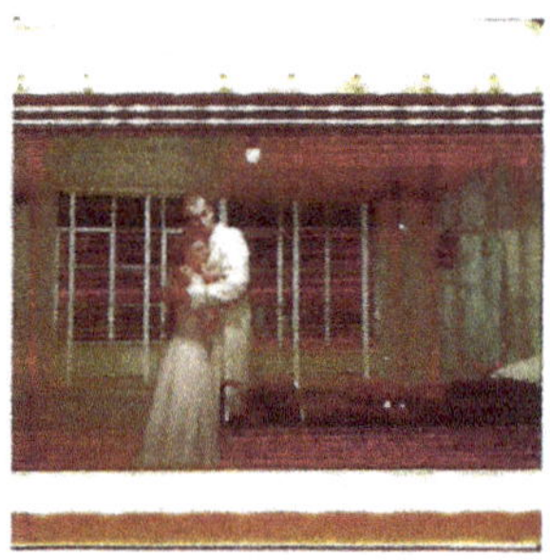

Masked down to 1.96:1

Battle of the River Plate (Odeon Leicester Square)

Strategic Air Command (Plaza)

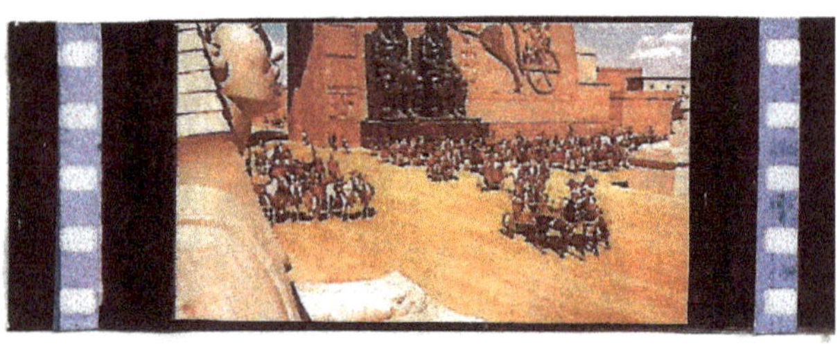

The Ten Commandments re-issued on 70mm

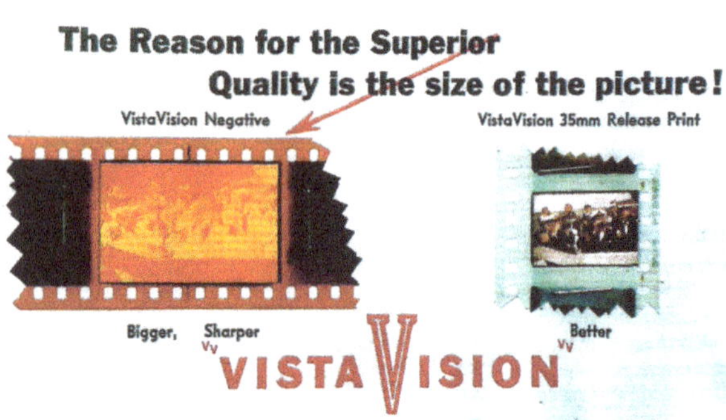

From VistaVision's original trade pack.

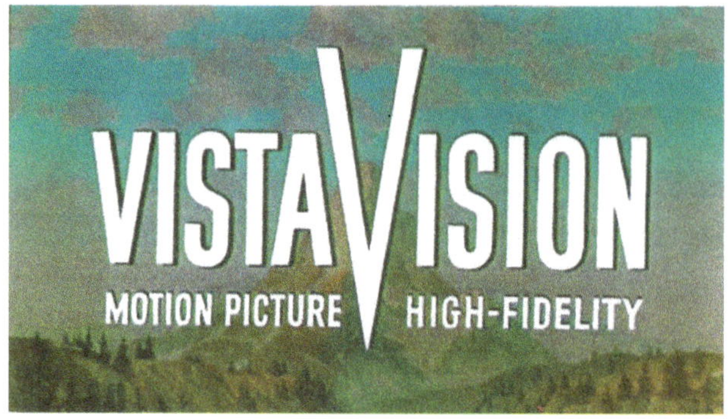

Back in the 1950s VistaVision was promoted as 'Motion Picture High Fidelity', but for today's viewers 'Motion Picture High Definition' may now be a better description.

Although this 'aperture controlled' form of widescreen appears to be the most simple to operate, it has led to much controversy and complaints. Even today it can cause a dilemma for those making new film masters, trying to determine the best framing at the 'correct' aspect ratio. The coming of wide screen to the cinema during the 1950s has left archivists and restorers many different shapes and sizes of film negatives to deal with, but fortunately for cinemas, these would only produce two new kinds of 35mm print. These would be either, the squeezed image 'Scope copies, introduced with CinemaScope's anamorphic lens process, or 'widescreen', which simply reduces the height of the existing Academy 1.37:1 frame to achieve its wider picture.

A format with issues

Although the masked-frame method may appear to be the easy way to a wider screen, it has led to much controversy, with both film-makers and the more pictorially aware members of the audience often complaining about its framing and the 'correct' aspect ratio. For today's projectionists, still running film, together with telecine and scanner operators, this method's variables can present an extra challenge when deciding the best way to show it.

Framing, with an eye for composition

Framing is no problem for Academy or 'scope, as all the picture area is shown on the screen. This doesn't apply to many widescreen prints, as the displayed area is now much smaller, in terms of height, than the image on the film. This means it can be shown well 'out of rack', without a frameline appearing on the screen to draw attention to the error. Although any spoiling of the picture's composition may only be a temporary annoyance during the showing of a projected print, now with the long-run systems making it last for the whole film, the mis-framing can become locked into a video copy or digital master, marring all their future viewings. There was help to find the best framing. When first released, many films came with specially designed leaders with markings to position the frame in the reduced height gate. Once running, slight adjustments could be made to allow the actors the correct headroom. It took care to try and judge the intentions of the camera operator, whose viewfinder guidelines are not visible on the print.

The final position also depends on the chosen height being shown, which may be different to the original recommended ratio. This too was sometimes indicated on the dedicated printed leader, but, unfortunately, for later reprints, the laboratory may have replaced the originals for a more current version without all this additional widescreen information. A film's aspect ratio was also sometimes given on its can or container, but again at risk of being lost on new ones, with their labels at best, stating it being in either 'scope' or 'flat' (non-anamorphic).

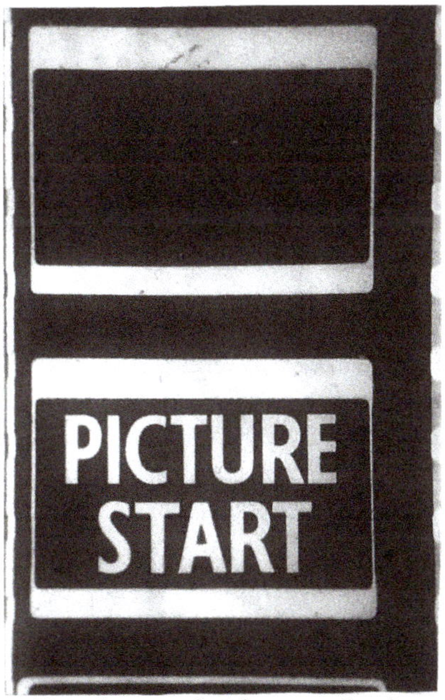

This design of widescreen leader helped to place the frame correctly in the gate and, when running, adjusted for minimum light spill

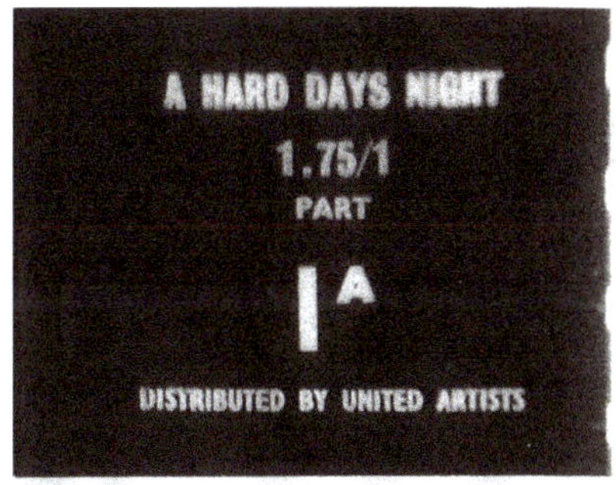

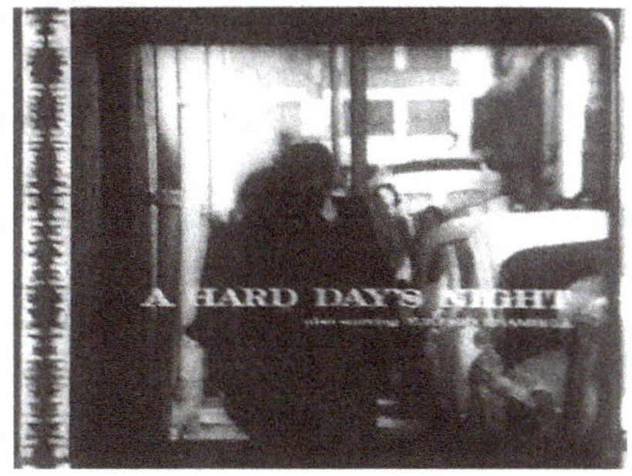

Some leaders stated the ideal ratio - useful if it is an unmasked print.

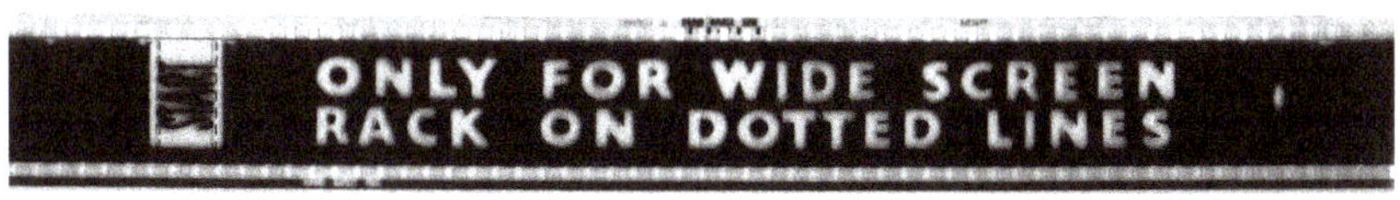

What aspect ratio?

After an initial period of chaos, America would soon settle for cropping the picture to give an aspect ratio of 1.85:1, which was extracted from across the centre of a still filled 1.37:1 Academy frame. Over here, the situation would be less certain. Although an early British Standard proposed that all our non-anamorphic films, again with a fully exposed frame, should be composed for projection at 1.75:1, not all producers and cinemas followed the recommendation. Although some, like the Rank Organisation, who had helped to arrive at the standard, adopted it for its films and cinemas, others would choose other ratios, with 1.66: 1 becoming equally popular. Although this lesser ratio was originally only intended as an interim measure, inflicting less harm to existing 4:3 films awaiting release, many continued to prefer it, giving a reasonable widescreen effect without sacrificing too much picture quality, wasting less frame area and valuable light during projection. Many cinemas, particularly the larger first-run theatres and in the West End, would have a full range of gate apertures, lenses and variable masking positions to show all the possible aspect ratios, including the 'old' 4:3.

4:3, reluctant to leave the cinema

Although newsreels and shorts would also begin to be framed to allow for cropping, most cinemas kept their 4:3 screen option to show a greater respect to revivals and foreign films. We would be close behind America on the road to widescreen, but other countries followed at their own pace. For example, Italy, hosting the production of many Hollywood widescreen epics, soon embraced both 'scope and widescreen for its own sword and sandal adventures and spaghetti westerns. Much slower would be East Europe and Russia, still shooting in 4:3 well into the 1960s. Before being raised up from the bottom of the frame, their subtitles could be a problem. Sometimes, obliged to show them in widescreen, the valiant efforts of the projectionist not to scalp the actors resulted in inadvertently only displaying the first line of the subtitles, making some continental arthouse films even harder to understand. When cropping the image was finally widely adopted, most would also be content with 1.66:1, with this ratio often referred to as 'European widescreen'. Unfortunately, cinemas, both

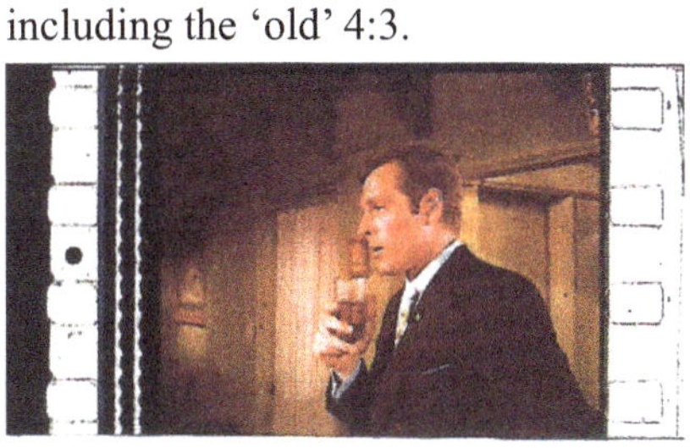

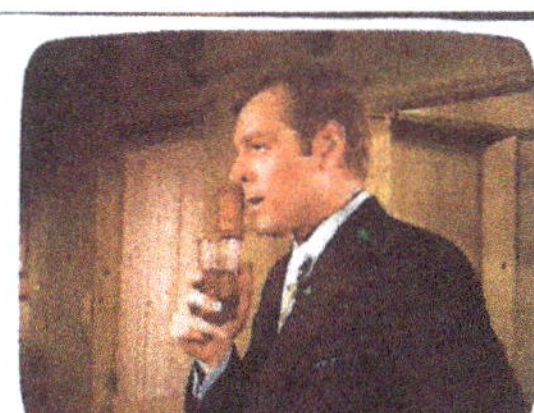

For previous 4:3 TV, a full-height widescreen frame could be raised to reduce the excessive headroom

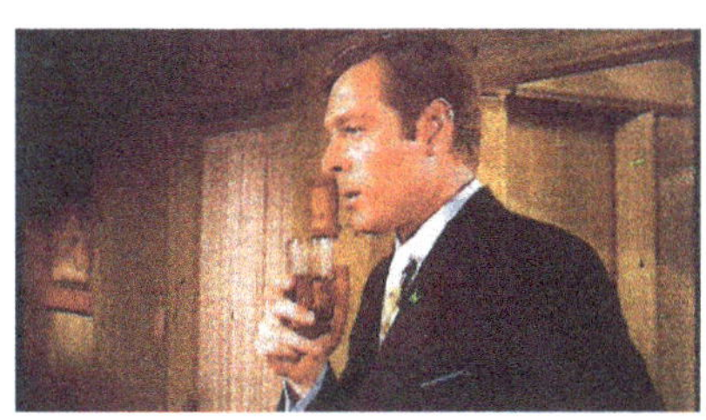

As seen in cinema, and now displayed on a current 16:9 (1.78:1) widescreen TV

home and abroad, with only 1.66:1 screens, would soon be in danger of seeing frame lines appearing on the screen.

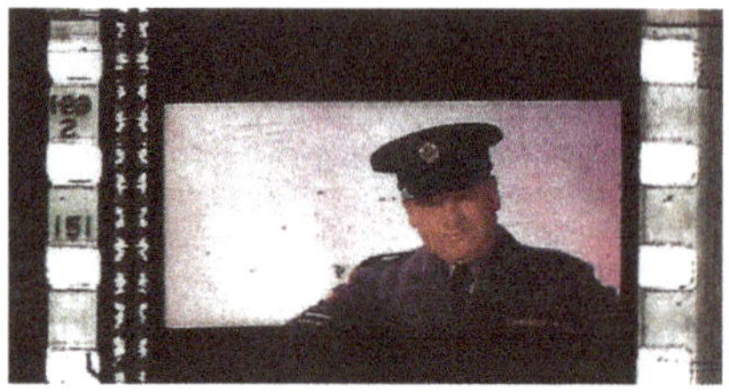

The first masked-down prints were conversions from CinemaScope for cinemas waiting to install the process. They continued as an option for 'scope trailers

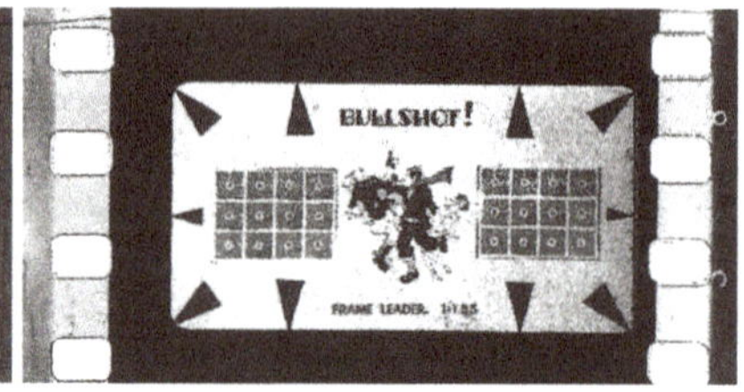

A studio 1.85:1 line-up leader corresponding to the guidelines in the film camera's viewfinder and on the video-assist monitor. Now also used to ensure the correct framing during the subsequent transfer to digital.

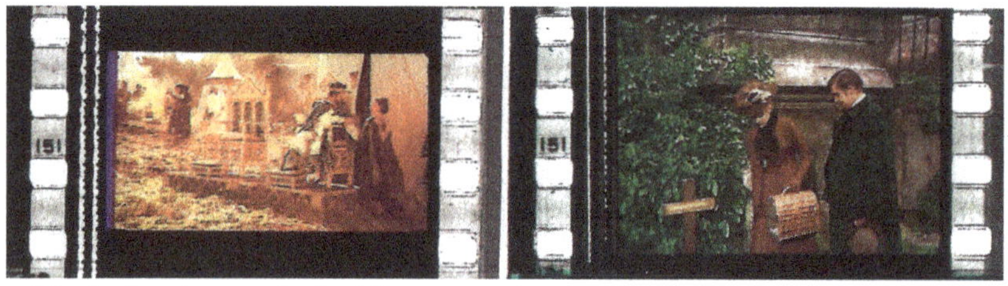

Masked and unmasked widescreen prints: both can be shown on the same 1.85:1 screen

The masked intruders

By the end of the 1950s, the consensus to keep the full frame filled was beginning to break down, with a growing number of films also using a reduced height gate in the camera. Despite concerns from exhibitors about losing their flexibility over the choice of aspect ratio, for many producers, this 'hard mask' had the advantage of imposing a minimum ratio with assured framing. A survey in the 1960s found that the most commonly used screen for non-scope films in the UK was between 1.66 and 1. 75:1, with the majority of our features shot using camera apertures masked to around 1.66:1 and the picture increasingly being composed for showing up to 1.85:1.

Thinking of the Viewers at home

Hard masking, without the full 4:3 frame for 16mm and 8mm reduction prints, didn't worry the original film-based home cinema enthusiasts, as they too were now toying with widescreen. They would soon have their own squeezed prints and anamorphic lenses, with the British made models of Bell & Howell 16mm projectors having an adjustable gate aperture to mask down the already small frames. However, with peace declared at the end of the cinema's war with television (the BKS became the BKSTS), broadcasters didn't welcome the masked-down prints. At one time, the European Broadcasting Union required that all 35mm prints destined for telecine use, should conform to the Academy 4:3 format. This meant that special optically printed TV versions had to be made. Scope had its notorious pan & scan copies, and widescreen would increase the magnification to push the intruding frame lines out of the picture, losing some of the image at the sides. This procedure was also used to produce some 'overseas' copies for territories which might object to a non-standard print.

Crop your own

Later telecines could do all this electronically, after the titles, zooming in to eliminate the frame lines. This was sometimes done to unmasked prints to lose the 'distant' look and excessive headroom of films composed for widescreen. Many of these now 4:3 versions, both film and video, are still on the shelves of archives and film libraries, and if mistakenly shown in widescreen, can in effect be cropped twice with a severe loss of picture information.

Some of the low budget, but still appreciated movie channels, have to show all kinds of available copies. For a 4:3 transmission (not just in the middle of a 16:9 picture) of a full-frame unmasked print, the 'aspect' button on a current 16:9 TV's remote can be used to crop and enlarge the image to see what it looks like in widescreen. Some DVDs and Blu-rays offer a choice of format, full-frame for the 'if it's on the film, I want to see it' viewers, or masked, as seen in the cinema. A recent example is the classic noir *Touch of Evil*, which looks much better in its intended 1.85:1, with greater intimacy and helping to draw you into the film.

Not wanted in the picture

Back in the cinema, projectionists had to cope with many types of widescreen prints. Back in the days of the big studio system, each had their own camera departments and could control the aspects of widescreen filming. If the Academy frame was still to be filled, there was always a strict 'shoot and protect' policy to ensure that the picture, outside the composed area, was kept free of microphones, lights, dolly tracks and other production paraphernalia, including the unscripted appearances of members of the crew. With the move to the four wall way of working, providing facilities for independent producers, they now rented the cameras. The hire companies, like Samuelson and Panavision, were happy to fit them with all manner of viewfinder ground glass markings and gate sizes. The choice of a masked gate allowed the sound recordist to keep the microphone closer to the actors, and the set designer no longer had to build higher sets, sometimes with a rarely seen ceiling. For some films the reduced height gate was only used in the principal studio camera, leaving the footage from the second unit and possible stock shots without the masking, which now comes and goes during the film.

Still creating framing problems was the opposite trend

to use the maximum height aperture in the camera, originally only intended for the anamorphic format. This 'universal' gate was chosen by some cinematographers to keep any dirt or hairs in the gate well away from the final projected area. Unfortunately, this increased the potential for mis-framing and the risk of seeing the microphone bobbing about for good measure. A compromise was to have the laboratory add the wider framelines. These were available to produce any requested aspect ratio and position relative to the original image. Unfortunately, later reprints often omitted the masking, sometimes revealing varying camera apertures and unwanted subject matter.

Spot the crew

A chance for the average viewer to appreciate the pitfalls of this form of widescreen was back in the 1980s during one of Barry Norman's film review programmes. It was prompted by a complaint letter objecting to many of the clips being shown with blank areas at the top and bottom of the then much smaller television 4:3 screen. The reason why was graphically illustrated by showing a masked off scene from *Dirty Dancing*. It was a dialogue sequence played out between the two principle characters. When the clip was shown again, without the masking, a third character made an unscripted appearance. He was the sound recordist lying on the ground, clutching his microphone. It was pointed out that he would never be seen (hopefully) on the cinema screen, as that part of the picture is not projected. It also gave the game away that they were not seeing extra picture at the sides, but less top and bottom. The programme went on to describe the anamorphic process, which actually does, but by then many non-technical viewers must have been left rather confused, and the distributors were about to complain about using their film to illustrate a perceived production failing.

More recently, at a 'Getting Technical' event at the NFT, a clip from a new print of Hitchcock's *North by Northwest* was shown. The action took place in a studio set representing the forest around Mount Rushmoor, this time including the tops of the truncated trees and lighting gallery. This may have been unfair to the camera crew who composed the image knowing that the original Technicolor VistaVision print would have blanked this off, and not in the future be regarded as sloppy camera work.

Widescreen and the censor, or now you see them and now you don't

The occasional sight of this unwanted subject matter may just be a mood destroying distraction, but sometimes more serious 'forbidden' images can be exposed. At the BBC, any suspect widescreen films were pre-viewed using a full gate to spot anything inappropriate. At a time, in the 1970s, when actual 35mm prints were transmitted, careful framing by the telecine operator was needed during the showing of an unmasked copy

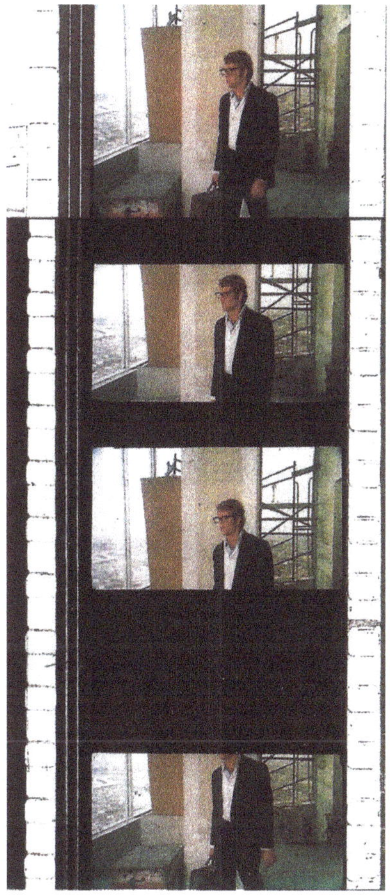

Exposed and printed full-height image composed for equal masking at the top and bottom to produce an aspect ratio of 1.85:1

Correct central framing

Limits of possible mis-framing and its effect on the projected image

Above: Using a full-height ('scope) gate in the camera for non-anamorphic widescreen films increased the potential for mis-framing

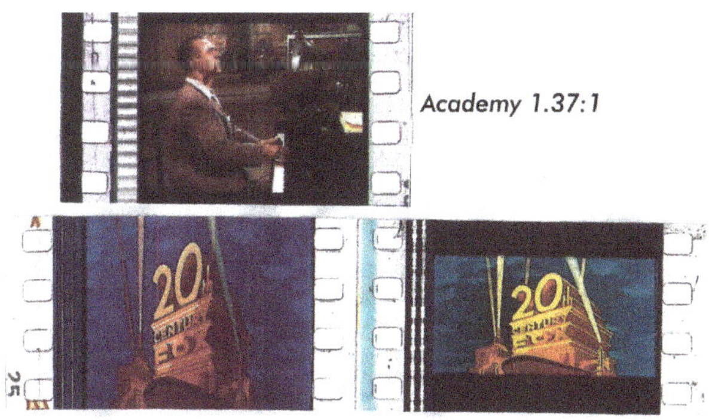

From 1953 the 35mm Academy format was joined by two other types of print. 'Scope and widescreen. If needed, one could be converted to the other

of *Don't Look Now* to prevent a full-frontal of Donald Sutherland reaching the eyes of viewers, a treat not even intended for cinema audiences. An ex-cinema projectionist colleague remembers, during the wide screen showing of certain full-frame 'exploitation' movies, he would keep hold of his racking knob to make sure his valued customers didn't miss anything. I once tried to find out about the British censor's viewing arrangements, thinking that the choice of aspect ratio and framing could affect a films classification. Sadly, I was told that all the goings on behind the BBFC doors were confidential, including the size of their aperture plates.

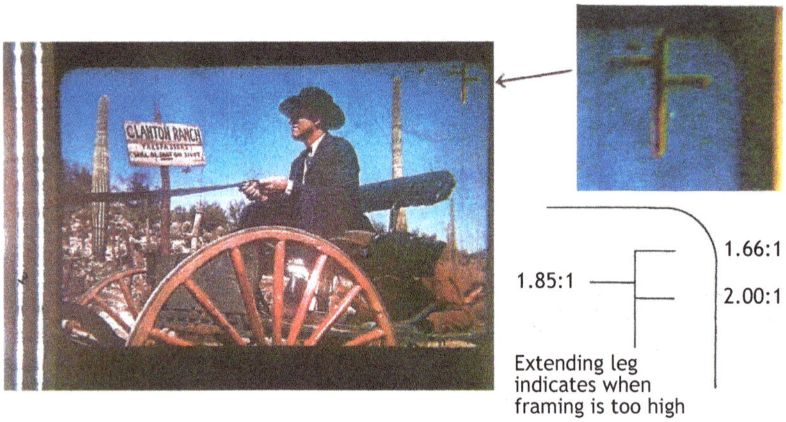

One aid to correct framing was Vista-Vision's Framing Index System. This was a pattern of lines which appeared briefly at the start of each 2000 ft reel in the top right-hand corner of the frame, in a similar manner to changeover cues. One of the horizontal lines was positioned to align with the top masking to give the correct framing for each specific aspect ratio. The frame shown, from Gunfight at the OK Corral was printed with the image already masked to 1.66:1

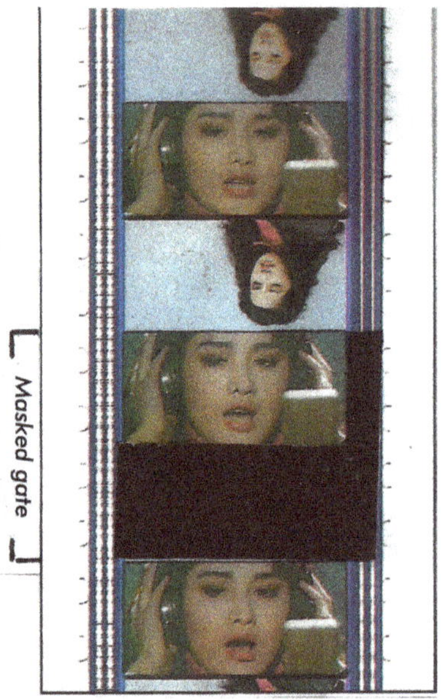

Another way to reduce the wasted picture area of the masked frame widescreen method was to use a 3-perf pull-down. Although occasionally used in the camera, it didn't prove practical for release prints. Saving film, but keeping 4 perf, was the proposed 'run both ways' print, with the other direction's frame and track masked off during projection.

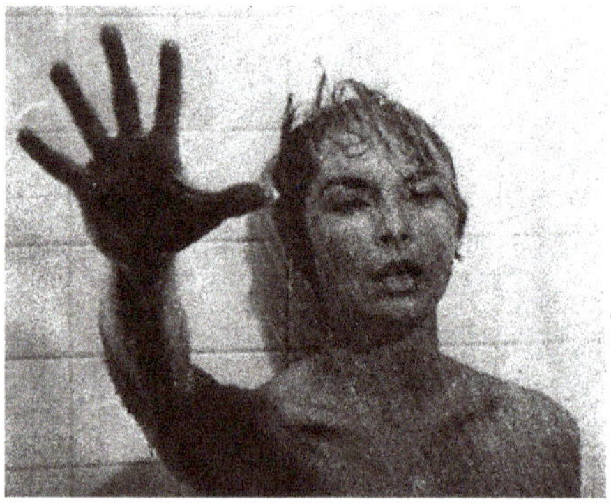

Hitchcock's PSYCHO was released with an Academy frame, but photographed for cropped widescreen. This particular shot in the shower scene had a black bar printed along the bottom, below the 1.85:1 projected area. This not for reasons of modesty, but to prevent the top of the flesh-coloured moleskin suit worn by Janet Leigh during the filming, from being seen if the complete 4:3 image is being shown. (A nude stand-in also appears in the scene.)

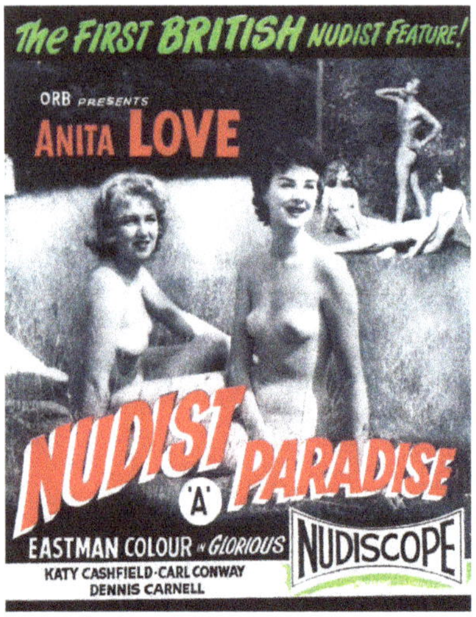

For some films, errors in framing and aspect ratio can hide what the audience has come to see. A highlight in the development of widescreen was 'Nudiscope', launched with Nudist Paradise. Its memory lingers on at the start of Carry on Camping.

Saving film with Skip Frame

The promoters of a short-lived idea called Skip Frame explained that with a 1.85 release print, only seven inches in every foot of film is actual picture content, with the other five inches being wasted by the amount of frame line spacing. A 50% saving in film stock was therefore possible if release prints were distributed in Skip Frame format. The idea behind Skip Frame was for the film labs to produce a release print with two parts of the film on the same reel, with a soundtrack on each side of the film. The first spool would have Reel 1 printed one way up and Reel 3 upside down, but both within a 4 perf frame. A new aperture plate size (0.375 x 0.7 inches) would provide a 1.85 ratio, requiring a smaller focal length lens in order to maintain the same picture size. However, this money saving idea is only viable where there are changeovers between two machines. A by-product of Skip Frame is that it is also a non-rewind system. For example, if parts one and three are on the same reel and part one is on the screen, then, after the changeover, when part one runs out, part three, which is on the same reel, can be laced up immediately in readiness for the next changeover from the other machine, which would be laced with parts two and four.

Disadvantages included having to move the projector sideways in order to adjust for centre line picture displacement and the need for extra care when framing, because of two frames of the film occupying the same picture aperture. The height of the 1.85 picture would be fractionally reduced, but as you have an optical soundtrack on both sides reducing the width of the frame, the 1.85 ratio would be restored. Obviously if the framing handle was moved you would be showing the other half of the frame which is upside down and back to front - tales from the revered Billy Bell told how during the projection of part one of a cowboy film, a slight movement of the framing handle caused horses in part three to be seen galloping upside down and backwards. Skip Frame loses all of its advantages when used with long playing cake stands and towers which were becoming used almost universally at the time of its introduction. It also required the presence of a projectionist in the projection room, something which the coming of digital projection was to bring to an end. Skip Frame has long since been forgotten and has been consigned, like many other filmic curiosities, to the dustbin of cinema history, but .

Whilst investigating the history behind the skip frame technique, cinema guru Dion Hanson spotted the similarities with the ingenious pre-war Harper system which used a 16mm film print (above right) carrying two optically reduced 35mm film reels with sound, the pictures being interlaced and upside down with respect to each

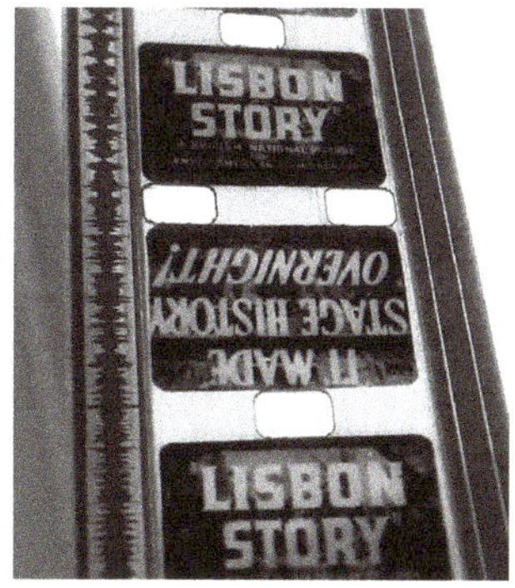

other. On projection after running the film through it was not rewound but transferred from the take-up to the feed spool and run through the projector a second time when the second film reel with its associated sound track would be reproduced. The equipment was designed and made by the Miles Aircraft Company.

Widescreen goes digital

The nature of the cinema's switch to digital, beginning with exhibition, meant it had to accommodate all of film's aspect ratios, including widescreen. Fortunately, for today's digital projectionist, all their presentation decisions have already been made and included in the digital file sent to the projector. This should, in theory at least, ensure a perfect image every time, without past problems and issues marring the picture.

Screen X - Wider than widescreen

Screen X is a multi-projection immersive cinematic platform which provides moviegoers with a 270-degree viewing experience by expanding the scene onto the side walls. The idea is that three sides of the cinema are used to express more of the story, the expanded space allowing for more creative possibilities so that the whole system provides a more immersive audience experience.

The system was created in 2012 by South Korean company CJ CGV, and uses an array of projectors (between 5 and 13 depending on the setup) and with proprietary Screen X software, blends multiple images into one seamless image extending from the central screen out. Screen X walls are covered with a fabric to ensure brightness and colour closely match the content on the main screen and extend the length of the auditorium. Strategically placed audio systems and speakers ensure that sound matches the immersive viewing experience.

A front to side ratio of between 1:1.5 and 1:2.0 is recommended, 'front' being the screen width of the auditorium, not the wall-to-wall width of the auditorium, and 'side' being the length of the auditorium from the screen edge to the last row of seats.

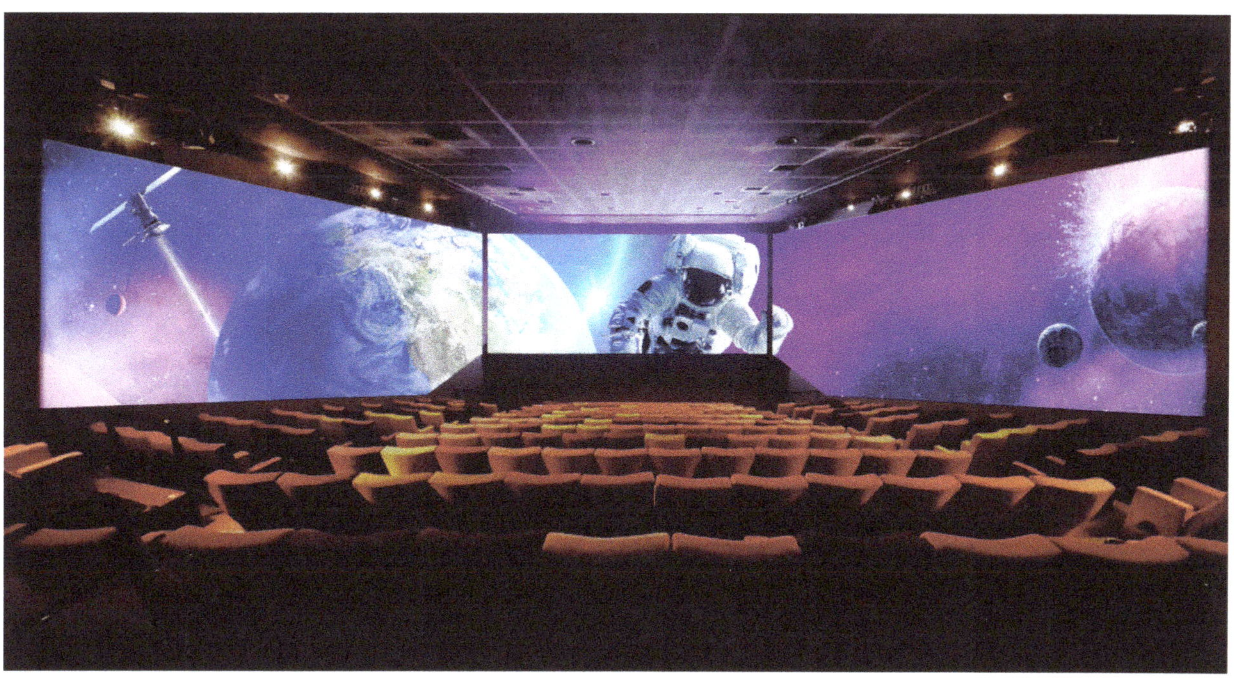

Rationalising Aspect Ratios - how cinemas and restorers cope with the multiplicity of different aspect ratios over the years

We have looked at the origins of the cinema's still popular 2.35:1 (2.40:1) and 1.85:1 picture shapes. Although inherited from the days of film, they have survived the switch to digital, with no general desire from either film-makers or exhibitors to abandon them in favour of, perhaps, a new single 'digital' ideal screen shape.

Keeping them in shape

The coming of digital projection has helped ensure that pictures are now displayed correctly, without the options presented when showing a film print, sometimes leaving the projectionist to make the final aspect ratio decision. With all of today's post production digital manipulation of the image, the picture on the screen can appear very different to that photographed through the film or digital camera's lens. However, its chosen aspect ratio and framing is now more likely to be preserved. Back in the all on film analogue days, it was left to the Director of Photography, with help from the laboratory, to create the style and look of the image reaching the screen, but its shape and the camera operator's careful framing was far less secure.

Less scope for spoiling 'scope

The anamorphic 2.35:1 format was in less danger of abuse. Apart from the loss of image when an optical track had to be added to the first CinemaScope films, originally photographed for their magnetic sound only 2.55:1 prints, most would go missing due to architectural problems, with cinemas trying to fit its wider picture into unsuitable prosceniums designed for the much smaller 4:3 screens, common before the 1950s big screen revolution.

Some would say goodbye to them altogether, often losing seats to build a new wider screen frame and curtains in front, now becoming the main centre of attraction and, like cinemas in the future, no longer having to compete with the auditorium's often elaborate decor of the past.

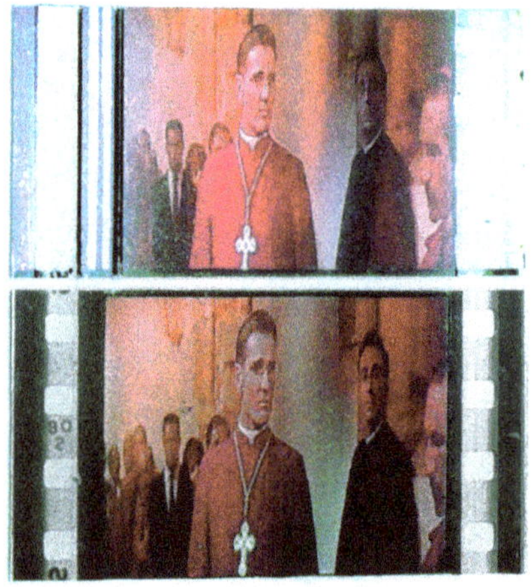

Adding an optical track to 'Scope's original 2.55:1 magnetic sound only format reduced it to 2.35:1. This squeezed image uses the full frame area, leaving very narrow frame-lines. In the 1970s.to reduce the risk of joins appearing on the screen, the height of the projection aperture was reduced a little to give the now also quoted 2.39:1 and 2.40:1

Unfortunately, some theatres didn't have the room to spread out, and even in some of the much later smaller and narrow auditoriums squeezed into the first multi screen conversions and multiplexes chose to reduce the width of their 'Scope picture to keep it a reasonable height. It was thought that few in the audience would notice that it wasn't wide enough, but more likely to complain that they hadn't left home and their TVs only to come to the cinema and watch another small screen.

Too many ratios to get wrong

In greater danger of complaints was the alternative masked-frame 'wide screen' method of producing a wider picture. When introduced, along with CinemaScope in 1953, three different amounts of cropping emerged, producing aspect ratios of 1.66:1, 1.75:1 and 1.85:1. Before long, Hollywood would settle on 1.85:1 as its ideal screen shape, but over here, despite a recommended standard of 1.75:1, our cinemas would continue to show all three. Most of the West End and other showcase theatres had lenses and aperture plates to present all the available ratios, but many local cinemas chose just one to suit their individual auditoriums.

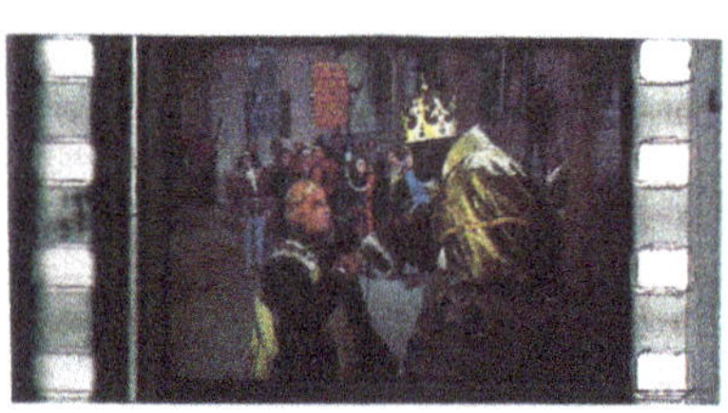

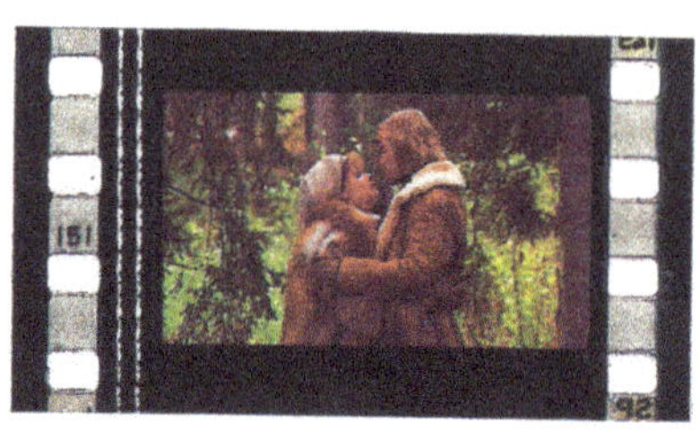

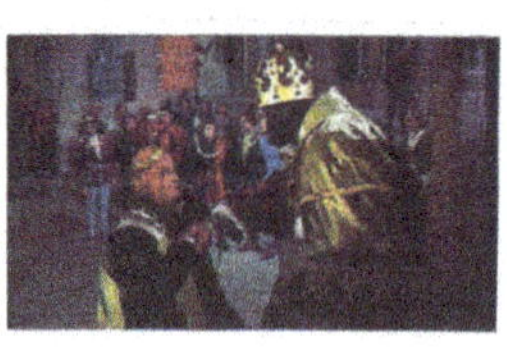

'Wide Screen' only projects a portion of the 35mm frame. Sometimes, only the chosen aspect ratio is photographed on the film.

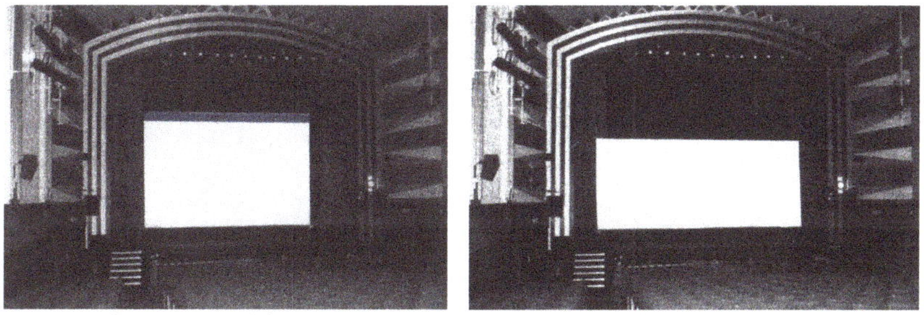

Some theatres couldn't present 'Scope to its best advantage, with 4:3 and Widescreen often appearing to be larger

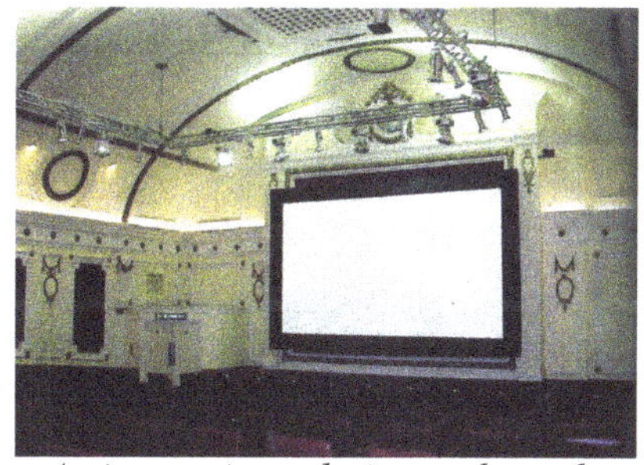

An interesting solution, to keep the '4:3' proscenium at the historic Electric Cinema in Portobello Road. The screen moves forward and expands sideways to provide for today's wide screen pictures.

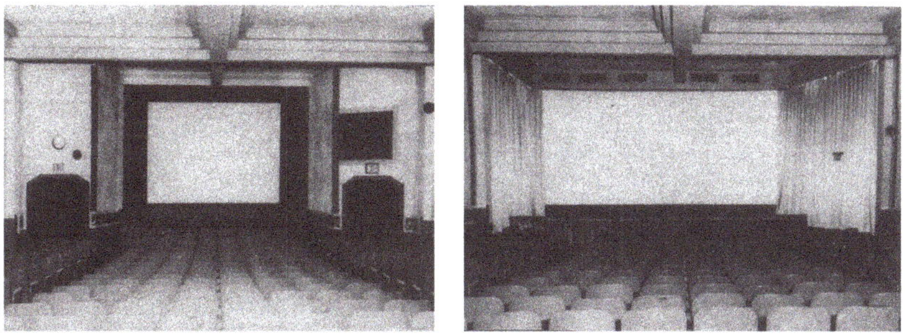

Many prosceniums didn't suit the new wider screens, so a new one was sometimes built in front, in this case also hiding the exit doors

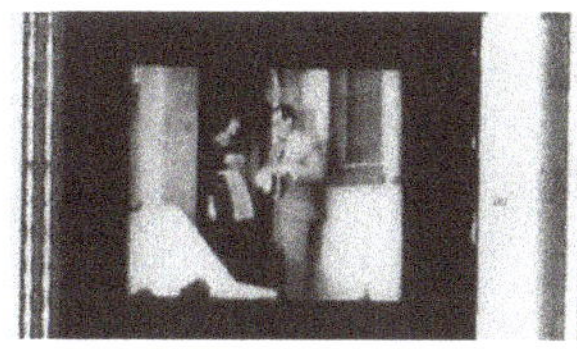

A reduced 4:3 picture, to prevent it from being cropped by a wide screen gate

Making the most of all the shapes

If space permitted, it was generally thought that a common height for all the ratios was the best arrangement, opening out from the occasional old 'small' 4:3 picture, through the selected wide screen ratio, to show 'scope to its best advantage. This favoured 1.85:1, but in theatres with restricted available width, they preferred to have movable top masking to allow for a larger 4:3 and wide screen picture. This time, it was 1.66:1 which gave a bigger image, sometimes with a greater area than 'scope.

On the production side, our non-anamorphic films were also being composed in different ratios. 1.66:1 remained popular during the 1960s. As an example, the sets for Stanley Kubrick's *Dr Strangelove,* including the famous war room, were designed for its higher frame. Although still in use in many cinemas, 1.75:1 would begin to lose favour as a filming format, with a growing trend to follow Hollywood's 1.85:l, particularly for films with international ambitions.

Before only 'scope's 2.35:1 could contain all their action, the first Bond films began modestly on 1.66:1 screens, but changed to 1.85:1 when they briefly shrank back to non-anamorphic filming during the 1970s. Also in the 1970s, many cinemas were giving up 1.66:1 after frame lines began to appear on the screen. Some widescreen films had used a masked down gate in the camera, but usually this had stopped at 1.66:1, with the image itself either composed for this ratio, or for further

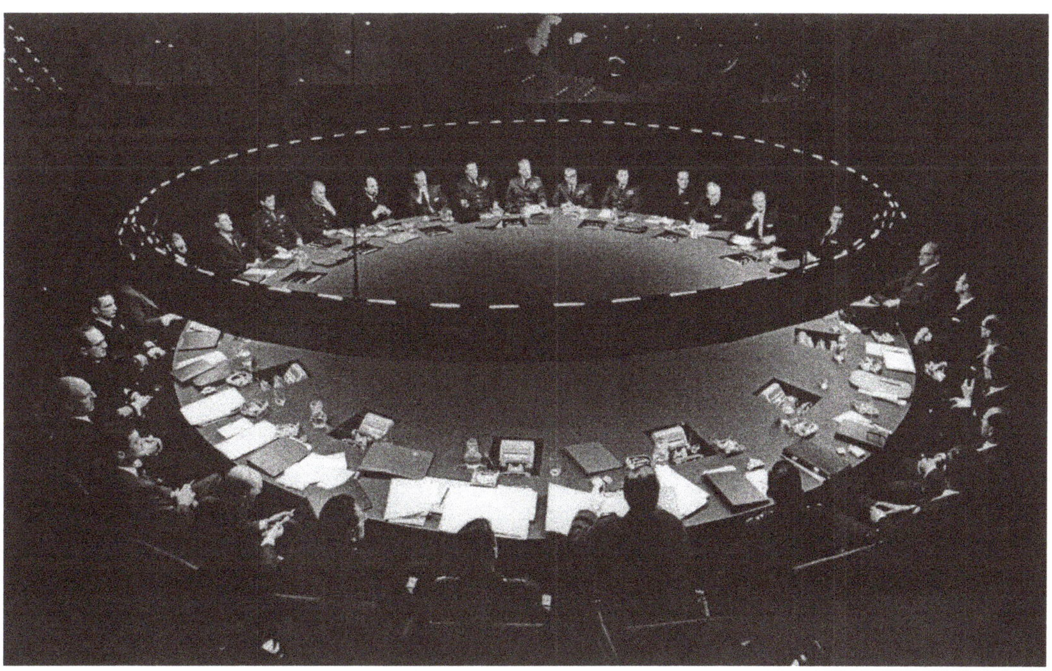

Ken Adam's incredible war room set in Dr Strangelove can be seen at its best in the film's intended 1.66:1 ratio

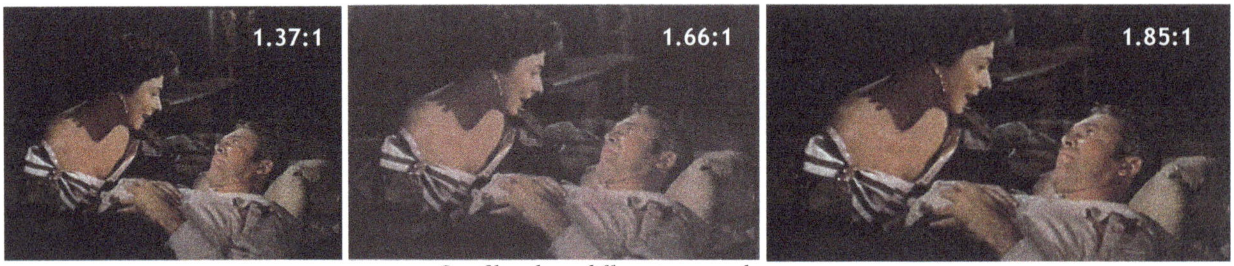

One film, three different screen shapes

cropping up to 1.85:1 during projection. Now this 'hard' masking on the print sometimes extended down to 1.85:1, a ploy-to impose this ratio with assured framing.

The move to 1.85:1 becoming the universal standard received a boost with the coming of the cinema's saviour, the multiplex. Apart from, perhaps, Screen one, their designers simplified the projection and screen arrangements by only providing for 2.35:1 and 1.85:1, banishing 4:3 and the other ratios forever. To save them from the chop, the few remaining 4:3 films, including a number of Disney re-issues, had to reduce the size of the image to make it fit into the centre of the reduced height 1.85:1 frame.

Clash of the ratios

All this seemed to go unnoticed by many film-makers. As late as the 1990s, published guides and manuals for cinematographers still suggested that they still had the choice to shoot in 1.66:1. Even new 35mm cameras, like the Arriflex 535, came with an 1.66:1 option built into its illuminated viewfinder guidelines. The lack of an agreed common ratio would inevitably lead to films being composed for one ratio, but shown in another. This can result in either 1.85:1 on a 1.66:1 screen with the headroom looking sloppily loose, and the risk of a microphone creeping into the picture, or more likely, 1.66:1 films at 1.85:1 with noticeably cropped head and foot room.

Don't shoot the projectionist

The end of the practice of including full aspect ratio information on the film's leader and can, together with a growing disconnect between the production and exhibition sides of the industry, would lead to many 'misunderstandings' about the 'correct' aspect ratio, often leaving the projectionist to take the flack. Busy Directors of Photography and their camera operators often only see the results of their work under the controlled conditions of daily rushes, crew shows and other special studio viewings, rarely venturing out to share the experience with other cinemagoers at local cinemas.

Film festivals often bring film-makers and projectionists together. Unfortunately, sometimes this leads to a director in a huff complaining that his film, often a revival, is being ruined by careless framing and in the wrong ratio. In defence of their presentation and showmanship skills, all that the projectionist can do is point to the can, which often just states that the aspect ratio is 'flat' or '1.85:1', used this time as a catch-all term to describe any film not in 'Scope. Given sufficient notice, every effort would have been made to project the print in the requested screen shape, even if special arrangements had to be made.

In other situations when a full range of screen shapes are available, but without instructions which to use, the projectionists must use their own judgement. As a rule, American films can safely be shown at 1.85:1. On rare occasions individual films come with different advice. Spielberg's *Duel* (originally a TV movie) and *E.T.* apparently look best at 1.66:1, but can be shown at others, 'not exceeding 1.85:1'. For our own past films, and those from abroad, clues to the ratio include the width of the frame-lines, the design of the titles, and the amount of headroom provided.

What's going on, or not, on the screen

At times over the years, interested parties, like the BKSTS and BSC, have expressed concern about the situation. In touch with its camera operator members, The Guild of' British Camera Technicians drew attention to the unhappiness felt by many of them that their fastidious framing· for the format being photographed could not always be appreciated by the audience.

Some of the last 1.66:1 films, like *Hope and Glory* and *Robin Hood: Prince of Thieves,* were being shown almost exclusively in 1.85:1. Fortunately, today's trend

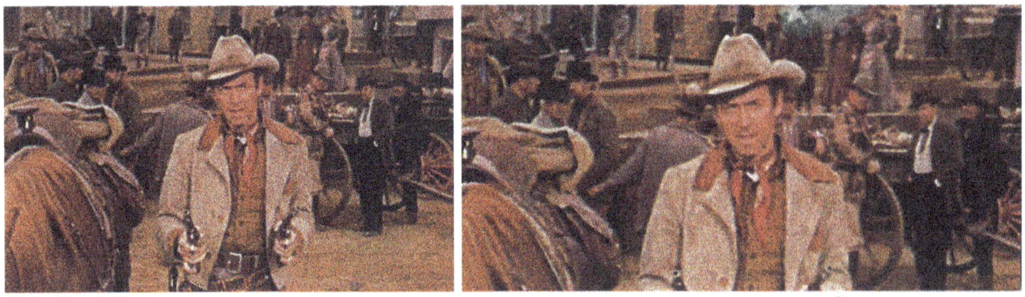

Ready to shoot in 1.66:1, but with the risk of being disarmed in 1.85:1

to much tighter close-ups makes this less noticeable. Even *Shirley Valentine*, also confirmed by its operator to be framed for 1.66:1, received its Royal Premiere in the wrong 1.75:1 ratio, although it is unlikely that all the celebs, including Charles and Diana, noticed the error. This was blamed again on the lack of information, and the inquest also revealed that even by the beginning of the 1990s, 50%, of Odeon cinemas were still projecting their non-anamorphic films on 1.75:1 screens.

Digital help on the horizon

Eminent cinematographers would also put their weight behind ways to end the conflict. Usually this involved, like the old 1.37:1, and the 2.35:1 anamorphic formats, only to photograph a tamper-free 1.85:1 image on the camera negative.

They had to convince others, including the distributors, who were sometimes willing to have the laboratory mask down the picture on the cinema prints, but still appreciated having extra image on the original negative for conversion to the aspect ratios of other presentation methods, from TVs at home to giant screen IMAX.

However, attention would soon turn to the challenges of digital imaging. There were suggestions that 1.85:1 should be changed to 1.78:1 to match the new shape of digital television, which was about to share the cinema's wider window on the world. In the end, it would be digital cinema which would put minds at rest, finally only sending a fixed protected image to the projector and out of the lens in the selected, perfectly framed, aspect ratio.

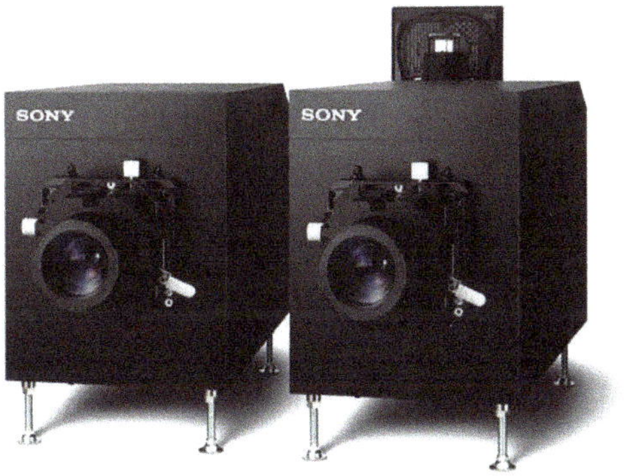

Who Invented 16:9?

The previous 'old' squarer 4:3 shape of cinema and television screens can trace its origins back to the birth of motion pictures when it was first seen in the Edison Kinetoscope peep show machine in 1893. Its one and three-eights of an inch (35mm) film was soon being projected onto a screen and would go on to become the industry standard.

The coming of wider screens in the cinema would leave TV with 4:3 for many years, until moves were made for its picture to go wide too, as part of the various competing proposals for high definition TV systems. One common suggestion was that their images should have the proportions of 16:9, and the final choice proved to be a committee decision made by an alliance of manufacturers and electronics experts, with little input from the artistic and creative community.

One justification for 16:9 was that it was an ideal 'middle' format, able, if necessary to display existing picture shapes from 4:3 to CinemaScope's 21:9 without too much wasted screen area. It was also suggested as a 'universal' shooting format which could readily be converted into all the other popular screen shapes.

In the diagram below, the outer 16:9 rectangle is the complete picture and if all the important action is kept within the inner, smaller 16:9 area then all the other formats could be successfully extracted. This may appear to be a good idea in the engineering sense, but few skilled and creative camera operators would tolerate this restriction, always preferring to compose their images carefully in just one chosen aspect ratio.

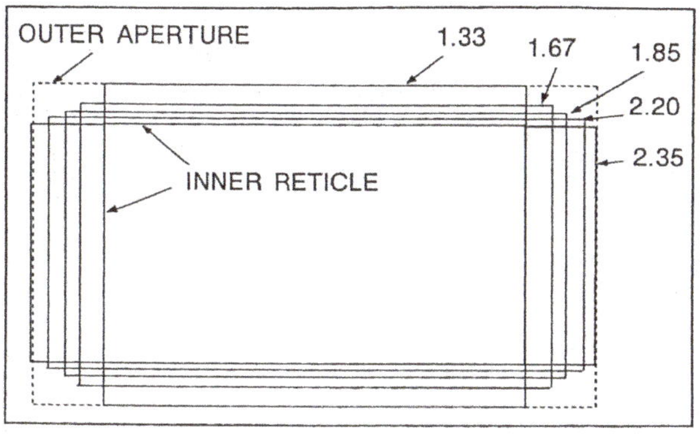

Coping with Curved Screens - a look at some of the solutions

When deeply curved screens were common, systems like the later 70mm single-lens version of Cinerama and Dimension-150 tried, at one time, to improve the picture for more viewing positions in the cinema by using a combination of 70mm prints with a modified image and special projection lenses.

Some of these solutions to the problem are shown below, but it is interesting to consider that with modern digital projection technologies the digital image could be modified as it is being projected to provide the optimum image on each part of the screen.

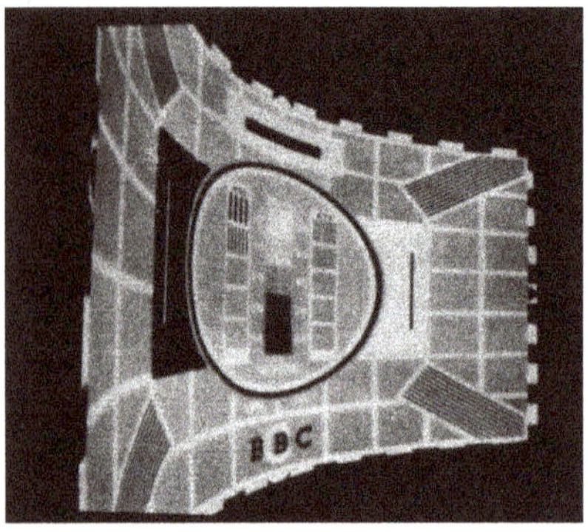

Computer prediction of a test pattern (including a circle and squares) as it would appear if projected onto a curved screen and viewed off centre away from the ideal position directly in front of the screen.

'Rectified' 70mm Cinerama print

The diagram shows a 'Rectified' 70mm print designed to counterbalance the stretching effect on the image when it is projected onto a deeply curved screen. Although the idea works reasonably well,

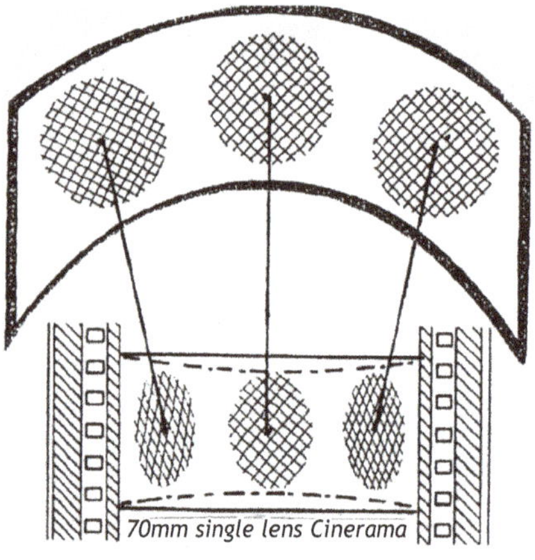

no single correction will restore the correct geometry for every viewing position. In addition, the print's non-linear squeeze was often apparent, particularly when the camera panned, giving the impression that the film had been photographed with a faulty lens.

The negative's x1.25 squeeze was redistributed, being around x1.18 at the centre of the picture, increasing to x1.33 at the sides. The total compression factor still added up to x1.25, so no image lost or gained. However, like all deeply curved screen systems, the image was severely cropped towards the centre of the frame when projected.

D-150 optically corrected 70mm print

The illustration showing how distortion is built in to the D-150 print has been somewhat exaggerated to make the effect on the image clearer.

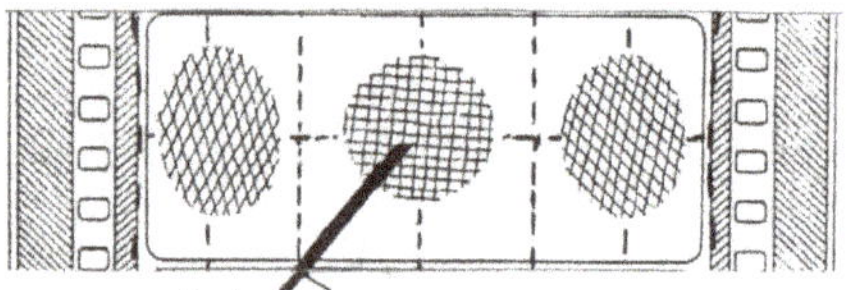

In practice, it was hardly noticeable and, in view of many independent projection experts, was of doubtful value and not worth the bother. D-150 was an excellent process and still looked good when using normal 'flat' 70mm prints.

The special corrected prints were probably included in the specification to make the system more unique and help justify the licensing fees. The aspect ratio of a D-150 screen is often quoted as 2,7:1, however, this figure is only notional and would apply only if the curved screen and its image was flattened out. The more relevant ratio is that actually 'seen' by the projector and most of the audience, which was nearer 2:1. The 2,2:1 70mm frame was made to fill the 2.7: 1 screen area by a combination of the cropped "butterfly" shaped projector gate and the stretching effect of the curved screen. The distortion was most noticeable by those viewing away from the line of the projector. By the end of 1966, rectified 70mm prints, along with Ultra Panavision squeezed prints, had largely been abandoned for the sake of compatibility.

Special lenses

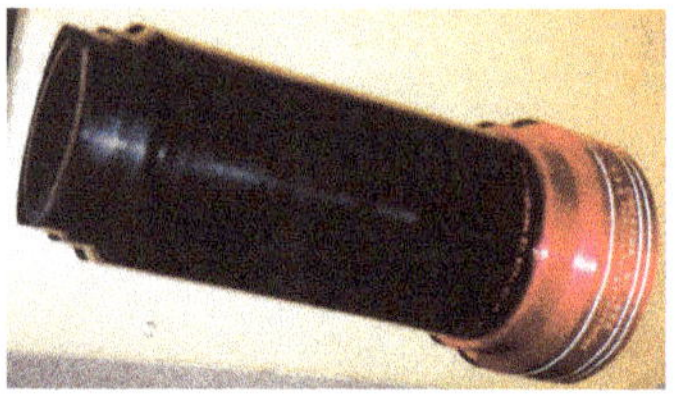

Cinerama and D-150 projection lenses were designed with a curved field of focus to keep their 70mm images sharp on the deeply curved screens.

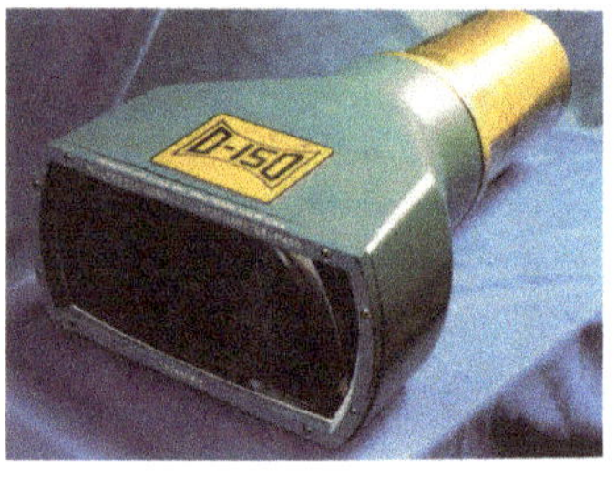

They also incorporated a small degree of pincushion distortion to help fit their images to the shape of the screen.

All shapes and sizes
- Getting along with television

Our story of movie formats and their restoration continues with a look at how film played a major role in the world of television and video.

While cinemas were happily running their movies at a fixed 24fps, television arrived and some of its viewers would soon be watching films at the wrong speed again.

The synchronisation circuits of television systems around the world were traditionally linked to each country's mains frequency. In Britain and Europe this is 50 Hz. It would have been convenient to adopt a frame rate for TV of 50fps, which would produce a smooth flicker-free image. Unfortunately, this would have consumed too much bandwidth, so it was halved to 25fps. To avoid flicker, each frame was displayed using two sweeps (fields) of the screen made up first of the even lines and then the odd lines interlaced together to form each picture. This brought the viewing frequency back up to 50, in effect, television's version of a film projector's two bladed shutter.

There was now a potential problem, the incompatibility with motion picture's 24fps. The chosen, easy way out, solution was simply to show the film one frame a second faster. In practice the change to the motion is imperceptible and the slight raising of the pitch of the sound is also not noticed by most viewers. Over the years this proved to be the case, with no complaints. However, this 4% increase does have a significant effect on running times, with an average feature film being three to four minutes shorter. This did lead to complaints from eagle-eyed viewers with stopwatches, who suspected that their favourite movie had been censored or cut to fit a specific programme slot. In many instances, complaints to broadcasters were justified, but the BBC for one had a standard reply ready, explaining that for 'technical reasons' films made for the cinema run faster on television.

America and Japan have a mains frequency of 60Hz and their television runs at 30fps. No easy way out this time. A corresponding speeding up of films would certainly be noticed, with the most gravelly voiced actor rushing around and speaking like a cartoon chipmunk. Their solution was the 2:3 pull-down system. The film runs at the normal 24fps but alternate frames are scanned with an extra field so, after a second, they still add up to 60. Although the film is running at the correct speed, there is the risk of a judder affecting the picture, but various ploys were adopted to reduce this, like camera pick-up tubes with a slow decay time to smooth out the motion.

Before videotape, and even after; before its cost came down, feature films were transmitted live, direct from telecine machines, complete with change-overs. In America most telecine set-ups used conventional intermittent projectors shining into a TV camera. For 16mm, some used special high speed movements which held alternate frames a fraction of a second longer to allow for the extra scan (field). For 35mm slower intermittents, one way was to use a pulse light to flash each frame, between the TV fields, onto a pick-up tube, again with a slow-decay 'memory' which held onto the image long enough for it to be scanned off while the projector moved the film to the next frame. These ran at a fixed 24fps.

One type of telecine which offered a variable-speed option was the 'polygon'. In these, the continuously moving film is followed by a rotating multi-facet prism, or a series of mirrors, which optically hold each frame stationary for a moment before dissolving into the next. With no shutter the image is visible all the time and independent of the TV scanning system. It would seem to be the ideal system, but its construction needs great precision and the complex optical path makes it difficult to match the picture quality produced by the other types. There have been attempts to use the principle for cinema projectors, a notable example being the German Mechau, known as the Arcadia in Britain.

Apparently at least one West End cinema gave it a try, but its spinning mirrors couldn't match the performance of a normal cross intermittent. The projectors were sold

Left: A camera looking at a TV monitor screen - a telerecording machine from the 1950s. Centre: Polygon telerecording machine based on the Mechau mirror drum. Right: The Bauer B14 - a popular choice of 35mm projector at the BBC way back in its film days

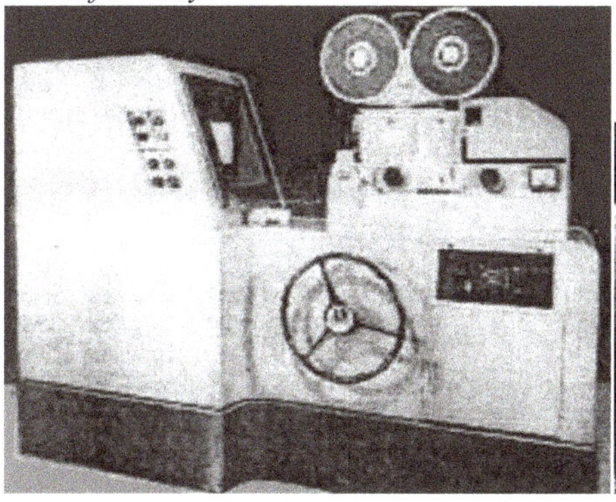

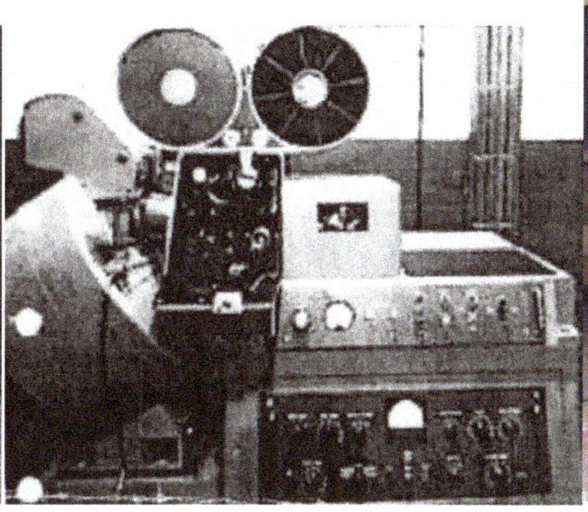

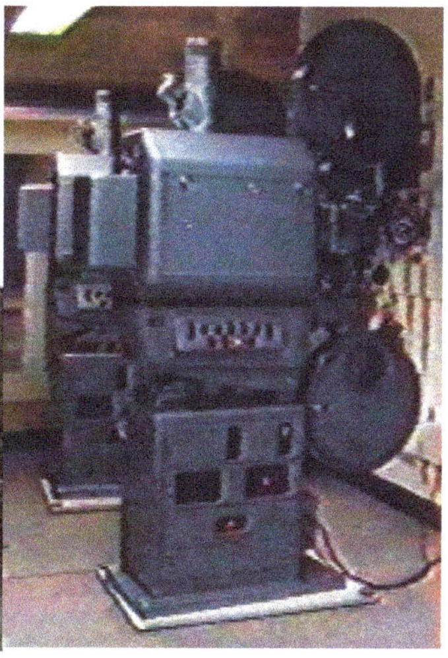

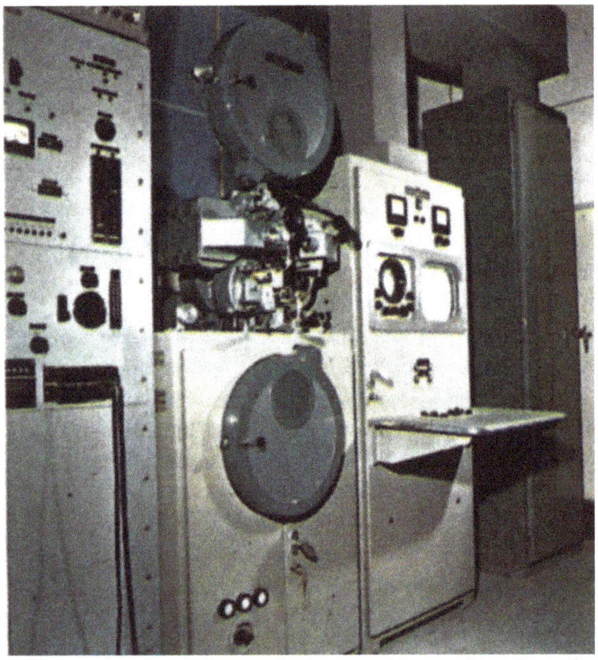

Above: Earlier 35mm telecine machines often shared parts with projectors, in this case a Bauer B14. Its enclosed spool boxes suggest it could safely run nitrate film.

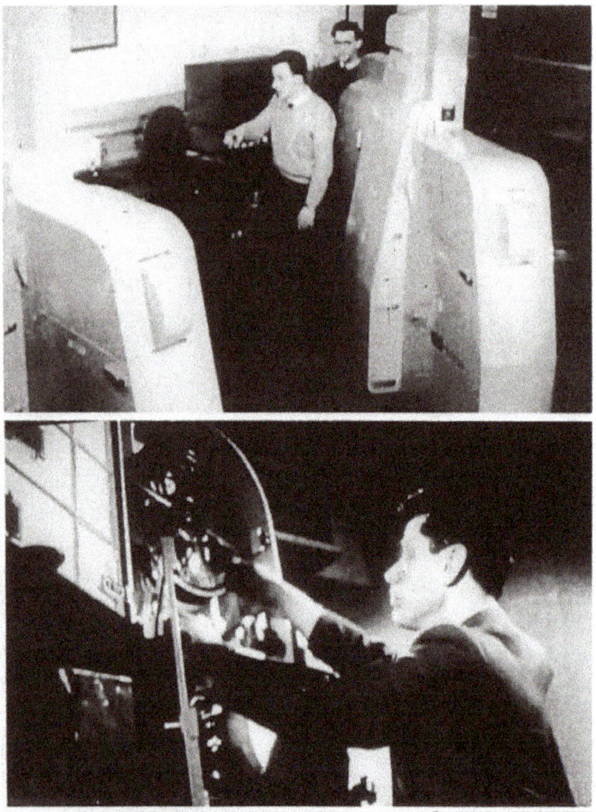

Early telecine areas had the look of a cinema projection room, but without portholes, and showed their film directly 'on air' to an even larger audience. It was necessary to have a pair of machines to allow for changeovers. Those illustrated, from 1959, are the 35mm Rank Cintels which had a family resemblance to the Kalee 21 projector.

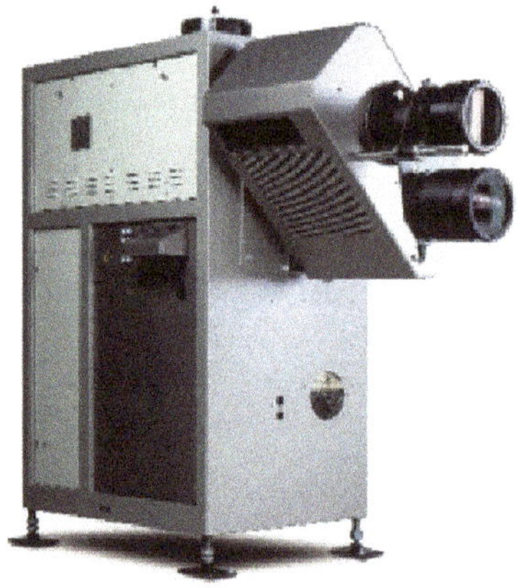

Examples of the first digital cinema projectors, dating back to the turn of the 21st century, may soon become sought after museum exhibits

off to the BBC in the 1930s and adapted for telecine and later film recording use. Polygon projectors did find an application in studios for multi-speed viewing and use in dubbing theatres. The most familiar use of the idea is in film editing and viewing machines, some of the latter now being fitted with a TV camera for making video copies.

In Britain's 25fps TV world, the most popular type of telecine was the flying spot. This reproduced the picture in much the same way as an optical sound track. The film moved continuously at a fixed 25fps, which also contributed to the scanning process. The image was scanned by a bright spot of light tracing out a blank TV picture (raster) on a cathode ray tube. This was focused on the film and picked up on the other side by a photocell. Usually twin lenses were used, the film passing the first for the even field, and then the second for the odd. When I joined the BBC Film Department in the early 1960s, I remember seeing an early Rank Cintel flying spot machine which had the look of a Kalee 21 projector, and even the sound head was the same.

Grab one while you can

I hope an example has been saved. Perhaps the National Media Museum in Bradford has managed to spirit one away in its warehouse. I know the Projected Picture Trust is also doing an excellent job saving historic cinema projectors and associated gear, but I am not so sure if there is an equivalent group of enthusiasts equally dedicated to preserving television's heritage, including tracking down its old equipment. It can be a difficult task. The previously mentioned Mechau non-intermittent 'flying mirrors' 35mm projector has so far eluded the Projected Picture Trust, with the only working examples believed to be in the hands of private collectors in Norway and the USA.

But the accelerating switch to digital cinema has offered new opportunities to rescue more recent 35mm projectors. Although it is said that there is no place for sentiment in business, many in the theatre chains' management and their chief engineers would much prefer finding good homes for their redundant 35mm analogue equipment, rather than seeing it end up in a skip, knowing that, as manufacturers cease production,

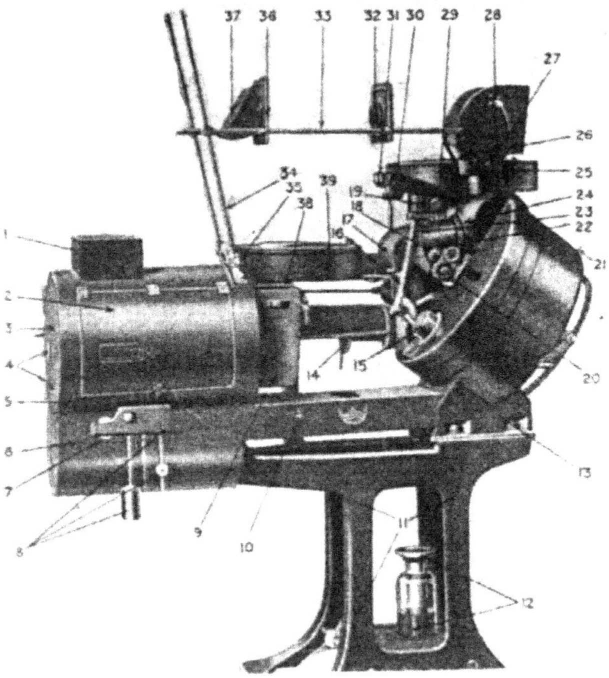

A strange beast, the Mechau / Arcadia continuous motion projector, from the 1930s. Looking for the spool boxes? These were horizontal, as was the film movement, with its non-intermittent dissolving images rotated to the vertical by the overhead projector-style lens/ mirror arrangement above. Not a success for use in cinemas, it cost over £1000, twice the price of a conventional intermittent projector at the time. However, the BBC purchased a few, which they adapted for telecine, and later telerecording use.

they will become harder to find in the future. All this is reminiscent of an earlier audio visual revolution, when schools and colleges threw out their 16mm machines in favour of video projectors and white boards. Cinema museums and collectors will soon be seeking out the first digital cinema projectors, many of which, after only ten years or so of service, are already being retired and of only historic interest.

Telecines go digital

The start of the digital revolution in the 1970s, particularly the ability to memorise and store video frames, gave an opportunity to simplify the design of telecines and film scanners which no longer had to produce an interlaced picture directly. The continuously moving film could now be scanned using a single in-line array of sensors. The progressively scanned image could be held in a frame store while being converted into an interlaced version. Digital manipulation could also be used for frame rate changes.

Spot the difference

Although most of the time, like the majority of viewers, I didn't notice the speeding up of cinema films on TV, on rare occasions my ears did detect a difference. I first viewed Hitchcock's 'Psycho' on TV and became used to the tempo of Bernard Hermann's strident score. When I finally had the opportunity to see the film properly on the big cinema screen, to me, the music seemed to be running slow. Inevitably, as I first listened to it on TV, I still prefer the slightly speeded up version!. Also, familiar actors voices on TV sometimes sound a little sharper when heard again when the cinema versions of their shows shot at 24fps, like *Dad's Army* and *Rising Damp* were subsequently shown on TV at 25fps.

Film material specifically shot for television, is usually shot at 25fps. There were a few exceptions. Filmed series, particularly those with significant world-wide sales, like *The Saint* and *The Avengers*, were usually filmed at 24fps, many on 35mm, in film studios. American film series, also at 24fps, ran shorter than their official running times when shown on British TV. All the film projectors at the BBC used for general viewing and in the dubbing theatres ran at 25fps, except for a pair of 35mm Ross machines at their Maida Vale studios, which were kept at 24fps. These were not only used for previewing feature films, but also for transferring their soundtracks onto audio tape for inclusion in radio film review programmes. TV documentaries often included footage shot abroad by hired 'stringer' crews who were instructed to film at 25fps. Inevitably, particularly from America, some arrived back shot at 24fps. All the dubbing theatres had an electronic pitch changer to raise that of the presenter or reporters' voices to match the home shot footage.

Telerecording memories

Another kind of 25fps television film was the telerecording made of electronic programmes and before video tape was used to keep and repeat live shows. These were basically a film camera photographing the image 'off the tube' of a TV monitor. Again the differences in the nature of film and TV images, particularly the latter's shorter period (blanking) between frames did present problems to overcome. The pull-down for 16mm film could be made just fast enough to capture all the 50 fields, but for the larger 35mm it couldn't keep up. The first tele-films, as they were originally called, were made in the late 1940s, again with the help of the Mechau projector's mirror-drum optical system. It was used in reverse, the TV monitor taking the place of the screen and a 35mm camera positioned at the projector's gate. Although its

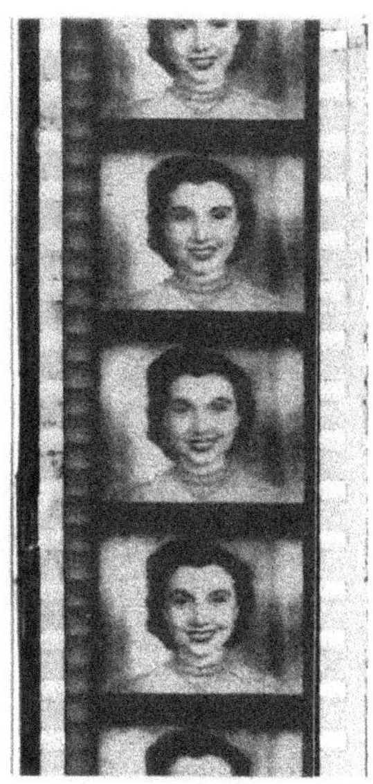

The first 35mm telerecordings were made in 1947

continuously dissolving imaging allowed both fields to be recorded, its overall quality wasn't too good. It was found better to have the camera looking directly at the TV screen, but its slower pull-down could only capture one of the fields with its lines made thicker to fill in the gaps left by the 'suppressed' discarded field. Although only recording half of the then 405 lines, the picture was considered more satisfactory, and was used to preserve the Coronation in 1953. All the early telerecordings were 35mm and the final improved method relied on the after-glow 'memory' of a special TV tube to record the field missed while the camera's shutter was closed.

The 35mm, and later 16mm, cameras used for telerecording also produced a combined optical track on the same film. For 35mm, a separate 35mm magnetic track was also usually recorded. Apart from its better quality it also made it easier if later the programme was tidied up by a film editor, who would also take the opportunity to replace any, now poorer quality, telerecorded film inserts with the actual original film and its mag track. As an example, the final copies of some episodes of the BBC's, still-remembered *Maigret* series from the late 1950s had more actual 35mm film, shot on location in Paris, than the still telerecorded studio footage with its optical track. This meant that only the separate magnetic track had the complete sound. However, for some all studio programmes the mag track was just a duplicate of the film's optical sound track.

Projection pitfalls

During my days as a BBC projectionist, I must admit that, knowing that telerecordings also had an optical track, for some lower-profile researcher showings we were tempted to take a gamble and try and save time by not bothering with the magnetic track. Usually we got away with it, but were sometimes caught out, when suddenly the sound was lost during an unexpected joined in film insert. If this kept happening, one response was to say a 'technical fault' meant we would have to start again, and this time quickly lace up the separate mag track, regaining our skilful reputation by miraculously curing the fault.

While working at the BBC's Lime Grove Studios, I noticed that the 16mm Bell & Howell 609 projectors could also be run at sixteen and two-thirds fps. I was told that this speed was used to show special in-house 'cheap and cheerful' telerecordings made of topical and other programmes which were not normally recorded, just in case they became the subject of a post-mortem. I learned that they were produced using a Siemens 16mm projector converted into a camera and enclosed in a wooden light-tight box looking at an ordinary production TV monitor. Its exciter lamp was replaced with a modulated glow-lamp to expose a variable density optical soundtrack. Already becoming interested in the technical history of film, I tried to find some examples to show again, but apparently, after the all clear they were junked. If any have survived, you would have to actually run them to spot the different speed.

Lost on video, found on film

Like other filmed material, telerecordings were useful for overseas sales, being independent of the different TV systems in use around the world. Later a few colour telerecordings were made, but by then video tape and electronic standards converters were taking over their role. However, as late as the 1970s, black and white telerecordings, or tape-to-film transfers, were still being made from colour-taped programmes for export, and still convenient for countries that were yet to introduce a colour service.

Even in today's digital age, old telerecordings still make news when copies are found to have been kept by far off broadcasters, private collectors, or rescued by the staff (I admit nothing!) of programmes thrown away by their original producers. Even black and white prints of colour programmes sometimes show traces of the dot pattern in the image which represents the original colour information, and, with the help of digital technology, we can also bring back the colour. A recent example was a missing, believed wiped episode of *Dad's Army*. This was not the first time colour was restored to a black and white telerecording. For an earlier discovery of lost *Dr Who* episodes, the colour was recovered from an otherwise poorer-quality American U-Matic video cassette. The idea of transferring electronic, now digital images onto film lives on in the guise of today's digital intermediates, and prints made from them could be described as posh telerecordings.

In America, telerecordings were known as kinescopes. In their case, fields were missed out to produce a 24fps print. However, for domestic use, their quality wasn't always considered good enough, so the networks shot their most popular shows and series on 35mm film. Even those with a live audience were also filmed on 35mm, using multiple camera set-ups, a technique pioneered by *I Love Lucy* in 1955. Alternative 16mm reduction prints were available for syndication and smaller TV stations, but for American series shown over here, we generally chose the 35mm copies. These were of excellent quality and, in later years, would show up our own rather grainy and wobbly 16mm, which was increasingly replacing 35mm, particularly after the introduction of colour had added to its cost. In America, there was always a reluctance to switch to 16mm, even

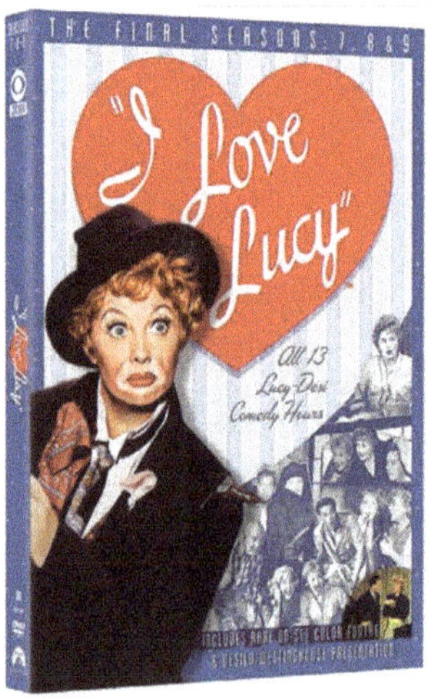

after its later dramatic improvement and development of Super-16. It was a while before HD video production took over the traditional role of 35mm film for American TV. A few TV films were shot at 30fps for direct transfer and distribution on videotape.

The speed of restorations

Digital speed corrections are now a regular part of the restorations of silent films and have greatly improved their transfer to DVD. It also proved useful for the latest restoration of Claude Friese-Greene's 'Open Road' colour films from 1924. Like the earlier Kinemacolor system, the black and white negative was shot at double the normal speed (32fps) through alternating colour filters, with Friese-Greene replacing Kinemacolor's red and green with red and a combination of yellow and white light. For the additive projection, he also eliminated the former's red and green filter wheel by staining alternate frames on the print the appropriate colours, which, at 32fps, blended together on the screen, or more accurately in the brains of the viewer, to produce a limited range of colours.

For an earlier all-film restoration by the National Film Archive, the negative's two filtered images were superimposed in their correct colours onto a single frame of modern colour film, reducing the running speed to 16fps. It was this footage which formed the basis of the TV series *The Lost World of Friese-Greene*, with the speed corrected during the telecine transfer. For a more authentic film presentation, with the original inter-titles and live music, selected footage was restored again digitally, but this time scanned back to a digital intermediate at 24fps to make the print easier to show on a normal fixed speed projector.

The digital version of stretch printing, the way silent films (16fps-20fps) were brought up to sound's 24fps by printing every other, or third frame twice, produces a much smoother and judder free result. Current interpolation programmes create new intermediate frames using information from the preceding and following images. Digital editing and restoration computer stations can play out the results at any frame rate and, if required, return them to film.

Living with analogue

Today's digital world will still have to accommodate left-over analogue technology for some time yet. For the moment, digital cinema has inherited film's 24fps, but it will be interesting to see if this is kept after the production on film eventually gives way to HD video. Already, some alternative programming makes use of higher frame rates for a smoother non-film look, with 60fps being a popular alternative.

The switch from film to digital has made it easier to increase frame rates, like the 48fps employed by the alternating left and right images in some 3D systems. With no physical shutter, a digital projector flashes each frame twice, or now more likely three times, onto the screen to provide the higher flicker-free viewing frequency.

The conflict between the different TV standards still adds a complication to the production of DVDs. Despite the availability of standards convertors, for the best quality film transfers two separate runs through the telecine are usually made, one at 24fps for the American NTSC 525 line 30fps master, and another at 25fps for the European PAL 625 line 25fps version. If necessary, the former can be shown using our own players, but the motion portrayal to some extent suffers from regular glitches and slight jumps as the machine reduces the disc's 30fps down to 25fps. If this artefact, most noticeable during slow pans, is spotted on a PAL disc, this is a clue that the image has, at some stage, passed through a convertor from a 30fps American master. Just in case of discrepancies, and to avoid trouble, the magic word 'approx' is now sometimes added to the stated running times.

The advances in digital processing have now largely de-coupled the link between the origination and display frame rates. One current example is, the latest modern miracle of the moving picture, the Blu-ray. All the discs run at 24fps, leaving the player and display devices to process them to fit their requirements. In theory the same disc can be replayed on any Blu-ray player or drive around the world, but in practice this can be thwarted by, to some, the curse of region coding.

To encourage the sales of Blu-ray discs a dual-format set is sometimes offered with a normal DVD included. If, for us, this is a separately mastered PAL disc, and you are a viewer in a hurry, then watch this one - it will finish sooner!

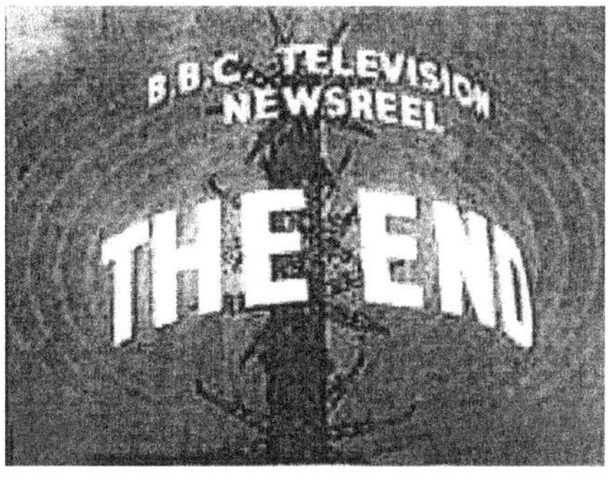

All shapes and sizes
- Television shapes up

There was a time when the world of cinema regarded television as a rival, but over the years, both their interests and technology have moved closer together. As film gives way to ever more sophisticated digital cinema, it is worth looking back to a more simple age, and the birth of television. This too, all began with relatively simple often do-it-yourself technology with its early viewers watching the first 'electric pictures' at a time when it was possible to build your own TV.

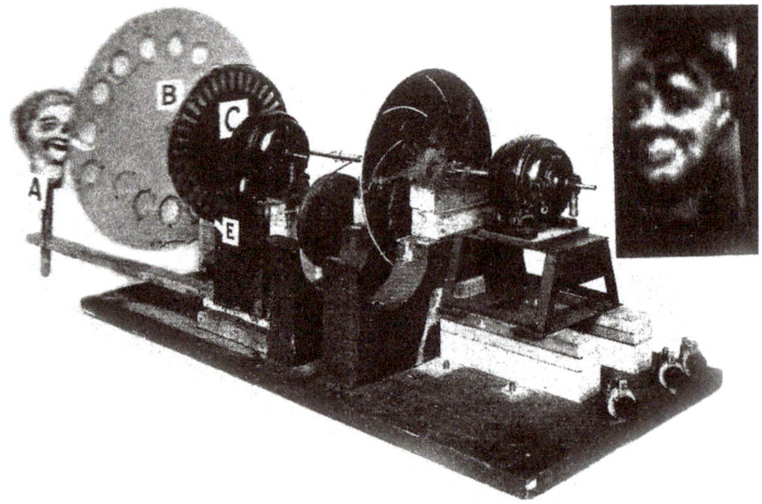

Baird's original makeshift apparatus (1925) and its first victim 'Stooky Bill'. The rudimentary image of his wooden performance didn't leave the building until the GPO granted Baird an amateur band radio licence so that he could show the outside world that the soon to be perfected wonder of 'seeing by wireless' was about to become a reality.

With cinemas keeping their 4:3 screens, at least for the time being, a new form of moving pictures would soon be capturing the imagination of the public. Television had arrived, offering smaller screen entertainment back at home.

Like the cinema, it all began with spinning cogwheels and shutters

It is sobering for us to think that for future generations, the projection of film prints may only be remembered as a rather primitive part of the earlier pre-digital history of the cinema. This is already the case for television, but unlike the cinema, which took well over a century to make its 'electronic' change, TV's own relatively simple and largely mechanical era would only last a mere ten years. During this time, beginning in the mid 1920s, it would be Britain which would lead the way, in the shape of Scotsman John Logie Baird. Although many TV historians would question the popular belief that he actually invented television, he was the first to actively promote and introduce TV to the public, leading to the first regular service. As with the birth of the cinema, which had to wait for the coming of flexible celluloid film, it would be advances in the technology of radio and electronics, particularly the means of amplification, which would enable Baird to put into practice the ideas and visions of earlier inventors and scientists, with many of their discoveries dating back to the 1800s.

What was needed

Unlike the images on film, which can be captured and presented as a series of complete frames, TV pictures have to be divided up into many tiny elements which can be sent to the viewer in a single continuous stream to be re-assembled at the receiver into a replica of the original image. This was achieved by a process of scanning and there were two mechanical devices already available at the time which could do the job and Baird would make use of both at various times.

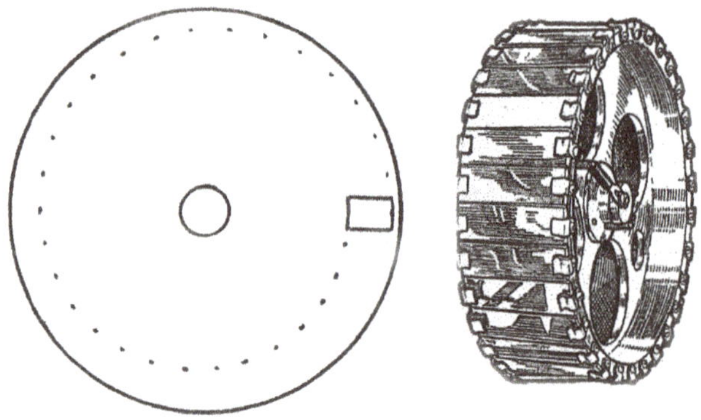

Baird's pictures were scanned into 30 lines using either a Nipkow disc or mirror drum

The first of these was the 'Nipkow' spinning disc (1884) which used a spiral of small holes to turn the image into a series of progressively scanned lines, each varying in brightness from point to point, depending on the tones of the subject.

Having much in common with reading the modulated light passing through a film's optical soundtrack, Baird's original apparatus directed the light from the subject passing through the moving holes in the disc onto a photoelectric cell (1873). This turned the fluctuating light into an electrical signal which could be sent by wire (closed circuit) or transmitted by radio to a receiver. Here it was amplified to control the brightness of a neon bulb, which if viewed through the spinning holes of a matching synchronised disc, in the same position as that at the transmitter, persistence of vision allowed the rapidly scanning point of light to trace out a coherent image in the mind of the viewer.

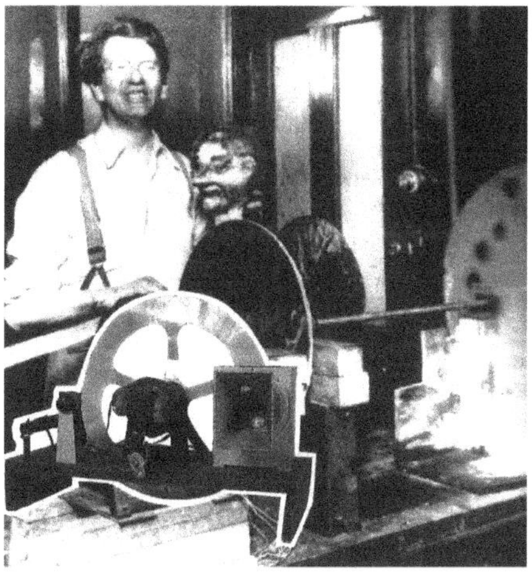

A happy Baird and Stooky Bill after creating their first TV picture. Inset is the later Televisor with its cabinet removed.

Making progress

At first, troubles making the early sluggish selenium cell react quickly enough meant he could only reproduce blurred brightly back-lit silhouettes, but work to improve its response and replacing the small holes in the disc with bicycle lamp lenses made it possible to change to very bright reflected light to send still rudimentary images, but now showing more detail and displaying gradations of light and shade. Baird's improving TV pictures were made up of 30 vertical lines with a frequency of 12½ pictures per second. Both were a compromise between detail and flicker, while keeping the amount of information, or bandwidth, low enough to be sent by ordinary telephone wires, medium wave radio, or even be recorded onto a gramophone record to create the first ever 'Phonovision' video disc.

As for the picture's aspect ratio, unusually, Baird deliberately chose a taller than wide 3:7 portrait format, which he said could take in faces and head and shoulder shots without wasting any space or lines, with the possibility later of full-length figures. In fact due to the blinding light still needed to produce a satisfactory picture, the first face transmitted belonged to the wooden head of 'Stooky Bill', a ventriloquist dummy who didn't complain about the intense heat and boredom during Baird's long hours of experiments. Although he did manage to bribe an office boy called William Taynton to endure it long enough to become the first live TV personality, he had to come up with another way, without cooking his future performers.

In the flying spotlight

The original meaning of the word "camera" was dark room or chamber, and Baird would now place his subjects inside one. Outside, a powerful 1000 watt lamp behind the spinning disc projected a scanning 'flying spot' of light through a hole in the wall into the darkened studio, with the variations of light reflected off the subject picked up by a bank of photocells. An added advantage was that he could now forget the lenses in the disc and return to the spiral of tiny holes which improved the detail. The field of view was a little larger, but the brightness of the spot only covered head and

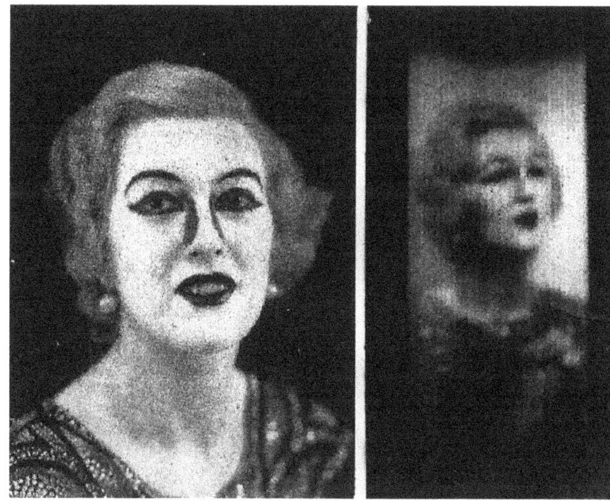

As in the early days of the cinema, when film stock was only sensitive to mostly blue light, TV's photo-cells had a similar response, so for the best pictures its performers would also use the same whitened faces and blue-black make-up to highlight their features so that they would look better on the screen.

shoulder shots. For a later more sophisticated 'spotlight' studio an even more powerful mirror drum projector was developed, which could illuminate a larger space. This scanned a much brighter spot of light, by reflecting it off a revolving drum of small mirrors, each set at a slightly different angle. (1889). Another improvement was to mount the photocells on moveable stands.

These could now be positioned, and their output adjusted, to alter the shading of the final picture. The concept may be easier to grasp if you imagine a normal floodlit studio in reverse, with the light now coming out of the camera and photographed by the lights.

What about films on TV?

Although losing the 'I see it as it happens' added advantage of TV, showing films could also become an attraction, without having to leave home to go to the cinema. However, showing films raised the problem of turning the intermittent nature of film presentation into a continuously scanned TV picture. Trying to scan the flashing on and off, with dark periods in between, film frames resulted in severe flicker, black lines, partial pictures, or none at all. One solution was to use a continuous motion projector, which produces an uninterrupted, always visible picture, optically dissolving from frame to frame. The only 35mm projector of this type available at the time was the German mirror drum 'Mechau' and Baird was persuaded to buy a second-hand one from a cinema in Charing Cross Road. This was converted into a device for televising cine film, or 'telecine' by illuminating its gate with a small flying spot projector and placing a photo-cell in front of its lens. Although it worked OK, ordinary 1.33:1 cinema films still suffered from being cropped to match Baird's taller picture and its low definition only allowed close-ups to be seen clearly, with long shots left to the imagination.

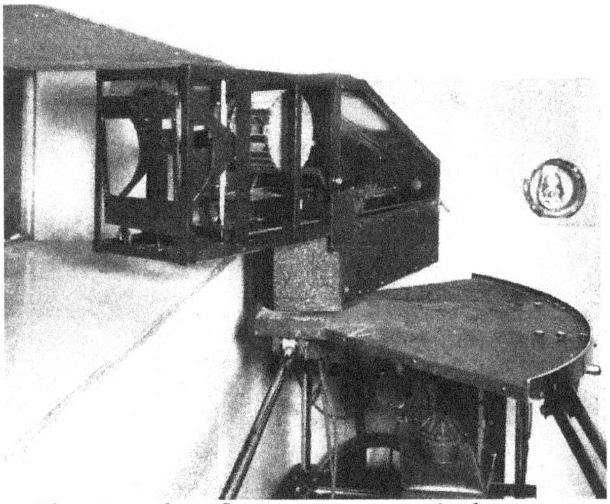

The mirror drum flying spot projector (with its cover removed) could pivot for panning shots.

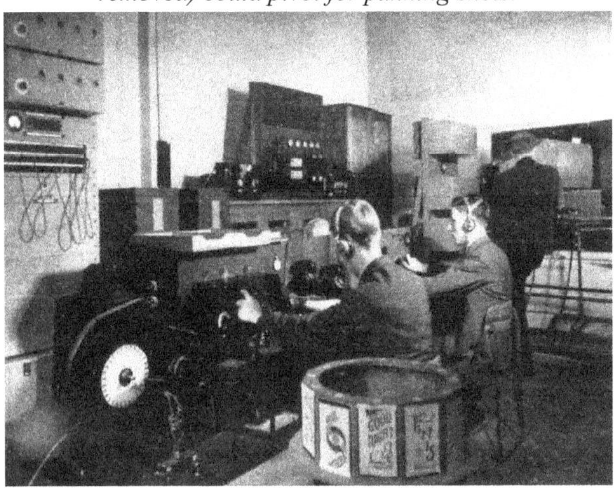

The picture from the projector above is shown in the background of this picture being operated by its projectionist ('cameraman') who is directing its scanning spot of light through the window of the BBC's first TV studio control room at Portland Place in 1935

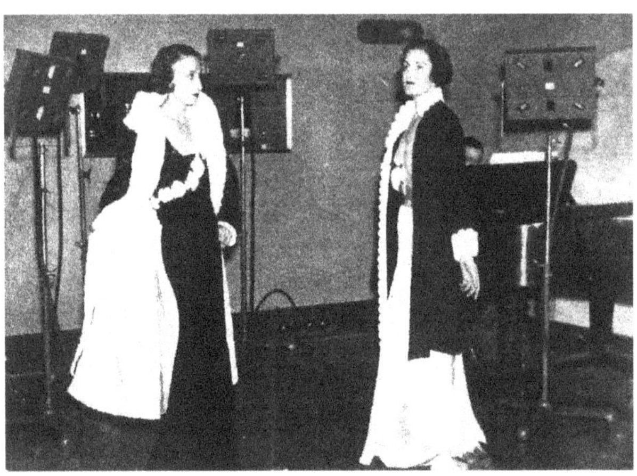

On the other side of the glass, with the lights up in the normally darkened studio to show it ready for a fashion show, when the models would only be illuminated by the moving spot of light from the projector, the reflected light being picked up by the photo-cells mounted on their moveable stands, which look like floodlights in a normal studio setup.

Fight to get on the air

Running in parallel with all his technical developments, Baird's talent for publicity had come into play to promote his TV breakthroughs with a series of high profile demonstrations and stunts. These had kicked off when Mr Selfridge Jnr paid Baird to show off his early efforts at his shop in Oxford Street. Baird would go on to excite interest in television by staging for the press various 'firsts'. Pictures were sent over ever increasing distances, including to America, seeing in the dark infra-red 'Noctovision', 'Telechrome' colour TV (a TV version of Kinemacolor) and he even added 3D. In the event, the actual results rarely lived up to all the hype, but did help to keep the possibilities of television in the public eye and was beginning to spur others, both in Britain and around the world to accelerate their own efforts to perfect TV. To keep one step ahead Baird would have to persuade the BBC, with their broadcasting monopoly, to transmit his pictures to a wider public. At first they resisted, even accusing Baird of fooling the public that TV was ready, but after much lobbying and the suggestion that Britain would be left behind, in 1929 the BBC agreed to provide a transmitter to begin a limited 'experimental' service.

Baird set up a studio at Long Acre in Covent Garden, and would now have to add entertainment value to just the novelty of TV. The talent included the Baird Concert Party of singers, conjurers, puppets and dancers, who all had to adapt their performances to the close-up coverage of the flying spot studio. One dancer made the best of it by, after giving the viewers a big smile, jumping up onto a table so they could see her legs and feet.

The chance to have your own 'telly'

To join in and see it all you could now buy your own 'Televisor', the first commercially marketed TV receiver. This was a simple Nipkow disc picture-only add-on device which you had to connect to the output of an existing radio set. It was available ready-assembled in a nice green tin cabinet for 25 guineas, but was more popular as a kit of parts for only 16. When tuned in, you could see the tall 30-line orange-red neon coloured picture magnified by a lens to about four inches high. Of the controls, the most important knob was the disc's speed control. To keep it in sync with that at the transmitter an extra low-frequency control signal was sent, but this was sometimes lost, so it needed constant adjustment to stop the picture from going out of rack, or in the worst case, disappearing into 30 unrecognisable stripes. One critic described it as a fruit machine, with, if you were lucky, winning the prize of a picture.

Keep listening, the picture will follow shortly

At first, with only one transmitter available, the viewing experience also suffered, because the picture and sound could not be sent simultaneously. The sound was broadcast first, followed by the picture, each sent in two-minute segments. If you didn't have a Televisor

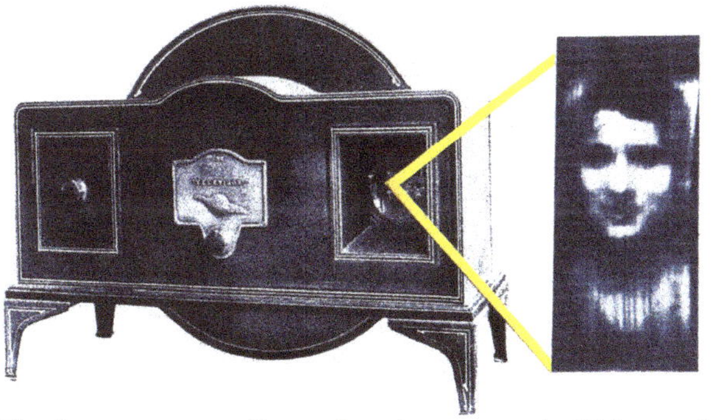

The first commercially produced picture-only 'Televisor' (1930) and an example of its tall aspect ratio (CinemaScope on its end!) 30-line images which were displayed at 12½ frames per second - definitely Low Frame rate!

you had to imagine what the picture looked like while listening to its humming sound. All this didn't put off the early adopters of television, as most were radio and TV enthusiasts, who felt more involved with this new medium, having built their receiver from scratch or from the many other cheaper kits put together by radio shops. After six months, a second transmitter became available, so, providing you now had two radios, you could watch the new in-sync programmes. From 1932 these were now being produced by the BBC themselves from a new studio in Broadcasting House. Even though it was stressed that it remained an experimental service and only guaranteed to keep going until 1934, other 30 line sets were being offered for sale. The most expensive, at 75 guineas, was the Baird / Bush de-luxe model. This was a self-contained floor standing set with the radio receivers built-in and a mirror drum which focused a beam of white light, from a 100 watt lamp, onto the rear of a 9 by 4 inch ground glass screen. Its brightness was varied by passing it through a Kerr Cell 'light valve' (invented in 1875) which modulated the light by directing it through a crystalline fluid, which rotated its plane of polarization in response to an electrical signal. (Thoughts of today's LCD displays.) Even as a rich man's toy, few, if any, of the 100 made were ever sold, so in an effort to get rid of them, the owners of Bush, who also had an interest in Gaumont British Cinemas, found a new home for many of them as an exhibit in their foyers.

Another type of receiver, which would point the way to TVs of the future, used a cathode-ray tube in which an electron beam was made to scan the 30-line picture onto a layer of fluorescent powder coated on the inside surface of its flattened face, which formed the screen. The first on the market was made in London by Gillavision Television who, for 55 guineas, offered a four foot high cabinet model with a five inch circular screen displaying a rather greenish picture. No reliable figures exist for the numbers of TV receivers in use in Britain during the years, between 1929 and 1935, of the first 30-line service.

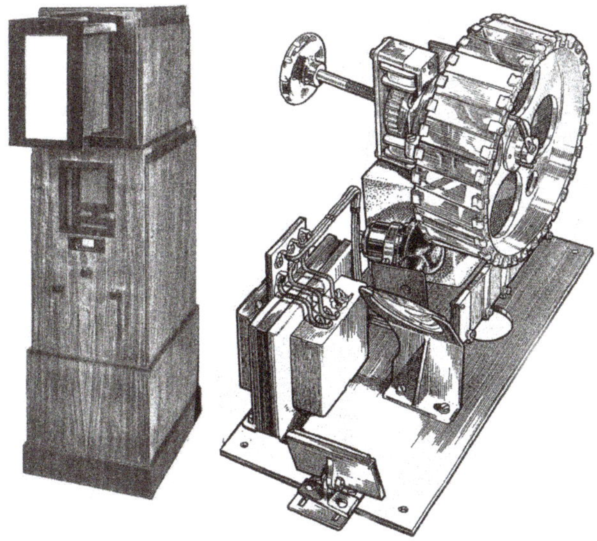

Above left: the Bush luxury 30-line mirror drum back-projection model (1933) with the picture and sound radio receivers built-in. Before switch-on, its 4 x 9 inch frosted screen was pulled out on its bellows to set the correct throw. The picture display part of the innards (right) was also available as a kit and also used in studio monitors.

'Television', the journal of the Television Society (which Baird helped to set up and fund to persuade people to join his campaign for the introduction of TV) estimated that, based on correspondence from constructors, 14,000 had been put together by the end of 1933. The Daily Express had a 'special offer' of TV kits during 1934 and ended up selling 5,000 of them. All these, together with the far fewer ready-assembled models sold, would suggest that at least 20,000 were eventually spinning away. One place to go to buy a TV was Selfridges, which would keep its pioneering role in 'selling' television by being the first department store to open a TV department.

Television and the cinema

Even before it actually became a reality, a sign that the idea of television was making an impression on the cinema was its early appearances in films. Among the first was Georges Méliès *La Photographie Electronique à Distance* (1908). In this trick film, an inventor invites an old couple to see themselves transmitted by TV. Obviously still to be perfected, as their anger after watching each other's grossly distorted 'monkey' faces on the screen results in them smashing up the machine, when, sadly, during all the chaos, the wife gets caught up in its flywheel. TV would often be depicted as a threat, like in *High Treason* (1929) when it was turned into a surveillance device (CCTV), reinforcing the fear that TV could be used to look back at, and spy on its viewers in their own homes. On the fun side, no science fiction serial of the 1930s would be complete without its super hero, like Flash Gordon, keeping in touch with its other characters and the rest of the plot by watching at least a simulation of a TV screen.

The road to digital cinema begins

What did 'film' people think of early TV? Looking at reports in "Today's Cinema" some dismissed the first receivers as little more than a novelty, equivalent in cinema history to the Kinetoscope and the end of the pier 'What the Butler Saw' Mutoscope machines, without even offering the latter's more stimulating subject matter. Others speculated that if television made the same rapid progress as early 35mm projection, then it might go on to find an additional role in cinemas.

With the BBC now taking over the production and transmission of programmes for the 'lookers-in' at home, Baird turned his attention to other ways to exploit TV, including a big screen version.

His first effort wasn't particularly big. It was 2 foot wide by 5 foot tall and, like a rather crude version of today's multiple LED advertising and stage displays, consisted of 2100 small light bulbs in thirty vertical rows of seventy. These were activated by a revolving metal brush making contact with a series of contacts in synchronism with the disc at the transmitter. In front of the lamps was a frosted screen which softened the dotty bright points of light, blending them into a larger version of his normal 30-line picture.

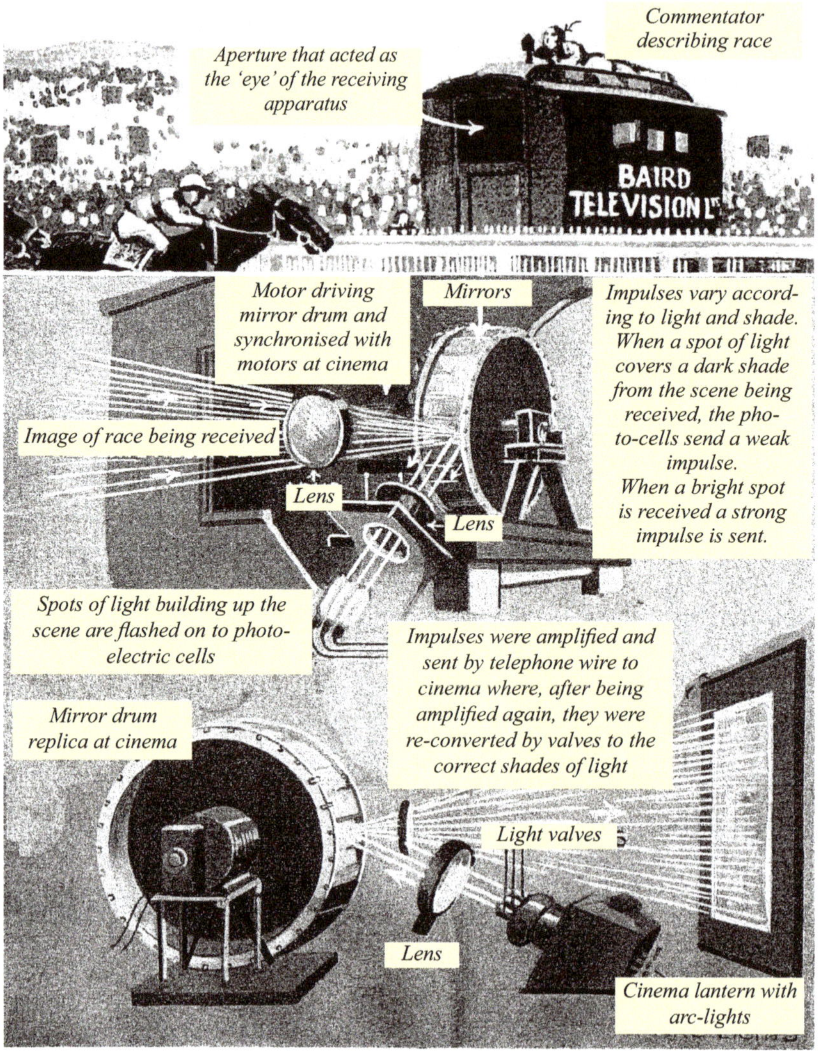

Based on a contemporary drawing showing the big-screen TV system used to transmit the 1932 Derby to the Metropole Cinema in Victoria, London.

Like the early days of the cinematograph, it became part of a 'turn' in a variety theatre. Its first performance, in 1930, was at the Coliseum in St Martin's Lane, where, as part of the act, personalities of the day back at Baird's studio were proved to be 'live' by members of the audience asking questions and urging them over the phone to make specific gestures. For its climax, music hall star George Robey, who had introduced the show, left the stage and dashed to the near-by studio to reappear again on the TV screen. While he was away, the Mechau telecine transmitted one of his short cinema films. It must have been considered a success as, after a two week run, the show was taken on a tour of European cities.

Perhaps the most famous of Baird's early big screen TV special events was a live broadcast of the finish of the 1932 Derby. The scene at the winning post was scanned by a mirror drum onto three separate photo-cells and sent by four telephone lines (one for the sound) in three 30-line sections to the Metropole cinema in Victoria. Here, before a full-house, a mirror drum projector with three light valves presented them side-by-side, Cinerama style, to form a complete 90-line 4:3 picture on a 6 by 8 foot rear projection screen.

At the same time, only the centre 30-line portion was relayed to the BBC for simultaneous transmission to its own viewers at home. Fortunately, the 'see it as it happens' excitement overcame the fact that the actual picture was very poor, with noticeable white dividing lines between the segments, which often differed in brightness. Although the horses flashed past the post as only a barely recognisable blur, the lower expectations of the audience at the time meant it was still considered to be a great success, with Baird appearing on stage to great applause. To see it all again, in much more detail, you could wait for the filmed newsreel coverage of the event shown later in the evening.

Even 'Today's Cinema' got carried away, convinced that 'Baird has at last hit on the very method which will bring television into the cinema'. Zone TV, as it was known, could offer cinema audiences the added attrac-

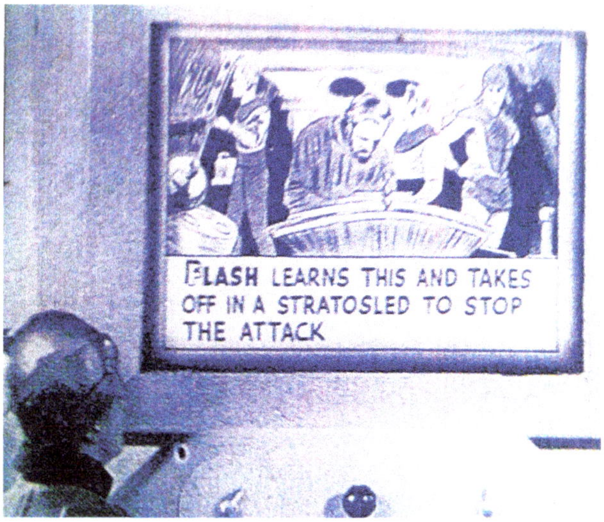

Left:
Catch up TV:
Flash Gordon's story so far...

Right:
Top of the bill in 1930: Baird's British invention, TELEVISION.

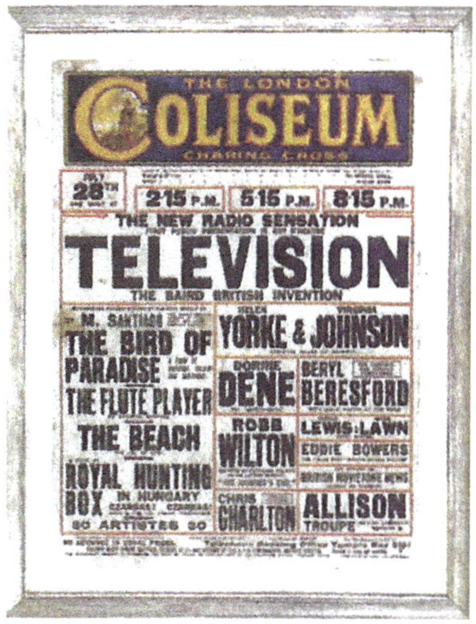

tion of seeing the complete picture on the big screen, with small screen viewers at home only receiving one of the sections, usually the centre, but with the possibility of switching between them, like an early form of pan-and-scan.

While all the discs and mirror drums continued to spin, others, with far less fanfare, were working on all-electronic TV systems and radio transmitters which could carry much higher definition pictures. Soon, mechanical television would be fighting to stay on the air.

Making progress by stealth

Our story of the birth of television and the first big screen 'electronic' pictures shown in cinemas back in 1932 has so far shown how the BBC had been persuaded to produce and transmit a limited experimental TV service using the largely mechanical Baird 30 line system. They were doing so reluctantly, knowing that the low definition flickering images, although well received by early TV enthusiasts, many of whom were happy just to get a picture on their home-built Televisors, would not be able to sustain the interest of the rest of the public once the initial novelty value had passed. However, Television would still have a future.

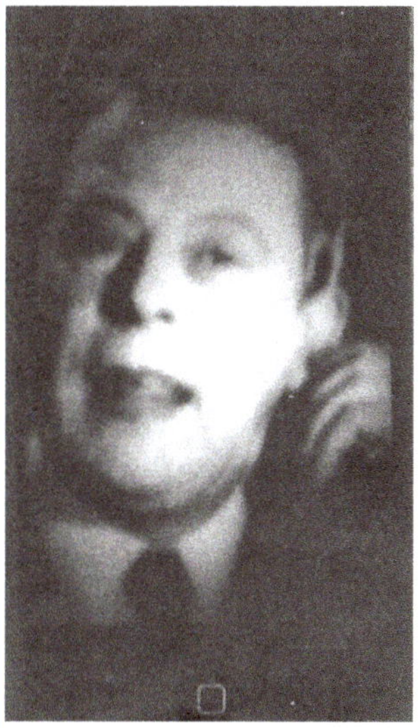

A recent discovery

On the screen in 1930, comic actor Seymour Hicks appearing in what he announces is the first 'talkie' film publicly transmitted by television, which is being directed by his friend Alfred Hitchcock.
In the event, it is believed that this specially shot for TV film may have been beaten to the tele-cine by a George Robey cinema film 'The Bride' 1929.

Working quietly behind closed doors, another company, EMI, was also developing TV, and after discarding their own earlier work using mechanical scanning methods, were ready to demonstrate an all-electronic system based on using cathode ray tubes for both generating and viewing the pictures. The Cathode Ray Tube (CRT) from 1907 had moved on from being an interesting scientific instrument to become the chosen way to display TV pictures, including those now beginning to emerge in other countries, even if, like Baird's they were still being scanned mechanically.

Magic rays

To produce a TV picture, the tube had an electron gun placed at the narrow end of its conical, or flask shaped, evacuated glass bulb, which fired a sharply focused beam of electrons to produce a small bright spot of light on a fluorescent screen coated on the inside surface of its wider and flatter other end. The signal was made to scan and vary its brightness, leaving the rapidly moving spot to use the moving picture trick of persistence of vision, to trace out the image in the mind of the viewer.

EMI's breakthrough was its new 'electronic eye' Emitron camera version in which a lens focused an image, through the glass, onto a plate covered with a mosaic of tiny photo-cells which became positively charged in proportion to the amount of light falling on them. These were then discharged in turn by a negative scanning electron beam, producing a signal of impulses on the plate, varying in strength depending on the tones of the image. Once wiped clean, the process was repeated to produce a stream of pictures many times a second.

240 - 405 line 'High Definition'

For their final system, EMI settled on a 405 line horizontally scanned picture displayed at 25 complete images per second. Then described as being 'high definition', the pictures were presented in the landscape proportions of 5:4, an aspect ratio of 1.25:1. The sight of these greatly improved pictures prompted the BBC to suggest dropping their low definition 30-line experiment, and to begin again with an improved system which would have

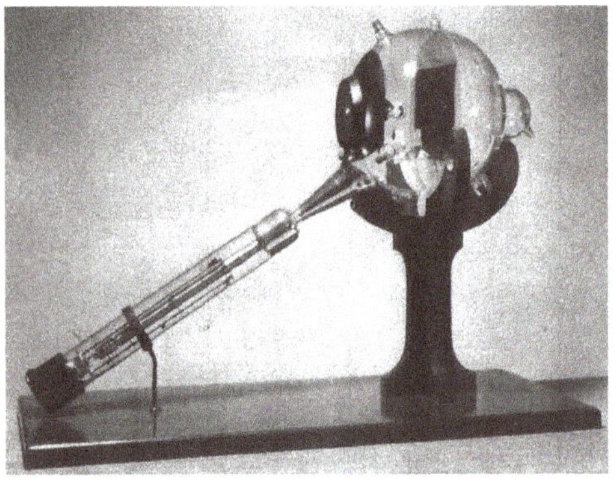

EMI's Emitron camera tube had an offset electron gun to pick the image off the front of its plate of photo-cells, giving the first TV cameras their distinctive shape.

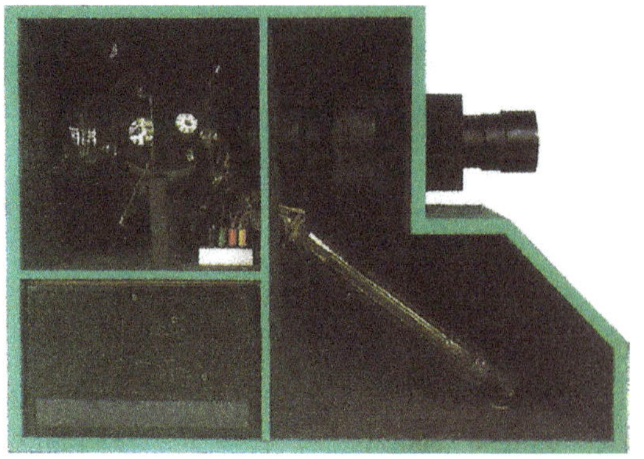

wider appeal and more entertainment value. To transmit higher definition pictures, the BBC would need new, high frequency (VHF) transmitters to carry the extra information. EMI had joined forces with Marconi, who had the technology to build them.

Let battle commence

When Baird got wind of what was going on he reacted by lobbying all those with influence, including the press, letting it know that, with access to the same transmitters, his company too could come up with a much better TV system. As part of his campaign, he even accused the BBC of being unpatriotic, prepared to reject a British system in favour of EMI's, which he claimed was based on technology developed by RCA in America; RCA had a major stake in EMI at the time. EMI fought back, maintaining that, although almost identical to RCAs Iconoscope version, their improved Emitron camera tube had been developed independently.

Attracted by the prospect of offering the public more watchable TV pictures, and to help quell the spat about the best way to provide them, the government set up a committee, which duly reported that indeed the BBC should start a new higher definition service. No specific standard had been chosen, but they defined HD at the time as not being less than 240 lines with a picture frequency of 25pps. This minimum specification was thought to have been chosen to give Baird a better chance to compete, the evidence being that, without an electronic camera available, this was the maximum possible using mechanical scanning.

How to close the gap?

After condemning his rival for allegedly using foreign technology, Baird would turn to a German company Fernseh AG, with whom he already had a connection, for ideas as to how to catch up. Fernseh had in fact beaten Britain to provide better pictures to the public by already operating a regular 180-line service, although this was not received by viewers on their own sets at home, but on cathode ray tube receivers set up in public viewing rooms. Like Baird, without access to an electronic camera, they derived their 180-line horizontally scanned images at 25pps from film, using a relatively simple but effective disc and photo-cell telecine. Unlike the usual Nipkow spiral arrangement, the holes in the spinning disc were placed at the same radius around its edge to perform the horizontal scanning, relying on the continuously vertically moving film to complete the process. Of course, just showing pre-shot film lost TV's main advantage of the sense of immediacy, but Fernseh had found a way to still use film but yet offer the viewer 'almost live' TV.

The amazing Intermediate film process

For this early method .of instant photography, the scene was captured on special 35mm Agfa film with a much thinner emulsion which could be processed more quickly and then easily washed off. It was formed into a continuous loop about 100 foot long, and after being exposed in the camera, together with a combined optical sound track, was fed into a processor to be rapidly developed and fixed to become a negative, which while still wet was then scanned into a TV picture. All was not over yet, as after this the emulsion was removed and the film dried and re-coated with a new sensitive layer before entering the camera again for another trip through the system. This remarkable setup only delayed transmission by about a minute, and although bulky, the whole apparatus could also be used for outside broadcasts, being installed in a 3½ ton Mercedes Benz truck, which was described as a film factory on wheels.

Baird's new system would also adopt the Fernseh design of telecine and a scaled down version of their intermediate film process. This no longer recoated a continuous loop of film, but had to be kept loaded with fresh rolls of stock. A switch to 16mm would have helped to keep down the cost but instead a new format was added to the history of film gauges by using the old idea of splitting ordinary 35mm stock down the middle to produce a more economical 17.5mm format with quarter size images.

First seen as the Birtac home movie system in 1899, the new up-dated version added a narrow optical soundtrack outside the perforations. This was exposed, along with the picture, in a modified Vinten camera mounted on top of the processor and disc scanner, all of which had to be firmly rooted to the spot, having to be plumbed into both the mains water and drainage, keeping it all well clear of the high voltages also passing through the machine. The 17.5mm film stock was supplied by Kodak, but its

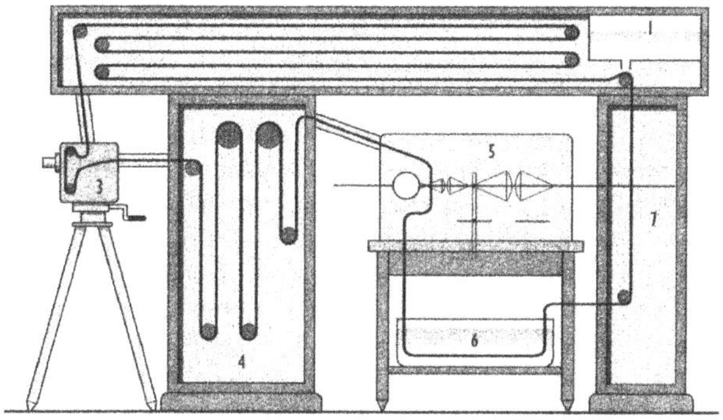

Schematic of the Fernseh full intermediate film process. After the endless loop of 35mm film was exposed in the camera, it was rapidly processed to a negative, and, after being scanned into a TV picture the emulsion was washed off and the base dried. It was immediately re-coated with a new sensitive layer which, when dry, entered the camera again for another trip.

special low contrast emulsion took longer to process, particularly the fixing, but by replacing the normal hypo with a somewhat more hazardous, but quicker acting cyanide solution, the time from exposure to scanning was reduced to only 54 seconds. Also helping to save time, the film's negative image could be turned into a positive TV picture electronically, without the need for further reversal processing steps. To reach the minimum 240 line 25pps standard, new faster scanning discs were designed. These were made with great precision by Fernseh in Germany, perforated with many more even smaller three thousandths of an inch hexagonal holes.

The complete system would still have a 'live' element. Although relying mostly on the intermediate film camera, another spotlight studio would also be available, which, along with the normal 'dry' 35mm telecine, could also provide the pictures. This was particularly useful when the machine had to stop to be reloaded with a fresh roll of film. The revolving mirror drum of the existing 30-line flying-spot projector ('camera') wouldn't stand up to being speeded up for the new standard, which meant a return to a Nipkow disc. An even more powerful arc lamp was needed to force enough light through its tiny perforations flying past faster than before. Even so, like the original flying spot studio, ten years earlier, the scanning dot of light was still only bright enough to illuminate the head and shoulders of an announcer or solo performer.

Shape change

For the change to 240 lines, the now horizontally scanned image no longer had the taller than wide portrait format of the first 30-line system, switching to an almost square 4½:4 (1.125:1) shape for the picture.

Decision time

A number of electrical and radio manufacturers submitted their plans for proposed TV systems, but only those of EMI and Baird had made sufficient progress to be considered. After numerous demonstrations, the

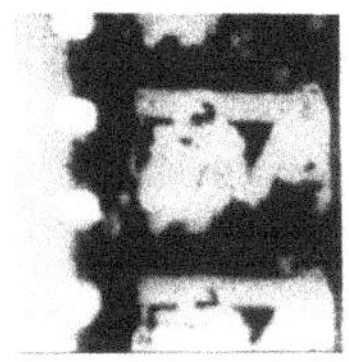

Birtac 17.5mm format from 1899

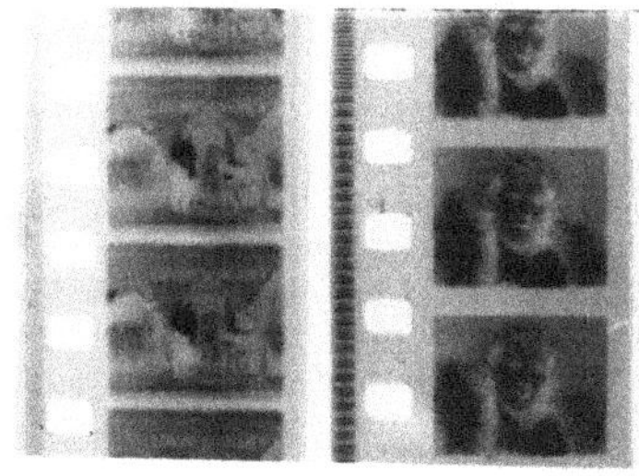

Baird's own 17.5mm format. Only developed to a negative for scanning into a TV picture.

Baird's simplified version used fresh film each time. To reduce the cost, 17.5mm film was used. This revived the idea of splitting 35mm film down the middle, which was first seen as the 'Birtac' home movie system in 1899, with a narrow optical track outside the perforations.

general view of the committee and the BBC was that EMI's was the most practical, that the era of mechanical TV was coming to an end, and that the future would be all-electronic. However, there was a reluctance to reject the Baird system out of hand. For the general public, the name was synonymous with television and there was also fear of a backlash from the pro-Baird press and his many political and celebrity supporters. In fact, Baird himself had had little to do with the actual construction of the 240 line system. Sometime before, his failing company had come under the control of Gaumont British, and he was now devoting most of his time to big screen cinema TV. The result of his latest efforts was the showing, using a mechanical mirror drum camera and projector, of live 120-line (162/3 pps) pictures, which included an introduction by GB star Will Hay, onto a rear 8 by 6.5 foot screen at the Dominion Cinema in London's Tottenham Court Road.
A few months later, he and his team returned with their equipment to the theatre and, during a normal evening performance, surprised the audience of three thousand with a demonstration of a colour version. Shown on

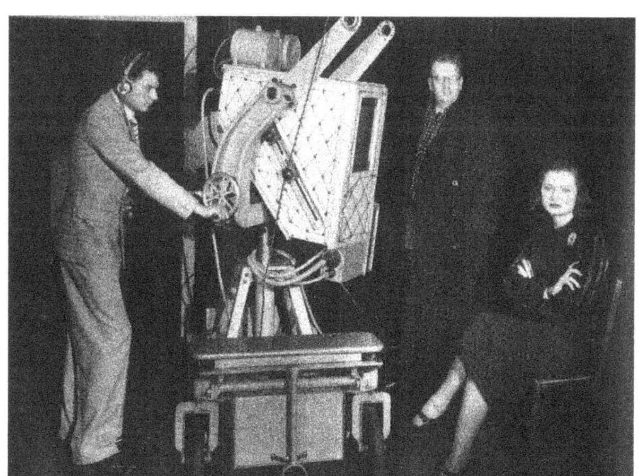

Baird (centre) with his 'mechanical' colour TV camera, for a big-screen show at The Dominion. Both camera and projector had a mirror-drum spinning at 6000rpm. The seated lady came from RADA as a model.

an even larger 12 foot by 9 screen, it was achieved' by simply adding a rotating, Kinemacolor-style, red and blue/green filter to both the mirror drum camera and projector.

Again, making news, this time perhaps fearing that improving TV might become a menace, the specialist cinema press was more critical. The colour image was said to be less bright than the earlier black and white show, with colour fringes and noticeable flicker due to the two-colour repetition rate being halved to only 8.33 per second. Trying to ignore TV's unique appeal of live pictures, it was suggested that projected colour TV would need a lot more work before it could match colour film, particularly the new 3-colour Technicolor prints beginning to appear on British cinema screens. As we know, it did take a long time, and it would be another 70 years or so, before, except on special occasions, electronic digital pictures would oust film from the screen.

Television's first switchover

Back to small screen developments. To avoid controversy, both the Marconi-EMI and Baird companies had been selected to join in at the start of the new television service. The committee had given the BBC eighteen months to prepare for the start of high definition transmissions, which would begin with a six month trial period when each system would be used during alternate weeks, after which a final choice would be made. Not long after the announcement, the BBC closed down its 30-line service, with the last of its over 1500 programmes going out in September 1935. Although only experimental, its loss would still mean that thousands of disappointed viewers would be stuck with useless Televisors. With no hope of converting them to higher definition, most ended up in cupboards or lofts, destined for destruction, with others taken apart by their constructors to use the bits for other projects. As a result, few have survived, becoming, like the cinema's own Kinetoscope, icons from television's early history and now sought after by both private collectors and museums.

Back from the dead

Some of this equipment has been brought back to life using today's imaging technology to help build a relatively simple 30-line Nipkow disc camera. A group of early TV enthusiasts formed the Narrow Band Television Association to exchange information and encourage its members to construct replica, or modern versions of the original equipment needed to produce and display the pictures. In keeping with their low-technology philosophy many transmitted them through the post, recorded on audio cassettes. Actual 30-line images from the days of mechanical TV have been recovered from Baird Phonovision 78 rpm discs and other home recorded pictures made by viewers at the time. Another find was a vision-only gramophone record of still 30-line pictures, made for Selfridges to give away to their customers who had bought Televisors so that they could try them out outside broadcasting hours. Examples of these restorations can currently be seen at the other end of the technology scale, on the Internet.

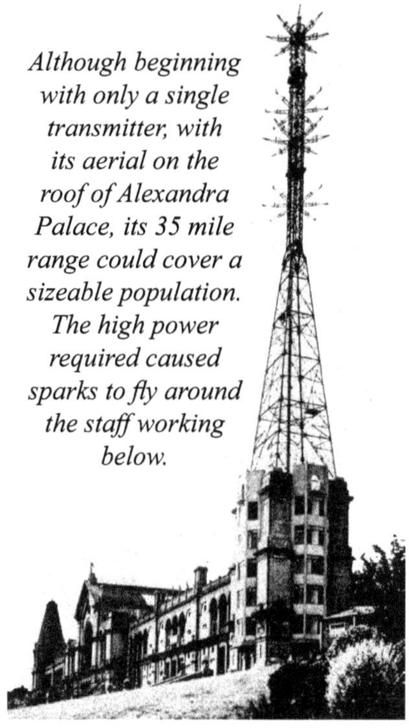

Although beginning with only a single transmitter, with its aerial on the roof of Alexandra Palace, its 35 mile range could cover a sizeable population. The high power required caused sparks to fly around the staff working below.

Getting it up and running

At the beginning of 1936, both companies began to install their equipment, including their own vision transmitters, at television's new home at Alexandra Palace, an ageing Victorian entertainment centre, high up in North London. The BBC had prepared the way by providing the shared sound transmitter and aerial mast on the roof, and its range of 35 miles covered a quarter of the population. Each system was provided with its own studio. Baird's would resemble those used to produce the first 'talkies', with its intermediate film camera firmly fixed in a sound deadening booth. It was able to pan through its bay window to cover three different sets and had the benefit of a turret with four lenses to change the angle of view. Unfortunately, without another camera to cut to, the viewer had to put up with the disruption to the image as it was being rotated.

Next door in the EMI studio, all was far more flexible. Their setup would become the pattern for all future TV studios, giving the viewer a smooth flow of well lit pictures captured from various angles by switching between a number of cameras. Although the Emitron only had a single fixed lens, it could be mounted on a film studio-type wheeled 'dolly' which could move around the floor to follow the action.

First looking at you

Both companies managed to get it all going by August, in time for the BBC to transmit demonstration programmes to RadiOlympia, the radio manufacturers' annual exhibition. The draw of seeing TV resulted in a record-breaking attendance of 100,000 visitors who filed past a display of newly developed cathode-ray sets to watch a mix of newsreels, feature film excerpts and hastily put together live programmes. These included the BBC's first big hit "Here's Looking at You", complete with a catchy song. For many, their brief look still had

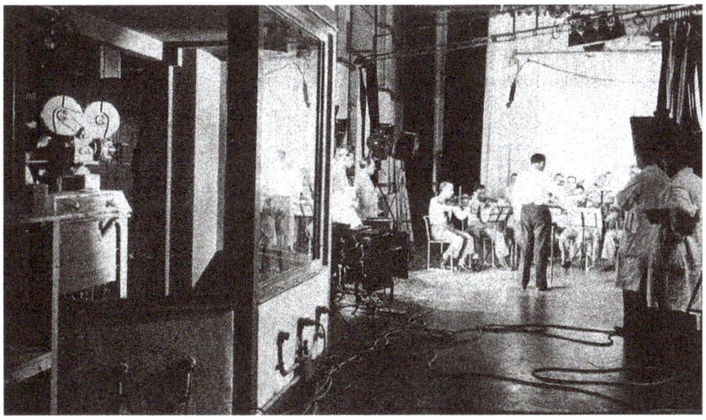

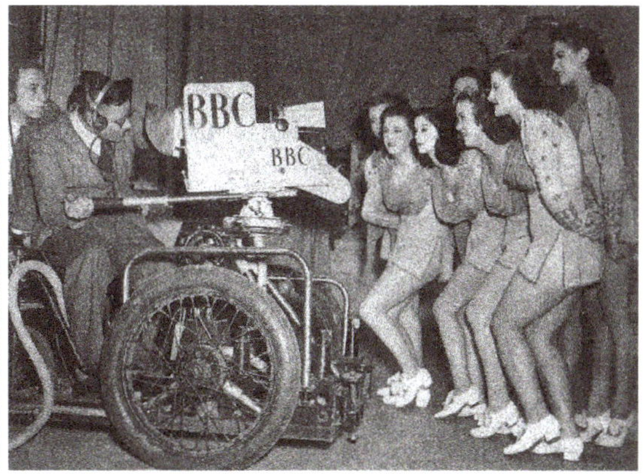

Baird's studio (left) resembled one from the early 'talkies', with its static intermediate film camera on top of its processor and scanner, confined to a sound-deadening booth. Next door, EMI's Emitron electronic cameras were more mobile, this one mounted on a 'dolly' made from an Austin Seven car chassis.

more novelty than entertainment value, and the showing of films wasn't considered to be real TV. Long-shots in particular, spectacular on a cinema screen, were turned to a confused fog when reduced to TV's smaller version. The Baird and EMI systems were used on alternate days, but near the end of the show, only EMI could present the first outside broadcast. A camera, at the end of its cable, on the steps of Alexandra Palace, treated lookers-in to the sight and sound of personalities saying goodbye before getting into their cars and setting off down the hill.

A camera was sometimes left outside on the studio's balcony to take in the view over London and watch the trains go by during the interludes between programmes. It would soon venture further at the end of a 1000 foot cable to present shows from the park. In less than a year the camera would shed its umbilical cord and take to the road in the BBC's first OB (Outside Broadcast) van, or 'scanner', using a radio link back to the studio to transmit live coverage of sporting and other special events. These would become one of TV's greatest attractions.

But whatever the first reaction was to seeing these early programmes, the receivers on offer, priced at between 100 and 150 guineas, the same as a car, were well out of reach for most aspiring viewers.

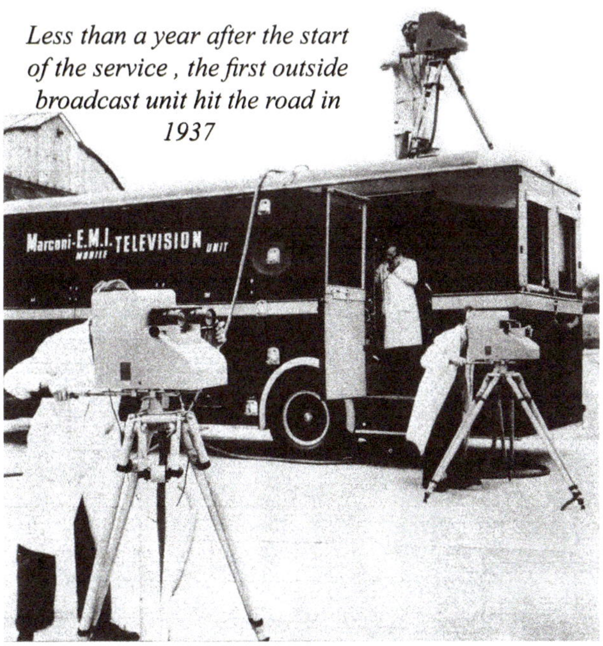

Less than a year after the start of the service , the first outside broadcast unit hit the road in 1937

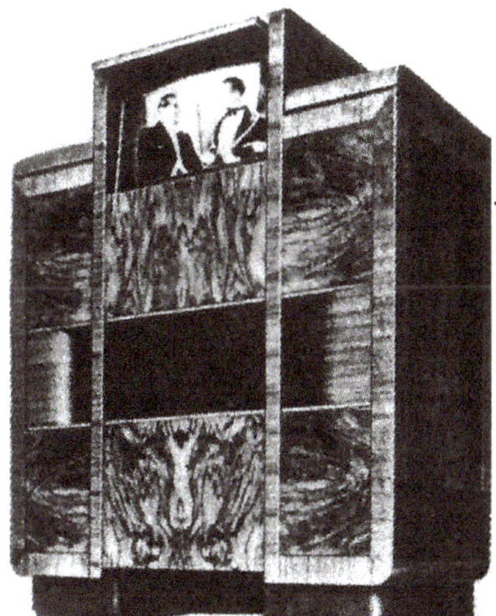

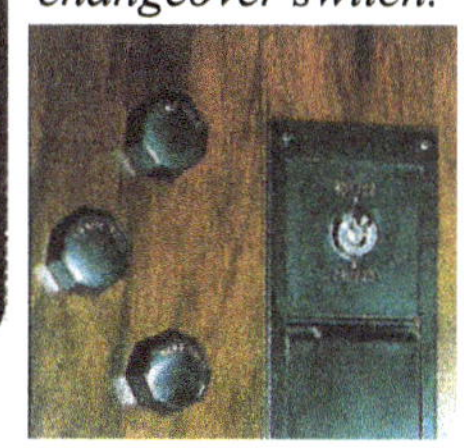

Early TV sets were very expensive, with small screens and large cabinets. The first models also had to be dual-standard, the controls including a 240/405 line changeover switch.

Vision on, Sound on

Shortly after, on the 2nd November 1936, Britain, or more accurately just London and the South East, beat the rest of the world with, as we would define, the first proper regular high definition public television service received by viewers on commercially-available sets in their own homes. Only an estimated 400 sets were switched on by their well-to-do viewers to watch the opening programmes for two hours a day, except Sundays of course. Remembering to flick the switch at the start of each week, the 405 and 240 line pictures looked much the same on their small, no bigger than 15-inch, screens.

Although both systems operated at 25 pictures per second, well below the threshold needed to prevent flicker, only Baird's progressively scanned pictures appeared to flicker. EMI's electronic scanning system was able to make use of RCA's idea (patented in 1933) of interlacing first the odd and then the even numbered lines during two separate sweeps of the screen, which doubled the effective viewing frequency up to a now flickerless 50.

Both systems would occasionally suffer their own particular faults. In EMI's studio, they had early trouble trying to keep the tonal range of their Emitrons constant and their sometimes bent pictures tumbled when switching between cameras.
Before this was fixed, the new role of 'Vision Mixer' had to gently fade them in and out, with each cut taking about eight seconds. Despite its fewer lines, Baird's best pictures, remaining square and stable, came from their spinning disc telecine. These were considered far superior to EMI's reproduction of film, which, at the beginning, relied on Emitron cameras looking at the gates of a pair of conventional 35mm projectors set to run at 25 fps. Apart from missing lines, due to dust getting into the Nipkow disc's holes, the spotlight studio's live pictures flickered more than those from the intermediate film's scanner, which, despite its smaller frames, could also produce quite good images.

Practical problems...

Unfortunately, the film's perforations often dragged down air bubbles into the scanner. Done through an optical glass window while the film was still underwater, these could cause its image to balloon, and add the sound of gurgling bath water to the track. Much like a frustrated film projectionist trying to get rid of a hair in the gate, all the cameraman could do was to give the machine a good kicking in the hope of dislodging the problem, if only in time for the next bubble to arrive. To save broken toes, a useful accessory was a cricket bat to give it a good beating. Perhaps not a wise move as it could fight back, with its discs spinning at 6000 rpm, 10,000 volts, and not forgetting the cyanide, which, if it leaked out, could turn the booth into a gas chamber!
It was never stated if the cyanide washed off the film was actually flushed down the drain; if so, it would have helped to keep the sewer rats below AP under control. Retreating to the canteen, situated under the high power signal leaving the aerial, may not have been much safer, judging by the sparks which, sometimes jumped between the knives and forks.

Early defeat

It soon became obvious that EMI's 405-1ine all-electronic system was superior technically and the most flexible for actual production. Even with the chance of tripping over their trailing cables, early TV performers much preferred appearing in front of the mobile Emitron cameras, which could follow the action. They came to dread working during Baird's alternate weeks, having to act to a fixed point. Shut up in the darkened spotlight studio, subject to its flickering gaze, announcers, still with white face and blue lips makeup, had to try and accommodate the late arrival of the pictures from the intermediate film camera. Its 1000 foot magazine of 17.5mm film only lasted 20 minutes, limiting the length of programmes. If quick, its built-in delay did give the chance for artists to find a monitor and watch the end of their act going out. Its magazine would run out of film for the last time when the 240-line system, always regarded as a waste of time by the BBC, was abandoned, ending after a variety show on the 13 February 1937. They would now continue using only the 405-line system, which would become the standard for British TV.

What remains of Baird's gallant effort?

The many thousands of feet of film running through the IF camera should have left us with a unique record of early TV programmes. Sadly not, apart from a few clippings, since to save costs all the exposed 17.5mm film was sent back to Kodak to be recycled, the images lost to recover the silver. If kept, it could have become a recording system to allow for repeats and to start an archive. This possible advantage didn't overcome the view then that the intermediate film method's 54 seconds delay wasn't true instant TV. It's interesting that few of today's viewer worry that their digital TV has returned to being no longer live, although its own intermediate compression coding and decoding processing only keeps us waiting for a couple of seconds.

Back to the analogue Alexandra Palace

With the rejection of the 240 line system, its hardware was also discarded, with no heritage group to rescue it. Events at another palace would also reduce the chance of finding original equipment. In 1933 the Baird company had relocated its operations, including workshops, studio and experimental transmitter to space at the Crystal Palace, only to see it all destroyed when the famous glass edifice burnt down in 1936.
Back before video tape recording, with its instant playback, rapid film processing straight after leaving a cine camera found other applications. It was used for timing and helped judges to settle appeals and objections without delay at sporting events, including from the patrol cameras at horse racing tracks. As we shall see next, the intermediate film process was also tried out to provide big screen cinema presentations of 'live' TV relays of special events.

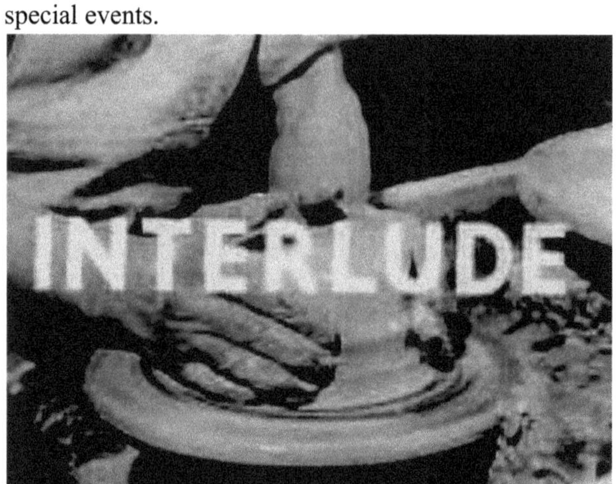

In these days of constant 24 hour TV on thousands of channels its hard to remember that many hours of TV transmission time in the early days were devoted to 'Interludes' like this one of the Potters Wheel.

More on cinema's early encounters with TV

Scanning systems

Back in 1937, the decision that Britain's new television service would continue using only the all-electronic 405-line system didn't immediately kill off the idea of mechanical scanning which was still thought by many to be the best for the reproduction of film and projection. Designs for new telecines would appear with their ever faster Nipkow-type discs, now spinning within a glass vacuum to prevent air turbulence and dust getting-into their tiny holes. Mirror drums also continued to revolve, but these too needed to be speeded up to cope with higher definition pictures.

A small company, Scophony, who specialised in projection TV, kept up by using a pair of drums, a relatively slow one for the vertical scanning and a small two-inch lightweight 20-sided polished steel polygon, spinning at 30,000 rpm, for the horizontal. To modulate the brightness of the spot of light coming from the projector's lamp, a new 'supersonic' light valve was developed. The video signal was made to send pressure waves along a column of constantly modulated fluid, using the resulting interference pattern to control the light. It was far more efficient than the original Kerr cell, being able to project more picture information at once. The system was first seen at the 1936 Radio Show, either incorporated into rear projection TV sets, which offered a bigger picture than rival cathode ray tube TVs, or an early form of home cinema projector paired with an even larger silver screen unit with a built-in speaker. Although few domestic models were ever sold, a more powerful professional version, using almost identical technology, was successfully used to show live sporting events in West-End cinemas.

Frightened by new technology

In more recent years, miniature rotating and reciprocating mirrors, again working inside a vacuum, returned as a way to scan laser beams. In the1990s it was predicted that these would soon be offering the ultimate in cinema projection. However, we are still waiting. Apparently, although lasers are already being incorporated into projector light sources, turned into normal white light before leaving the lens, actually shooting a high power sharply focused scanning laser into the auditorium has been held back due to health and safety concerns. Not knowing the specific dangers, this conjures up thoughts of death rays passing over the heads of the audience on their way to set fire to the screen! Of course, safely bouncing ordinary light off moving mirrors is already happening in many of today's projection rooms. Now reduced to a microscopic scale, they are busy twitching away on the image-forming chips found at the heart of DLP digital projectors.

Returning to the pre-digital days of the 1930s, our hero of mechanical television, John Logie Baird, disappointed at the rejection of his 240-line system, moved on to continue his work on projected and colour TV. He would abandon his earlier mirror drum big screen cinema projector to join the all-electronic route and adopt a method also being chosen for projection TVs. For this, a small cathode-ray tube, typically between 2 and 7 inches in diameter, was driven at a much higher voltage to produce an intensely bright image on its face which, if combined with a large wide aperture F1.5 lens and high gain silver screen, could provide an adequately bright picture, at least for smaller cinemas.

The Baird company developed their own 'teapot' projection CRT operating at 40kV compared to the 5kV used to drive the average direct vision home TV tube. The bigger frame size of a cinema TV projector meant that their wide aperture lenses were also large and heavy,

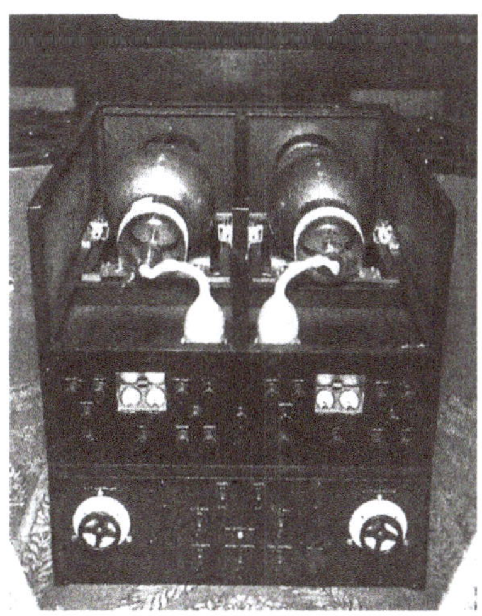

Baird TV projector with its 'teapot' tubes. High-voltage over-run tubes had a short life so everything was duplicated in case one died during an unrepeatable live show. Using both at once would have offered the opportunity to experiment with two-colour red and blue/green video projection.

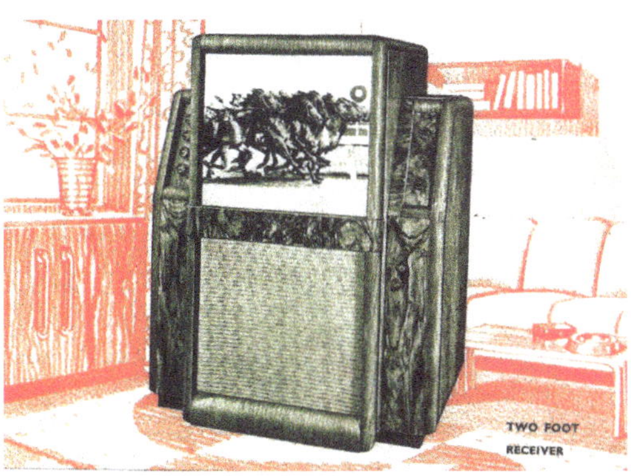

Home cinema in 1938. Scophony used high speed rotating mirror drums to project the pictures, either in rear-projection TVs or using stand-alone projectors with a separate screen unit

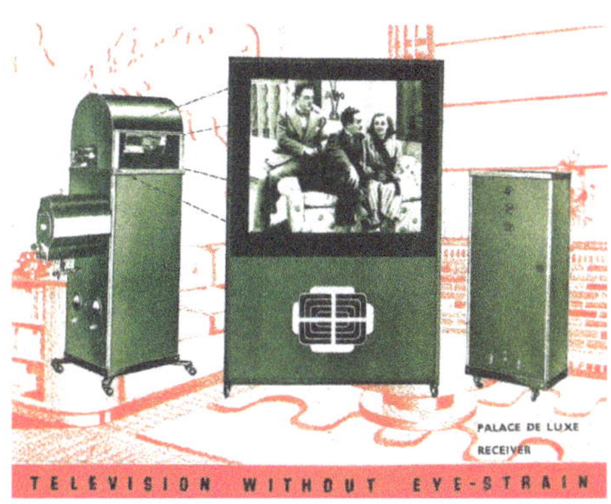

with a 'normal' 12 inch being around 9 inches in diameter. The growing physical size of longer focal lengths would restrict them to shorter throws.

There was an alternative 'faster' optical layout known as the Schmidt system. Instead of the face of the tube, with its bright image, facing the lens, it looked back into a larger diameter concave mirror which reflected it back through an additional distortion correcting lens element onto the screen. This arrangement gave the same light efficiency as using an unachievable F0.7 conventional lens.

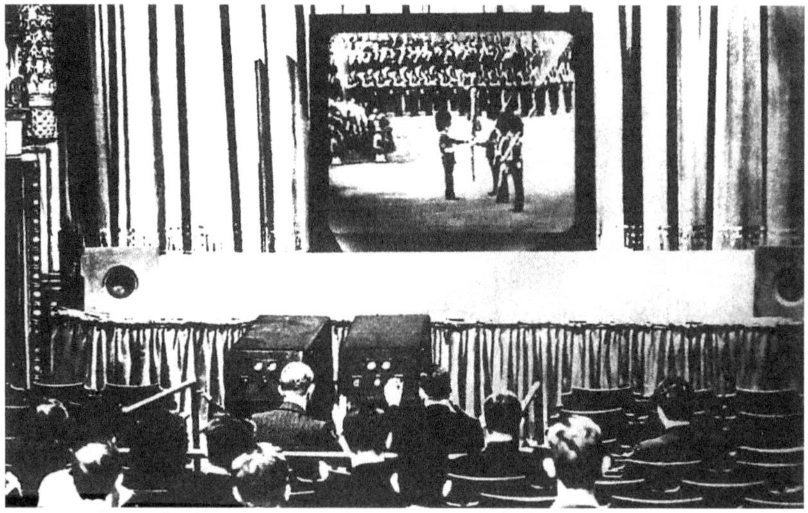

A pair of Baird tube projectors (in case one failed) presenting a show at the Tatler cinema in 1938.

This system too required a short throw, having to be installed closer to the screen, either at the front of the circle or in the stalls. These were not popular locations, having to lose seats,

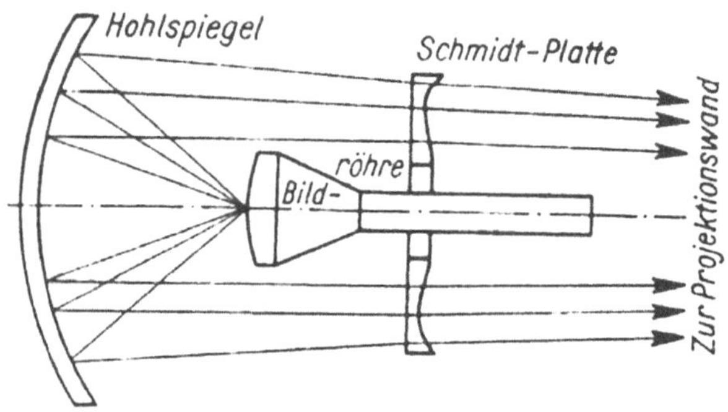

A diagram of the Schmidt optical system using a high intensity tube facing back into a large concave mirror

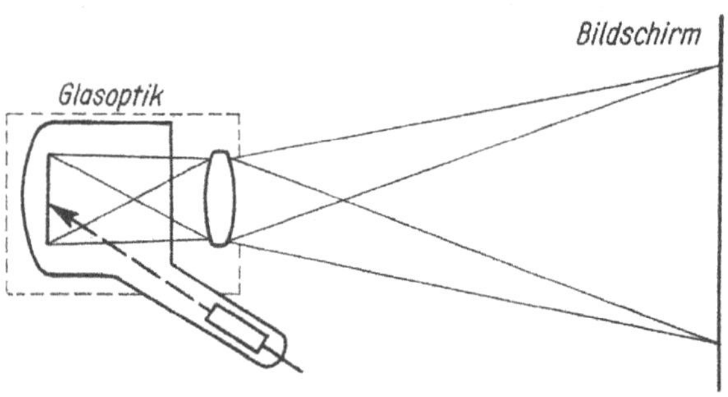

Another type of projection tube produced an even brighter image on a metal plate inside the cathode ray tube

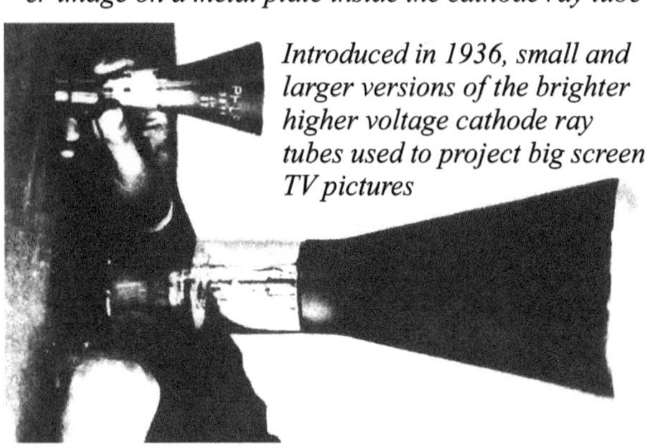

Introduced in 1936, small and larger versions of the brighter higher voltage cathode ray tubes used to project big screen TV pictures

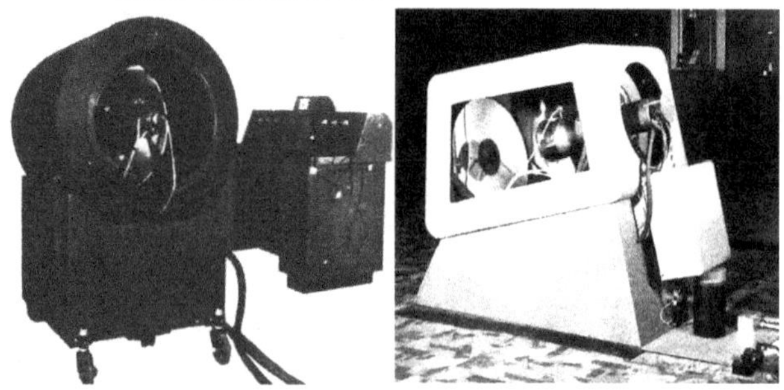

Early Schmidt-type RCA and Cintel tube projectors employing 30 and 27 inch mirrors respectively. Both angled to look up at the screen from the stalls.

not only to make room for the projector, but also to keep the audience well away from its high voltages. If space allowed, a safer position was on the stage behind a rear projection screen.

Later, a new home would be found for them, hanging from the ceiling. Hiding the projection gear within the auditorium is becoming a new challenge for those designing the layout for 'boothless cinemas'.

Let me in

After all these big screen developments, would TV's electronic pictures be welcomed into cinemas? Early on, much of the industry was beginning to see TV as a threat and future competitor. A couple of studios were slightly less hostile. Gaumont British was allowing the BBC to transmit its newsreel, and Disney, completing its switch to all-colour production, was happy-to provide its earlier B&W cartoons, now considered to be of lesser value for showing in cinemas.

Back at Alexandra Palace, the technicians running them were known as 'Film Assistants' and this title would become the official name for BBC projectionists right up to the 1990s, when, like film itself, they were phased out.

Flirting with the enemy

Gaumont British would continue to be the most interested in exploiting TV. The Tatler, their news theatre in Charing Cross Road, was kitted out with Baird tube-type projectors to see if this new form of alternative programming would attract an audience. With few sets in people's homes, the shows proved very popular, relaying the BBC's coverage of state occasions and sporting events. The greatest draw was live boxing, when every available Baird and Scophony projector filled the screens at other West End cinemas to help satisfy the demand for tickets. Suddenly, all this came to an end when the BBC withheld its permission to show its programmes. This was probably in retaliation to the cinema industry's growing boycott, which would keep most mainstream English language films off the small screen for at least the next 20 years.

Going it alone

Gaumont British responded by planning to introduce its own TV service, using a transmitter and aerial at Crystal Palace to send its signals directly to cinemas. They formed another company, Cinema Television Ltd, to produce the programmes and manufacture the projectors which would be installed in 70 of its Greater London cinemas. The shows couldn't be 'pirated' by viewers at home as they would use a different higher line standard. It was suggested that around 800 lines would be needed to match the quality of a typical 35mm print of the time. Unfortunately, this too all came to nothing as the company was refused a broadcasting licence. They did go on to build equipment for use at the interface between film and television. This included 'Cintel' video projectors and, most notable, their flying spot telecines, which would soon be at the BBC, greatly improving their often criticised reproduction of 35mm film. These also helped to put an end to any thoughts of returning to mechanical scanning. Now the flying spot of light came from a small CRT displaying a bright white blank screen which was projected through the moving film onto a photo-cell. In fact, twin lenses, closely following each other, allowed the frames of the continuously moving film to be scanned twice, first with the odd and then the even lines of the interlaced picture.

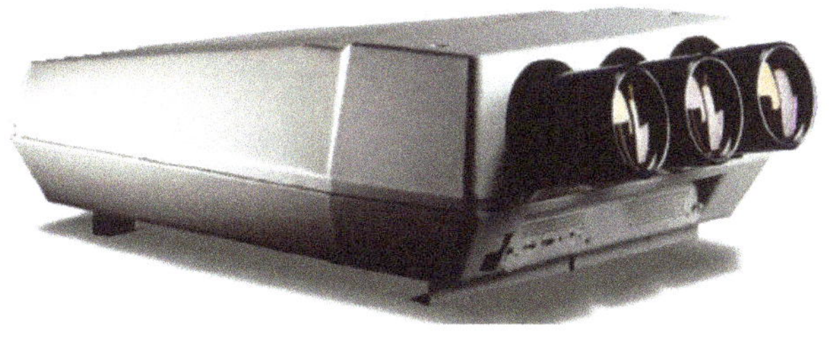

Video projectors, many designed to be unobtrusive, may be forgotten altogether when it comes to saving examples of cinema heritage

Tube-type video projectors, both stand-alone and built into rear projection TVs, became the most common until the switch to LCD, SXRD, DLP and other forms of digital projectors. Back in the pixel-free analogue days, these too were capable of producing high definition pictures. Given a suitable source, they were limited only by the size of the particles used in the tube's fluorescent coating. When colour arrived, they effectively became three projectors in one, now with the tubes producing the red, green and blue images. These were either superimposed on the screen coming from three separate lenses, or optically combined before leaving a single lens. To aid registration, they usually shared much of the same circuitry.

Video projectors, harder to love

For many of us with an interest in preserving the technical history of the cinema, these earlier video, and even today's digital projectors, don't seem to evoke the same fascination as old film equipment. Despite the undoubted magic going on inside, they always tended to end up looking like just a box with a lens, or lenses, poking out. This made them less attractive to collectors and as exhibits in museums. Even so, for one, the Cinema Museum in Kennington, South London, has given a new home to one discarded unloved three-eyed monster, although lack of space means it is currently used in the cafe to put things on. Left to last and top of the bill, were a couple of big screen video projection techniques which did have a better chance of capturing the imagination.

Where's the oil can?

Film projectors need to be kept well-oiled to keep them running smoothly, but there was a video projector which

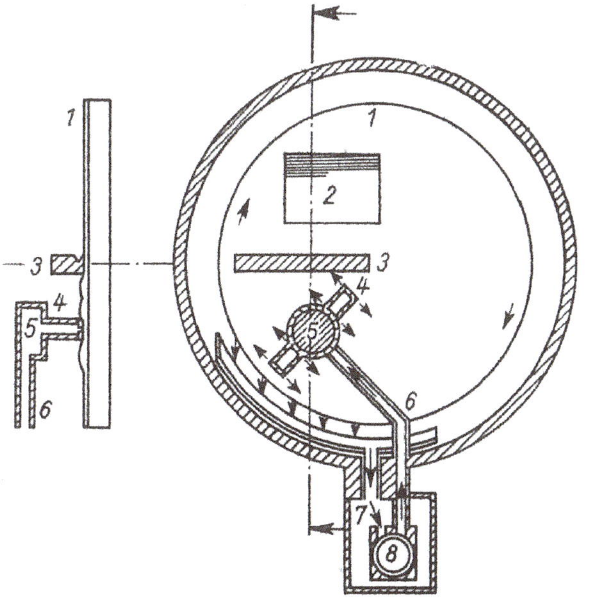

The system used by the Eidophor projector to continuously create a thin film of oil on its mirror, which was spun to help to spread it out and keep an even coating. The modulated picture area occupied only a small portion of the mirror.

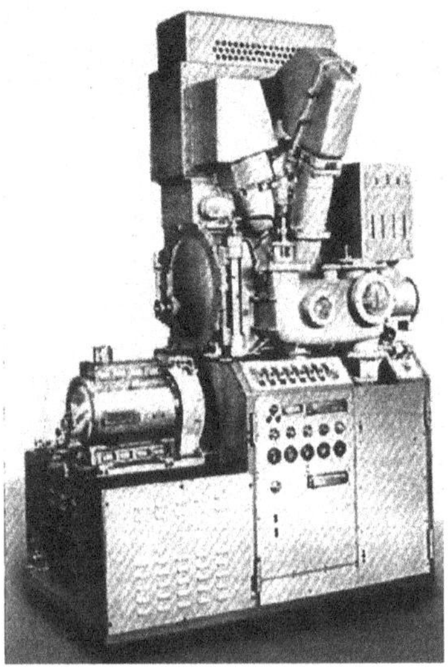

Top left:
The first Eidophor projector from 1943, using a carbon arc lamp.

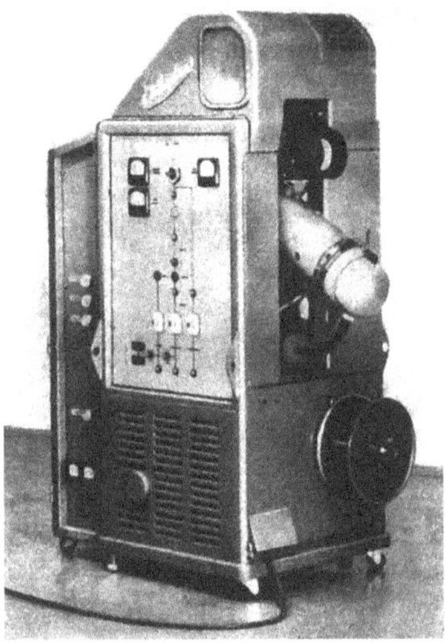

Below left: Later version using a xenon - for 'the projectionist of tomorrow'. Although occasionally used in cinemas and other large venues, the Eidophor was notable for being chosen to fill the big screens behind closed doors of military war rooms, and, more openly, at NASA's space mission control centres during the 1960s and 1970s.

actually used the oil to help create the picture. It was the Eidophor, first demonstrated in 1939. A powerful arc lamp illuminated a concave mirror inside a special cathode ray tube which was kept coated with a thin film of oil. After bouncing off the mirror through the oil, the light was interrupted by a second semi-silvered mirror made in the form of a fine grid. With no signal present, the optical system was aligned not to allow any light to escape through the gaps. However, when the scanning cathode ray caused deformations in the oil, some of the light was diffracted and was able to pass through the grid to the projector's lens and onto the screen. Along with its brighter images, another advantage for cinema use was that it could be used with longer throws so could be installed safely back in the normal projection room.

Eidophor tales

On a personal note. When, back in the good old real film days, the author was working as a projectionist (Film Assistant) in the dubbing and preview theatres at the BBC Television Centre, a short cut to the studios tea bars, a chance to mix with TV stars and dancing girls, took you past the Scenic Projection Department's equipment cage. Often seen parked next to their normal 35mm Mitchell BP machines was the BBC's own Eidophor, used when electronic back projected images were

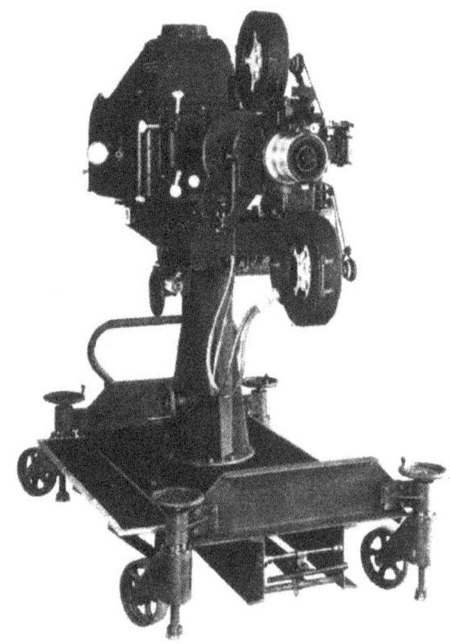

Unfamiliar to most cinema projectionists was the studio Mitchell BP projector. It was a quiet-running 35mm full-frame (silent) machine with a camera-type claw and register-pin intermittent, for maximum steadiness. Its carbon arc lamp usually employed condensing lenses instead of a mirror in order to help to avoid a hot spot on the translucent back-projection screen.

required. Back beside my own projector, I was sometimes caught looking at the BBC' s wonderful 'Technical Stores Catalogue'. Listed among: the cleaning and lubricating fluids (most now banned), was 'Eidophor Oil'. Before I learned about its inner secrets, I often wondered why an electronic video projector also had to be topped up with oil. In later years, I was reacquainted with an Eidophor (possibly the same one) when it became an exhibit at the top of the stairs leading to the cinema within the BFI's long gone MOMI (now NFT3). It never seemed to have a description, so perhaps nobody at the museum knew what it was. I hope it escaped the skip, and is now resting in a museum's warehouse somewhere, not forgetting a can of life blood oil in case it is ever brought back to life.

Film lends a hand

Digital cinema has made it easier to show alternative content using the same projector. However, there was an earlier method which allowed the theatre's existing 35mm film projector to show video pictures. Enter the return of the intermediate film process. This time, the programme material was displayed on a TV monitor, usually with the tones of the image electronically reversed to produce a 'negative'. This was printed onto film by photographing it directly off the screen by a film camera (including a combined optical sound track) and then immediately feeding the exposed film into a

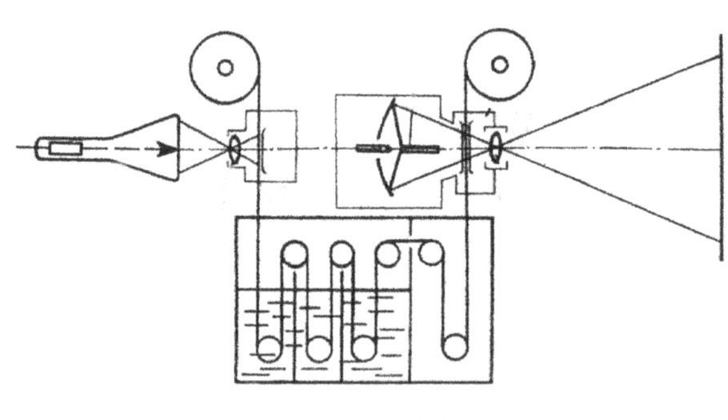

An application of the intermediate film system to turn video into film for large screen projection.

processor where it was rapidly developed and fixed to provide the positive print which, when dry, passed to the normal 35mm projector, reaching the screen in less than a minute after the event.

Although, seemingly to be the most impracticable, it was actually used on occasions when the largest and brightest pictures were required. An example was, in 1953, when such a system was installed at the Plaza in Piccadilly, with a view to using it to show live coverage of the coronation. Although there is no evidence that it was actually used on the big day, the public did have the chance to see it demonstrated during the premiere of 'The Story of Gilbert and Sullivan', when the already seated audience could watch, on the big screen, the later arrival of its stars and VIPs relayed from a TV camera set up in the foyer. If quick, when taking their own seats, they were able to see themselves still coming up the stairs. (In this case 38 seconds earlier.) This would have given the game away that the pictures were not actually 'live'.

Not really live...

In today's digital world, there are now no truly live TV and video pictures. Apart from the digital compression delay of a couple of seconds or so, some programmes are deliberately held up for even longer.

Some live reality shows are slowed down long enough to give censors the chance to cut out any inappropriate behaviour. A recent example is the new feed from the Court of Appeal, which is delayed by 75 seconds to stop inadmissible evidence from reaching the outside world.

Big screen...small screen

We have seen how in the 1930s there were many attempts to put television's electronic pictures onto cinema screens to offer audiences a new form of alternative content. These were largely unsuccessful, but so was trying to get early television into people's own homes. Although the cinema's new small screen rival was drawing a crowd at radio shows and department stores, the first TV sets were well out of reach for most of the general public. Like today, you had to pay a high price to become an early adopter of new technology. The cheapest model was around £60, rising to £150 for one with a built-in wireless and gramophone. This may not seem much today, but in the mid-1930s this was the same as a car, and for £600 you could buy a nice three-bedroom semi in the London suburbs to put it in. Remember too, this was a time when the average wage of a British worker was £2.70 a week.

Make room for 'the box'

For the few who could afford one of the first TVs, they also gained a new piece of furniture. Before the days of printed circuits and microchips, the 12 or 15 inch picture tube had to share a large cabinet with other bulky hand-wired components, including up to 20 valves which took a minute or two to warm up before it all came to life. Some designs of cabinet reduced the depth by mounting the much longer tubes of the day vertically and viewing the picture via a mirror fitted inside a lift-up lid. A less publicised advantage was that if the early thinner glass tube should implode, any flying debris would pepper the ceiling and not the viewer. Even if it stayed intact, the tube's life was shortened by particles falling off its fluorescent screen onto the electron gun below.

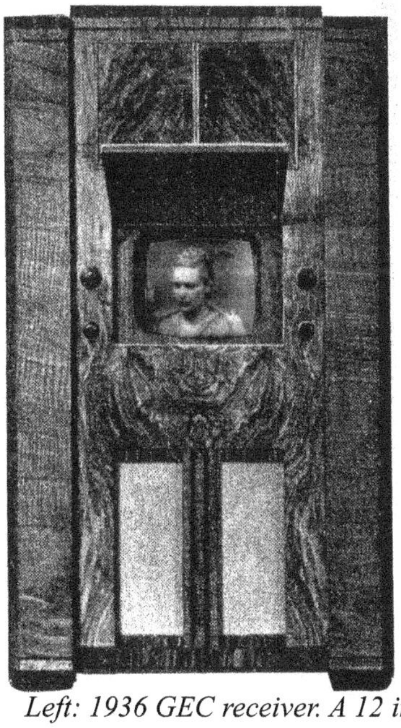

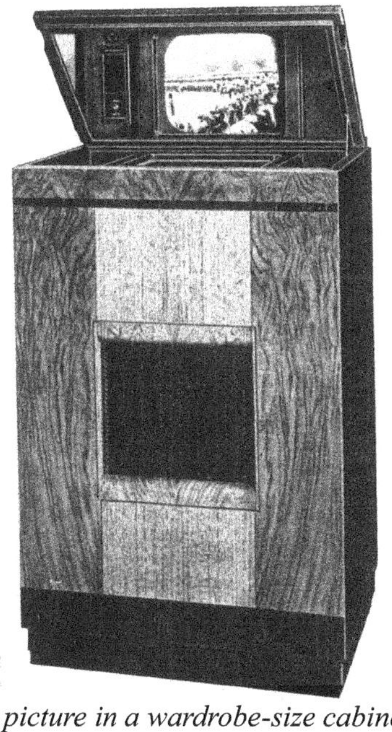

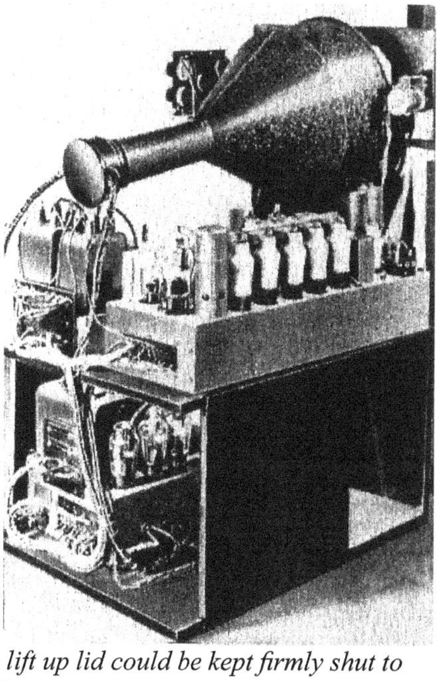

Left: 1936 GEC receiver. A 12 inch picture in a wardrobe-size cabinet. A lift up lid could be kept firmly shut to prevent your servants wasting time watching it. Centre: 1937 HMV TV with a vertical tube viewed via a mirror in its lid. Right: The innards of the 1937 HMV TV showing its long tube and its many valves - long before integrated circuits.

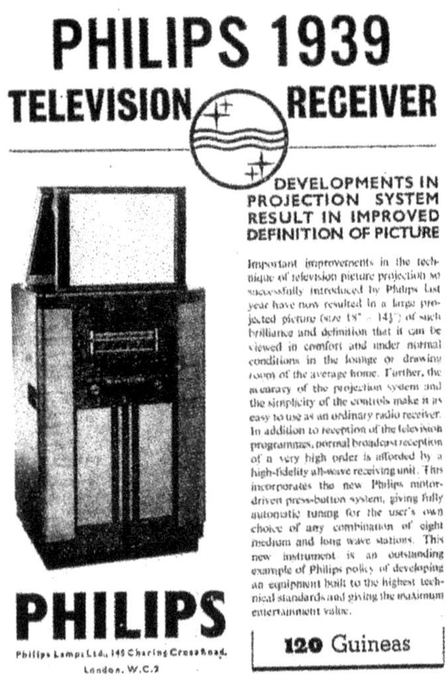

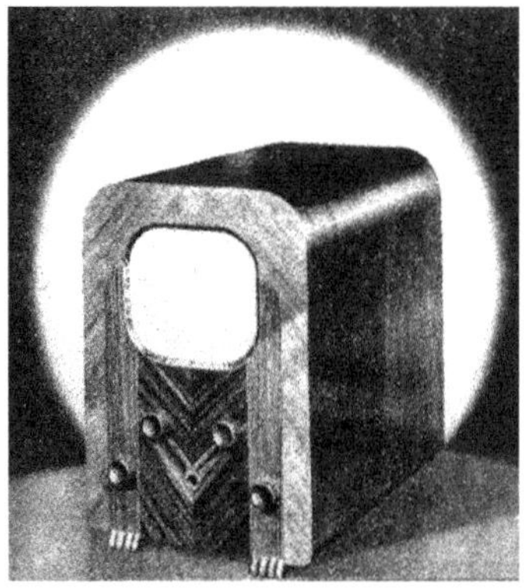

Left: This 1939 Philips projection set cost 120 guineas, almost a year's pay for some British workers in the 1930s. For the less well-off there was (above) this 5-inch vision-only model - the sound signal had to be fed to the owner's radio. (1938)

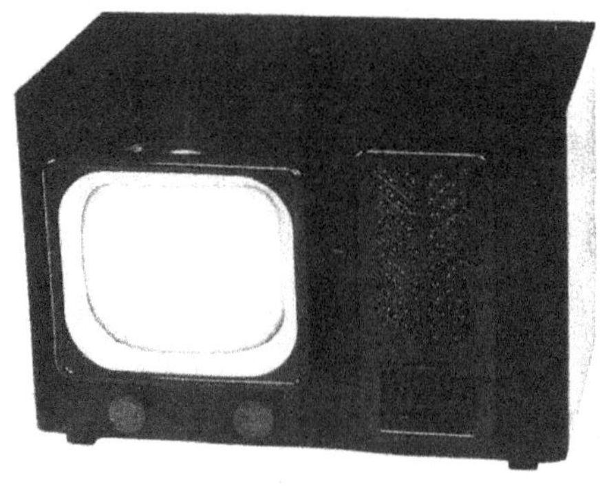

By the late 1940s more affordable models became available. Advances in electronics during WWII resulted in the choice of smaller less expensive TV sets like this Pye 9-inch table-top model in a plastic (Bakelite) cabinet (1948).

Cathode ray tubes, here to stay

It is interesting that many manufacturers of TVs thought that the CRT as a display device was just an interim measure. "We didn't really believe that this huge vacuum envelope, a cumbersome sort of thing, would last". As we now know, it did, taking another 70 years before a satisfactory alternative was found in the form of today's various types of flat panel displays. These are growing ever larger, helping to bring the cinema experience into the home. Although the bulk and weight of a glass CRT would limit screen sizes to around 30 inches, Baird in the 1930s actually enquired about the possibility of producing a steel version eight foot in diameter for use in Gaumont cinemas. Although long gone from dealers shelves, some stuck-in-the-past viewers are still happy watching their old CRT sets, believing that for standard definition at least, they produce the best looking image and motion compared with the often over processed and still somewhat directional LCD screens. Even some professionals are reluctantly saying goodbye to their CRT grade one monitors. Studio control rooms were among the last to welcome in their flat panel replacements.

Never mind the picture, hear the sound

Often forgotten is that television introduced the wider public to anything approaching 'Hi-Fi' sound. The large cabinets also provided the space for a decent size speaker, reproducing the sound coming from the same VHF transmitter needed to carry the wider-bandwidth picture. The sound benefited with a rise in its upper frequency, much higher than the optimistic 8 kHz of the existing medium-wave radios, records,and even the cinemas' optical tracks.

It took ten years to catch up when, in Britain, Decca launched its 'ffrr' (full frequency range recording) records and pick-up with a 14kHz top frequency. The BBC followed, in 1952, with its radio VHF FM service and shortly after, for some lucky cinemagoers, the arrival of magnetic soundtracks.

No threat yet to the cinema

By the end of 1937 only 1500 TVs had been sold, one for every 7000 people living within the 40 mile range of the BBC's single Alexandra Palace transmitter. To encourage sales, prices were cut and new lower-cost models introduced. Those waiting for bigger pictures would be disappointed as screens actually became smaller with 5, 7 or 9 inch diameter tubes in much cheaper wood or plastic (Bakelite) table-top size cabinets. Trying to build down to a price, it was said that designers were told to keep taking out 'unnecessary' less vital components until the set stopped working and then put the last one back in again.

Loudspeakers also shrank, degrading the sound, which would soon gain its reputation as being the picture's poor relation. Some sets had no sound at all, returning to the old Baird Televisor idea of having to be connected to an add-on radio or gramophone to hear the sound. History seems to have repeated itself, as today' manufacturers have all but given up trying' to get good sound out of their current no-cabinet flat panel TVs, suggesting seeking outside help now in the form of add-on home cinema sound systems, sound bars or bases to make the most of the sound.
Potential 1930s viewers could now buy a set for less than 30 pounds, However, the well-to-do, with up to 200 to spend could still own a luxury 'entertainment centre' model complete with a radiogram and drinks compartment, all built into a fine piano-finish floor standing cabinet. Like today's high priced communication tech, it could be 'locked', to prevent unauthorised use; in this case, a real lock and key to keep its lid and flaps firmly shut to stop the servants using it.

Television's poor take-up was also blamed on the BBC, who were accused of not taking TV seriously. Only transmitting for 2½ hours a day, the live sporting and other outside broadcasts of special events were well received, but less popular were the boring discussion programmes and dreary plays in between. Even these were once taken off the air when the service was closed down to allow the TV staff to go on holiday. When back at work, they were urged to be less 'middle class' and, like the cinema, provide more low-brow content for the masses. The BBC did respond with more light entertainment, creating its own TV stars and personalities. These, now appearing in more popular programmes, helped to attract new viewers and the sales of sets began to take off. By 1939, there were over 20,000 in people's homes, at last catching up with the number of, mostly home-built receivers operating at the end of the first 30-line mechanical era.

Forced to sit out the war

No sooner had it got going, television became the first casualty of WWII. Unlike the cinema, which had a good war, TV screens stayed blank, abruptly switched off halfway through a Disney cartoon, the government fearing that the transmitter might become a homing device for German bombers. On the other side, Germany's burgeoning TV service kept going, but now only to receivers in hospitals and barrack rooms, helping to keep up the morale of its troops. This too was killed off at the end of 1943 when its Berlin transmitter was destroyed by Allied bombing. However, another in occupied France, on top of the Eiffel Tower, continued to broadcast right up to the liberation in 1944. One avid viewer this side of the channel was a British intelligence officer, watching in a top secret shed on Beachy Head, with the most popular programme being the newsreel which sometimes unwittingly gave away the results of raids by the RAF.

War over, the small screen returns to its fight for viewers

Television re-opened in June 1946, when pre-war sets, switched off for 7 years, were tentatively warmed up again to be greeted with 'Mickey's Gala Premiere', the cartoon which was rudely interrupted back in 1939. No new TVs were ready, the manufacturers having been busy with their war work building military radio and radar equipment. When peace came, this would help some potential new viewers with little money but plenty of remaining 'make do and mend' spirit and a soldering iron, to also become set owners. Like the first TV enthusiasts you could again build your own at home. For only a few pounds, kits became available making use of government surplus components, including ex-radar CRTs, which, if you could get it all to work, gave a nice round green picture.

To put all this kit in, some dealers bought up empty cabinets left over from never-completed pre-war models. The idea of putting new stuff in old boxes has returned.

Old TVs catch the eye again

Like many of us giving, or fighting the temptation to give, a new home to historic old film gear, there is another happy band out there of old telly collectors. Also looking out for them, are museums, for their social history exhibits, production designers dressing period sets, and some have even returned to people's own retro-style living rooms. Although probably condemned by dedicated restorers, many are displaying a picture again by removing their original 'unsafe' innards, leaving a shell with enough space to fit in a modern small screen TV.

I regularly pass by one old B&W 405-line receiver in a local retro shop's window which has been brought back to life, now in 'living colour'. I remember that when the BFI's Museum of the Moving Image was still up and running, they had a display of vintage TVs, showing contemporary programmes, helping to illustrate their influence on the cinema (the coming of CinemaScope etc.). Unfortunately, they soon had to put protective Perspex screens in front of them because 'over enthusiastic' restorers were walking off with the control knobs.

Talked about but not seen

Among the early post-war BBC output was the first regular film programme. 'Film History' began in. 1947 and was introduced by historian and author Roger Manvell, who would later become the first director of the British Film Academy, now BAFTA, having embraced the even newer art of television.

Unfortunately, his efforts to encourage an appreciation of the cinema weren't being reciprocated, as the ban on the showing of newsreels and feature films continued. The filming of the BBC's own newsreel became the first job for its newly created Film Unit, but it would have to rely on foreign films to help fill the gaps between its live programmes. Just before the wartime close down, in 1939, the BBC had managed to show a small number of features, including Michael Powell's *Edge of the World*, but after the war the other 'war' with the cinema industry intensified.

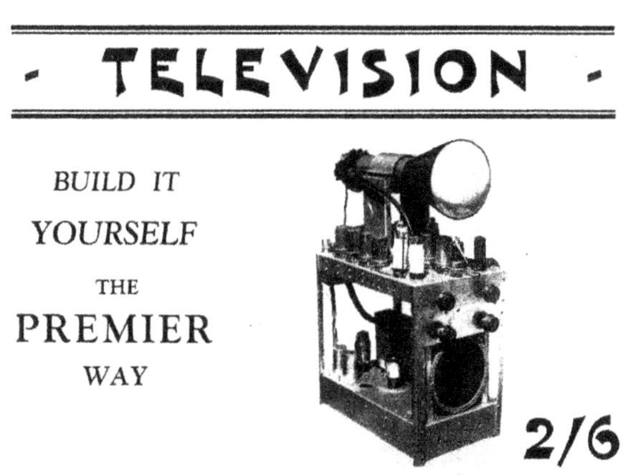

Cheaper than buying a set was to build your own. Cover of the guide booklet available for such a construction project.

Apart from sneaking *Renfrew of the Mounties* and a few of Tex Ritter's B-westerns onto the small screen, the 1940s and 50s would become great viewing for world cinema fans. Silent classics were also revived. In 1947, *The Birth of the Nation* was screened, complete with a live commentary by Roger Manvell and the original score coming from musicians in the studio playing along with the telecine, which was said to be running at the 'correct speed'.

The tide of war changes

By the mid-1950s cracks began to appear in the boycott. Still looking after the interests of its members today is the Cinema Exhibitors' Association, (although renamed to become the UK Cinema Association) which was originally formed to help keep films off television. Soon in trouble with the CEA was producer Michael Balcon, condemned for selling out to the enemy when, in 1955, he sold both his Ealing Studios and back catalogue of early films to the BBC. The corporation added another hundred to their collection when they also bought the British TV rights to most of the RKO library, which included the Astaire/Rogers musicals and King Kong. When the RKO studio closed down, it fell into hands outside the cinema industry, who were happy to make money from its old films, which were rarely, if ever, shown again in theatres.

When ITV started in 1955, the BBC had a rival looking for films, Joining the fight to keep their hands off them was the Film Industry Defence Organisation (FIDO) who used a levy on cinema admissions to buy up films so they couldn't be sold to TV. This was aimed principally at the smaller independent producers tempted to unload their old B-features. One critic of the scheme resented the large sums of money being paid for 'downright awful' films, which TV wouldn't want anyway. Even so, by the end of 1959, FIDO had locked away almost 60 features. The major studios didn't see any of the cash, as they were expected to hold out for the good of the industry. For the good of some of the smaller British studios, they found work making the first filmed for TV series, like *The Adventures of Robin Hood* and *The Buccaneers*.

FIDO would occasionally bite. Producer Daniel Angel (*Reach for the Sky* and *Carve Her Name with Pride*) was blacklisted for a time for dealing with TV. The threat of 'you'll never work in this town again' didn't frighten veteran Hollywood independents David O. Selznick and Samuel Goldwyn who were among the first to break ranks and offer some of their films to TV. Most of the major Hollywood studios would become divisions of large corporations, who also wanted to make the most of their assets. They found a loophole which didn't break the promise to shun TV. This only applied to their own films, but apparently, there was no objection to selling other people's, so they began to buy each other's libraries. With the freedom to deal in 'acquired' films, Paramount's would move home to Universal, Warner's to United Artists and other collections would regularly change hands over the coming years.

New battles to fight

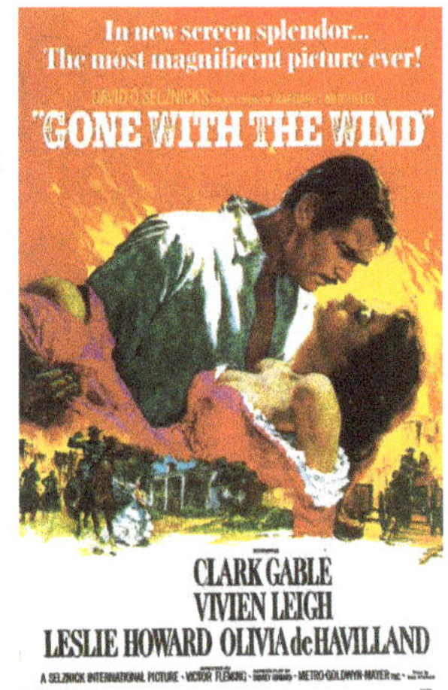

By the mid-1960s the war with TV was coming to an end. The initial flood of mostly pre-1948 films meant that the BBC and ITV could take their pick at reasonable prices, but soon a new bidding war broke out between them, when the more recent and the still making money held-back classics became available. During the crazy days of the late 1970s and 80s, literally millions would be paid for audience grabbing titles like *The Sound of Music* and *Gone With the Wind*, by the BBC, and *Jaws* and the Bond movies by ITV. They were usually kept ready to become the much anticipated 'Christmas film'. To get these blockbusters, like cinema bookings in the 1930s, they also had to take a block or package of other, sometimes less desirable titles. It was not unknown that some of these, at the end of the lease period, were returned without ever being shown, or being given a single last-minute airing, before disappearing back into the vaults. Fortunately for old films on TV fans, many of these did see the light of TV screens again with the arrival of Channel 4, which, in its early years, filled its afternoon and late night schedules with films rarely shown today. The BBC had its own library of oldies and its second channel was giving more opportunities to let them out for an airing.

This golden era for film buffs coincided with the availability of home video recorders. They could now build up their own library, either by buying the new pre-recorded tapes or by recording them off the TV. I knew one collector who used up 2,500 VHS cassettes recording films transmitted across all four channels. It wasn't all heaven, as many of the films had been cut to fit specific programme slots, a sin mostly perpetrated by ITV, and there was the added bother of having to be poised over the pause button ready to cut out the adverts. At a time when actual film prints were transmitted, it was hoped that the editor would reinstate the missing footage in time for the next showing, when you could try again.

Still more cuts

Of course, most TV viewers would prefer to watch new films, but the price of peace included an agreement that none of these would be shown until five years after their original release date. After paying big money for them, they had to stay on the shelf, hoping that their stars would still be as popular and any 'adult' scenes and bad language, would be more acceptable in living rooms. So as not to miss a sale, the studios could sometimes provide a 'sanitised' TV version, already cut, or with specially shot 'tamer' alternative scenes, more suitable for prime-time viewing, leaving the cinema original for late night showings.

Persecuting heroes

FIDO gave up the fight in 1965, but this didn't mean freedom for its films (not all awful) which would still be kept off TV screens for decades. With TV no longer in their sights, the cinema industry's defence organisations would take on other foes, including the tax-man and pirates. A less just war was waged by the KRS (Kinomatograph Renters' Society) who targeted private film collectors and their 35mm and 16mm prints. Some suffered the full force of the law, accused of being in possession of stolen goods.

One high profile defendant was the comic Bob Monkhouse. Among his multi-talents was film collecting, and he had accumulated literally shed loads of film prints and video tapes. Sadly, like other obsessive collectors, he didn't live long enough to be recognised as a hero of film and TV preservation, having saved many films and TV programmes, which their original producers had wiped or thrown into the furnace. At a BAFTA tribute event in March 2004, stars gathered to watch previously thought lost early performances which were also featured in a documentary telling the story of his collection. You can still find the video of this moving tribute evening on YouTube at *http://www.youtube.com/watch?v=qr0BewZu49Q*
Now less likely to be sued, collectors can still help in the search for lost films and TV programmes. But owning a catalogue of film titles, doesn't always mean it comes with a collection of good quality copies.

Clearing them

With the changing fortunes within the industry, the question of the ownership and rights to films can become quite complicated, with the theatrical, TV and video/DVD rights each controlled by different organisations. There are even squabbles over the prints and video copies of the so called 'orphan' copyright-free public domain films.

Worth a look

These have become the staple fare of the welcome 'terrible old films' channels (the same often applies to the picture quality too) which surface in the digital backwaters – but they are worth keeping an eye on, just in case a gem pops up. If not already disposed of, the cost cutting BBC still owns outright the TV rights to hundreds of old films, including those from their original RKO deal. These are the ones chosen first to fill the odd early morning slot. It was a pity that when the BBC chose to close

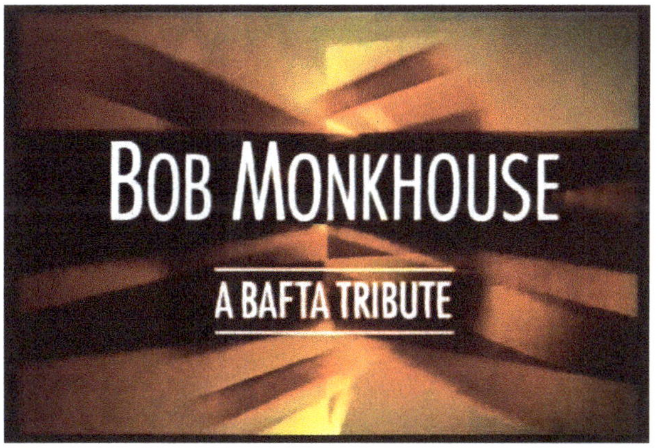

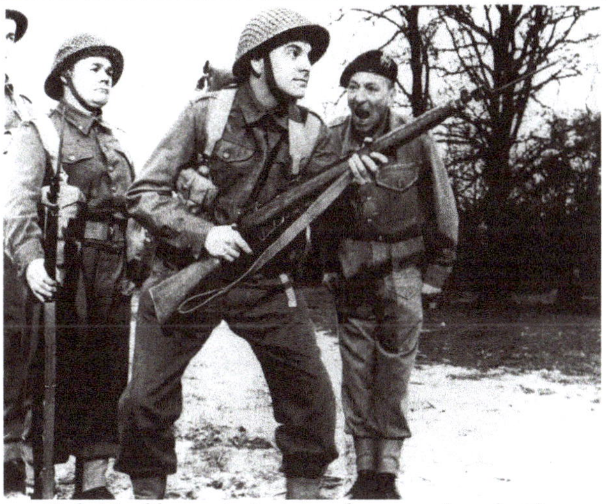

Bob Monkhouse in training for a previous battle - 'Carry on Sergeant'

down the BBC Three broadcast channel (it went internet only) they didn't make better use of this resource and launch a replacement, much cheaper, channel, dedicated to vintage movies. I'm sure this flight of fancy from an old film fan (both meanings) would be greeted with 'It's not as easy as that – it wouldn't attract a large enough audience – would risk the BBC's reputation for quality programming'. But I dreamed on and was delighted when the Talking Pictures TV channel was launched in 2015, a vintage film nostalgia channel which shows many older British films from classics to B-movies.

Back in shape

This look at the background history of television's first electronic pictures, the forerunner of today's digital cinema, provides a reminder that television also had to choose between aspect ratios, whilst being far more constrained than cinema about what was possible. It must be remembered that, at the time, cinemas were projecting a 1.37:1 picture, in practice onto a screen with the proportions of 4:3.
TV's choice would, in time, influence changes to cinema screens and these in turn have led to a new shape for today's TV. When, in 1936, EMI's 405-line system was selected for British TV, it came with a 5:4 (1.25:1) picture shape. This was chosen to just keep a landscape format whilst remaining nearer to a square, to make the most efficient use of the earlier circular faced tubes.

Below: 1940s TV with its masked off circular tube.
Centre: American Zenith TV from 1950. Its 2-in-1 screen offered the choice of two picture shapes, 'Giant Circle' or rectangular type at the touch of a switch.

Right: Classic Pye TV from the early 1950s. A pale colour screen surround, illuminated by stray light from the tube, was often chosen to make the picture look bigger. This idea has occasionally been given a try for cinema screens.

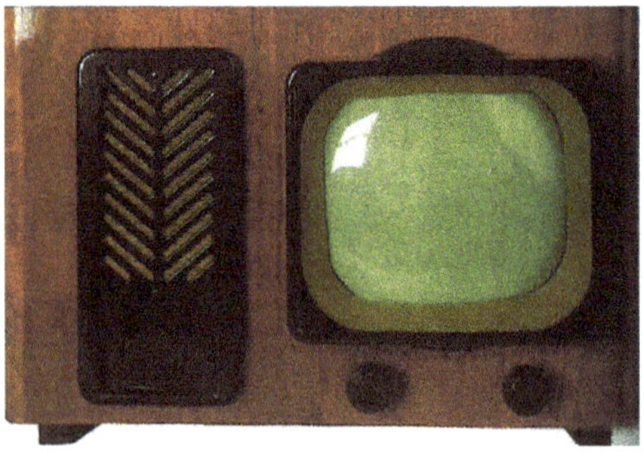

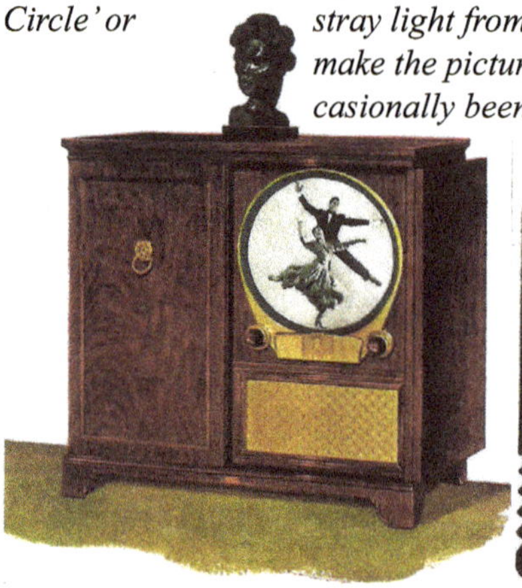

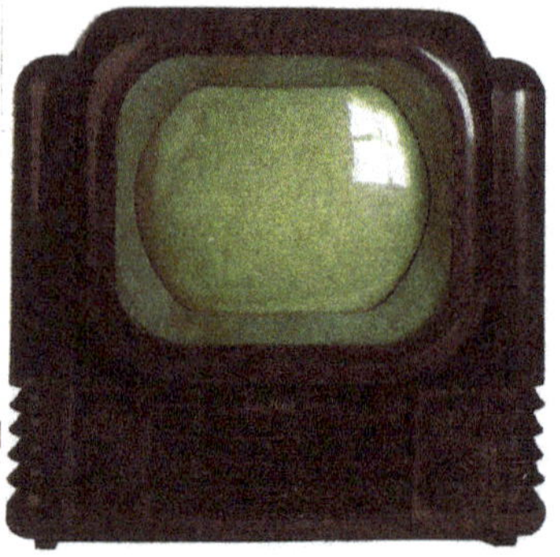

America decides

For many Americans, TV all began when this new invention was first demonstrated at the 1939 World's Fair in New York. Despite America's significant progress and contributions to electronic TV, the start of a national service was being delayed by various disputes, mostly with RCA who controlled many of the basic patents (fortunately shared with its partner EMI in Britain).

The Federal Communications Commission was allowing some experimental transmissions and sets could already be bought to receive them, including NBC's first 'telecasts' from an aerial on top of the Empire State Building. However, the FCC would not allocate frequencies for full-scale regular services until agreements were reached, including common technical standards. The manufacturers helped set up the National Television System Committee (NTSC) to come up with a single TV system for American TV. The front runner was RCA who had raised its 343 lines to offer a 441-line interlaced 30pps (linked to the country's 60Hz mains supply) system. Rival company Philco did better with a 605 line proposal, so not wishing to favour a specific company the NTSC did adopt the basic RCA system but changed the number of lines to 'somewhere in-between' - 525, ready for the FCC's go-ahead in 1941.

Like the beginning of our own TV service, America's also made a slow start, delayed first by their entry into WWII and then by the task of setting up a national distribution network, which then would rely mostly on the invention of the coaxial cable. Fortunately, here in Britain, it was possible to spread the BBC's first single channel across the bulk of the country using only four high-power transmitters, although it would take over fifty smaller ones to complete its final 95% coverage.

In the best shape

As for the aspect ratio, the NTSC had looked at 31 emerging TV systems around the world. The most popular shape was 4:3 used by 19, followed by 7, including Britain, choosing 5:4. The NTSC went for 4:3, one reason given was to follow motion picture practice; this permitted the scanning of film without waste. Although a rectangular 4:3 or 5:4 picture left the transmitter, not all of it was usually visible at the receiver end. The shape of viewers' screens varied, depending on the individual manufacturer's decision on making the best use of the still circular tubes. For the biggest picture a few left the whole tube visible, displaying a severely cropped round image but with an optional switch to see more of a reduced sized version. Mostly, sets had a more rectangular mask or frame in front of the tube, giving the familiar rounded cornered 'TV-shaped' picture. A popular compromise was to slice off the top and bottom of the circle leaving the sides curved, producing the other popular 'pumpkin' screen.

Jobs in danger

With the increasing demand for TVs at the beginning of the 1950s, the earlier circular CRTs, made by hand, or, more accurately, the mouths and lungs of glass blowers, were being replaced by mass-produced mechanically pressed more rectangular shaped tubes. In 1952, the BBC decided to take the opportunity to change to a 4:3 aspect ratio. This was done quietly within the industry, without bothering the viewers at home with such technicalities. It was unlikely that many noticed that their favourite performers became a little slimmer overnight. This was put right the next time the TV repair man was called out – he would slightly over-scan the picture before leaving. Many today fear that the job of a cinema projectionist may become a dying trade. Already gone are the army of TV repair men who, in earlier times, visited homes up to an average of three times a year. Set owners lived in constant fear of hearing the dreaded expensive words "sorry, the tube's gone." Although new TVs now had roughly 4:3 screens, over the coming years a few would still appear showing only 5:4 images.

Colour so real, you'll think you are there!

The first attempts at full-colour TV used synchronised spinning red, green and blue filters in front of a normal

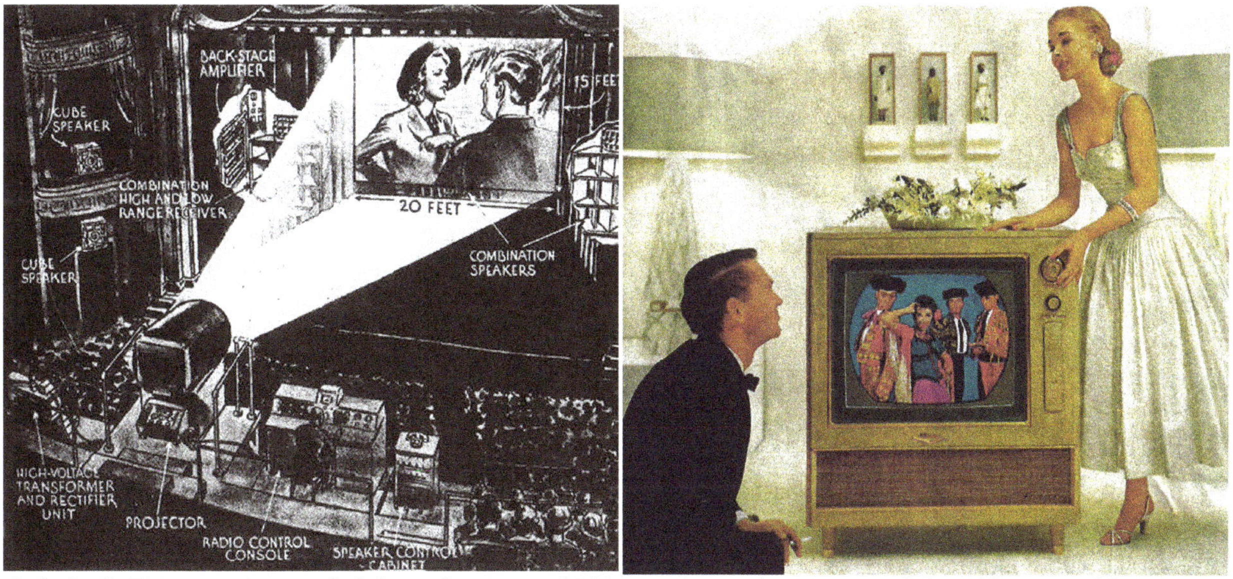

Left: RadioVision movies invaded the auditorium in 1946, complete with stereo sound. Possibly inspired by Disney's Fantasound which accompanied the first showing of Fantasia in 1940.
Right: 1950s-style ad for one of the first RCA colour TVs with its 'pumpkin'-shaped picture.

black and white camera and receiver. Although seemingly rather crude, this arrangement can produce quite good pictures at the expense of reduced brightness and needing a higher picture frequency to prevent flicker and colour fringes appearing around rapidly moving subjects. Here in Britain, Pye demonstrated such a system at the Radio Olympia exhibition in 1949.

Although more suitable for closed circuit applications, the same year the FCC in America approved a more sophisticated field-sequential version developed by CBS, who began transmitting colour programmes in 1950. These couldn't be viewed on existing B&W sets, so after three years the decision was revoked, in favour of a new compatible system proposed by RCA.

This exploited the phenomenon that if you add low definition colour to a normal B&W picture, both appear to the eye to be equally sharp. The extra colour information could be fitted into the normal B&W signal, which still produced a good picture on a B&W set. It wasn't perfect, as in practice the colour part of the signal could become distorted, particularly when picked up further away from the transmitter, resulting in either a poorer greenish or purple image. The picture (right) shows the effect. To try and correct it, colour sets needed an extra 'Hue' control knob to fiddle with. Despite this, in 1954, a re-convened NTSC adopted it as America's new NTSC colour system, which some thought meant 'Never Twice the Same Colour'.

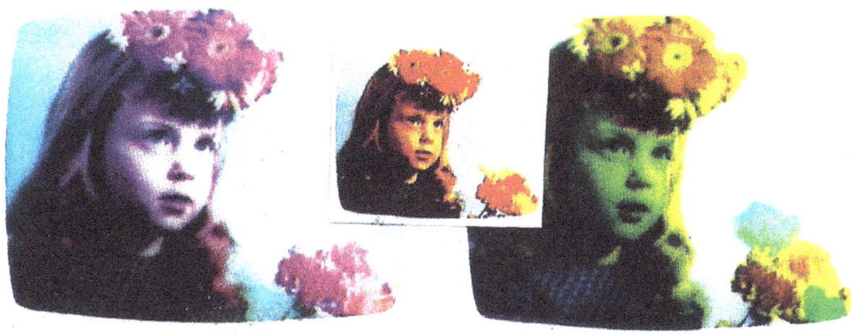

NTSC's 'never twice the same colour' hue shifts. Later NTSC capable TVs still had a hue (tint) control, now well down the list in its picture menu, but much tighter specification production and delivery standards meant that the control rarely, if ever, needed adjusting.

Although future colour TV would now be all-electronic, the comparatively ancient idea of a rotating filter disc in front of a black and white camera would live on into the space age. NASA chose the method as the most convenient way to transmit the first colour TV pictures from the surface of the moon, although on one trip, the tube camera was killed off when its astronaut cameraman accidentally pointed it at the sun. Fortunately, Hollywood stepped in to re-enact what was going on up on the moon in the studio to help fill the screens of the disappointed viewers back on earth. Many of these were now watching in colour on a new kind of TV screen.

The CRT lives on in colour

To display the results, RCA had also introduced its 'shadow-mask' colour cathode-ray tube. Instead of the normal overall B&W fluorescent coating, the screen was now in the form of a regular pattern of red, green and blue phosphor dots. The first 21-inch tubes had a million of these, which were fired at by three separate electron guns. Before reaching the phosphor dots the beams had to pass through a metal shadow-mask positioned a short distance in front of the phosphors. The mask

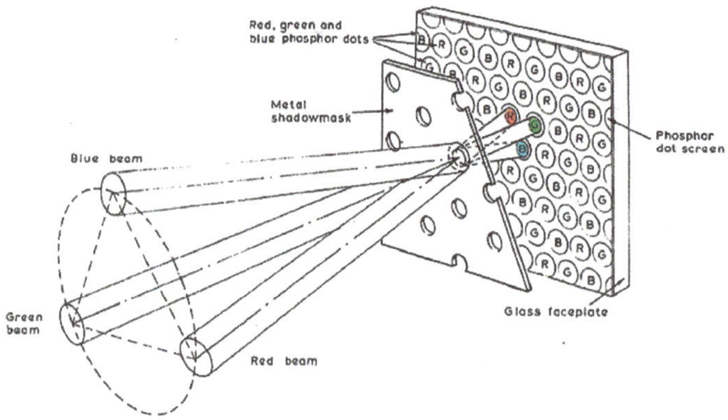

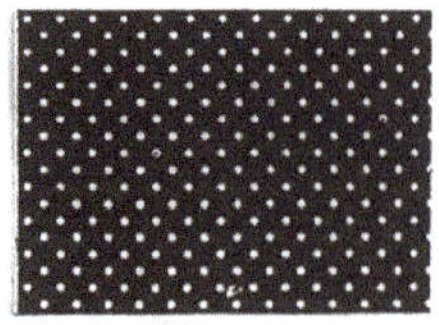

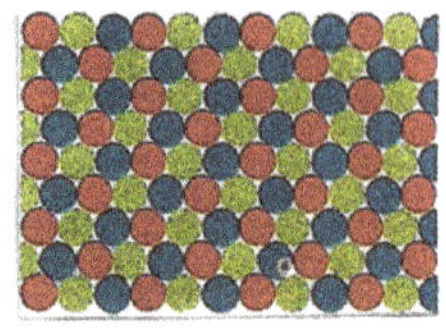

Top: Principle of the shadow-mask colour CRT with its perforated mask and pattern of phosphor dots.

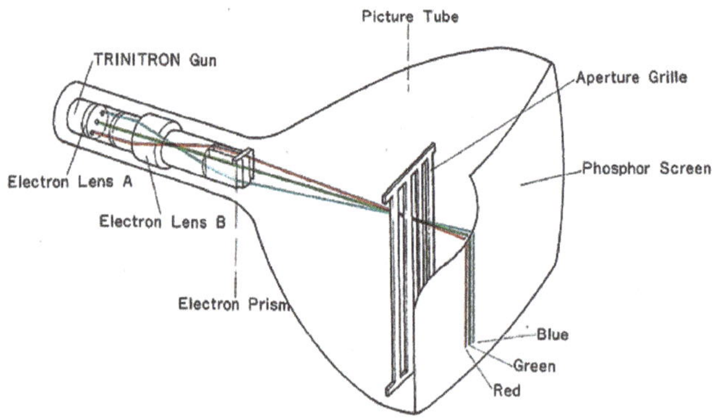

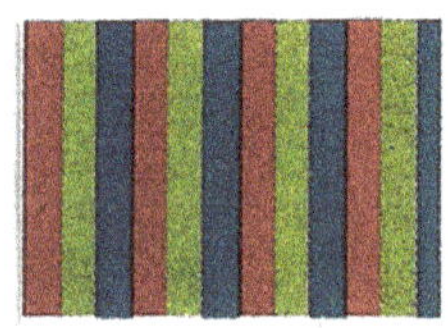

Left: Sony's 'Trinitron' version with an aperture grill and phosphor stripes.

was perforated with over three hundred thousand small holes, which ensured that each beam passing through at a slightly different angle could only 'see' its own appropriate set of dots. Unfortunately, the mask wasted at least two-thirds of each electron beam, which needed to be driven at a much higher voltage to match the brightness of a monochrome tube. It also had to be kept de-gaussed to stop stray magnetic fields deflecting the beams on to parts of the wrong dots, spoiling the purity of the colours.

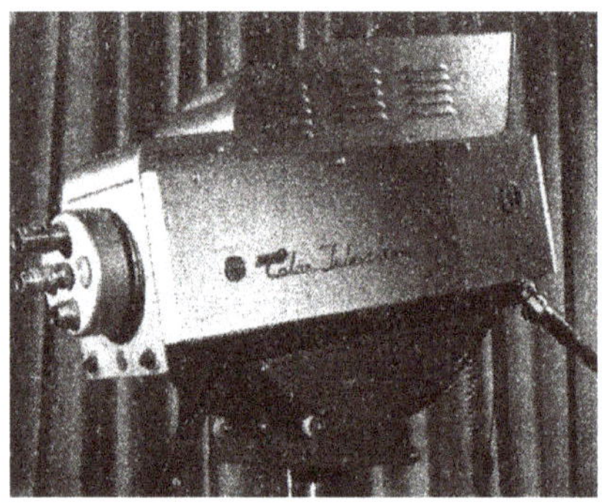

RCA's first commercially available triple tube TV camera.

To add to the complexity, an array of coils and magnets on the tube had to be adjusted to stretch, squeeze, bend and twist the three individual colour images to keep them in register on the screen. Manufacturing problems keeping the purity of the colours stable, as the tube and its mask heated up, meant a return to a longer (70 degree) circular faced tube and a return to the pumpkin and often 5:4 pictures.

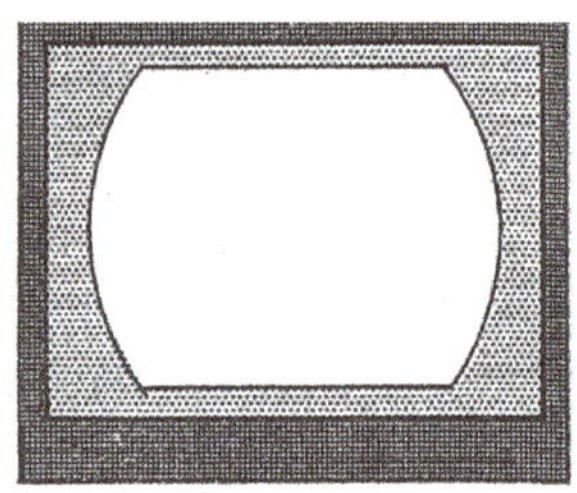

The different shapes of home TV screens required much smaller 'safe areas' for camera viewfinders.

Keeping everything in view

Although leaving the studio in a 4:3 format, the possible loss of picture information on earlier TVs, with their differently shaped screen frames and masks, led to both electronic and film cameras, involved in making television programmes and TV movies often having viewfinder markings showing a much smaller 'safe area' than recommended for shooting 4:3 cinema films. This was particularly important for titles and even more so when framing TV commercials, to make absolutely sure the product and its name would always be visible, even on poorly-adjusted sets. Earlier filmed TV shows and movies were characterised by their rather loose composition, with plenty of space around the subject.

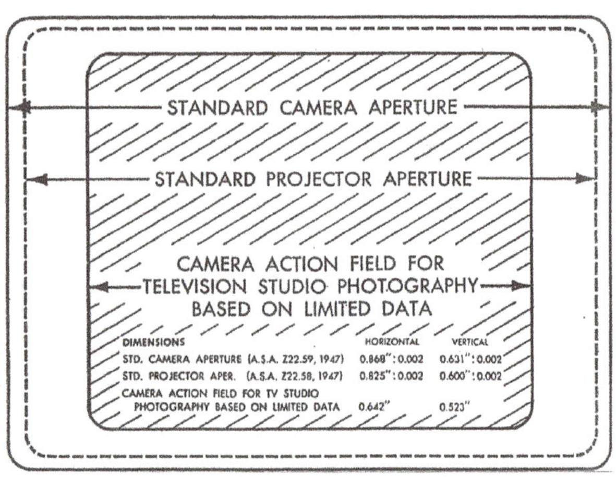

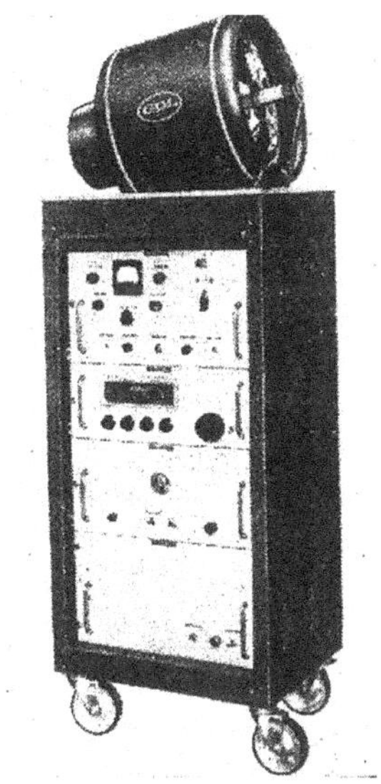

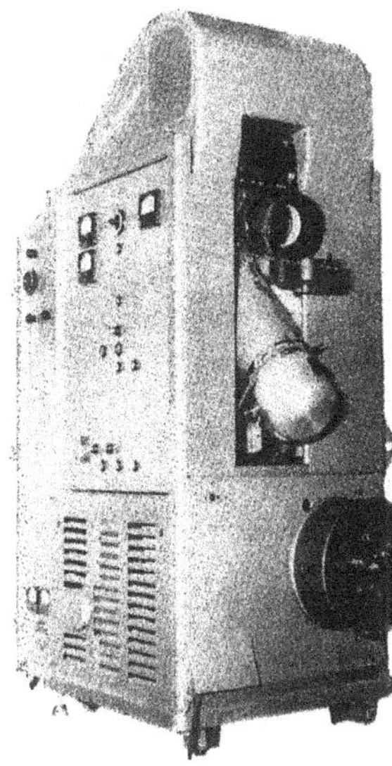

Left: Until relatively recently TV and video projection relied on tube-type projectors such as the tube-type from the 1950s (far left) and the oil-film based Eidophor (left).

Right: The 'near miracle' intermediate film TV projection system made it into the newsreel, but not to the 1953 Coronation, which carried on without it.

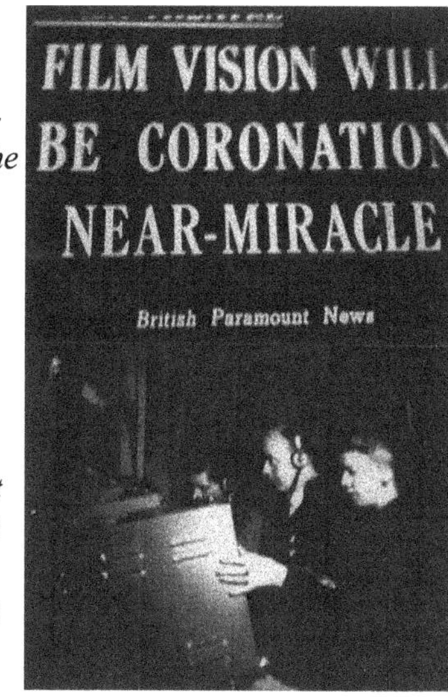

More brief encounters between cinema and TV

The prospect of TV in colour would now challenge one of the cinema's unique added attractions, a weapon needed all the more to hang on to its audiences, who were staying away in increasing numbers, many at home watching television, which was finally taking hold at the start of the1950s. Here in Britain Gaumont-British's early interest, during the 1930s, in bringing TV's electronic pictures into cinemas had waned somewhat after they had been taken over by Rank. At one time, the Postmaster General had been persuaded to reserve a number of frequencies exclusively for the cinema industry, but with falling interest and opposition, particularly from many exhibitors, these were withdrawn.
Even so, their own Cintel tube-type TV projectors, along with Eidophors, were occasionally installed in cinemas to relay live prize fights and topical events, not least the long queues waiting to see the Coronation on the big screen in 1953.

In America it was Twentieth Century Fox and Paramount who would show the most interest in using big screen television to help win back audiences. It would be an even greater lure if this extra live content was in colour too. TCF hosted demonstrations of a colour version of the Eidophor projector, first at its maker's factory in Switzerland and then at their New York preview theatre. Colour had been added to its already complicated modulated oil image and optical system by using a sequential field system with a spinning segmented RGB filter wheel, rather like today's single chip DLP video projectors.

The light loss meant that its colour pictures could only be half the width, typically around 15 feet, of its equivalent B&W images. Even so, it was reported that some easily impressed visitors thought they were watching a Technicolor movie. A boost to the future of the Eidophor came with the news that Fox was about to order 500 for its theatre television project. The results were encouraging enough for Fox to help facilitate a gathering in New York of 60 top studio executives to consider the future of theatrical television. They discussed the methods of the production of these alternative 'Radio Movies' and the quality and reliability of the available projection systems. A highlight was an Eidophor presentation at the Plymouth Theatre in the Bronx of a live dress rehearsal of a stage show sent across the city from the Roxy, featuring their Roxyettes troop of high kicking dancing girls.

Despite their attraction, attention would turn to technical changes taking place in their own world of film. Important among these was the introduction of Kodak's Eastman Color single-strip colour film, which would simplify colour filming and make the new 3D, widescreen and stereo sound movie systems under development more practical, and which might become a better weapon in its fight to offer something different to the ever growing TV audience staying at home.

Unfortunately, the Eidophor too would lose out in the search for audience grabbing innovations, when Fox, spurred on by the success of Cinerama, decided a better bet was to go for a bigger and wider shaped screen, snapping up the French, long neglected 'Hypergonar' anamorphic lens, discussed elsewhere in this book.

Among Paramount's big screen TV efforts were tests of an intermediate film projection process. For this, the incoming video picture was photographed off a TV screen, rapidly developed and continuously fed to a conventional 35mm projector, reaching the screen in an almost 'live' minute or so. One of its try outs was over here at their Plaza cinema in the West End. It was considered as a way to put the BBC's coverage of the Coronation on the big screen. As many predicted at the time, this rather bizarre near-miracle proved impractical; there was little hope of changing its B&W film stock to colour, which required longer and more complex processing. It brings to mind Polaroid's short-lived 'instant' Super-8 colour system from the 1980s. With much in common with

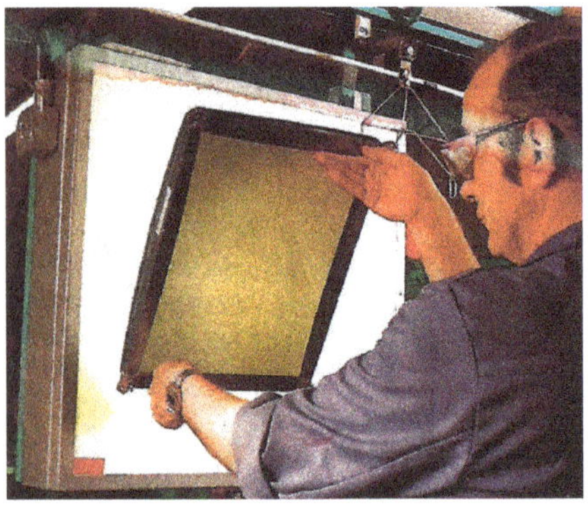

Inspecting a shadow-mask, showing the neutral density filter effect

the old Dufaycolor additive process, it used a 'quick to develop' black and white film, which was exposed and projected through a fine pattern of red, green and blue filter elements formed on its base. The final, processed to a positive image, together with the filter layer, made the print rather dense, so it stayed sealed up, together with the remains of its processing chemicals, in its cassette, for showing in a bright small-screen back projection viewer.

Unfortunately, the shadow-mask colour CRT proved unsuitable for projection, with the need for a small ultra-bright image. Most subsequent designs would rely on three separate high-intensity tubes to provide the red, green and blue images, usually projected by their own wide aperture lens and superimposed in register on the screen.

Other colourful and bright ideas

The shadow-mask tube did have some rivals. Paramount, perhaps with a view to its use for projection, helped in the development of a simpler, more efficient type of colour cathode ray tube known as the Chromatron. This only had a single gun, and instead of the triads of phosphor dots, the screen was made up of alternate red, green and blue vertical stripes, which were able to cover its surface more effectively. Replacing the shadow-mask was a more transparent grid of fine wires, through which flowed a high voltage switching signal which, in response to the colour information, deflected the single beam from moment to moment onto the required colour stripe.

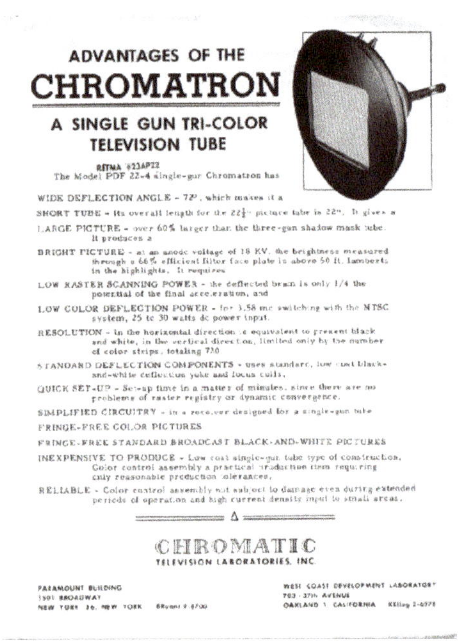

ADVANTAGES OF THE

CHROMATRON

A SINGLE GUN TRI-COLOR TELEVISION TUBE

RETMA #23AP22

The Model PDF 22-4 single-gun Chromatron has

WIDE DEFLECTION ANGLE - 72°, which makes it a

SHORT TUBE - Its overall length for the 22½" picture tube is 22". It gives a

LARGE PICTURE - over 60% larger than the three-gun shadow mask tube. It produces a

BRIGHT PICTURE - at an anode voltage of 18 KV, the brightness measured through a 66% efficient filter face plate is above 50 ft. lamberts in the highlights. It requires

LOW RASTER SCANNING POWER - the deflected beam is only 1/4 the potential of the final acceleration, and

LOW COLOR DEFLECTION POWER - for 3.58 mc switching with the NTSC system, 25 to 30 watts dc power input.

RESOLUTION - in the horizontal direction is equivalent to present black and white, in the vertical direction, limited only by the number of color strips, totaling 720

STANDARD DEFLECTION COMPONENTS - uses standard, low cost black-and-white deflection yoke and focus coils,

QUICK SET-UP - Set-up time in a matter of minutes, since there are no problems of raster registry or dynamic convergence.

SIMPLIFIED CIRCUITRY - in a receiver designed for a single-gun tube

FRINGE-FREE COLOR PICTURES

FRINGE-FREE STANDARD BROADCAST BLACK-AND-WHITE PICTURES

INEXPENSIVE TO PRODUCE - Low cost single-gun tube type of construction. Color control assembly a practical production item requiring only reasonable production tolerances.

RELIABLE - Color control assembly not subject to damage even during extended periods of operation and high current density input to small areas.

CHROMATIC TELEVISION LABORATORIES, INC.

PARAMOUNT BUILDING
1501 BROADWAY
NEW YORK 36, NEW YORK BRyant 9-4700

WEST COAST DEVELOPMENT LABORATORY
703 - 37th AVENUE
OAKLAND 1, CALIFORNIA KEllog 2-4778

Another variation was the 'Zebra' colour tube. This too had stripes and a single gun, but the wires were replaced by an additional 'index' layer on the back of each stripe which emitted UV light. This was picked up by an optical photomultiplier inside the tube and helped to provide the control signal to switch the beam between the red, green and blue components of the scanning image as it crossed the appropriate stripes. In the event, these beam index designs didn't manage to displace the shadow-mask colour tube, as their simplicity was more than offset by the quantity and complexity of the circuitry needed to switch between their colour stripes. Hopes that they could be made bright enough for single tube cinema projectors were also dashed. However, it wasn't the actual projector technology which was holding back electronic cinema. In America, like here in Britain, the authorities refused to grant the industry the frequencies needed to carry their own exclusive programming. In the days before access to satellites, the added cost of renting cables from telephone companies made the idea uneconomic.

The Chromatron lives on, to leave a legacy

The Chromatron CRT still had its advantages, which led to it being seized upon by the US military for use in the field where a small, bright and sharp display was required for portable equipment. It would also be chosen for Sony's first colour TV, a 9 inch portable, introduced in 1961. To reduce the switching demands they adopted a line-sequential system, only changing to a different

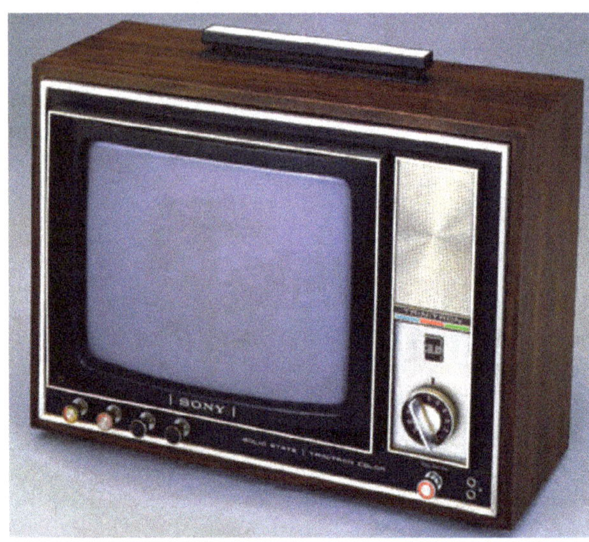

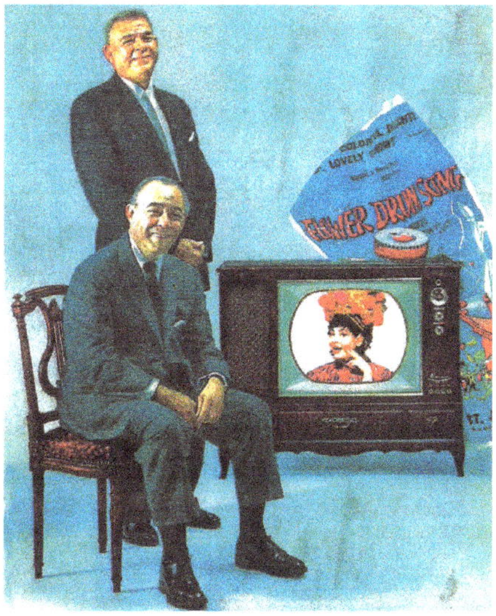

Left: Rodgers and Hammerstein with their second most prized possession, an RCA colour TV, beaten only by the colour ad for their latest musical.

Right: Laurence Olivier's feature 'Richard III' was first seen in America on NBC colour TV.

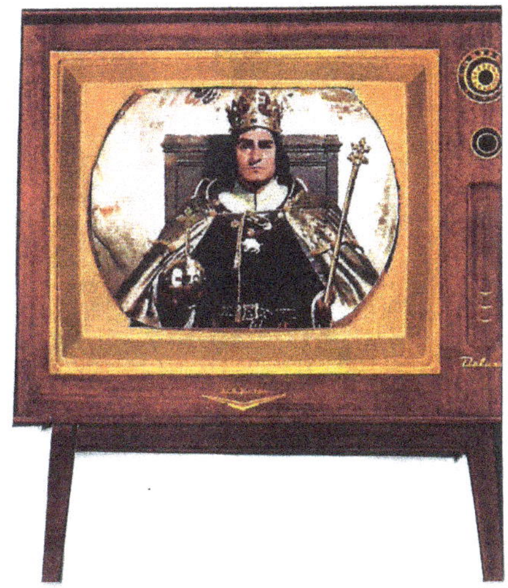

colour stripe at the end of each line. This reduced the vertical colour definition, but still produced a good bright picture on its small screen. After this model, Sony used some of its features for its own famous 'Trinitron' shadow-mask tube. This kept the striped screen and had a new type of single gun with triple cathodes producing three side by side beams. These passed-through an 'aperture grill' mask of vertical slits, resulting in a 30% brighter picture than a conventional shadow-mask. The profile of the screen's surface was a portion of a cylinder instead of a sphere, and fears about its strength would initially restrict them to smaller screens, which again could only show a 5:4 picture, meaning either a slightly squeezed, or over scanned image.

Getting colour through the door

After the false start in 1951, using the CBS semi mechanical colour wheel system, America's colour TV service was re-launched using the NTSC system in 1954. The big publicity push, particularly by RCA and its broadcasting company NBC, would employ a full line up of high profile entertainment and sports stars to promote the new 'now in living color' programmes. Interesting among them were Rodgers and Hammerstein, whose RCA Victor colour TV was now one of their most prized possessions, second only to a plug for their latest musical *Flower Drum Song*. On a smaller stage, their television production of *Cinderella* had apparently received rave reviews, including its colour. R&H would prove to be quite free with their recommendations, as they were also praising the cinema's new 70mm big screen Todd-AO as the only process grand enough to allow the filming of another of their musicals, *Oklahoma!*.

Still in monochrome, Britain would also join in and contribute to the birth of electronic colour. Laurence Olivier's feature 'Richard III' was given its US premiere on NBC colour TV. Ironically, it was filmed in VistaVision, another one of the cinema's widescreen systems introduced to combat TV. The first British TV series filmed in colour for American viewers was *The Adventures of Sir Lancelot*, which switched to Technicolor halfway through its 30 episodes after it had been picked up by NBC.

Despite our help, there wasn't a rush for colour, with most American viewers content for the time being watching in compatible black and white. It would take a decade before colour TV broke free of the trap of poor sales discouraging the production of more colour programmes, in turn reducing the incentive to buy a new more expensive set.

Never mind the colour, what about the definition?

Although the BBC began its own colour tests in 1955, many thought it should be kept on hold until it could be added to an improved basic black and white picture. When first seen in 1936, our 405-line image was described as 'high definition', but by the end of the 1950s, we had found ourselves stuck with the lowest line standard in the world.

Bringing yet more colour into our lives - the march of television continues

Waiting for colour

The BBC began the first of its series of colour tests in 1956. After giving the press a sneak preview, experimental programmes were regularly transmitted from Crystal Palace, which came back to life in colour after its normal late night close down. The BBC was using the American NTSC colour system but with the extra colour signal fitted into our own 405-line picture, which could still be watched in black and white on existing sets. This was all to gain operational experience and allow the experts, and more typical viewers, to judge the quality of the pictures, both in colour and compatible black and white. These were coming from an old vacant studio at Alexandra Palace and included 'live' pictures. The Marconi company had built a pair of 3-tube colour cameras based on those developed in America by RCA. Being much larger than the normal B&W cameras, they were soon being referred to as 'coffins', perhaps ready for the performers and crew about to drop under the intense lighting, which, at 350 foot-candles, was about ten times that of a monochrome studio. Even at their best, apparently achieved by not fiddling with the knobs on the cameras, the colour pictures were thought by many of the BBC engineers, always striving for the best possible images, to be on the borderline of quality. At the time, the best colour TV was coming from 35mm film running on a new Cintel colour telecine. On today's TV, it is B&W pictures which are unusual, but back then, most people were amazed at seeing colour TV for the first time and were far less critical of the technical quality. Encouragement also came from visiting American technicians who expressed astonishment at our excellent pictures. This reflected on the situation back in the U.S. where the variable quality of their colour TV, together with the less stable and unreliable receivers were holding up its progress. In fact, the production of colour programmes actually declined throughout the rest of the 1950s.

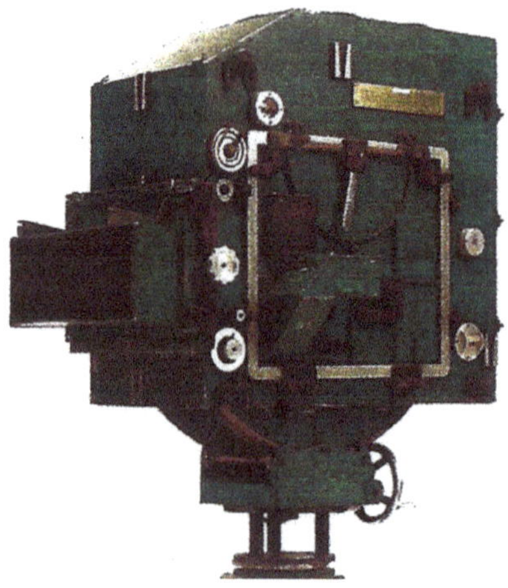

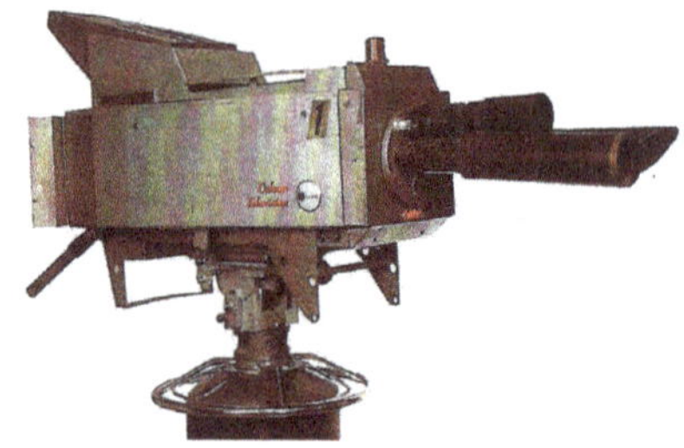

By 1955 we were seeing the end of one camera technology, the Technicolor 3-strip camera, shown in its green 'icebox' blimp, and welcoming 'the coffin', Marconi's early colour TV camera, used by the BBC for its first colour tests at Alexandra Palace.

Not ready yet to bring colour into British homes

The BBC's colour tests also helped the manufacturers designing and building prototype receivers, with the first of these being used to give demonstrations to MPs and other decision makers looking to the future of television. These early sets and monitors had to use the imported very long (70 degree) and circular-faced shadow-mask tubes, and most of their makers made it known that they wouldn't contemplate introducing new domestic versions, as the much larger cabinets needed to house them would not be welcome in Britain's smaller living rooms. They would wait until new colour tubes could be made to match the dimensions and shape of the then current B&W CRTs. These were already becoming slimmer with the arrival of the wider scanning angle 110 degree versions. At first, these could only be constructed with a more bulbous and rounded screen which could only display a 5:4 image, but advances in their manufacture soon allowed a return to a flatter 4:3. For now these would remain in monochrome as the general opinion was that, despite our pioneering spirit in the history of television, this time we should not rush into colour. Both the set-makers and the viewing public were already preoccupied with the launch of ITV, so thoughts would turn next to making our B&W pictures look better.

TV in other theatres of life

Apart from television's place in the home and occasional appearance in Cinemas, it was also finding a role in industry and education. Among the first to adopt colour was the field of medicine. In 1949, students at the University of Pennsylvania in the USA were able to watch a surgical operation live and in colour on a big screen. It had been sent by microwave transmission using the CBS field sequential system, with its red, green and blue filter wheels spinning within the cameras, monitors and TV projector. It was sponsored by the drug company Smith, Kline and French, who began running similar events in the UK. The first in colour on a big screen was seen in 1957. At St Bartholomew's Hospital in London the bulky triple tube colour camera was able to keep its distance while covering the surgeon's work in close up by using an angled mirror above the operating table. Again via a microwave link, the operation, together with comments from a panel of experts, was presented to an audience of doctors gathered behind a three tube 'Schmidt' optical system video projector set up in the Great Hall of the Royal College of Surgeons, which allowed them all to follow the knife on an 8ft by 6ft screen. Like other projectors of this type, the projectionist had to arrive

Big screen medical television was the first to adopt colour, making life-saving operations more life-like. The pictures from 1958 (below) show the operating theatre at St Bartholomew's Hospital in London, when a large colour TV camera followed the scalpel for the benefit of other doctors at the Royal College of Surgeons, who watched the operation using three linked CRT projectors superimposing their separate RGB images onto a big screen. It is interesting to note that today we have cameras that are small enough to send colour pictures from the inside of a patient's body.
Other medical shows made use of a Xenon powered colour Eidophor projector (right). Its sequential RGBs images modulated on an oil film were projected through a spinning filter wheel. This type of projector gave much brighter and larger pictures.

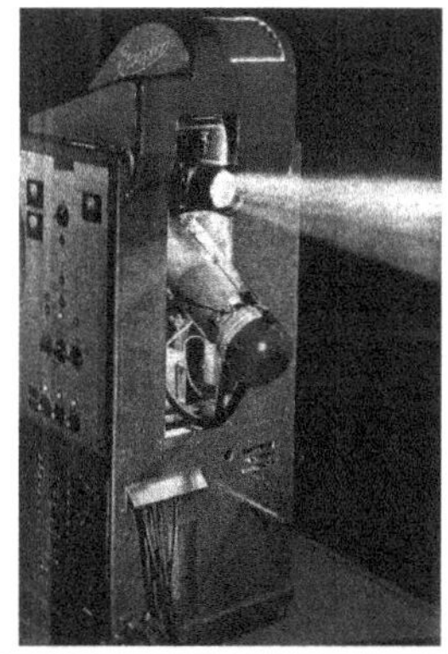

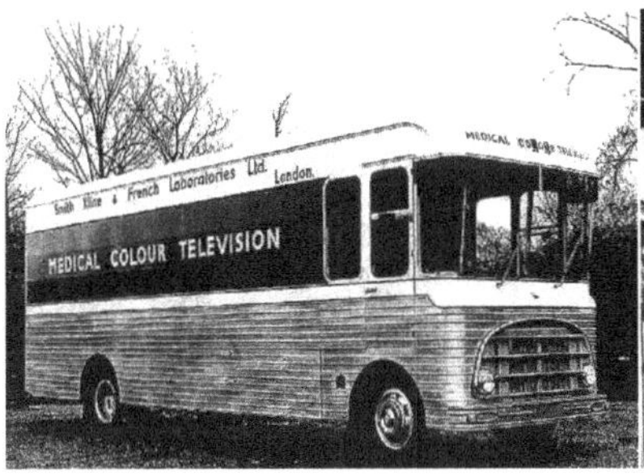

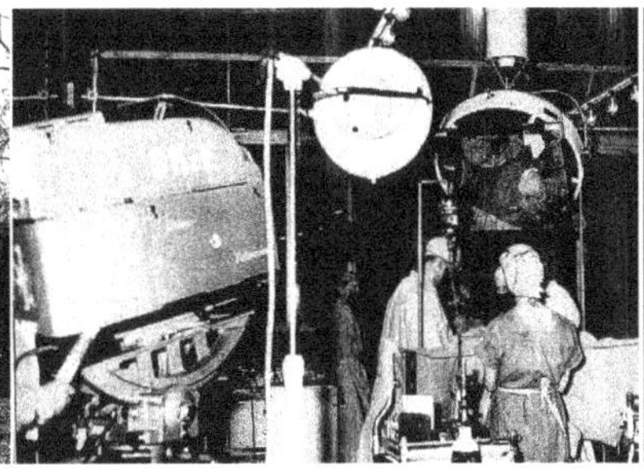

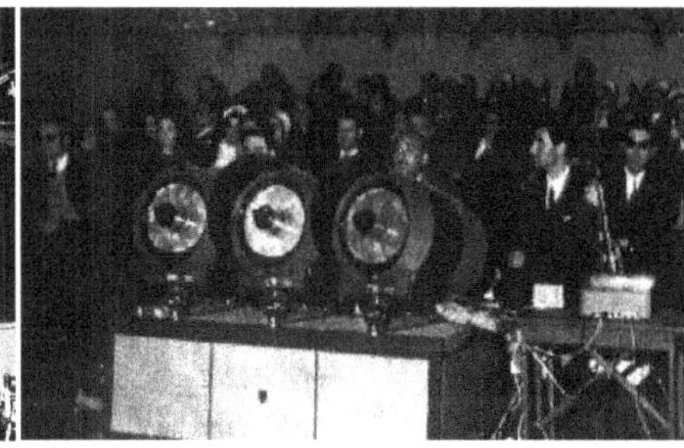

early to switch it on well in advance for everything to warm up and stabilise. Also, the separate red, green and blue images had to be accurately aligned on the screen to produce an acceptable picture without serious colour fringes. Other big screen operations employed the CBS system and a much brighter colour Eidophor projector, although on one occasion, at the Hammersmith Hospital, the show had to be interrupted when the heat of the extra lights needed for the filter disc camera began to warm up the hypothermia induced patient. How times change, today it's now routine to relay colour images from actually inside the patient's body. Out of hospital and back home in the 1960s, our TV pictures were about to look even healthier, and in colour too.

Keeping up with technology

One downside of leading the way into the television age was a reluctance to incorporate later incompatible improvements, fearing the public's reaction to making their existing receivers obsolete. (Perhaps future candidates may be the earlier and less efficient 1990s technologies of SD Freeview and DAB radio!) Although many of today's generation seem more willing to discard their high priced technology for the latest model, back in the 1950s it was far more risky to upset viewers who were happy with their long-saved-up-for sets. Many were still paying the instalments on the 'never-never', the popular term for the hire-purchase scheme, which along with the coming of ITV, had given a boost to TV ownership.

No need to throw it away yet

Fortunately, although aiming to buy a new set was best, it was still possible to pick up the new ITV, broadcast using VHF's higher band III frequencies, by using the first of the saviour of old tellys, a set-top box. The cheapest of these simply dropped the frequency to join the BBC in the lower band I. Unfortunately, fitting it in sometimes caused interference and you ended up watching both at once. At this time, the most popular screen

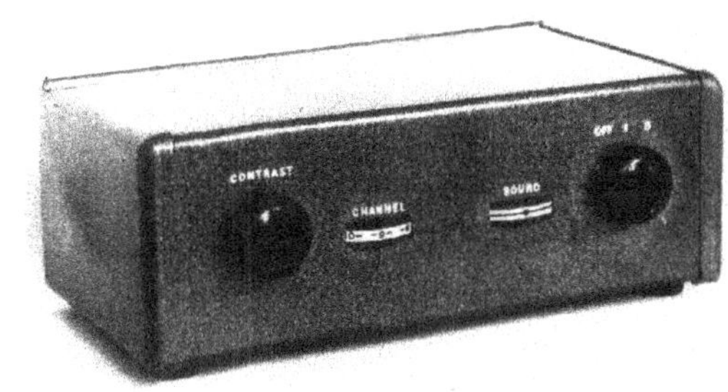

Helping to keep up with the technology changes was the first of the set-top boxes, called an ITV convertor in those days. It enabled older BBC-only TVs using Band I to tune in to the higher Band III frequencies used by ITV.

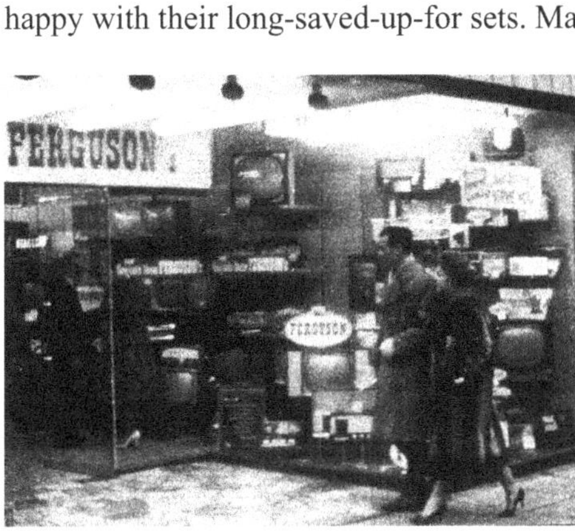

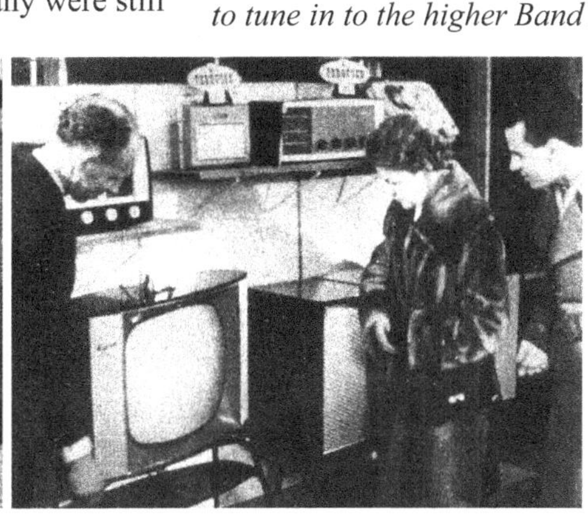

It is interesting that cinema advertising was actually used to sell television sets. These frames from a 1958 cinema ad show a couple about to buy a new, slimmer 110 degree tube TV.

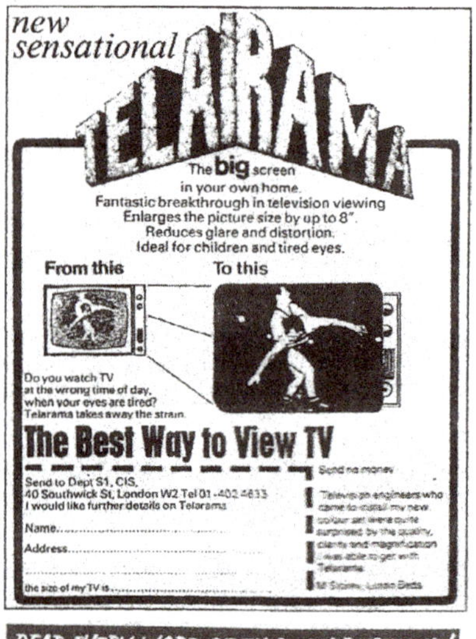

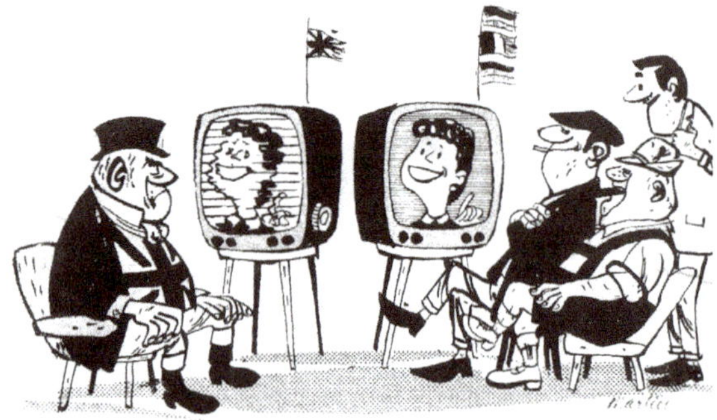

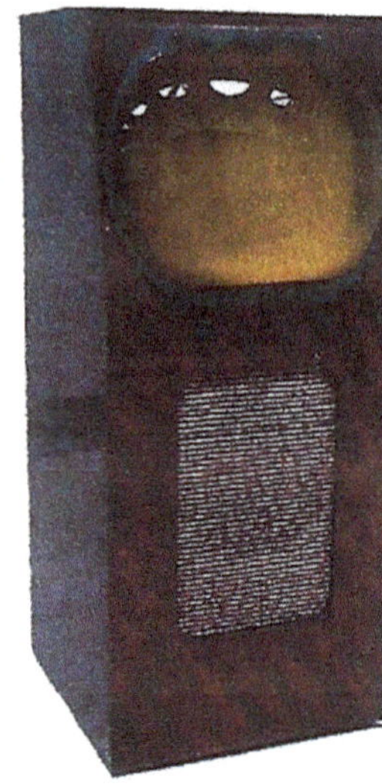

Above: Cartoon showing poor British John Bull having to watch an inferior 405-line picture whilst Johnny Foreigner enjoys a much better one. This appeared in 1958, supporting a change to a higher line standard. Right: Size has always counted! This 1949 nine-inch screen TV gained a much bigger picture with the aid of an add-on screen magnifier.

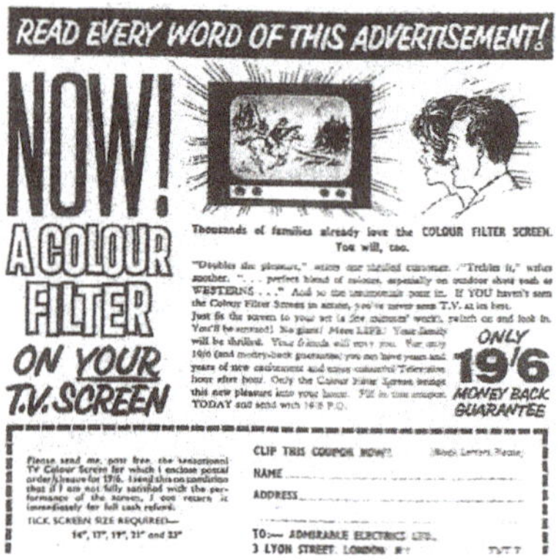

Left: Easy ways to add big-screen colour featured in many contemporary advertisements!

size in British homes was 17 inches; anything larger and, if you sat too close, you could see the lines of our 405-line picture (only 376 actually visible). As we have noted previously, our early work as TV pioneers meant that by the end of the 1950s we (along with viewers in Hong Kong) were watching the lowest definition TV in the world.

Others following us into the rapidly growing invasion of television were choosing much higher line standards. Countries, like Canada and Japan, had followed America with 525, with most of Europe and many other areas adopting the even higher 625-line standard recommended in 1951 by the International Radio Consultative Committee (CCIR). One notable exception was France, knocking on HD's door with 819 lines, the greatest number which would fit into the internationally agreed TV bandwidth. In 1960, the Postmaster General appointed a committee to consider the future of British television, including possible technical advances.

While waiting, why not do-it-yourself?

Some viewers had already taken matters into their own hands. For those impatient for colour, they could buy an add-on colourisation filter to stick over the screen. These had a one-fits-all range of graduated colours, with typically a sky blue band across the top, becoming a flesh tone in the middle and then brown and green along the bottom. Tired of your small picture, why not blow it up with a magnifying lens attachment - some even had the colour built in.

Just thinking it's in colour

The broadcasters too occasionally came up with their own, often mind bending looks into the future. Long before today's 'contains flashing images' warnings, ITV viewers were startled by an 'OXO' commercial which appeared to be in colour on their black and white sets. A following science programme gave the secret away. The brightness of the various parts of its abstract images pulsated at different rates, fooling the brain into thinking it was seeing colours. It did more or less work, particularly if you 'wanted' to see the colours. It reminded me, when on a car journey I discovered you could enjoy another multi-colour psychedelic trip using only the sun flashing through the trees.

Other added dimensions

3D wasn't neglected. One experiment for younger viewers caused a run on Woolworths ladies' small handbag mirrors to make a 'Blue Peter' cereal packet stereoscopic viewer. Once the glue was dry, it was ready to watch the following week's split-screen 3D demonstration. Fortunately, I was able to save money, having learned how to cross my eyes for the unaided viewing of stereo side-by-side images.

This trick of superimposing images was also useful to make the changes stand out when trying to solve a pair of 'spot the difference' pictures. For another all-in-the-mind 3D experiment, we were asked to put a sunglass filter over one eye to view pictures taken by a camera constantly tracking sideways at a calculated speed, which now appeared to have added depth. The theory, this time, was that the uncovered eye retained its brighter image longer than the darkened one, so you were able to make out a separated pair of laterally displaced images, giving the impression that the scene was in 3D. I remember that it was tried out on TV with the camera moving around a pop group, and another time with a static shot of an aquarium with fish swimming across the screen.

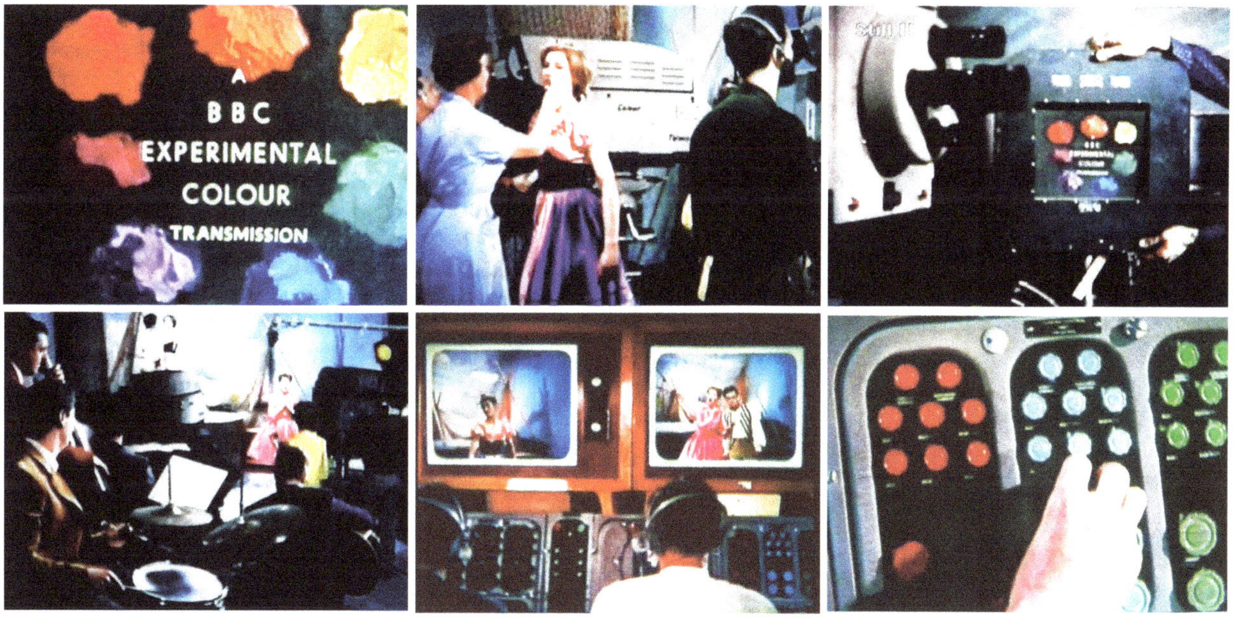

A series of shots from the early BBC experimental colour test transmissions. The pictures are taken from the 1950s BBC Black and White documentary 'This is the BBC' which burst into colour at the end to feature the after-hours tests that were taking place at Alexandra Palace - interesting to note that they used only simulated colour TV pictures on the monitors! An award winner in 1959, this was very much a film of its time. There is a reluctance to show it today, as it shows mostly posh people making the programmes, which included 'The Black and White Minstrel Show'.

Back to reality in finer detail

The committee's report in 1962 recommended a step by step transition to 625 lines using UHF bands IV & V. This would start with the BBC's planned second channel, which would only go out on 625 lines. No help this time from a set top box. A completely new dual-standard set was required to also watch the existing BBC and ITV programmes, which would continue on 405 lines until being duplicated on 625 as soon as possible. The government reassured the ten million licence holders that these would remain available on 405 lines for at least ten years; in fact the last transmitter wasn't switched off until 1985, when the last 405-line only set sold would have been 20 years old. The freed up frequencies were now ready for the next big thing, the mobile phone. BBC2 was launched in 1964, but unfortunately, even in better quality 625-vision, its early mix of 'innovative' and minority interest programmes didn't attract a mass audience, leading to both being described as 'the great unwatched'. It would take the success story of colour to finally establish 625 lines.

Testing a wider choice of colour

Moving from Alexandra Palace to Lime Grove, the BBC resumed its 405-line NTSC colour tests in 1962. The first in 1956 had been well past my bedtime, but now I could dash home from college to catch them in glorious black and white. No live studio this time, but for an hour or so in the afternoon you could watch interesting sponsored shorts supplied by the likes of BP and Shell. As an extra treat, feature films were also shown, but there was only time for a single reel per session. It was a chance for the BBC to make better use of the colour prints in their previously acquired RKO film library. I remember it took a couple of weeks to sit through 'She Wore a Yellow Ribbon'. It amused me to imagine when another, 'The Boy with Green Hair' was being run, the engineers reaching for the colour balance controls. It recalled the old story of Technicolor lab technicians desperately trying to turn a green Irish post box red! An aid to natural colour reproduction would be the BBC's 'TARIF' system. Unfortunately, this Television Apparatus for the Rectification of Indifferent Film, could only improve the film's colour, but not its content.

Our set-makers were also getting ready for colour. One of my favourites among the test films came from tube maker Mullard, working with Philips, showing the construction of their new rectangular 90 degree shadow-mask colour tube and how to adjust its convergence and colour balance, which to me seemed that it would take even an expert all day. I still remember most of the other films, and there is a group of even keener TV 'test card' historians who have traced and logged them all, and even identified the music played while the nice colour slides of flowers and smiling ladies were on the screen waiting for the next film to be laced up. Now familiar with colour TV, I sometimes have to remind myself that back then I was only watching them on a B&W set; even so, it was still quite exciting to imagine what they looked like in colour and envying the lucky few in front of the early receivers and monitors.

You always remember the first time

For a sight of the real thing, I set off on a pilgrimage to the Radio Show at Earls Court for the BBC's first

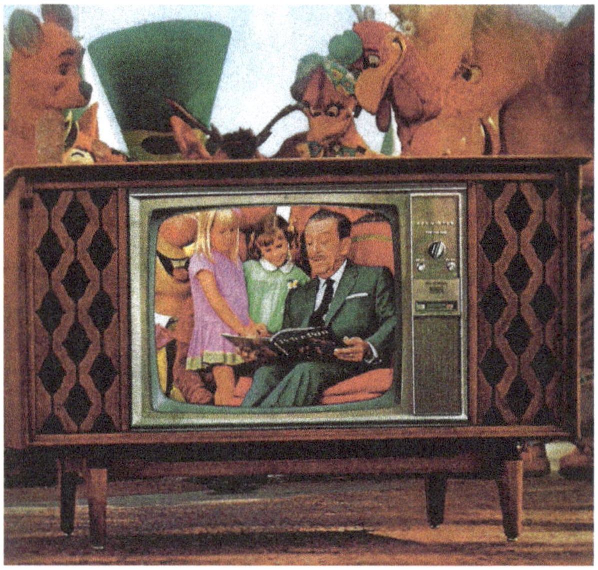

Walt Disney, who was a pioneer in the use of colour in the cinema, used his 'Wonderful World of Color' programme to help fill the screens of America's early colour receivers. He is shown here in a 1961 ad for one of RCA's first sets with a rectangular tube.

public demonstration. Although fascinating, having been brought up watching Technicolor films in the Cinema, this new form of electronic colour seemed rather pale and looked different on each of the row of models on display. At this time, in the early 1960s, colour TV in America was about to stage a second coming. Although beginning in 1954, its poor take-up meant that less than half of its TV stations had equipped themselves for colour. But now able to buy more affordable and reliable sets, colour TV finally caught the imagination of American viewers. For those interested in past U.S. television programmes, it was at this time, around 1965, that many long-running series switched over to colour.

Battle of the systems

Even by 1965, no technical standards had been agreed, the advisory committee only indicating that it should be on 625 lines and compatible, for those still viewing in black and white. At one time, the BBC favoured the NTSC system on 405 lines, which could be ready to celebrate the 20th anniversary of the re-opening of television after WWII. ITV was also in favour, this time its greater VHF coverage being more attractive to its advertisers. Fortunately, wiser minds thought that this was a retrograde step, and that colour should only be added to 625 lines. After waiting for colour, three systems arrived at once, each with its own merits. For its full three-colour image, the American NTSC system only needed to fit two 'colour difference' signals into the basic B&W picture, which now also represented the total RGB colours. Using this information, the set's decoder could do the maths and calculate the separate red, green and blue voltages for the tube's triple electron guns. NTSC sends these additional difference signals together and any distortion, or loss of phase between them, can cause the 'Never Twice the Same Colour' hue shifts, leaving it up to the viewer to adjust an extra 'Hue' or 'Tint' control on their receiver to try and correct it.

The colour information wasn't completely hidden within the compatible B&W image, being visible as a pattern of fine dots in highly coloured areas. Following NTSC, two competing variations were developed, which eliminated the problem of changes in hue. From France, in the process of down-scaling its 819 lines to join the 625 club (1963), came SECAM (Sequential Colour with Memory). To avoid any colour distortion, the difference signals were sent separately on alternate lines, being brought back together to be decoded by a delay-line memory device. A third system, PAL (Phase Alternation line) was developed in Germany. It was again basically NTSC, but if any hue shifts occur, the false colour is reversed on alternate lines. In the first 'simple' version, the effect was actually displayed on the screen, leaving the viewer's eyes to average them out to produce a corrected image. A later version, to which Britain made a significant contribution, used a delay-line again to enable this to be done within the circuitry of the set, to provide the viewer with an already correctly balanced picture on the screen. The BBC began its final series of on-air colour tests, alternating between the competing systems. This prompted a following year trip to Earls Court for another look. They also showed the results at various international conferences, but despite the CCIR's valiant efforts to arrive at a common standard, the intense rivalry between SECAM and PAL meant that, apart from both being on 625 lines, they had to let countries go their own way. France, naturally, supported its own SECAM, along with Russia and other eastern bloc countries. We would join Germany and the rest of Western Europe and adopt PAL.

Making better connections

Jumping forward for the moment to today's digital world, it is worth noting that the NTSC, SECAM and PAL systems are still very much with us and most current TVs and video projectors are designed to deal with them. The PAL 'composite' system does have one noticeable flaw, the occasional spurious patterns caused when the frequencies chosen to squeeze in the colour clash with the similar frequencies in the picture representing striped or checked fabrics. This led to other ways to send video pictures between TVs and other types of equipment. 'S-Video' splits the colour and B&W signals, using a pair of connections, or three can be used to carry the separate RGB 'component' parts of the image. These legacy analogue connections can still be useful, although due to 'copying issues', the manufacturers of more recent Blu-ray players have agreed to banish them, leaving the only choice of a well-protected HDMI socket.

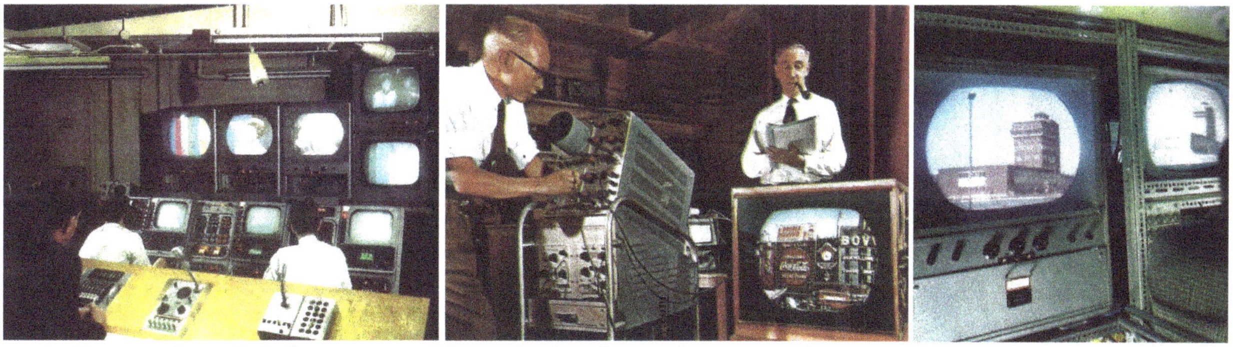

L-R: Keeping the right balance at Lime Grove Studios during the BBC's colour tests in the 1960s. Colour TV boffins deciding on the best system to use. A Cintel colour monitor from the 1960s. still using a circular-faced tube.

Back to the later 'in colour' years of the 1960s

The BBC planned to launch colour on BBC2 in December 1967, but on the news that France, Germany and Russia all intended to start earlier, they jumped the gun to be first with a pre-launch service, beginning with Wimbledon tennis in July. Early adopters paid around £350 (over £2,000 in today's money) to own one of the few, still dual-standard, colour sets, knowing that for most of the time they would be watching the more popular BBC1 and ITV in 405-line monochrome, their pictures often inferior, with a slight colour cast and fringes, compared to an equivalent £50 B&W receiver.

At least they were ready for the official launch in December, the most popular programme shown during the opening weekend being *The Black and White Minstrel Show*, moved from monochrome BBC1 for the occasion. The BBC's first costume drama in colour was *Vanity Fair*, which prompted a comment at the time, that this was history repeating itself as, back in 1935, the cinema's first full-length 3-strip Technicolor film was *Becky Sharp*, based on the same Thackeray novel.

While all this was going on, I had joined the BBC as a Film Assistant (projectionist) and during a stint at the Television Centre I was able to pop into the new colour studios' viewing galleries. Here you could watch their output on splendid top of the range teak veneered

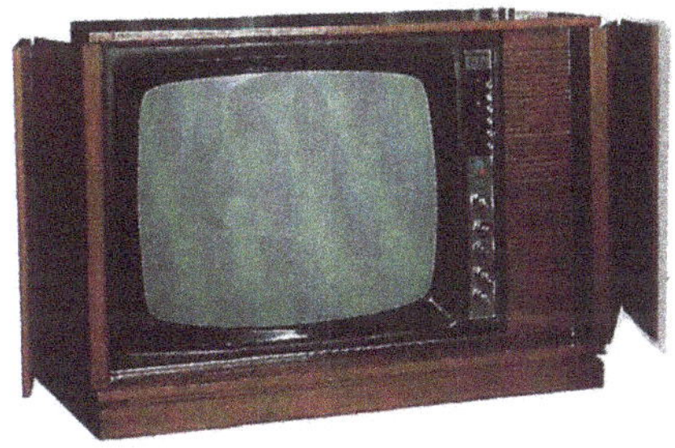

A British world first in colour television - the first all-transistor large screen colour TV from 1967.

Deccacolour domestic receivers, complete with folding doors and a 'do not touch' notice.

After this sight of well-adjusted colour, I persuaded the family back home to join the colour TV set. This was made possible by the popular option of renting, free of worries over maintenance and obsolescence. This enabled a change from our first set, with valves in, and often visited by the repair man to clean its troublesome multi-pole mechanical system change switch, to another British first, a more reliable large screen (22 inches!) all-transistor model with a more stable colour picture.

I must admit, that on occasions, when no one was looking, I had made unauthorised entries into the back of the set to adjust its colour balance. Watching the 'alignment' film during the earlier colour test transmissions, had taught me that a good grey scale on its black & white picture meant the colour image would be good too.

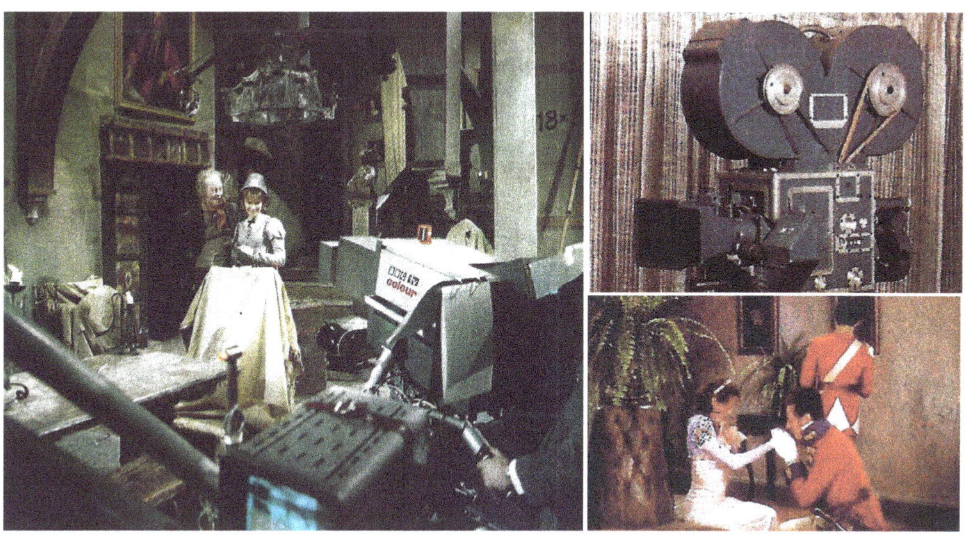

Film and television share a long history together. The shot from on the set of the BBC's first colour costume drama 'Vanity Fair' in 1967 reminds us that it was the same old story, since this had much earlier become the first feature-length Technicolor three-strip film. 'Becky Sharp', adapted from the same novel by Thackeray.

Pride of ownership

For my own first colour set, I saved up for one of Sony's early Trinitrons. Trying to stop me were Telefunken and EMI who controlled the PAL patents. In an effort to resist a Japanese invasion, they had refused Sony a licence to build PAL sets. This didn't put off Sony (or me), who simply eliminated the PAL feature, effectively turning it into a NTSC receiver. It only used the colour information from alternate lines, reducing the vertical colour definition, but the picture on its brighter Trinitron 13 inch (5:4) screen was excellent. It had a NTSC hue 'tint' control, but that rarely needed to be moved from its centre position. My pride of ownership extends to today. After 45 years, I still have it, and with the help of a set-top box it lives on into the digital age. It must have other admirers, as it is now an exhibit in London's Science Museum, considered a milestone in television technology. On later models the extra hue knob wasn't needed, as the developers of PAL relented, allowing all future sets to use it, fearing that any resulting poorer colour would rebound on the reputation of PAL itself.

Colour TV's golden age

The final boost for colour came in 1969, when both BBC1 and ITV became available on 625-lines and in colour. Unfortunately, no sooner had ITV burst into colour, it reverted back to black & white, when its technicians imposed a colour bar, wanting more money to operate the more complicated cameras and other colour gear.

After three months, the colour returned. As 625-line coverage increased, set-makers could begin to make less expensive single-standard receivers, many being exclusive models for the rental companies. The British public would lead the way in embracing colour TV. During a twelve month period between 1972 and 1973, over three million sets were welcomed into viewers' homes. Here they soon became the accepted way to enjoy TV, and the initial fascination and excitement was over.

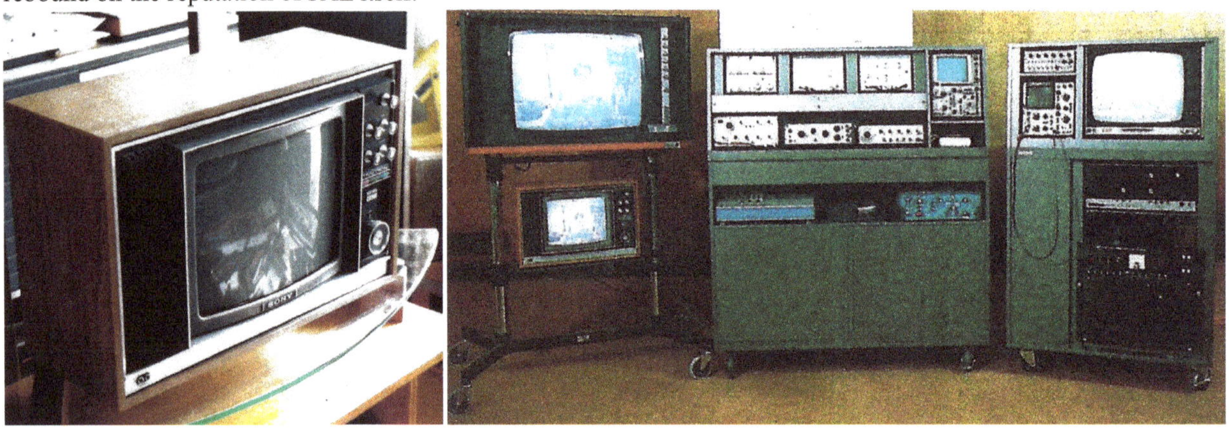

Grant's 45 year old Sony Trinitron, initially produced to get around the PAL patents, and a picture of the equipment that was assembled in 1983 to prove to a high court judge that the French hadn't also invented the basic PAL colour TV system.

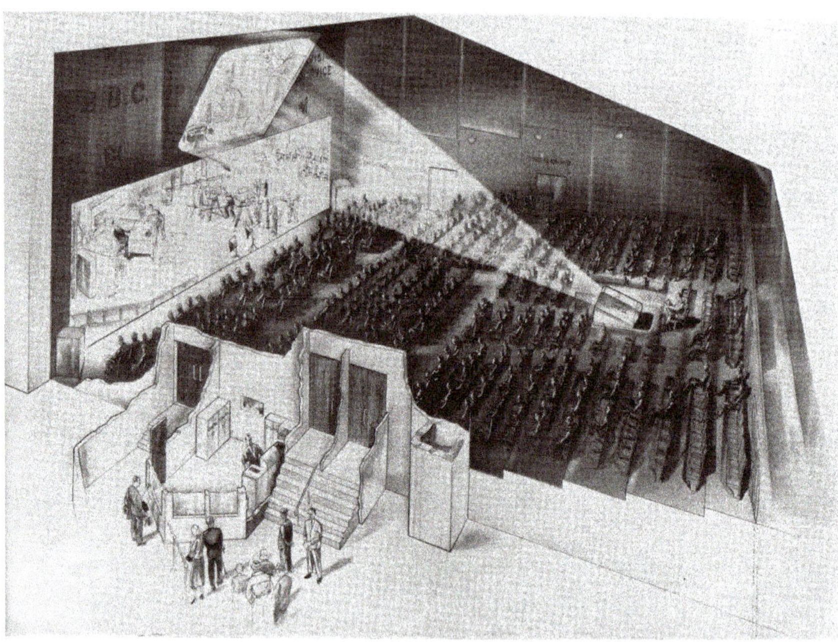

The National Radio Show at Earls Court in 1953 featured a studio-theatre. Visitors could study production techniques through the glass-panels of the studio (left) and could sit in the theatre and watch the picture recorded by the camera, transmitted over the BBC network, projected onto the screen above by the Cintel system which had been developed for cinemas. Those in the front rows who couldn't comfortably see the big projected image could instead see the images from Gaumont-Kalee teleprojectors installed at the sides of the glass panel to the studio. (The Ideal Kinema, August 1953).

Competing with TV - Cinema aims for something different and looks again at film in two different lights

At the end of the 1940s, cinema was experiencing one of its occasional slumps, with many theatres closing. Cinema-goers were losing the habit of a regular trip and only leaving home for well publicised 'big' pictures. Taking its share of the blame, along with other competing leisure activities, was television, which was finally attracting a growing stay-at-home audience. One solution, apart from making better films, was to make the cinema-going experience as different as possible from television. Perhaps it was time to look again at the many 'new' innovations and screen processes, which had previously been passed over when times were good and would be difficult to duplicate on the small screen back home.

A showcase for possible candidates would be the 'Telekinema', the BFI's futuristic cinema being built for the 1951 Festival of Britain, an event celebrating the best of post-war design and technology. During its planning in 1948, its designers considered all the then-available cinematic enhancements. First in the queue to be chosen were stereoscopic movies, soon gaining the tag '3D'.

Most of today's 3D systems are simply more sophisticated and easier to operate versions of the basic methods worked out, and employed at various times, dating back to well-before the birth of moving pictures. The aim of them all is to produce a left- and right-eye viewpoint of a scene, and then ensure it can only be seen by the appropriate eye of the viewer.

Capturing the pair of images is relatively easy. Two cameras can be mounted together with their lenses pointing forward or looking at, or through, an arrangement of mirrors to provide the, required 2½in lateral displacement, the same distance apart as the human eyes. Provision is normally made to reduce the spacing for close-ups and to move further apart to give extra depth to long-shots. An alternative is to use a single camera with two lenses, or an optical attachment, including mirrors and prisms, to place the pair of images, usually reduced in size and orientated in various ways to fit into the space of a normal frame. Either type can be used with both film and digital cameras, but today it's possible to eliminate them altogether.

Digital magic can now turn any ordinary film, both old and new, into 3D. This uses the additional depth clues found in their 'flat' pictures to generate a pair of simulated stereo images. This is not necessarily the easy way, as the process still needs, despite computers, a lot of work from human hands and eyes. So if a 3D version of a new film is planned, it's often best to shoot in 'true' 3D in the first place.

Revealing it all to watching eyes

Much more demanding has been finding the best way to present this added third dimension to the many pairs of eyes in a cinema audience looking at a big screen. One early method was simply to copy the established 'Stereoscope', popular in Victorian parlours for viewing 3D still pictures, and show the pair of images side-by-side on the screen, with viewers holding a mirror device to direct them to the appropriate eye. Unfortunately, this didn't suit a large audience, all at different distances from the screen, and requiring individually adjusted Stereoscopes.

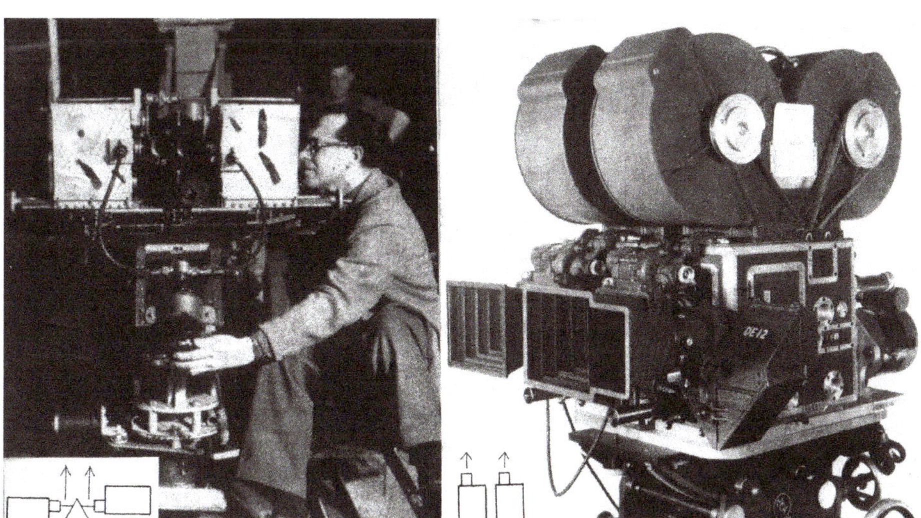

The two different camera systems used to produce the Festival of Britain's 3D films. The BFI's (left) with a pair of cameras facing each other through 45 degree mirrors, shooting the ballet film The Black Swan and (right) two Technicolor 3-strip cameras looking ahead with their 'eyes' too far apart (9½in), so restricted to distant views taken from a boat moving along the river Thames to produce Royal River, in excellent 3D.

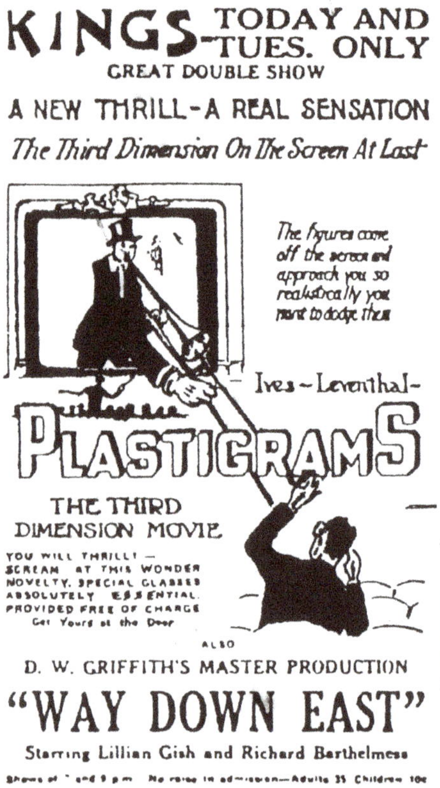

In 1921 the 'Plastigrams' anaglyphic shorts received top billing, and were a greater attraction than the main feature.

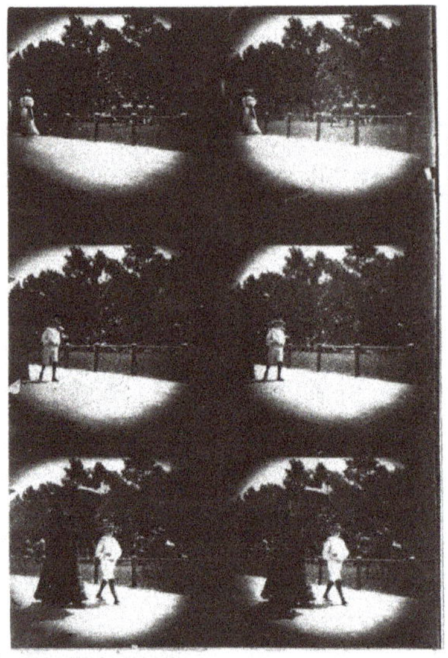

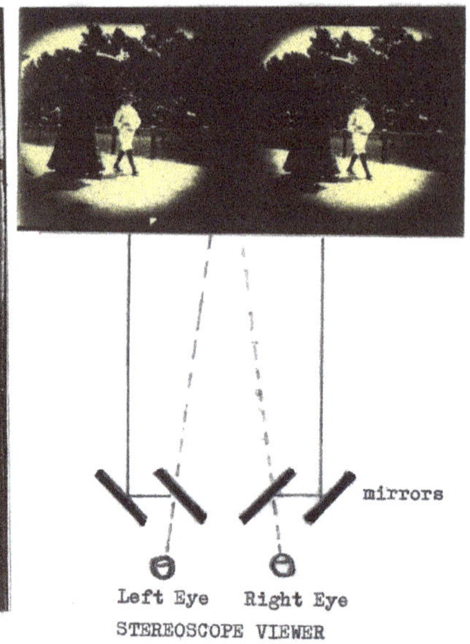

Above:
The 3¼in lantern slide-sized pair of pictures produced from Friese-Green's camera/projector could have been viewed with the aid of a stereoscope-type viewer.

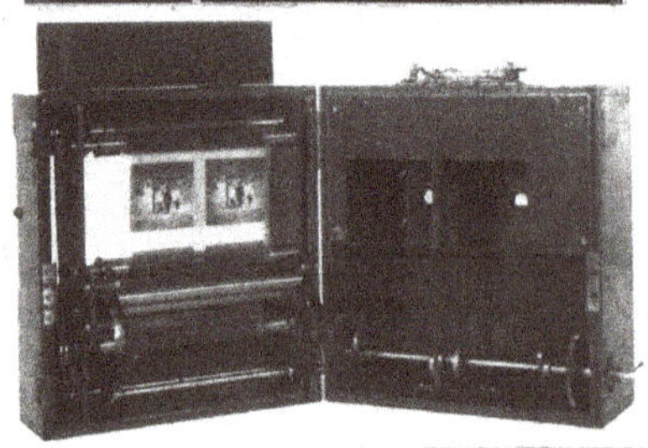

Friese-Green's moving (only just, at best 6fps) camera/projector.

THE BIRTH OF THE 3D IMAGE:

The anaglyph system had also already been applied to stereo still photographs and lantern slides. For this, two images are superimposed in complementary colours, usually red and blue-green (cyan), and viewed through filters with the same combination of colours. Actually, it is the blue-green image which is given a visible density by the red filter, the red being 'washed out', and vice versa.

The first anaglyphs, dating back to soon after the birth of photography in the mid-1800s, had to be projected through filters. But by the 1920s, the arrival of early Technicolor and other two-colour processes made it possible to produce the already superimposed coloured images together on a single film. In the world of 3D, anaglyphs are often dismissed as just a cheap and cheerful novelty, but they require no special projection equipment, the audience enjoying the fun through the cellophane filters of their disposable cardboard glasses.

Sight for sore eyes

It was important superimposed images were accurately aligned, particularly vertically, as our separate eyes don't like to look up and down at the same time. Unfortunately, some viewers can suffer from eye strain and headaches caused by 'retinal rivalry' as the two eyes have to look at a different colour for long periods. Although a few full-length features have been presented this way, the anaglyph system is usually reserved for shorts or 'it's now time to put on your glasses' inserts into the occasional fantasy film, or adding an extra dimension to a horror film's scary moments. Using colour to achieve the separation into each eye was generally thought to restrict anaglyphs to black and white films, but it was later successfully applied to colour films and the odd 3D experiment on television.

These 'polybiochromatic' shows sometimes used a different combination of colours (e.g. blue and light orange), sacrificing some of their efficiency, with a greater risk of each eye seeing a 'ghost' image of the wrong eye breaking through, in exchange for watching a picture in a reasonable range of colours. Whatever the pair of colours chosen to separate the images, there must be a close match between those on the print and in the

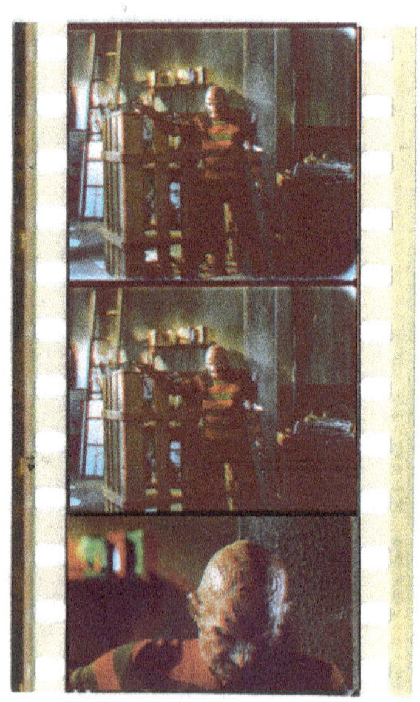

Freddy's Dead (1991). The last ten minutes of the final nightmare was shot in polybiochromatic 3D.

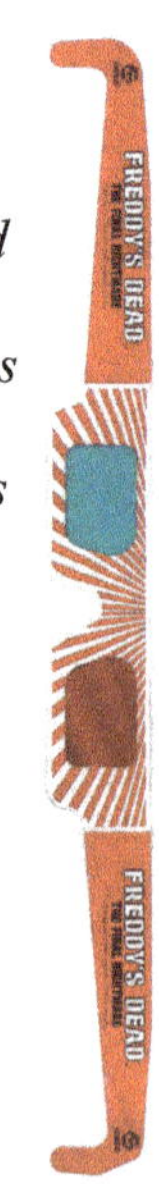

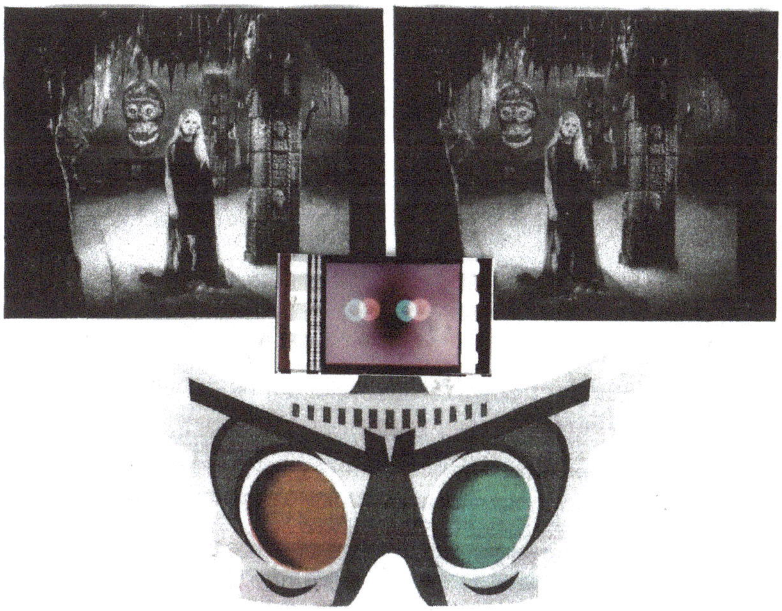

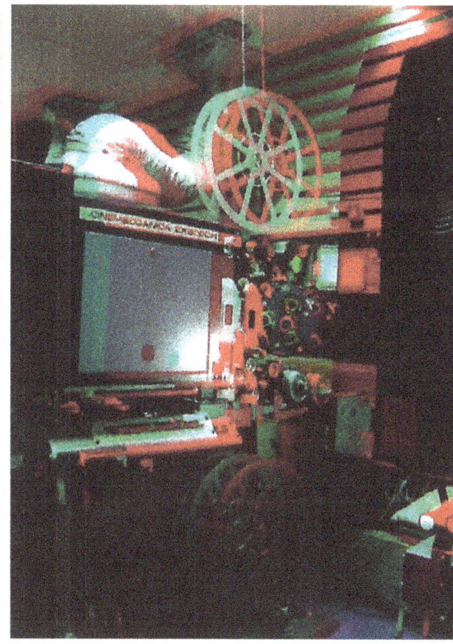

The Mask (1961) included four 3D sequences, shot with dual cameras and converted to single film duo-colour anaglyph. AKA 'The Eyes of Hell', these popped out of the screen with the aid of the novelty mask design red and cyan glasses. The side-by-side on-set pictures can be viewed in 3D by those who can superimpose them by crossing their eyes. Right: Anaglyphic image for viewing with left-over red and cyan 3D glasses.

glasses. Sadly, for 3D archivists, original copies made on the less stable, pre-1980s Eastman Color print film have now faded, leaving only a mostly one-eyed red image.

Recent advances in filter technology have led to the return of a form of anaglyph using the full colour spectrum. It is now possible to sub-divide it into even narrower bands and share them out between the two images, with each eye of the viewer seeing a slightly different shade of the colours in the scene. Although this trick can provide the required separation, it is not apparent to the viewer, whose brain adds it all back together for a normal colour picture. Unfortunately, this very subtle spectral-splitting can't be successfully reproduced on colour film, or even on today's digital projectors, so more costly fine-cut filters have to be employed in both projector(s) and glasses, with the latter now far too valuable to be given away as a memento. Other well-guarded viewing devices use the 'active-shutter' principle. Among the few duo-colour anaglyph shows during the early 1920s was '**Teleview**'. This replaced the coloured glasses, the audience now watching through a rotating shutter which exposed each

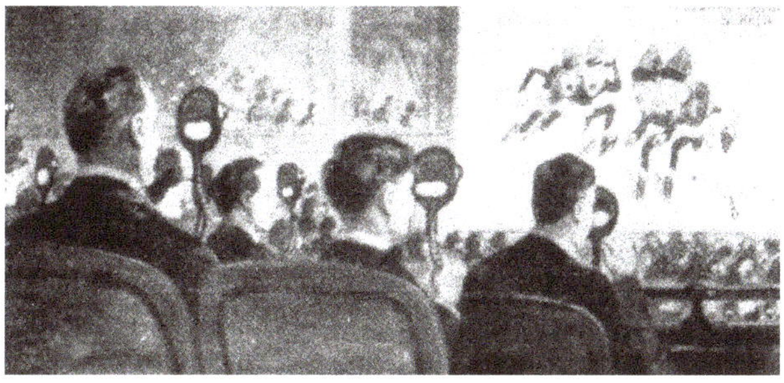

Watching Teleview in 1921 through its seat-mounted shutter viewing devices that rotated at 1,500 rpm.

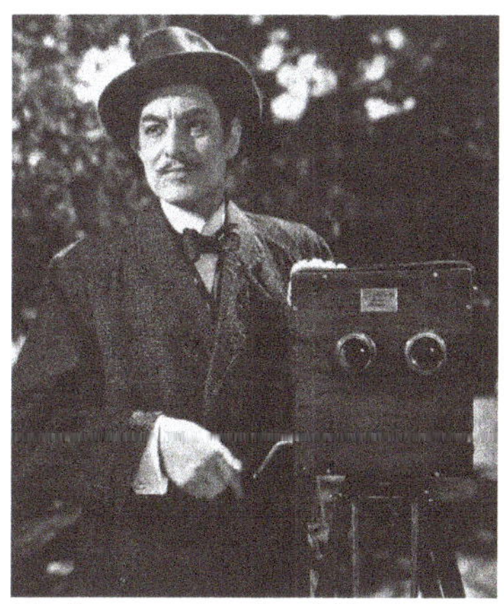

The British film industry's contribution to the Festival of Britain was 'The Magic Box'. A feature film starring Robert Donat as moving picture pioneer William Friese-Green, shown here operating his twin lens camera in 1893. At a time when stereoscopic picture viewers were popular, he thought his first movies should be in 3D too. In the film, the camera, now being used as a projector, only shows one of its pair of images. Although it was shown at the Telekinema, the film's producers weren't brave enough to make it in 3D.

eye in turn to rapidly-alternating left and right images. There were two ways to project them onto the screen. A dual projector method used two prints, one laced a frame behind, with the shutters and intermittents timed to show them in sequence as the other was pulling down.

Another method stacked the pair of stereo images on a single film. Smaller than normal, they were not placed directly one above the other, but offset to allow the blades of an additional special shutter, sweeping across, to again project them in sequence. This now had to be done using a prism attachment to keep them super- imposed on the screen. Although small for the time, the motor and other parts of the mechanical viewing device weren't small enough to wear on the head, so were mounted at eye-level on the seats. They also had to be hard-wired to the projector(s), with all their motors running in step on the same alternating current.

Crystal Gazing

Centuries ago, those studying the nature of light determined that a light beam vibrates in all directions at right angles to its direction of travel. Proof of this was an observation that light passing through a certain kind of crystal emerged vibrating in only one direction, described as being 'polarised'. The crystal acted like a kind of optical grating and if the now-polarised light were to be interrupted again by a second crystal set at the same axis, with its own 'grid' parallel to the first, it could pass through, but, if turned, the light gradually diminished, until at 90 degrees it was blocked altogether. Looking through the same crystal, it was also discovered that light reflected off the surface of glass or water, at a precise angle (54 degrees) had also become polarised. With the coming of photography, it was suggested that differently polarised light could be used to present stereoscopic lantern slides. In 1891, this was demonstrated using prisms fabricated from large crystals, but these were far too expensive and fragile to be practical at the time. It wasn't until 1932, that Edwin Land (of later instant-camera fame) introduced his synthetic 'Polaroid' polarising 'filter. He had found a way to embed millions of microscopic needle-like polarising crystals in plastic (originally celluloid) and the process of extruding it into very thin sheets pulled them all into alignment. This thin film filter material could be used in cheap viewers, or laminated between glass to stand up to the heat of projection. They were also neutral in colour, so the first demonstrations in 1936 could use the newly launched 16mm Kodachrome.

The shows had little effect on the cinema industry, even after a stand-out presentation at the 1939 New York World's Fair. The event also introduced the American public to a future rival attraction, television. The big queues, however, were at a motor industry exhibit where a pair of projectors, fitted with Polaroid filters set at 90 degrees, showed a stop-motion stereoscopic film of a Chrysler apparently building itself without the help of human hands. This feat was seen in greater depth through car-shaped cardboard viewers, with matching oppositely opposed filters. While waiting for 3D to jump out of the screen, most Polaroid viewing would be through sunglasses, helping to reduce the polarising element in its reflected glare.

There is a price to pay

Although not a problem for sunglasses, light loss of polarising filters results in 3D pictures considerably less bright than normal. Less than 50% gets through filters on the projectors, a further 20% is lost by the glasses. The usual matt white screen scatters the light, destroying the polarisation, so must be replaced by a metallised 'silver' version able to maintain polarisation. The higher reflectivity of this type of screen helps compensate for the filter's light loss - but at a cost of being more directional and less suitable for ordinary films, particularly in auditoria with wider viewing angles. The audience, too, has to co-operate by sitting up straight. Tilting the head can let some of the wrong eye image through. The risk of seeing a double image could be reduced by slanting the polarisation or adding extra diffracting crystals which can twist it into a left or right spiral, the now circular pattern allowing for greater head movement and fewer ghosts.

Crystals on the move

Another way to produce a polarising filter was to suspend the crystals in plastic while still in its fluid state and use an electro-magnetic force to hold them in alignment while it hardens into a solid. If the crystals are kept in a liquid, it is possible to produce an electrically controlled light valve, or a switch to turn it on or off rapidly. For example, if a layer of randomly dispersed crystals is placed between two opposing polarising filters, the light is still blocked, but in response to an electrical signal, the crystals move in a way to rotate the already polarised light from the first filter now to match the direction of the second, allowing the light to pass through.

This, together with advances in micro-electronics, made it possible to make lightweight remote-controlled shutter glasses for an updated sequential 3D system. The polarised light effect is only used in the glasses to blind each eye in turn in sync with the alternating frames, which can now be projected onto a normal white screen. Such sophisticated 'active' glasses are more expensive than the existing types and require more maintenance and management by the cinema, so have become a less popular option.

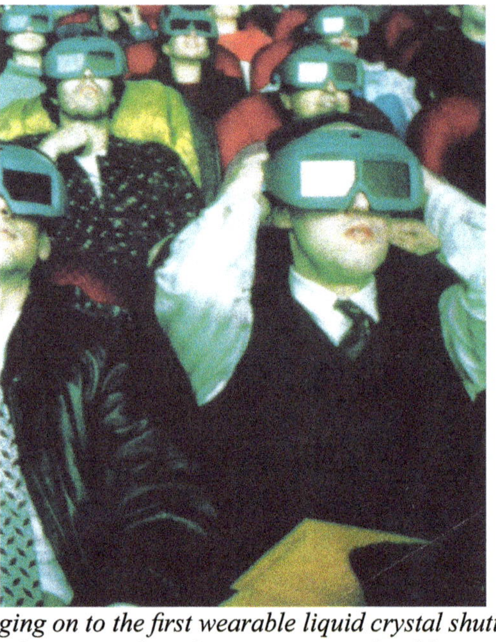

Hanging on to the first wearable liquid crystal shutter 3D glasses. Modern designs are considerably more lightweight, fortunately.

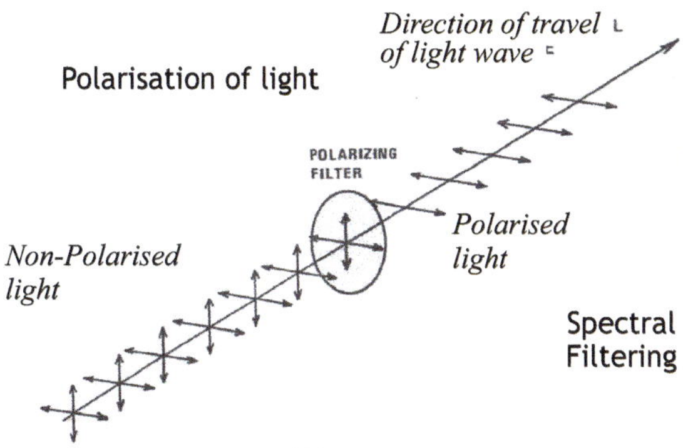

Old style glasses which can also give depth to comics and 'pin-up' magazines

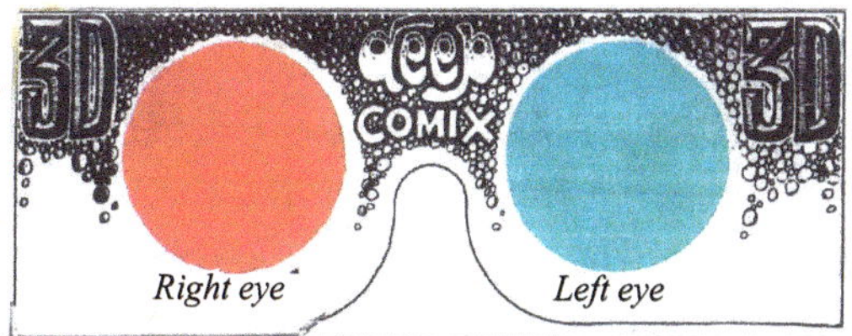

Spectral Filtering

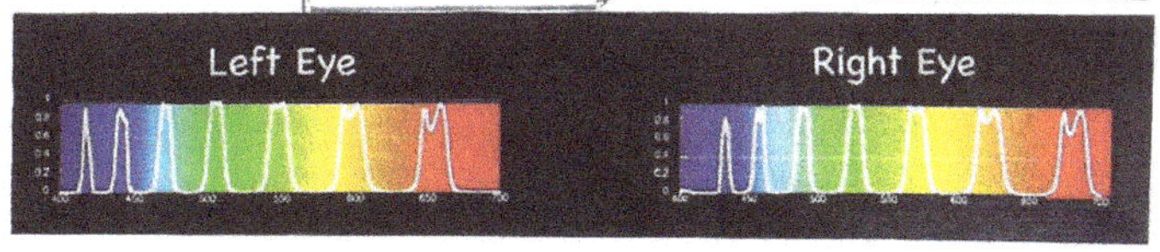

The current most popular 3D projection methods use either the polarisation of light or an updated version of the original red and green anaglyph system, now dividing the whole spectrum into two different sets of narrower colour bands, either by multi-layer filters or by adjusting the wavelengths of a pair of RGB laser light sources.

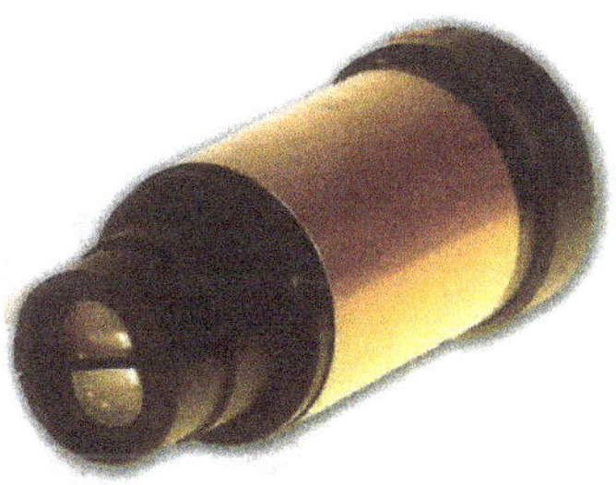

Some digital single projector (SXRD) 3D shows also have to stack a pair of smaller images within the normal area of their imaging chips. 3D TV can also be transmitted in a similar way.

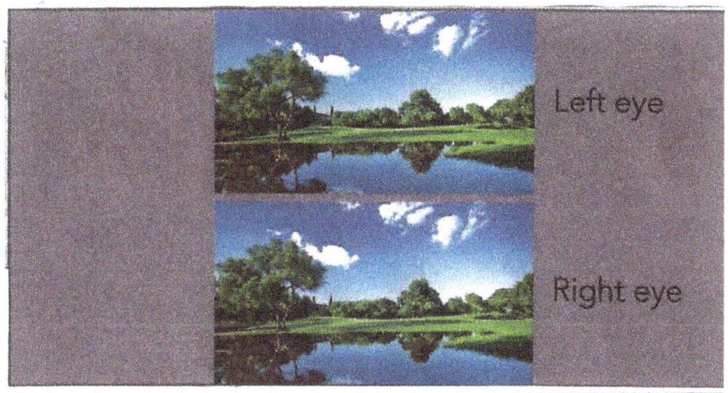

For today's single projector digital cinema, sequential 3D is now the most common system, but with the alternating left and right pictures now being individually polarised back in the projection box. This is achieved using either a synchronised filter wheel or by projecting the image through an LCD filter panel, its crystals being moved to change the direction of the polarisation instantly for each of the images as they are shown on a silver screen and viewed using cheaper, ordinary 'passive' polarised glasses. Some digital projectors (SXRD) can't provide the high picture frequencies needed for successful sequential 3D, so have to go back to the old film idea of placing two smaller stereo images within the space of the chip's normal frame area and use a lens attachment to polarise each and superimpose them on the screen.

Every lumen is sacred

Many accounts of 3D history end with the prospect of new lenticular and holographic systems appearing from around the corner to banish the glasses. Although the developers and promoters of today's 3D presentation systems think that everybody is happy wearing their well-designed and comfortable glasses, they are still a bit of a nuisance, and need looking after by both the cinema and the audience. Although enjoying the fun of the 3D experience, it comes at the cost of a far dimmer picture without its normal punch and sparkle.

As it looks like we are stuck with the glasses for some time to come, much work is being done to squeeze as much light as possible through them. If it can be paid for, by increased ticket sales, the 'brute force' method of using dual projectors with even more powerful light sources can approach the screen brightness of normal 2D films shown on the same size higher gain screens. These too have received much attention to try and make them more compatible, reducing centre hot spots and the fall off of the illumination when viewed from the side.

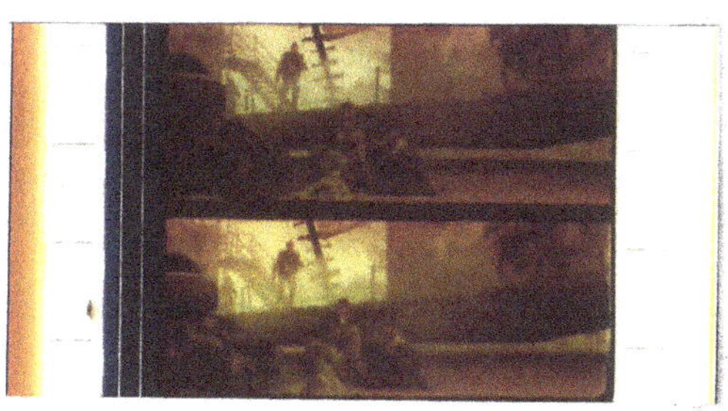

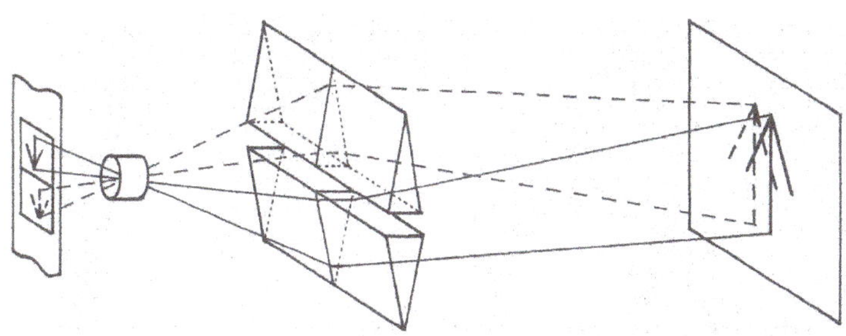

The dual projector system of the 1950s short-lived 3D boom had, by the 1970s, given way to the more convenient single film format with over and under stacked images. Shown with a special twin lens, or a beam-combiner in front of the normal lens, which if too close, the prisms of some, could produce unwanted 'ghost' images (not indicated) above and below the screen which had to be masked off. Current types of polarising attachments try to recover wasted light to make the 3D pictures brighter (less dim).

Ghost-busting

Apart from damaging them, pushing higher levels of light through the filters also risks seeing signs of the other eye breaking through. Circular polarisation, particularly when combined with the single projector switching panels, or modulators, is not as good as plane polarising filters at blocking the light, typically 10% less efficient. For digital shows, the pair of images can receive extra 'ghost-busting' processing to make the problem less visible. The relative brightness and contrast between each eye's picture is modified from moment to moment to cancel out the ghosting. When heavily applied, it can reduce the overall contrast of the final complete 3D image, which is not always appreciated by those producing the best original mastered images. The alternative spectrum-splitting 'wavelength multiplexing' colour filter system has been able to benefit from the latest big thing in projection, laser light sources. The brightest combine the light from triple red, green and blue laser units, to produce normal high-intensity white light. Although still needed in the glasses, the multi-coated (up to 30 layers) filters in the projector can be replaced by tweaking two separate sets of RGB lasers to achieve the slightly different range of colours for each eye. For alternating single-lens 3D, the mechanical spinning spectrum-splitting filter wheel, which also absorbs some of the light, can now be replaced by, for one option, a shutter to switch between the two different light sources. If the glasses become cheaper, the advantages of this system, including keeping a white screen, will make it a greater challenge to the polarising methods.

Fighting for every ounce of light

The latest big thing for the rival polarising systems is the idea to recover the light left behind by the filters on the projector. A special beam-splitter, incorporating the polarising filter, is included in an optical system of prisms and mirrors to form a matching polarised secondary image, made up from some of the normally lost light, superimposing it on the main picture to gain an extra percentage of light. It isn't that easy, as the separate beams emerge from the periscope-style attachment at different angles. Care is needed to register them accurately on the screen without spoiling the definition. On the latest models, the angles are reduced by showing the secondary image, in two halves, closer above and below the main beam, and blending the join on the screen.

Back to the Telekinema

All these future 3D developments were yet to come in 1951, so a system using basic twin-interlocked projectors, fitted with crossed Polaroid filters was chosen for showing the Telekinema's (sometimes called the Telecinema) stereoscopic films at the theatre built on the South Bank for the Festival of Britain. A programme of shorts was produced, including a ballet film, a Technicolor trip up the river Thames, a light-hearted look at how 3D works and, perhaps the most memorable, Norman McLaren's pair of abstract animations, one with floating hand-painted patterns and the other featuring figures formed on a cathode-ray tube. The carbon arcs of two BTH projectors provided a well-lit picture on a modest-sized silver screen. Although this was 20ft wide, the actual image only occupied 15ft of it, leaving a border which was illuminated by diffused light constant-

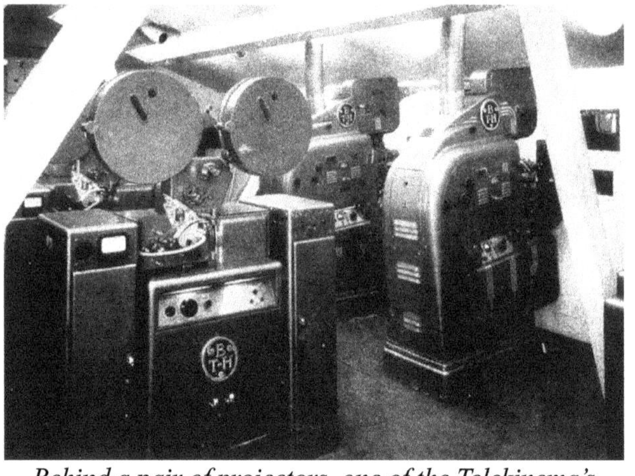

Behind a pair of projectors, one of the Telekinema's four-track magnetic sound recorder / reproducers

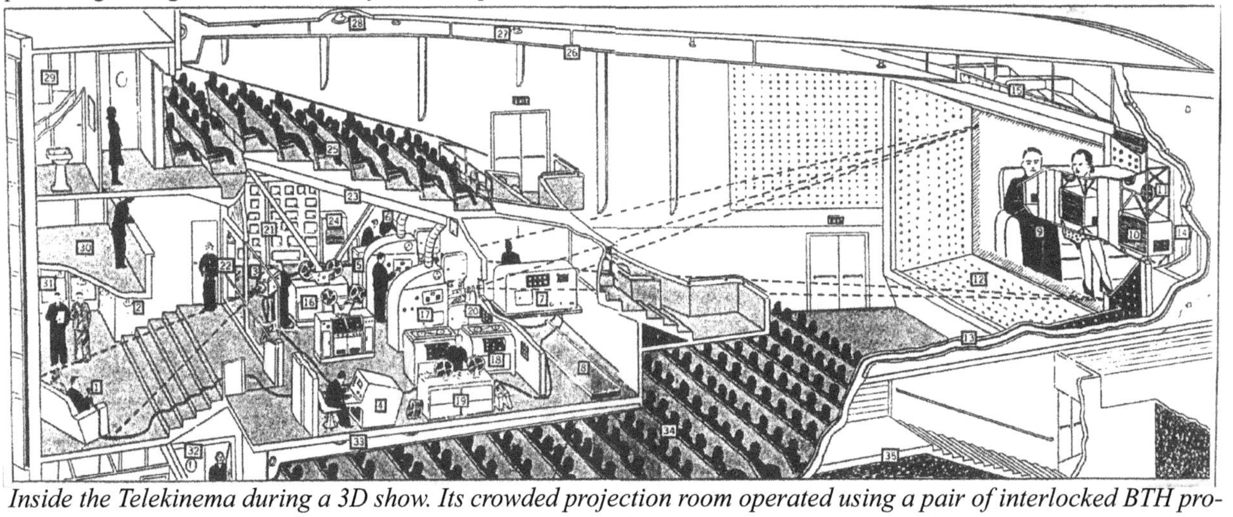

Inside the Telekinema during a 3D show. Its crowded projection room operated using a pair of interlocked BTH projectors and separate magnetic sound reproducers. Out in front is the video projector fed mostly from a TV camera looking through the glass rear wall back down the stairs to the foyer.

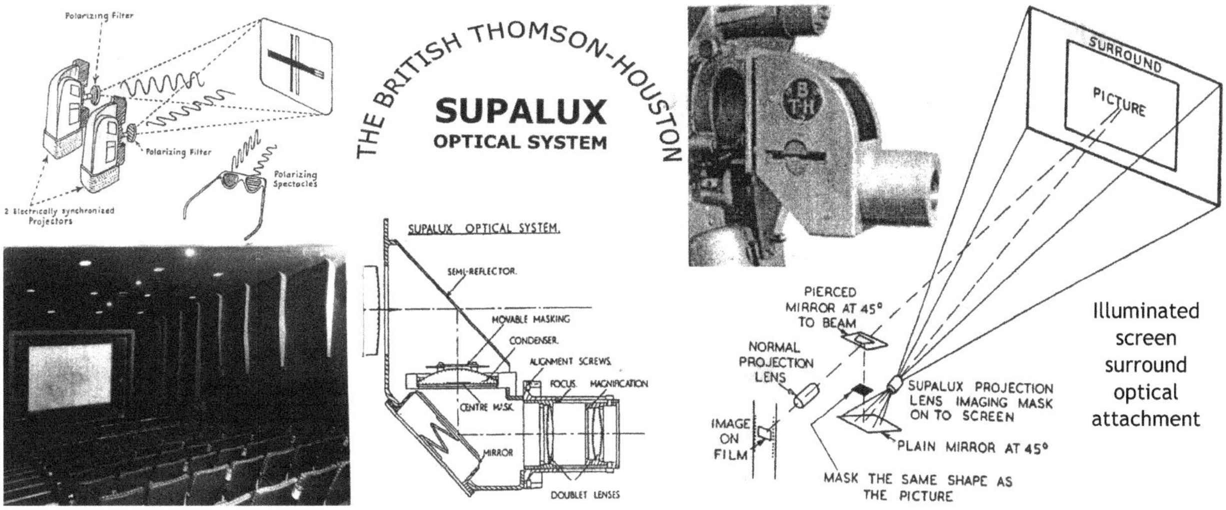

Diagram showing the synchronised dual projector set up and the Supalux illuminated screen optical attachment

ly changing in brightness and colour to match the film's picture. This was achieved using a BTH 'Superlux' attachment, which took some of the light from the beam and projected a masked-off portion through its own lens to create the pool of light around the picture. Although available to give ordinary films a 'bigger look', it was thought at the time to be particularly useful for 3D, which wouldn't be confined by a hard-edged window of black masking.

Giving a rival some space

As the theatre's name suggests, the screen was sometimes filled by big screen television, but its video projector wasn't allowed in the box. Needing a shorter throw anyway, it had to stay outside on an enclosed veranda in front, able to be pushed aside when the films were being shown. The still-crowded projection room was situated under the circle and had a glass rear wall so visitors coming up the stairs could see the equipment and all that was going on to prepare for the show. Staring back at them was a TV camera with a view looking back down to the foyer. This provided much pre-show amusement, as many in the audience rushed out again to wave at friends, who watched their antics on the big screen.

Hearing in 3D too

As well as a treat for the audience's eyes, the Telekinema also offered the first chance for their ears to experience high- fidelity stereophonic sound. Running in step with the projectors were a pair of new BTH magnetic recorder/reproducers. These had been built with the help of EMI who had already gained some experience of stereophonic sound for the cinema when, back in 1936, their inventive genius Alan Blumlein demonstrated his twin stereo optical soundtrack. At the Telekinema, the 35mm fully-coated magnetic film had room for four tracks, three driving speakers behind the screen, the fourth feeding others around the auditorium. As magnetic sound was only just beginning to replace optical for original studio recordings, the Festival's film soundtracks, including music, had to be recorded on machines at the Telekinema itself. Amazingly, McLaren also 'drew' the stereophonic sounds to accompany his hand-painted animated 3D images, which had to be transferred to the magnetic film.

A good space to see and hear it all

The auditorium too, looked to the future. Gone was the 'picture palace' decor, in favour of a muted colour scheme leaving the eyes to concentrate on the screen. This had perfect sightlines from all its seats, even from those at the back of the steeply raked circle. Although there were only 400 seats, nearly half a million people enjoyed its 45 minute 3D shows.

Following the Telekinema's success

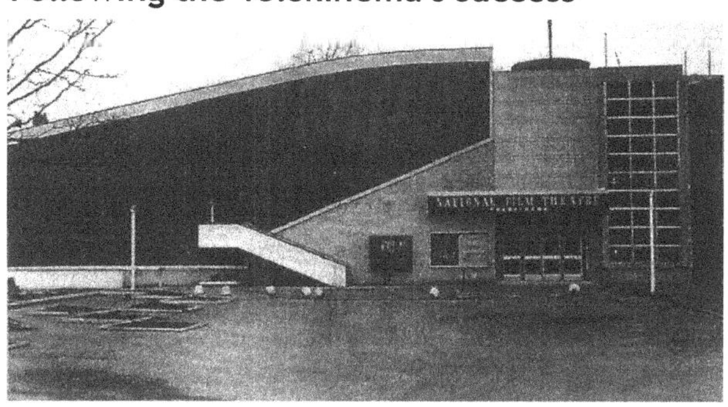

After the 1951 Festival of Britain the Telekinema became the first National Film Theatre, before being rebuilt under Waterloo Bridge in 1957

The crowds at the Telekinema went largely unnoticed by the mainstream cinema industry, but other independent minds saw the possibilities of 3D. In the USA, the 'Natural Vision' Corporation built a 3D camera based on the Festival's layout of a pair of cameras facing each other, picking up the scene at right angles reflected off 45 degree mirrors. In their case, the compact, silent cameras were replaced by standard Mitchell studio models enclosed in a huge blimp for sync sound shooting. Test footage was shown to the major studios, but their bosses still thought 3D was okay as a novelty programme filler, but audiences wouldn't put up with wearing special

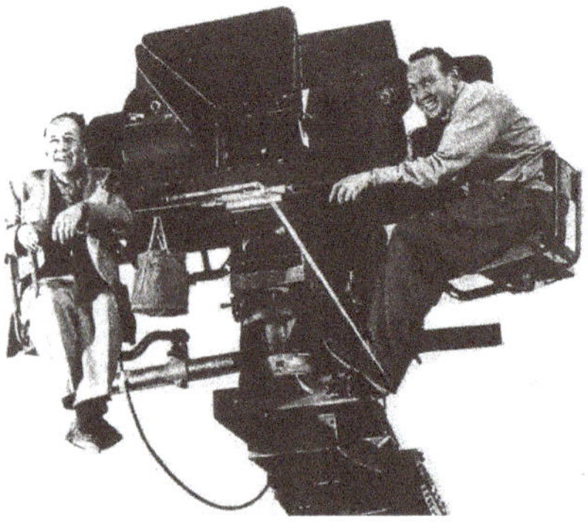

Having fun operating the 'Natural Vision' 3D camera used for both 'Bwana Devil' and 'House of Wax'

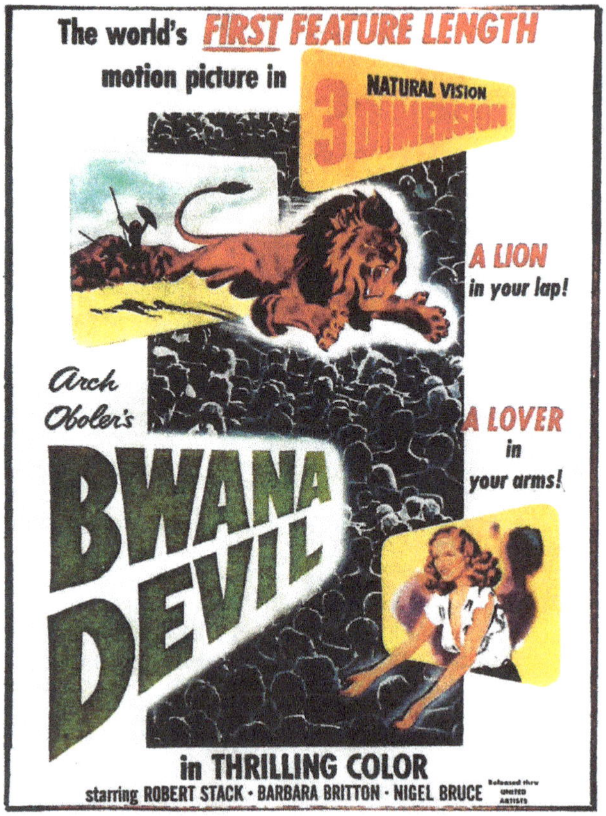

glasses for a complete performance. It was pointed out that the Telekinema had been fully booked throughout the Festival and everybody seemed happy in glasses. Among those seeing the test material was Hollywood writer/director Arch Oboler. He was planning a low-budget feature based on the exploits of a real-life 'white hunter'. In the 1920s and 1930s, they were celebrities of their day, with the public thrilled at tales of killing lions and tigers, with the odd elephant too. By the 1950s, this had become more acceptable if the animals had first become man-eaters, in this case, a couple of lions making a meal of workers building a trans-African railway. On Oboler's return to the USA, he did a deal with Natural Vision to film all the carnage in 3D, with the hills above Malibu in California standing in for Africa. Bwana Devil was released in 1952 to great disdain from the critics - 'Do you want to see a good film, or a lion in your lap?!' Judging by the queues around the block, audiences preferred lions leaping out of the screen. The success of Bwana Devil, among the indifferent films only remembered today because they were 'in something', launched the first of the recurring 3D booms. Over the following year or so, more than 60 films had various objects popping out of the screen with most, both in colour and black and white, using the dual-film polarised method. Some were shown with separate magnetic sound.

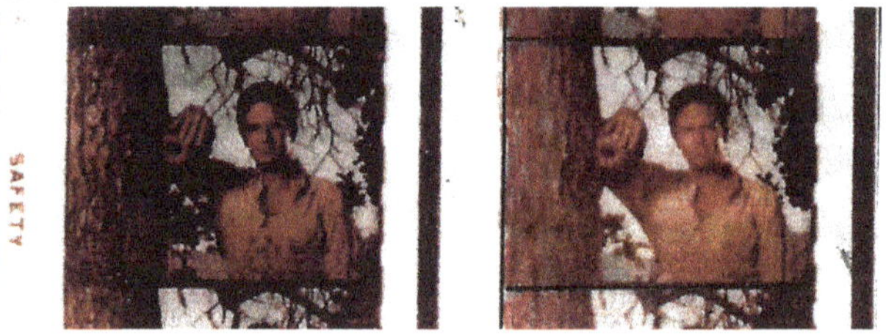

Left and right frames from 'Bwana Devil' transposed for unaided cross-eyed viewing. Released in 1952 this film was shot full frame as some of the first showings used separate magnetic (mono) sound.

An example, often quoted as the first 3D feature, was House of Wax. Made by Warner Bros, it was one of the best and came with '**Warnerphonic**' stereo sound. This was quite complex. Its separate 35mm magnetic film had three tracks, two for the music, the other for the dialogue, which was moved between the three screen speakers by sub-audible control tones. The system was completed with the rear auditorium speakers fed by one of the print's optical tracks, the other track carrying the full soundtrack as a stand-by, or for theatres without magnetic facilities.

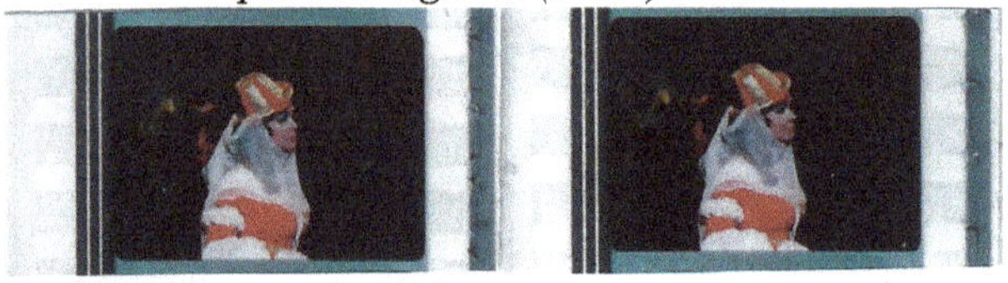

'Kiss me Kate' with three-track magnetic sound.

As in all subsequent periods of enthusiasm for 3D, it sooner or later retreats back into the screen until it again becomes time to offer a new generation of cinema-goers the chance to have fun experiencing big screen 3D. Fortunately, each time we are left with improved and/or more convenient technology, with many of today's digital cinemas now always ready, at the flick of a switch and a cupboard full of glasses, to show the next 3D film to come along.

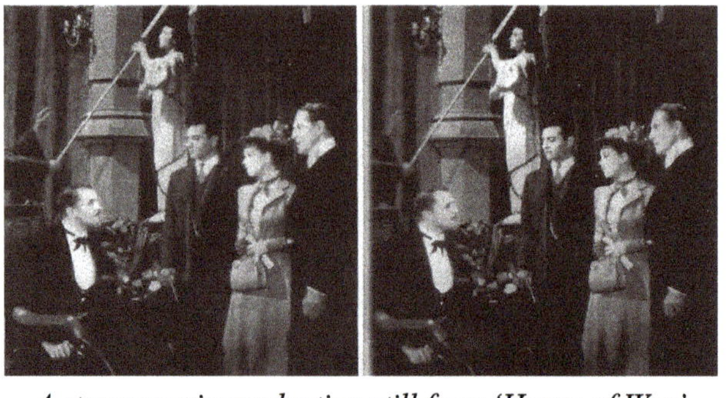

A stereoscopic production still from 'House of Wax'. Provided for those with the knack of un-aided stereoscopic viewing

That's what I call Showmanship

the success of the cinema business has always depended on making a visit something to remember

The Magic Of The Cinema Casts Its Spell - Grant Lobban reminisces

My interest in the technical side of the cinema began while I was still at school during the 1950s. Back then, I always looked forward to family trips up to London. These usually included a visit to Hamleys toy shop, before lunch at the Quality Inn (days before McDonald's) and then, in the afternoon, enjoying a matinee at the Palladium or Cinerama. The latter always got my vote and in the souvenir programme the "What is Cinerama?" section, with its intriguing diagrams and pictures of the 3-eyed camera, soon captured my imagination, and I was hooked.

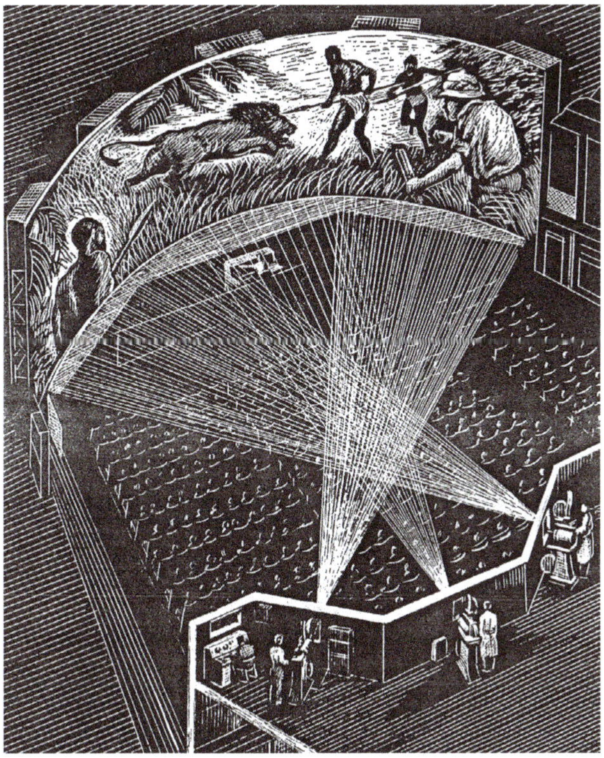

I eventually saw all of Cinerama's triple-panel films and the early ones had a live overture played by the London Casino Orchestra. When the film's new fangled 'magnetic' stereophonic sound took over, it sounded just as good. As an extra treat, when *South Seas Adventure* came to an unexpected halt, we were shown the behind-the-scenes 'breakdown' film on a smaller screen before the problem was fixed and the adventure continued on the giant curved screen.

Back home in Reading, I eagerly awaited the arrival at a cinema in the town of the latest widescreen epic, particularly if it was in a new 'scope, 'rama or 'vision. If my eyes ever wandered from the screen, it was to look back at the projection box to try and spot the spools going round, or a face at the window during a change-over. Books borrowed from the library, including The Complete Projectionist, had taught me about watching out for the cue dots and then waiting to see the beam jump to another porthole. I would have a long wait today.

Despite this fascination, I was never to work in a cinema projection room, but I did join the BBC's Film Department as a studio projectionist. Many of my colleagues had come from cinemas so, over the years, I heard many stories about life in a 'proper' projection box. Also, projectionists were on the circulation list for the trade papers like Today's Cinema and Kine Weekly. Apart from keeping up with any new screen 'process', many of which were sadly only inventions of the film companies' publicity departments and poster designers, my favourite section was the 'Showmanship' page. I soon learned that this term didn't only mean dimming the house lights and opening and closing the curtains at the right moment, but also included the many gimmicks and publicity stunts dreamed up to tempt punters into the theatres. Every week, there was news of super wheezes, not only 'official' ones devised by the film's distributor, but also those thought up by local managers and cinema staff with a heightened sense of showbiz.

Roll up, Roll up

For me, the most memorable stunts were those which would now be considered to be in poor taste or non-PC. I enjoyed seeing pictures of 'volunteers' from a cinema's female staff going around the town wearing only bikinis and offering free tickets to any young ladies who would come to see *Bikini Beach* (1964) similarly attired,

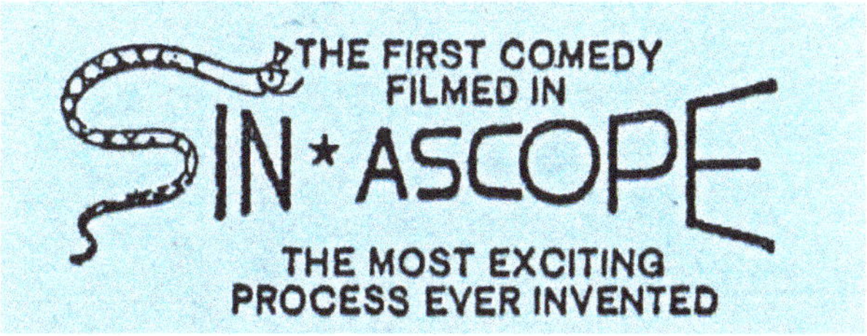

You won't find this exciting movie process in the technical books - it was only invented for use on the ads for 'Happy Anniversary' (1959)

and become an added attraction for male members of the paying audience. Another of my favourites, was the manager and projectionists dressed up as Nazi officers demanding to see Saturday shoppers' identification papers before handing out flyers advertising *Where Eagles Dare* (1968). I did worry a little at the time that an elderly veteran with a weak heart, who had survived WWII might have become a late casualty at the sight of an old enemy coming round the corner. Particularly popular with children was the use of exotic animals. I remember a reluctant camel helping to promote *Carry On Follow That Camel* (1967), although it didn't seem to want to go anywhere. A source for moonlighting wild animals was a visiting circus, at a time when no Big Top show was considered complete without its lions, tigers, elephants and other animal acts. I now feel a little guilty that I enjoyed these the most back then when you could still go and see a 'real' circus.

Tony Tenser, British producer of sexploitation and horror films (Tigon) during the 1960s and 1970s, began his movie career as a cinema manager. Back in 1949, he had already shown a gift for PR and exploitation when, at the Central Cinema, Cambridge, he staged a sheepdog trial to promote *Challenge to Lassie*.

Distributing bogus newspaper supplements with headlines linked to a film's plot has been used a few times. Theatre staff, acting as newspaper sellers, handed out a fictitious 'Graphic Gazette' warning that *Behemoth the Sea Monster* (1959) was on the loose. If this didn't cause panic in the streets, the film's campaign material suggested the use of a loudspeaker van broadcasting 'Britain in peril - Behemoth is heading this way'. Another mock paper, 'The Daily Globe' carried the headline 'Panic as Gorgo Approaches' for another British colossal creature feature *Gorgo* (1952), our answer to a more famous man in a rubber suit monster, *Godzilla*. Also provided were stencils to paint giant footprints on the pavement leading to the cinema, 'if local bye-laws permit'.

Enter if you dare

Once enticed into the cinema, you might not be left in peace to enjoy the show. A depiction of what you could be in for in the way of added showmanship can be seen in the projectionists all time favourite *The Smallest Show on Earth* (1957) when the boiler at the Bijou is turned up to enhance the viewing experience while watching the latest 'desert' picture. The rising temperature, with its threat of heatstroke, was also good for business, encouraging the sweating audience to buy more ice creams. In the real world, it was to be horror films which would inspire showmen to do their worst.

Way back in 1931, the opening of Universal's *Frankenstein* carried a warning that the film was not suitable for those with 'feeble nerves'. Faint-hearted patrons, who decided to risk it anyway, were made even more nervous at the sight of a strategically placed ambulance outside the theatre and out of work actresses playing the part of nurses available if needed during the performance. This ploy proved popular over the years, including for some of the early showings of Hitchcock's *Psycho* (1960). The 'Showmanship' page reported similar medical cover, but on a lower budget, when the ice-cream girl did a quick-change act into a nurse between sales intervals to stand at the back of the auditorium in case of heart attacks during a scary movie. I wondered what would have happened if a member of the audience was genuinely taken poorly and all the 'nurse' could offer in the way of treatment would have been a nice Eldorado choc ice or a Kia-ora orange squash! (Included to show my age.)

Don't worry, we have got you covered

If all help failed and the worst did happen during *Frankenstein's Bloody Terror* (1972) at least you got a free burial.

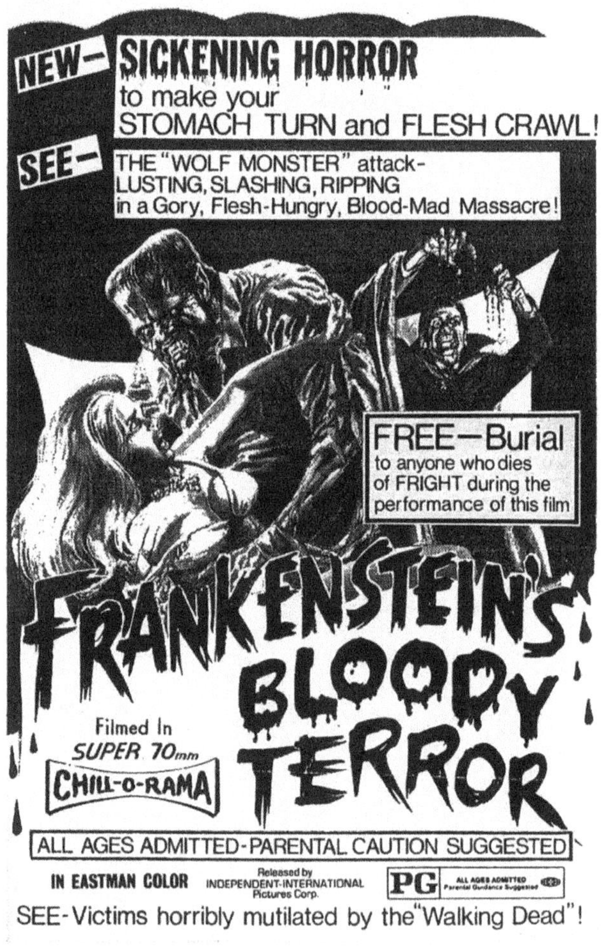

A visit to see Roger Corman's *The Pit and the Pendulum* (1961) included life insurance cover to the tune of £10,000 payable to the first person who died of fright.

This fringe benefit was also on offer from the king of the gimmicks, producer/director William Castle. He became known as the 'Hitchcock' of the B-movies, also appearing in his own trailers and prologues promising all kinds of 'horrors' while watching some of his films. For his

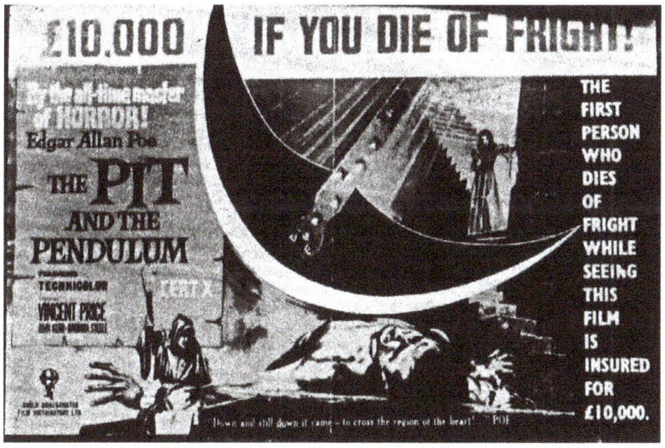

Macabre (1958) the price of the ticket included a Lloyds of London insurance policy to cover being scared to death. At £1000 it wasn't so generous, but there was no restriction to the number of deaths. I never heard of any claims, but I'm sure the producer's investigator was ready to prove the death was caused by boredom and not covered.

Skeletons might fly

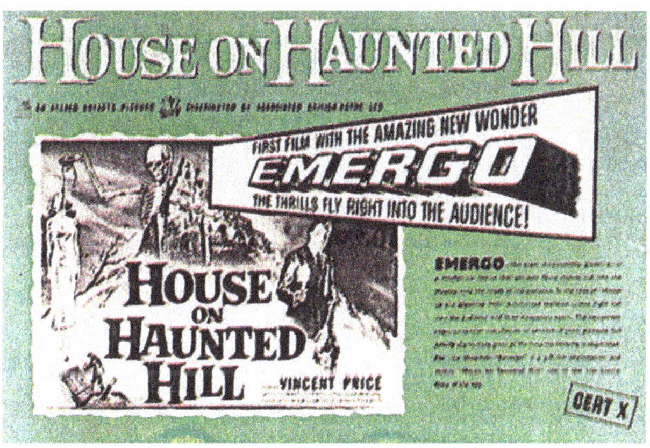

More famous on William Castle's roll of gimmicks was the luminous skeleton which floated over the audience during *House on Haunted Hill* (1958). Called Emergo, it emerged on cue from a black box by the side of the screen and travelled on a wire strung across the auditorium, either hand operated or the deluxe motor-driven push button model. I have spoken to many people privileged to have seen Emergo in the flesh, or more accurately without any, and their opinions differ about its effectiveness, form and even flight pattern. Some said they were scared, but only of it falling on them. Others thought it was 'a bit of a joke' particularly on a Saturday night, when the more unruly element among the audience refused to enter into the spirit of the apparition. On many occasions, Emergo was more frightened of the audience, soon scurrying back to the safety of its box under fire from a hail of discarded ice cream tubs. There were also differing views of its construction. Was it a relatively heavy *'Doctor in the House'* medical student-type skeleton, or a lighter plastic or even a blow-up version which would have been far safer if it was ever shot down? Using my contacts in the world of movie memorabilia collectors and museums, I tried to

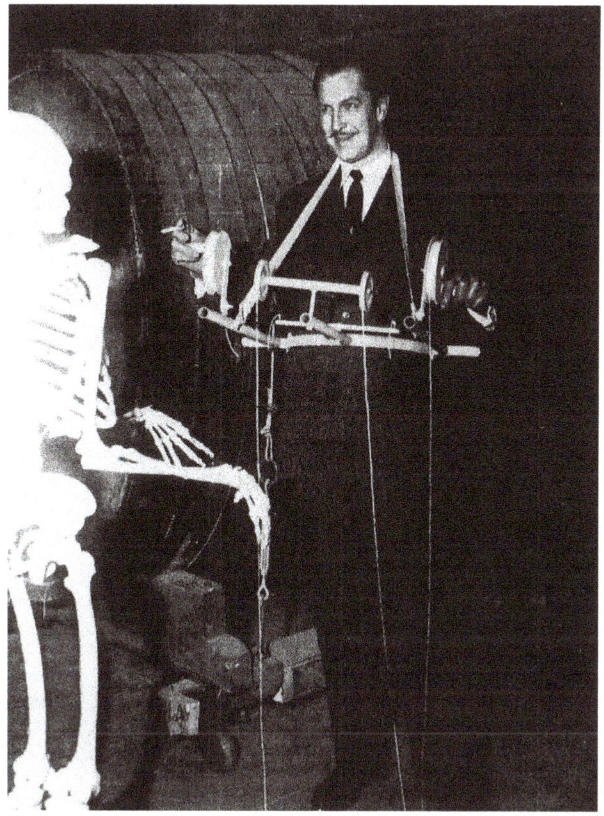

find an original Emergo to examine its bones and see if they still glow in the dark, but no luck. I haven't given up hope, so if you know of any old ex-projectionist with a skeleton in his cupboard, it may be an Emergo. If any readers were ever Emergo's 'roadies' or helped set it in motion, let me know.

As an update, I discovered, in an early 1991 issue of Cinema Technology, an account by Alan Ashton of the day the Emergo roadshow arrived at the Lyric, Wellingborough. At the time he was the Chief and thought it was all 'hilarious', except perhaps the disruption with Emergo's hideout and fittings being bolted to the walls, and its control system needing a hole right through into the projection box. Before it was ready to go, the local Licensing Authority had to inspect the setup to make sure the stretched out wire couldn't be reached by any member of the audience. Alan described the skeleton as being inflatable, and in case of anything sharp coming from the enemy below, its first aid kit included a puncture repair outfit. This information has made me think that finding an original Emergo may be even more difficult, as they may by now all have literally perished.

I looked forward to the CGI enhanced remake of *House on Haunted Hill* (1999), hoping that Emergo would appear again in a modern hi-tech form, like a projected hologram hovering above the audience, but I was disappointed.

Our seats are shocking

Close on the heel bones of Emergo was 'Percepto', another of William Castle's physical off-screen processes, dreamed up this time for *'The Tingler'* in 1959. The

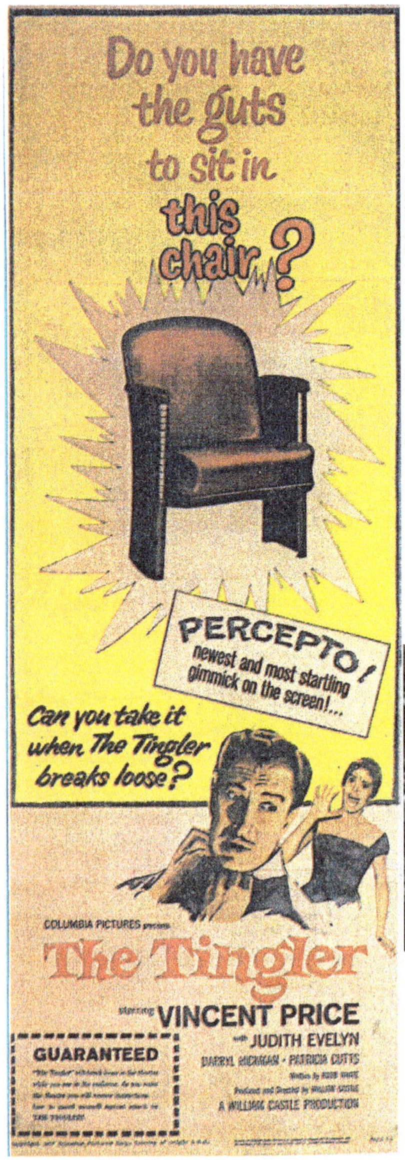

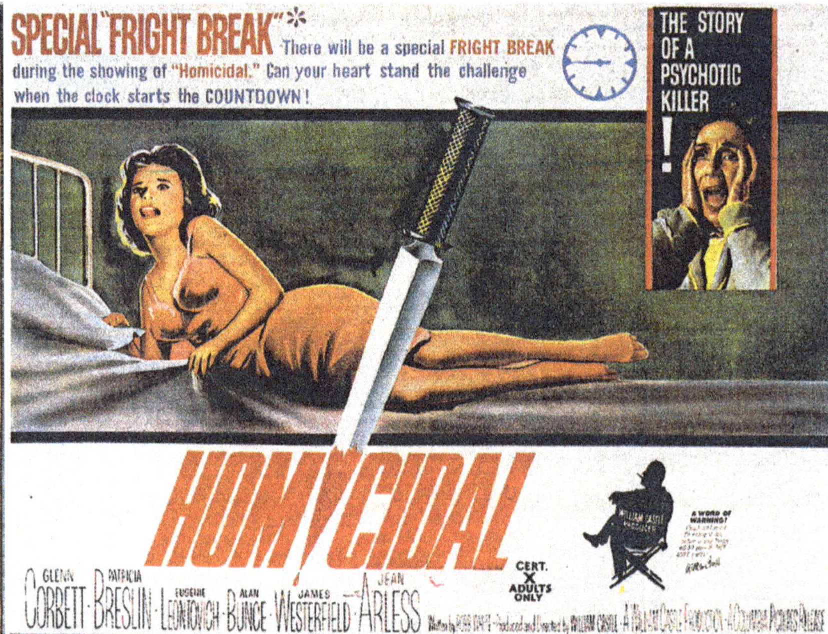

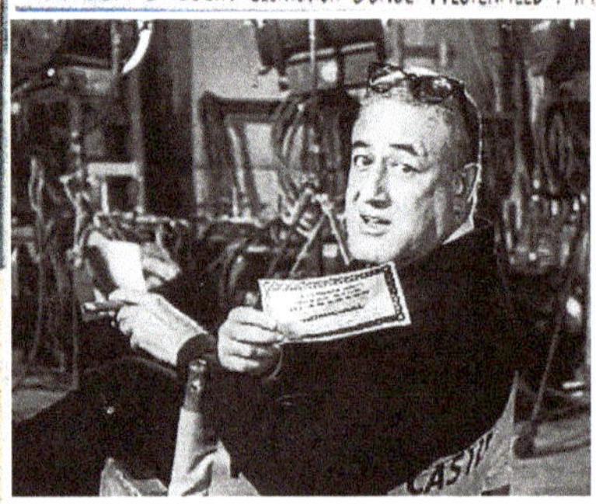

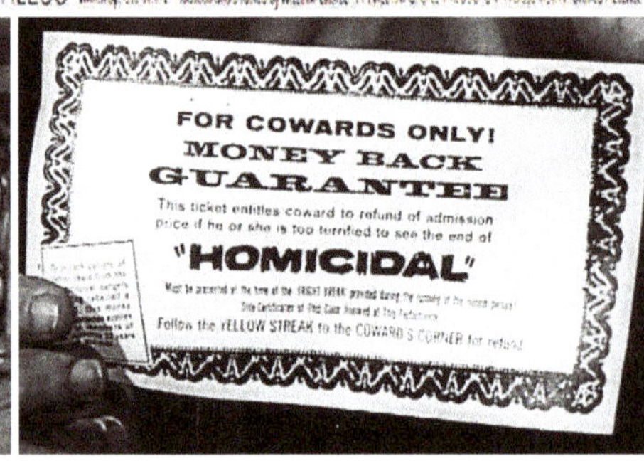

film featured a lobster-like creepy crawly which grew on the spine of its victims when in a state of fear. The unwelcome parasite could only be removed by screaming for your life. While on the loose looking for another host, the creature runs amok in a cinema. To share in the horror of it all up on the screen, a few members of the audience were given an actual tingle by a buzzer/vibrator device attached to their seats. Many believed that they were given an electric shock, but even before Health and. Safety, this wasn't risked, just in case a more delicate soul received a deadly jolt. A prologue to the film warned that 'it could be you', so everybody was on the edge of their seats, just in case. Just before the switch was thrown, the screen went blank and at the big moment, the sound of screams in the darkness made most of the audience jump out of their seats, whether tingled or not. It was soon realised that there was no need to go to the trouble and expense of wiring up any seats, just use a 'planted' screamer in the audience and leave the rest to auto-suggestion and mass hysteria. To help, the film's soundtrack provided standby screams and cries like 'Help! it's got me'. *The Tingler* had an extra gimmick for your money. Although the film was only in black and white, the blood was coloured red in a scene showing a bath full. For his last film *Bug* in 1974, William Castle planned to use a variation on Percepto. The bugs of the title were a cross between a cockroach and a beetle and could turn red hot to burn their victims to death. This time, the seats would have motor driven 'leg strokers' to make selected members of the audience think that one of the little monsters was crawling up their leg. Nothing came of the idea. If it had ever been put into practice, a few innocent men may have been taken away in a police van, after sitting next to a lady (or gent), unaware that they were actually being molested by their seat.

You have been warned

Included in *Homicidal* (1961), William Castle's answer to Hitchcock's *Psycho*, was the 'fright break', and this was the first of his gimmicks I was able to experience for myself. The film marked a milestone in my movie-going career, being my first 'X' film, showing on a double-bill with the gimmick free *Terror of the Tongs*. The fright break was a Countdown type clock which was displayed on the screen just before the shocking finale. It ticked away for 45 seconds to give the faint hearted time to leave the theatre. At some shows they were then presented with a 'Certificate of Cowardice', which could be kept or exchanged for a refund. I was brave enough to stay in my seat to see, as far as I can remember, a severed head rolling down stairs. I sometimes wish that I had suffered the shame of fleeing, just to get hold of the certificate, as I'm now sure that this cinematic white feather is worth big money on ebay. I have since thought of a flaw in this money-making device for the theatre owner. If you had already seen the ending, you could enjoy the rest of the show again for free by running out during the fright break and getting your money back.

Another collectors item was the promotional sick-bag (unused) distributed to patrons about to see the 'Likely to upset your stomach' *Mark of the Devil* (1970).William Castle's showmanship inspired Joe Dante's *Matinee* (1993), in which a producer of exploitation movies tries to persuade a theatre owner to run his film-within-a-film *Mant*, together with its associated gimmick 'Rumblera-ma'. Another warning device could be seen and heard in *The Chamber of Horrors* (1966). It was the 'horror horn' and 'fear flasher' (not Dracula in a mac). The story involved a serial killer, known as the 'Butcher of Baltimore' who is apprehended but escapes his shackles by cutting off his own hand. He then continues his killing spree, making good use of his replacement hook. Before the hand chopping and subsequent murders, the screen flashed red and a horn sounded, much like a car alarm going off. Although given a cinema release, the film was originally made for TV, when the warning proved useful, letting you leave the room to make the tea knowing that if you heard the horn sounding, you could rush back to see the best bits.

It's all in the mind

The use of hypnotism in the cinema, at first thought a sinister addition to the show, in practice never became a threat to movie-goers' state of mind, except perhaps to question their judgement in choosing to go and see the mind bending films in the first place. One of these was *The Hypnotic Eye* (1960) which featured 'Hypnomagic'. This was no more than showing a spinning spiral wheel on the screen to try and mesmerise the audience during a scene when an evil hypnotist uses his powers to induce his female victims to mutilate themselves. The rival 'Hypnovision', employed for *The Maniacs are Loose* (1971), included a prologue with a warning that during the film you would be made to believe that you are actually surrounded by maniacs and monsters. The promised moment came when in the film, maniacs escape from an asylum, decapitating anyone who gets in their way. As before, a kaleidoscope pattern appeared on the screen as theatre staff, dressed and made up like the marauding lunatics, ran down the aisles attacking screaming 'plants' with fake axes. Similar 'live' stunts were performed during other films, including *The Texas Chain Saw Massacre* (1974). This time, it was particularly popular in drive-ins, when a masked character wielding a cardboard chain saw ran between the cars banging on the roofs to disturb the occupants, whether they were watching the film, or doing something else. Although an R-rated film, one local reviewer remarked, 'great fun for the kiddies'. I must admit, that during some over-long films, which have failed to capture my imagination, I have been 'put under' without the aid of hypnotism.

Beware! ... a flasher in the theatre

Another assault on the sanity of the audience was to control their thoughts using subliminal images which are too brief to be noticed, but send messages into the viewers subconscious mind. These, for good or ill, can be superimposed on a few frames of the film, or flashed onto the screen using a separate strobe projector. In *My World Dies Screaming* (1960), presented in 'Psy-chorama', the heroine's nightmares included subliminal images of a crawling snake to suggest hate, a skull for terror, and, during the more passionate moments, a pair of fluttering hearts for love. One wonders what images might be flashed at us in these more permissive times. Supposedly, the idea has since been banned, after advertisers used it on TV to make us buy things we didn't think we needed. Some of them must be breaking the rules, as I've got a lot of stuff I never use! One cinema-related urban myth is that much of the success of *The Exorcist* (1973) was due to subliminal images. The producers have always denied any hidden messages were included. After its release on video, some believers have spent many hours going through the film frame-by-frame looking for the evidence, but,without success. This hasn't satisfied the conspiracy theorists who say that any extra nerve jangling clues were removed after its initial release. In theory, the subliminal idea could be applied to the film's sound track, with a faint message hidden below louder sounds, being sent directly to the brain without us realising we have ever heard it. I have never heard of 'Psychosound' ever being used, but I suppose we are not to know?

What a stinker

Adding smells to the show (on purpose) has a long history. The US trade paper Variety reported that for showings of *'Lilac Time'* in 1929 the manager of one theatre spilled lilac perfume into the plenum of the ventilation system, timed to reach the audience as the titles hit the screen. Soon after, the trick was used again during the song 'Orange Blossom Time' in MGM's *Hollywood Review*, when the aroma of oranges drifted into the auditorium of another US cinema. Like many of us with a long history of cinema-going, I can remember that older theatres often had unique 'atmospheres' made up of stale tobacco, dust and their own odd individual aroma. All this was despite the fact that among the ads was one boasting that 'This Theatre is Disinfected with Jeyes Fluid', (showing my age again). Today, cigarette fumes and yellow screens have been replaced with the smell of popcorn.

The first proper 'with smells' production was the documentary *Behind the Great Wall* (1959) which was presented in 'AromaRama'. A timing device fed 72 oriental odours into the auditorium using the normal air circulating system. They included incense and smoke at

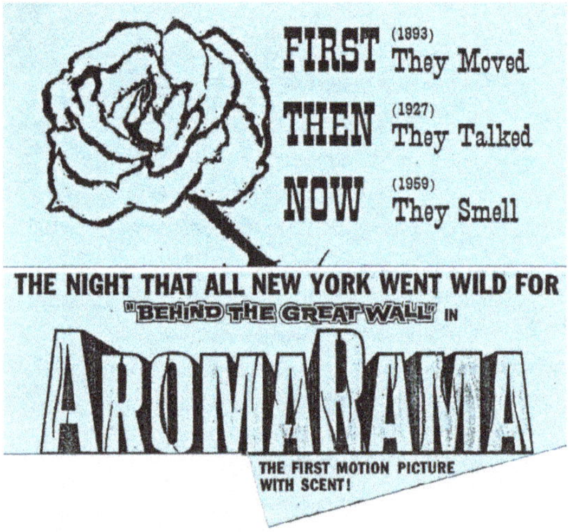

The AromaRama card and both sides of the Odorama scratch card

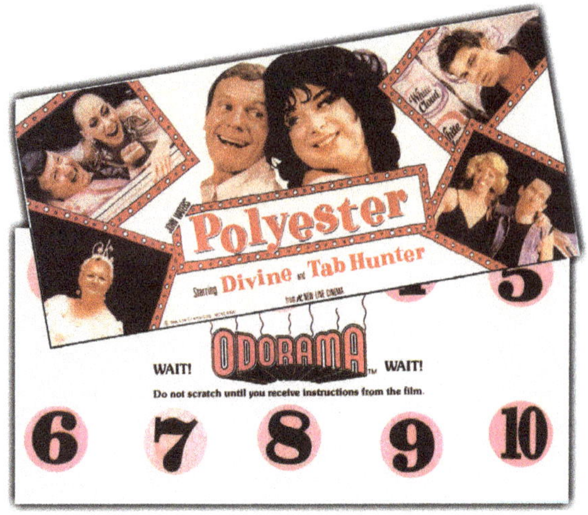

a Hong Kong night club, spices and 'mystic' fumes at a Buddhist temple, and the less exotic smells of a farmyard full of geese. In the prologue to the film, AromaRama was hailed as an equal milestone to the coming of sound, colour and wider screens, and which you-must-breathe-it-to-believe-it.

Unfortunately, it was difficult to expel each smell before the next was due, so by the end of the film, the mixture smelt like the waste bin at the back of a Chinese restaurant and the audience looked forward to heading for the 'Way Out to fresh air' sign. The film on its own without smells went on to become an award winner showing, in 'scope and colour, life in China that was less familiar to audiences at the time.

More sophisticated was 'Glorious Smell-O-Vision', which was paired with Mike Todd Jr's 70mm production *'Scent of Mystery'* in 1960. It offered a choice of 30 scents contained in pressurised phials on a rotating magazine. A smell track on the print sent each smell on cue to the noses of the audience via a network of tubes ending up at the back of each seat. After each discharge, a neutraliser killed each smell ready for the next. The film itself was directed by Jack Cardiff and starred Denholm Elliott and Peter Lorre trying to stop an heiress from being murdered. During the film you could smell roses, baking bread, garlic, leather, gun smoke and coffee. Among the many more were the distinctive smell of a particular perfume and pipe tobacco which were clues to solving the mystery. Smell-O-Vision cost 30,000 dollars to install, so was only smelt in three American theatres on a roadshow basis. A smell-less version of *Scent of Mystery* was released under the title *'Holiday in Spain'* and shown in Cinerama theatres, always on the lookout for 70mm product.

For low-budget smells, those about to enjoy John Walter's *Polyester* (1981) were handed an 'Odorama' scratch-and-sniff card, with instructions to WAIT! until a number appeared at the corner of the screen before scratching and sniffing the appropriate patch on the card.

In keeping with the rather sleazy plot, the smells were not always the most fragrant, including pizza, old shoes and something nasty from 'No. 2'. The thought of it takes me back again to my schooldays, when stink bombs were thrown during Saturday Morning Pictures. In later years, while watching the 'passing wind' cowboys enjoying their baked beans around the camp fire in Mel Brooks's *'Blazing Saddles'* (1974) I had the mischievous idea that they could be thrown again 'officially' to cause a stink at the right moment and add the film to the list of smellies.

In your face showmanship

Kids matinees also introduced me to 3D movies. I remember the excitement when the cardboard glasses were given out to watch *Metroscopics*. By the time the film began, many had been bent, squashed, or fingers poked through the cellophane filters. I kept mine safe and managed to resist losing them to my more resourceful and forceful fellow minors (bullies) who had spoiled theirs. I saw eye-popping scenes of a fireman's ladder coming out of the screen and dodging the contents of a burning building being thrown out of a window at me. I went home happy, but with a bit of a headache, and the treasured glasses which I failed to hand back. This was a sin I never overcame, so I now have a drawer full, many smuggled out via the fire exit.

The heyday of 3D in the cinema was in the early 1950s, before the easier on the eyes CinemaScope and other widescreen systems took over, which you could see without 'special glasses'. The best 3D films have the left and right eye images on separate films or next to each other on a single print which are sent to the correct eyes of the audience via oppositely orientated polarized filters. This, until digital projection came along, remained the most practical method and was used in Imax and other special venue theatres which gave a more permanent home to 3D. Stereoscopic films occasionally made a comeback every ten years or so, to give a new generation a chance to enjoy 3D again before the novelty wore off. Even the producers of 'serious' 3D films found it hard to resist including the odd 'comin' at ya' shots, which are always the most memorable. These usually involved ducking to avoid arrows and tomahawks in westerns, but also fun for me was Grace Kelly's hand at the end of my nose,

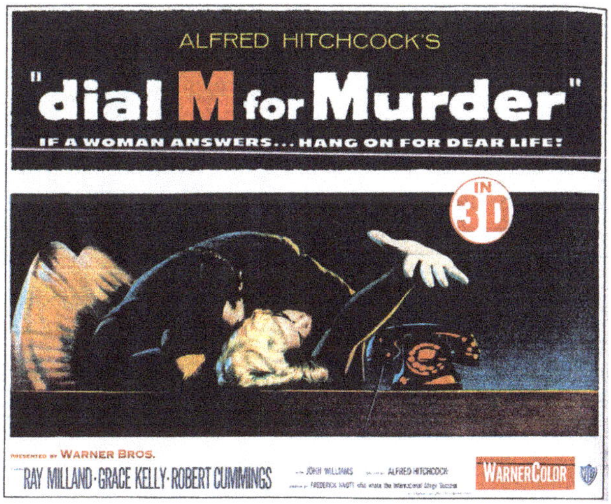

before she grabs a pair of scissors to plunge into the back of her assailant during Hitchcock's rarely seen in 3D, *Dial M for Murder*.

The more gimmicky use of 3D is usually as short sequences within a film and using the cheap and cheerful anaglyph method, needing no special equipment, polarised filters or silver screen. The time to put on the red and green glasses is normally built into the plot, like in *The Mask* (aka *The Eyes of Hell*), when the principal character puts on an ancient cursed mask and we share his mad dreams.

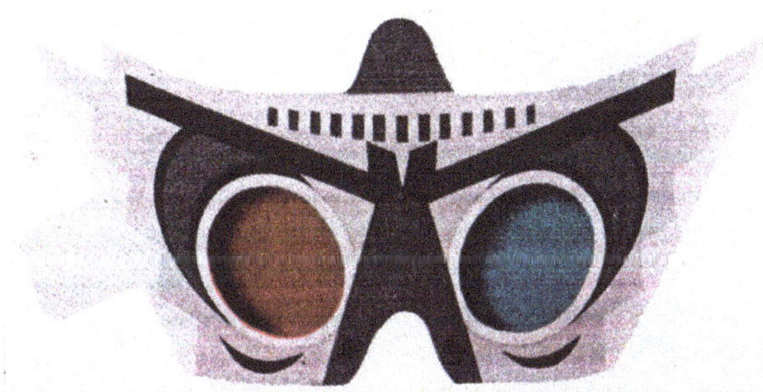

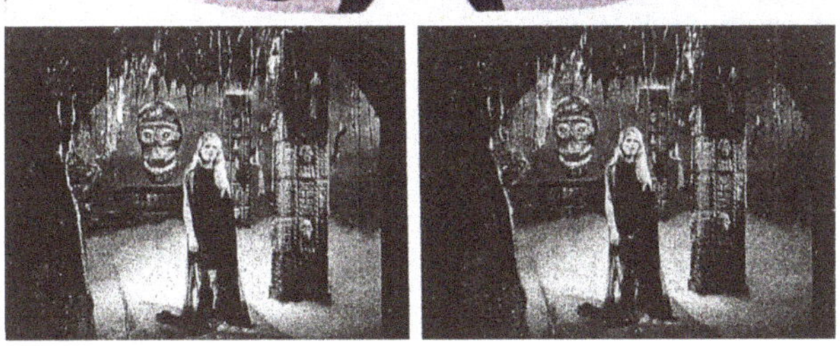

Dual film left and right eye images from 'The Mask' - for projection they were tinted red and green respectively and superimposed onto a single film.

The stereoscopic photography in the film was supervised back in 1960 by Charles W. Smith who, before his death in May 2004, was the cinema industry's authority on everything you might want to know about 3D. He is shown here with Bernard Happé at the NFT in 1957. Both were my heroes and I tapped their knowledge at every opportunity.

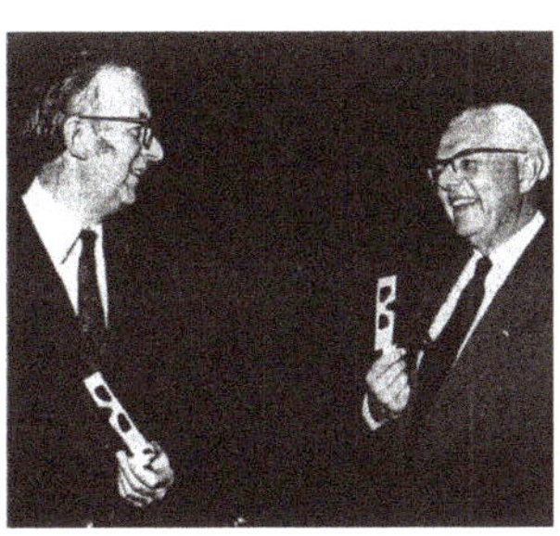

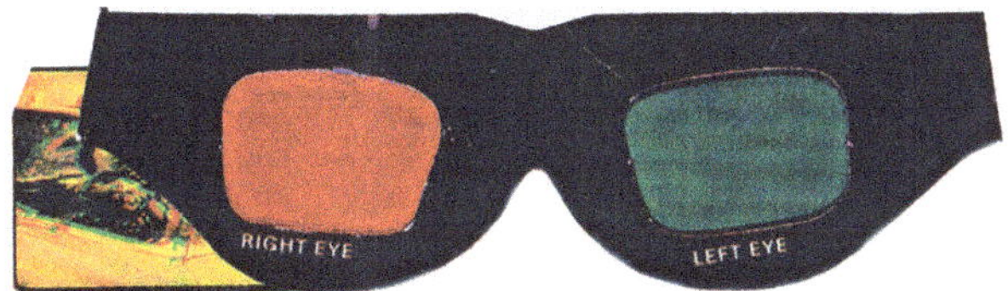

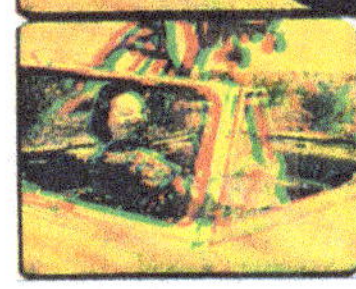

Black and white anaglyphic 3D was used in films such as 'The Mask", also known as 'Eyes of Hell'. Clips below.

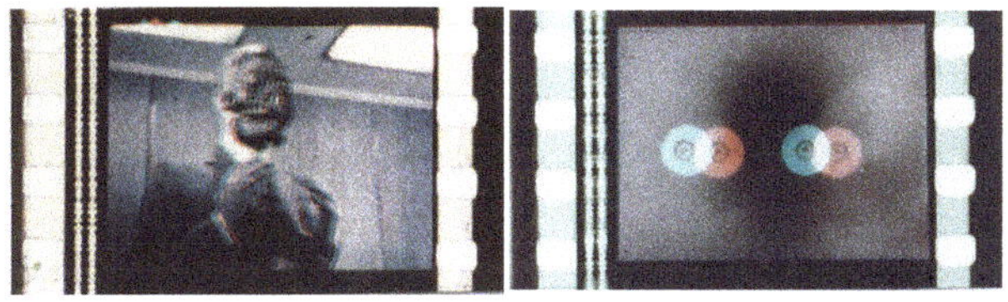

Although anaglyphic 3D using red and blue/green images and glasses was once considered only suitable for black and white films, the principle was also applied to colour movies.

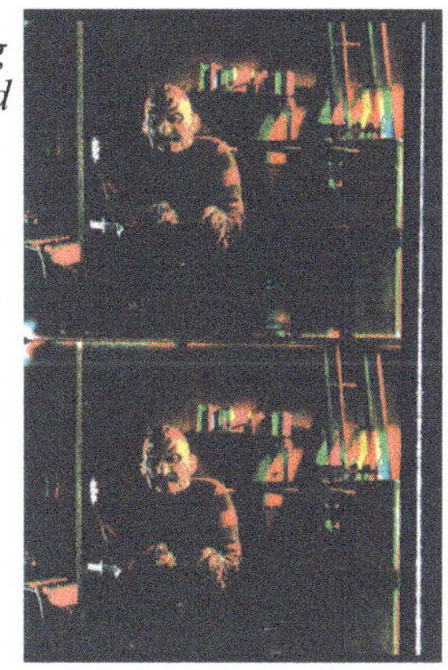

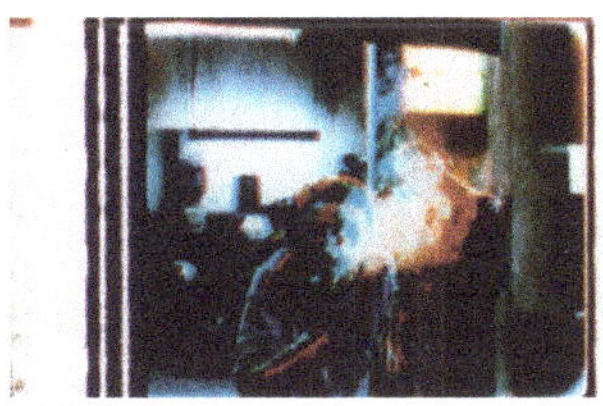

The purity of the original colour is degraded somewhat when distracted by the stereoscopic action. 'Freddy's Dead' clips proved to be a good example.

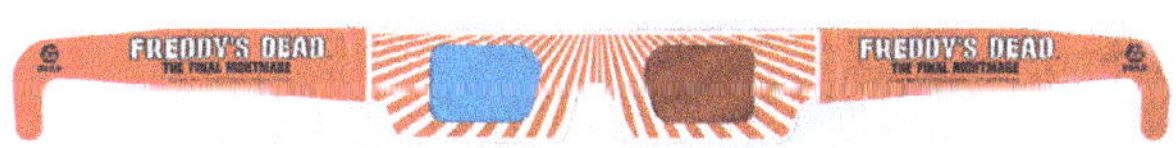

Another British contribution to exploiting 3D, were the four anaglyphic segments in the skin flick *3 Dimensions of Greta* (1971), the extra dimension making her attributes stand out more and provide greater relief. Also claimed, or ashamed, to be British was the earlier *Paridiso* (1962) in which a dirty old professor uses his 'magic' lens (time to put on your glasses again) to see naked ladies in 3D.....OO-ERR!

Having several times been impressed by the 3D film finale to *Freddy's Dead: The Final Nightmare* (1991) I kept my glasses ready for the film to appear on TV. When it did, I waited patiently before the heroine and I both put on our glasses for the 3D mayhem, but it was only in one-eyed 2D. Perhaps the broadcaster was worried that viewers, not in the know and without glasses, would be more terrified that their TV picture, now with a double image and red and green fringes, had developed a convergence fault.

Added anaglyphic 3D sequences continue to be popular, a more recent example being in *Spy Kids 3* (2003), allowing younger movie-goers to share the thrill of 3D as the kids in the film enter the world of a reality computer game.

Now you see them... now you don't

To give William Castle a final encore, I must give a mention of 'Illusion-O'. This too employed a red and blue viewing device, but this time it was designed to allow both eyes to see through each filter at once, to enable those watching his *Thirteen Ghosts* (1960) to see them or not. The film was in black and white, but the ghosts were printed in blue which appeared through the red filter and disappeared through the blue. This feature is sometimes mistakenly listed as being in 3D, but in fact, it may deserve its place on the list, as it was found that due to some optical fluke, if the viewer was turned through 90 degrees and each eye looked through only one of the filters at the same time, the ghosts could still be seen, but now floating in front of the screen.

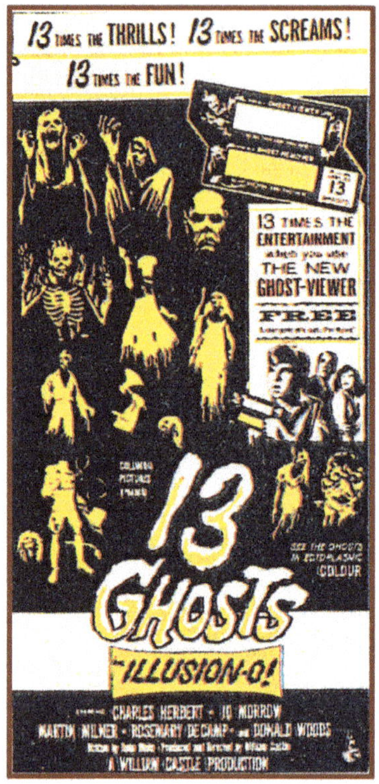

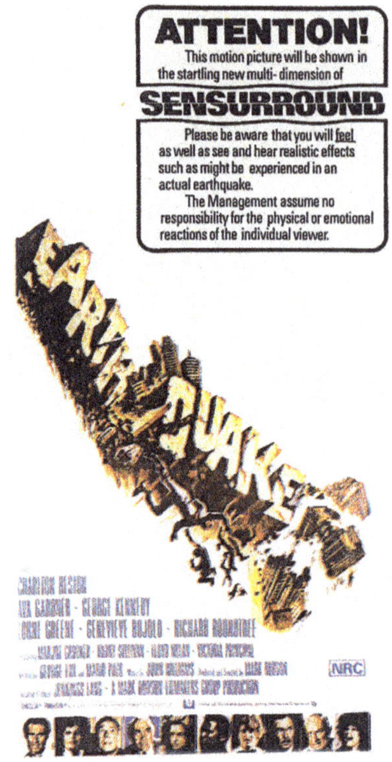

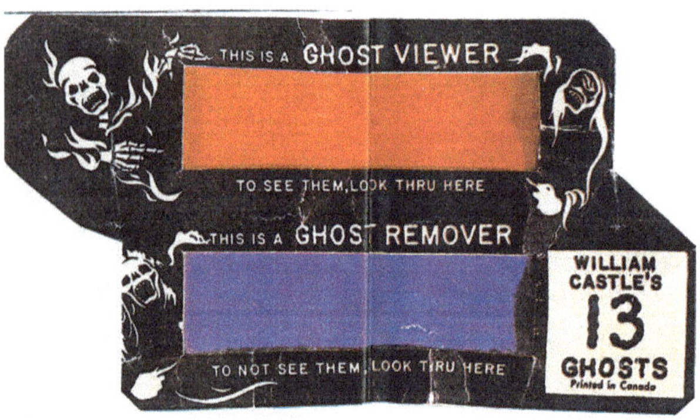

All shook up

I also remember the 'feelie' system Sensurround. In 1974, audiences could feel the effect of being at the epicentre of *Earthquake* when high power sub-audible pulses of 'sound', at around 16 to 20 Hz, coming from large auxiliary speakers below the screen, shook up their stomachs. For many of the first showings, the low frequency rumbles came from a separate generator and, in some cases, were a little too realistic, with rattling light fittings and lumps of plaster falling from the ceiling, before the level had to be turned down to a lower point on the Richter scale. Later, all the low frequencies were recorded within the film's normal sound track. The effect was so successful it was used again to put you in the thick of it during the *Battle of Midway* (1976), and make you hang onto your seat on an out of control theme park ride in *Rollercoaster* (1977). Rival shake-you-up processes, like MegaSound and Vibrasound, followed and soon Sensurround also gave birth to Dolby's 'baby boom', adding a dedicated bass channel to cinema sound systems. This is now a common feature in all of today's digital systems, with sub-woofers thumping away in theatres and home cinema systems.

I only remember it was in something

We don't see, hear or feel many gimmicks these days. Most of a film's publicity budget goes on sending its stars and director around the world to plug it on endless talk shows and film review programmes. To cash in on all the hype, the film usually gets a blanket release and can be seen straight away in a nearby multiplex. In the past, you may have had to travel to a big city 'first-run' theatre to see it first, or wait sometimes many weeks for it to arrive at your local cinema, when the extra publicity of a good gimmick or stunt could help revive interest. Many of the films mentioned in this story are only remembered today, by me at least, because they were shown in some special 'process', or other gimmick.

Not always a serious business

Although I have always enjoyed writing and talking about the more 'important' developments in the history of cinema technology, this look at some of the silly stuff reminds me that all the years of invention and engineering effort have been in the cause of helping to entertain the public and giving them a good show, whether they like it, or not.

The title of this piece was inspired by a Barbra Streisand film, *For Pete's Sake* '1974), when during a madcap chase sequence, cattle are released from a market and career down the street. Some enter the rear of a cinema, which just happens to be showing *'How the West Was Won'*, and at the moment a stampede scene is being shown, the animals burst through the screen into the auditorium, prompting one startled patron to comment, "That's what I call showmanship".

Keeping the magic

Some of the old tricks that cinema managers used to make a customer's visit memorable have been given a modern makeover...

For most cinemagoers, the main attraction is still the film itself, but modern cinema managements have learned how to use today's ever improving technology to add even greater realism to the fantasy worlds being created around them.

Using technology to keep cinema special

As digital cinema has already given us enough audio channels to totally immerse audiences in all-around sound, industry innovators, like Dolby, IMAX and the various projector manufacturers, are now turning their digital skills to further enhance the image. Also welcome, is a desire to use the latest technical advances to help keep the overall cinema-going experience something special and not just another way to watch a film. Once the cinema only had to lure the public away from their televisions, but now there are many more screens to watch films on, both at home and on the move.

Screens everywhere

Apart from the thriving home cinema market, the coming of digital projection, without reels of film to deal with, has encouraged and made it easier to set up pop-up shows both indoors and out, be they on land, water, or up on the roof. For communities who have lost their local cinema, specialist distributors can now clear the rights and provide DVDs or Blu-rays of recent releases for showing in nearby pubs, clubs and village halls. Even if you are stuck in hospital it is good to know that some are now finding space for a free volunteer run Medi-Cinema able to show current DCPs to patients, who are sure to be made to feel better by not having to stay in bed and watch films on the over-priced pay-as-you-go hospital TV.

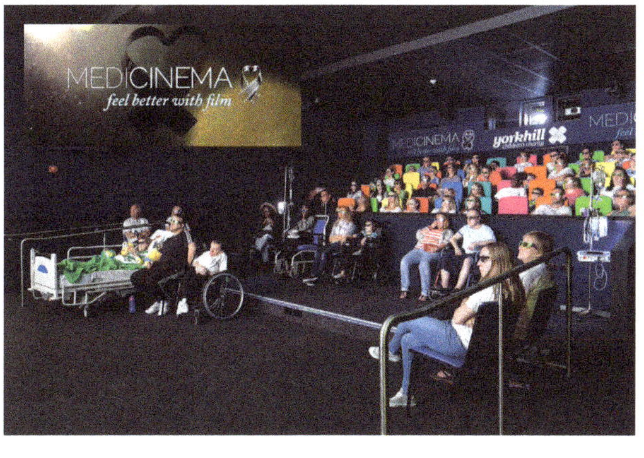

For the well-off, who choose to stay in, cinema architects have found new work designing luxury well equipped mini cinemas, not only for multi-millionaires mega basements, but now an extra facility for residents of up-market apartment blocks and hotels.

Enjoy it first in a real cinema

In response, multiplex operators now have the opportunity to employ the latest methods to ensure they keep, and sometimes bring back, the old cinema magic and showmanship. This can begin before reaching the doors. Many of the early characterless warehouse-looking multiplex exteriors can be livened up with a new, eye-catching, easily changed electronic billboard. It's becoming rare that a brave member of staff has to climb up to change the letters on an old style canopy. Also going is its opportunity, when out and about, to catch a fellow projectionist up a ladder and ask if you could have a look around. Sometimes, particularly for films expecting a long run, an elaborate display was constructed

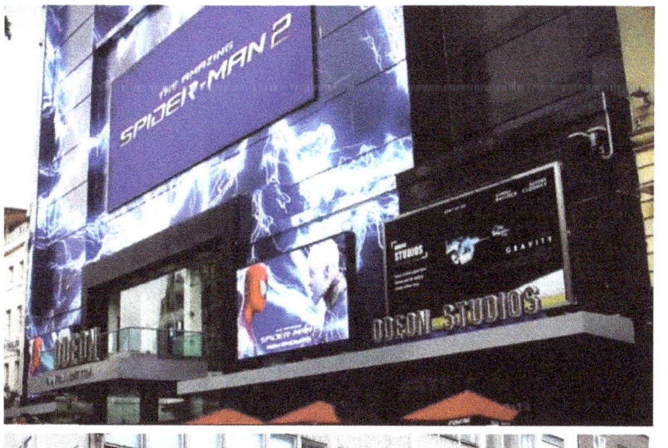

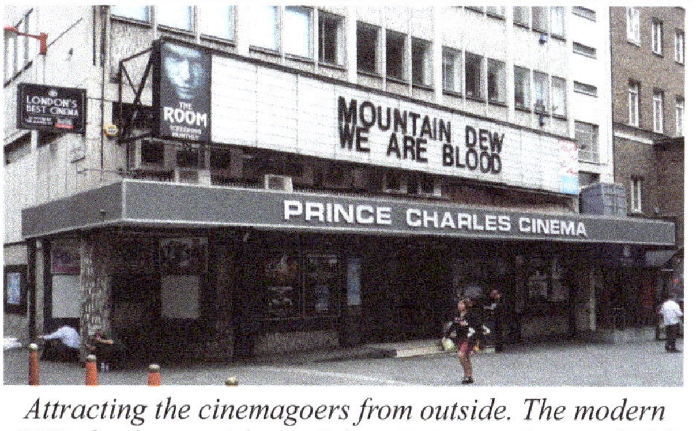

Attracting the cinemagoers from outside. The modern LED display outside the Odeon Leicester Square (NEC Display Solutions and Beaver Group) measures 107 sq. metres. The nearby Prince Charles cinema, still a haven for 70mm film enthusiasts, keeps its traditional letters on an old style canopy.

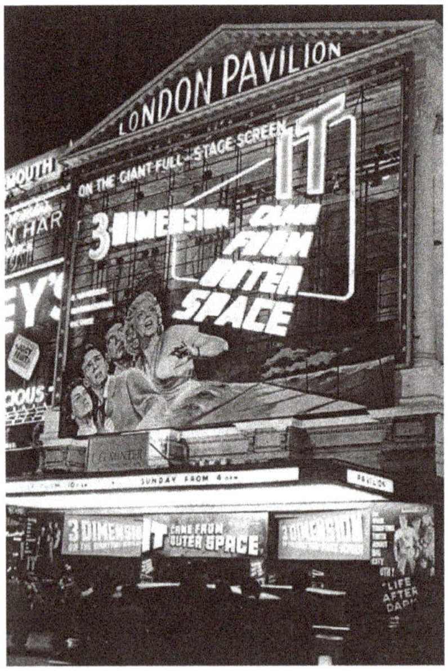

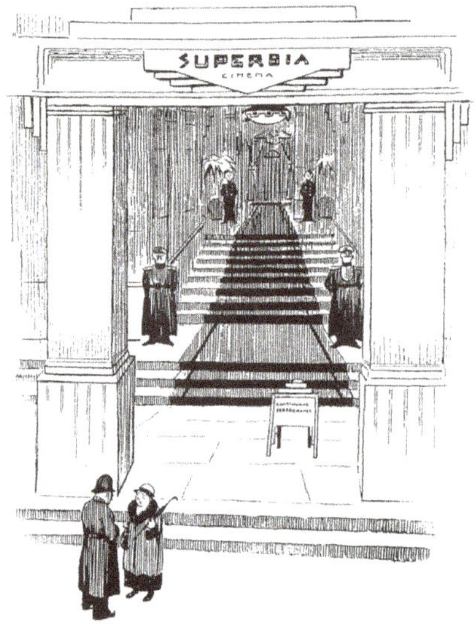

" Can **anyone** go in there? "

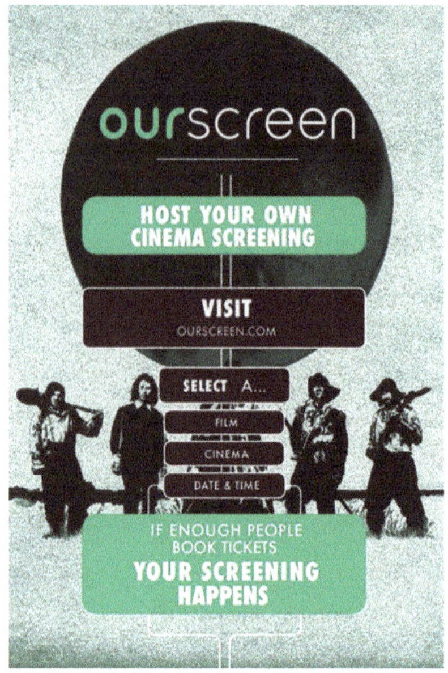

Left: No chance of missing what's on, with almost all of the front of the cinema covered in the art of wood, metal, paint, and neon. Centre: Need to take care that the plush surroundings don't put off the ordinary cinemagoer. Right: Organise your own cinema showing for a group of friends via social media

on the front of the cinema, with some, looking back to their fairground roots, including movement and special effects. A memorable example, back in the 1950s, was a giant mannequin of Marilyn Monroe in a dress, which was suddenly blown up by a blast of air, tempting the public to come in and see the real thing in *The Seven Year Itch*. Like the latest digital displays, which can also feature movement, this is now discouraged, as it may distract passing drivers. Before LEDs replaced wood, metal and neon, a hoarding on the facade of the Odeon Leicester Square was made even more spectacular with jets of flaming gas until waiting cinemagoers had to scatter when fire engines arrived to stop the theatre from burning down.

Who says showmanship is dead?

At one time, it took some time for a big film to reach the smaller local cinemas, so their managers, often frustrated showmen, were free to reignite some of the original hype. Many had fun involving the staff in organizing related events, competitions and publicity stunts. Today, the audience is encouraged to help promote the film by using the latest word of mouth way of spreading the news. Even before the showing is over, social media can be buzzing, telling friends and the world how much you have enjoyed the film.

Something different, now and then

However you get to know about it, the choice can now include 'Event Cinema', using the normal digital projector to show live relays of opera, plays and concerts. This too, brings back memories of earlier alternative content. Before every home had a TV, cinema screens would sometimes go live when patrons in the stalls had to keep well away from the thousands of volts passing through the earlier analogue short throw video projectors, temporarily installed to screen important national events, with

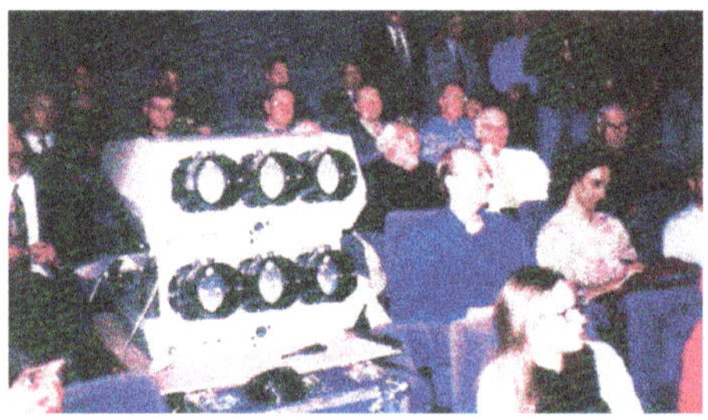

Earlier, short-throw pre-digital video projectors had to share the auditorium with the audience

royal occasions and prize fights drawing large audiences. For an actual live performance, some theatres still had a cinema organ, many a survivor from the silent era, when it was a cheaper alternative to a full orchestra. This wondrous instrument and its organist could rise up and keep audiences happy during intervals and were available to accompany visiting entertainers.

In towns without a suitable venue, the film projectors were also given a rest when the auditorium hosted live acts. During the 1950s and 60s, a cinema was often

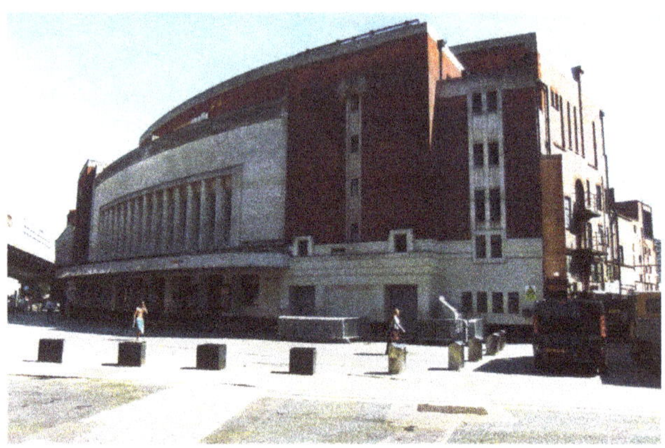

The Gaumont, then the Odeon, and now the Apollo Hammersmith. A 'Super-Cinema' that escaped a multi-screen conversion or being pulled down by becoming a prominent music venue.

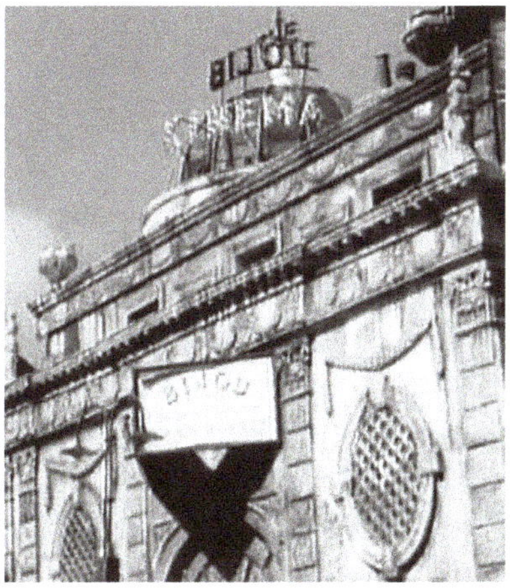

The Smallest Show on Earth 'Bijou' fleapit. Not a good example for today's designers to follow.

borrowed for a full house of fans standing on the seats to scream at the latest touring pop star or group. A few large capacity and well appointed cinemas, which had avoided a multi-screen conversion, would finally give up showing films altogether, becoming prominent music venues. Among those now gone was the Astoria Charing Cross Road, now the new Tottenham Court Road tube station. But still going strong is the former Odeon Hammersmith, which is also remembered by us 'old' film fans, when it played the part of the 'Grand' cinema rival trying to put *The Smallest Show on Earth* Bijou flee-pit out of business.

More recently, Disney revived the Cine-Variety idea of combining a film with live acts, when it offered to present a pre-film mini-musical before a couple of its animated features. These were so successful that they have now expanded into full-scale stage musicals, without the film.

Cinemas' new look

Probably going to be missed the most by film memorabilia collectors and dealers, is the possibility that down-loaded images on video screens will eventually replace paper posters and the already gone portraits and cut outs of the stars, and the display boards with their 'Now Showing' and 'Coming Soon' stills and lobby cards. Today's foyers are being praised for their clean uncluttered look, with the air of a well-furnished airport departure lounge, rather than the traditional cosy plush of a high street cinema's foyer, often with its own adjoining cafe or restaurant. The dominant feature of a modern foyer is its food and concession counter. This is also playing the role of an information point and the box office for the on-the-door tickets, not already booked on line or issued by a machine. During quiet periods, some multiplexes boast that they need only one person, with an eye on CCTV, to look after their customers. However, like many West End theatres, others still think it is worthwhile to spare a well-informed member of staff, with a friendly smile, to meet and greet its visitors at the door. As well as directing them to their chosen screen, via the popcorn of course, they can talk about the films on offer and even be able to answer any 'technical' questions about the latest presentation methods being

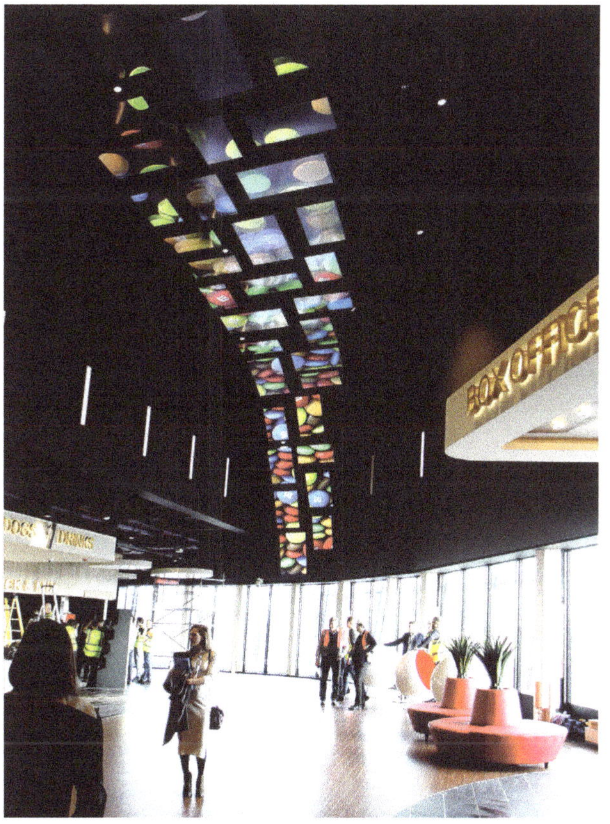

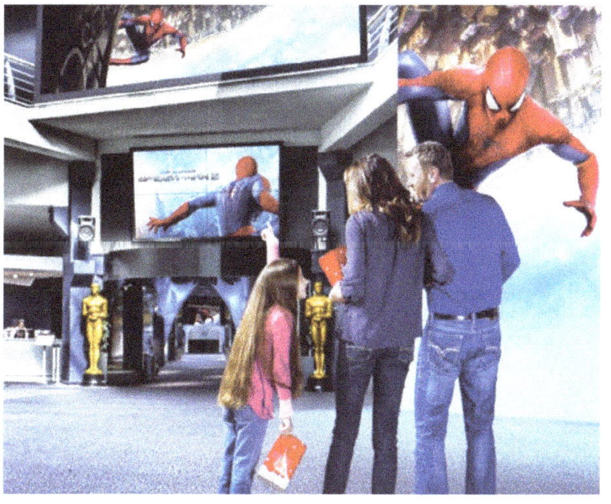

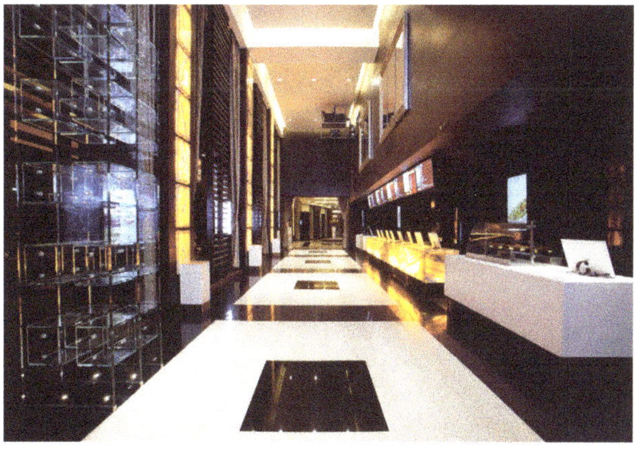

Cinema lobbies can be digitally transformed to deliver the magic of sight, sound and social media, making for a great experience before you ever come near the auditorium.

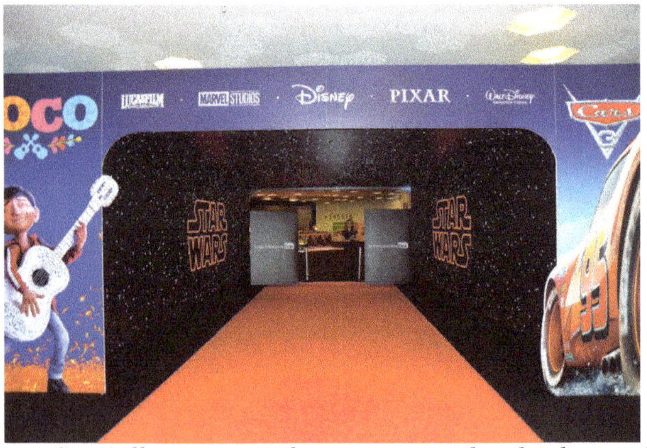

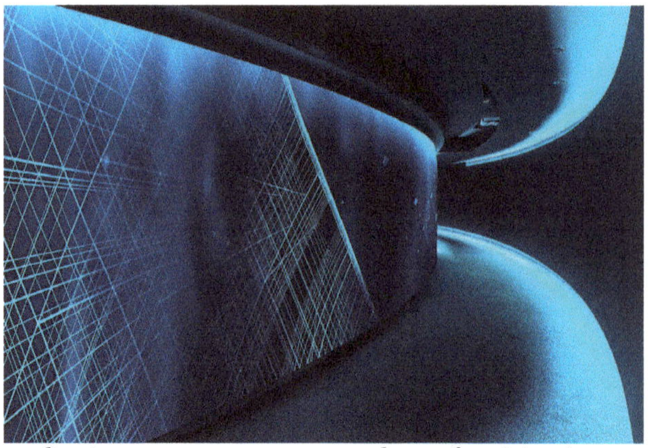

Specially constructed entrance corridors leading to the auditorium can create an atmosphere of anticipation

used to show them. This harks back to the days when the manager, in a suit and bow tie, would sometimes come out into the foyer and join the commissionaires to give ordinary cinemagoers a VIP welcome.

A more modern welcome

The most recent multiplex designs have more in common with the architectural style of the shopping complexes, in which many are now situated. Even so, their designers put much effort and imagination into creating attractive high-tech spaces which are more familiar and welcoming for today's, mostly younger, audiences, than entering the quiet hallowed atmosphere of the old picture palaces and cathedrals of the movies. This is even more likely to be blown away, with the latest idea of adding to the pre-show experience with the chance to play related video games and plans to try out virtual reality headsets.

After all this, some are bringing back a degree of theatrical ambiance, by finally reaching the screen along a more atmospheric, specially lit corridor or tunnel to get you in the mood before entering the auditorium.

Watching the film need not be just sitting in silence in front of a bare screen at the end of a once typical multiplex plain black box studio style auditorium. Although technically this may provide the ideal conditions when actually projecting the film, once the lights come up, they can appear rather soulless, with only its rows of speakers along the walls to look at. No need to call in artisans to add some decorative plasterwork, creating a more theatrical look may only involve fitting examples of the latest fully controllable mood lighting panels and fixtures, some of which can include the speakers.

It's even possible to retro-fit the screen with curtains and variable masking. As most current mainstream films use the 2.35:1 format, they look much better if properly masked and not just across the centre of a previously fixed 1.85;1 screen, leaving the audience to wonder where the rest of the picture has gone.

Don't stop the music

Music too, can play its part in creating the right mood. Known as the non-sync back in the days when no projection room was complete without its turntable and pile of records, the music, possibly from the film's soundtrack, can be played unobtrusively while the audience take their seats. Then, after the ads and trailers are over, it can return at greater volume with the lights half-dimmed to create a roadshow-type overture before the illuminated tabs, real or a projected virtual version, open. Perhaps the distributors could provide an optional specially prepared overture for their latest blockbuster. This can add to the sense of anticipation before the main event and suggest it's time to put the mobile away. All this takes imagination and showmanship, together with a projectionist still available to programme it all each time into the now common computer controlled automation.

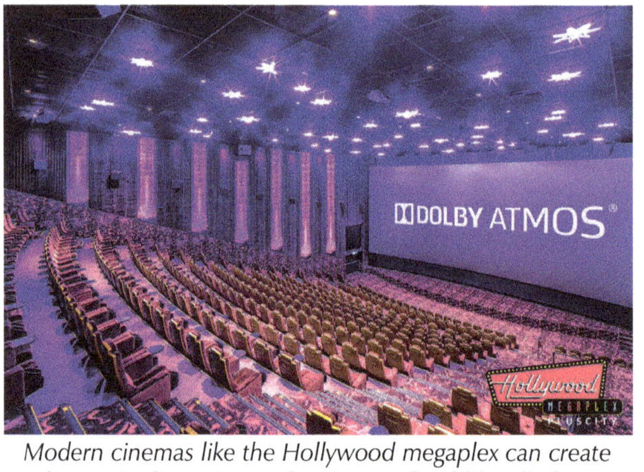

Modern cinemas like the Hollywood megaplex can create the magic that going to the cinema should be all about

All this, and then some

In an extra effort to compete with the ever growing size of TVs at home, audiences are being tempted to pay more to enjoy the film in one of the various 'Premium Large Format' systems now being offered in a number of multiplexes' main auditoriums, perhaps in an effort to make PLF recreate the splendour of 70mm in digital form.

High Wide and Handsome - could PLF be the new 70mm?

The past present and future of large formats

The cinema is often described as the big screen, but with ever-larger TV screens being squeezed through the door at home, cinema is trying to prove that size still matters by offering even more eye-filling Premium Large Formats. This has pleased those who, although they appreciate the value of the latest sound systems, still think that a good picture is worth a thousand extra speakers.

What is PLF?

The term appears to have a broad definition and several categories based on providing 'the optimal configuration of sight and sound and seating experience.' This has always been the main aim of the various special venue systems found at and supported by museums, science centres and theme parks. Here they present specially produced, usually short, films on various flat, curved, domed and all-around screens, with some viewed while 'riding' on moving motion-controlled seats. For long periods, they would be the only opportunity to see big screen 3D.

Many of their ideas are now inspiring more adaptable 'multiplex' versions to give normal commercial features the same enhanced degree of audience participation. Before the general switch to digital projection, many would make use of the cinema's original premium large format, 70mm film.

What is 70mm?

Back in the 1890s and the birth of the cinema, wider film gauges were common, but all had disappeared by the time the more popular smaller 35mm size was adopted as the industry standard. Wider formats did return briefly at the end of the 1920s and early 30s when Hollywood first tried to introduce bigger and wider screens. This time they were killed off by the depression, and the new Talkies were already drawing in the audiences. In a case of third time lucky, wide film finally came to stay during the cinema's switch to wider screens in the 1950s.

The current 70mm format was launched with the Todd-AO process, its name a combination of producer and showman Mike Todd and the American Optical Company which turned his ideas into reality. Todd was involved in making the first 3-strip Cinerama film, but thought its triple 35mm projector system was far too complicated and costly for normal film-making and cinemas. Despite its great success, he was determined to find a much simpler way to fill a similar large deeply curved screen but using only a single film and projector.

Announced at around the same time as CinemaScope, Fox's 35mm anamorphic lens response to Cinerama, which reached the public just ten months later, Todd-AO would take almost three years to develop. For the photography, a 65mm camera, left over from the earlier 1930s widescreen experiment, was fitted with a range of lenses, with one having an ultra-wide view approaching that of Cinerama. To make it an attractive proposition for many more theatres, its projector would be multi-purpose, also able to show normal 35mm films, including CinemaScope, as well as the new 70mm prints. These were a little wider beyond the perfora-

Todd-AO and other compatible 70mm prints have a frame area 2½ times that of a 35mm CinemaScope magnetic sound copy and also have applied stripes to carry stereo sound tracks.

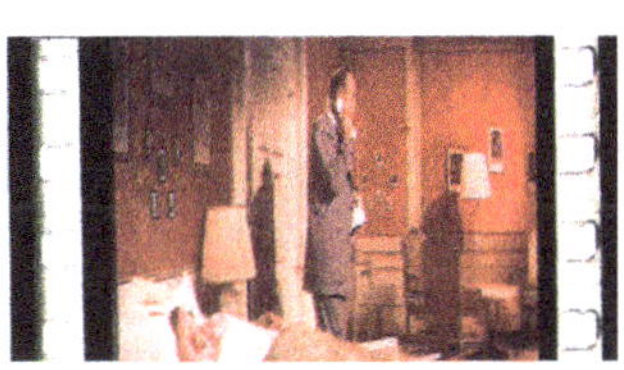

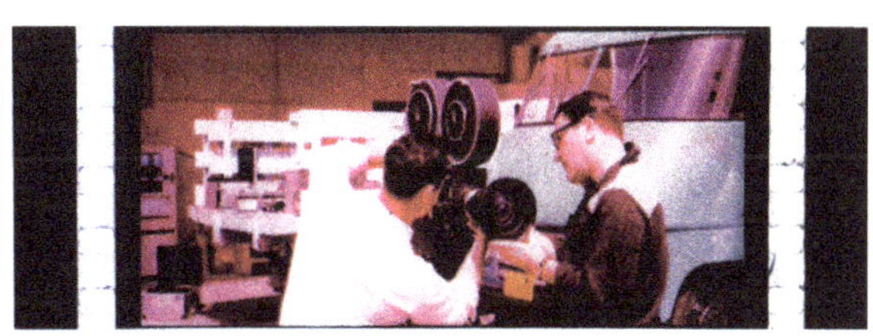

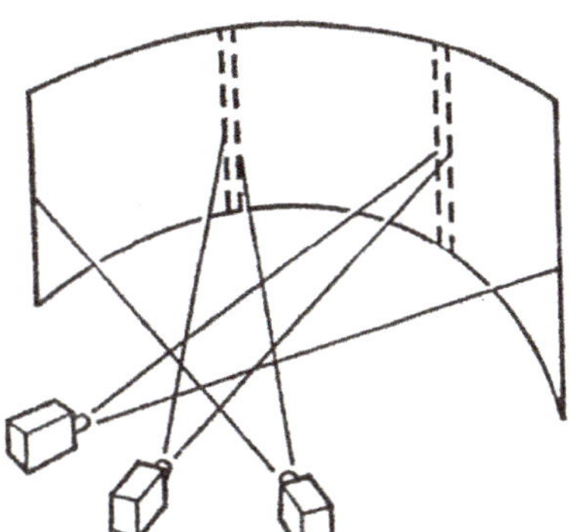

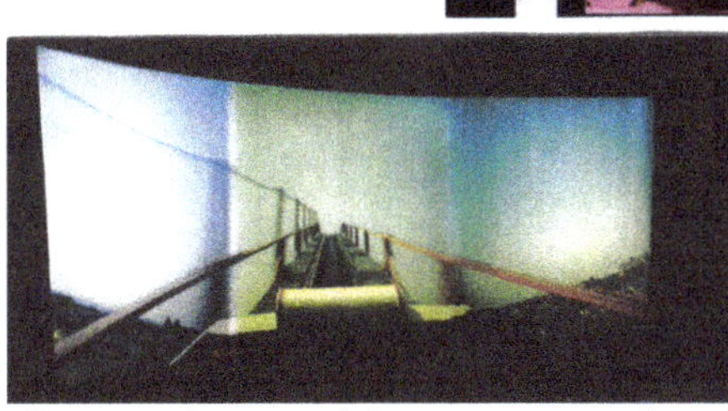

Cinerama's original three projectors shared the deeply curved screen.

Cinerama's louvred screen could give the picture a streaky appearance

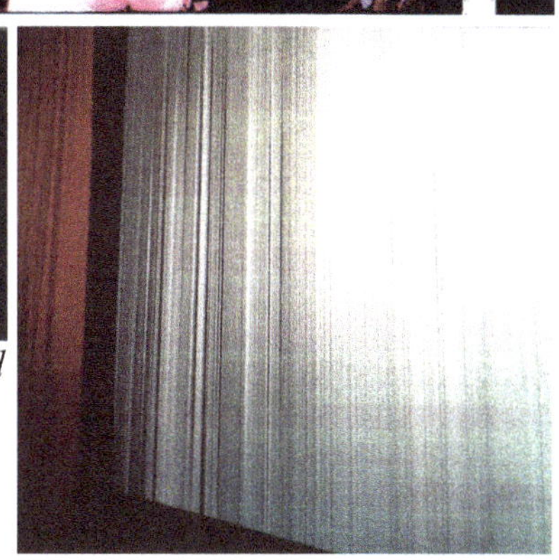

tions, to follow CinemaScope's idea of finding room for multi-channel magnetic stripes.

The first Todd-AO films would also feature HFR (Higher Frame rate), the frame rate increased from 24 to 30 to reduce flicker and smooth out the action on the intended brighter and bigger screens. To make it easier to install, the theatre's normal projection room could be used even if it was high up at the back of the circle. Cinerama used level projection, with each of its projectors only having to cope with a third of the curve.

A single wide film image from above sags in the middle so, long before digital help, an ingenious optical printer arched the image on the print to counter balance the effect. Unfortunately, it wasn't entirely successful and together with a poor print, marred the premiere and early shows of *Oklahoma*, the first film in the process, resulting in 70mm being given the thumbs down by both the critics and trade press. Fortunately, the film itself was a smash hit and drew attention away from Todd-AO's shortcomings. Also, it had been simultaneously filmed in 35mm CinemaScope just in case of trouble and for later general release.

Too good to lose

To give 70mm another chance, the 'bent' prints were abandoned and projection rooms relocated lower down to reduce the distortion on the deeply curved screen, before these too were largely discarded in favour of a normal flat or only slightly curved screen. Todd personally produced the second Todd-AO feature, the star-studded *Around The World In 80 Days*, which could now display the great advantages of its larger frame. The 2.2:1 aspect ratio suited the biggest possible screen, with at least the width of CinemaScope but with extra height, and all achieved with less magnification, resulting in a sharper, brighter and steadier picture.

70 mm was first seen in Britain, when the third Todd-AO production, *South Pacific* opened at the Dominion Tottenham Court Road. By now, the frame rate had been reduced to the normal 24 fps, so the same 65mm negative could be used to make 35mm reduction prints. Sadly, just as 70mm was taking off, Mike Todd was killed when his private plane crashed on the way to New York to receive the Showman of the Year award in 1958. Fox would acquire Todd-AO and Todd's widow Elizabeth Taylor also retained an interest in the process and helped ensure that *Cleopatra* was shot in it, rather than the originally intended CinemaScope. This film would be among the many large scale epics and big screen musicals photographed on 65mm film for an initial 70mm release. Todd-AO's specifications and dimensions would become a new 65mm/ 70mm international standard. One variation came from MGM, who teamed up with anamorphic lens attachment maker Panavision to add a low power (x 1.25) version to both the camera and projector for its Camera 65 process which increased the width of

A selection of 70mm print variations

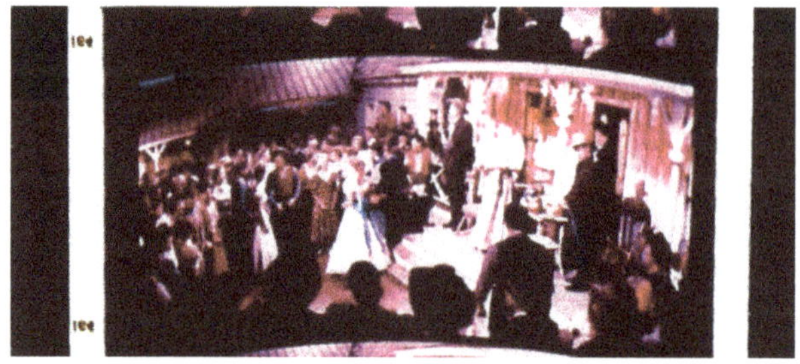

Abandoned Todd-AO 'arched' copy (Oklahoma)

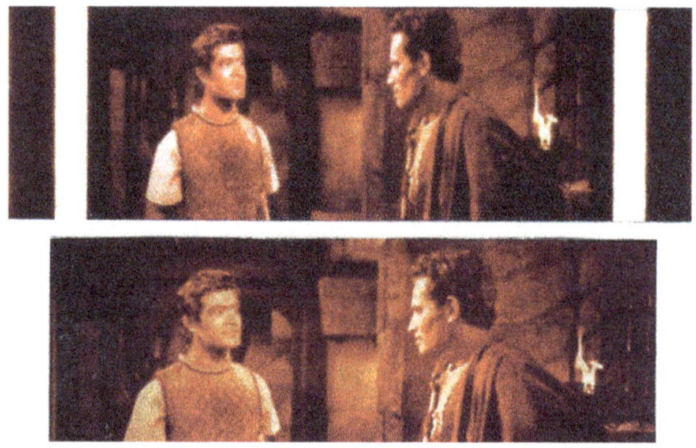

MGM Camera 65 squeezed print for a wider 2.75:1 screen (Ben Hur)

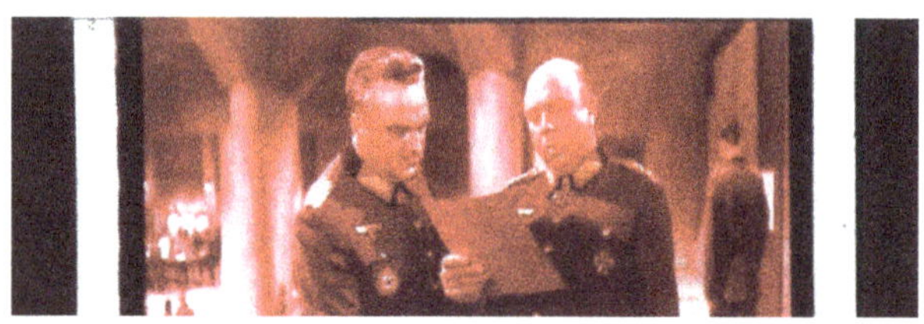

Ultra Panavision rectified version for Cinerama screens (squeeze greater at the sides of the frame)

Blow-ups not filling the frame

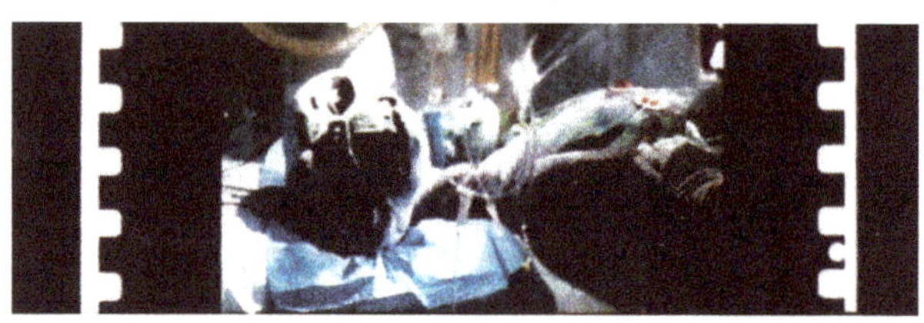

E.T. 1.66:1

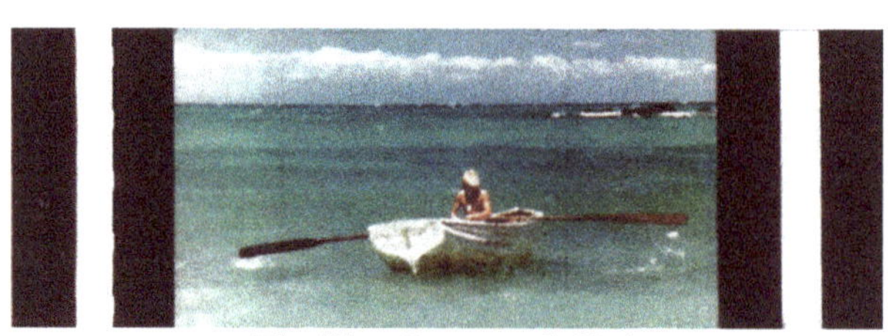

The Blue Lagoon 1.85:1

the screen to provide an aspect ratio of 2.75:1. It became available to other studios as Ultra Panavision 70 and another, Super Panavision 70 using normal lenses was the same as Todd-AO.

Like today's PLF shows, installing 70mm gave cinemas the chance to re-model and up-grade the auditorium and offer a different more theatrical style performance.

The 70mm Roadshow

When 70mm arrived, most cinemas operated on a continuous performance basis. Once the doors opened, cinemagoers were free to enter the auditorium at any time with, if necessary, an usherette with a torch waiting in the dark to guide you to your seat. You could then enjoy the show until the 'this is when we came in' moment came around again, or stay in the warm until the national anthem and everybody had to leave. A roadshow presentation was a special occasion. Chosen seats could be booked in advance for a separate performance of a film which came complete with an overture, intermission and a souvenir brochure to take home and treasure. People would travel great distances to the West End and other big city theatres to see the film first in the splendour of 70mm.

Unfortunately, more recent attempts to revive the idea, like the special 70mm showings of *The Hateful Eight*, left some viewers, unfamiliar with the etiquette of roadshows, rather bemused. Originally, most overtures were played with the curtains closed, the music coming from tracks recorded on blank film at the start of reel one. Even back in the glory days of 70mm, some did project an image on the screen just in case the unenlightened in the audience thought that the film had actually started but perhaps the bulb in the projector had blown. An unexpected intermission can also leave modern audiences sitting in silence wondering what to do next. In the past, sales staff were soon coming down the aisles with trays of drinks and confectionery delivered directly to your seat.

The rise and fall of 70mm

All projector manufacturers would soon be producing dual 70mm/35mm models and 70mm would soon

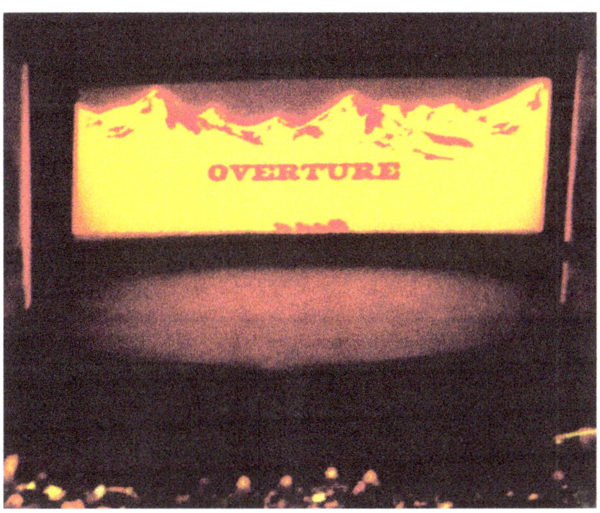

The on-screen announcement during the playing of the overture to The Hateful Eight

become an added attraction in many more cinemas. To ensure a continuing flow of 70mm prints to show, many began to be made by enlarging 35mm films. At first, these came from anamorphic CinemaScope-type negatives, their 2.35:1 images a reasonable fit to 70mm's 2.2:1. Although not a match to 65mm shooting, if carefully done, the results were more than satisfactory with early results, like *Doctor Zhivago*, showing their worth. The average viewer didn't notice the loss of image quality and could still enjoy the other benefits of 70mm projection, including its magnetic stereo sound. Many dedicated 70mm enthusiasts didn't consider these 'blow ups' to be true 70mm and even more so, when they began to be made from various shapes and sizes of non-anamorphic 35mm negatives, with most, in an effort to retain their original aspect ratios, no longer filling the complete 70mm frame. However, in terms of print numbers, the 1980s and most of the 90s would become the heyday of 70mm, with mostly blow-ups being 'Presented in 70mm', before a combination of improved film stocks, the coming of optical Dolby stereo to 35mm prints and the smaller auditoriums and screens in multiplexes, would lead to a decline in 70mm.

Keeping to the curve

Also to be missed by many was the practice of showing 70mm on deeply curved screens, which have been in and out of fashion over the years, (out at the moment). Most cinema higher gain screens have a directional effect and are slightly curved to improve the distribution of light being directed back to the audience. There have always been advocates for going further and to use

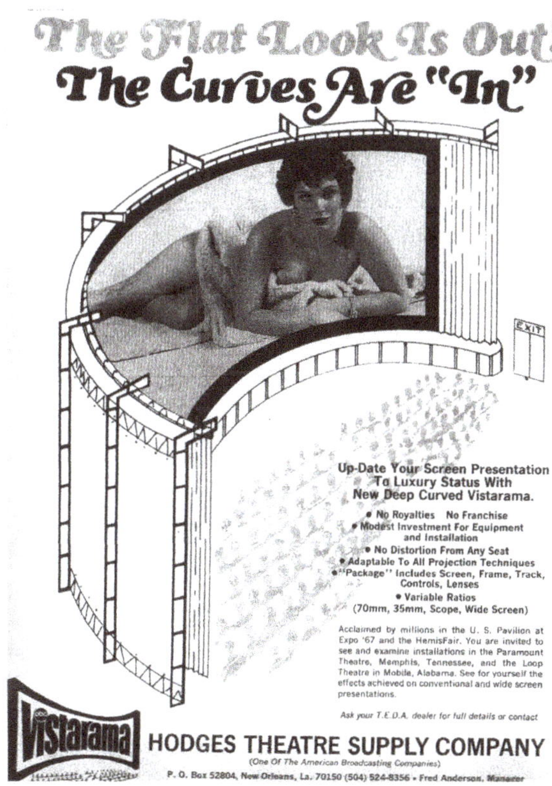

Ad for the deeply curved Vistarama screen - a different age!

a much greater depth of curve, thinking it can give an extra sense of involvement and drawing the viewer into the picture. Unfortunately, if very deep, one side of the screen can see the other and cross reflections can spoil the contrast of the picture. A special screen was an integral part of Cinerama, which solved the problem with its louvered screen, the slats angled to allow stray light from the other side to pass through the gaps and out to the back of the screen. Todd-AO's early screens embossed their reflective surface with ribs which changed in profile as they moved away from the centre, all trying to keep the light going in the right direction. Even at a distance both the vertical ribs and slats gave their pictures a streaky look which, in the case of Cinerama, helped to disguise the seams between its three panels. Even so, they would keep this type of screen even after switching to its single lens version showing 70mm prints.

A rival deep curve system, **Dimension-150**, relied on using a relatively low gain screen to help keep cross reflections to a minimum. Higher contrast 70mm prints were sometimes used to keep the picture looking good. Both the new 70mm Cinerama and D-150 kept to level projection and used lenses with a curved field of focus to keep their images sharp. They could also provide laboratories with special printer lenses to modify the image on the print to help reduce the remaining distortion, including the stretching effect at the sides of the screen.
All this was not good enough for one prominent director. The London showcase for D-150 was the Odeon Marble Arch and when it hosted the 1989 70mm restoration of *Lawrence of Arabia*, David Lean didn't like its effect on his desert landscapes, so the curved screen was replaced with a flatter one. The original was sadly missed, as is the theatre itself.

Today's digital distortion correction and screen technology has improved the performance of deeply curved and other forms of concave screens, but at the moment these

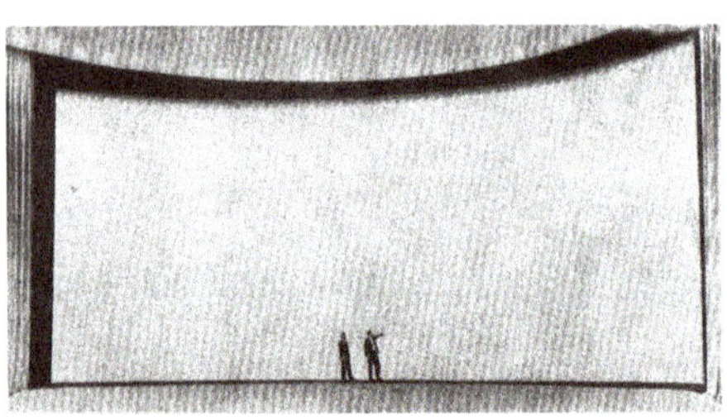

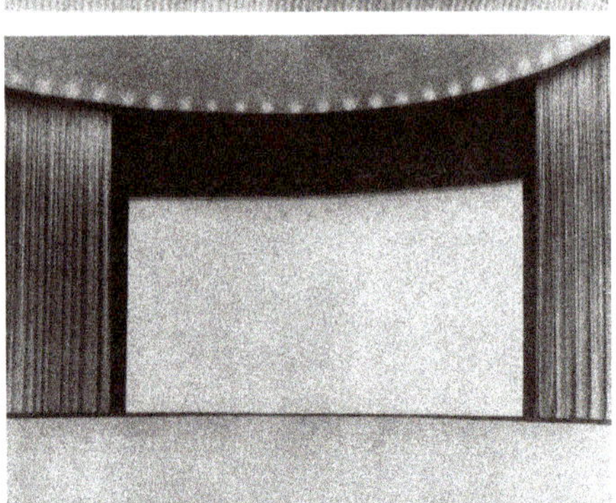

Unlike many of today's PLF giant screens, the D-150 70mm presentation system could mask down its curved screen and adjust the curtains for better-looking 35mm showings

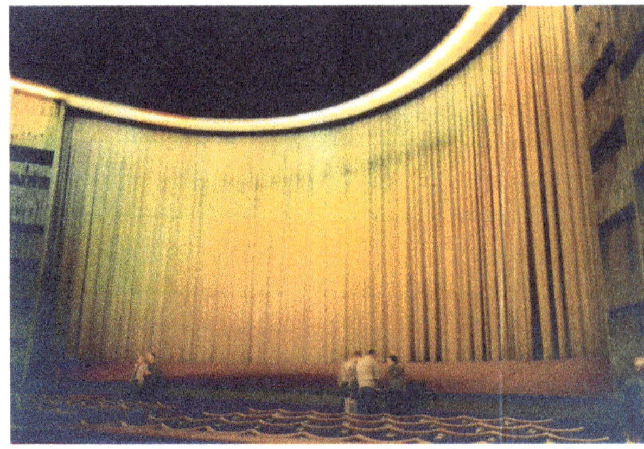

Although the D-150 screen at the Odeon Marble Arch was removed, the curtains remained, showing its original size and profile.

are only benefiting a few special shows and training simulators. The last 65mm/70mm film presented under the Todd-AO banner was in 1970 and Cinerama in 1974, but a new name would soon become familiar to the public and synonymous with giant images.

Behold, IMAX®

The special venue side of the industry would also seize on 70mm. Some would use the same 5 perforation high theatrical frame, but others would change it to suit their various shows and rides. One of these, IMAX, was first seen back in 1970. It was the invention of Canada's Multi-screen Corporation, which as its name suggests, provided the expertise and technology for the multi-screen displays popular at the time at events like major exhibitions, world fairs and expositions. It was premiered in the Fuji Group pavilion at Expo 70 in Japan.

This time, to reduce the number of projectors required, a single 70mm film was turned on its side with a 15 perf. frame, shown using a unique compressed air 'rolling loop' projector, much kinder to the film as it moved through at three times the normal speed. The emphasis was still on multi-images, with up to three 65mm or nine 35mm, printed within its large, now 3:4 frame. However, a 65mm 15 perf. camera was constructed for the occasional full frame image. These were so impressive on the 60 foot screen, they would set the pattern for future IMAX theatres, characterised by their steeply raked seats to keep every member of the audience close to the vast screen which filled their complete field of vision. IMAX would go on to produce a domed screen version, sometimes combined with a planetarium, photographed and projected via fish-eye lenses and even a 'Magic Carpet' show with another screen under your feet.

At first, IMAX was mostly found showing short films at museums and other institutions These were often of an educational nature, and for many, unlike Cinerama, didn't always exploit the giant screen to the full. When they did, IMAX produced some amazing sights, particularly when the camera was taken up in the air, under

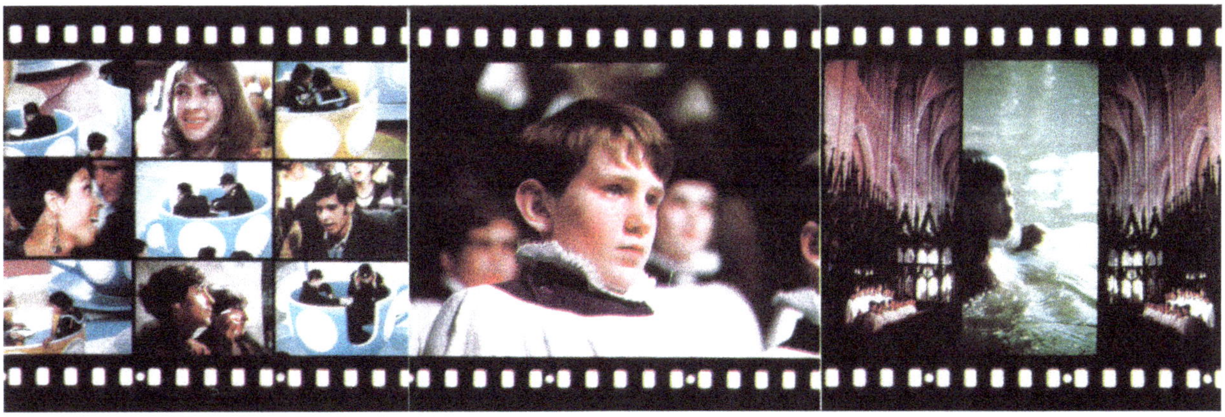

The first IMAX film TIGER CHILD at Japan's Expo 70 was mostly multi-image with an occasional full-frame image.

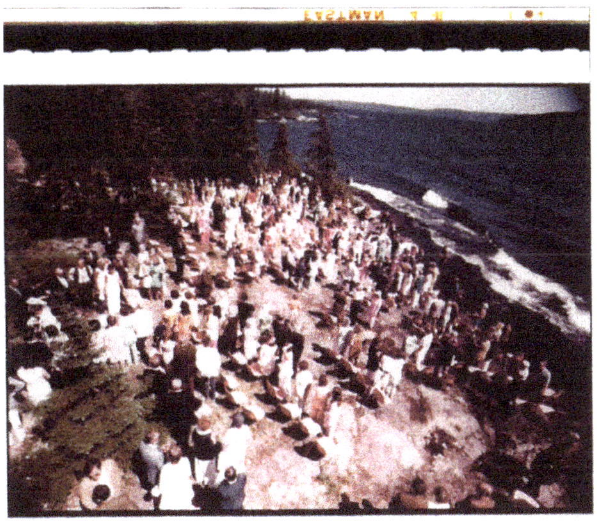

IMAX's large negative allowed the viewer to pick out the smallest detail.

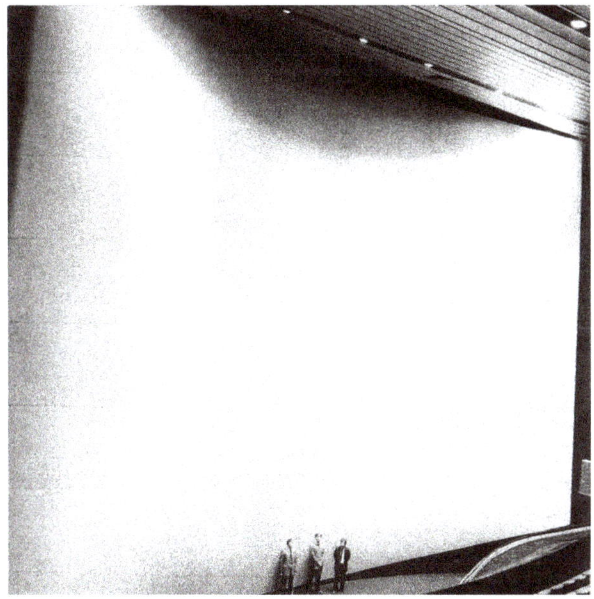

Traditional giant IMAX screen at Bradford's now National Science and Media Museum

the water and out in space, when its huge negative area allowed the viewers eyes to roam over the vast screen, picking out the smallest detail. They would also lead the way to bringing back 3D to the big screen.

IMAX at a theatre near you

IMAX would take a similar path to Cinerama to attract a wider audience by showing normal 'entertainment' films on its giant screen. After Cinerama's series of travelogues had run out of places around the world to visit, the 3-strip system was used for a couple of story films. Although one, *How The West Was Won*, was very successful, most film- makers weren't prepared to be restricted by its fixed 146 degree angle of view.

An important factor in giving its sense of involvement, the switch to the narrower views of 70mm increased the range of films to show, but lost some of the original magic. Features, like *Grand Prix* and *2001*, suited the curved screen, but to make the most of others intended for an initial Cinerama release, their widest possible camera lens was fitted to include an occasional 'Cinerama-type' sequence. Some were at the start to show off the screen, for example, *The Battle of he Bulge* began with a hold on to your seat flying sequence over the battlefield and *Khartoum* set the scene with a mini-travelogue taking in the ruins of ancient Egypt.

As digital techniques became available to cinema, IMAX's own efforts to broaden its appeal could now use digital help. They developed their DMR (digitally re-mastered) process for blowing up 35mm films to its 70mm 15 perf. frame. The negative is scanned at the highest possible resolution, the image 'optimised' for the big screen, and transferred onto the film print. To bring them to more theatres, a simpler more compact projector, with moving rollers replacing the compressed air to form its rolling loop, was built to fit in alongside their normal projectors. Space also had to be found for the 6ft platter carrying the up to 9 miles of 70mm film now needed for the average full-length feature.

The auditorium was sometimes re-styled with new steeper stadium seating to ensure a good view of the screen, which isn't as tall as the original, but most DMR copies from 'Scope and widescreen films don't fill the complete 4:3 IMAX frame.

The next step, which would see its name on many more multiplexes, was to show its optimised image directly us-

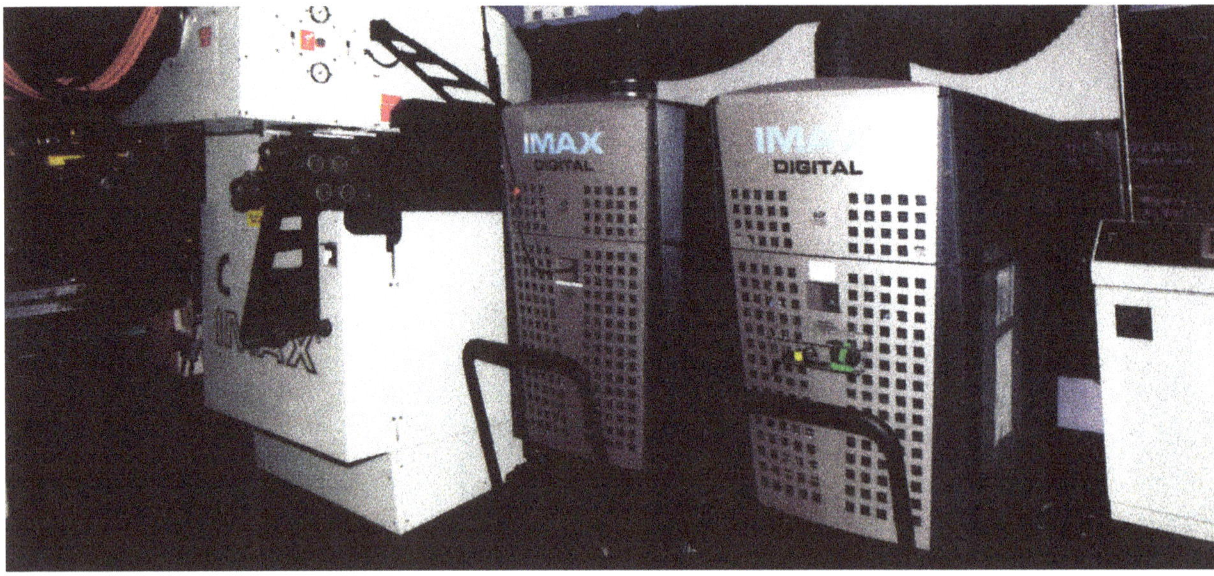

Like a few of the other original IMAX theatres, the BFI have kept their film projector alongside its new digital pair for occasions when a 15/70 print comes along. An extra digital projector is also provided for non-IMAX showings.

ing digital projectors. Without IMAX film frame size DLP chips available to reflect the amount of light required, two projectors superimpose a pair of auto-aligned images on the screen to achieve sufficient brightness. They are also available to project 3D's separate left and right eye images, and a further move to replace xenon with even brighter laser illumination has allowed the previous polarised filters to be replaced with a less light hungry spectral splitting colour separation system. The shape of digital IMAX is 1.9:1, making the best use of the full area of current DLP chips. If possible, today's films, originated on both 35mm film and digital, are re-formatted to fit, but if they keep their original ratios they can leave much of the vast unmasked screen blank.

Keeping bigger looking better

On typical size screens, digital projectors are producing excellent pictures, which for many are just as good, and more consistent than film. However, without the advantages of the larger 70mm and IMAX film frames, their nearer to 35mm size 2K and 4K chips are being pushed to fill the new PLF giant screens. As well as a pair of projectors working together to maintain the same level of illumination, some also add extra visual tricks and artefacts to their images to keep them looking good and help them to stand up to the greater magnification and closer viewing distances.

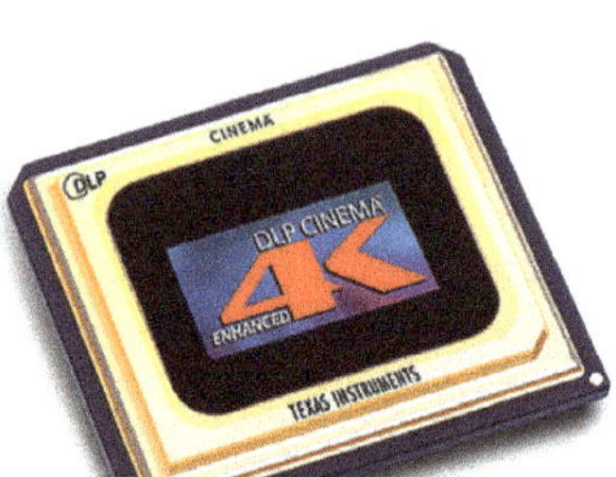

Current digital image forming chips are nearer to the size of a 35mm frame. With the growth of PLF screens, perhaps a larger version could be made to fill them using a single new '70mm' digital projector.

Film vs digital

In terms of definition, even 4K is less than 35mm. A recent comparison suggests that a 'Scope frame is around 6K, 70mm (from a 65mm negative) is 12K and the original IMAX film 18K. Arriving at an exact figure is complicated by the fact that film and digital record and display their images in a different way.

Unlike digital's fixed pattern of pixels, film has the benefit of its moving grain, with a better chance of capturing

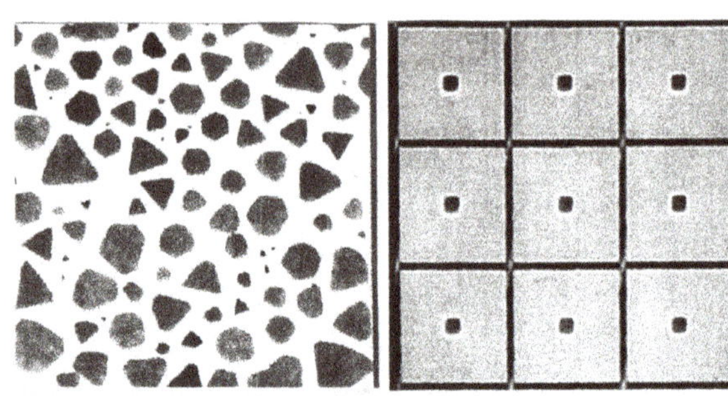

Film's random 'moving' grain can display much finer detail than a fixed array of pixels.

the finest detail, if missed by one frame it may be picked up by the next. A hint of visual grain can also make film appear sharper. It's all in the eye of the beholder, but some 70mm lovers think that it's not like it used to be, blaming modern film stocks for being too good, with their grain-free velvet texture lacking the punch and sparkle remembered from the past. Although high definition is important, particularly for extra large screens, it's only one factor for producing good quality pictures. A phenomenon that the latest HDR (High Dynamic Range) systems exploit, is the well known observation that a well-lit picture with a wide contrast range can 'look' much sharper than a higher definition one that has a dim flat lower contrast image.

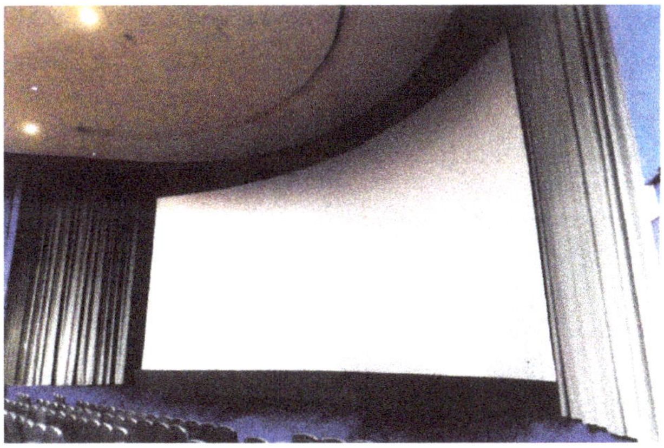

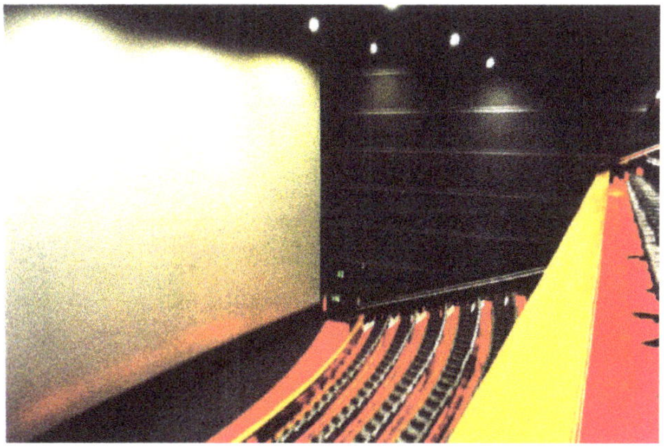

The changing fashions for big screens - out go curves and curtains, in comes plain and flat

On the edge

Some film processing methods accentuate an edge effect with increased contrast just along the edges of the image, which again adds to the apparent sharpness (denser parts steal some of the developer's strength from the edge of adjoining lighter exposed areas). Video and digital have their own versions to also make their finer detail stand out. SD video often put a white line around it, and one form of digital 'definition intensification' increases the relative contrast between adjacent pixels along the boundaries, with the amount applied depending on the nature of the image.

Looking for something different

Film and digital can offer different viewing experiences. Some think that digital lacks some of the 'magical' look of film and is more like watching big screen TV in the dark, even more so with the prospect of large active LED cinema screens. Back at home, analogue audio is making a comeback, with today's digital generation willing to put up with the odd click and plop from their 'new' vinyl records in exchange for the chance to hear a less clinical more friendly sound coming from their speakers. Perhaps now is a good time for them to re-discover the different look of analogue film projection and encourage them to again make a journey to see a 'Special Edition' 70mm show.

Fortunately, real film lovers, like Christopher Nolan and Kenneth Branagh have helped keep 70mm and IMAX film alive, while waiting for a wider revival. Apparently, other film-makers are waiting in a queue to use Panavision's remaining Super 70 65mm cameras, and the search for new old 70mm projectors continues, together with the skills to run them. Often their refurbishment doesn't include the sound head, as new 70mm films can no longer be accompanied by the appropriate analogue sound. With the print's magnetic stripes now long gone, the sound is coming from a separate digital source.

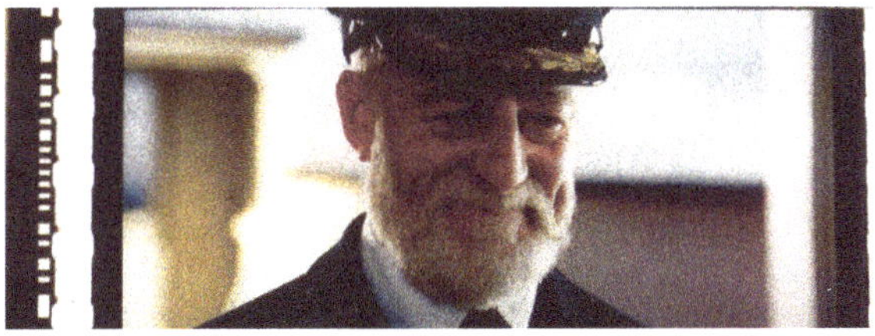

Later 70mm prints said goodbye to the wonder of analogue magnetic sound, using an optical control track keeping the film sound in sync with a separate digital system.

At best, with digital cinema firmly established, 70mm may find a place as another form of Event Cinema, recreating its memorable roadshows of the past.

The screen's still the thing!

70mm remains an occasional treat, but many more multiplex auditoriums are being turned into digital IMAX and other Premium Large Format screens. There currently don't appear to be any minimum requirements to gain the title, such as the size and shape of the screen, or how much it should fill the viewer's field of view. In practice, most feature increasing the size of the screen relative to that of the auditorium and arranging the often new 'premium', sometimes motorized, reclining seats so every member of the audience can appreciate it. To rival IMAX, it should be wall to wall and floor to ceiling. This can be a challenge for designers, sometimes having to raise the screen so those in the retained original shallower seating can see the bottom of it. Sometimes, a section of the screen has to be moveable, just in case the now covered emergency exits in the front wall are ever needed. The new giant screen can dominate the auditorium. Those who can still remember entering an old Cinerama theatre, with their vast curved red curtains, find being confronted with a looming plain giant flat screen less welcoming. At least one IMAX theatre is said to have fitted equally huge curtains to give it a less 'cold' theatrical ambiance.

Some of the first digital PLF systems struggled to maintain the same rich and sharp image, but recent technology, like HDR and laser light sources, have helped them to keep up with the growing screens. Both film and digital cameras are capable of much higher resolutions, but the final screen image is limited by the projector's pixel count. When asked to fill bigger than normal screens, the resulting pictures could be compared to the earlier 35mm films blown up to 70mm, with a good bright larger image, but without its full potential.

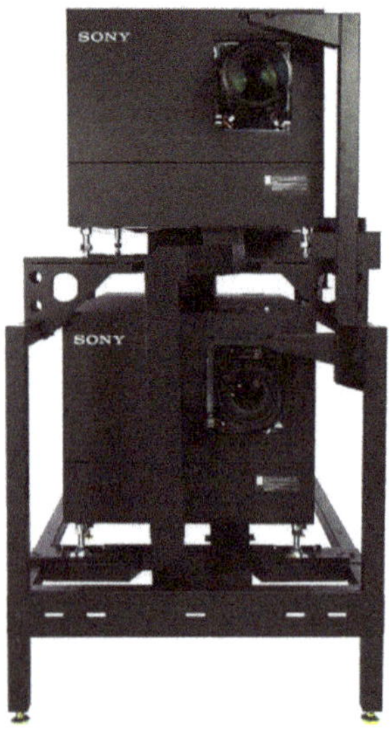

Sometimes, especially in the absence of laser projection, when it comes to filling the largest PLF screens two projectors are better than one.

The film's the thing too

The success of a PLF screening can also depend on the film's subject matter and style of photography. Plenty of action and all-embracing wide shots can add to the excitement and draw the audience into the heart of the action. However, quieter, more intimate stories, can end up with a rather distracting over-blown look, with its in your face close-ups better observed from a little further away with less visual intensity. For the leading systems, the choice of suitable films also involves the film-makers and distributors. IMAX, for example, currently produces its own DCP, incorporating its optimised image which may have been re-formatted to make the best use of the screen. Another, Dolby Cinema, hides Dolby's own enhancements, including its Dolby Vision version of HDR, within a normal DCP, which looks good on any size screen.

Create your own PLF

The principal branded PLF systems use their own customised, or specified digital projectors, with usually a pair needed to help fill the largest screens, together with the obligatory immersive sound. However, there's nothing to prevent any cinema from creating its own bigger screen auditorium, using their own choice of technology and thinking up a good name for it - IHS Markit recently established that there are currently 72 brands worldwide. Names already promising a premium viewing experience in the UK and beyond include Impact, Isense and Finity which, like those from the past with '70' in the title, mean that cinemagoers are again in for something special – which can only be good!

The ultimate in PLF for the future?

Samsung installed its first commercial Cinema LED Screen at Lotte Cinema World Tower in Korea. The High Dynamic Range (HDR) LED (Light Emitting Diode) Cinema LED Screen provides direct viewing (no projection involved!) with distortion-free images and no projection artefacts. It generates sharper and more realistic colours, increasing the 'immersive' effect for viewers, and the 10.3m (33.8ft) wide LED Screen accommodates a variety of configurations and aspect ratios. The HDR pictures are 4K resolution (4,096 x 2,160) with peak brightness levels up to 146fL, some 10 times greater than standard projector technologies. The flat screen can offer low-tone grey-scale settings to showcase the brightest colours, deepest blacks and most pristine whites at a nearly infinite contrast ratio.

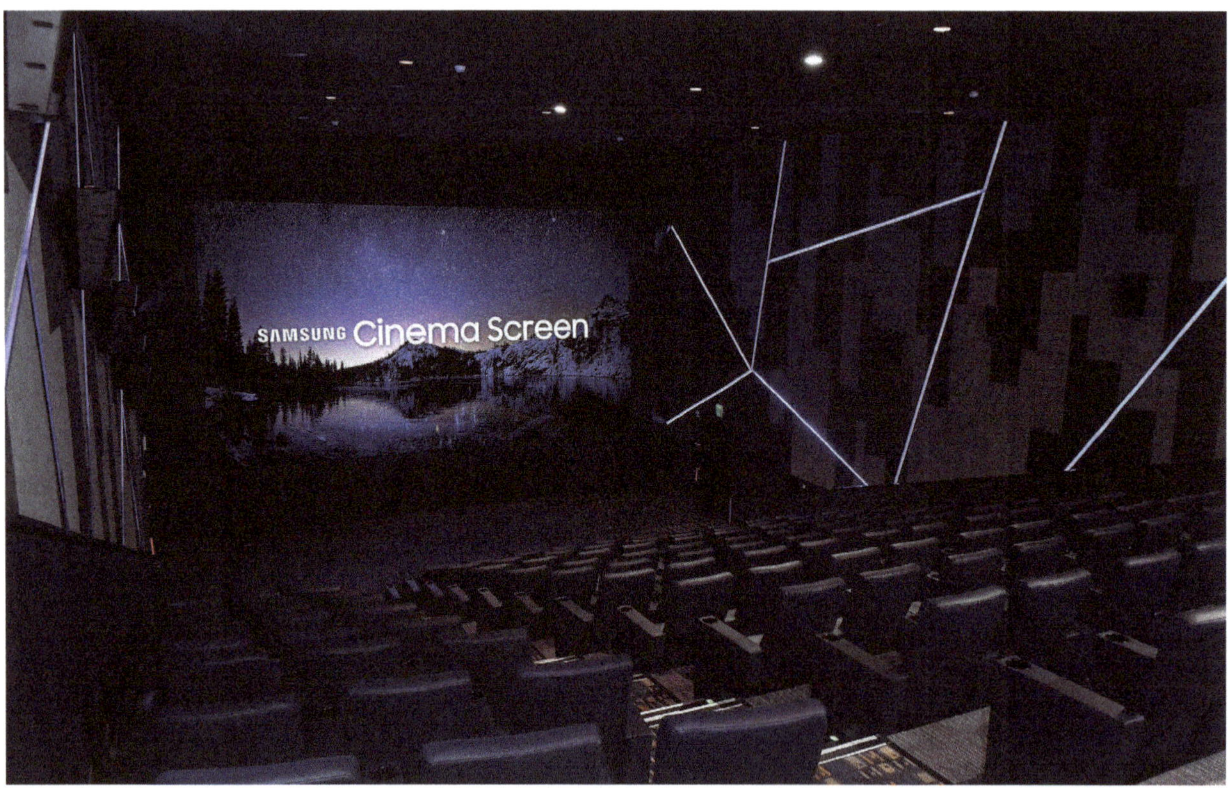

Never mind the film - look at the premium extras

A recent survey looking at the cost of going to the cinema around the country found, for example, that the same film could be seen for as little as £5 on certain days in Cardiff and Truro, but could cost up to £25 in London's Leicester Square. Apart from the higher West End prices, like many other theatres, cinemas around the country are now offering cinemagoers willing to pay more the chance to enjoy extras like pre-show entertainment, even more comfortable seating, 3D, and giant screens. These can be either in 'upper class' areas within the normal auditorium, or in a new separate Lux or Super screen.

Seats at all prices

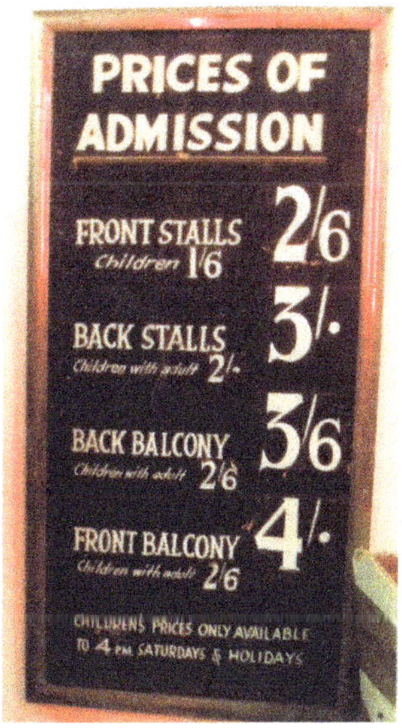

Back before the multiplex, most cinemas had a range of seat prices. The degree of comfort, or lack of it, was usually the same but they differed depending on their location in the larger auditoriums. Unlike a live theatre, the cheapest were at the front of the stalls. Today, IMAX® and other premium large format shows try to arrange their seating so viewers are literally on top of the screen. In earlier times, sitting too close to the screen was thought to be bad for the eyes, so many preferred to pay a bit more to sit further back in the stalls or up in the circle.

Seats of desire

Looking back at the social history of cinema going, the back row became the premium choice for so called 'courting' couples. Some enterprising cinema owners even installed special double seats to allow the customers to get closer, relying on an usherette, armed with only a torch, to stop them going too far. Stories from cleaners suggested that evidence was sometimes found indicating that they had not always been successful! Apparently, particularly during wartime, some cinemas gained a reputation for catering for couples less interested in actually watching the film. Like later 'specialist' theatres, they soon attracted the attention of the licensing authorities and even undercover policemen ready to put a stop to any lewd behaviour both on and off the screen. Sadly, at times of falling audiences, some respectable cinemas had to resort to showing less wholesome exploitation films to stay in business.

Lay back and enjoy it

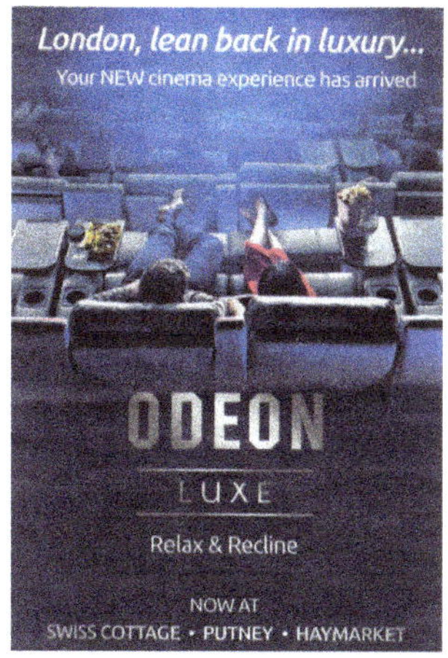

Back to today's multiplex, where all audiences can now expect the best in sound and vision experienced in ever greater comfort. Some can now pay more to put their feet up in the latest luxurious fully reclining motorized seating, joining the other premium options of sofas, sinking in cushions or sitting up to enjoy a meal during the show in a dining screen. To make it easier to eat and drink without missing any of the film, some have brought the bar and food counter into the auditorium.

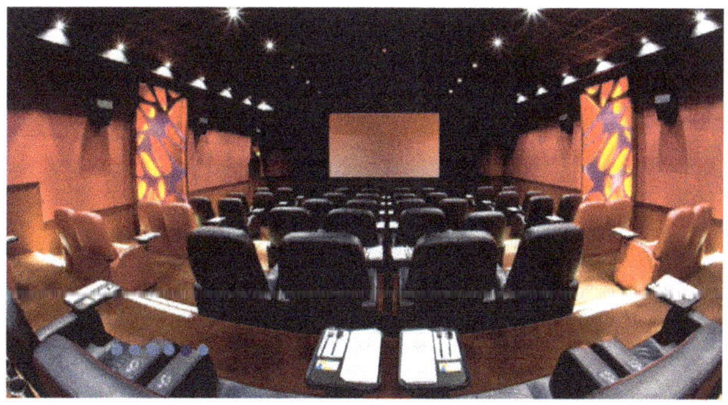

Eating while you watch a film in luxury at The Odeon, Whiteleys, London.

A better show in every sense

It can be fun speculating what other of the body's senses could be stimulated to boost ticket prices. Although most possible 'new' cinematic innovations have been tried before, the latest technologies may give them another

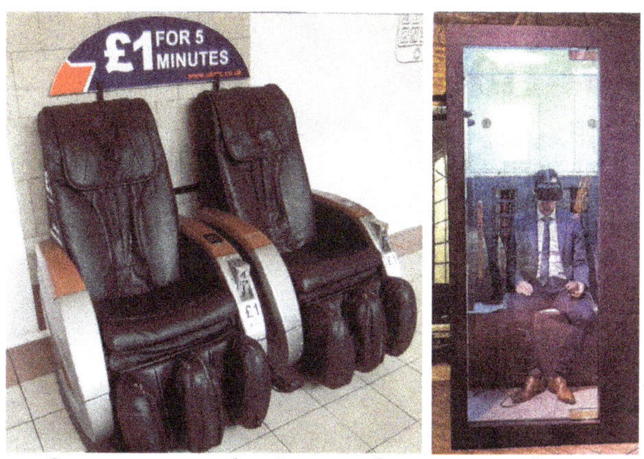

On your way to the cinema, why not stop to have a massage? Or chill out in a sensory pod?

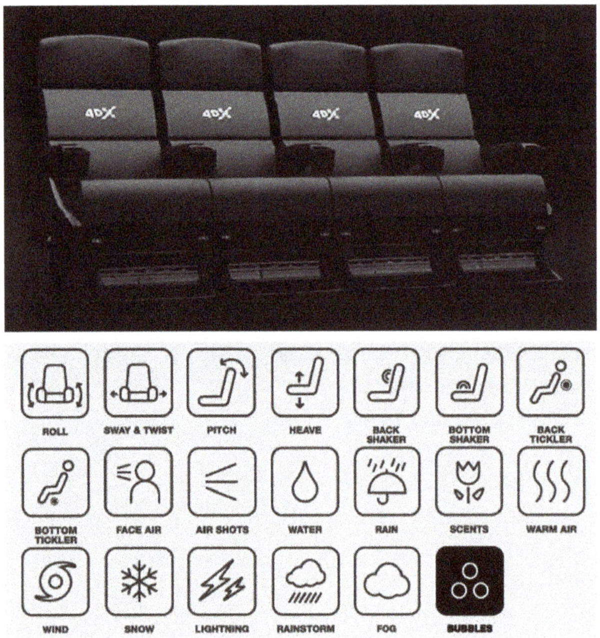

4DX from South Korean company CJ 4DPLEX, allows a motion picture presentation to be augmented with a wide range of environmental effects such as multiple seat motions, wind, rain, fog, lights, and scents.

chance, just as the switch to digital projection made the return of 3D more practical and easier to operate.

A performance that moves you

The motor driven reclining seats could be made even smarter, offering a relaxing massage before the show and then shaking you up during suitable moments in the film. This could range from a gentle sway for a romantic boat trip up the river, to being thrown about to share the even greater danger and excitement of car chases and other fast moving action. This could help bring the idea of a 4D experience into the multiplex, the extra dimension being physical effects. In its more violent theme park home, the viewer, or rider, hangs on for dear life in moving seats, either mounted in cars or on hydraulically operated platforms, motion controlled to match the action on the large immersive screen. To add to the sense of reality, the short ride films are often in 3D with fans blowing wind and spray in your face, and this can include suitable smells. Multiplex versions of 4D are already starting to become popular and could provide individual control of this moving experience, including a pause button to prevent it coming to life unexpectedly and sending drinks and popcorn flying into the air.

Blowing hot and cold

Playing with the temperature may be a less welcome addition to the sense of reality. Audiences are less likely to pay extra to either shiver so they can share the discomfort of the on-screen characters fighting for survival in the frozen wastes, or queuing up for fans and iced drinks to suffer the burning heat of the desert. In the past, having to keep your coat on for films like Scott of the Antarctic and other snow bound adventures, was not the new wonder of Chill-0-Vision, but the cinema's heating

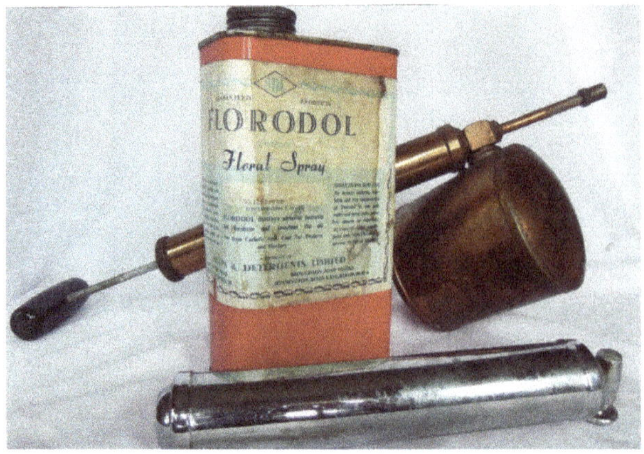

system breaking down during the depths of winter. A more comic situation up on the screen, was when, for its latest desert picture, *The Smallest Show On Earth*, Bijou flea-pit's boiler was turned up full in order to sell the sweltering audience more ice creams.

There's something in the air

Apart from the occasional stink bomb thrown during kid's Saturday morning pictures, the lingering smell of earlier cinema-going was cigarette smoke. The magic flickering beam from the projection box was clearly visible as it passed through the haze onto a screen slowly turning yellow. When widescreen arrived, it was recommended that after the show the variable masking was left fully open so all the different screen shapes suffered the nicotine staining equally. To avoid buying a new one, some screens received a coat of aluminium paint, improving the picture but having the sound spoilt by blocked perforations. Sometimes, the audience too was freshened up when an usherette came down the aisle spraying a scented disinfectant at them. This was often supplied free in exchange for an ad on the screen praising the brand for improving the atmosphere both at the cinema and back home. Fortunately, by the end of the 1980s, the cinema led the way by first restricting lighting up to certain areas of the auditorium and then banning it altogether, with its smell now replaced by, for many, the equally unpleasant aroma of popcorn.

The search for the sweet smell of success

Over the years, the idea of actually polluting the atmosphere on purpose to add to the sense of reality has generated much publicity but few successful presentations. The challenge isn't producing a suitable range of smells, but introducing them in sync with the images on the screen and then clearing the air ready for the next. Although critics had fun describing them as 'stinkers', a couple of aromatic processes did reach the noses of the public.

Around 1960, the short-lived AromaRama added the scents via the cinema's air conditioning and the now legendary Smell-O-Vision sent them along pipes to the back of the seats.

Twenty years later, the simplest, Odorama, left the audience to do most of the work - on seeing a number displayed on the screen they had to scratch and sniff the

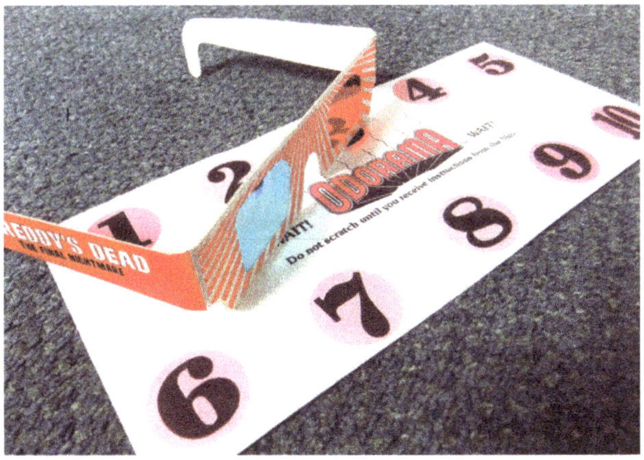

appropriate spot on a card given away with their ticket. Like the old cardboard 3D glasses, you were welcome to take the card home as a souvenir.

Today, smells, both fragrant and not, are making a comeback, this time also augmenting the new worlds of virtual reality and even being used to trigger the memories of dementia patients.

VR, the cinema's friend or foe?

The key to enter virtual reality is its headset, a high-tech stereoscopic viewer which allows its wearer to move around a 360 degree image, either computer generated or live action stitched together from multiple cameras. Although being in a world of your own is without the communal spirit of a cinema auditorium, some well-known names in the industry, like IMAX®, are looking at the potential of VR, both within cinemas and as separate attractions. 20th Century Fox created VR experiences to support its sci fi film The Martian. Most headsets are being aimed at gamers and are offering new opportunities for tech start-ups. One idea is to place escape rooms or booths in shopping centres, stations and other public spaces, ready to transport stressed out workers to their own enchanted forest or tropical island. Some play with more of the body's senses than the VR headset alone. Motion control can allow users to experience floating in an open boat while being brushed with warm or cool air.

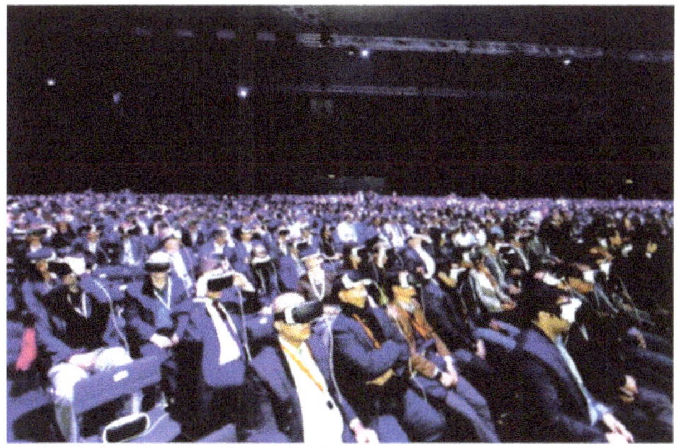

Will this be the shared VR cinema experience of the future?

The smell of another premium extra

4D shows and VR experiences have made it worthwhile to give 'Smell-0-Vision' another go. Scent cartridges and phials are again being made to release smells like, burning wood, salty sea air, chocolate and coconut, a freshly cut lawn and even elephant dung for a walk with elephants in the African Savannah. Also on the list, is one to induce a 'euphoric state of mind'? Some headsets include sensors which feed back the user's heart rate and temperature so as to adapt the experience.

Now is the time to put on your VR headset

Although a VR booth or pod may find a place in the foyer, it is interesting to think of ways in which VR might be let into the auditorium and become part of a normal show. Unfortunately, some cinemagoers are already not too keen on having to wear ordinary 3D glasses for a couple of hours, so are unlikely to want to swap them for a heavier headset with a high 'sweat factor'. Except for the most dedicated video gamer, 20-30 minutes of VR is considered the limit before the participant can become uncomfortable or even sick. One method might be to adopt the idea from some early 3D films which only had certain sequences in 3D. The audience had to wait until a voice on the soundtrack, or it was indicated in the plot, that now was the time to put on your 3D glasses. These could now be VR headsets, either available to all the audience, or just those who had paid extra for them and sitting in swivel seats allowing the full 360 degree experience. The rest of the audience would be left to

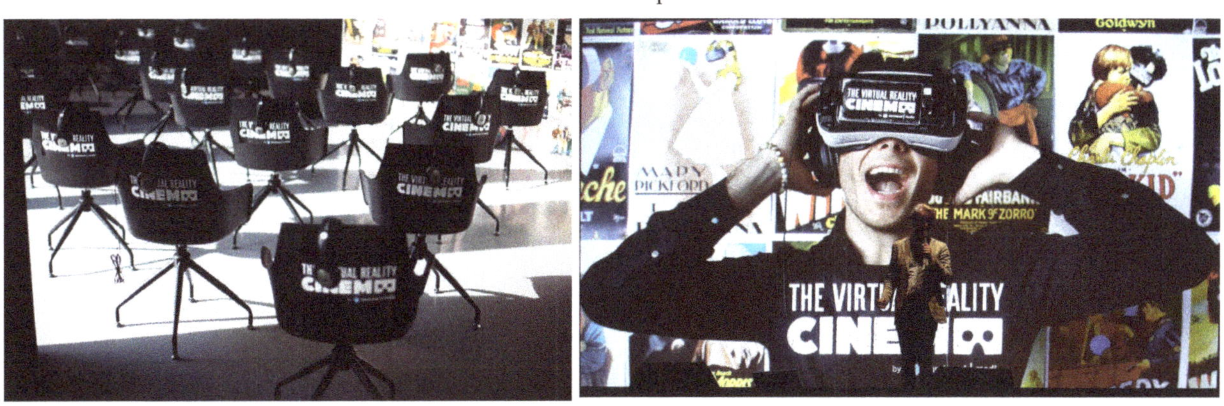

Cinema experiences of the future? An experimental 'virtual cinema' where all the seats can be swivelled through 360 degrees and (Right) the virtual reality cinema experience at Cine Europe.

share the continuing normal picture on the screen, which may be in old fashioned 3D. The film-makers would have to provide a VR version of the chosen scenes, which may have to include picture or sound cues to make sure that for any significant action, those now in their own 360-degree VR world are looking in the right direction.

More entertainment going to your head

Other forms of new headgear may also have an effect on the cinema. AR, augmented reality, which can add virtual reality content to the real world, could usurp the director and give the viewer a choice of what and who they see on the screen. Those without a special large format screen nearby might choose to stay at home and don the latest visual headphones. Using what looks much like a VR headset, they can simulate watching a Blu-ray or streamed movie on a giant screen with immersive sound. At the moment, all these head mounted devices can't match the resolution and picture quality of a big cinema screen, and like all the other premium extras, can only help a good film which, as always, has the innate ability to make audiences forget the real world, with or without the added gimmickry.

What's a blow-up?

A 'blow-up' is the term used to describe a print made by enlarging or 'blowing- up' images from smaller formats to larger ones. It usually involved enlarging images from 35mm film to make 70mm prints, but such prints have also been derived from 16mm and even 8mm originals. When the first 35mm to 70mm blow-ups appeared there were concerns that these weren't 'proper 70mm prints, which, like the original Todd-AO process, has to be photographed on 65mm negative with the same large image area, but eventually the high quality of some of these blown-up images became recognised by all but the most pedantic of 70mm purists.

Unlike 70mm prints from 65mm negatives, which can be simply contact printed by laying the negative onto the unexposed print film and illuminating it, blow-ups are made using an optical printer. In essence this uses a projector (35mm, say) which focuses its image onto the gate of the 65mm camera. As well being able to change the size of the image it is possible for the optical system to include an anamorphic lens to squeeze or unsqueeze the image.

It is generally accepted that the first blow-ups to hit the cinema screen were the 70mm prints made from Technicolor's Technirama horizontal 8-perf 35mm negatives. The height of the Technirama negative already matched that of a 70mm frame, so only a 50% horizontal enlargement was needed to restore the systems squeezed image, as it was photographed using the camera's x1.5 anamorphic lens, in order to produce the 70mm copy.

In later years the term blow-up was generally used to mean the creation of 70mm prints from standard 4-perf 35mm anamorphic (CinemaScope-type) negatives, and this was augmented later by the printing of various image areas onto normal 35mm 'flat' (non-anamorphic) originals.

By the early 1960s, ever-improving film stocks meant that optical conversions could be used to enlarge and un-squeeze anamorphic negatives, often 35mm Panavision, up to a 70mm print. Despite the smaller original negative area, in practice the resulting 70mm prints were generally judged to be more than satisfactory, and helped to increase the supply of product in the rapidly growing number of 70mm installations.

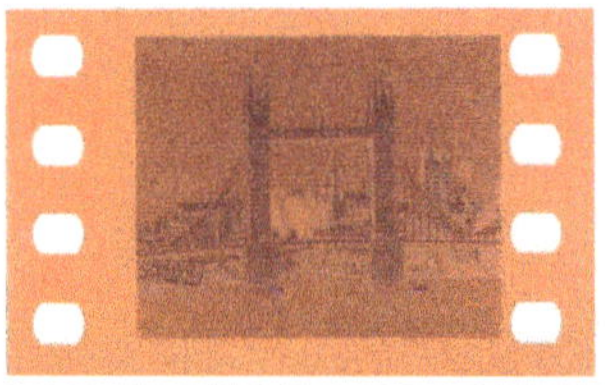

70mm prints are often made from anamorphically originated 35mm. They are usually printed full height, clipping the surplus from the sides.

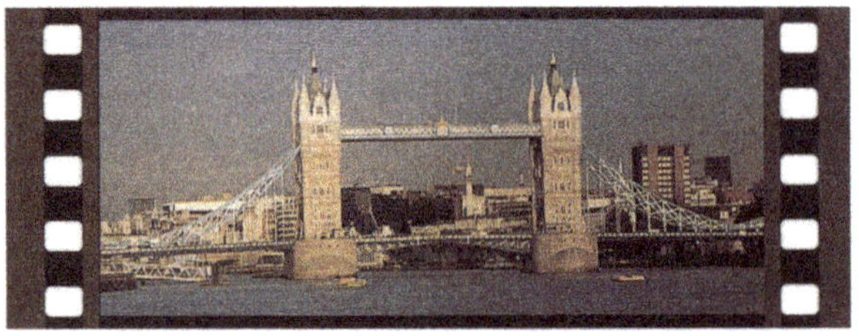

Other reasons why the 35-70mm blow-ups produced excellent on-screen images were that the 70mm prints required less magnification to fill the screen, resulting in brighter and steadier pictures, and that the image from the 35mm negative was usually transferred to 70mm film via a high-quality printer lens (Micro-Panatar) compared to the possibly less than perfect projector anamorphic attachment used when showing a 35mm 'Scope print.

Although 35mm anamorphic negatives were the most suitable for a blow-up, losing little of the 2.35:1 image when enlarged to 70mm's 2.2:1 aspect ratio, some spherical non-anamorphic 1.85:1 films were also blown up, sometimes being enlarged to fill the full frame of the 70mm print (or nearly so) which meant losing some of the vertical composition.

This led to some directors and cinematographers, fearing that their composition might be compromised, only agreeing to a blow-up if the original intended aspect ratio – usually 1.85:1 – was kept. This meant that the optical printer's magnification was reduced, leaving unused areas at the sides of the 70mm print. Less often to be seen were 70mm prints masked down vertically to retain the aspect ratios of originals wider than 70mm's 2.2:1 including several 2.35:1 films and, exceptionally, *Seven Brides for Seven Brothers*, which recreated the old 2.55:1 CinemaScope screen shape from 4-track magnetic sound days.

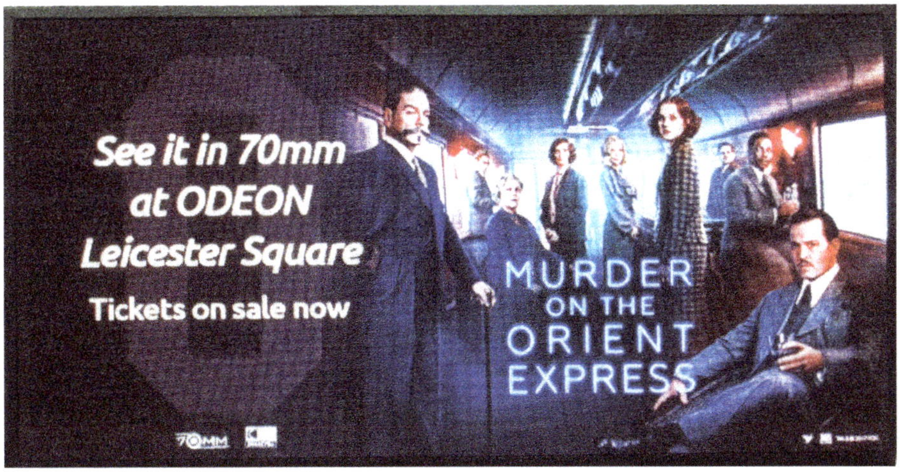

Interesting to see how in the new world of digital cinema, the showing of an actual film print, particularly if 70mm, is itself now a special event - this picture taken from the huge LED advertising screen outside the Odeon Leicester Square

PART THREE

GRANT'S GEMS

A somewhat random collection of technical pieces from Grant Lobban illustrating many different aspects of how technology has always been used to make a visit to the cinema something special and something to remember.

Confessions of a BBC projectionist...

Life in the projection room wasn't dull, as illustrated by these stories to frighten any health and safety officer, including artificial suntans, and even sex tips for projectionists.

Memories of the Bell & Howell 609

The projection gear at the BBC during the heyday of film was different from that in the average cinema, and I have memories of operating this wide range of equipment. One of my early favourites was the Bell & Howell 609. This was a carbon arc 16mm projector mounted on its own trolley-type stand, complete with rectifier and amplifier. Apart from its mag/opt sound heads, a selsyn motor system allowed it to keep in sync with one or more separate magnetic (or optical) tracks, run on sound 'bays'. These, also known as 'followers' were usually nearby in the same area, but in the case of Ealing Studios dubbing theatres they were situated in a far removed 'repro room', which, for one of them, was across the road.

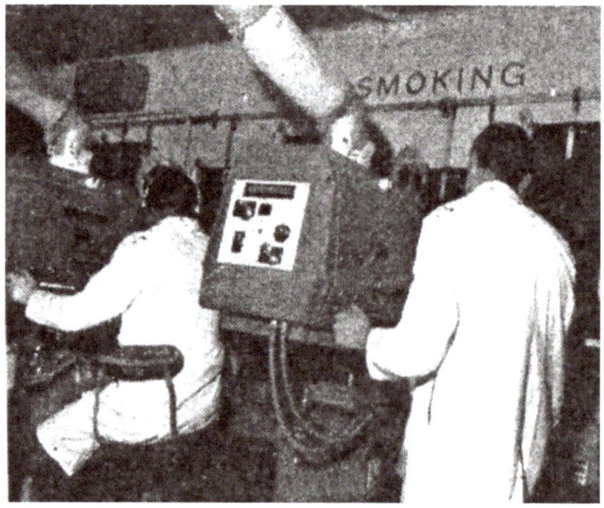

BBC projectionists had the option of wearing white coats. Most didn't bother, not wanting to be confused with doctors!

Bell & Howell 609 carbon arc 16mm projector. Amplifier under the arc Rectifier on lower shelf.

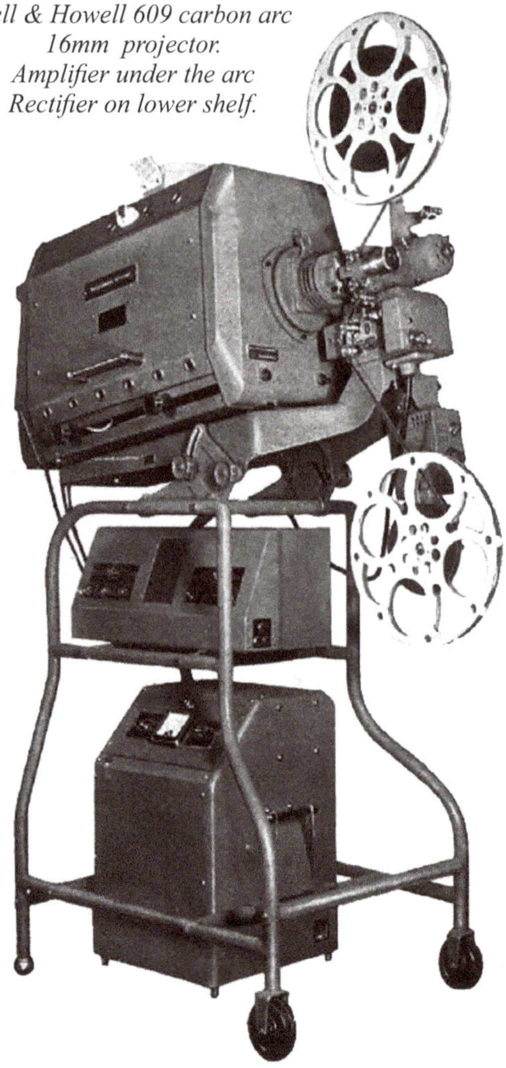

I started my training course at Ealing in 1963. I always remember the year, as I started when 'Dr Who' did - the programme was filming on one of the stages during my first day tour of the studios. Back then, the 609s could be found in both the preview and dubbing theatres, and I had the chance to operate them for a while before the German invasion, of Bauers. These first made their appearance soon after, bought as a package to equip the Film Department's new dubbing and preview area in the recently built East Tower at the Television Centre. I think they were chosen because both the 35mm and 16mm Bauers could run both forward and backwards at either normal (25 f.p.s.) or double speed. This was a useful feature, particularly in what would become the BBC's first "rock 'n' roll" dubbing theatres, with the projectors kept in sync with the separate tracks using Bauer's Synchrostart system. This took over from the

The Bell & Howell 609 and their range of portable projectors used the same mechanism

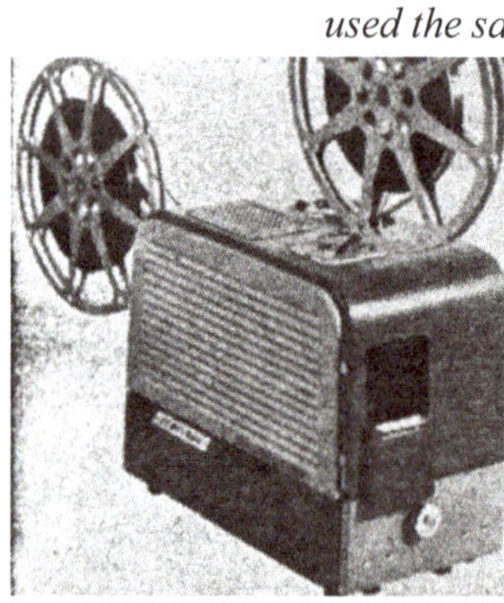

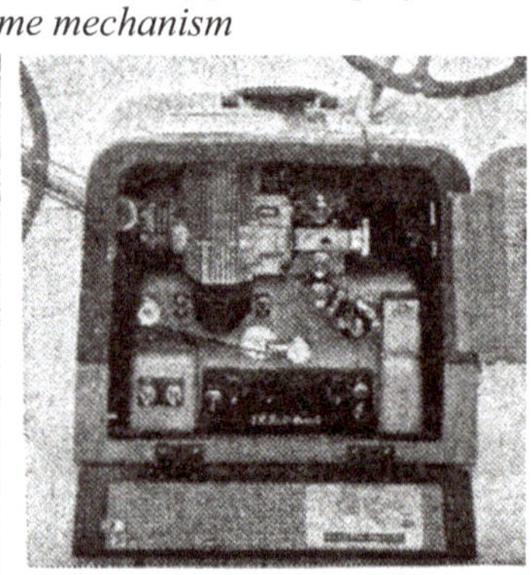

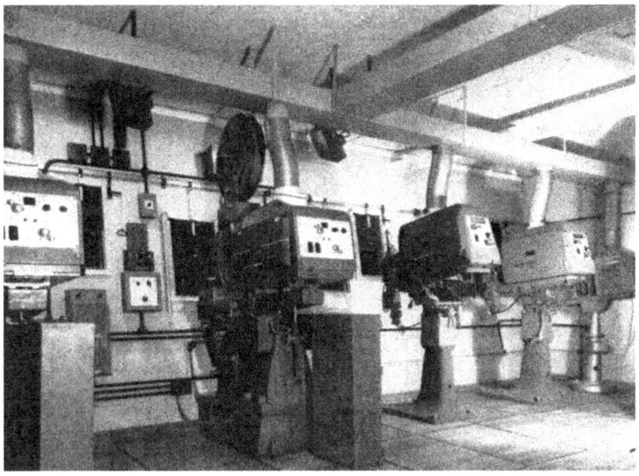

A pair of Bell and Howell 609s were included in the original line up of Gaumont Kalee equipment at the National Film Theatre. Seen on the right, their 609s were mounted on more substantial bases than those at the BBC

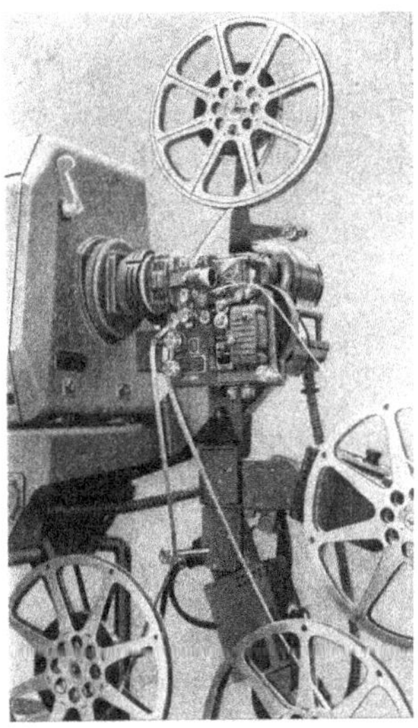

Bell and Howell 609 equipped for double band running of a separate track on the same machine. This shared the sprocket directly below the gate with the picture, which was diverted to its own take up spool. The track then continued through the projector's normal sound head and lower sprocket onto an additional take up arm and spool

normal 3-phase mains supply, generating its own version with a rising or falling frequency rate, between zero and fifty cycles per second, to control the speed of all the machines' synchronous motors during the run-up and stopping in sync.

Don't stop running

Before the invaders reached Ealing, the projection areas were largely based on GB Bell & Howell and Kalee equipment, together with quick-to-lace Ross GC 35mm projectors in the still non-rock 'n' roll dubbing theatres.

Back to the 609s. These had the same basic mechanism as all the then current Bell & Howell l6mm models, including their portable sound projectors. I was already familiar with these, having been a volunteer projectionist at school. The intermittent used a high speed claw, which was sprung to be as kind as possible to the film. If it failed to engage a sprocket hole, it rode over the film until it found one to pop into.

This made it possible, if you dared, to lace up the machine while it was actually running! This was a useful trick in the dubbing theatres. If the sound mixer made an error, the cue buzzer sounded for us to stop. Then, as quickly as possible, the picture and sound tracks had to be unlaced, rewound and threaded up again in order to start all over again. To reduce the pressure on the mixer, the rolls were usually limited to around ten minutes. These were often full of joins, either in the form of cutting copies, or even more valuable edited 'show prints' of topical stories shot on reversal film and later used, in sometimes only a matter of minutes, (at Lime Grove and Alexandra Palace) for transmission.

Although tape joins were becoming common practice, transmission copies often still had narrow cement splices to make them less visible on TV. Should one of these come apart during the dubbing process, we were reluctant to stop the mix, particularly if near the end of the roll. Provided that the print was still on the top sprocket, to keep it in sync, the film could be slipped back into the gate and pulled through, helped by the sprung claw, until the top loop was the correct size. The dowser was then opened again, and we could be back on the screen within a few seconds, the mixer in the meantime having continued to mix using just his cue sheet and the footage counter under the screen. You then had a choice of what to do with the film now emerging from beneath the gate. It could be quickly placed on the still turning bottom sprocket, the inevitable larger loop accommodated by the open layout of the 609, and then wound onto the take-up spool, trying not to produce too much of a fold in the film. An alternative was to quit while you were ahead and call for 'the bin' and let the film spill into its cloth bag, careful not to drop the end in and lose it. During these emergency measures, it was inevitable that some of the film ended up on the floor, which was kept spotless just in case. Any signs of this, or any other extra handling, was treated before transmission by the film editor who cleaned the print using now eco-unfriendly carbon tetrachloride, and disguised any scratches with a coating of 'Mr Sheen' furniture polish.

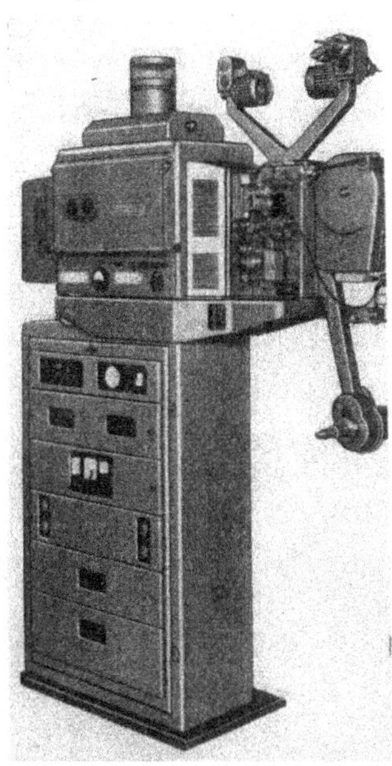

The Bauer Selecton double band xenon projector was the BBC's principal 16mm machine from the mid 1960s. They gave good service for over 35 years and some were later modified to run Super-16 prints

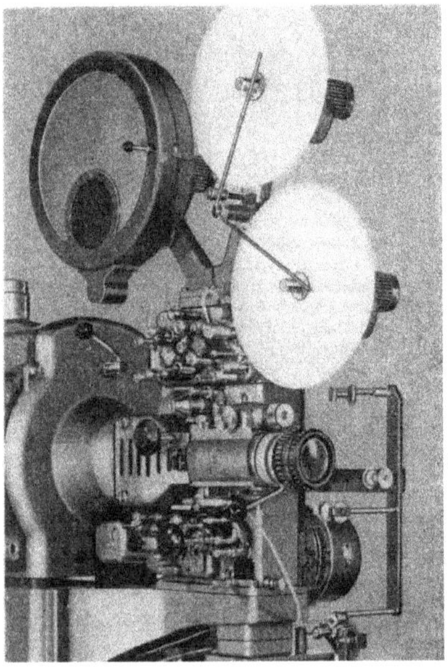

There was a double-band attachment available for the 35mm Bauers (B14s) which ran the separate track through its penthouse magnetic head, but this was never chosen by the BBC.

Playing with fire

I was fascinated by carbon arcs - striking and observing the naked flame through the smoked glass spy-hole made me think of the mysterious power source driving the Nautilus in '20,000 Leagues Under the Sea'. The Kalee lamp on the 609 did have one flaw. Although the projector had a film capacity of over 2000 feet, enough to run a typical BBC 50 to 55 minute documentary, the arc, even with a new pair of carbons, only operated 'correctly' for 45 minutes. The carbons were long enough, but the screw thread automatic feed mechanism came to an end too soon. Again a trick was needed to keep the show going before the light went out. Just before this happened, the lamp-house door was opened and a pair of pliers was used to loosen the hot holder and, while racking back the feed mechanism, the positive rod was tapped through with a piece of wood maintaining the gap to keep it burning for the rest of the film. I remember that, after taking your head out of the lamp-house, you couldn't see properly for the next five minutes and the box was full of the smell of smouldering wood and, if not careful, singed hair. I learned from my ex-cinema colleagues that this knocking through of the carbons was often used to help make sure that every available inch of carbon was turned into valuable light.

The price of this light included extra maintenance. Once a week, the department's ancient vacuum cleaner, held together with camera tape and often producing sparks almost as bright as the arcs, was used to suck up the hopefully harmless white powder-like fall-out produced by the burning carbons. The lamp-house also had a sand tray, like a bird cage, which caught the molten drips as the carbon's copper coating melted and fell from the burning tips. With projectionists acting like gold prospectors, the nuggets were sifted out, and kept in a bag. When full, the treasure was sold for scrap, using a scheme which, at the time, sent the profits to the Cinema & Television Benevolent Fund.

Extra-curricular

I did see the carbon arcs being used for a couple of non-film projection purposes. The last reel before a meal break was a good time to slip a few mince pies into the lamp-house - they would be nice and warm and ready to eat by the end of the show! One of my fellow projies kept up his tan by burning up short-ends with the door open and soaking up the UV rays. Another, at the end of the day, couldn't get his motorcycle going, and came back holding its flat battery. Before we locked up, he placed it in the lamp-house between the positive and negative carbons and turned on the rectifier. After 30 seconds or so, he stopped the rapid charging process (45 amps), and carried off the still boiling battery. Shortly after, I heard the bike start up and off he went.

Safer all round

After saying goodbye to the 609s, showing l6mm became a little less exciting, but much safer. Nobody risked losing their fingers trying to lace up the Bauers while they were running, and their xenon lamp-houses were kept firmly shut with a lock and key to keep our heads out.

I enjoyed being a BBC, projectionist, much better than having to find a proper job! At one time, there were over 80 of us, enough to staff a whole cinema chain. However, we were all needed to man all the various projection areas, with many on shift to get through all the work and cater for late night programmes. Before video took its toll, the amount of film stock consumed by the Film Department was tremendous. I remember the rep. from Kays Laboratories telling me that their BBC work paid for all the lab's overheads, with their other customers providing the profits.

After thoughts

My unjustified inference that being a BBC projectionist wasn't a proper job came about after, at one of our lunchtime shows (too wet to go out) we ran a British feature called *The Family Way* (1966). In the film, Hywel Bennett plays a cinema projectionist newly married to Hayley Mills. Unfortunately, he is unable to consummate the union. On seeking advice, the marriage councillor, after learning that he is a projectionist, suggests that his problem could be over if he gives this up and gets a 'proper job'. He does, and it is - but what a high price to pay!

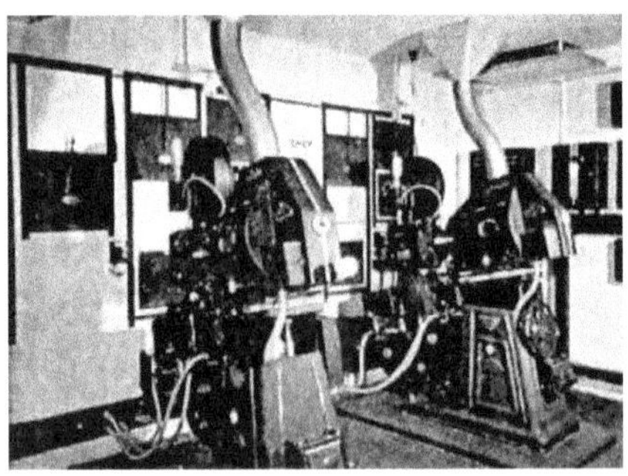

Earlier days - BBC Alexandra Palace projection room for dubbing theatre - around 1950. Two Ross GC1 35mm projectors with carbon arcs.

Cyan tracks of yesteryear

- It had all been seen before!

In traditional optical sound systems for film, light passes through the modulated track onto a photoelectric cell which is mostly sensitive to infra red light. A black and white film's 'silver' track has a high density to IR, but a dye-only track on a colour print would appear almost transparent, resulting in poor sound. These prints normally have an extra processing step just for the sound track area, so as to provide greater density and contrast. To avoid having to do this, later optical tracks on 35mm prints, both analogue and digital, were printed in only cyan dye, and in order to enhance their sensitivity and improve the sound signals, projectors were retro-fitted with a new type of diode - the 'red reader'. In film colour technology the three primary colours, red,green and blue, have three 'complementary' colours, cyan, magenta and yellow. Each colour sees its complement as black, so cyan is seen as black when a red light is used, hence the move to cyan tracks.

The moves towards the adoption of cyan dye sound tracks that came about shortly before digital projection took over the projection booths were eco-driven, the aim being to avoid creating the waste silver products and toxic chemicals that result from standard film processing. The use of cyan tracks in the early 2000s brought to mind some much earlier colour release prints which had cyan coloured tracks, but for different reasons.

During the 1940s almost all colour films were made in Technicolor, with its 3-strip colour and dye-transfer prints. However, there was the option of using a cheaper 2-colour process, such as Magnacolor or Cinecolor.
They employed a simpler bi-pack camera to produce only a red and blue-green pair of black and white separation negatives.

The prints were made on duplitized positive stock, with separate black and white emulsions coated on both sides of the base. After the negatives had been printed onto opposite sides of the film, the black and white images were chemically coloured, the blue-green to red-orange, and the red to blue-green (cyan). Although this combination produced fairly acceptable prints, with a limited range of colours, they were always inferior to Technicolor's 'full-colour' prints made from a complete set of red, green and blue separation negatives.

On 2-colour prints, the soundtrack was usually printed on the cyan side of the film, but, unlike the later pure dye tracks, their cyan image was created by iron metallic toning. Fortunately, like a normal silver track, it provided the high infra-red density required by a traditional tungsten exciter lamp and photocell sound-head.

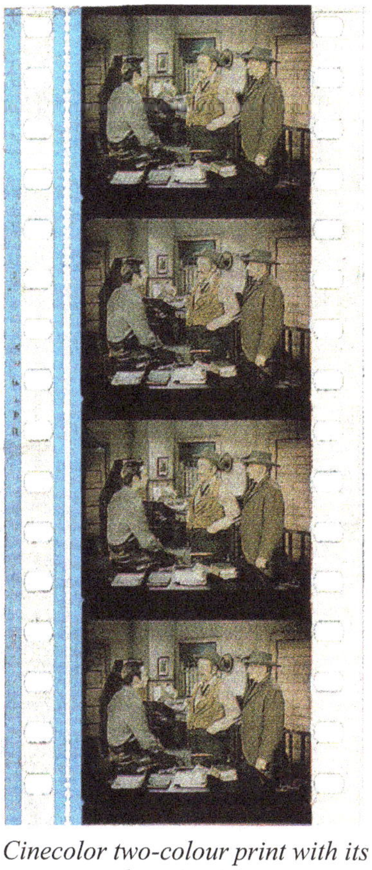

Cinecolor two-colour print with its cyan toned track. They remained available until 1954.

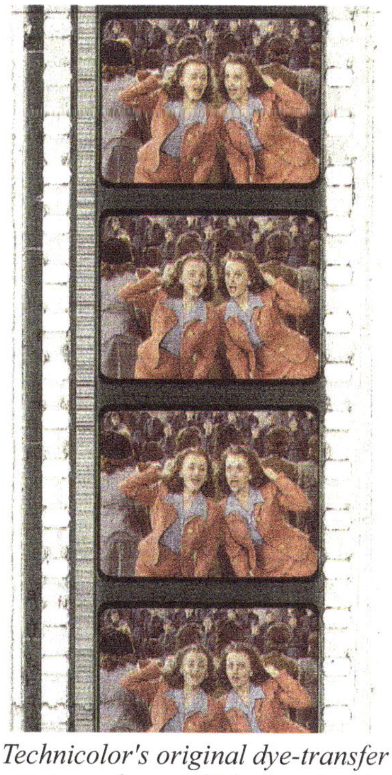

Technicolor's original dye-transfer prints used special black and white positive stock as its blank, on which a silver track was printed before the magenta, cyan and yellow dye images were transferred. Dye-transfer colour prints were available from Technicolor until 1978.

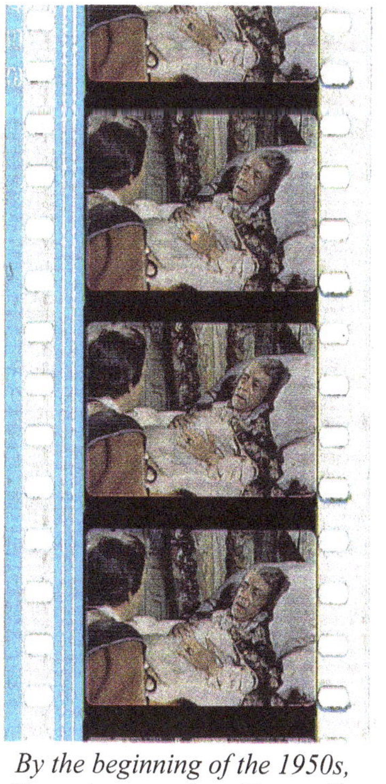

By the beginning of the 1950s, Cinecolor was also able to offer the option of three-colour prints (SuperCinecolor) by adding the third colour, yellow to its existing double-coated prints, retaining the cyan toned soundtrack (1950-1954).

Shrinking film formats

why some aren't always the size you expect

The BKSTS Film Gauges and Soundtracks wallchart includes not only the latest digital cinema sound systems, but also more rare and unusual film formats from the early years of cinema. As one of the principal aims of the chart is to help identify unknown formats, all the examples on that chart are illustrated life size, as they are today. But it is interesting to note that the late Harold Brown, who spent nearly 50 years at the National film Archive, working with all shapes and sizes of film, and who is now renowned for his knowledge of old film formats, told me that in the case of some of the older formats the images appear smaller than the nominal dimensions given in the captions. The reason seems to be that these are either based on original descriptions given by their creators or promoters, or that the descriptions use the most often quoted figures published over the years, which can be less reliable.

Regarding their dimensions, he notes that the width of early films, particularly those from the first 20 years of motion pictures and before the adoption of rigid standards, was often only nominal in the first place. Since then, the old nitrate stock has also been subject to shrinkage, so surviving examples are now usually significantly less than the width quoted, typically around 5%. Some dimensions published over the years, would seem to have been based on the measurement of actual samples, without taking into account the effect of shrinkage. Harold also points out that many of the pioneers, particularly those in the USA and Britain, worked in terms of inches. For example, Edison, who is given the credit for introducing the 35mm format, first used in his Kinetoscope viewing machine way back in 1893, always described the film as being 1¾in. wide. It was only when his and other inventor's films were used or copied in Europe that they came to be referred to in millimetres, usually to the nearest round figure. It was only after seeing Edison's Kinetoscope, together with its film, that the Lumieres created their own 35mm format for projection onto a screen in 1895. Incidentally, all the film widths quoted on the current wallchart are in millimetres. Some formats were copied exactly, or inspired others from different manufacturers.

For example, the British Prestwich company offered a 2¾in. wide film, broadly similar to the French Demeny 60mm format. At first sight, particularly when only comparing single frames, they look identical. In fact, the Prestwich version had four perforations on each side of the frame, unlike the Demeny, which did not have an integrated number of perforations per frame, but had 15 perforations for each four frames. This was possible because the perforations were not involved in the intermittent mechanism, which used a 'beater' movement, with each frame being pulled down by an eccentrically mounted roller. This arrangement became immediately apparent when trying to make copies using the perforations for registration.

This contemporary drawing illustrates the most popular formats available 120 years ago

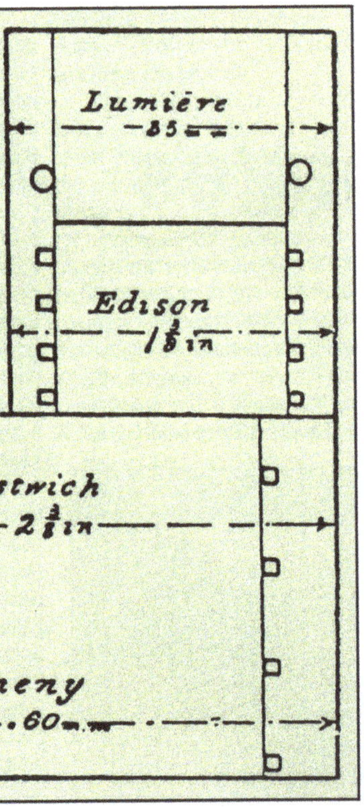

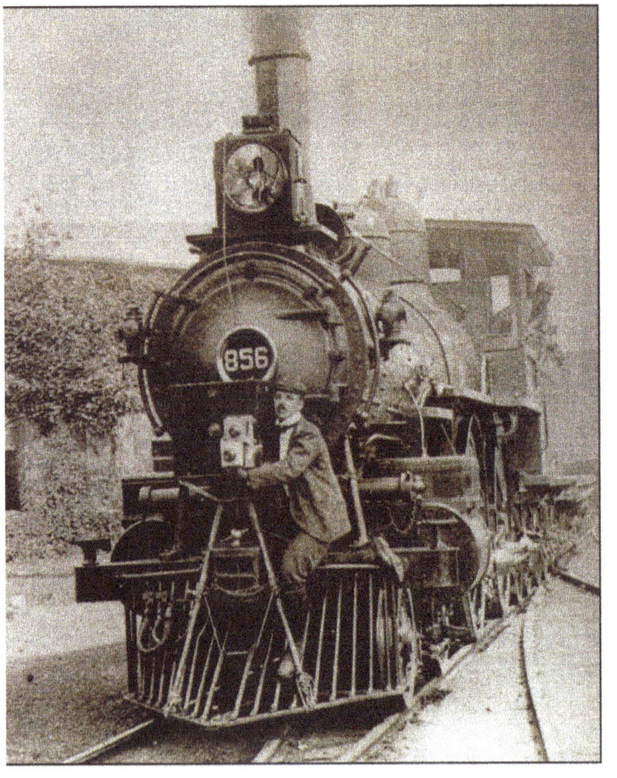

Shrunken large screen

As an aside, looking at some film material that had shrunk considerably led to the discovery of an interesting large format that has only rarely been commented on before. This format was used on an American Biograph wide film camera mounted on a locomotive for filming a Point of View sequence in 1897.

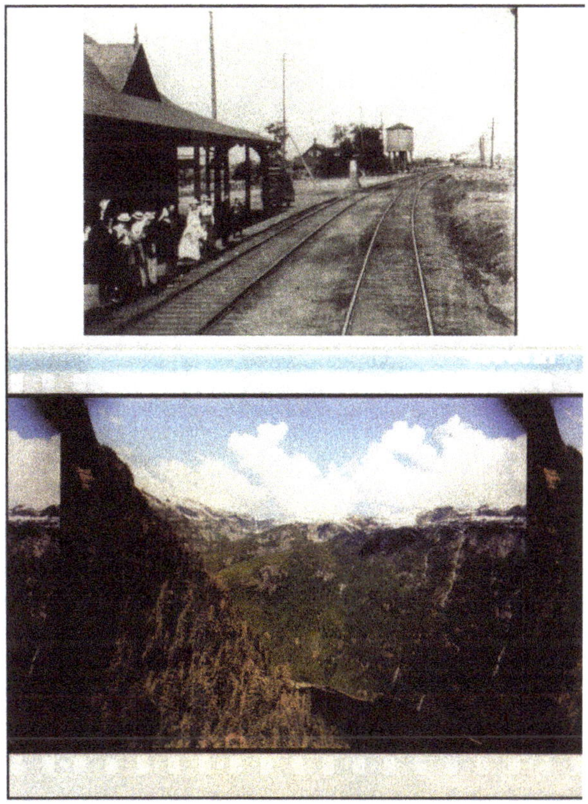

The 'IMAX' of its day, (film size shown underneath, for comparison) the resulting frame had a nominal width of 2¾ in. and was projected on large screens at the rate of 40 frames per second without the aid of perforations.

Variously described since, as being between 68mm and 70mm, this particular surviving frame is currently down to 66.5mm, or should we say two and five eighths inches.

Modifications to post production equipment can help in the preservation process

When cellulose tri-acetate film begins to degrade, acetate ions react with moisture to form acetic acid. Once degradation begins it cannot be halted, but optimising the storage conditions can help. The acid attacks the film base, causing it to shrink. Consequently, the perforation pitch shortens, the film becomes shorter and narrower, sometimes warped to the point where it can no longer be played back on normal reproducing equipment.

The Chace company in California, an audio post production facility well known for sound preservation and restoration, developed several techniques to cope with such damage, and as long as the film emulsion or magnetic coating has not parted from the base, good reproduction can be achieved even when the shrinkage has reached up to about 4%.

Capstan drive machines where the film is held between a capstan and a rubber roller aren't generally suitable since they can cause speed and synchronisation problems, so the answer is to match the shrinkage by using special sprocket wheels with reduced pitch and diameter. Although the film has become shorter and the pitch is smaller, the number of sprockets on the driving wheel is unchanged, therefore the synchronisation is unaffected.

Shrinkage also changes the film width, 3% shrinkage reducing the width by 1.05mm. When you consider that with film optical sound one stereo track is only 0.97mm in width, special measures have to be taken to compensate for the variations in track width and to bring the soundtrack to the correct position with reference to the sound reader element. Special optical sound heads use spring loaded idler flanges to locate the film to the reference edge, independent of its width. Azimuth and gap position are also adjustable.

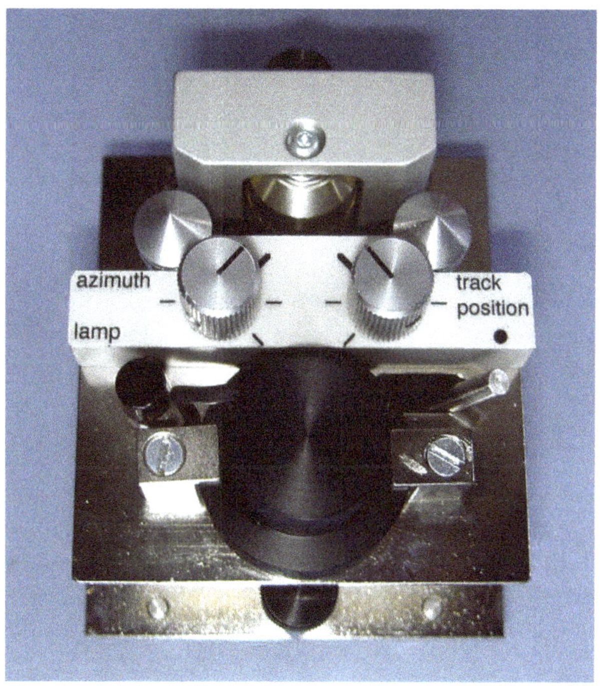

Chace 35mm optical head-block showing the adjustable azimuth and track position controls

A Distorted View of Todd-AO

- a sideways look at the history of this magnificent 70mm format

The wide screen revolution in home entertainment has been much slower than was the cinema's rapid change to larger and wider screens in the 1950s. Their have been numerous widescreen cinema processes over the decades and, arguably, they began with Cinerama, first seen in 1952, then Cinemascope, which followed in 1953, and VistaVision in 1954. Here I would like to take a look at aspects of Todd-AO, which successfully introduced the 65mm/70mm format which was to become adopted as an industry standard for theatrical 70mm.

The success of the Todd-AO system owed much of its initial success to its original projector, the much-loved Philips DP70. This Oscar-winning machine, together with the other 'multi-purpose' dual-gauge 35mm/70mm projectors it inspired, made the adoption of 70mm a practical proposition. There were, however, other original aspects of Todd-AO which were less successful and which, for a while, jeopardised its future.

Walter Siegmund is rightly credited as the originator of Todd-AO. Back in 1953, Walter was a young optical science graduate who was recruited by Dr. Brien 0' Brien at the American Optical Company to help bring producer Mike Todd's conception of a simplified version of the three-projector Cinerama system to the screen. One of Walter's first tasks was to go and see Cinerama. He reported back that the huge ultra-wide angle image coming from three separate 35mm projectors and blended together on its deeply curved screen was a "WOW"! Strangely, this reaction didn't prompt the Doctor to immediately set off to see it for himself. If he had, he might have appreciated more the difficulties which would lie ahead trying to keep to Mike Todd's brief that every thing must come out of "One Hole". If Cinerama's inventor, Fred Waller, had been able, during the ten years it took to develop, to produce the same image using only a single film and projector he surely would have done so, rather than having to end up using the cumbersome and costly triple-lens system.

Mike Todd had been associated with Cinerama, but wanted his new process to be easier to install with less disruption to the theatre's normal operation. Cinerama required that three new carefully positioned projection boxes be built at the rear of the stalls to provide near level projection of the three films onto the screen, sharing out the deep curve. For Todd-AO, the single 70mm projector was to be installed in the theatre's existing projection room, even if this was situated high up above the balcony.

Any film hitting the screen from a steep angle shows the familiar 'keystone' effect caused by the increasing magnification towards the bottom of the screen as it becomes further away from the projector. This is usually hidden by masking off the over-spilling image by using a specially shaped aperture plate and sometimes by tilting the screen back to face the projector. If the screen is also deeply curved, the distortion is much more serious, with the picture curving up at the sides. This is far more noticeable to the audience, with curved horizons and strange effects, like ships sailing uphill.

Walter joined the team given the job to find a solution to the problem. The method finally chosen was to purposely distort the image on the 70mm print to counter-balance the distortion on the screen. The picture on the film was bent up into an arched shape to correct the sagging effect caused by the screen.

To achieve this, a special 'secret' continuous optical printer was devised. A normal intermittent optical printer takes the form of a projector head projecting its images via a lens system into the gate of a camera. It is slow but very versatile; for example it can print from a different sized original and change the size or shape of the image, e.g. anamorphic conversions. A high speed continuous printer simply runs the negative and positive films together over a common sprocket with the exposure made using a narrow slit of light. Less common is a continuous optical printer which separates the two films with the image-forming slit relayed to the print stock by a lens. It can be used to copy shrunken film which will not run over a common sprocket, with the optical system adjusted to restore the size of the image.

Todd-AO"s variation was to slightly reduce the magnification of the image-forming slit as the negative and print stock moved the distance of one frame. This produced the required distortion, and the amount of change could be adjusted for the different intended projection angles. The lens system had to be reset between frames, so the printing process was relatively slow.

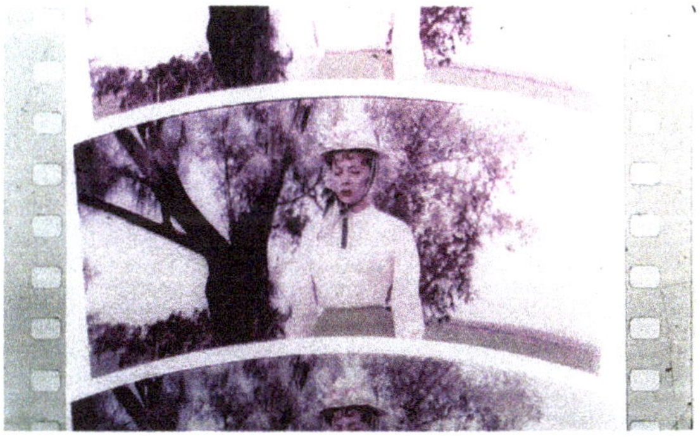

Example of a Todd-AO distortion-correcting print

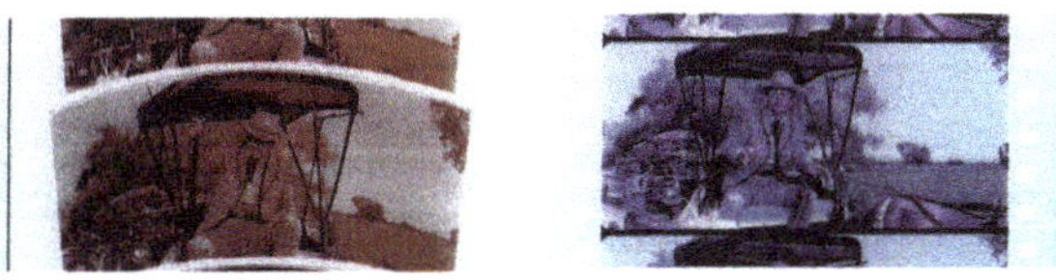

A scene optically printed with distortion (left) and a normal contact print (right). Sadly the poor quality of the clips is due to fading, not looking back at history through rose-coloured glasses.

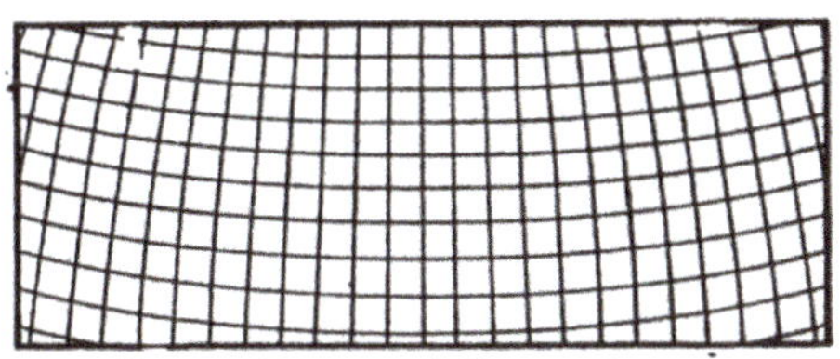

Above - Distorted Screen Image
Below - distortion-correcting print

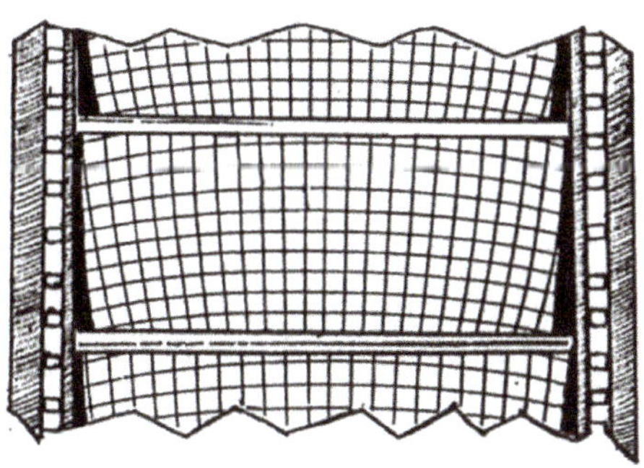

Corrected Screen Image - below

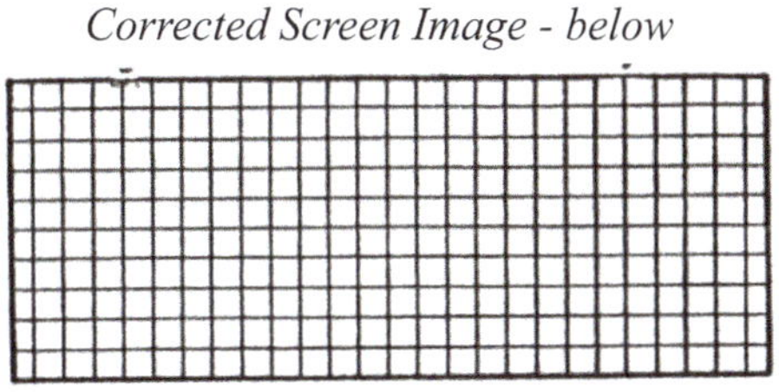

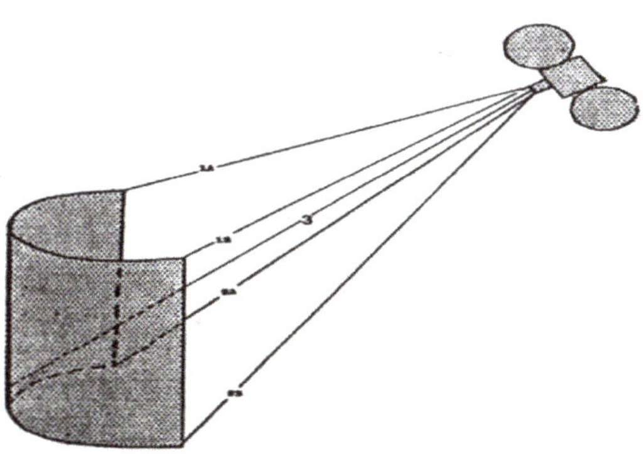

The idea of altering the shape of the image on the film to counter balance the effect of projecting it onto a deeply curved screen was tried again some ten years after the introduction of Todd-AO. Special 70mm 'rectified' prints were made as an option for showing in the later single-lens version of Cinerama and its rival Dimension 150. Both used level projection, so the correction was confined to just squeezing up the image towards the sides of the frame to compensate for the stretching effect of the concave surface of the screen.

Although this gave a better picture for those sitting at the sides of the auditorium, when viewed head-on the built-in distortion was still noticeable and worse than watching a normal print. In general, these special prints were considered more trouble than they were worth, particularly so if later reissued and shown on flat screens. The apparent non-linear distortion was sometimes blamed on the film being photographed or projected with a dodgy lens. The result was rather like the 'Panoramic' option on a widescreen TV, when a 4x3 picture is progressively stretched out at the sides to make it fill a 16x9 screen. This ploy usually looks OK, until the camera pans and gives it away.

Optically modified prints

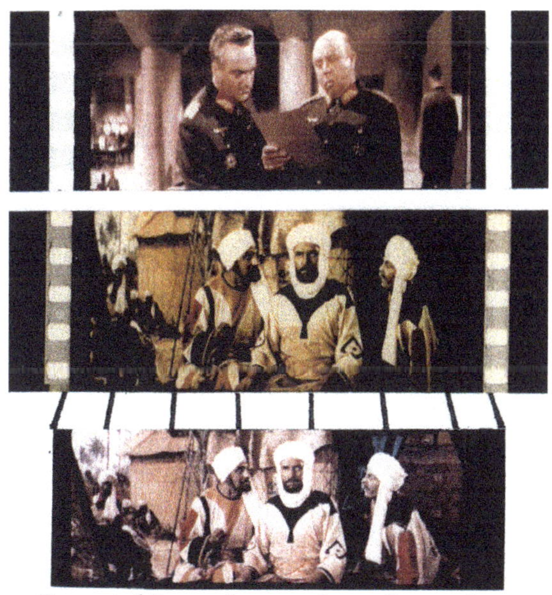

Corrected Screen Image - shown flattened out

If deeply curved screens ever become fashionable again in this new era of digital projection, the balancing distortion could be done electronically in the projector and fine-tuned for the best compromise when viewed from different angles, although, in theory anyway, any corrections will only work for a single viewing position.

Although a clever idea, its use was going to spoil Todd-AO's debut. The printer was used to provide the print destined for the premiere of the first Todd-AO feature *Oklahoma* at the Rivoli in New York. The deadline prevented the printer from being fully perfected. For example, it had no method, like a liquid gate, to suppress the visibility of scratches and other blemishes, and in fact the specular nature of the optical system accentuated them. As a result the print shown 'sparkled' with white specks. To add to this, the degree of distortion correction didn't quite match the theatre's rake, so the picture still looked bent. Although the film itself received good reviews, Todd-AO got the thumbs-down, with critics suggesting that its developers go back to the drawing board to correct its flaws. Walter and the team at American Optical had also failed to find a reliable way to manufacture a highly reflective single-sheet screen with different directional characteristics across its width, so a lower gain deeply curved screen had to be used, which was far less successful than Cinerama's louvred design at reducing the cross reflections. Soon the decision was made to give up trying to emulate Cinerama and to project normal prints onto a flat or only a slightly curved screen, and when necessary relocate the projection box down to a lower level.

In its new form, Todd-AO went on to be a success in its own right, now clearly showing the advantages of 70mm presentation. Its superb images ensured that it shared in the Oscar-winning acclaim of the second Todd-AO feature, Mike Todd's *Around the World in 80 Days*, in 1956. A year later, the process received an Academy Scientific and Technical Award, shared by the Westrex Corp. for its equally superb sound.

Walter Siegmund's own story of the development and launch of Todd-AO is fascinating, with many more details of the technical aspects and personalities involved. Although some of his memories are tinged with failure, he still enjoyed his time working alongside the many film people he met, before, like his boss, Dr. 0' Brien, he left the world of showbiz to continue his career working on other optical projects.

Much more information about Todd-AO and 70mm cinema can be obtained by pointing your web browser at *www.in70mm.com.*

Although the Philips DP70 was the first commercially available Todd-AO projector, during the development of the process old equipment from an earlier failed attempt to introduce wide-film systems was brought out of retirement. The camera was a Fearless Super Film camera made by the Fearless Camera Corp. in 1930. It was used back then to photograph a 65mm version of *The Bat Whispers*. When acquired by Todd-AO, it had already been recycled for an unsuccessful colour process, Thomascolor, in 1947.

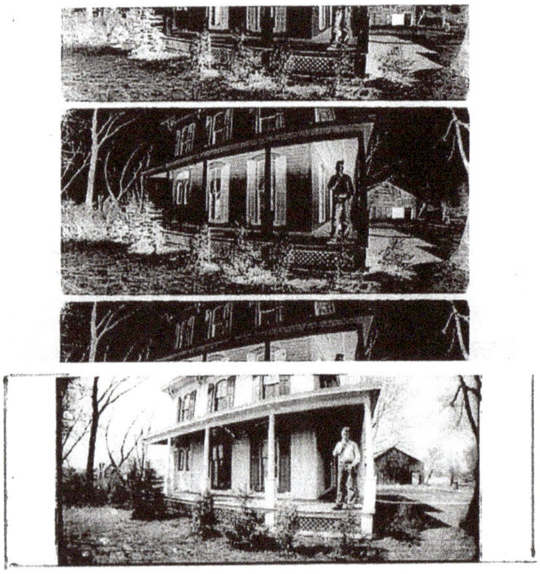

An early black & white test of Todd-AO. The camera was fitted with a 128 degree 'bug-eye' wide-angle lens to try to match Cinerama's 146 degree angle of view. The severe 'barrel' distortion limited its use when used later in actual productions.

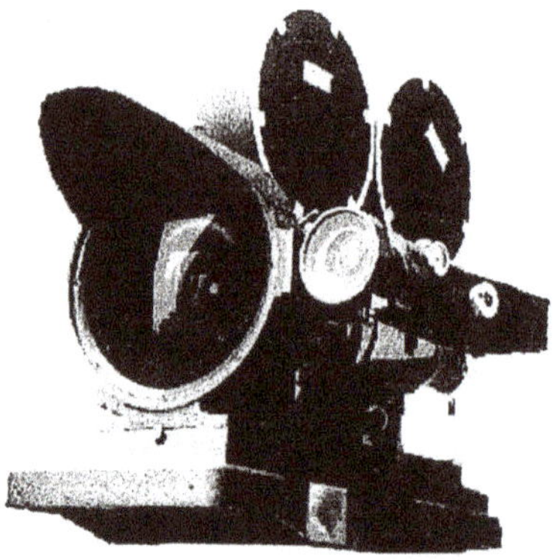

Interchangeable gates for 35mm and 65mm

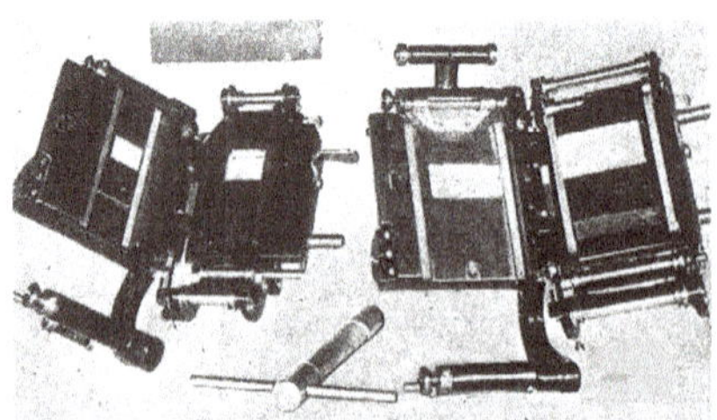

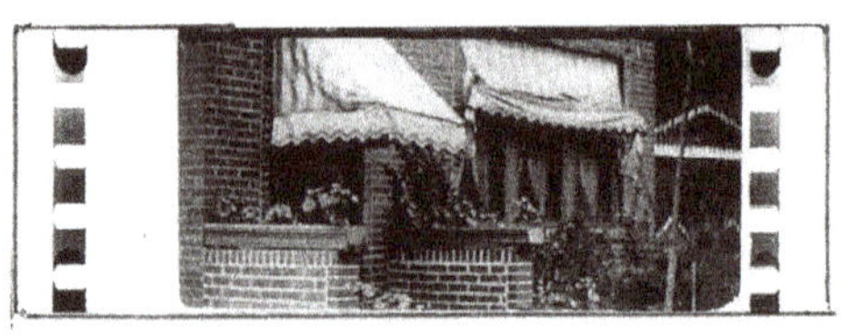

This and earlier footage was shown using an Ernemann 'combination' machine, originally supplied to Paramount for their 1930 65mm wide-film process.

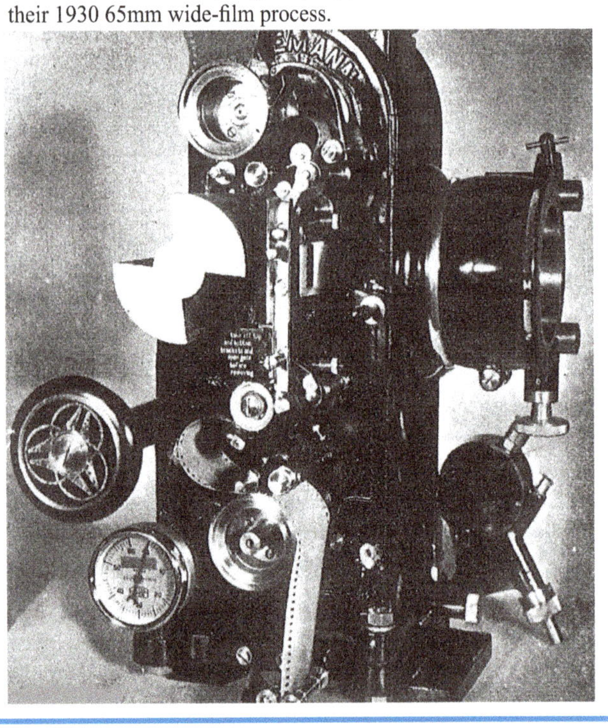

Out of the Lens Cupboard

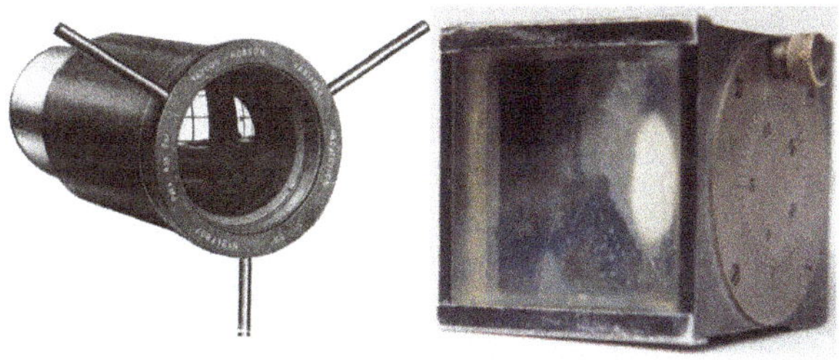

Left: Taylor Hobson 'Magnascope' variable focus projection lens. Right: Hypergonar Anamorphic lens.

Grant has always been fascinated by unusual and historically interesting lenses from the past, ranging from the 'Magnascope' variable focus projection lenses, which enlarged the image during spectacular scenes, to early anamorphic types, which helped bring wider pictures to the cinema screen.

The quest for depth

The so-called deep-focus lenses claimed to offer cinematographers a way to increase the depth-of-field without the need to stop down the lens or change to one with a shorter focal length. This could be considered an advantage, particularly in the studio, when smaller apertures meant increased lighting costs and wide angle lenses often came with possibly unwanted distortion, exaggerated perspective, and their greater field-of-view requiring the building of larger sets

Not perfect, but well-balanced

On a personal note, after leaving school, I began a full-time course on photography at the Berkshire College of Art. One of my well respected tutors, who knew all about the construction of lenses, and their use in practice, always said that there was no such thing as a perfect lens. Their designers often had to correct one kind of aberration by compromising on other aspects of its performance. For example, printer lenses have high resolution but often lower contrast, while for some early video lenses, the opposite was desirable. In my student film making days, I was advised not to be tempted to buy cheaper 'video' lenses, which also fitted my C-mount 16mm Bolex, but to save up for proper cine lenses, which were optimized for film.

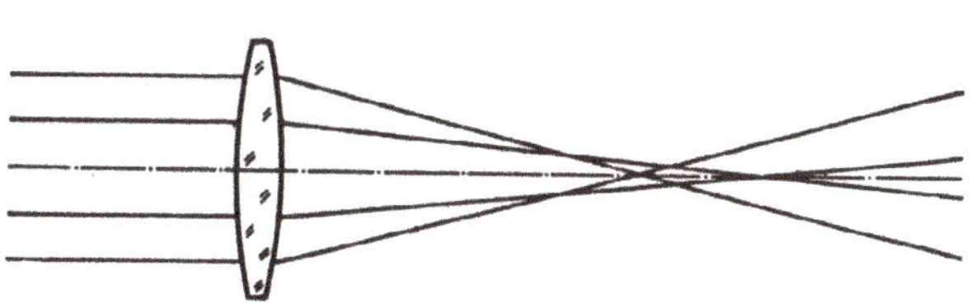

Spherical Aberration
Rays passing through the lens away from the centre are focussed on different planes, reducing the definition. Rather than fully correcting the 'fault', it can be exploited to balance the loss of some of the potential resolution in favour of apparently greater depth of field.

Wild lifelike images

Around this time, I had the chance to see a banned film called *The Wild One*, starring Marlon Brando as a motorcycle gang leader. The opening titles carried the intriguing credit, 'Filmed With Garutso Balanced Lenses'. I enjoyed the film, being a fellow, if not quite so wild, motorcyclist, but to me, the picture on the screen didn't seem any different from any other well shot black and white feature. Although it was now the early 1960s, the film was originally released in the U.S. during 1954. I quizzed my expert tutor if he remembered anything about the lens, but he knew nothing about it so, for a while, it was to remain a mystery.

Secrets exposed

I learned later that the Garutso lens was an example of these strange deep-focus lens systems. In fact, without knowing it, I had already been taught about some of the possible principles involved. Some special 'soft-focus' portrait lenses have intended built-in spherical aberration. Along with the softer definition, another symptom of the 'fault' is the sometimes greater than expected depth-of-field. Could this be applied to a deep-focus lens? I had also been shown how to use a large format studio technical still camera for taking portraits and products appearing in magazines and catalogues. I remember the depth-of-field of a 10x8 in sheet film camera, with its relatively longer focal length lenses, was almost nil and required high lighting levels and small apertures to try and keep everything in focus. To help, the camera had a swinging lens panel and back which could be adjusted to tilt the plane of focus to match the position of the subject(s), arranged to give the composition greater depth.

There may be an 'alternative' way

Not found in the operating manuals, was the curious suggestion that you could actually move the focus setting during the exposure, or take multiple exposures each focused on a different part of the scene. Surely this would only result in fuzzy pictures, but apparently not, or at least not noticeably so.

Believe it or not?

The theory is that if you superimpose a sharp image over a softer version, the in-focus one is reproduced as brighter points of light over the top of the spread out and now dimmer larger discs of light (circles of confusion) representing the out-of-focus image. The effect, as recorded by the film's emulsion and perceived by the eye, is that the sharper image predominates and literally overwhelms the softer one. Although the definition is reduced somewhat, it is spread out more evenly throughout the depth of the picture....well, that's the idea. To keep the visibility of the out of focus contribution to a minimum, it is possible to light the chosen planes of depth separately and only illuminate the one having its in-focus exposure. Even if these ploys are worth trying, they would only seem possible for still, static photography, but in the past, they have all been applied to the movies.

Way back in 1936, cinematographer Hal Mohr ASC (who later shot *The Wild One*) described his 'Universal Focus' lens system based on the still camera swinging back principle. He mounted a 50mm lens in a ball-and-socket type mount which allowed it to be tilted relative to the film plane to adjust the line of sharp focus through subjects at different distances from the camera. For example, a figure very close at one side of the frame could be of equal sharpness to another in the distance. He used his lens for certain scenes in *The Green Pastures* and *Bullets or Ballots* shown the same year. It didn't generally catch on, as it was restricted to carefully composed scenes.

Pan-focus, the talk of Hollywood

By the beginning of the 1940s, deep-focus had become a hot topic, with articles and correspondence appearing in professional magazines like 'The American Cinematographer' discussing the new 'Pan-Focus' technique and how to achieve it. Much of this interest was sparked off by Gregg Toland's wide-angle and deep-focus style adopted for *Citizen Kane* (1941). This was achieved using the traditional combination of small apertures, (f/8 - f/16) and shorter focal-length lenses (28mm & 24mm), made easier by the newly introduced faster stock (four times the speed) and coated lenses to increase the light transmission and reduce the flare, a particular problem in early wide-angle lenses. It should be said that some big close-ups in the film, like others, were matted into their backgrounds using Linwood Dunn's optical printer. (An optical printer consists of one or more film projectors mechanically linked to a movie camera, allowing filmmakers to re-photograph one or more strips of film. The optical printer is used for making special effects for motion pictures, or for copying and restoring old film material.)

The chance of gaining extra depth-of-field was welcomed by some Directors of Photography working on low-budget features. To speed up production, it was common to shoot dialogue scenes in one long take with all the characters included in the frame. Like today, there are different opinions on how to handle the focus. Some preferred all the actors to be in focus, thinking that continual focus-pulling back and forth as each spoke can become a distraction for the viewer, and sometimes dialogue coming from an out-of-focus character can be even more disconcerting. The shallow-focus supporters believed that the changing focus helped to isolate and concentrate attention on the performance.

There are always exceptions, but the everything-sharp wide-angle photography became more popular in the

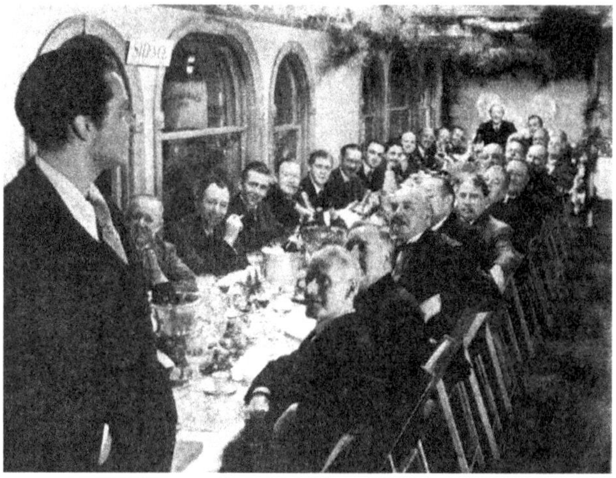

Citizen Kane (1941) pioneered the deep-focus style of photography

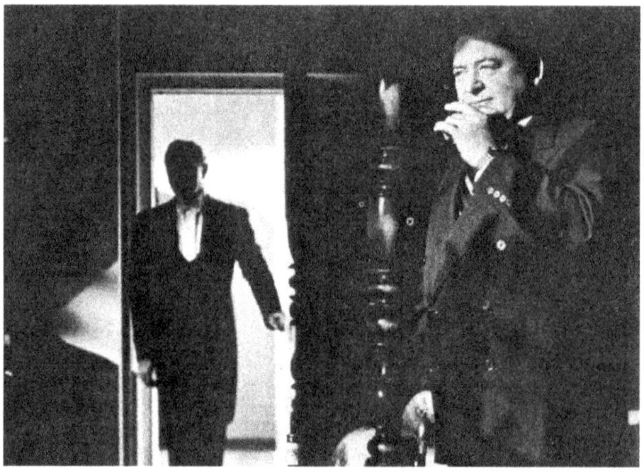

Eyes in the Night' (1942)
Example of hard-edge, low-key and deep style of 'Film Noir'

1940s, compared to the often softer diffused 'Glamour' lighting of the 1930s. Sometimes the extra cost of lighting the larger sets captured by the wider lenses was avoided by leaving much of them unlit, resulting in the much discussed 'Film Noir' style of photography, with its dark shadows adding to the sense of mystery. Even more mysterious, behind the scenes were the strange lens systems being described and promoted to help create this greater depth. Most of them used the sharing-out-the-focus idea.

The American Bausch and Lomb Company described a lens in which the focus was rapidly changed by moving one of its elements at the rate of 20,000 times a second. A similar 'Detra' lens was a feature of the 'Electroplane' camera, with the oscillating internal focusing element driven by an electro-mechanical arrangement, much like a loudspeaker's voice coil. Switching both the focus and lighting between different zones of focus was the basis of the bizarre 'IR' system described in 1942. Up to four areas of the deep set were lit with flashing strobe lamps synchronised to rapidly changing lenticular 'Dif-fo-Plates' which rotated behind the lens to change the focus to match each zone as it was illuminated, many times a second.

There must be an easier way

Although not so much fun, there are much simpler means of manipulating the apparent depth-of-field. One is a split-field diopter. This is nothing more than cutting a supplementary close-up lens in half. It can be placed in front of a normal lens to produce a split-screen effect in terms of focus. They are still occasionally used today, and I can remember spotting one being used while watching Brian de Palma's *Carrie* (1976), keeping John Travolta at the front of a classroom in focus as he plays out a scene with an equally sharp student at the back of the class. To be successful, the trick is to hide the fuzzy dividing line and make sure the foreground subject is big enough to obscure the out-of-focus background behind it, as can be seen in the example shown from 'Blow-Out' (1981).

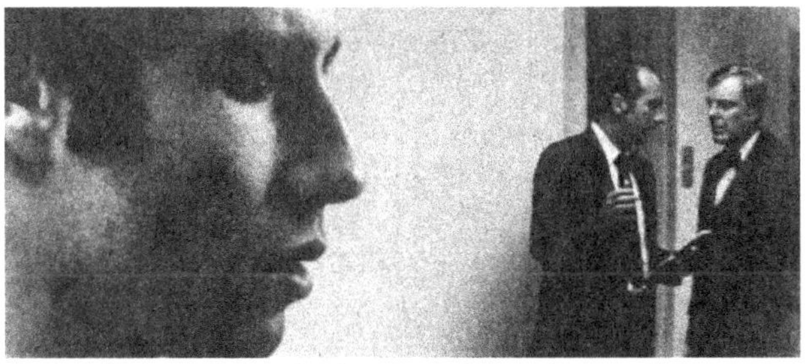

Split-diopter shot of John Travolta as he overhears conspirators in 'Blow-Out' (1981)

Behold, a sharper picture

Another way to cut up a lens element is to make a hole in the centre to form a ring shaped lens. If included in a lens system, it can be made to produce two superimposed images of the subject, one focused as set by the original lens, and another modified by the supplementary element. Again the blend of differently focused images can give a greater 'look' of depth, far more than the normal lens alone, set at the same wide aperture. This was the idea behind the Garutso lens, which had originally made me look at the subject in greater depth.

Mr. Garutso modified a series of existing lenses, using a combination of manipulating the spherical aberration and sometimes adding annular elements to 'balance' their characteristics, trading off some loss of definition to give greater apparent depth. When first introduced, they were treated with scepticism by some lens experts saying that deliberately spoiling the definition of a lens was not on, and even he couldn't break the natural laws of optics and make a mockery of long established depth-of-field tables. It was all in the eye of the beholder, with some believers thinking that, as most lenses have higher resolution than can be recorded by the film's emulsion, particularly using stocks available at the time, some resolution could be sacrificed in the interest of greater depth. Any visible softness was actually promoted as a benefit, claiming, 'Great depth is gained without the hard contrasty effect of stopping down the lens.'

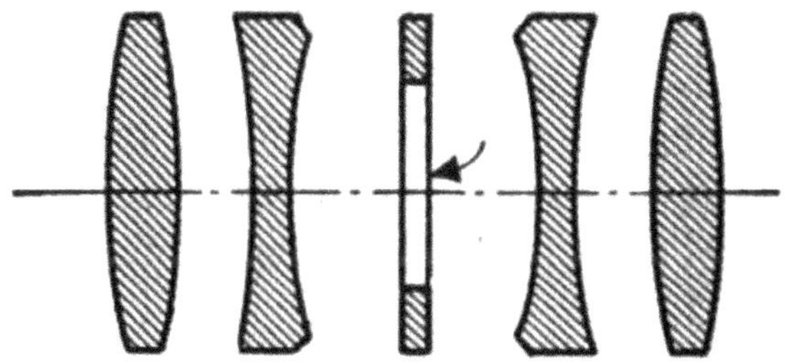

Garutso Lens: Stephen Garutso invented the 'optical balance', a round lens with a hole in the centre (arrowed). Placed between the front and rear elements it produces a massively increased depth of focus and corrects much of the spherical aberration.

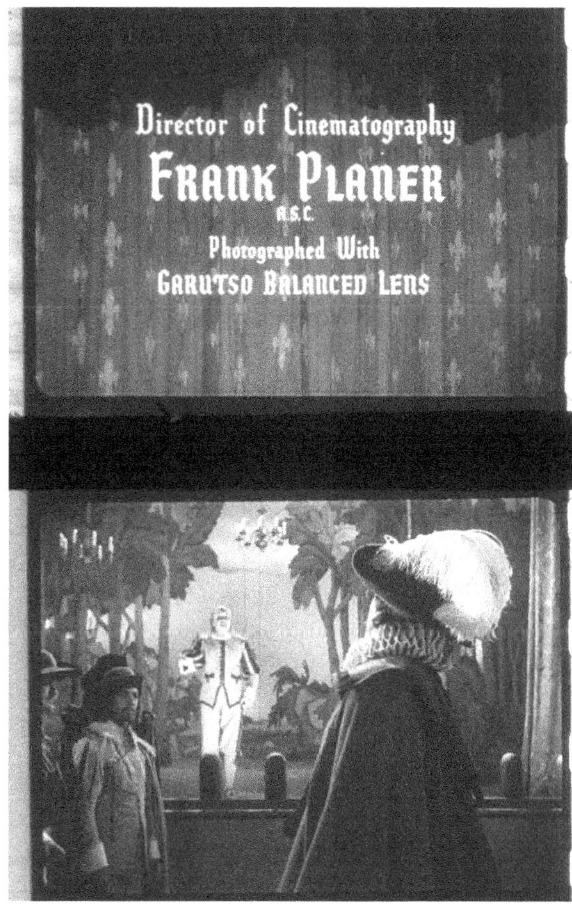

Frames from 'Cyrano de Bergerac' (1950) showing credit for the Garutso Balanced Lens which claimed to give greater depth of field at wide apertures

Remembered on the credits

Although the advantages of a Garutso lens were questioned by the technical press, non-expert reviewers praised its sharpness and clarity, some suggesting it produced a stereoscopic effect. It had enough support to be used commercially, first for a few now forgotten B-westerns, including *Apache Chief* and *Deputy Marshal* from the late 1940s. Later, apart from *The Wild One*, it was given a credit on a couple of other Stanley Kramer features, *Cyrano de Bergerac* (1950) and *The Four Poster* (1953). The Garutso lenses were last heard of being used in Germany under the name 'Plastorama' by noted director and cinematographer Eric Pommer in 1955. By the end of the 1950s, all of these black art aids

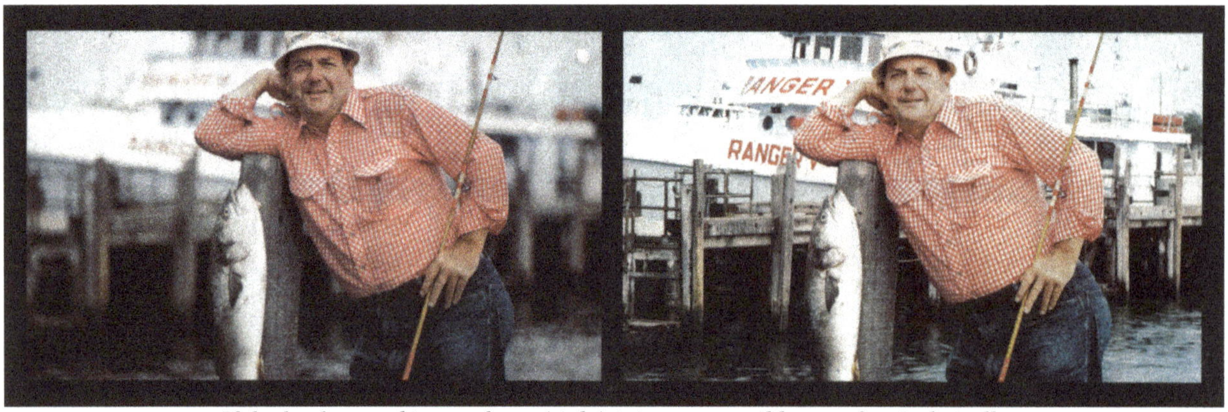

If the background is too sharp (right) it is now possible to soften it digitally.

to greater depth had been forgotten, as further increases in film speed had given cameramen more freedom to choose the depth-of-field without technology restrictions getting in the way. However, in 1970, Popular Photography reported that Pathé in France had patented an oscillating gate system which, at the cost of slight image degradation, would free Super-8 users from the chore of focusing.

Other solutions

Achieving any desired depth-of-field on 35mm presents few problems today, but for smaller formats, like Super-16 and 2/3 inch video cameras, the quest is sometimes for a shallower depth-of-field. For the equivalent field-of-view, they use shorter focal-length lenses, and special measures may be needed to avoid the everything-in-focus look. Control of depth-of-field can be a selling point. High on the list of the desirable features offered by Arri's D-20 digital camera, is its larger chip, the same size as a 35mm frame, which provides the same control over the depth-of-field. As the brochure states, this 'is one of the essential aesthetic tools for dramatic expression'. Even after the results are in the can, the focus decisions, like other of the cinematographers dramatic expressions, can now be changed in post production. If you don't like your all-in-focus image, an electronic matte can be traced around the areas to stay sharp and the rest can be digitally thrown out of focus.

Hand crafted at Cooke

Turning glass into gold!

The process of making lenses of the highest possible quality is the same as it always has been, and it is interesting that the process of turning the glass blanks into finished lenses is sometimes called 'turning glass into gold', a great example of adding value to a product by working on it. Although lenses for hobbyist and professional photographers are these days made on computer controlled machinery, with the big Japanese companies churning out thousands each day, the process of making top-quality lenses for cinematographers is still reliant on craftsmanship and hand and eye skills that have been honed over generations.

Companies like Cooke Optics build each lens by hand and individually calibrate each one. The company buys in moulded glass blanks from companies such as Schott and Ohara, and these are then ground and polished in a fascinating mixture of old and new technologies. Some of the grinding and polishing machinery is of the latest Computer Numerical Controlled design but Cooke also use polishing machines from as far back as 1913, simply because they are the best for the particular job that needs doing. After a lens has been ground to shape in a CNC machine it is polished to the final shape in a cup or dome shaped iron tool of the correct curvature using an abrasive slurry. The curves come from precision glass gauges that are the 'master' shapes, which have been precision ground to the tremendous accuracy of half an optical interference fringe - close to the wavelength of light. The final process is to coat the glass with several chemical layers which provide a more durable surface and provide anti-reflection properties.

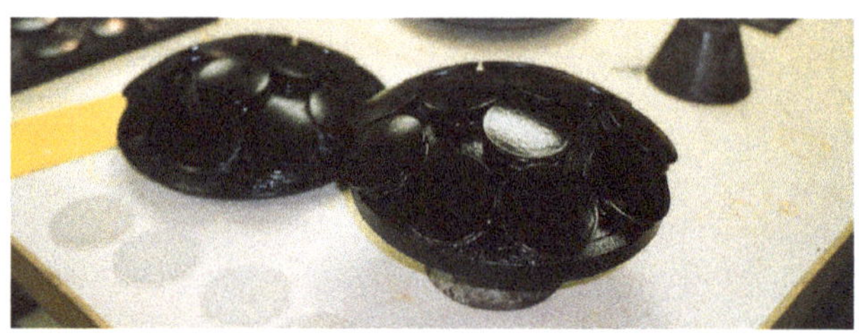

Lenses mounted in groups ready for the grinding process

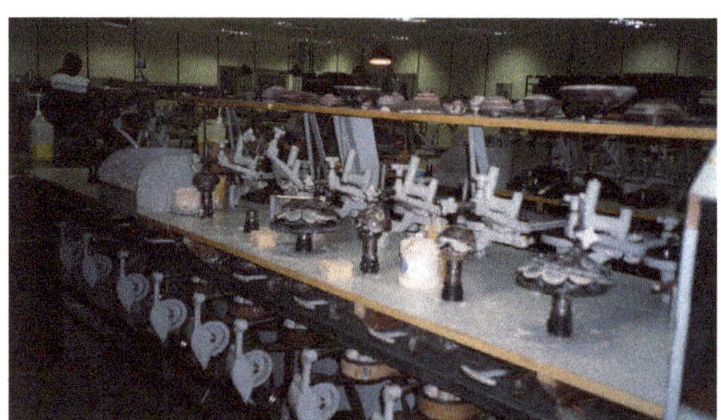

Traditional lens polishing machinery

Fun with The Varamorph

Helping to restore and preserve old cinema equipment needs a combination of skills and, in the case of 35mm projectors, I soon learned that foremost of these was an interest in the techniques of weight lifting! Also useful is a knowledge of mechanical engineering, electrics and optics. Hopefully, at some stage during a projector's repair, the mechanics can be seen working, so are easier to understand. However, except for the basics, electronics have remained a mystery to me, often resulting in the smell of burning, blown fuses and the occasional electric shock. In the past, I consoled myself with the belief that these were good for you and a stimulus to the heart, but I now try not to play around with things best left to the experts.

Much safer to deal with are projection lenses, which have become a particular fascination for me, especially the old and unusual ones, like the special wide-angle types for rear projection, 'Magnascope' zooms, which were popular in the 1920s and 1930s, to enlarge the image during spectacular scenes, and the various forms of anamorphic attachments which soon became a must-have item for every theatre wishing to join the cinema's widescreen revolution back in the 1950s. Being smaller and easier to rescue and carry off, I have managed to save a few early examples which were among the first to arrive in British cinemas.

The most common of these use cylindrical lens elements arranged to provide an added extra degree of magnification (x2) in the horizontal plane only, to stretch out the squeezed-up image on the film and restore it back to its wider 'CinemaScope' proportions on the screen. Although, at the start, Bausch & Lomb supplied large numbers of cylindrical lens attachments in the U.S., most over here seem to have come from Zeiss, sometimes carrying the official 'CinemaScope' logo, and Isco. I have an early model called a 'Vidoscope', from long before digital projection and all things video invaded the projection box.

Other optical principles can be used to un-squeeze the image, and another kind of attachment used a pair of curved mirrors to achieve the same effect. In some ways this reflection method was superior to a conventional lens system and was capable of excellent results, being free of the aberrations which can affect refracting lens systems. One unique advantage was that it could be deliberately misaligned to counter-balance the picture distortion resulting from using a steep rake onto a curved screen. There were disadvantages, the exposed front-silvered mirrors collected dust and the constant cleaning often shortened their useful life. Their periscope-like design also displaced the light beam by about 5 inches, sometimes needing modifications to the portholes.

I was lucky to find an example, still with good mirrors, of the most often seen model, the Delrama, designed by Old Delft in Holland. It was distributed by Frank Brockliss and regularly appeared in 1950s ads for Philips projectors, which they also imported. I have since seen a similar device advertised by Cinepanoramic in France and it is worth looking out for.

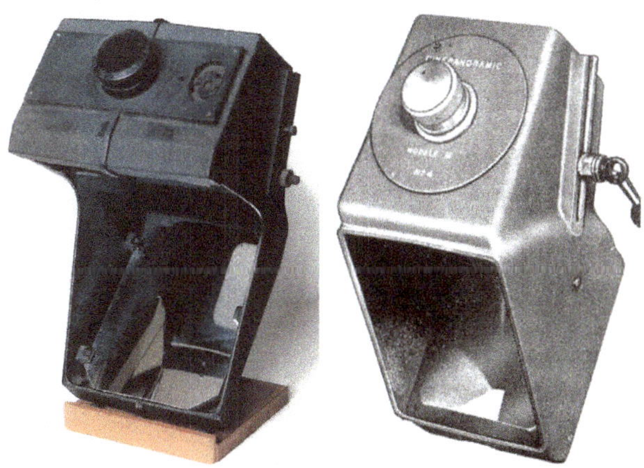

Mirror anamorphic attachments - (left) the Delrama mirror anamorphic attachment. For some, this is now worth more for its aluminium scrap value, but for many of us an historic optical device worthy of preservation and display and (right) the Cinepanoramic unit.

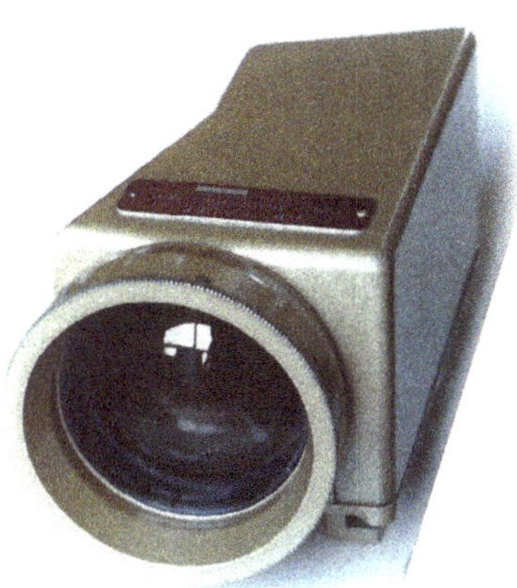

Rank Taylor Hobson fixed x2 prismatic attachment

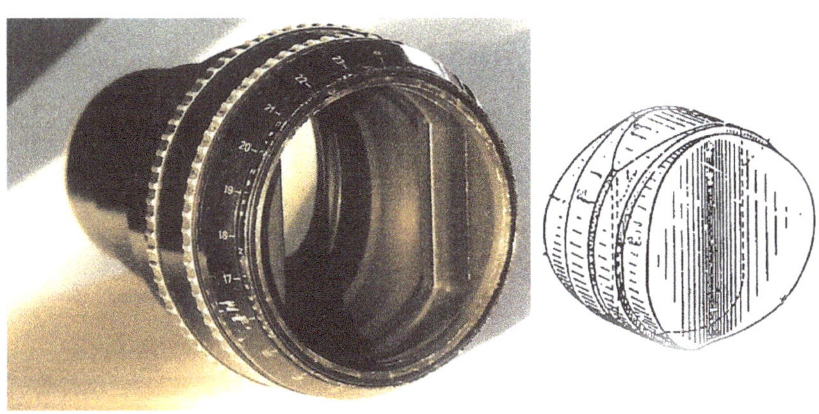

Early Zeiss attachments with the more usual cylindrical elements

There was yet another form of anamorphic system, this time using a pair of wedge-shaped prisms set at an angle to give the required amount of expansion. They were initially very popular, being cheaper to produce without the need for the more sophisticated lens grinding machines used to make accurate cylindrical elements. Like the elements in cylindrical attachments, each prism was made up of separate sections using different types of glass to correct distortion and colour aberrations, including fringing. Prisms alone will only produce a sharp image at infinity, in practice OK for long throws, but most designs included additional spherical lens elements in front to focus them closer. British lens makers, like Ross and Taylor-Hobson, favoured the prismatic principle with their 'Expandascope' and 'Type P' respectively, both providing the x2 expansion ratio.

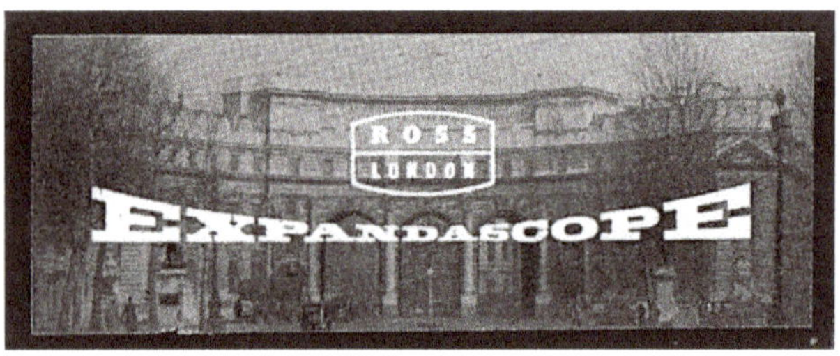

My first experience of prismatic anamorphic attachments came when I joined the BBC at Ealing Studios as a trainee projectionist. The 35mm preview theatres were equipped with GB-Kalee 21s, complete with Taylor-Hobson 'Varamorphs'. As the name suggests, the expansion ratio could be changed by operating a knob on top, connected to pivots which changed the relative angle between the prisms. At the time, in 1963, this seemed to be a superfluous feature, as all the anamorphic prints we showed had the same x2 compression ratio, whatever widescreen process had been used to photograph the film. However, back in 1954, when the Varamorph was first introduced, there was the possibility that prints would be available with a different amount of squeeze to that of CinemaScope's x2.

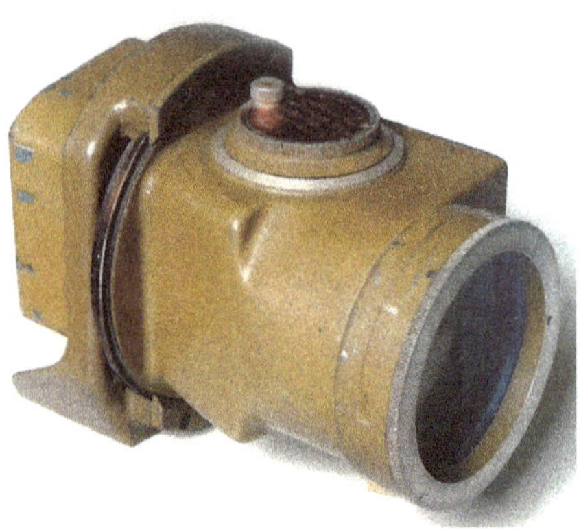

A Varamorph lens and (below) its optical layout

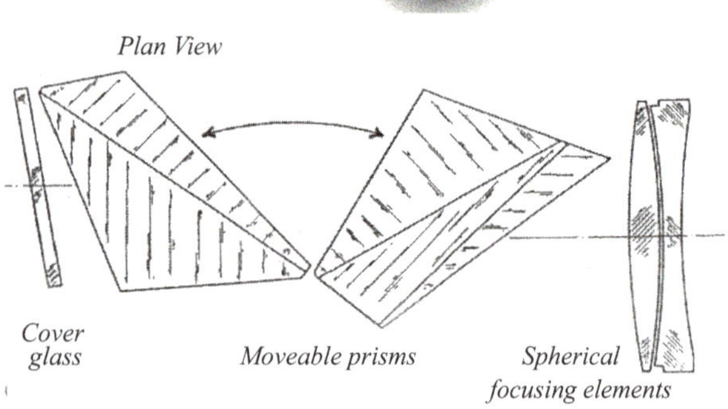

Another early variable prismatic attachment was the Tushinsky Superscope. It was launched in collaboration with RKO, which also announced its own widescreen process, also called Superscope.
This was an optical printing process which converted a masked-off portion of a conventionally shot negative (full-frame or Academy) to produce an anamorphic print with a compression factor of x1.5, half that of CinemaScope's x2. The final aspect ratio of the picture on the screen varied, depending on the height of the projector's aperture, between 1.66:1 and 2:1.

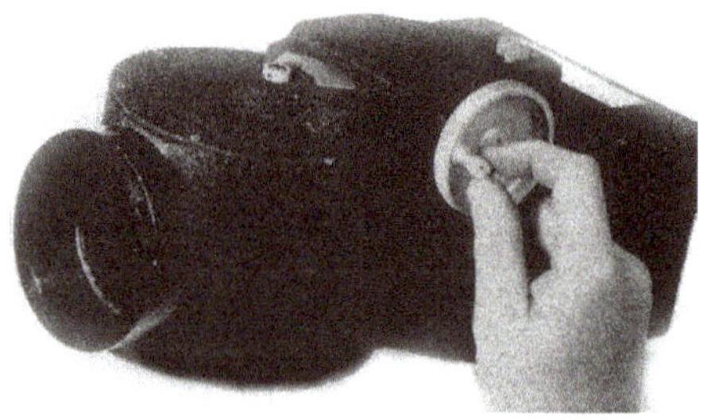

A Tushinsky Superscope

Soon, there were other x1.5 squeezed print formats being proposed. The principal release format from Paramount's VistaVision large-area 35mm 8-perf horizontal negatives was to be 35mm reduction prints with a normal non-anamorphic image which was composed to allow it to be masked down to provide aspect ratios from 1.66:1 to 2:1. In the interest of light conservation, at the maximum 2:1 ratio, it was planned to offer alternative prints with this ratio squeezed (x1.5) within an academy frame. Although MGM had adopted Fox's CinemaScope, they too had an idea to offer similar non-compatible x1.5 conversions of their CinemaScope films for theatres which couldn't accommodate the original full-width picture.

All this activity was welcomed by other manufacturers of variable prismatic attachments. These included the Hilux-VAL and the Gottschalk Ultra-Panatar. The latter was made by a new company called Panavision who would later become better known to cinema-goers on the other side of the portholes when they entered the photographic side of the industry. Interestingly, the first of their camera anamorphic lenses also included prisms to

A Varamorph line up film, anticipating Superscope and Vista-Vision x1.5 squeezed prints

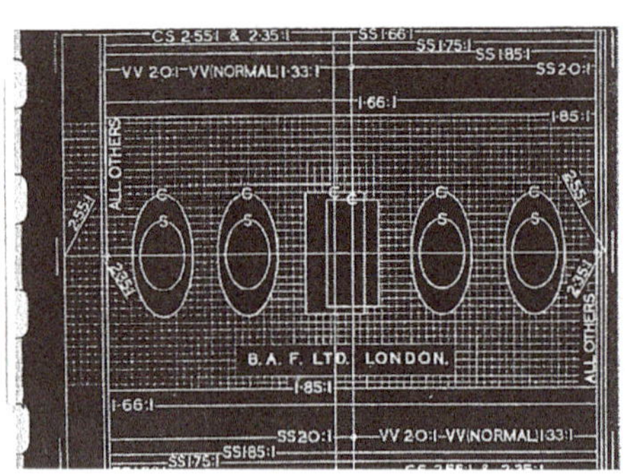

impart a slight squeeze (x1.25) to the 65mm negatives of MGM's 'Camera-65' process. This format evolved into the Ultra Panavision 70 system, with the lenses changed to cylindrical types which made possible wider fields of view. This was useful to Cinerama, who adopted the process for its first single-lens version.

Back to 1954, when, although many exhibitors had chosen to invest in the variable types, many more had fixed cylindrical attachments and with the distributors wishing to avoid adding to the number of different print formats already being circulated, the x1.5 squeezed prints were abandoned. Before any releases, Superscope changed its squeeze factor to x2 to match CinemaScope. It still retained the original maximum 2:1 aspect ratio, leaving

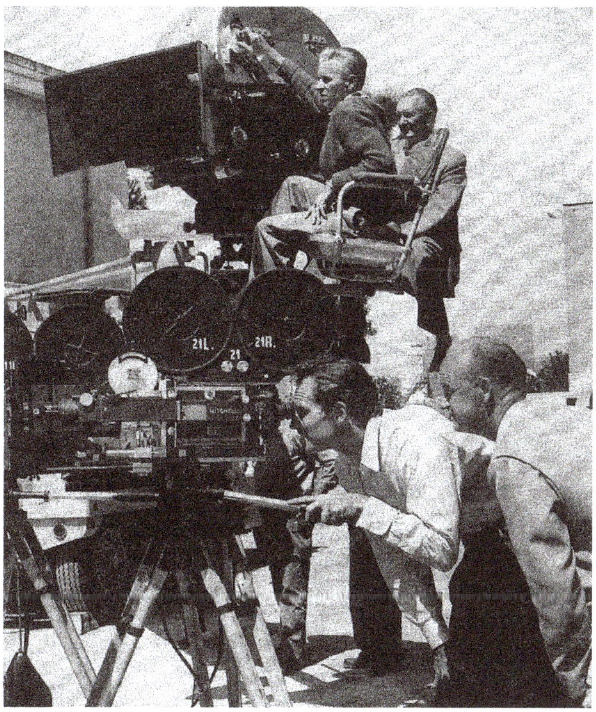

MGM 'Camera 65' 65mm cameras with Panavision x1.25 prismatic anamorphic lenses

unused blank areas down both sides of the frame. In this form, also known as RKO-Scope, it had a fair amount of use.

A later version, which extracted the full 2.35:1 area from a full-frame negative and produced prints compatible with CinemaScope, was introduced as Superscope-235 and is still with us today, now called Super-35. MGM only made a few of its 'ScanaScope' x1.5 versions of its early CinemaScope films, including *Forbidden Planet*, and Paramount too decided not to pursue its VistaVision squeezed print option.

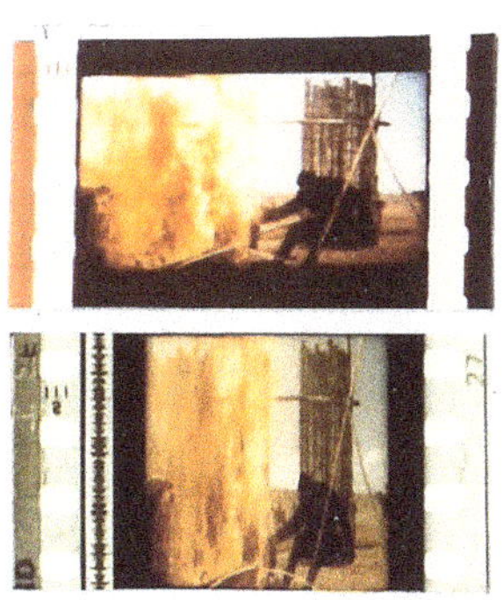

Superscope conversion to squeezed print

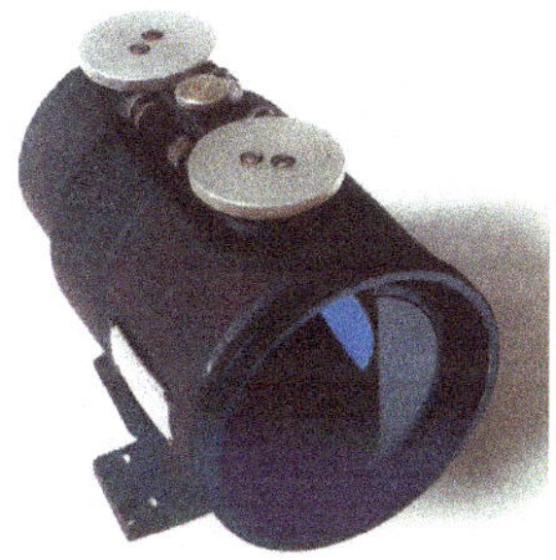

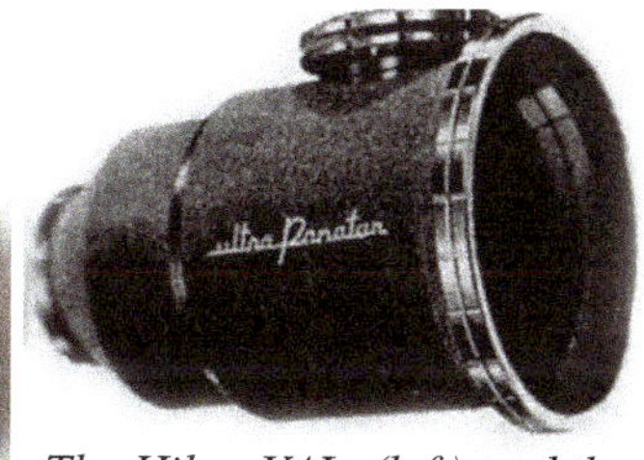

The Hilux-VAL (left) and the Ultra Panatar

The Rank Organisation, having fallen out with Fox over its 'CinemaScope only with stereo sound' policy, had adopted VistaVision and used it at Pinewood for a couple of years. In 1957 they considered reviving the VistaVision squeezed x1.5 print idea, with a 1.75:1 image within a normal 'Scope aperture. At the time, this was considered a practical proposition as almost all of their Odeon cinemas were equipped with Varamorphs, which could be adjusted to show the non-compatible prints. However, after a few trial squeezed copies were made of *Doctor at Large* and *Dangerous Exile*, (printed at Denham Labs on Eastman Color, instead of the usual Technicolor dye-transfer prints) Rank had settled their differences with Fox and given up VistaVision altogether in favour of CinemaScope.

Not wishing to lose a valuable selling point, variable anamorphic attachments were then promoted with the possibility of leaving them permanently in position. The projectionist could then show ordinary films, such as the cartoon and newsreel at zero magnification and then, with the turn of a knob, present a CinemaScope film. It was also suggested that the theatre owner could set the control to less than x2 and make the projected picture less wide and so use a smaller 'less expensive' screen!

For many, the thought of deliberately showing audiences a distorted picture was appalling. In practice, it was found that the eye is quite tolerant to viewing partly squeezed images, remembering that those sitting at the side of the auditorium see a slightly elongated picture anyway. I remember watching a slightly squeezed 70mm Ultra Panavision print of *Mutiny on the Bounty* at the NFT which was being shown without an anamorphic lens (x1.25). I'm sure, apart from me, few other patrons noticed that the ship always had an oval wheel. This would still seem to be true, judging by the number of viewers happy to watch distorted pictures on their widescreen TVs. However, what was not mentioned, was that leaving the unit in place for standard films served no purpose except to reduce the definition and light output. Light passing through a typical prismatic attachment had to fight its way through a lot of glass, with a loss of around 30%, compared to the 10% of a contemporary cylindrical lens. The Varamorph didn't provide a zero setting, the minimum mark on its dial being x1.38, to discourage this practice.

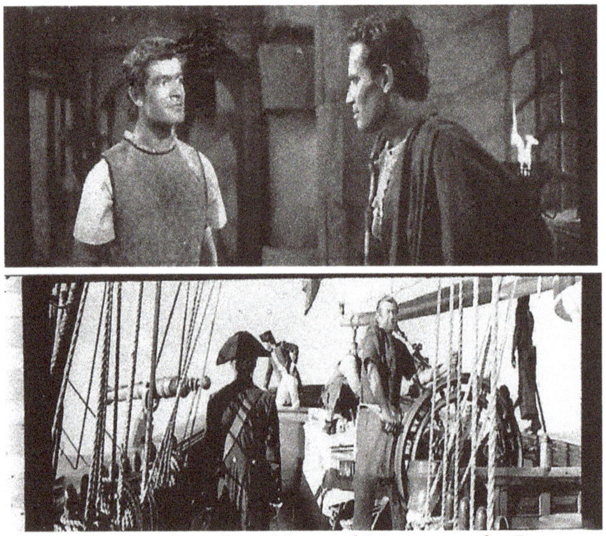

70mm frames from Ben-Hur and Mutiny on the Bounty with slightly squeezed (x1.25) images. Note the distorted ship's wheel. Grant says that he has seen both films without an anamorphic lens and is sure that few people noticed.

Although now largely redundant, the control on the Varamorph still fascinated me. While still only a trainee, I did what I was told and left it alone. However, being a born knob-twiddler, I eventually gave in to temptation and gave it a turn and enjoyed seeing the effect of expanding out the picture and back again. Inspired by the old Magnascope process,

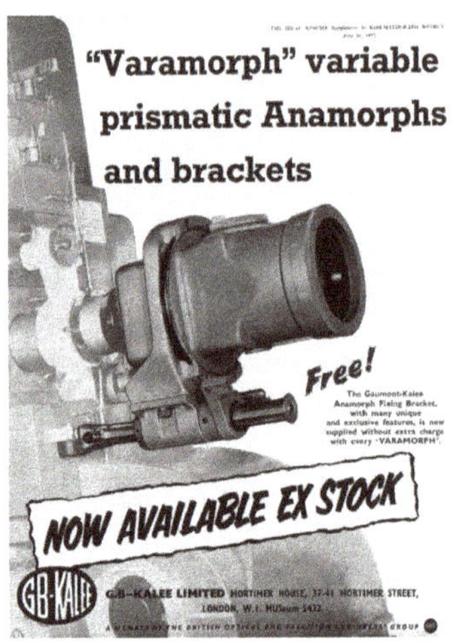

I invented my own called 'Stretch-O-Rama'. I would run a normal film at the minimum setting, but would be ready to give a landscape, or any other scene I thought suitable, the full widescreen treatment until people, who seemed to have suddenly put on weight, appeared and I would sneak it back again. I remember showing an episode of Kenneth Clark's *Civilisation*, which was particularly effective. I'm sure I played havoc with their classic proportions, but the Greek and Roman architecture looked splendid in their new panoramic dimensions and looked like scenes from *The Fall of the Roman Empire*. (During the early days of colour TV, the BBC shot many of its prestige documentaries on 35mm colour negative.)

Due to all this, the Varamorph became one of my favourite anamorphic devices. The quality of the picture was excellent and more than a match for the Zeiss attachments supplied with the Bauer B14 35mm projectors which were used alongside the Kalees from the mid-1960s. The high light loss wasn't a problem for us at the BBC. It actually helped to reduce the light on our smaller screens. Like other anamorphic attachments, focusing down for shorter throws needed special measures. The end-stop screw, at the minimum distance, was removed and the front element unscrewed to its last thread, and taped up to stop it falling off.

I once had a chance to see inside a Varamorph. While I was working at Lime Grove Studios, one developed a fault. Like other old lenses, I think it had something growing in it! While the side plate was off, I was able to watch the magic prisms moving. The work was done by resident engineer, Bob Dyer, who was one of my early technical heroes. In his office/workshop he kept his collection of books on projection and other associated equipment, which he let me borrow, and helped to spark my interest in the technical history of the cinema. He told me an anecdote about the Varamorph. Before joining the BBC, he was a B.A.F / Kalee engineer and helped install the GB-Kalee equipment used to show the film *Around the World in Eighty Days* (1956) at the Astoria, Charing Cross Road. The film was shot in Todd-AO, but as 70mm projectors had yet to arrive in Britain, a presentation system called 'Cinestage' was devised to make the best possible use of 35mm film. The multi-channel sound was on separate magnetic film running on reproducers locked in synch with the Kalee 21s using selsyn motors. This left the maximum available space between the print's Fox-hole perforations for the picture. This was reduced from the 65mm negative using a non-standard x1.56 squeeze, calculated to retain all the picture information and produce a screen aspect ratio of 2.2:1, the same as if an actual Todd-AO 70mm print was being shown. The special anamorphic projection lenses were provided by the American Optical Company, but during the run, doubts were expressed about their performance. Apparently, this was demonstrated to visiting Todd-AO representatives by comparing them with Varamorphs set to give the same squeeze ratio. All agreed that the image looked better and a switch to using the Varamorphs was allowed for the final weeks of the run, providing no publicity was given.

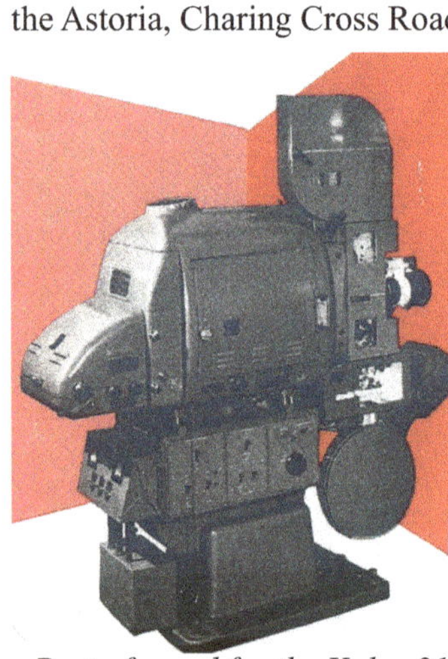

Part of an ad for the Kalee 21 'Cinestage' presentation, subtitled 'Around the World in Eighty Days'

Another piece of related wide screen trivia was the '34mm' ploy. To avoid the then current quota regulations, which would have meant a break in the run, in order to show a British film, one millimetre of the Cinestage print was shaved off the right hand edge. This

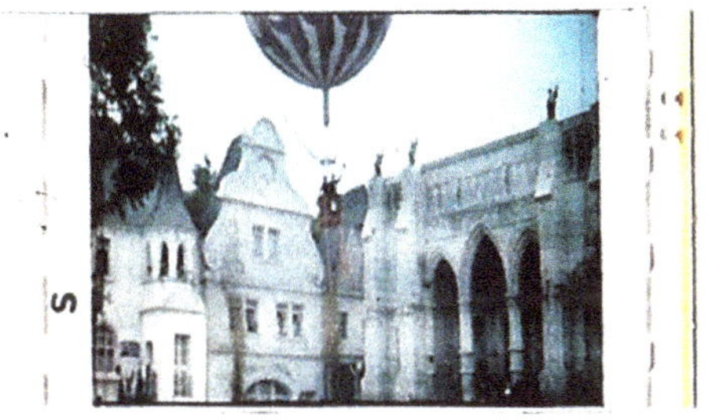

34mm picture showing a x1.56 squeeze. (Not actual size)

exempted the film from the quota, which only applied to professional cinemas showing 'standard' 35mm film. According to Mr. Harding, the Chief at the time at the Astoria, Customs and Excise, who policed the quota, sent their men to the theatre twice during the run to confirm that the 34mm print was still being used. When 70mm finally arrived, it was also exempt, being over the width of standard 35mm. The regulations continued until 1983 and some 35mm features were blown-up to 70mm just to avoid the quota. One example was *A Bridge Too Far*.

Even more trivia for wide screen fans. Two 65mm negatives were shot of *Around the World in Eighty Days*, one running at 30 fps for the 70mm Todd-AO prints and the other at 24 fps for making the high quality 35mm reduction prints for general release. The special Cinestage prints must have been made from the 24 fps version as Bob said the Kalee 21s used standard motors and gearing. Like ours at the BBC, they were mounted on what he called 'studio' bases which included the extra control switches for the selsyn locking system.

The last film projection theatre at the BBC was in Centre House, across the road from the TV Centre. When I left in 1993, it still had a pair of Kalee 21s with the less often seen fixed prisms version of the Taylor Hobson anamorphic attachment. When I last paid a visit, just before it closed, they had been replaced with what I call modern gold ones with cylindrical elements. After asking what happened to the originals, they were found languishing in the stores cupboard under a pile of camera tape. Needless to say, (with permission) I transferred them to one of my cupboards at home for preservation. They joined a Hilux-VAL that I had saved from the old Bijou preview theatre in Wardour Street. It had ended its working life on a 16mm projector, before ending up on the 'of no value' pile when the theatre closed down and the rest of the equipment found new homes.

Learning of my interest in early anamorphic lenses, Nigel Wolland, now MBE, then still chief engineer at the Odeon, Leicester Square, found me not only a Varamorph but a Delrama as well. I collected them from the theatre, but I forgot to ask if they were ever used at the theatre and if any famous 'Scope films received their royal premiere through them?

I'm still looking out for examples of a Superscope and Panavision's Super and Ultra Panatar variable prismatic projection lens attachments. I must find a computer and check if the PPT have any on their collection database.

Even harder to find, must be the Taylor Hobson/Kalee anamorphics made for use on their horizontal 35mm 8-perf 'VistaVision' projectors, when showing contact prints from Technirama negatives. This was basically the same format as VistaVision but photographed with a x1.5 squeeze (via a reflecting Delrama anamorphic Camera lens) and primarily intended for making high quality 'Scope reduction prints. The x1.5 projection attachments were unusual in that they were designed to restore the image by compressing it vertically, instead of expanding it horizontally. As, I believe, only six horizontal projectors were commissioned, these attachments must be very rare. I think they were only used to show a Technicolor Technirama demonstration film, *The Curtain Rises on Technirama*, at trade shows held at the Odeon Leicester Square and introduced by Jack Cardiff. I include a picture of one taken from Kalee's 'Horizontal Equipment' brochure in case you ever spot one.

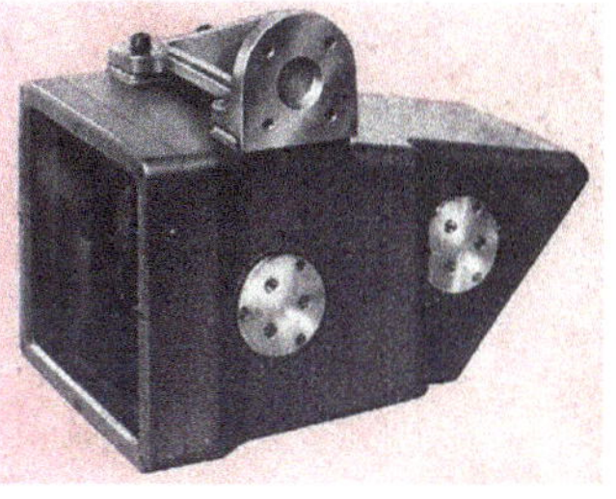

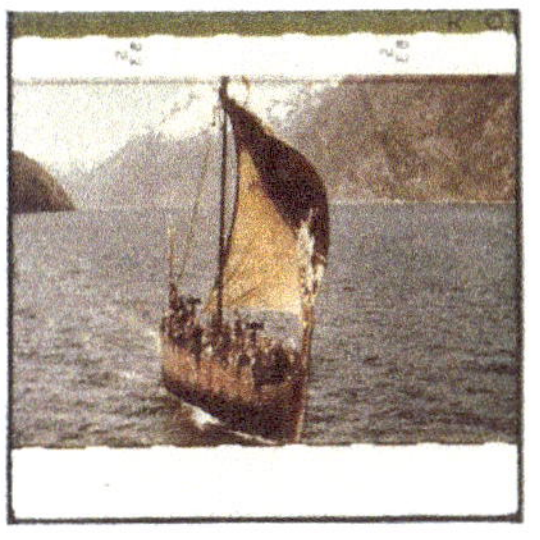

Technirama x1.5 attachment for use on the Kalee horizontal projector. Technirama contact print.

All of today's theatres still running 'real' film need anamorphic lenses for showing the 2.35:1 squeezed print format, which remains popular with film makers. However, their continued use in the digital future is less certain. To make the most efficient use of all the pixels on the squarer 4x3 chipsets found in earlier digital cinema projectors, anamorphic lenses were often employed with powers calculated to produce both the 1.85:1 and 2.35:1 screen ratios. Although still an (expensive) option, the wider format chips in the latest models allow for the two formats to be accommodated by small amounts of cropping, so anamorphic projection lenses may eventually become part of cinema history. However, it could be an opportunity to produce an up-dated 'digital' version of the old variable anamorphic lenses. This would make it possible to choose any screen aspect ratio and still use all of the chip's full vertical and horizontal resolution, whatever its own 'native' aspect ratio. In the case of 16x9 chips, the lens would now need a less than zero (compression) setting for ratios less than 1.78:1, including when showing 'classic' academy 1.37:1 films.

In the meantime, if a projector has to go to the scrap yard, always remember 'save the lens', particularly if it has got knobs on!

Circles of confusion

Anamorphic camera lenses are to blame...

Many people wonder why some types of camera anamorphic 'squeeze' lenses throw bright points of light into the ellipses often seen in the out of focus backgrounds of 'CinemaScope' films, while others turn them into circles, like normal spherical lenses. This is sometimes described as the BOKEH effect. It is interesting that they never appear in squeezed prints derived from original spherically shot 'flat' negatives such as Super-35. Conversely, in the good old days of regular showings of 70mm prints, the sight of these ellipses on the screen gave the game away that we were being fobbed off with a blow-up from a 35mm anamorphic negative, rather than 65mm photography, using spherical lenses.

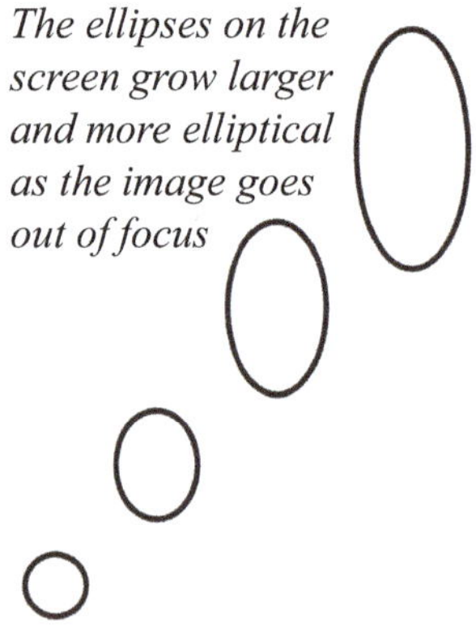

The ellipses on the screen grow larger and more elliptical as the image goes out of focus

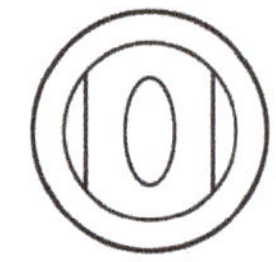

Which all goes to show what curious optical devices anamorphic lenses can be

A conventional spherical lens focuses the light from the scene into infinitely small spots, known as circles of confusion. Moving away, in either direction from the plane of focus, they grow larger, until the image is said to be out of focus. Between these limits is the lens's depth-of-field, which varies depending on the distance on which it is focused, its aperture and focal length. Anamorphic lenses have effectively two focal lengths, the horizontal being half that of the vertical, each with differing depth-of-fields. (The vertical figure is the one used for classification and calculating the depth-of-field.) When in focus, anamorphic lenses record an ellipse of confusion, its shape corresponding to the 2:1 compression factor. This is restored back to a circle, when projected through the complementary anamorphic (x2) lens on the projector. (Projection lenses are not affected, as they only have to deal with single planes of focus.)

However, away from the plane of focus, anamorphic lenses tend to go more out of focus in the vertical plane, than they do in the horizontal, with the ellipses of confusion becoming more elliptical, far greater than

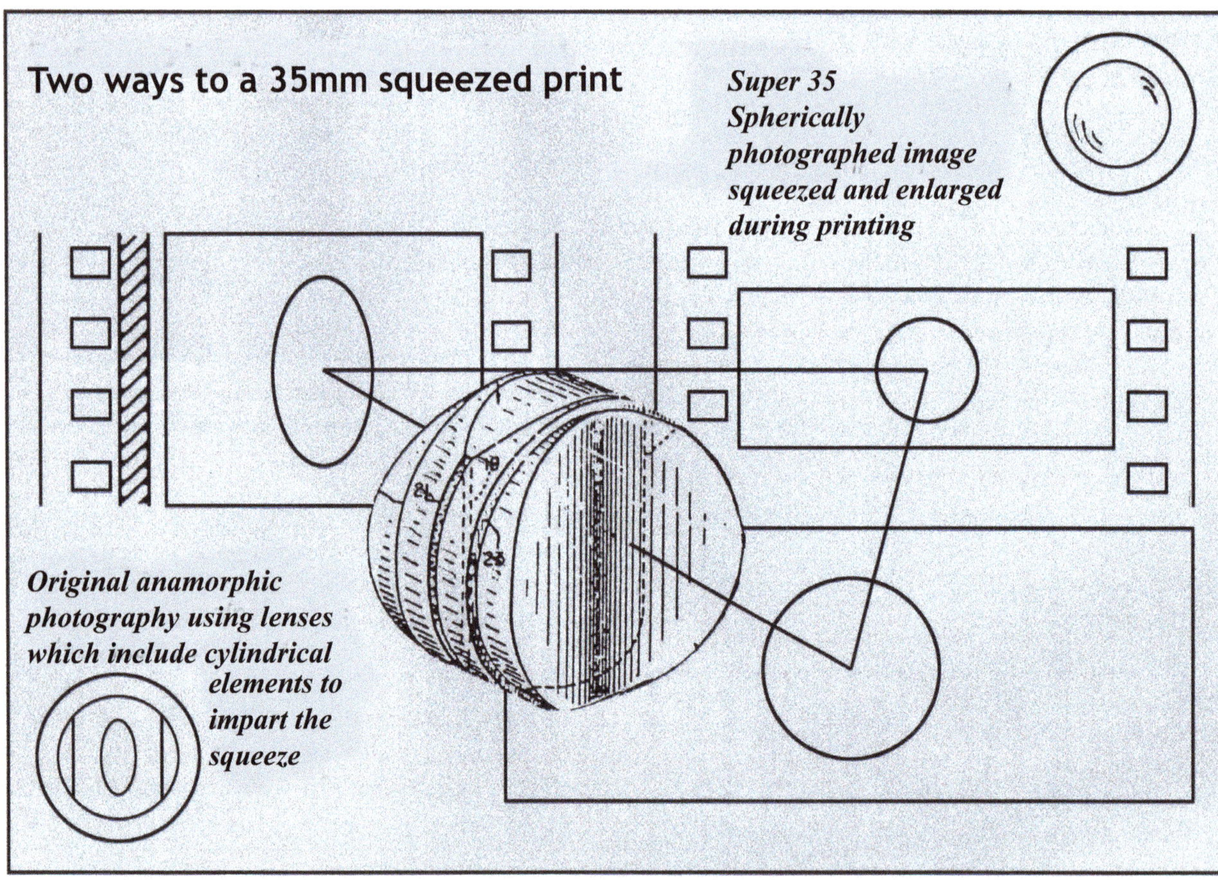

can be fully restored by the projector lens. Even if the ellipses can't be spotted, the out of focus areas often have a streaky look, due to being more out of focus in one direction than the other. This is actually a form of astigmatism, which would not be tolerated in a spherical lens, but is accepted as a 'characteristic' of most anamorphic lenses. The effect has become more noticeable, with the trend over the years to using wider apertures. The compression factor, or size difference between the two planes, can also differ in the out of focus areas. This shows up during rapid changes of focus, when the image is seen to be pulled back into shape.

Why then, do some anamorphic camera systems only produce circles of confusion on the screen? Anamorphic lenses are made up of a combination of both spherical and cylindrical elements, with the latter imparting the squeeze. Most anamorphic prime and shorter range zooms have these cylindrical elements at, or near, the front of the lens and they play their part in forming the image. It is this type of design which produces the notorious ellipses, to a more or lesser extent, depending on the positioning of the cylindrical elements and the focusing method employed. However, some longer focal length telephoto lenses and wider range anamorphic zooms are in fact ordinary spherical lenses, with an anamorphic converter placed at the rear. This squeezes up the image before it reaches the film, but after it has been completely formed by the spherical elements at the front.

This is rather like the optical equivalent of Super-35, and is free of screen ellipses. This arrangement is often used to reduce the weight and size of larger anamorphic lenses, but usually at the cost of resolution and speed. These sometimes strange optical characteristics of anamorphic lenses are not generally considered to be a problem, and are not noticed by the average movie-goer. In fact, the current resurgence in the use of the format continues, together with a constant demand from film makers for the best quality lenses available. Supporters of the system, including the writer, like the format not only for its larger negative area, but also for its more 'natural look'.

This is hard to define, but may be due to the way anamorphic camera lenses record perspective. They seem to have the ability to extend the horizontal field of view, but with less exaggeration of the perspective, when compared with the shorter focal length lenses needed to cover the same angle on the smaller Super-35 negative. This has the effect of further separating the subject, in the foreground, from its background, which is pushed back into the distance. In theory, the apparent perspective should be the same when using both methods, after the

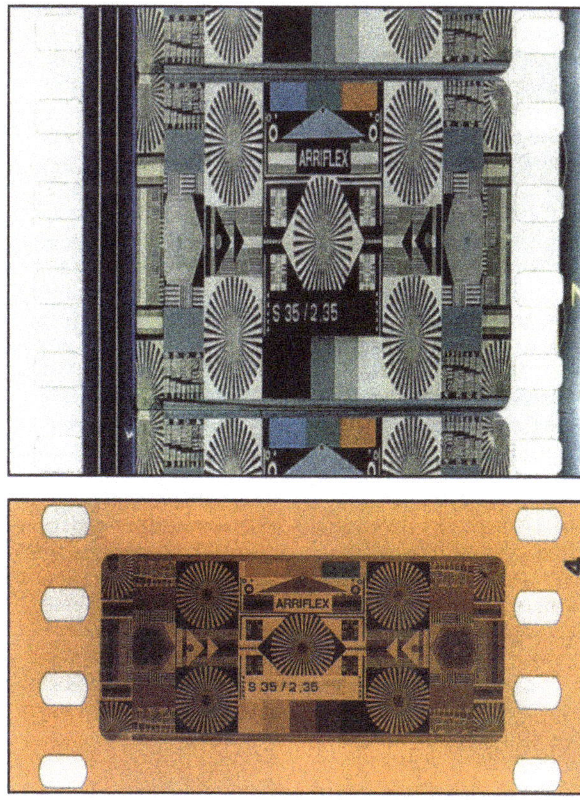

For those who don't like using anamorphic lenses, there is the option of Super-35, but at the cost of a reduced negative area (Courtesy Arri)

extra magnification, (via its conversion to a compatible squeezed print), needed to project the Super-35 image onto the same width screen. In practice, the two ways to a squeezed print still 'look' subtly different, which all goes to show what curious optical devices anamorphic lenses can be.

Many Directors, and Directors of Photography like the wider 2.35:1 anamorphic format, but hate the anamorphic lenses themselves. These have improved greatly over the last 60 years or so, but the basic laws of optics still make them heavier, having more geometric distortions and reduced overall resolution, when compared with comparable spherical lenses. The Super-35 format is available as an alternative, using a wider range of potentially superior spherical lenses, but this time at the cost of a greatly reduced negative area.

This has been a somewhat simplified (I hope!) explanation of the peculiarities of camera anamorphic lenses, which like their construction, is actually far more complex, so much so that even the most learned textbooks on photographic optics prefer to ignore the subject. This is surprising, considering their continuing popularity and the important role they still play in the photography of today's motion pictures.

A rare 'hands-on' chance

Grant's report on the sale of the historic Samuelson collection provided yet another example of his love for all things cinema. He enjoyed attending the pre-auction viewing days, not wishing to miss out on a unique opportunity to handle and 'play with' all this historic equipment.

A rather special sale took place at Christie's South Kensington on 22nd November 2006. The Sale of Cameras, Photographs and Optical Toys included the Samuelson Brothers Collection of Motion Picture Cameras. The Samuelson Brothers Collection was regarded as one of the world's most important collections of historic movie cameras, and comprising some 70 lots, the collection was expected to make up to £75,000, with estimates for individual items ranging from £100 to £12,000.

The collection was assembled by BKSTS Past President David W. Samuelson in the mid-1960s. Along with his brothers, he ran the well-known British firm of Samuelson Film Services (Sammy's) in Cricklewood, the world's largest supplier of motion picture cameras for hire, and over the years built an extensive collection of motion picture cameras. These were made available on long-term loan to the British Film Institute and the collection formed a key part of the Museum of the Moving Image on London's South Bank, from1988 to 1999.

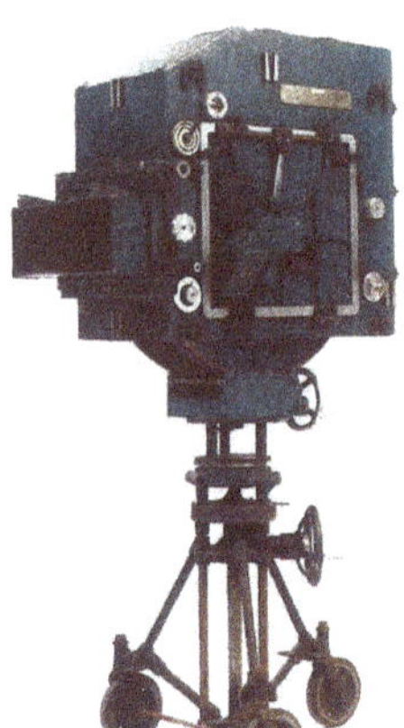

Of particular interest to Grant was the Technicolor 3-Strip camera and blimp, (right and on catalogue front) which was sold to an anonymous buyer for £11,000. The camera was one of one of only 30 made and the only example in private ownership in the world. Grant commented that both he and Cinema Technology magazine were quoted in Christie's catalogue as expert reference sources relating to the Technicolor camera. Technicolor camera number DE13 (DE stood for Drama England, in case you ever need the information for a pub quiz!) was given to the Samuelson brothers by Technicolor, and the blimp was acquired in a separate transaction.
Grant's other favourite items included the Bausch and Lomb
'monobloc' CinemaScope lenses that were used to photograph The Bridge on the River Kwai (1957). This historic set of CinemaScope lenses (50mm, 40mm, 35mm) - picture right - used by Jack Hildyard for his Oscar-winning cinematography stayed in Britain, after a bid of £1200.

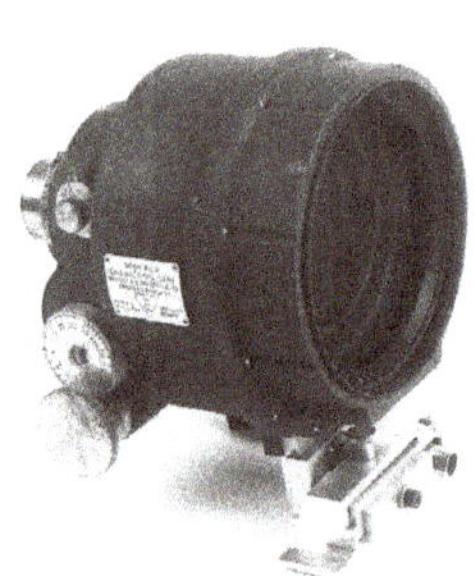

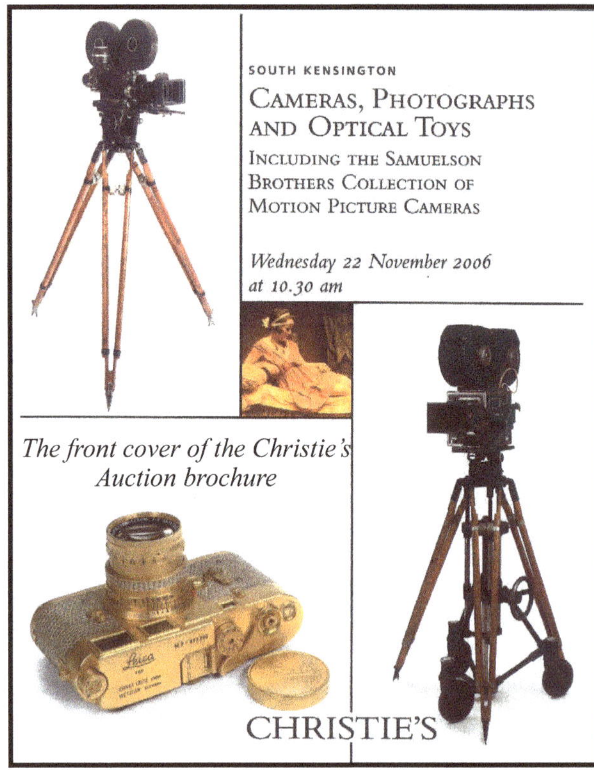

The front cover of the Christie's Auction brochure

Les Zellan of Cooke Optics bought the world's first zoom lens for the company and intends to refurbish it. The 1930s Cooke Varo was the first non-telescopic zoom lens and the world's first production zoom lens - more of a variable prime, some claim. The lenses were made by Bell & Howell who owned Taylor Hobson at the time.

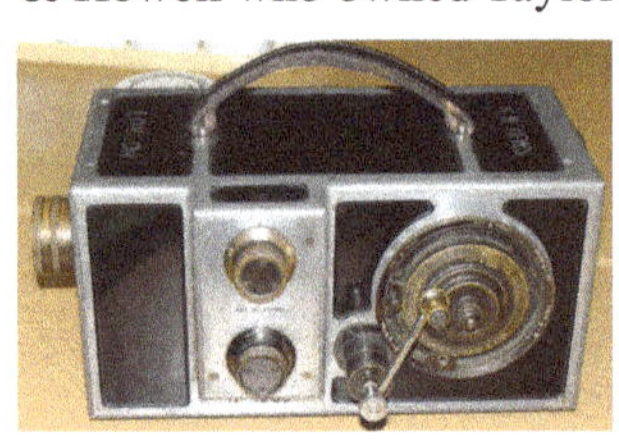

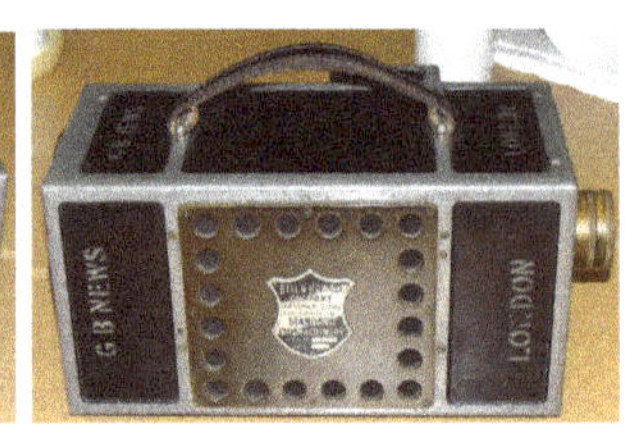

Other highlights of the collection included:

- The Caméreclair reputedly used by Jean Renoir
- A 1906 Prestwich camera
- A 1912 Moy Aerial camera with gyroscopic stabilisation
- The first production Arriflex camera serial no. 500

The Samuelson Brothers collection included early projection mechanisms, as well as equipment made for the amateur movie market such as a rare Schalie Collée 16mm camera, and the only known example of the first British made 16mm projector, the Thornton-Pickard 'Ruby'.

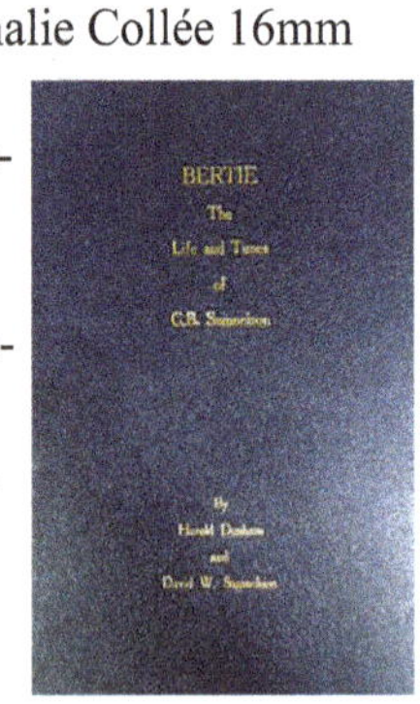

The proceeds of the Samuelson Brothers Collection went towards funding a book about prominent producer and director of the silent movie era, "Bertie": The Life and Times of G.B.Samuelson.

Index

Other publications by the authors

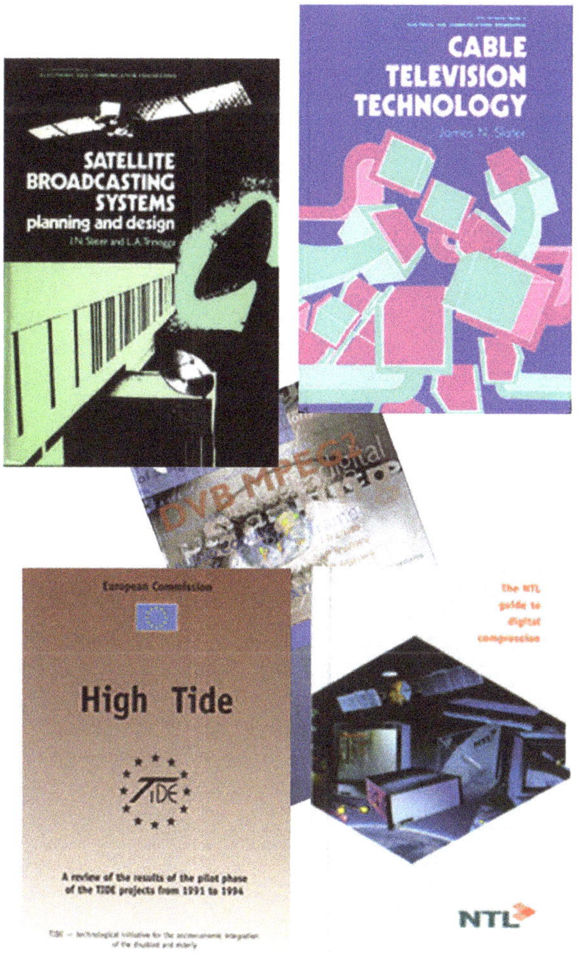

Satellite Broadcasting Systems: Planning and Design (Ellis Horwood series in electrical and electronic engineering)
J.N. Slater, Lothar Alfred Trinogga
Published by Ellis Horwood Ltd , (1985)
ISBN 10: 0853128642 ISBN 13: 9780853128649

Modern Television Systems - to HDTV and Beyond
J.N.Slater
Pitman Publishing, Longmans 1991
ISBN-10: 0273031228

Cable Television Technology
J.N.Slater
Ellis Horwood Limited, John Wiley & Sons, 1988
ISBN 0 7458 0108 0

The NTL Guide to Digital Compression
J.N. Slater (Ed.) 1995'
Publisher: NTL

High Tide - A review of EC TIDE Research Projects
J.N.Slater (Ed.) 1998
Publisher: OOPEC, European Commission

Lightning Source UK Ltd.
Milton Keynes UK
UKHW051148050122
396605UK00002B/113

9 781789 821499